eMarketing eXcellence

Planning and optimizing your
digital marketing

eMarketing eXcellence

Planning and optimizing your digital marketing

Third edition

Dave Chaffey and PR Smith

AMSTERDAM • BOSTON • HEIDELBERG • LONDON • OXFORD • NEW YORK
PARIS • SAN DIEGO • SAN FRANCISCO • SINGAPORE • SYDNEY • TOKYO
Butterworth-Heinemann is an imprint of Elsevier

Butterworth-Heinemann is an imprint of Elsevier
Linacre House, Jordan Hill, Oxford OX2 8DP, UK
30 Corporate Drive, Burlington, MA 01803, USA

First published 2002
Reprinted 2003 (twice)
Second edition published 2005
Third edition published 2008

British Library Cataloguing in Publication Data
A catalogue record for this book is available from the British Library

Library of Congress Cataloguing in Publication Data
A catalogue record for this book is available from the Library of Congress

ISBN 978-0-7506-8945-8

For information on all Butterworth-Heinemann publications
visit our website at http://elsevierdirect.com

Typeset by Charon Tec Ltd, (A Macmillan Co) Chennai, India
www.charontec.com

Printed and bound in Slovenia

08 09 10 11 12   10 9 8 7 6 5 4 3 2 1

Working together to grow
libraries in developing countries

www.elsevier.com | www.bookaid.org | www.sabre.org

ELSEVIER   BOOK AID International   Sabre Foundation

Contents

Preface

Why eMarketing eXcellence?

E-marketing impacts all aspects of marketing from strategy and planning through the marketing mix, marketing communications and buyer behaviour to marketing research. *eMarketing eXcellence* highlights the most significant opportunities, pitfalls and defines the new marketing approaches needed. It highlights best practice in applying digital media to support a range of organizational goals based on the 20 years' plus combined practical Internet marketing experience of the authors. Best practice is exemplified by a selection of the leading pureplay and multichannel organizations who have exploited the unique characteristics of digital media.

E-marketing impacts all organizations. *eMarketing eXcellence* shows you how to assess your current use of e-marketing and then develop and resource an effective plan.

E-marketing does not exist in a vacuum. Planning must ensure that e-marketing integrates with the marketing objectives and the corporate aims of moving towards e-business. *eMarketing eXcellence* shows how to develop a plan that achieves this integration.

The e-marketing imperative is further indicated by success stories from leading adopters of e-marketing such as Alliance and Leicester, BMW, Dell, CIPD, Diageo, E-consultancy, ING Direct, Tektronix and TUI, who have found e-marketing to be effective and who are substantially increasing their online marketing expenditure to double-digit percentages of total marketing communications spend.

How is eMarketing eXcellence structured?

eMarketing eXcellence has been developed to help you learn efficiently. It has supported students on many university and college business and marketing courses and a range of specialist qualifications in digital marketing offered by the Chartered Institute of Marketing, E-consultancy/Manchester Metropolitan University and The Institute of Direct Marketing. It is structured around ten self-contained chapters, each of which supports learning through a clear structure based on sections with clear learning outcomes, summaries and self-test questions. The E-marketing Insight boxes give varied perspectives from practitioners and academics while the E-marketing Excellence boxes give examples of best practice. We have also included numerous tips and best practice checklists for you to compare your e-marketing against and to help you develop a plan.

Chapter 1 Introduction to e-marketing

This chapter introduces e-marketing and its benefits and risks. It describes the difference between e-commerce, e-business and e-marketing; the alternative digital communications channels, the dangers of sloppy e-marketing; how to present a business case for increasing your online activities and the benefits – Sell, Serve, Save, Speak and Sizzle.

Chapter 2 Remix

The digital world affects every aspect of business, every aspect of marketing and every aspect of the marketing mix. Some argue that physical distribution, selling and pricing absorb the biggest impact. In fact all the elements of the marketing mix are affected by this new world. This chapter shows you exactly how to evaluate the options for varying your organization's marketing mix.

Chapter 3 E-models

The business world is changing faster than ever before. Old approaches and models are being turned on their head. In this chapter we show how to assess your online marketplace, review new business, revenue and communications models and develop budget models.

Chapter 4 E-customers

This chapter looks inside the online customer's mind. We explore customers' issues, worries, fears and phobias, as well as other motivators for going online … and how marketers can respond to these behaviours. We also look at on-site behaviour, the online buying process, web analytics and the many influencing variables. We finish with a look to the future, your future and how to keep an eye on the e-customer.

Chapter 5 E-tools

This is where the online world begins to get really interesting. Once we move beyond the PC and into the wireless world of pervasive technology, a whole new vision appears. Always on, everywhere, easy to use, contextual, integrated marketing is exploiting these new technological tools to reach and satisfy customers in new ways.

Chapter 6 Site design

This chapter will make you think about web sites a little differently. We go beyond best practice in usability and accessibility, to show how to design commercially-led sites which deliver results. Commercially-led site designs are based on creating compelling persuasive experiences which really engage visitors through relevant messages and content, encouraging them to stay on the site and return to it.

Chapter 7 Traffic building

Sadly it's not always the best products that succeed, but rather reasonably good ones that (a) everyone knows about and (b) everyone can easily find when they need them. The same is true of web sites. This chapter shows you how to build traffic – how to acquire the right visitors to your site in order to achieve the right marketing outcomes for you. You will receive a briefing on the different digital communications channels, including search engine marketing, online PR, online partnerships, interactive advertising, opt-in e-mail and viral marketing. We will also show you that to succeed with your online communications also means gaining different forms of visibility on partner sites which are themselves successful in traffic building.

Chapter 8 E-CRM

Online customer relationship management is packed with fundamental common sense principles. Serving and nurturing customers into lifetime customers makes sense as existing customers are, on average, five to ten times more profitable. At the heart of this is a good database – the marketer's memory bank, which if used correctly, creates arguably the most valuable asset in any company. In this chapter we show how to develop integrated e-mail contact strategies to deliver relevant messages throughout the customer lifecycle.

Chapter 9 E-business

The dot-com disasters still scare many professionals. Clicks and mortar companies generally outperform pure-play Internet companies. Why didn't these new e-businesses survive? Where did they go wrong? The answer is that they weren't e-businesses. They weren't even businesses, since many were ignorant of business essentials such as the need to integrate front-office systems with back-office systems, keep close to customers, deliver real added value, have clear propositions, carefully target the right customers, etc. This chapter clarifies what is meant by e-business; a much abused concept.

Chapter 10 E-planning

E-marketing planning involves marketing planning within the context of the e-business e-environment. So, not surprisingly, the successful e-marketing plan is based on traditional marketing disciplines and planning techniques, adapted for the digital media environment and then mixed with new digital marketing communications techniques. This chapter shows you how to create a comprehensive e-marketing plan, based on the well-established principles of the SOSTAC® Planning System (PR Smith, 1993).

WHO IS THIS BOOK FOR?

Marketing and business professionals

- *Marketing managers* responsible for defining an e-marketing strategy, implementing strategy or maintaining the company web site alongside traditional marketing activities.

- *Digital marketing specialists* such as new media managers, e-marketing managers and e-commerce managers responsible for directing, integrating and implementing their organizations' e-marketing.
- *Senior managers and directors* seeking to identify the right e-business and e-marketing approaches to support their organizations' strategy.
- *Information systems managers and Chief Information Officers* also involved in developing and implementing e-marketing and e-commerce strategies.
- *Technical project managers or web masters* who may understand the technical details of building a site, but want to enhance their knowledge of e-marketing.

Students

This book has been created as the core text for the CIM e-marketing professional development award and the Institute of Direct Marketing Digital Marketing Qualifications. As such, *eMarketing eXcellence* will support the following students in their studies:

- *Professionals studying for recognized qualifications.* The book provides comprehensive coverage of the syllabus for these awards.
- *Postgraduate students on specialist masters degrees in electronic commerce, electronic business or e-marketing and generic programmes in Marketing Management, MBA, Certificate in Management or Diploma in Management Studies* which involve modules or electives for e-business and e-marketing.
- *Undergraduates on business programmes* which include marketing modules on the use of digital marketing. This may include specialist degrees such as electronic business, electronic commerce, Internet marketing and marketing or general business degrees such as business studies, business administration and business management.
- *Postgraduate and undergraduate project students* who select this topic for final year projects/dissertations – this book is an excellent source of resources for these students.
- *Undergraduates completing work placement* involved with different aspects of e-marketing such as managing an intranet or company web site.

MBA – we find that this book actually gives non marketing people a good grounding in marketing principles, business operations and of course emarketing.

WHAT DOES THE BOOK OFFER TO LECTURERS TEACHING THESE COURSES?

This book is intended to be a comprehensive guide to all aspects of deploying e-marketing within an organization. It builds on existing marketing theories and concepts and questions the validity of these models in the light of the differences between the Internet and other media, and references the emerging body of literature specific to e-business, e-commerce and e-marketing. Lecturers will find this book has a good range of case study examples to support their teaching. Web links given in the text and at the end of each chapter highlight key information sources for particular topics.

LEARNING FEATURES

A range of features have been incorporated into *eMarketing eXcellence* to help the reader get the most out of it. They have been designed to assist understanding, reinforce learning and help readers find information easily. The features are described in the order you will find them.

At the start of each chapter

- *Overview*: a short introduction to the relevance of the chapter and what you will learn.
- *Overall learning outcome*: a list describing what readers can learn through reading the chapter and completing the self-test.
- *Chapter topics*: chapter contents and the learning objectives for each section.

In each chapter

- *E-marketing Excellence boxes*: real-world examples of best practice approaches referred to in the text.
- *E-marketing Insight boxes*: quotes, opinions and frameworks from industry practitioners and academics.
- *E-marketing Best Practice Checklists*: to enable you to evaluate and improve your current approaches or plan a new initiative.
- *Practical e-marketing Tip*: Do's and don'ts to improve your website, e-mail or database marketing.
- *Definitions*: key e-marketing terms are highlighted in bold and the glossary contains succinct definitions.
- *Web links*: where appropriate, web addresses are given for further information, particularly those to update information.
- *Section summaries*: intended as revision aids and to summarize the main learning points from the section.

At the end of each chapter

- *Summary*: also intended as revision aids and to summarize the main learning points from the chapter.
- *References*: these are references to books, articles or papers referred to within the chapter.
- *Further reading*: supplementary texts or papers on the main themes of the chapter. Where appropriate a brief commentary is provided on recommended supplementary reading on the main themes of the chapters.
- *Web links*: these are significant sites that provide further information on the concepts and topics of the chapter. All web site references within the chapter, for example company

sites, are not repeated here. The web site address prefix 'http://' is omitted for clarity except where the address does not start with 'www'.

- *Self-test questions*: short questions which will test understanding of terms and concepts described in the chapter and help relate them to your organization.

At the end of the book

- *Glossary*: a list of definitions of all key terms and phrases used within the main text.
- *Index*: all key words and abbreviations referred to in the main text.

Preface to the third edition

The innovation in digital technologies and the ways in which we interact with them have continued relentlessly since the second edition of *eMarketing eXcellence*.

The most dramatic changes have been in user participation facilitated by the new Web 2.0 digital technologies and evolving Web 3.0 approaches. Today, and into the future, consumers don't only go online to save time and money while selecting and purchasing products, they go online via web or mobile to spend time, to socialize and simply for entertainment. The rise of the now familiar social networks such as Bebo, MySpace, Facebook and in the business arena, Linked In and Ecademy are now where many of us spend time, sometimes discussing brands, but for most of the time just socializing. And of course when we're socializing, we mostly don't want to be interrupted by marketing messages – so customer engagement has become a key challenge. Systems to tell others what we think about products and brands are also important and user generated content generated on rating platforms such as Delicious, Digg, YouTube and the shopping comparison sites are only going to increase in importance.

Many of the forecasts that we made have proved true. We forecasted that customers would start to consolidate their choices to better, added value sites and services. We also described the growth of blogs and the emergence of interactive Web 2.0 applications. And that the role of comparison intermediaries would increase, although it has taken longer than we thought for customer behaviour to change.

We also said that being customer centric online was essential to create real value added customer experiences that nurture customer satisfaction and ultimately, highly profitable, repeat business. Nothing too surprising there, you might say. What is surprising is that many organizations are only at an early stage of developing their online marketing capabilities. Many have not implemented or refined many of the core digital marketing techniques that we describe in this book such as search engine optimization, partner marketing, personalized web recommendation, A/B and multivariate testing and automated e-mail contact strategies.

Many of the permission-based approaches to e-marketing we recommended in earlier editions are now legal requirements due to European and US privacy laws such as the European Community Electronic Communications Directive and the US 'CAN-SPAM' laws. E-marketers also now have to make sure their web sites are accessible to be compliant with the Disability and Discrimination Act (which is good practice since it also assists with search engine optimization).

Despite all of this, the fundamental principle remains the same (we said this in the second edition) – stick close to customers. Talk to them. Listen to them (in communities and social networks). Understand them better than they understand themselves. Become customer experts. Be crystal clear about the target markets, who they are, how you access them, why you are going after them.

Use marketplace analysis and modelling to understand your offering and how you compare to competition, both in reality and in customers' perceptions. Then develop credibility before raising visibility. After that, strong and clear value propositions help to win customers' and prospects' permission (permission marketing). Use e-marketing analysis techniques such as surveys, audience data and web analytics to refine your online offering. You can then refine your proposition and develop relations (relationship marketing) through effective, usable web sites and timely reminders (whether by opt-in e-mail, text messages, direct mail or even telephone (permission allowing).

Many readers will be moving from their initial e-plans onto the next generation of e-plans or developing a long-term e-marketing roadmap to introduce new approaches. We hope this book helps to move you along the evolutionary path towards e-plans that really help to boost performance in an integrated way. Although the benefits of e-marketing span right across an organization's functions (customer feedback, customer service, product enhancement, sales, finance/payment, delivery, administration and marketing), we tend to link it strongly to marketing communications plans. The reality is that any e-marketing plan needs to be part of a Marketing Communications Plan and it also should be part of a broader Marketing Plan. Needless to say the e-plan should fit in with the overall business plan and goals.

Enjoy the read, enjoy the digital ride and let us know what you think via our sites.

Dave (www.davechaffey.com/E-marketing) and Paul (www.prsmith.org)

Acknowledgements

Our thanks to our many friends and colleagues who have helped us in many ways. In particular, Paul Smith would like to thank Alison Bowditch, Martin Burke, Lou Burrows, Peter Hurst, Jan Klin, Mike Langford, Martin Lindstrom, Gerry McGovern, Paul O'Sullivan, Steve Saunders and John Twomey. Dave Chaffey would like to thank the following for e-inspiration: Bryan Eisenberg, Ashley Friedlein, Avinash Kaushik, Neil Mason, Jim Novo, Richard Sedley and Jim Sterne.

All web site screenshots included in this book are examples of best practice. We thank all companies who have agreed to have their sites included and offer our apologies to those it has not been possible to contact.

Finally thanks to the Smith clan: Beverley, Aran, Cian and Lily and the Chaffey clan: Sal, Zoe and Sarah.

Chapter 1

Introduction to e-marketing

'Scarcely a day goes by without some claim that new technologies are fast writing newsprint's obituary. Yet, as an industry, many of us have been remarkably, unaccountably complacent. Certainly, I didn't do as much as I should have after all the excitement of the late 1990's. I suspect many of you in this room did the same, quietly hoping that this thing called the digital revolution would just limp along.

Well it hasn't . . . it won't. . . . And it's a fast developing reality we should grasp as a huge opportunity . . .'.

Rupert Murdoch (News Corporation, 2005)

OVERVIEW

This chapter introduces e-marketing and its benefits and risks. It describes the difference between e-commerce, e-business and e-marketing; the alternative digital communications channels, the dangers of sloppy e-marketing; how to present a business case for increasing your online activities and the benefits – Sell, Serve, Save, Speak and Sizzle.

OVERALL LEARNING OUTCOME

By the end of this chapter you will be able to:

- Describe the development of the electronic marketspace
- Outline an approach to developing an e-marketing plan
- Describe the key benefits of e-marketing.

CHAPTER TOPIC	LEARNING OBJECTIVE
1.1 Introduction	Outline the benefits and risks of e-marketing
1.2 The wired-up world	Outline the characteristics of the new marketspace
1.3 B2C, B2B, C2B and C2C	Identify different forms of collaboration between marketplace members
1.4 E-definitions	Describe the difference between e-commerce, e-business and e-marketing
1.5 Sloppy e-marketing	Avoid basic e-marketing mistakes
1.6 Objectives	Outline the five basic e-marketing objectives
1.7 Objective – Sell	Define objectives for selling to the customer online
1.8 Objective – Serve	Define objectives for serving the customer online
1.9 Objective – Speak	Define objectives for speaking to the customer online
1.10 Objective – Save	Define objectives for saving online
1.11 Objective – Sizzle	Define objectives for enhancing the brand online
1.12 Introduction to e-strategy	Outline approaches to achieving e-marketing objectives
1.13 Tactics, action and control	Outline e-marketing tactics, actions and control

1.1   Introduction

This chapter introduces you to the world of **e-marketing**; its background and its benefits. It explores the current e-marketing situation, e-marketing definitions and examples of good and bad e-marketing. Chances are your organization is already engaged in e-marketing, so in this chapter, and throughout the book, we give you a planning framework and checklists to evaluate and improve your current e-marketing practices or plan new initiatives.

The chapter is structured using a simple *aide-mémoire*, called **SOSTAC**®. SOSTAC® is used by thousands of professionals to produce all kinds of plans (marketing plans, corporate plans, advertising plans and e-marketing plans). In later chapters and, in particular, Chapter 10 we provide a step-by-step guide to creating an e-marketing plan. In this chapter, we'll use SOSTAC® to provide a structure for an initial review.

INTRODUCING SOSTAC® PLANNING FOR E-MARKETING

SOSTAC® stands for Situation Analysis, Objectives, Strategy, Tactics, Actions and Control (Figure 1.1). It is described in more detail in Smith (1998, 2001) and Smith *et al.* (1999, 2004) who note that each stage is not discrete, but there is some overlap during each stage of planning – previous stages may be revisited and refined, as indicated by the reverse arrows in Figure 1.1. For creating an e-marketing plan, the planning stages are:

- **Situation Analysis** means 'where are we now?' (In the context of this chapter, this includes definition of 'e' terms, growth in users and change in the marketplace, as well as examples of good and bad e-marketing.)
- **Objectives** means 'where do we want to be?' Why bother going online, what are the benefits, what is the purpose of going to all of this effort? We describe five main objectives, reasons or benefits of being online which you should exploit.
- **Strategy** means 'how do we get there?' Strategy summarizes how to fulfil the objectives. What stage of 'e'volution and level of database integration is required, what segments and positioning should drive the overall marketing mix and the promotional mix, right down to the different **contact strategies** for different segments, and which e-tools should be selected? Getting your e-strategy right is crucial. As Kenichi Ohmae says (Ohmae, 1999), 'there's no point rowing harder if you're rowing in the wrong direction'.
- **Tactics** reviews the tactical e-tools and the details of the marketing mix which is covered in Chapter 2 and the communications mix which is covered in Chapters 6 and 7.
- **Actions** refers to action plans and project management skills – essential skills we won't go into in this chapter.
- **Control** looks at how you know if your e-efforts are working, and what improvements can be made – again, we won't delve in too deeply in this chapter.

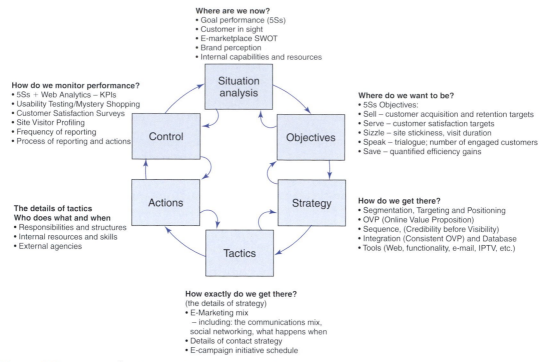

Where are we now?
• Goal performance (5Ss)
• Customer in sight
• E-marketplace SWOT
• Brand perception
• Internal capabilities and resources

How do we monitor performance?
• 5Ss + Web Analytics – KPIs
• Usability Testing/Mystery Shopping
• Customer Satisfaction Surveys
• Site Visitor Profiling
• Frequency of reporting
• Process of reporting and actions

Where do we want to be?
• 5Ss Objectives:
• Sell – customer acquisition and retention targets
• Serve – customer satisfaction targets
• Sizzle – site stickiness, visit duration
• Speak – trialogue; number of engaged customers
• Save – quantified efficiency gains

The details of tactics
Who does what and when
• Responsibilities and structures
• Internal resources and skills
• External agencies

How do we get there?
• Segmentation, Targeting and Positioning
• OVP (Online Value Proposition)
• Sequence, (Credibility before Visibility)
• Integration (Consistent OVP) and Database
• Tools (Web, functionality, e-mail, IPTV, etc.)

How exactly do we get there?
(the details of strategy)
• E-Marketing mix
  – including: the communications mix,
  social networking, what happens when
• Details of contact strategy
• E-campaign initiative schedule

Figure 1.1 SOSTAC® planning framework. SOSTAC ® is a registered trade mark of PR Smith (www.prsmith.org)

Introduction

The SOSTAC® planning framework is used to structure this chapter. SOSTAC® is:

- **Situation analysis** – where are we now?
- **Objectives** – where do we want to be?
- **Strategy** – how do we get there?
- **Tactics** – which tactical tools do we use to implement strategy?
- **Actions** – which action plans are required to implement strategy?
- **Control** – how do we manage the strategy process?

1.2 Situation – the wired-up world

Let's consider the current situation of e-marketing – where the marketplace migrates into the **electronic marketspace**. How significant is this change? The Internet is continuing to grow rapidly and seamlessly across borders and into an online world already inhabited by over a billion customers. Given its scale and the benefits it offers to these customers and businesses, it is a big part of the future of all businesses. The Internet is far more than 'just another channel to market' – a misguided phrase that is heard surprisingly frequently. We will explain how the Internet can and should be used to transform how a business communicates with its audience and delivers enhanced brand experiences.

Despite the vast number of people (and businesses) buying online, don't you think it's a little weird when you consider that millions, billions and even trillions of dollars, pounds and euros pass seamlessly through wires interconnecting lots of devices all around the world? Google has built a billion dollar business simply by charging for mouse clicks, some costing up to $50! Perhaps it's even weirder when you consider that in future a lot of it will be wireless. In China there are already more mobile phone subscribers than the population of the US, while meanwhile in Japan, surveys by Comscore show that usage of the web by mobile nearly equals that by PC.

Some say it's 'surreal' others say it's 'sublime' and others again say 'ridiculous' when you consider that the direction of many of these millions, billions and trillions will be determined by **robots, info-bots, shopping-bots, portals** and **infomediaries**. The future Weird Wired World may sound like a wonder of convenience when our refrigerators negotiate the best price for new supplies or a washing machine chooses the best utility supplier for any particular wash – courtesy of embedded chips complete with Internet access. Or is it introducing unnecessary complexity for which demand is limited? Consumers often take longer to embrace new ideas than technologists or some marketers expect.

THE CONNECTED WORLD

And it's not just washing machines, but rather anything and everything can be wired up, or connected, to the Internet. The most common way of accessing the Internet remains the desktop computer or laptop. What are the up-and-coming ways of accessing the Internet? **Interactive digital TV**, interactive radio, interactive kiosks, mobile phones, palm tops, planes, trains and automobiles all access the Internet. The **convergence** of these new digital access devices is described in more detail in Chapter 5. In fact the average luxury car today has more computing power in it than the rocket that landed on the moon. Cars can also be 'connected' so that they can alert roadside repair companies to your location before you actually break down. Just about anything can be wired up, courtesy of the powerful combination of computer chips and cordless or wireless technology, including higher speed data transfer protocols such as **3G**, HSDPA (High Speed Data Packet Access), **WAP** technology (Wireless Application Protocol) for rendering simple content and **Bluetooth** for data transfer between mobile phones and other hand-held devices.

RESEARCH, TRENDS AND FORECASTS

To effectively plan your e-marketing to predict your results, you need to tap into the wealth of research about current Internet usage and future trends. In Table 1.1 we summarize a selection of free and paid for services to help you analyze your e-marketplace. In Chapter 3 on e-models and Chapter 4 on e-customers we explain how you should analyze your online marketplace to help understand and exploit the online potential.

Table 1.1 Tools for assessing your e-marketplace

Service	Description
1 **Alexa** (www.alexa.com). Free tool, see also www.compete.com. Also use the Google syntax related:domain.com to find related sites.	Free service owned by Amazon which provides traffic ranking of individual sites compared to all sites. Works best for sites in Top 100 000. Sample dependent on users of the Alexa toolbar.
2 **Hitwise** (www.hitwise.com). Paid tool, but free research available at http://weblogs.hitwise.com.	Paid service available in some countries to compare audience and search/site usage. Works through monitoring IP traffic to different sites through ISPs.
3 **Netratings** (www.netratings.com). Paid tool.	Panel service based on at-home and at-work users who have agreed to have their web usage tracked by software. Top rankings on site gives examples of most popular sites in several countries.
4 **Comscore** (www.comscore.com). Paid tool.	A similar panel service to Netratings, but focusing on the US and UK. A favoured tool for media planners.
5 **ABCE Database** (www.abce.org.uk). Free tool. (Choose ABCE Database).	The Audit Bureau of Circulation (Electronic) gives free access to its database of portals (not destination sites) who have agreed to have their sites audited to prove traffic volumes to advertisers.
6 **Search keyphrase analysis tools. Compilation available from** www.davechaffey.com/seo-keyword-tools.	Tools such as the Google Keyword tool and Google Traffic Estimator can be used to assess the popularity of brands and their products reflected by the volume of search terms typed into Google and other search engines.
7 **Forrester** (www.forrester.com).	Paid research service offering reports on Internet usage and best practice in different vertical sectors such as financial services, retail and travel. Free research summaries available in press release section and on its marketing blog (http://blogs.forrester.com).
8 **Gartner** (www.gartner.com).	Another research service, in this case focusing on technology adoption within companies. Also see Jupiter research (www.jupiterresearch.com) who often have good reports on e-mail marketing best practice.

Table 1.1   *(Continued)*

Service	Description
9 **IAB** (US:www.iab.net, UK:www.iab.uk.net, Europe: www.iabeurope.eu).	The Internet or Interactive Advertising Bureau has research focusing on investment in different digital media channels, in particular display ads and search marketing. In 2007, the UK was leading in online ad expenditure, accounting for over 15% of ad investment.
10 **IMRG** (www.imrg.org).	The Internet Media in Retail Group has compilations on online e-commerce expenditure in the UK which, as of the time of writing, was averaging around £5 billion per month or over 10% of all retail spend.

SECTION SUMMARY 1.2

Situation – the wired-up world

More customers are spending an increasing part of their lives in the virtual world. They are using automated tools to find the products that best meet their needs. Marketers need to analyze demand by consumers for online services and respond to customers' needs in this new wired-up world.

1.3   Situation – B2C, B2B, C2B and C2C

The options for digital communications between a business and its customers are summarized in Figure 1.2. Traditionally, the bulk of Internet transactions are from business-to-business or industrial and commercial markets known as **B2B** (business-to-business) and consumer markets known as business-to-consumer (**B2C**) markets (like cars and cola).

B2B AND B2C

This is where the bulk of online business occurs. Most estimates suggest that B2B companies will reap ten times more revenue than their B2C counterparts. Once upon a time marketing used to learn from the **FMCG** manufacturers like Guinness, Coca-Cola and Heinz, while industrial marketing, or B2B marketing, was considered by some to be less exciting. This is now no longer the case.

In the online world, B2B is already much bigger than B2C. Almost ten years ago General Electric made the decision to procure $1 billion worth of purchases online in year one,

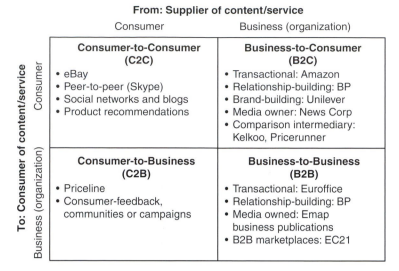

Figure 1.2   Options for online communications between an organization and its customers

followed by $3 billion in year two, followed by total procurement online. Cisco systems announced many years ago that they will no longer do business with suppliers who can't take orders over the web. Major organizations, such as government councils, are also moving online, e.g. from 2005 the British Government's Local District Councils only procure their goods and services online.

Several years ago Ford and General Motors combined forces through the **B2B marketplace** Covisint (www.covisint.com) and moved their then $300 and $500 billion dollar supply chains online. This created great hype about the potential of online B2B auctions which didn't really realize expectations. Today, Covisint is no longer an open marketplace used by a handful of motor manufacturers, instead it is a software provider which helps over 30 000 companies in automotive and other sectors, such as Healthcare, manage communications with their suppliers. In 2003, Covisint sold its auctions business to Ariba which now has 120 000 suppliers in its network – a surprisingly small number for the largest online network. Auctions or 'sourcing events' are only part of a range of 'spend management solutions' available to buyers. Today the benefits of online B2B commerce are more about identifying products in electronic catalogues from a range of suppliers, selecting the best option and then managing the paperwork and workflow electronically. The eBay auction model has not really taken hold in B2B, although eBay do have their own B2B auction facility (http://business. ebay.com, Figure 1.3) selling products as diverse as tractors and office furniture, where there is an annual turnover of $2 billion in goods. But this is a small fraction of all products sold which had a Gross Merchandized Volume (GMV) of $52 billion in 2006. Remember that eBay isn't just about auctions, with 40% of its turnover now arising from fixed price sales. However, the marketplace model isn't dead, it just didn't grow as quickly as many anticipated.

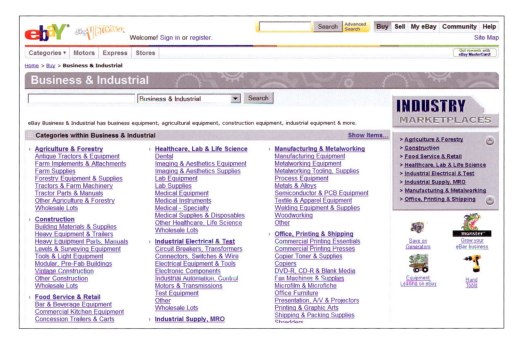

Figure 1.3 Product categories at eBay business (http://business.ebay.com)

C2C AND C2B

Whether B2C or B2B, don't forget C2C and C2B. C2C models have proved one of the most disruptive examples of online business technology. An early indication of the popularity of C2C was the growth of online consumer auctions at eBay and niche communities focusing on interests such as sport, films or pastimes. More recently, a dramatic growth in C2C interactions has been fuelled by the growth of **social networks** such as Bebo, Facebook and MySpace and their business equivalent LinkedIn which we examine in more detail in Chapter 3. Social interactions are now so important that they are reducing consumption of other forms of digital media and traditional media, so all companies need to develop a strategy to engage these consumers.

Customer-to-business models may play a significant role in some B2B or B2C sectors. In this model, a potential buyer approaches a marketplace of sellers who then compete for the sale. In the consumer market Priceline (www.priceline.com) and other price comparison sites such as Kelkoo follow this model. In B2B, the Covisint and Ariba services referred to above have C2B options. C2B also involves customers developing their own content online, which is known as **user generated content (UGC)** where businesses facilitate it. For example, many smaller travel companies, such as Supabreaks (www.supabreaks.com) and TravelRepublic (www.travel-republic.co.uk) have exploited the approach originally adopted by Trip Advisor (www.tripadvisor.com). Do you have a plan for UGC?

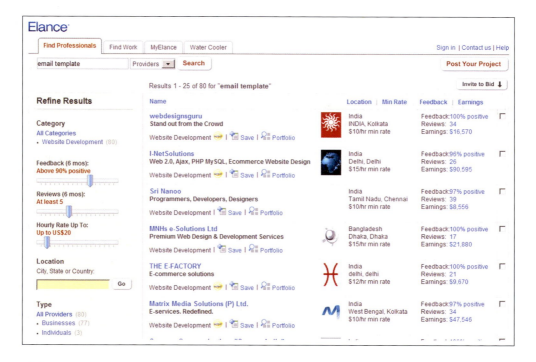

Figure 1.4   Selecting a freelance e-mail template designer at elance (www.elance.com)

TYPES OF ONLINE PRESENCE

When assessing the relevance and potential of e-marketing for a business, remember that different business types offer different opportunities and challenges. Chaffey *et al.* (2006) identify five main types of online presence or components possible as part of a site:

1 **Transactional e-commerce site**. Manufacturers or e-retailers provide products available for purchase online. The main business contribution is through sale of these products. The sites also support the business by providing information for consumers who prefer to purchase products offline.

Visit these examples: an end-product manufacturer such as Vauxhall (www.vauxhall.co.uk) or online retailers such as Amazon (www.amazon.com).

2 **Services-oriented relationship building web site**. Provides information to stimulate purchase and build relationships. Products are not typically available for purchase online. Information is provided through the web site, along with e-newsletters, to inform purchasing decisions. The main business contribution is through encouraging offline sales and generating enquiries or leads from potential customers. Such sites also help by adding value for existing customers by providing them with information of interest to them.

Visit these examples: B2B examples are management consultants such as PricewaterhouseCoopers (www.pwcglobal.com) and Accenture (www.accenture.com). A B2C example is the UK portal for energy supplier British Gas (www.house.co.uk). Most car manufacturer sites may be services-oriented rather than transactional.

3 **Brand-building site**. Provides an experience to support the brand. Products are not typically available for online purchase, although merchandise may be. The main focus is to support the brand by developing an online experience of the brand. They are typical for low-value, high-volume, fast-moving consumer goods (FMCG brands).

Visit these examples: Tango (www.tango.com) and Guinness (www.guinness.com).

4 **Portal or media site**. These **intermediaries** provide information or news about a range of topics. Portal refers to a gateway to information with a range of services such as a search engine, directory, news, shopping comparison, etc. This is information both on the site and links through to other sites. These are the three different types of **destination sites** described above. Portals have a diversity of options for generating revenue, including advertising, commission-based sales and sale of customer data (lists).

Visit these examples: Yahoo! (www.yahoo.com) (B2C) and FT.com (www.ft.com) or Silicon (www.silicon.com) (B2B).

5 **Social network or community site**. A site enabling community interactions between different consumers (C2C model). Typical interactions including posting comments and replies to comments, sending messages, rating content and tagging content in particular categories. Well-known examples include Bebo, Facebook, MySpace and Linked-In. Other startups also have a social network element such as Delicious (social bookmarking or rating web pages), Digg (comment on blog postings), Flickr (image tagging), Technorati (blog postings) and YouTube (videos). In addition to distinct social network sites such as these, they can also be integrated into other site types, in particular into media owned sites. Large social networks such as Facebook or MySpace are effectively media owners and advertising is their main revenue source.

Note that these are not clear-cut categories of Internet sites since many businesses will have sites which blend transactional, services-oriented, brand-building, media and social network components, depending upon the range of products they offer. Virgin (www.virgin.com) is an example of one such company.

> ### E-MARKETING EXCELLENCE
>
> **Argos and RS Components exploit new markets**
>
> When catalogue retailer Argos (www.argos.co.uk) launched its web site, it found that sales were not limited to its core B2C market. Around 10% of the site's customers were B2B – the web provided a more convenient purchase point than the previous retail chain. It has since changed its product offering to accommodate this new segment. Conversely B2B company RS Components found a significant proportion of sales were B2C, so reaching new customers via its online presence.

SECTION SUMMARY 1.3

Situation – B2C, B2B, C2B and C2C

E-marketing involves collaboration between different parties that can be characterized by four main interactions:

- B2C – business-to-consumer (B2C e-tail is arguably the most talked about)
- B2B – business-to-business (less talked about, but with the most transactions)
- C2C – customer-to-customer interactions (best known as consumer auctions, but can also be achieved as B2C and B2B social networks or communities)
- C2B – customer-to-business (novel buying models where customers approach the business on their own terms or generate content to support the business).

1.4 Situation – e-definitions

There are many terms with the e-prefix and many different interpretations. Within any organization, developing a common understanding for terms such as e-commerce, e-business and e-marketing, and how they interrelate and who will manage them, is important to enable development of a consistent, coherent strategy.

E-commerce is primarily about selling online or the ability to transact online. This includes e-tailing, online banking and shopping – which involve transactions where buyers actually buy and shoppers actually shop. Some suggest that e-commerce includes all online transactions such as a responding to an enquiry or an online catalogue search.

E-commerce itself does not include the marketing nor the back office administration processes that are required to actually run a business. **E-business** has a broader perspective. It involves the automation of all the business processes in the value chain – from procurement or purchasing of raw materials, to production, stock holding, distribution and logistics, sales and marketing, after sales, invoicing, debt collection and more. Companies such as Covisint and Ariba, who we referred to earlier, provide e-business services. **E-business** creates the ability to run a business online. This includes e-marketing and e-commerce.

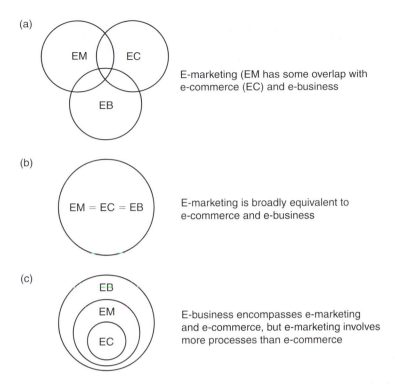

(a)

E-marketing (EM has some overlap with e-commerce (EC) and e-business

(b)

E-marketing is broadly equivalent to e-commerce and e-business

(c)

E-business encompasses e-marketing and e-commerce, but e-marketing involves more processes than e-commerce

Figure 1.5   Three alternative relationships between e-marketing, e-commerce and e-business

E-marketing is at the heart of e-business . . . getting closer to customers and understanding them better, adding value to products, widening distribution channels and boosting sales through running e-marketing campaigns using **digital media channels** such as search marketing, online advertising and affiliate marketing which we will explain later in this chapter. It also includes using the website to facilitate customer leads, sales and managing after sales service. As with mainstream marketing, e-marketing is a way of thinking, a way of putting the customer at the heart of all online activities, e.g. getting different user groups to test your web site on different browsers in different settings on different connections.

Figure 1.5 summarizes the definition of e-marketing, e-commerce and e-business. It considers three of the possible alternative relationships between e-marketing, e-commerce and e-business. Which do you think is most appropriate? We would suggest (c) is most appropriate although often the terms are used interchangeably.

E-MARKETING – THE DYNAMIC DIALOGUE

Simply put, e-marketing is marketing online whether via web sites, online ads, opt-in e-mail, interactive kiosks, interactive TV or mobiles. It involves getting close to customers, understanding them better and maintaining a dialogue with them. It is broader than e-commerce since it is not limited to transactions between an organization and its stakeholders, but includes all processes related to marketing.

This dynamic dialogue is at the heart of good marketing. E-marketing builds on the database (of customers and prospects) and creates a constant flow of communications between customers and suppliers and between customers themselves. Dynamic means what it says. Dynamic does not mean static web pages. It's a two-way flow of communications – an ongoing discussion between customer and supplier. Remember that e-marketing also involves using electronic communications to manage the internal marketing process and better understand customers, including marketing research and analysis.

What David Siegel said in the dot.com days still holds true:

> *'E-marketing is not about building a web site, but building a web business . . . harmonizing the power of customers'. Siegel (2000)*

E-marketing can help create a business which is customer led . . . where the customer participates – through a constant dialogue, a dynamic dialogue, expressing interests, requesting products and services, suggesting improvements, giving feedback . . . where ultimately, the customer drives the business.

PRACTICAL E-MARKETING TIP

Do you right touch?

Savvy web marketers understand the importance of building an integrated multi-channel **touch or contact strategy** which delivers customized communications to consumers by search ads, e-mail and web recommendations and promotions. Every customer interaction or response to a communication should be followed up by a series of relevant communications delivered by the right combination of channels (web, e-mail, phone, direct mail) to elicit a response or further dialogue. This is contextual marketing, where the aim is to deliver relevant messages which fit the current context of what the customer is interested in according to the searches they have performed, the type of content they have viewed or the products they have recently purchased.

We call this **right touching**:

Right Touching is:
*A **Multi-channel Communications Strategy***
*Customized for **Individual Prospects** and **Customers** forming **segments***
*Across a **defined customer lifecycle***
Which. . .
*Delivers the **Right Message***
*Featuring the **Right Value Proposition** (product, service or experience)*
*With the **Right Tone***
*At the **Right Time***

> With the **Right Frequency** and **Interval**
> Using the **Right Media/Communications channels**
> **To achieve. . .**
> **Right balance of value** between both parties

You can see that Right Touching is not easy; all the permutations mean that businesses often get it wrong. That's why we think it's one of the biggest challenges for companies across both customer acquisition, retention and growth. For now, review how well you 'right touch' your prospects and customers. You should review aggregate open rates, clickthrough rates and sales rates across different segments over a long-term period of 3-months-plus to see how well you engage different audiences. We return to this topic in Chapter 8 on E-CRM where we explain how to develop the right contact strategy.

E-MARKETING CHECKLIST – RIGHT TOUCHING

To what extent are you incorporating right-touching into your e-marketing? Use this checklist from customer acquisition to retention:

☑ 1 *Search marketing:* when a prospect uses a search engine to search for a company or brand name or a specific category or product, a paid search ad from the company or an affiliate should explain an appropriate value proposition and direct them to the right product page. Alternatively, if the site is well optimized a relevant message featuring your brand should feature high in the natural search results, as explained in Chapter 7.

☑ 2 *Behavioural targeting or online advertising:* when a prospect interacts with content on a media site or searches on a specific term, a sequence of follow-up ads known as **behavioural retargeting** should be displayed as they visit other sites within a network and the destination site of the merchant paying for the advertising.

☑ 3 *Multi-touches across different digital media channels for acquisition.* Use tracking through **web analytics** to understand the sequence and combination of different digital media channels (search, **affiliates**, display ads or **aggregators**) which generate the most cost-effective response. How do you allocate the channel to the outcome? Do you simply do 'last click wins' or do you weight across the different touch points as we discuss in Chapter 3?

☑ 4 *Customer lifecycle model and welcome strategy*: when a prospect subscribes to an e-mail newsletter, enquires about a service or makes a first purchase, a welcome communications strategy should be in place which uses a sequence of e-mail and possibly personalized web recommendations, direct mail and phone communications to educate the customer about the brand or product and generate the initial sale. This should aim at building a relationship and then developing commitment from first time visitor, to repeat visitor to qualified prospect, to first time customer and then a repeat customer, so increasing customer lifetime value.

☑ **5** *Reducing online attrition*: when a shopper abandons their shopping basket, a combination of communications should seek to win them back. Alternatively, after a quotation, for example for a car policy, follow-up e-mails should remind customers about the benefits of taking out the policy.

☑ **6** *Delivering relevant recommendations for retention and growth.* When an existing customer returns to a site, a personalized container should be available on every page to deliver relevant personalized promotions. Amazon recommendations are the best known examples, another is office supplier Euroffice (www.euroffice.co.uk, Figure 1.6) which uses OpenAds, an open source 'promo server' to deliver relevant recommendations to prospects and customers according to their position in the lifecycle, segment and previous purchases. Similarly panels within e-mails can achieve the same.

☑ **7** *Following up on customer product or promotion interest.* When a customer clicks on a link in an e-mail or interacts repeatedly with content on a site is there an automated workflow triggering an e-mail, direct mail or phone reminder about the offer?

Figure 1.6   Euroffice Office Supplies serving B2C and B2B markets (www.euroffice.co.uk)

☑ 8 *Getting the frequency right*. Effective Right Touching requires that messages stay engaging, relevant and do not become too intrusive or too repetitive. So you should put limits on the maximum number of e-mails that are sent in a period (e.g. one a month or one a week) and the interval between them (e.g. an interval of at least 3 days).

☑ 9 *Getting the channel right*. Right channelling means using the best channel(s) for the customer, which fits their preferences and the right channel for the company, which gives them the best combination of cost and response. It means that for some customers you may be able to upweight e-mail communications because they interact and respond to them, so reducing costs of direct mail. But other customers on an e-mail list may not respond to or dislike e-mail and so direct mail is upweighted to them.

☑ 10 *Getting the offer right*. Offers will vary in effectiveness according to the audience targeted and this will be indicated by their profiles and customer journeys indicated by the media and content they have consumed. Can you identify the Next Best Product for previous purchasers? So right-touching requires that testing is built-in to deliver the right messages and right sequences of communications for different audiences.

THE CUSTOMER-LED BUSINESS

Now we can leave B2B and B2C models and see where e-marketing creates a new dynamic C2B model. A customer-to-business (C2B) model is one in which customers drive the business, freely communicate and are involved with new product suggestions, pricing, design and service. The customers help to shape the future of the business.

Although some different business models and marketing models are emerging, the same basic marketing principles apply whether online or offline:

- get close to customers, listen to them
- involve them
- serve them
- add value
- find the best ones
- nurture them into lifelong customers and replicate them
- and of course test, test, test, measure and improve.

To help define e-marketing in more detail, let's look at what marketing is. The UK Chartered Institute of Marketing define marketing as:

> *'The management process responsible for identifying, anticipating and satisfying customer needs profitably'.*

> ### What does e-marketing involve?

Now let's consider how e-marketing can fulfil the definition of marketing, if properly implemented. Let's break up the definition into manageable chunks:

E-marketing can identify, anticipate and satisfy customer needs efficiently.

Taking a web site as a major part of e-marketing, consider how a web site can fulfil the definition of marketing (identify, anticipate and satisfy customer needs profitably). It can:

- *Identify* needs from customer comments, enquiries, requests and complaints solicited via the web site's e-mail facility, bulletin boards, chat rooms and of course, sales patterns (seeing what's selling and what's not), and observing new customer groupings identified by data-mining through customer data, sales and interests (recorded using **web analytics** which reveal insights into interests determined by pages visited). Even **online surveys** asking how to improve the site or requesting suggestions for product improvements or new products identify current and sometimes future customer needs. Finally there is a proliferation of online secondary sources of research, many of which provide free in-depth insights into customer needs.

- *Anticipate* customer needs by asking customers questions and engaging them in a dynamic dialogue built on trust. And of course a little bit of what Amazon call **collaborative filtering** helps Amazon to identify and anticipate what customers might like given that buyers of similar books have similar interests. Customers often welcome suggested books from Amazon. And today's sophisticated profiling techniques allow many companies to do their own **data mining** to discover and anticipate buyers' needs, like Tesco's feta cheese, beer and nappy sales. This is old technology. More recent sophisticated **profiling** technology allows some companies to analyze your interests without even knowing your name – courtesy of the **cookie** – a bit of code sent to your PC (with your permission) when you visit certain sites. So without knowing your name, it knows your interests. It recognizes your PC and records which types of sites (interests) you have. So when you visit a web site and an unusually relevant banner ad drops down, this is no coincidence – cookies have anticipated your desires and needs.

- *Satisfy* needs with prompt responses, punctual deliveries, order status updates, helpful reminders, after sales services and added value services combined with the dynamic dialogue. The dialogue maintains permission to continue communicating and then adds value by delivering useful content in the right context (right time and right amount).

- *Efficiently* means in an automated way (or partially automated) . . . an efficient, yet hopefully not impersonal, way (i.e. it allows tailor-made technology to increase the marketer's memory as the relationship effectively blossoms during the customer's life – increasing **lifetime value**). 'Efficiently' probably should mean efficiently and effectively, as otherwise it could alienate the vast armies of not-for-profit marketers.

And if the web site is integrated with customer relationship management (**CRM**) systems and **mass customization** then the relationship deepens and needs are completely satisfied in a very efficient automated two-way process. This also, of course, provides some protection from the inevitable onslaught of competition.

The IDM defines digital marketing

You will often hear e-marketing and digital marketing used interchangeably. Practitioners often refer to e-marketing or Internet marketing. But digital marketing is increasingly used by some agencies and trade publications such as *New Media Age* (www.nma.co.uk) and *Revolution* (www.revolutionmagazine.com). The IDM (www.theidm.com) has created qualifications in digital marketing ratified by its Digital Marketing Council who have defined digital marketing as follows. You will see the similarity with our definition of e-marketing.

Digital marketing is:

Applying . . .   Digital technologies which form online channels to market . . . (web, e-mail, databases, plus mobile/wireless and digital TV and more recent innovations including blogs, feeds, podcasts and social networks

to . . .   Contribute to marketing activities aimed at achieving profitable acquisition and retention of customers . . . (within a multi-channel buying process and customer lifecycle)

through . . .   Recognizing the strategic importance of digital technologies and developing a planned approach to improve customer knowledge (of their profiles, behaviour, value and loyalty drivers), then delivering integrated targeted communications and online services that match their individual needs.

The first part of the definition illustrates the range of access platforms and communication tools that form the online channels which e-marketers use to build and develop relationships with customers. E-marketers have to keep up to date to select the most relevant e-tools such as **Web 2.0** or even **Web 3.0** which we review in Chapter 3. Web 2.0 refers to a collection of web services which facilitate certain behaviours online such as community participation through **social networks** such as Facebook and MySpace together with creation of user-generated content, rating and tagging.

The second part of the definition shows that it should not be the technology that drives e-marketing, but the business returns from gaining new customers and maintaining relationships with existing customers. It also emphasizes how e-marketing does not occur in isolation, but is most effective when it is integrated with other communications channels such as phone, direct mail or face-to-face. Online channels should also be used to support the whole buying process from pre-sale to sale to post-sale and further development of customer relationships. The final part of the definition summarizes approaches to customer-centric e-marketing. It shows how it should be based on knowledge of customer needs developed by researching their characteristics, behaviour, what they value, what keeps them loyal and then delivering tailored web and e-mail communications.

Situation – e-definitions

E-commerce generally refers to paid-for transactions, whether B2C or B2B, but others include all communications between customers and business. E-business is broader, including e-commerce, and is a means to optimize all business processes that are part of the internal and external value chain. E-marketing is best considered as how e-tools such as web sites, CRM systems and databases can be used to get closer to customers – to be able to identify, anticipate and satisfy their needs efficiently and effectively.

1.5   Situation – sloppy e-marketing

Identifying, anticipating and satisfying customer needs is all simple common sense. Yet common sense is not common. Sloppy e-marketing has become commonplace . . . broken sites, delayed deliveries, impersonal responses, non-responses.

Whether it's unclear objectives, lack of strategy or simply lousy execution, good e-marketing is still relatively rare.

Take a well known American toy company. Many years ago they were allegedly sued for late fulfilment at Christmas. Several families who purchased online were disappointed by the non-arrival of Christmas presents. They sued. The site lost sales, irritated customers and damaged the brand. However, today, many online marketers have improved their fulfilment to avoid these problems as the report below shows.

E-MARKETING INSIGHT

E-commerce fulfilment improves

However, a recent report (Snow Valley, 2007) suggests that fulfilment has improved. Over half of the retailers we assessed delivered orders within two working days as part of their standard delivery service. This was a major improvement on 2006. Over 90% of orders arrived within the timeframes given on the retailer's website. Nearly two thirds now give the customer a choice about when their goods will be delivered, whether offering a next-day service or a choice of specific dates and times.

Many other web sites damage the brand when they don't respond. They invite e-mails through the web site, but then do not respond quickly. Many top companies don't reply quickly to incoming e-mails and in some cases they never reply at all.

Other sites frustrate customers with poor navigation or not answering visitors' typical questions on the site. When they turn to e-mail, responses are often slow or inaccurate. Look at these figures from Tranversal (2006) surveys of two sectors:

1 Travel: Average number of questions answered online: 1.35 out of 10 (2005 findings: 1.2); Percentage of companies that responded to e-mail correctly: 40% (2005 findings: 2%); Average e-mail response time: 66 hours (2005 findings: 42 hours); Percentage with customer search: 50% (2005 findings: 30%).

2 Banking: Average number of questions answered online: 2.5 out of 10 (2005 findings: 3); Percentage of companies that responded to e-mail correctly: 40% (2005 findings: 55%; Average e-mail response time: 22 hours (2005 findings: 17 hours); Percentage with customer FAQ pages: 50% (2005 findings: 60%); Percentage with customer search: 60% (2005 findings: 40%).

Research shows very high attrition rates of customers successfully completing purchases due to different causes of sloppy e-marketing (Figure 1.7). The web sites of 80% of Britain's top 50 retailers perform inconsistently with slow response times, timeouts and errors (Leyden, 2004). Despite online sales outgrowing offline sales in many sectors, separate research reveals that 40% of the UK's top retailers spend too little on maintaining and developing their online operations (Armitt, 2004).

Chapter 3 on changing e-models shows why many of the old world models, business models, marketing models, distribution models, pricing models and advertising models do not fit the new world of e-marketing. New models are required and the e-models chapter invites you to create some new models and examine other new emerging models. Whether marketing offline or online, do not forget the basics of good business – carefully thought-through ideas, attention to detail and excellent execution can be the difference between success and failure.

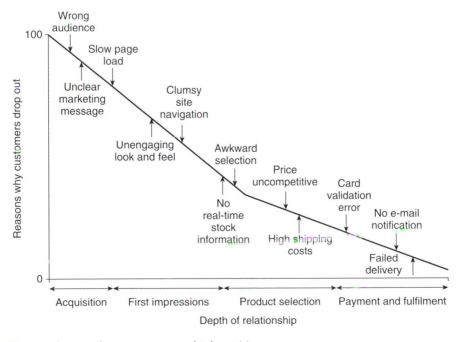

Figure 1.7   E-marketing sloppiness causes high attrition rates

Situation – sloppy e-marketing

There are many examples of poor e-marketing. This may result from unclear objectives, lack of strategy or simply lousy execution. Marketers should assess and minimize the risks before embarking on e-marketing.

1.6 Objectives

One reason why many new businesses, and in particular new e-businesses, go horribly wrong is often because objectives are not clearly agreed and companies keen to get on with it jump straight to tactical e-tools (such as web sites and banner ads) without first agreeing clearly defined objectives and razor sharp strategies.

The following sections on objectives cover the purpose or reasons why businesses go online. They examine the kind of clear objectives and goals that will drive good e-marketing.

So before making the change to e-marketing first be clear: Why do you want to go online? What are the objectives? What advantages and benefits are expected?

You must be clear why you're getting into e-marketing and the areas on which you want to focus as you improve your e-marketing. What are the objectives? Apart from competitive paranoia? What are the benefits? There are five broad benefits, reasons or objectives of e-marketing:

- Grow sales (through wider distribution, promotion and sales).
- Add value (give customers extra benefits online).
- Get closer to customers (by tracking them, asking them questions, creating a dialogue, learning about them).
- Save costs (of service, promotions, sales transactions and administration, print and post) and so increase profits on transactions.
- Extend the brand online. Reinforce brand values in a totally new medium.

There is a section on each of these 'objectives'.

All these e-marketing objectives can be summarized as the 5Ss – Sell, Serve, Speak, Save and Sizzle. These are covered in the next five sections. Once you have defined (and quantified) 'where you are going' (your objectives), you can then decide 'how to get there' – Strategy. First consider objectives.

You should set specific goals for objectives in each of the five areas, as shown in Table 1.2.

Table 1.2   Objectives for the 5Ss of e-marketing

Benefit of e-marketing	How benefit is delivered	Typical objectives
Sell – Grow sales	Achieved through wider distribution to customers you can't readily service offline or perhaps through a wider product range than in-store or lower prices compared to other channels.	• Achieve 10% of sales online in market • Increase online sales for product by 20% in year
Serve – Add value	Achieved through giving customers extra benefits online or inform product development through online dialogue and feedback.	• Increase interaction with different content on site • Increase dwell time duration on site by 10% (sometimes known as stickiness) • Increase number of customers actively using online services (at least once per month) to 30%
Speak – Get closer to customers	This is creating a two way dialogue through web and e-mail forms and polls and conducting online market research through formal surveys and informally monitoring chat rooms to learn about them. Also speak through reaching them online through PR.	• Grow e-mail coverage to 50% of current customer database • Survey 1000 customers online each month • Increase visitors to community site section or increase ratings/reviews and discussions by 5%
Save – Save costs	Achieved through online e-mail communications, sales and service transactions to reduce staff, print and postage costs.	• Generate 10% more sales for same communications budget • Reduce cost of direct marketing by 15% through e-mail • Increase web self-service to 40% of all service enquiries and reduce overall cost-to-serve by 10%
Sizzle – Extend the brand online	Achieved through providing a new proposition and new experience online while at the same time appearing familiar.	• Add two new significant enhancements to the customer online experience • Rework online value proposition messaging • Improve branding metrics such as: Brand awareness, Reach, Brand favorability and Purchase intent

Ultralase grow visits and sales through clearly defined objectives

Ultralase (www.ultralase.com, Figure 1.8), is a company offering laser eye treatment – a high value consumer service. In 2003 their market was characterized by intense competition with other suppliers such as Optimax, Optical Express and AccuVision. Ultralase had relatively low brand awareness and was struggling with a long sales cycle and relatively uninformed customers. The main communications disciplines used were:

- Press
- Direct mail
- PR
- Brochures.

From 2004 onwards, they increased their digital expenditure and in 2006 at Ad Tech presented their achievements through their agency, Agency.com. These included:

- 10 million site visits per year
- 3.7 billion ad impressions (Jan to Sept 2006)
- Reach between 18 M and 22 M unique users per month
- Now the dominant online brand with a high brand awareness and a shorter sales cycle.

To achieve this, they developed clear objectives and used a customer-centric website focused on generating response through online leads or phone enquiries. They also invested in digital media channels to hit their growth targets including:

- Affiliate marketing
- Paid search marketing
- Display advertising
- E-mail marketing based on permission-based lead generation through offers on their website
- DVD brochures.

As we review the 5Ss we will relate them to Ultralase.

SECTION SUMMARY 1.6

Objectives

Organizations need to be clear about the objectives of e-marketing, so that the appropriate resources can be directed at achieving these objectives. A useful framework for developing objectives is the 5Ss of Sell, Serve, Speak, Save and Sizzle.

Figure 1.8   Ultralase web site (www.ultralase.com)

1.7   Objective – sell – using the Internet as a sales tool

Just about anything can be sold online, from books to bikes, jobs to jets, turbines to toys and chemicals to kidneys. A young boy recently tried to auction one of his kidneys on eBay. Bidders were waiting but fortunately the deal was scrapped when the online auction house realized what was happening. Therein lies one of the many cyber challenges – regulating what is reasonable and proper to sell. Although just about anything can be sold online, the Internet impacts some industries more than others, particularly education, entertainment and advisory services – many of which can be digitized and delivered down the line.

But even this is changing, as cyber sales rocket across industry sectors and types. We all know that companies like Dell and IBM sell millions of dollars of PCs online every day. In parallel, more and more industrial buying is shifting online. General Electric buy billions of dollars worth of raw materials only online. Ford and GM are merging their buying power to buy online. Companies must be able to sell or transact online to meet these customers' new online needs. A key objective to set is the **direct online revenue contribution** for different products and different markets. This defines the proportion of sales transactions completed online. For example, a bank might try to achieve 15% of its insurance sales online in the UK.

But remember that many other products and services are partly bought online. Shoppers browse online collecting information, prices and special offers before visiting stores and showrooms or picking up the phone to negotiate better deals. So **mixed-mode selling** is a must! Organizations have to be able to sell both online and offline. Therefore it is essential to accommodate those that want to buy online and those that want to just browse. Already BMW find approximately half of their test drives are generated from their web site, although a much smaller number of customers would want to purchase online. 'Clicks-and-mortar' organizations offer customers reassurance of a real presence (building/mortar) along with the easy accessibility of the net. So another objective to set is the **indirect online revenue contribution** – the proportion of sales that are influenced by digital communications. Ultralase will have objectives for the number of leads generated from the website either directly or by phone. A similar objective is the **reach** of the web site within its target audience. Ultralase will be able to work back to assess the number and cost of leads generated by different channels, such as paid search and display advertising.

E-MARKETING INSIGHT

Tagging value events to assess the influence of a website and digital channels on sales

The key types of outcomes or 'value events' such as Ezine registrations, enquiries or sales on a site that will be useful for a business should be defined. These value events are particularly important for a business-to-business vendor, or a consumer brand with non-transactional sites which don't sell products online. Pages on which these value events occur can be tagged through web analytics systems. For example, the free tool Google Analytics (www.google.com/analytics) allows you to set up 'conversion goals' by indicating which page(s) are valuable and you can then attribute a dollar value to each, e.g. $1 for a newsletter signup. You can then see which referring channels and content on the site influence sales and other goals. Alternatively, other web analytics systems allow scripting (coding) within the HTML of a page, sometimes known as '**spotlight tags**', to indicate whether it is a valuable page.

Typical value events include:

- Sale (by tagging a sales confirmation page)
- Lead (by tagging enquiry or document download form)
- Newsletter registration (tagged confirmation page)
- Searches (tagging a search results page)
- Product page views (tagging product pages)
- Product document downloads (tagging document download pages).

Don't forget offline value events such as sales generated by phone numbers. You should aim to track these through using unique phone numbers, perhaps for different parts of the site.

So why not take it to the next level and offer the web visitor who wants a real test-drive delivery of the vehicle for the weekend? Assuming the visitor is screened and fits the ideal profile and suitable insurance is taken out, wouldn't this close the sales cycle and accelerate mixed mode selling?

The real crunch may come when businesses realize the power of the Internet's potential for distribution – extending the availability of many products and services without physically having to display a product. Take British Airways London's Eye. The service could be extended and distributed to a much wider audience than London's immediate tourist market. Anyone around the world could log on to a live web cam (camera) and take the 30-minute virtual ride to enjoy stunning views at night or by day. This service could be revenue generating whilst promoting tourism simultaneously. Equally, the Louvre, the Pyramids and many more attractions can now extend their distribution of both the point of purchase (i.e. buying a ticket) and the point of consumption (enjoy the view from your home). Sales and distribution opportunities abound.

So online sales will continue to grow. But there are other additional benefits or objectives for e-marketing including serving, speaking, saving and sizzling. You can explore each of these at your leisure.

SELLING WHAT TO WHOM

There is a tendency, when setting online sales objectives, to use a low-risk approach of selling existing products into existing markets. This is the market penetration approach shown in Figure 1.9, which you may recognize as the Ansoff matrix – used by marketers for over 40 years to determine strategic priorities. We will see in later chapters that objectives should also be set for selling new digital products into new markets as appropriate.

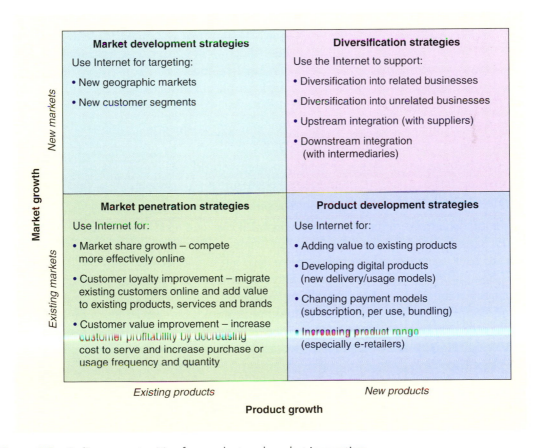

Figure 1.9   Online opportunities for product and market innovation

E-MARKETING EXCELLENCE

EasyJet sell

EasyJet was founded by Stelios Haji-Ioannou, the son of a Greek shipping tycoon, who reputedly used to 'hate the Internet'. In the mid-1990s Haji-Ioannou reportedly denounced the Internet as something 'for nerds', and swore that it wouldn't do anything for his business. However, he decided to experiment with a prototype site, and sat up and took notice when sales started to flow from the site. Based on early successes, easyJet decided to invest in the new channel and proactively convert customers to using it. To help achieve this they set an initial target of 30% of seats by the year 2000. By August 2000, the site accounted for 38% of ticket sales and by 2001 over 90% of seats. In 2007, phone sales were down to just single digit percentages, but significant enough for the phone channel to be retained. Of course, this success is based on the relative ease of converting direct phone-sale customers to online customers (Figure 1.10).

Figure 1.10   EasyJet site from 2001 showing incentive for online booking

SECTION SUMMARY 1.7

Objective – sell

The clearest benefit of e-marketing is the capability to sell from an online presence. Although this may not be practical for all products, an online presence is still important in supporting the buying decision leading to sales through traditional channels. You should use your web analytics system to tag different types of value event web pages which indicate your goals are being achieved. An online presence also offers opportunities to sell into new markets and reach particular segments.

1.8   Objective – serve – using the Internet as a customer-service tool

Another e-marketing objective is serving or adding value. How can a web site help customers, improve their experience or add value to their experience? Take newspapers. Newspapers can allow readers to create their own newspapers through personalization. They are no longer constrained by publication times, but can be accessed at any time. Their readers can set up alerts to notify them by e-mail as soon as an event breaks.

Ultralase provide a range of information to serve their audience and answer their questions as shown in Figure 1.8. These include a suitability checker, an online forum, a Q&A service, an info pack on a DVD and, of course, an appointment booker.

Another example: for customers who like their wines, the Marks & Spencer web site tests their visitors' knowledge of labels and grapes. And if, having chosen a wine, you're unsure of what to eat, Ragu's web site offers free recipes (and encourages visitors to send the recipe to a friend).

If, after dinner, you're not sure which toothpaste to use, visit the Mentadent web site where visitors can get sample toothpaste and free oral care advice. Visitors can even e-mail questions to a resident dentist.

And if life gets really interesting you might join a virtual club of fun seekers who not only give their permission but actually welcome e-mails from specific airlines informing them of last minute unsold seats on airline trips for the weekend. Or wouldn't it be nice if the 07.06 train to London is late or, worse still, cancelled, and someone texts you or calls you? This may save you a lot of time and frustration. Time is an increasingly scarce and valuable commodity. Some technology allows you to shift time, e.g. TiVo type or Sky Plus technology allows TV viewers to watch what they want when they want and not be subject to the limitations of a TV schedule.

E-MARKETING EXCELLENCE

Assessing online customer engagement

How effectively you serve and speak to your online audience is indicated by measures of online **customer engagement**, an important concept we will refer to throughout *eMarketing eXcellence*. You should assess customer engagement both for web site visitors and e-mail subscribers and break it down by different online segments such as different audience types and visitors referred from different sources such as search engines or online ads.

You should assess online customer engagement using the checklist shown in Table 1.3.

Table 1.3 Measures of online customer engagement

Engagement metric	Engagement tactic
1 **% of non-home page entry visits:** Your home page isn't necessarily the most important page on your site. People might arrive on other pages so make sure your messages are distributed throughout the site.	**Use run-of-site OVP messages:** Use promotional messages across the site that explain the essence of your offer (not just on the homepage).
2 **Bounce rate:** The percentage of visitors who enter a site or page and leave immediately.	**Use a run-of-site signup:** Place value-based messages and calls-to-action prominently throughout your site. For example see the newsletter sign-up on www.thomson.co.uk.
3 **Duration:** Duration on site, or better, pages per visit.	**Use heatmaps or overlays to assess engagement:** Tools like ClickDensity show what people click on and how soon. Helps you refine the clarity of your messages and calls-to-action.
4 **Marketing outcomes:** Assign values to outcomes/events and use them to assess the success rate, e.g. newsletter sign-up, 2 points; register CV, 5 points, etc.	**Get your scent right:** Experiment with design or language variations in hyperlinks and images to see what is attractive to visitors. For example, Dell have menu options to appeal to different business sizes.
5 **Micro or step conversion rates:** Assess the effectiveness of your site and drop-off at every stage of the customer acquisition-to-conversion lifecycle.	**Interactive sales advisors:** Replicate the steps you would use in a physical sales situation, considering types of questions asked, etc., and tailor responses to visitors accordingly. If a visitor dwells on a page offer for a long time encourage them to enter a chat session.
6 **Brand search term strength:** Assess the number of people searching on your brand name or URL through time to assess how powerful your brand is in attracting new and repeat visitors.	**Generate awareness:** This could be through above-the-line advertising online or offine or sponsorships, for example, to generate awareness. But previous visitors and customers will also search on your brand if they have had a favourable experience.

Table 1.3 *(Continued)*

Engagement metric	Engagement tactic
7 **E-mail activity level:** Use e-mail communication for on-going engagement with customers. Check levels of activity and response.	**Refined touch strategy:** Develop a strategy that looks at message type, triggers, outcomes required, the right medium for messages and the right sequence, etc.
8 **Define activity levels or hurdle rates (for different activities):** Set metrics to review different types of user activity, e.g. number of new users in last 60 days, number of active or dormant users, etc.	**Personalize by activity or lifecycle of content in web or e-mail pods:** Offer users different messages depending on their status, i.e. message for new visitors will differ from message to regular, registered users.
9 **Emotional response:** Conduct benchmarking research with users to assess their emotional responses to aspects such as look and feel, design, messaging, etc.	**Multivariate testing:** Test different permutations of buttons, messaging, etc., to see what the highest uplift is.
10 **Outcomes:** Beyond the use of analytics tools, play programmes to find out what people think, including aspects such as relevance, believability and likeability, etc.	**Use secondary navigation to highlight next steps:** Use a combination of images and text for menus to invite users to do something else on your site.

SERVING THE B2B AUDIENCE

Examples of excellent added value, online, can also be found in B2B markets. Companies like Fedex, GE and Dell add value through their web sites all the time. They also build switching costs as customers become more and more locked into their excellent services.

Take GE Power Systems – they have created a web based tool called a 'turbine optimizer' which enables operators of any GE turbine to measure their machine's efficiency by comparing its performance against any similar turbines anywhere in the world. The tool then shows the operator how to improve the turbine's performance (and how much money the improvement is worth). It then helps the turbine operator to schedule a service call to make the improvement happen. This used to take weeks, in the online world it takes seconds.

Dell adds value by integrating its web help system into a customer's own Enterprise Resource Planning system (ERP). This means that, when a customer orders online from

Dell, this triggers both Dell's system and the customer's own system simultaneously, which in turn updates both systems as to orders, approvals, budgets, stock, etc. This also makes switching suppliers more difficult.

Intel add value by sharing relevant information with their customers. They track their stocks (inventories) second by second and make this information available to their customers. Customers return the favour with information about their own stocks.

Fedex go one step further and give customers a free PC loaded with software that tracks the customer's packages around the world. The PC can also be used for non-Fedex purposes. While adding value it also creates switching costs, because should the customer ever want to switch to another supplier they have to return the PC.

Real added value leaves customers tingling. Take the London Eye. It could add real value to the customer experience by offering to record the customer's experience (and comments) via a web cam installed in each capsule. It could be delivered to the customer's PC, TV or mobile phone instantaneously.

A web site's main purpose is to help customers (and other stakeholders such as suppliers and distributors). The big question to ask is: 'How can my web site help my customers? How can I add extra value?' The search for new ways to add value is continuous.

Added value, extra service, call it what you want, becomes part of the product or service. Web sites can become part of a product or service. Do you agree?

E-MARKETING INSIGHT

Patricia Seybold on adding value to B2B services

Seybold (1999) defines eight success factors to achieve e-marketing. Two of these refer to adding value and they still ring true today. She says:

- '*Let customers help themselves*'. This 'customer self-service' can be enquiring about delivery of a product or obtaining after-sales support.
- '*Help customers do their jobs*'. Give information about best practice to help professionals complete their day-to-day work.

E-MARKETING EXCELLENCE

EasyJet serve

When easyJet customers have a query, the easyJet contact strategy is to minimize voice calls through providing carefully structured Frequently Asked Questions (FAQ) and e-mail forms.

SECTION SUMMARY 1.8

Objective – serve

A web presence can be used to add value for customers at different stages of the buying process, whether pre-sales, during the sale or post sales support.

1.9   Objective – speak – using the Internet as a communications tool

A web site can be used as a new communications channel to increase awareness, build brand, shape customer opinion and communicate special offers. The box 'EasyJet Speak – using the web as a PR tool' illustrates some approaches. As well as speaking to customers, the Internet provides a tool to listen to customers – to get closer to them. In the last 100 years marketers have got worse at knowing customers. We've become separated and distanced by middlemen, distributors, agents, retailers, advertising agencies and market research agencies. The world of e-marketing opens up the opportunity to get close to customers again . . . to speak to them and to listen to them in ways that were not previously possible.

E-marketers can enjoy direct access to customers, their attitudes, their interests and their buying patterns through chat rooms, questionnaires, web logs and databases.

Chat rooms offer a new approach to focus groups (small groups of customers who discuss your product, pack, advertisements, etc.). Although they are not classified formally as focus groups, they do have many similarities. MTV, the music channel, claim they have 'year long focus groups' where customers discuss their products freely (bands, videos, DJs). This is invaluable information. Chat rooms can be moderated by a facilitator (just like face-to-face focus groups) or unguided (or un-moderated) in a free flowing manner.

Questionnaires, on the other hand, are more structured and guide the respondent through specific questions. Online questionnaires can annoy web visitors, since they take time. The e-marketer either keeps them short (and builds the questions across pages) or wins permission to ask for the respondent's time and information by rewarding them with a suitable incentive. Do not put a pop-up or lengthy questionnaire on your opening page as it will drive traffic away from your site.

Having said that, open questions, like 'how can we help you'? or the opportunity to key in what you're looking for (into an onsite search engine) helps customers and simultaneously allows the e-marketer to see what is of interest to the visitor. It also reveals how customers may categorize things differently. This is invaluable information.

┌───┐
│ **Using digital media channels to speak to your audiences on other sites** │
└───┘

Online marketers have a fantastic range of communications tools that they can use to speak to their audience when they are not on their site, and to encourage them to visit the site as we detail in Chapter 7. In Chapter 7, we review the 6 main options for traffic building shown in Figure 7.11. For now, we will just introduce these key digital media channels.

1 **Search engine marketing** (SEM) – placing messages on a search engine encouraging clickthrough to a web site when the user types a specific keyword phrase. The two main disciplines are Search engine optimization (SEO) to boost a companies position in the natural search listings and Paid search marketing which uses sponsored ads, typically on a Pay Per Click (PPC) basis.

   Search marketing is great for targeting audiences at the moment of intent. It can help create a level playing field where small companies can be listed alongside well-known brands to increase their awareness and drive response. That's if the small companies can get SEO right or afford to compete in paid search.

2 **Online PR** – Maximizing favourable mentions of your company, brands, products or web sites on a range of third party web sites such as media sites, social networks and blogs, which are likely to be visited by your target audience.

   Online PR can offer a low-cost route to increase awareness of your brand, it can also help attract visitors and increases **backlinks** to a site, which as we will see in Chapter 7, is useful for SEO.

3 **Online partnerships** – Creating and managing long term arrangements to promote your online services on third party web site or e-mail communications. Different forms of partnership include link building, affiliate marketing, online sponsorship and co-branding.

   Smart online marketers realize the value of partnerships in extending their reach into their audiences via other sites.

4 **Interactive advertising** – Use of online display ads such as banners, skyscrapers and rich media ads to achieve brand awareness and encourage clickthrough to a target site.

5 **Opt-in e-mail** – Renting opt-in e-mail lists, placing ads in third-party e-newsletters, making deals with third parties for co-registration or co-branding of e-mails, or building your own in-house e-mail list and sending e-newsletters or e-mail campaigns.

   The main aims of e-mail marketing for acquisition is to generate awareness of brands or offerings or direct response to achieve registration or leads.

6 **Viral marketing** – Viral marketing is effectively online word of mouth – messages are forwarded to help achieve awareness. The message either contains, or has a link to a site containing, videos, pictures, games, jokes, information

Selecting the mix of digital media channels which give you the best reach and most cost-effective response is one of the biggest challenges of e-marketing. Ultralase has found that a combination of display ads, affiliates and PPC are most effective, but the optimal mix will differ for every company.

And of course the database behind the web site is a warehouse full of valuable information about customers and their patterns of purchasing, responses to promotions and much more. **Data mining** the **data warehouse** can reveal intriguing insights into buyer behaviour. Did you know that a significant number of frozen food buyers also have motor bikes? And the majority of nappy (diaper) buyers after 6 p.m. are male? What do you do with this data? Well one supermarket placed beer beside nappies and beer sales increased.

Combine the database with **collaborative filtering** (or rules such as 'if buy product "A" then likely to want product "C" ') and the e-marketer has a very powerful weapon . . . the dynamic dialogue.

Speaking to customers, monitoring their purchases, suggesting other relevant products and all in a helpful, non-intrusive manner. If your local delicatessen remembers your name and asks if you'd like to try some particular paté because they remember you bought a particular type of cheese last time, then you welcome this dialogue. The same applies here except this can be automated. This helps to create a dynamic dialogue with the customer.

E-MARKETING EXCELLENCE

EasyJet speak – using the web as a PR tool

EasyJet are active in using the web as a PR tool, some examples:

- EasyJet jets were emblazoned with oversize 'www.easyJet.com' logos.
- EasyJet ran a competition to guess the losses of rival airline GO and received 65 000 entries and also enhanced press coverage.
- Owner Stelios Haji-Ioannou has a personal views page, 'message from Stelios'.
- Standard press releases pages are regularly updated.

SECTION SUMMARY 1.9

Objective – speak

One of the many benefits of e-marketing is getting close to customers again. Speaking to them. You can explore the other benefits (selling, serving, saving and sizzling) now or later.

1.10   Objective – save – using the Internet for cost-reduction

Another e-marketing objective is 'saving'. This is what will catch the financial directors ear together with sell, since the two together increase profitability. Saving money, time and effort. Savings emerge in digital media channels, customer service, transactional costs, and of course, print and distribution.

Good systems help customers to service themselves. This obviously saves money, and if done in a simple, speedy and efficient manner, increases customer satisfaction.

Fedex estimated they save between $2–5 when they service customers via the web site rather than over the phone. This saves many millions of dollars per annum. Similarly,

Dell showed they saved between $5 and $10 per customer which adds up to many millions. Cisco save hundreds of millions of dollars every year now through their web-based customer services.

Other estimates suggest that transactional costs have huge savings when completed on line. For example, the cost of an over-the-counter transaction in a bank is over $1 compared to 1 cent when completed online.

Ultralase saves money in a range of ways – first by using the most cost-effective digital media channels such as affiliates and paid search which are pay for performance media. Then it uses its site to qualify visitors, since visitors can self-serve that means fewer inbound phone calls to manage and phone conversations can focus on the customers who need or prefer this type of service. It also saves money through sending e-mails rather than post (remember right touching).

In addition to efficiency gains of e-systems, many businesses negotiate better deals online (from suppliers anywhere in the world). These businesses can also enjoy new economies of scale from the higher purchasing power emerging from the new online purchasing alliances like GM and Ford, mentioned in Section 1.7.

Other savings are found in print and distribution. Annual reports, sales literature, user manuals and much more can be stored and distributed electronically – saving storage space, paper, trees, fuel (transport) and of course, money and time.

Some companies find other savings by using the Internet for cheaper phone calls. Other companies find savings by soliciting cost-saving ideas from their employees, customers and even general visitors to their web sites.

Other companies find their web operations not only save money, but also generate extra revenues through banner advertising. Busy sites attract traffic. Advertisers need audiences, so some sites allow advertisers to advertise on their web sites, for a price.

Introducing allowable cost per acquisition (CPA)

CPA is crucial in controlling media and is often used to control the level of bids. For example, to control online advertising or paid search marketing it is vital you calculate and define a target or **allowable cost per acquisition** for different types of product.

Your actual CPA will be dependent on a combination of conversion rate and cost per click.

$$\text{Cost per Acquisition (CPA)} = (100/\text{site conversion rate}) * \text{Cost Per Click}$$

This can be simplified to :

$$\text{Cost per Acquisition (CPA)} = \text{Cost Per Click}/\text{conversion rate}$$

For example CPA is £40, with a CPC of £2.0 and a conversion rate of 5%.

To set target goals for allowable CPA depends on the value delivered by the customer acquisition across their lifetime, i.e. we also need to factor in the revenue generated from an individual product sale, total basket size or predicted lifetime value, typically over a 5 year period as explained in Chapter 3.

A final note on CPA is that you need to take into account telephone sales influenced by the website and the contribution the media channel makes to developing brand awareness, familiarity and favourability. For example, display advertising may be not be justified in terms of CPA alone, but it may support sales through other digital channels such as paid search.

E-MARKETING EXCELLENCE

EasyJet save on callcentre expansion

The Internet is important to easyJet since it helps to reduce running costs, important for a company where each passenger generates a small profit. Part of the decision to increase the use of the Internet for sales was to save on the building of a £10 million contact centre which would have been necessary to sustain sales growth if the Internet was not used as a sales channel.

As an example, a 1999 sales promotion offered 50 000 seats to readers of *The Times*. The scalability of the Internet helped deal with demand since everyone was directed to the web site rather than the company needing to employ an extra 250 telephone operators.

SECTION SUMMARY 1.10

Objective – save

So e-marketing saves money in many different ways. Of all the benefits of e-marketing (selling, serving, speaking, sizzling and saving), saving is the one that will help to present any business case, as the financial fraternity relate to savings very quickly. The other benefits of e-marketing (selling, serving, speaking and sizzling) will strengthen your business case.

1.11 Objective – sizzle – using the Internet as a brand-building tool

The Internet offers new opportunities to build and strengthen the brand. To add some 'sizzle' to the brand. To add extra value (or 'added value'), extend the experience and enhance the image. Ask yourself 'what experience could a web site deliver that would be truly unique and representative of the brand?' A newspaper that allows you to build your own newspaper and have it delivered electronically, or a car manufacturer that allows you to build your own car, or a camera company that allows you to learn how to use its cameras by simulating taking photographs with different settings and allowing you to compare and contrast the results (and also gives you tips on how to maintain your camera and protect your films

Figure 1.11   Bacardi add some online sizzle (www.bacardi.com)

and photos, and invites you to send your best photos in to a competition). A travel company that gives you a 'virtual friend' – after you tell them what your interests are (via an online questionnaire) the 'friend' suggests ideas for things you would like to do in the cities you choose to explore. Cosmetic companies offer online games, screensavers, viral e-mails, video clips and soundtracks to enhance the online brand experience. See the Tango e-marketing insight box in Section 2.7. This extra sizzle can enhance the brand in a way that can only be done online.

Drinks brand Bacardi (www.bacardi.com, Figure 1.11) sizzles online by maintaining the club scene atmosphere with their OVP including a pulsating beat, BAT radio, video clips and cocktail recipes although delivered through a Flash rich media application – search engine optimization doesn't matter too much to them since the brand is so strong!

Brands are important as they build trust, recognition, and, believe it or not, relationships between the buyer and the supplier. Sometimes brand imagery is the only real differentiator between products.

The brand is affected by both reality and perception: the *reality* of the actual experience enjoyed (or suffered) when using the brand, the *perception*, or image, associated with the particular product. In addition to the real experience, these perceptions are built through advertising, sales promotions, direct mails, editorial exposure (PR), exhibitions, telesales, packaging, point-of-sale, web sites and the most potent communications tool, word-of-mouth.

All of these communications tools work both online and offline. For example, banner ads, incentives, offers and promotions. E-mail campaigns (**opt-in e-mail** campaigns) are also increasing.

And since many consider the Internet to be a new publishing medium, editorial opportunities abound. From chat rooms to bulletin boards, to newsletters, to e-zines there are a host of new PR/editorial opportunities. There are also virtual exhibitions and call-back technology (a button on a web site which allows the web site visitor to request a telephone call from the company).

And packaging and point-of-sale are still required in the online world as some sites recreate the shopping mall experience. As the visitor selects stores and aisles, packaging and point-of-sale skills are still required.

These all contribute to the brand. As does the experience – the quality of the experience, both online and offline. Remember sloppy web sites damage the brand. Slow e-mail responses damage the brand. Non-responses can kill it.

There is no doubt that e-marketing can help to build the brand. Many analysts see e-marketing as a way to build both the brand image and the overall company value. Yet another benefit of e-marketing. You can see the other benefits or objectives of e-marketing – adding value, getting closer to customers, selling and saving – whenever you need to build your business case.

Ultralase (Figure 1.8) has worked hard at developing its content and online services so that it now offers much more than a brochure site, with detailed technical information, a forum and a Q&A service.

E-MARKETING EXCELLENCE

Oasis sizzle

Several years ago, the pop band Oasis launched a free CD attached to *The Sunday Times* newspaper who advertised the fantastic sales promotion heavily. The CD contained older tracks that could be played on a CD player plus four new tracks from the new album. These were encrypted so they could only be played four times on a PC and then the user was automatically directed to HMV.co.uk to buy the album. The CD also contained an interview with the band, the video for the album's single, The Hindu Times, and links to the Oasis web site www.oasisinet.com with HMV donating 50p to the communications agency, Spero's favourite charity, Big Time Cultural Bank.

SECTION SUMMARY 1.11

Objective – sizzle

Objectives should also consider how to enhance a brand by adding value online. This can include adding to the experience of the brand through interactive facilities. Protecting the brand through achieving trust about security and confidentiality is also important.

1.12   Introduction to e-strategy

Strategy summarizes how you achieve your objectives. Strategy is influenced by both the prioritization of objectives (sell, serve, speak, save and sizzle) and of course, the amount of resources available.

You should think of e-marketing strategy as a channel strategy where electronic channels and digital media support other communications and distribution channels. It requires clear prioritization of how the channel should be used. Your e-marketing strategy should identify target markets, positioning, Online Value Proposition, the choice of mix of digital media channels to acquire new customers, and contact strategies to welcome and develop existing customers.

E-channel strategies are most effective when they are creating differential value for all parties to a transaction compared to other channels. But e-channels do not exist in isolation, so we still need to manage channel integration and acknowledge that the adoption of e-channels will not be appropriate for all products or services or generate sufficient value for all partners.

Key elements of an e-channel strategy, which we explore in more detail in Chapter 10 are:

1 It delivers against the goals that we have set through the 5Ss.
2 Defining and communicating the specific benefits of why customers should use the e-channel which we refer to throughout this book as the **online value proposition (OVP)**. For B2B office supplier Euroffice (Figure 1.6), the OVP centres on the Next day delivery, Price Guarantee and Rewards programme which are promoted prominently on their site. For Ultralase (Figure 1.8), the OVP is the services and content available to help visitors decide on the best treatment and supplier.
3 Prioritize audiences for whom e-channel adoption is most appropriate. Online services will not be equally effective for all customer segments, so decide which you will target. Ultralase needs to serve both fast customer leads where customers decide to enquire relatively quickly and more considered leads where the customer does a lot of research before deciding to ask for further information.
4 Prioritize products sold or purchased through e-channel. Some will be more appropriate.
5 Specify the mix of digital media channels used to acquire new customers against targets of sales revenues and profitability. This will be constrained by the objective of cost of customer acquisition. So, e-channel strategy guides the choice of target markets, positioning and propositions, which in turn guide the optimum marketing mix, sequence of e-tools (such as web sites, opt-in e-mail, e-sponsorship, viral marketing), service level and evolutionary stage. The evolutionary stages of e-marketing are indicated in the box: 'Evolutionary stage models and e-strategy'. Chapter 9 illustrates similar evolutionary stage models for e-business.

E-strategy also affects the traditional marketing mix as the **product** can be extended on line, the **place** of purchase can be expanded, not to mention web **price** transparency, online **promotions** and the **people** who service the web site enquiries, the automated **processes** and the importance of having a professional presence or **physical evidence**. The remix required for e-marketing is examined in Chapter 2.

One essential part of e-strategy is the development of the dynamic dialogue and the eventual full use of the integrated database potential. Regardless of how the customer comes into contact, he or she must be dealt with as a recognizable individual with unique preferences. The fully integrated database is essential so that the customer's name, address and previous orders are recalled and used appropriately. This requires careful planning, as described in Chapter 8.

So the components of e-strategy include:

- Crystal clear objectives (what you want to achieve online)
- Target markets, positioning and propositions
- Optimum mix of tactical e-tools (web site, banner ads, etc.)
- Evolutionary stage (what stage you want to be at)
- Online marketing mix (particularly service levels)
- Dynamic dialogue (ongoing with the customer)
- Integrated database (recognize and remember each customer whether via web or telephone).

Strategy is crucial. As Kenichi Ohmae observed (Ohmae, 1999):

> *'There is no point rowing harder if you are rowing in the wrong direction'.*

This is just a brief glimpse at e-strategy. It is examined in more depth in Chapter 10.

E-MARKETING INSIGHT

Evolutionary stage models and e-strategy

Quelch and Klein (1996) developed a five-stage model referring to the development of sell-side e-commerce. For existing companies their stages are:

1 Image and product information
2 Information collection
3 Customer support and service
4 Internal support and service
5 Transactions.

Chaffey *et al.* (2003) suggest there are six choices for a company deciding on which marketing services to offer via an online presence (Figure 1.12):

- Level 0. No web site or presence on web.
- Level 1. Basic web presence. Company places an entry in a web site listing company names, such as www.yell.co.uk, to make people searching the web aware of the existence of the company or its products. There is no web site at this stage.

- Level 2. Simple static informational web site. Contains basic company and product information sometimes referred to as 'brochureware'.

- Level 3. Simple interactive site. Users are able to search the site and make queries to retrieve information such as product availability and pricing. Queries by e-mail may also be supported.

- Level 4. Interactive site supporting transactions with users. The functions offered will vary according to company. They will be usually limited to online buying. Other functions might include an interactive customer service helpdesk which is linked into direct marketing objectives.

- Level 5. Fully interactive site supporting the whole buying process. Provides relationship marketing with individual customers and facilitates the full range of marketing exchanges.

Discussion of relevant stages and their sequence can be used by any company to help define their e-strategy.

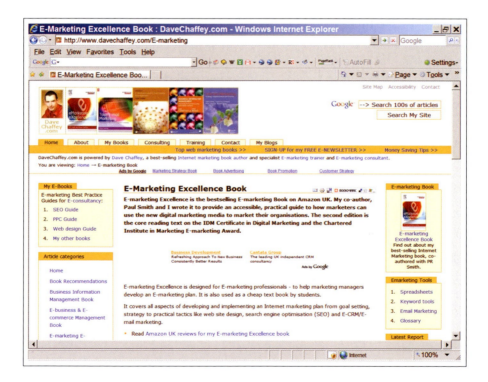

Figure 1.12   Dave Chaffey's e-marketing portal (www.davechaffey.com/E-marketing).

SECTION SUMMARY 1.12

Introduction to e-strategy

E-strategy defines a company's approach to achieving its e-marketing objectives. It should include the range of tactical e-tools and a revised marketing mix.

1.13   Tactics, actions and control

Tactics are the details of strategy. Tactical e-tools include the web site, opt-in e-mail, digital media channels such as paid search and display advertising, virtual exhibitions and sponsorship. Tactics require an understanding of what each e-tool can and cannot do. Tactics may also involve where and how each tool is physically used, whether with a kiosk, interactive TV, mobile or alternatives (such as microwave).

Each one is a mini project requiring careful planning, good project management skills combined with tactical 'nous' and creativity. Action, or implementation, also requires an appreciation of what can go wrong from cyber libel to viruses, mail bombs, hackers and hijackers, cyber squatting and much more . . . contingency planning is required. What happens when the server goes down or a virus comes to town? What happens if one of the e-tools is not working, or is not generating enough enquiries? Something has to be changed.

But how do you know if it's going well? Performance is measured against the detailed targets. Time has to be made for a regular review of what's working and what's not. Good marketers have control over their destinies. They do not leave it to chance and hope for the best. They reduce risk by finding what works and what doesn't – so that e-tactics, or even the e-strategy can be changed if necessary.

Real marketers also want to constantly improve. Which tools are giving the best return on investment? Why? Other control mechanisms include measuring number of hits, number of unique visitors, number of conversions (visitors that purchase/subscribe), churn rate (number of people who ask to be taken off the subscription list or database).

Some companies ask managers to present 'Learnings' alongside their actual performance. Learnings mean anything they have learned from the marketplace during the last period. This forces a culture of constant improvement.

Finally, control also includes **competitive intelligence** – monitoring your competitors – what they're doing; what they're repeating; what works for them; what they're stopping.

Good marketers also have contingency plans or practise risk management. What happens if plan 'A' doesn't work? What happens if competition cut prices? Or worse still, what happens if the server goes down and your network crashes? Do you have a second server? Good marketers think things through.

Whither web analytics

Developing a good system of **web analytics** is vital for controlling your digital communications. Web analytics help you check whether your objectives are achieved and should be used for ongoing improvements.

Web analytics also provide tactical insights such as the opportunity of seeing what are the most popular pages (i.e. what's of interest to customers) and how long they spend on specific pages. Web logs, or web stats, also track customers as they search on site so that the e-marketer can see how visitors' minds work – how they search and how they process information (how they move from page to page). Comparing enquiries (visitors) to sales (customers) reveals conversion ratios. How good are you at converting an enquiry into a sale or a sample? This ratio is important and should be watched carefully. High traffic (visitors) and low sales gives a low **conversion ratio** and suggests the web site needs to be improved whereas low traffic and high sales give a high conversion ratio which suggests the web site design is fine but perhaps more resources need to be spent on generating traffic.

Web analytics, chat rooms and questionnaires can work together. For example, the analytics system can reveal items or pages that are not popular. The chat room facilitator can ask 'why'? and a questionnaire can later check to see if the chat room reasons are valid with a wider audience.

So to conclude: e-marketing will continue to grow despite the vast array of sloppy sites and services. Winners will address these issues. Winners will plan strategically for both the evolutionary stages and the specific e-marketing objectives: sell, serve, speak, save and sizzle.

SECTION SUMMARY 1.13

Tactics, action and control

Tactics are the details of strategy. Tactical e-tools include the web site, opt-in e-mail, banner ads, virtual exhibitions and sponsorship. Actions include project planning and implementation while control involves assessing the results against objectives.

CHAPTER SUMMARY

1 SOSTAC® is a planning framework suitable for e-marketing and can be used for developing all types of plans, including e-marketing plans. It stands for Situation, Objectives, Strategy, Tactics, Actions and Control.

2 The wired-up world connects businesses to consumers using an ever-increasing range of devices from PCs to phones to TVs to fridges and cars.

3 E-marketers need to assess the particular relevance of B2C, B2B, C2B and C2C marketing to their organization.

4 E-marketing and e-commerce are a subset of e-business that involve the automation of all business processes. E-marketing can assist in all elements of marketing – providing new techniques to identify, anticipate and satisfy customer needs efficiently.

5 Sloppy e-marketing can arise from poorly defined objectives, lack of strategy or poor execution. Risk assessment can minimize the risks of this occurring.

6 Clear objectives are required for e-marketing in order that resources can be directed at achieving these objectives and we can measure whether our targets are achieved.

7 The first of the 5S objectives is 'Sell'; using the Internet as an additional sales channel to reach new and existing customers.

8 The second of the 5S objectives is 'Serve'; using the Internet for customer service and adding value. Value can be added using a range of techniques including 24/7 access to support information and online tools.

9 The third of the 5S objectives is 'Speak'; using the Internet as a communications tool for inbound, outbound and social communications integrated with other media.

10 The fourth of the 5S objectives is 'Save'; using the Internet to increase efficiency and so reduce costs.

11 The fifth of the 5S objectives is 'Sizzle'; using the Internet as a brand building tool, by increasing brand awareness and enabling interaction with the brand. Your Sizzle is communicated through your Online Value Propositions (OVPs).

12 E-strategy entails defining approaches to achieve e-marketing objectives using a range of tactical e-tools and a revised marketing mix.

13 Tactics are the details of strategy. Tactical e-tools include the web site, opt-in e-mail, banner ads, virtual exhibitions and sponsorship.

References

Armitt, C. (2004) High Street Bandits don't take entailing seriously. *New Media Age*, 15 October.

Bossidy, L. and Charan, R. (2004) *Execution – the discipline of getting things done*. Crown Business.

Chaffey, D., Mayer, R., Johnston, K. and Ellis-Chadwick, F. (2006) *Internet Marketing: Strategy, implementation and practice*, 3rd edition. Financial Times/Prentice Hall, Harlow.

DTI (2003) *Business In The Information Age – International Benchmarking Study 2003*. Department of Trade and Industry. Based on 6000 phone interviews across businesses of all sizes in eight countries. Available from www2.bah.com/dti2003.

Hill, S. (2004) Etailers offer poor customer service. *New Media Age*, 2 September.

ITU (2004) Internet Reports 2004. International Telecommunications Union (www.itu.int).

Leyden, J. (2004) Wobbly Shopping Carts Blight UK e-Commerce. *The Register*, 4 June.

Marden, E. (1997) *The Laws of Choice. Predicting customer behaviour*. Free Press, New York.

Mazur, L. (2004) Poor Profiling. *Marketing Business*, February.

News Corporation (2005). Press Release. Speech by Rupert Murdoch to the American Society of Newspaper Editors. April 13, 2005. http://www.newscorp.com/news/news_247.html.

Ohmae, K. (1999) *The Borderless World: Power and Strategy in the Interlinked Economy*. Harper Business, New York.

Quelch, J. and Klein, L. (1996) The Internet and international marketing. *Sloan Management Review. Spring*, pp. 61–75.

Seybold, P. (1999) *Customers.com. Century Business Books*. Random House, London.

Siegel, D. (2000) *Futurize Your Enterprise. Business Strategy in the age of the e-customer*. John Wiley, New York.

Smith, P.R. (2003) *Great Answers to tough marketing questions*, 2nd edition. Kogan Page.

Smith, P.R. and Taylor, S. (2004) *Marketing Communications: an integrated approach*, 4th edition. Kogan Page, London.

Smith, P.R., Pulford, A. and Berry, C. (1999) *Strategic Marketing Communications*. Kogan Page.

Snow Valley (2007) e-Delivery in the UK 2007. How UK online retailers are handling the delivery of orders.

Transversal (2006) *Survey of online customer experience*. www.transversal.com

Further reading

Chaffey, D. (2004) *E-Business and E-Commerce Management: Strategy, implementation and practice*. Financial Times/Prentice Hall, Harlow, 2nd edition. Chapter 8 introduces the concept of e-marketing and its relationship with e-commerce and e-business.

DTI (2003) *Business In The Information Age – International Benchmarking Study 2003*. Department of Trade and Industry. Available from www2.bah.com/dti2003.

Web links

ClickZ (www.clickz.com) has articles and statistics on a wide range of e-marketing tactics.

DaveChaffey.com (www.davechaffey.com, Figure 1.11) is a portal with articles and links to update you on the latest developments in digital marketing. See http://www.davechaffey.com/E-marketing for links related to this chapter.

E-consultancy (www.e-consultancy.com). Detailed insights and events about e-marketing best practice.

E-marketer (www.emarketer.com). A compilation of research reports showing trends in Internet adoption and usage.

E-marketing Excellence Book homepage (www.davechaffey.com/E-marketing). An index of all e-marketing links for each chapter in this book.

The Interactive Media in Retail (www.imrg.org). Trade body for e-retailers reporting on growth and practice within UK and European e-commerce.

International Telecommunications Union (ITU) (www.itu.int/ti/industryoverview/index.htm). Choose Internet indicators. This presents data on Internet and PC penetration in over 200 countries.

Marketing Sherpa (www.marketingsherpa.com). Case studies and news about e-marketing.

New Media Age (www.nma.co.uk). A UK digital marketing trade weekly.

New Media Knowledge (www.nmk.co.uk). Articles and events about new media developments.

Net Imperative (www.netimperative.co.uk). Updates and reports on the UK new media landscape.

Revolution magazine (www.revolutionmagazine.com). Keep up-to-date on e-marketing best practice for the range of new media with the UK trade monthly for digital marketing.

UK Netmarketing (www.chinwag.com). The premier e-mail discussion and advice list for insiders in the UK e-marketing industry.

Self-test

1 Summarize each element of the SOSTAC® framework.

2 Describe how customers and companies are becoming interconnected.

3 Assess the potential for B2C, B2B, C2B and C2C interactions via your online presence.

4 Devise a diagram outlining the difference between e-business, e-marketing and e-commerce.

5 List your experiences of sloppy e-marketing.

6 Describe the need for objectives and the characteristics of suitable objectives.

7 Outline 'Sell' e-marketing objectives for your organization.

8 Outline 'Serve' e-marketing objectives for your organization.

9 Outline 'Speak' e-marketing objectives for your organization.

10 Outline 'Save' e-marketing objectives for your organization.

11 Outline 'Sizzle' e-marketing objectives for your organization.

12 Summarize e-strategies to achieve the objectives you have described in Questions 7 to 11.

13 Summarize the main tactical e-tools used by your organization.

Chapter **2**

Remix

'A marketer is like a chef in a kitchen . . . a mixer of ingredients'.

Frederick Bartels (1963)

OVERVIEW

The digital world affects every aspect of business, every aspect of marketing and every aspect of the marketing mix. Some argue that physical distribution, selling and pricing absorb the biggest impact. In fact all the elements of the marketing mix are affected by this new world. This chapter shows you exactly how to evaluate the options for varying your organization's marketing mix.

OVERALL LEARNING OUTCOME

By the end of this chapter you will be able to:

- Understand the online implications of each element of the marketing mix
- Extend each element of the mix into the online world
- Begin to plan each element of the mix in the online world.

CHAPTER TOPIC		LEARNING OBJECTIVE
2.1	Introduction	Identify the different elements of the marketing mix and where they fit into the e-marketing plan
2.2	What is the marketing mix?	Appreciate the many different approaches to the marketing mix
2.3	Beyond the mix	Identify the marketing skills required to take you beyond the mix
2.4	Product	Assess the full potential of extending any product online
2.5	Price	Review your pricing and consider some dynamic pricing models
2.6	Place	Identify the online distribution issues and challenges
2.7	Promotion	Discuss the problems and opportunities of the online communications mix
2.8	People	Analyze why online service requires a delicate balance of people and automation
2.9	Physical evidence	Identify the digital components that give 'evidence' to customers and check that your web site has them
2.10	Processes	List the components of process and understand the need to integrate them into a system
2.11	An extra 'P', Partnerships	So much of marketing today is based on strategic partnerships, marketing marriages and alliances that we have added this 'P' in as a vital ingredient in today's marketing mix

2.1   Introduction to Remix

The **marketing mix** is a well-established conceptual framework that helps marketers to plan their approach to each market. At worst, it provides a checklist of decisions which marketers must make. At best, marketers integrate, or mix, these decisions together and allocate their resources accordingly. In this chapter we examine how the mix applies today. Online developments affect every aspect of business, every aspect of marketing and every aspect of the marketing mix. So do we have to throw out the old marketing mix concept or can it still be applied? Is a radical remix needed?

There is a debate amongst marketers about which mix is the most appropriate, regardless of online or offline. Some feel that the traditional version of the mix simply misses the mark. There are others who feel it is a useful starting point. Some argue that physical distribution, selling and pricing absorb the biggest impact from the Internet. In fact all the elements of the mix are affected by the online world.

The e-marketing mix is changing as products become services, services become customer driven, and customers create communities that extend the brand into new online experiences. It's a new type of mix. While 'people', or staff, used to do all the customer service, today, there are 'new people' (customers), who help each other in creating new customer experiences. These new people are users who generate new products (see Constant Comedy), new promotional materials including advertisements, reviews and ratings (positive and negative as for automotive companies Chrysler and Honda, although they are moderated); new customer services such as 'ask and answer services' where customers share answers to other customers questions (as offered by www.TheHomeDepot.com).

Although an extra element of the mix is suggested at the end of the chapter, this chapter does not seek to create a new mix, but examines how the old mix is radically changed by the fast-changing digital environment. Figure 2.1 summarizes the main elements of the marketing mix and key issues of how the mix is changed in the digital environments that are explored in this chapter.

The overall balance of the marketing mix is strategic and the details of the mix are tactical. For example, deciding whether to heavily discount prices and raise a high profile in a broad array of down-market web sites and communities is strategic. The tactical details would list the sites and communities and relevant prices in detail.

Of course, a balanced mix itself is not enough to ensure success. Too many clever start-up companies and many existing companies do not have all of the facets required to run a business. To ensure a business (or even just the new online aspects of a business), actually works (for the customer), you need to ensure firstly that there is a market and secondly that you can supply it, i.e. that the basic business is fit for purpose and that the appropriate technology, product/service design, production process and marketing process, sales process, delivery process, cash flow process and after sales support process are all in place along with the resources (men, money and time) required to service it. All of this must be 100% in place at the same time, because if any single element fails then so does the whole.

However, customers don't care about an organization's facets or internal processes they just want the right product/service to be available to them at the right time, in the right place

Figure 2.1   Keys aspects of the 7Ps of the classic marketing mix

and at the right price. The old 4Ps all carefully balanced. And since increasingly all products are becoming services (as they also offer online product experiences) we need to add the remaining 3Ps for services – people, processes and physical evidence – to the required mix online.

SECTION SUMMARY 2.1

Introduction to Remix

The marketing mix is a well-established conceptual framework that helps marketers to structure their approach to each market. It should be re-examined and reapplied for the online world.

2.2   What is the marketing mix?

The **marketing mix** rose to prominence in the early 1960s, although it was first referred to in 1949 at an American Marketing Association conference. Around the start of the 1960s, Canadian Jerome McCarthy (McCarthy, 1960) coined the term the '4Ps': **product, price,**

place, promotion. The four Ps are controllable variables which, when planned and carefully mixed together in the right way, satisfy customers. In 1963 Bartels said:

'A marketer is like a chef in a kitchen . . . a mixer of ingredients'.

So what are the ingredients that marketers need to mix together to satisfy customer needs?

Some of the controllable factors include: product quality, product availability, product image, product price and service.

EXTENDING THE MIX

Since that time many have argued that the **4Ps** worked for products rather than services. American academics Booms and Bitner then developed the **7Ps**, sometimes known as the service mix (Booms and Bitner, 1981). They considered the extra Ps crucial in the delivery of services – people, processes and physical evidence. People create and deliver a service – if they aren't happy the service falls apart. Processes are even more important as the process of production is not behind closed doors (as in the case of products), but open for all to see. Finally, when buying intangible services, many customers rely on cues given from physical evidence (such as uniforms, badges and buildings).

Some feel that for interactive marketing Peppers and Rogers' **5Is** should replace the **7Ps** in the information age. Do your online efforts support:

- *Identification* – customer specifics
- *Individualization* – tailored for lifetime purchases
- *Interaction* – dialogue to learn about customers' needs
- *Integration* – of knowledge of customers into all parts of the company
- *Integrity* – develop trust through non-intrusive marketing such as **permission marketing**.

The 5Is do not supplant the 7Ps, but rather are complementary to them since the 5Is define the process needed, whereas the 7Ps are the variables that the marketer controls.

Another explanation of the mix emerged when Frenchman Albert Frey suggested that the mix of marketing variables could be categorized into two groups:

- The offering (product, packaging, service and brand); and
- The methods/tools (distribution channels, personal selling, advertising and sales promotion).

MIXING THE MIX

Regardless of the approach to the mix, the same principle applies – stick close to customers; use marketing research to learn what they need and supply it better than the competition by mixing the right mix.

Marketers mix the mix in different ways, sometimes with astonishing degrees of success. The mix can be mixed in different ways to satisfy different segments.

But the increased price transparency made possible through price comparison sites means that it can be difficult to compete online as a trusted brand differentiating on premium service quality alone. Customer Management (2007) reported in a survey of UK online shoppers that almost half (48%) failed to remain loyal to a favourite brand if a competitor was running a special offer. Only 28% say they would remain loyal to a brand regardless, although the behaviour reported by consumers may be different to their actual behaviour.

Consumer behaviour seems to be to start with the product and then select supplier on price, but with a preference for known brands where there is a higher level of trust. Sites now start with reviews of products with alternative listings of suppliers listed by price. For example Reevoo (www.reevoo.com, Figure 2.2,) rates products according to individuals' opinions, but information on retailers at the time of writing is limited to price and whether the brand is known.

Figure 2.2   Revoo (www.revoo.com) consumer product rating site

Online shopping comparison site Bizrate (www.bizrate.com) has a different approach, with more in-depth ratings by consumers of online stores based on a broad range of variables from: 'ease of ordering; product selection; product info; price; web site quality; on-time delivery; product representation; customer support; privacy policies and shipping and handling'. The trick is knowing which variables are most important for the ideal customer. You need to know what your targeted 'ideal' customers base their decisions on: is it best price, best quality, best delivery, service, best image, best environment?

So today's dynamic customer communities give guidance which other consumers find trustworthy.

Sometimes tough decisions mean chopping and changing the mix. For example, faster and wider distribution might mean more money spent on stock and delivery vehicles and less money spent on advertising.

SECTION SUMMARY 2.2

What is the marketing mix?

Marketing touches every part of the corporation. One way of structuring, or categorizing, the set of decision variables is through the marketing mix. There are several different approaches including the 4Ps and 7Ps. These have to be re-evaluated for the new media. The 7Ps which are explored in this chapter are:

- Product
- Price
- Place
- Promotion
- People
- Physical evidence
- Processes.

2.3   Beyond the mix

The previous section showed that there are many different approaches to the marketing mix such as the 4Ps, 5Is and 7Ps. On top of all of this, today's marketers need skills that go beyond the basic mix. By the end of this section you will know what skills you need. Although the mix provides a useful framework for marketers, other factors also need to be considered. Decisions on the mix are not made until marketing strategy first determines **target markets** and required **brand positionings**.

Because of its origins in the 1960s, the marketing mix suggests a push marketing which does not explicitly acknowledge the needs of customers. Conseqently, the marketing mix can lead to a product orientation rather than a customer orientation. To mitigate this effect,

Lautenborn (1990) suggested the 4Cs framework which considers the 4Ps from a customer perspective. In brief, the 4Cs are:

- Customer needs and wants (from the product)
- Cost to the customer (price)
- Convenience (relative to place)
- Communication (promotion).

In our discussion of the online value proposition we add to these elements of the mix to reference specific issues that are important online, such as the quality of content, delivery of personalized messages and participation in social networks. In Chapter 4 we explain how, from a customer-centric point of view, you should review your digital activities against the 6Cs of Content, Customization, Community (and participation), Convenience, Choice and Cost reduction.

Marketers also need to know how to manage alliances (partnerships and marketing marriages), databases and how to build customer relationships that give lifetime value.

Everything today is about relationships. The choice of mix should help to grow relationships:

- Relationship marketing means keeping customers happy for life.
- Strategic alliances and partnerships are all about relationships.
- Supply chain management is increasingly built on relationships – sharing data and systems and budgets.
- If the trends towards **consolidation** (customers choosing fewer suppliers) and **commoditization** (competition producing similar products) continue, then much business will be won and lost depending on the relationship between buyer and supplier.

Marketers have to understand relationships and how to make them work – whether online or offline – with customers and suppliers.

As we will see in Chapter 8 on e-customer relations management, relationships blossom when important things are, first, remembered (like your name and preferences) and, second, acted upon (such as your birthday or wedding anniversary). As organizations become accessible 24/7/365 through a wide range of devices and people, an integrated database can help remember names, needs, events and a lot more (in both B2C and B2B markets).

E-MARKETING INSIGHT

Segmentation and positioning according to Professor Peter Doyle

Doyle on segmentation – Segmentation is the key to marketing. If there is one golden rule for upcoming marketers then it is segmentation. Why? For two reasons. First people are heterogeneous. Different customers want different things. So to satisfy customers you have to provide different solutions for different customers. The second reason is that people are prepared to pay different prices.

Doyle on positioning – Positioning is central to marketing strategy. Positioning refers to how a brand is perceived in the minds of a target group of customers. Positioning is the encapsulation of two key concepts. The first is the target market – what is your choice of segment? Second – what will make the customer prefer your product to competitors'? How can we achieve a differential advantage?

(*Source*: PR Smith 2002).

SECTION SUMMARY 2.3

Beyond the mix

Before choosing the marketing mix, marketing strategy first determines target markets and required brand positionings. Then excellent marketers think beyond the short term mix and think 'long term'. This means choosing a mix that nurtures 'lifetime customers'. Ask how each marketing mix decision affects customer relations. Relationship marketing permeates all the decisions marketing managers have to make about the mix. Excellent marketers have database skills, partnership skills and relationship skills built into all their decisions regarding the marketing mix . . . whether 4Ps, 5Ps or 7Ps.

2.4   Product

By the end of this section you will understand online value propositions, be able to assess the potential of extending your product online and spot opportunities for other products online. You will also be able to begin to assess your overall business as a result of the online opportunity.

> *'Destroy your business.com'*

That's what Jack Welsh, ex CEO of General Electric, told his managers. The implication being rethink your product before the online competition does it for you. In fact Jack used to say that the new CEO would have to go further – and recreate GE all over again.

The online world offers a host of new opportunities and prompts these product-related questions:

- What benefits do you deliver to your customers?
- Can they be delivered online?
- What other benefits might your customers like?
- Can these benefits be delivered online?
- What is your business? Can it be delivered online?

DIGITAL PRODUCTS

Ghosh (1998) suggested companies should consider how to modify product and add **digital value** to customers. These are huge questions that can reshape your whole business.

E-MARKETING INSIGHT

Digital value

Ghosh talks about developing new products or adding digital value to customers. He urges companies to ask:

1 Can I afford additional information or transaction services to my existing customer base?

2 Can I address the needs of new customer segments by repackaging my current information assets or by creating new business propositions using the Internet?

3 Can I use my ability to attract customers to generate new sources of revenue such as advertising or sales of complementary products?

4 Will my current business be significantly harmed by other companies providing some of the value I currently offer?

He suggests you need to analyze each feature of your product or service and ask how can each of these features be improved or adapted online.

These changes can be substantial – one such example is Hughes Christenson, an oil drilling tool company, who discovered they had a much more lucrative online oil drilling advisory service.

There is no doubt that every product or service can find some added value online. Even for soft drinks such as Pepsi and Tango there is a shift from physical interactions to non-physical brand experiences.

So it's not just digitizable products and digitizable services that extend themselves into the online world, but any products from any business.

Obviously the entertainment, education and advice services are ideal, but surprisingly so are complex industrial products (witness the GE turbine optimizer referred to in Chapter 1). In fact the more complex the product, the more online opportunity since there is a need to educate, train, test, install and service – most of which can be integrated online. Figure 2.3 shows how the online presence can be used to communicate the options for a complex product selection. The site visitor selects their requirements and suitable models are indicated using a **Rich Internet Application (RIA)**, in this case based on a technology known as Adobe Flex which is based on Flash. While these applications can provide a compelling customer experience, care has to be taken with respect to search engine optimization (SEO), since the search engines may not readily index and link to specific product pages.

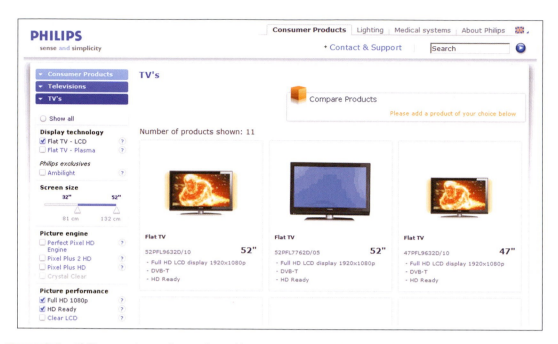

Figure 2.3   Philips product selector (http://www.consumer.philips.com/)

Even less complex but high involvement consumer purchases such as cars can be aided online through 'mixed mode' purchasing.

Remember to keep asking 'How can I help my customer'?, 'What information do my ideal target customers seek'? 'How can I save customers' time'? 'How can I add value to their online experience when they visit my site'? Ultimately, ask, 'How can I help my customers'? 'How can I excel at giving them this online'? Communities of customers can be tapped into to help answer this question. This is the idea of the **prosumer** – the proactive consumer who participates in the design of products/services.

The product or customer experience is increasingly important online as there is a school of thought that suggests that all products eventually become services. Cohen *et al.* (2006) from Harvard Business School believe that 'all products become services' as the after sales market opens up new opportunities. But many organizations still treat the aftermarket services as an afterthought. Perhaps because the 'after market' is deemed to be complicated or outside of the safety zone and therefore deemed to be difficult to manage. But they point out that many US organizations will generate their growth primarily from the 'after market' by add-ing services, updates and upgrades, consultancy, installations and training.

Products are consumed (and created) differently – many customers want to interact with the brand and with other customers in new found communities of kindred spirits who want to share information, ideas, problems, challenges and solutions, and maybe even friendship. Perhaps the online need for communities is a reflection of the offline breakdown of communi-ties. Some customers like membership privileges, exclusive areas. Chapter 4, e-customers, suggests that the couch potato may only be a slothful slob because of the absence of interactive technology, which today allows hundreds of thousands to interact with online programmes, as demonstrated by BBC's new guidelines for new programmes: 'find, play, share' (Chapter 5). 'Find' embraces distribution or place – ensuring viewers can find the content easily. 'Play' means the product itself and 'Share' combines product with promotion and distribution, as programmes and their communities of interest are nurtured to extend the product experience online, to talk to each other, to tell each other and ensure relevant people can access it wherever they congregate. Although this is for digital products, this fresh approach for a product brief may extend into many other non-digital products.

> *Companies that don't understand digital communities will die.*
>
> *Economist (April 2005)*

> *It is so huge, it's the biggest change since the industrial revolution (social networking).*
>
> *Business Week (June 2005)*

> *Person Of The Year: digital communities.*
>
> *Time Magazine (2006)*

Some companies set their production processes according to UGC. Consider the t-shirt company whose customers post their designs online, the community votes for the most popular designs and the company manufactures accordingly.

Of course customers have been determining products' functionality for many years now as mobiles are used for texting and taking photos (in fact mobile photos are now outstripping photos taken by cameras). Customers also consume vast quantities of entertainment via their phones (in fact more than the whole of Hollywood movies in cinemas; see Chapter 4).

And don't forget that in the IT business sector, as a new product spreads into a market the same fundamental product will not satisfy the second and third segments that adopt it later, as demonstrated by Geoffrey Moore's *Crossing The Chasm* (1999).

Finally, digital product and service portfolios can expand to meet the growing diversity of tastes being generated online by the many customer niches online otherwise known as *The Long Tail* (Anderson 2006).

E-MARKETING INSIGHT

Alvin Toffler and the prosumer

The prosumer concept was introduced in 1980 by futurist Alvin Toffler in his book *The Third Wave*. According to Toffler, the future would once again combine production with consumption. In *The Third Wave*, Toffler saw a world where interconnected users would collaboratively 'create' products. Note that he foresaw this over ten years before the web was invented!

Alternative notions of the prosumer, all of which are applicable to e-marketing, are catalogued at WordSpy: www.wordspy.com/.

1 *A consumer who is an amateur in a particular field, but who is knowledgeable enough to require equipment that has some professional features ('professional'+'consumer').*

2 *A person who helps to design or customize the products they purchase ('producer' + 'consumer').*

3 *A person who creates goods for their own use and also possibly to sell ('producing' + 'consumer').*

4 *A person who takes steps to correct difficulties with consumer companies or markets and to anticipate future problems ('proactive' + 'consumer').*

An example of the prosumer idea is illustrated by BMW, who, prior to the launch of a new model set up an interactive web site where users could design their own dream roadster. The information was stored automatically in a database and as BMW had previously collected data on its most loyal customers, the database could give a very accurate indication of which combinations were the most sought after and should therefore be put into production.

THE EXTENDED PRODUCT

Online opportunities for enhancing product value can also be identified. Ask 'how can I move beyond the core product?' The different elements of **extended product** can be highlighted or delivered online. What other products and services would a customer really value? Which of these services can be produced cost effectively and better than competitors?

The extended product also includes incorporating tools to help users during their use of the product. An example of this is the Carbon Neutral Calculator which BP provides for drivers (Figure 2.4).

Figure 2.4   Carbon footprint calculator from BP target neutral (www.targetneutral.com)

The extended product contributes to perceptions of quality. Quality and credibility are inextricably linked. 'Develop credibility before raising visibility' makes sense, otherwise you end up making a lousy low-profile company into a lousy high-profile company. Credibility requires quality products and services – these can be demonstrated by:

- Endorsements
- Awards
- Testimonies
- Customer lists and numbers
- Customer comments
- Warranties
- Guarantees
- Money back offers.

View the e-consultancy e-marketing portal (www.e-consultancy.com) to see how these are integrated into the site, alternatively view the site of CRM software vendor Salesforce (www.salesforce.com, Figure 2.5) which shows use of customer comments and numbers to show its scale.

Remember also – you need to analyze competition continuously. What is their core and extended product offering? That's the easy bit. Increasingly, the hard bit is knowing who your competition is, as boundaries and categories collapse. Witness Yahoo offering electricity and Virgin offering telephone services; it seems there are no boundaries, just shares of wallet based on relationship marketing. This means that once a supplier wins a customer's trust it is possible that the customer will consolidate their number of suppliers and start to buy a wider range of products and services from the same supplier. If the relationship is right the share of wallet can grow. This brings us back to the online value proposition – what exactly is being offered to the customer? Can you summarize your company's OVP?

ONLINE VALUE PROPOSITION

The **online value proposition** (previously called Internet value proposition) should be different to the offline proposition. Ideally, the proposition should exploit some of the unique advantages of being online which include: immediacy, interactivity and depth of content, faster, more convenient, easier, as well as cheaper to buy online, faster to buy online and better experience online, new experiences online, more resources/information online . . .

The OVP must somehow reinforce core brand values and clearly summarize what a customer can get from you online that they cannot get elsewhere (including competitors and offline offers). This is quite a task and requires very careful consideration of customer needs, competitive offering, company strengths and resources available. Many sites, in fact most sites, do not achieve this. Observe competitors' sites and their offerings, can you distinguish between them? A cleverly created advertising strap line appearing on a web site can

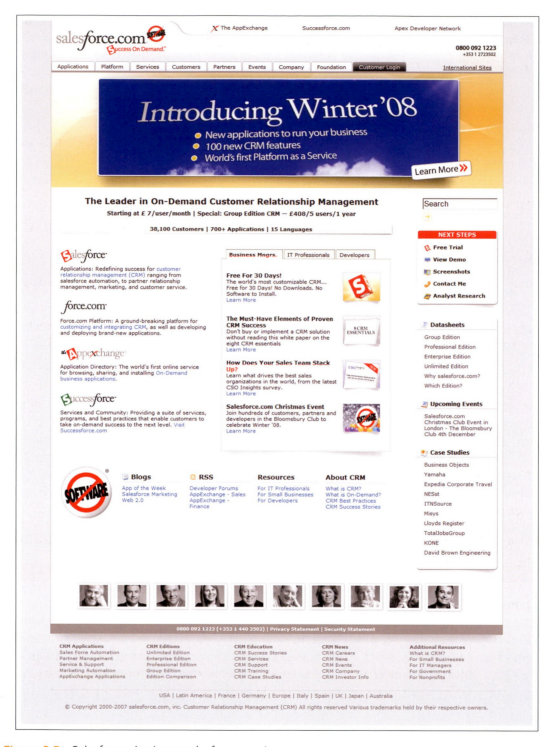

Figure 2.5   Salesforce site (www.salesforce.com)

summarize the offering. More detailed pages in offline communications or on the web site (e.g. under the 'About Us' option) can describe the proposition more fully.

Here are a few OVPs that appear to match the strap lines:

- Autotrader – The biggest and best car site on the planet – www.autotrader.com
- Boosey and Hawkes – A world of music – www.boosey.com
- EasyJet – The web's favourite airline (which suggests cheapest tickets) – www.easyJet.com
- Flickr – Share your photos. Watch the world. – www.flickr.com
- Kelkoo – Compare. Buy. Save. – www.kelkoo.com
- MUtv – The television channel dedicated to Manchester United – www.mutv.com
- WordTracker.com Find the keywords you need to succeed online www.wordtracker.com/
- YouTube – Broadcast yourself – www.youtube.com

Interestingly, Amazon use the line 'Top Seller' instead of their previous 'Earth's biggest selection at competitive prices' – www.amazon.com

Web guru, Jakob Nielsen, has an interesting exercise which assesses whether a web site communicates effectively during the first ten seconds:

Guideline 1

1 Collect the taglines from your own site and your three strongest competitors.
2 Print them in a bulleted list without identifying the company names.
3 Ask yourself whether you can tell which company does what.
4 More important, ask a handful of people outside your company the same question.

Guideline 2

1 Look at how you present the company in the main copy on the home page.
2 Rewrite the text to say exactly the opposite.
3 Would any company ever say that?
4 If not, you're not saying much with your copy, either.

The OVP is more than the sum of features, benefits and prices; it should encompass the complete experience of selecting, buying and using the product or service. The traditional categories of the different elements of the marketing mix are beginning to blur as proposition merges with product experience. About time too, as all of the mix must be seamlessly integrated.

Since the OVP is a core digital marketing concept, we refer to it throughout this book. In Chapter 4 we explain how, from a customer-centric point of view, you should review your site against the 6Cs of Content, Customization, Community (and participation), Convenience, Choice and Cost reduction.

Product

Find the ideal product that you can deliver, can afford, are good at, can protect and go for it. The online world allows you to create a whole range of new versions, variations and even new products and services. Finally, play to your strengths and exploit your distinctive competitive advantage by having a strong and clear OVP.

2.5 Price

Pricing and **price models** are being turned upside down by the Internet. In 2007, UK pop band, Radio Head, recently launched their CD online with a 'pay whatever you want' price tag. Reports suggested that many downloaded the album for free. Have you noticed how price models are changing online? Imagine being paid one day and the next day having to pay for delivering the same service? AOL used to pay ABC News for content. Now ABC pays AOL to place its content on AOL pages. It's also happened in advertising. Audiences used to pay for the media, now the media pay audiences to watch their ads.

In this section you will see why you need to review your prices and your pricing models regularly as transparent and dynamic pricing impact all markets.

NEW PRICING APPROACHES

New **buying models** require new pricing approaches.

Name-your-price services such as Priceline (www.priceline.co.uk), transparent pricing and global sourcing (particularly by giant procurement mergers like Ford and Chrysler) are forcing marketers to radically rethink their pricing strategies.

Companies who can offer digital products such as written content, music or videos now have more flexibility to offer a range of purchase options at different price points including:

- *Subscription*. This is a traditional publisher revenue model, but subscription can potentially be offered for different periods at different price points, e.g. 3 months, 12 months or 2 years.
- *Pay Per View*. A fee for a single download or viewing session at a higher relative price than the subscription service. Music service Napster offers vouchers for download in a similar way to a mobile company 'Pay As You Go' model.
- *Bundling*. Different channels or content can be grouped at a reduced price compared to pay per view.
- *Ad supported content*. There is no direct price set here, instead, the publishers main revenue source is through adverts on the site. (Either **CPM** display advertising on site using banners ads and skyscrapers or **CPC** which stands for 'Cost Per Click' more typical of Search ad networks such as Google Adsense (www.google.com/adsense.com) which accounts for

around a third of Google's revenue.) Other options include **affiliate** revenue from sales on third party sites or offering access to subscriber lists. The UK's most popular newspaper site, the *Guardian* (www.guardian.co.uk), trialled an ad free subscription service, but like many online publishers has reverted to ad-supported content.

For all of these it is necessary to have a sound **digital rights management (DRM)** solution in place to minimize copying.

A growth in competition is caused partly by global suppliers and partly by globalized customers searching via the web, which puts further pressure on prices. Many online companies enjoy lower margins with more efficient web-enabled databases and processes. They also cut out the middleman and his margin. So they revel in the ultra-competitive nature of online global markets.

And there's more . . . barter, countertrade, strategic alliances, technology transfer, licences, leasing as well as auctions, and reverse auctions where sellers compete to supply a buyer, counter auctions . . . are all putting downward pressure on prices. On the other hand, web sites can track customer segments and their sensitivity to prices against their activity on the site, or past purchase habits recorded in host databases or stored in cookies held on the user's computer (with their permission), e.g. if a customer's history shows two visits to a particular product page, then an automatic online coupon might nudge the unsure customer to buy. In theory, marketers with well-managed databases can tailor prices to discrete segments at optimum prices.

PRICING UNDER PRESSURE

Pricing is under pressure through the continual trend towards **commoditization**. Something new is commoditized almost every day. Once buyers can (a) specify exactly what they want, and (b) identify suppliers, they can run **reverse auctions**. Qualified bidders undercut each other – for both business and consumer products. Colvin (2000) reported that through MedicineOnline.com elective procedures such as laser eye corrections or plastic surgery required by a particular customer are fought over by rival practices.

Price transparency is another factor. As prices are published on the web, buyer comparison of prices is more rapid than ever before. Storing prices digitally in databases potentially enables shopping bots and robot shoppers to find the best price. Price comparison sites have been around for many years now, in different sectors, for example insurance quote site Screentrade (www.screentrade.co.uk, Figure 2.6). This site was originally a neutral intermediary launched by Misys in 1999/2000, but the brand and consumer demand wasn't strong enough, it was later purchased by Lloyds TSB as a **countermediation** strategy. Other comparison sites launched later when consumer demand was higher, such as Moneysupermarket (www.moneysupermarket.com) whose flotation on the London Stock Market in 2007 was valued at over €1 billion.

So, such comparison sites create customer empowerment which leads to further downward pressure on prices. This is what happens when customers want to take control of the relationship rather than the other way around.

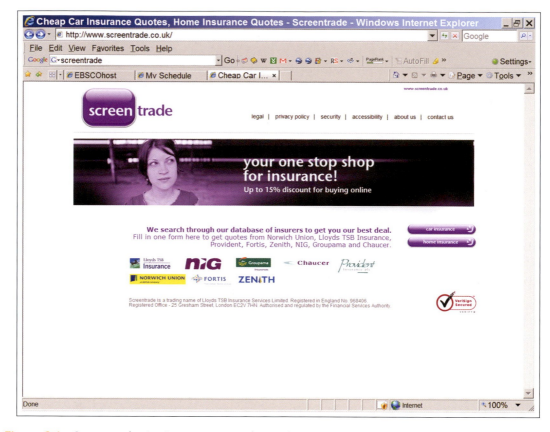

Figure 2.6 Screentrade site (www.screentrade.com)

And it's not going to get any easier to sustain old prices. A prototype next generation e-commerce server from the University of Washington uses gaming strategies to decide when to bargain even harder during the negotiation of complex contracts.

Prices are complex; options for the price package include:

- Basic price
- Discounts
- Add-ons and extra products and services
- Guarantees and warranties
- Refund policies
- Order cancellation terms
- Revoke action buttons.

Ironically, the money-rich and time-poor customers in B2C markets may be much slower than buyers in B2B markets where transaction values are often higher, so savings are more significant. B2B marketplaces such as EC21 (Figure 2.7), known as exchanges or hubs, and auctions will grow in significance.

Figure 2.7   EC21 global B2B marketplace (www.ec21.com)

Much routine and repetitive buying will be carried out in these B2B exchanges. Major corporations are already buying through online exchanges and auctions.

Marketers (and buyers) will need new skills – defining the strengths and weaknesses of various exchanges and auctions.

Experienced business people know the impact of buying efficiencies. Martin Butler estimates that a 5% saving in procurement equals the same contribution as a 30% increase in sales for many manufacturing companies (Butler, 2001).

Marginal costing may be required – for many digitized products the marginal cost is almost zero. Some companies (such as software vendors) are redefining their business, becoming service providers and giving the product away at cost. They make their money on selling the add-ons and extras. A very different pricing model or just a traditional loss leader approach? Some call it **second layer selling**. For example, companies sell end-of-term cars from corporate fleets, contract hire and leasing companies and car rental companies to affinity groups such as large employers. The cars themselves are sold at cost while the add-ons and extras make a profit – insurance, finance, recovery services.

Interestingly, many of the most successful brands are not the cheapest in their category. Customers are prepared to pay premium prices for perceived quality. In addition recent research (Apollo 2007) reveals that exposure to television commercials reduces shoppers' sensitivity to price changes.

One final pricing consideration is moving from fixed prices to rental and leasing prices. Cars, computers, flight simulators and now even music can be hired or leased.

E-MARKETING EXCELLENCE

GlaxoSmithKline reduces prices through reverse auctions

Healthcare company GlaxoSmithKline started using online reverse auctions way back in 2000 to drive down the price of its supplies. For example, it bought supplies of a basic solvent for a price 15% lower than the day's spot price in the commodity market and Queree (2000) reported that on other purchases of highly specified solvents and chemicals, SmithKline Beecham is regularly beating its own historic pricing by between 7 and 25%. She says: 'FreeMarkets, the company that manages the SmithKline Beecham auctions, quotes examples of savings achieved by other clients in these virtual marketplaces: 42% on orders for printed circuit boards, 41% on labels, 24% on commercial machinings and so on'.

The reverse auction process starts with a particularly detailed Request for Proposals (RFP) from which suppliers ask to take part and then selected suppliers are invited to take part in the auction. Once the bidding starts, the participants see every bid, but not the names of the bidders. In the final stages of the auction, each last bid extends the bidding time by one more minute. One auction scheduled for two hours ran for four hours and twenty minutes and attracted more than 700 bids!

SECTION SUMMARY 2.5

Price

The Internet is changing pricing for ever. Prices are under pressure. Pricing structures and options are becoming more complex. It is crucial to get the pricing right in the short, medium and long term. Review new price structures in your markets driven by customers looking for lower prices available through a range of online tools including reverse auctions, customer unions, commoditization, cybermediaries, intermediaries, infomediaries and shopping bots.

2.6   Place

To understand the significance of place, consider which is the most successful **brand** in the soft drinks markets? The answer is Coca-Cola not Pepsi. It is readily available almost whenever and wherever customers could need it. Their excellent **distribution** gives them the edge.

This logic also transfers to the electronic marketspace. Esther Dyson says:

> '*You put coke machines in places where you think people might want to drink a coke. On the Internet you put Amazon buttons in places where there might be people inclined to buy books*'.

Place and promotion overlap when organizations extend their presence online with links from other sites or with microsites in relevant places as the brand gets wider promotion, and simultaneously increases its distribution as the brand is, effectively, available for purchase more widely online. Place means the place of purchase, distribution and, in some cases, consumption. Some products exploit all three aspects of place online, for example digitizable products such as software, media and entertainment.

But it's not just digitizable products and services – all products and services can extend themselves online by considering their online representation for place of purchase and distribution. Even perishable goods such as food and flowers are sold online as customers like the increased convenience and reduced cost of ordering online, often using delivery partners for offline fulfilment.

WHICH PLACE? REPRESENTATION

Berryman *et al.* (1998) highlighted the importance of place in e-commerce transactions when they identified the three different locations for online purchases shown in Figure 2.8. When many companies think about making their products available online, they tend to think only of selling direct from their web site (a). However, other alternatives for selling products are from a neutral marketplace (b)? such as EC21 (www.ec21.com) and also through going direct to the customer (c). An example of this is a business-to-business auction such as that described for GlaxoSmithKline in Section 2.5 where the supplier goes to the customer's site to bid. Companies need to consider the alternatives for online **representation**.

NEW DISTRIBUTION MODELS

So place is vital and an explosion of radically new ideas has occurred in the online world of distribution in the last five years. Here are a few:

- *Disintermediation* – This is removing the middleman to deal direct with customers instead of through agents, distributors and wholesalers. Note that this can create channel conflict

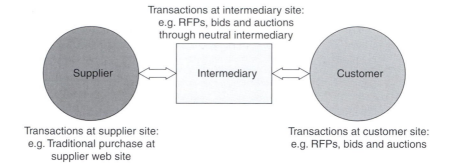

Figure 2.8 Alternative representation locations for online purchases

as middlemen feel the squeeze. For example, Hewlett Packard sell a lot of equipment to hospitals. But, when hospitals started going directly to the HP site firstly for information and then secondly to place orders, it posed a big question: do we pay commission to the sales representative for this?

● *Reintermediation* – This is the emergence of new types of middlemen who are brokers, such as Bizrate, who unite buyers with sellers.

● *Infomediation* – A related concept where middlemen hold data or information to benefit customers and suppliers.

● *Channel confluence* – This has occurred where distribution channels start to offer the same deal to the end customer.

● *Peer-to-peer services* – Music swapping services such as Napster and Gnutella opened up an entirely new approach to music distribution with both supplier and middleman removed completely, providing a great threat, but also opportunity to the music industry.

● *Affiliation* – Affiliate programmes can turn customers into sales people. Many consider sales people as part of distribution. Others see them as part of the communications mix. Amazon.com sees its 400 000 affiliate partners as a huge asset which creates part of their Distinctive Competitive Advantage.

One last way of extending an organization's reach or distribution (and promotion channels) is to create a **widget** (covered in more detail in Chapter 7) and make it available for other organizations to embed the widget on their own site to add value to their customers. Google Gadgets offers many free widgets ranging from Einstein Quotes, to calendars, to changing photos. YouTube is a classic widget that allows (and encourages) other web sites to seamlessly link YouTube content into the other organization's web site.

This approach is sometimes called **atomization** to suggest how the content on a site is broken down into smaller fundamental units such as features, blog postings or comments, which can then be distributed via the web through links to other sites. Widgets are another aspect of atomization where data can be exchanged between the widget and the server on which it is hosted. The syndication and distribution of content from one site to other sites or readers which access via **RSS feeds** are another example of atomization.

Excellent distribution requires a deep understanding of when and where customers want products and services. Partnership skills are also required as much distribution is externally sourced whether order fulfilment, warehousing, logistics or transport.

Place

Distribution, or place, is crucial to the success of any enterprise. Assuming your organization has a reasonable product or service, online or offline the principle is the same: increase your representation and make it widely and readily available to target customers. Marketers today need to think of multi-channels for distribution to ensure they make their products and services easily available to as many ideal customers as possible.

2.7   Promotion

The Internet extends and integrates all ten online communications tools. This section summarizes the opportunities and the challenges of online communications that are explored in more detail in Chapter 7 on traffic building. First we consider the range of online promotion tools that are available. We then give guidelines as to how these tools can be best exploited.

ONLINE COMMUNICATIONS TOOLS

Online promotion is continuing to grow in importance and gaining an increasing share of marketers' budgets and efforts – whether a text message that changes behaviour immediately or key words that attract more enquiries or contextual banner ads that change attitudes, or viral marketing that makes people talk about a brand. Online channels can do things that offline communications simply cannot, e.g. some web sites can promote, communicate and create a brand experience which is unique to the online users. Take the soft drink, Tango; it is renowned for its irreverence and fun approach. Tango.com brings the irreverence alive in a way that only the Internet can with games such as 'The Shocking Adventures of Nylon Neddie' (see e-marketing insight box).

The complete promotional mix or communications mix – the ten communications tools (advertising, selling, sales promotion, PR, sponsorship, direct mail, exhibitions, merchandizing, packaging and word-of-mouth) – can be used to communicate or promote in the online or offline world. They can all be extended online in new and dynamic ways. Think about their online equivalents. Table 2.1 summarizes the online equivalents of these established communications tools.

Although web sites can be considered a separate communications tool, they are best thought of as an integrator of all ten tools shown in Table 2.1.

Table 2.1   Online executions of different communications tools

Promotional mix	Online executions
1 Advertising	Interactive display ads, pay per click search advertising
2 Selling	Virtual sales staff and chat and affiliate marketing
3 Sales promotion	Incentives, rewards, online loyalty schemes
4 PR	Online editorial, e-zines, newsletters, social networks, links and virals
5 Sponsorship	Sponsoring an online event, site or service
6 Direct mail	Opt-in e-mail using e-newsletters and e-blasts plus **web response**
7 Exhibitions	Virtual exhibitions and whitepaper distribution
8 Merchandizing	Promotional ad serving on retail sites, personalized recommendations and e-alerts
9 Packaging	Virtual tours, real packaging is displayed online
10 Word-of-mouth	Viral, affiliate marketing, e-mail a friend, links

E-MARKETING INSIGHT

e-marketing insight

Chevrolet's Tahoe advertisements needed to escape the tightly controlled, painstakingly monitored, woefully predictable confines of the 30-second TV spot and roam the online jungle. But everybody's doing that now. So, Chevy marketers thought, let's take this thing a notch further – let's have an online contest to see who can create the best TV ad for the new Tahoe. The wikification of the 30-second spot.

The contest ran for four weeks and drew more than 30 000 entries, the vast majority of which faithfully touted the vehicle's many selling points – its fully retractable seats, its power-lift gates, its relative fuel economy. But then there were the rogue entries, the ones that subverted the Tahoe message with references to global warming, social irresponsibility, war in Iraq and the psychosexual connotations of extremely large cars. On its own Web site, the Tahoe now stood accused of everything but running down the Pillsbury Doughboy. . . . Attack ads piling up on its site, spilling over onto YouTube.

'Right now, consumers are engaged with new forms of media in a way they haven't been before and probably won't be forever, 'That is an opportunity'. says Ad Agency senior executive, Ed Dilworth.

The Tahoe campaign has to be judged a success. The microsite attracted 629 000 visitors by the time the contest winner was announced. On average, those visitors spent more than nine minutes on the site, and nearly two-thirds of them went on to visit

Chevy.com; for three weeks running, Chevyapprentice.com funneled more people to the Chevy site than either Google or Yahoo did. Once there, many requested info or left a cookie trail to dealers' sites. Sales took off too, 25% market share, outpacing its nearest competitor, the Ford Expedition, 2 to 1. In March, the month the campaign began, its market share hit nearly 30%. By April, according to auto-information service Edmonds, the average Tahoe was selling in only 46 days (as opposed to four months).

'When you do a consumer-generated campaign, you're going to have some negative reaction', Dilworth says. 'But what's the option – to stay closed? That's not the future. And besides, do you think the consumer wasn't talking about the Tahoe before?' They were, of course; the difference is that in the YouTube era, the illusion of control is no longer sustainable.

More and more, however, consumers are doing this stuff on their own. YouTube is full of unsolicited Chevy 'ads' that are far more sophisticated than anything the Tahoe Apprentice campaign yielded, pro or con.

Consumer-generated advertising has led to some seriously upside-down behaviour. Brands that once yelled at us now ask what we have to say. No longer content to define our identity (Gap kids, the Marlboro man), they ask us to help define theirs.

Source: Rose, F. (2006) And Now, a Word From Our Customers, *Wired* 14 December.

GUIDELINES FOR EFFECTIVE PROMOTION

The online promotional challenges marketers need to respond to can be summarized by the six key issues of mix, integration, creativity, interaction, globalization and resourcing.

1 Mix

E-marketers need to mix the **promotional mix**. This involves deciding on the optimum mix for different online promotional tools. Think about whether you use the full range of promotional tools in Table 2.1 and whether you are using the most cost effective techniques for acquiring your target customers.

E-MARKETING INSIGHT

Tango online

'*Clever, interactive, cool and wild*' is how the judges described the tango.tv web site, which was redeveloped by Grand Union. The purpose of this redevelopment was to make the site a central part of Tango's marketing activity. It had previously been used to post content, including viral games and TV ads, and to collect customer data.

Objective

Tango is renowned for its quirky TV ads and wanted to use the web site to build interactivity and participation around these, and create more enduring brand awareness among its target audience of teenage boys and girls.

Strategy

Grand Union developed three core campaigns for Tango to encourage kids to get involved online, including a game titled 'The Shocking Adventures of Nylon Neddie', which centred on a character who builds up static electricity by rubbing his nylon-clad thighs. This added interactivity to the TV ads as they corresponded to each level of the game. Tango also used the site to extend the reach of its 'The Big Drench' promotional roadshow, which ran in cities across the UK, and featured several games, including 'Drench Roulette', in which players had to stand underneath a 30 ft-tall apple-shaped installation filled with water. An online 'soak-'em-up' game gave teenagers who couldn't make it to the events a chance to get involved and win prizes.

Results

Tango said that the investment in the site helped the brand grow 15.5% in terms of volume (litres) and 17% in terms of value last year. This corresponded to an increase in sales representing a growth in value of £5.7m. The judges commented that the site fits very well with both the Tango strategy and audience, and were impressed with the integration of the web site into the campaigns as a whole.

(*Source:* New Media Awards 2004).

---

2 Integration

Both online and offline communications must be integrated. All communications should support the overall positioning and **online value proposition** which the e-marketing strategy defines.

A single consistent message and a single integrated database are needed – which recognizes and remembers customers' names and needs regardless of which access devices are being used (TV, telephone, PC or hand-held device).

Online integration is difficult enough. Online and offline integration requires even more management skills.

E-MARKETING INSIGHT

Ten golden rules of IMC

1 Get management support for IMC (integrated marketing communications) by ensuring they understand its benefits to the organization.

2 Integrate at different levels by putting IMC on the agenda of different meetings; horizontally between managers in different functions such as distribution and production and ensure that PR, advertising and sales are integrating their efforts.

3 Maintain common visual standards for logos, typefaces and colours.

4 Focus on a clear marketing communications strategy. Have clear communications objectives. Have clear positioning statements. Link core values into every communication.

5 Start with a zero budget – build a new communications plan by specifying the resources needed and prioritizing communications activity accordingly.

6 Think customers first. Identify the stages before, during and after each purchase and develop a sequence of communications activities that help the customers through each stage.

7 Build relationships and brand values. All communications should strengthen customer relationships. Ask how each communication tool enables you to do this. Customer retention is as important as customer acquisition.

8 Develop a good marketing information system which defines who needs what information when. IMC defines, collects and shares vital information.

9 Share artwork and other media. Consider how advertising imagery can be used across mail shots, new releases and the web site.

10 Be prepared to change it all. Constantly search for the best communications mix.

(*Source*: Smith and Taylor, 2004).

3 Creativity

Today's marketer can exploit the vast untapped creative opportunities presented by the Internet. The only limitation is your imagination. Imagine sponsoring a virtual experience.

Or sending opt-in e-mails that make customers sit up and take notice.
Or developing the ultimate virtual exhibition.
Or . . . moving into virtual immersion . . .

Of course creativity must fit the overall communications strategy – communications impact is most powerful in the new context.

4 Interaction

Next comes the extra layer of creativity – interaction. This enhances the experience and deepens the communications impact (and can also collect customer data). This is where the online opportunity can really create some 'sizzle'.

5 Globalization

Then of course there are the added complications of a global audience. Web sites open your window to the world. When global audiences look in (to your site) they may not like what they see. See the e-marketing excellence box for some examples of the cultural and business practices that need to be considered for the Japanese market. Also see Chapter 4, e-customers, for examples of localized brand names that restrict sales in international markets.

E-MARKETING EXCELLENCE

Adjusting the offering for the Japanese market

These are the many issues Clifford (2000) reported that Priceline (www.priceline.com) should be considering for a different culture:

1 Web site design – Japanese read from right to left.

2 Profit margins – Japanese negotiate fiercely. They do thorough research. Priceline may not get as good margins in this market.

3 No cancellations policy – Contracts in Japan 'are not perceived as final agreements. Traditionally, if either party has remorse there are renegotiations'.

4 One-hour acceptance or rejection of bids – Japanese don't like to make snap decisions.

5 Bargain hunting – Bargaining and price hunting is not talked about. Talking about haggling is tacky.

6 Customer service – 'At times you need to pretend that you are sure that your Japanese friend or colleague has understood you, even if you know this is not the case. This is important for maintaining a good relationship'.

7 Giveaways – 'In Japan, avoid giving gifts with an even number of components, such as an even number of flowers in a bouquet. Four is an especially inauspicious number; never give four of anything'.

---

6 Resourcing

The online communications opportunity is infinite. However resources to design and maintain the content, interactions and the database are not infinite. Resources are also needed to service customer enquiries whether online or offline.

Even ensuring consistent use of the brand requires time, energy and money.

Finally, remember all communications are wasted if the rest of the mix is wrong, for example a poorly targeted product.

SECTION SUMMARY 2.7

Promotion

All ten communications tools should be reviewed for how they can be extended and enriched online. Online communications challenges include: mix, integration, creativity, globalization and resourcing. Take advantage of the characteristics of the new media through promotion that is: dynamic, carefully targeted, highly relevant and helps build an ongoing relationship based on the permission and trust of the customer. Use the checklist in Table 2.2 to assess how integrated your communications are.

Table 2.2   E-marketing checklist – **integrated communications**

1	Does senior management support integrated marketing communications and the importance of the brand?
2	Do you integrate at different levels by putting IMC and the brand on the agenda of different meetings; horizontally between managers in different functions such as distribution and production, the web master and the sales team, etc.?
3	Do you have design guidelines or a brand book which maintains common visual standards for logos, typefaces and colours?
4	Is there a clear marketing communications strategy with clearly defined brand values, brand positioning and brand personality which is linked into the core of every communication?
5	Do you start from scratch with a zero budget and define exactly what is required – build a new communications plan by specifying the resources needed and prioritizing communications activity accordingly?
6	Do you think customers first and identify a contact strategy (a sequence of communications) for different customer segments who are at different stages in the customer lifecycle?
7	Do you build relationships and brand values with all communications? Do you ask 'how does this help the customer? Does this strengthen my brand?
8	Do you have a good marketing information system which defines, firstly, who needs what information when and, secondly, which communications tools are working better than others?
9	Do you always consider how campaigns and traffic generating ideas can be integrated with other tools and techniques? Do you share artwork across all the communications mix – both online and offline?
10	Are you prepared to constantly improve by closely monitoring what works and optimizing the best communications tools?

2.8 People

In services marketing people, or staff, are considered a crucial element of the marketing mix. As more products add online services to enhance their offerings 'people' become more and more important. By the end of this section you will understand how service needs a balance of people and automation and what the key management challenges are.

WHY ARE PEOPLE IMPORTANT?

Think about why so many clicks-and-mortar companies outperform pure dotcoms. As well as experience of the marketplace, people (and process) are key – real people, real buildings and established integrated systems that deliver goods and services. People are important since everyone in your organization is an ambassador and a sales person for your company.

Given that everyone represents the company, you can see the importance of having happy staff.

Happy Staff = Happy Customers = Happy Shareholders

The challenge, of course, is to recruit the right people, train them and reward or motivate them appropriately. This is a real issue as highlighted in Chapters 4 and 8, we have got worse at customer service. We are sitting on a customer service time bomb. This is in a turbulent environment where customer expectations are rising and often times satisfying these rising expectations is not enough to keep customers loyal. However, we ignore customer service at our peril.

DELIVERING ONLINE SERVICE

Remember the 90:10 ratio? Some suggest that web sites should adopt the 90:10 ratio as the value or service to sales pitch ratio. This implies that the bulk, 90%, of your web site should be designed to service customers.

In the online world much service can be automated. How well does your site make use of the following?

- **Autoresponders**. These automatically generate a response when a company e-mails an organization or submits an online form.
- **E-mail notification**. Automatically generated by a company's systems to update customers on the status of their order: for example, order received, item now in stock, order dispatched.
- **Call-back facility**. Customers fill in their phone number on a form and specify a convenient time to be contacted. Dialling from a representative in the call centre occurs automatically at the appointed time and the company pays, which is popular.
- **Real-time live chat**. A customer support operator in a call centre can type responses to a site visitor's questions. For example a widely deployed technology such as LivePerson (www.liveperson.com).

- **Frequently asked questions (FAQs)**. For these, the art is in compiling and categorizing the questions so customers can easily find (a) the question and (b) a helpful answer.
- **Ask and Answer services provide** a moderated service where customers help each other by answering each other's questions.
- **On-site search engines**. These help customers find what they're looking for quickly and are popular when available. Some companies have improved conversion-to-sale greatly by improving the clarity of the results the search engines return. Site maps are a related feature.
- **Co-browsing**. Here the customer's screen can be viewed by the call centre operator in combination with callback or chat.
- **Virtual assistants**. These come in varying degrees of sophistication and usually help to guide the customer through a maze of choices.
- **Customer reviewers and assistants**. Online social media enable organizations to recruit customers to help shape their service for other customers through reviews and comments.

IS AUTOMATION ALWAYS BEST? INBOUND CONTACT STRATEGIES

The concept of '**customer self-service**' or 'web self-service' is prevalent in e-marketing. Customer self-service enables the customer to obtain the information they need faster and saves the business money. However, we need to pause and ask whether all customers want to conduct all their interactions online.

Think of buying an air ticket via the web. This is fine if you have a particular flight in mind, and it is available. If it is not, our experience is that it is quicker to talk to a customer representative who is knowledgeable about the alternatives available.

Some online customer segments just want to browse, others want to find specific information and others again want to buy or get customer support. Of the segment that wants to buy, a sub-segment want to buy offline and need personal contact either via phone, letter, or personal visit. Alternatively they cannot find the information they need online in the **FAQ** or via the online search engine. At this point the customer will want to contact the company by e-mail or phone. Inbound contact strategies aim to control the volume and medium of enquiries and responses. Responses may be by **autoresponder**, e-mail, phone or real-time chat with sales staff as shown in Figure 2.9. As in this example, clear indications have to be given of when the service is available and to manage demand services are often only promoted when visitors are more engaged with the site. Some companies offering complex products have found a benefit in displaying a chat window automatically after a customer has been on a page for a certain length of time.

Many companies, such as the Nationwide bank (www.nationwide.co.uk), use an **inbound contact strategy** of customer choice or '**customer preferred channel**'. The easyJet e-marketing excellence box in Section 1.7 shows that you can give customers a choice, but steer them towards using the web as a contact tool.

A key figure for measuring the effectiveness of your inbound contact strategy is the average number of contacts to resolve an issue. Remember that many questions will not be

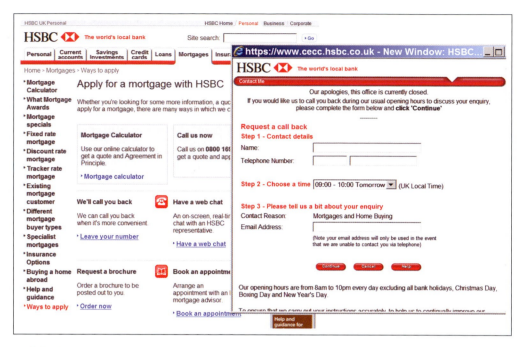

Figure 2.9 Real time chat with HSBC (www.hsbc.co.uk)

answered by the first e-mail. Companies need to decide whether the best strategy is to switch the customer to phone or online chat to resolve the issue, rather than bouncing multiple e-mails between customer and contact centre. Two-way interactions such as voice, online chat and co-browsing (where the customer's screen can be viewed by the call centre operator) will be more effective in resolving an issue immediately.

KEEPING CONTENT FRESH

Many organizations now have many thousands of web pages, often across separate web sites and different technology platforms. To keep the content fresh, up-to-date and relevant to the customer has significant management and resource implications. We will see in Section 6.7 how **content management systems (CMSs)** are essential to the consistency and management of any large site, since it will enable **content owners** in different parts of the organization to update the content they are responsible for. They also provide workflow facilities which can automatically prompt a content owner to update content and use e-mail to remind other staff to review and authorize publication. But having the right technology is only part of the story. Managers of content owners must have strategies to keep content fresh. These may include:

1 *Regular update dates* such as start of month for some content types like news or promotions.
2 *Triggers for publication.* Every new press release or product or price change must go on site.
3 *Ownership of content in job description.* The quality of content, including freshness, is part of staff performance appraisal (this is a 'stick' approach).

4 *Explaining benefits of content update to content owners*. Showing that updates will save the content owner time, e.g. in explaining things on the phone or by helping them sell more (this is a carrot approach).

5 *Using the CMS to set content expiry dates*. For certain content types, expiry dates can be set and an e-mail alert sent to the content owner.

6 *Publish dates of when pages on site were last updated*. Some organizations use a chart to show which pages are updated least frequently to shame staff into taking ownership!

7 *Real-time content delivery* taking articles or items from a database, so partially automating the update process (the database still needs to be updated).

TRAINING AND RESOURCING

Of course staff need to be trained and motivated whether they man the web site, the telephones, the field sales or the reception. What happens if a web transaction fails and the customer calls the centre? Can call centre staff access the web database to complete the transaction, or do they have to collect all the details again? A seamless, integrated contact database is required.

A key resourcing issue is whether to identify specific staff to handle contacts from different channels or empowering staff to answer questions from a variety of channels. Current thinking suggests the latter approach is best since this increases the variety of work and results in more knowledgeable staff who can better answer customers' queries.

It is worth investing in continual staff training as well as in online tools. Benchmark research from Harvard (Kotter and Heskett, 1992) revealed that companies who invest in all three key stakeholders (employees, customers and shareholders) outperform those that invest in only two or less (say customers and shareholders).

A final point is that although some consider the Internet 'marginalizes the role of direct customer contact', it is also used to recruit quality staff. Most potential recruits these days check out web sites as a matter of course. If they don't they're probably not management material!

SECTION SUMMARY 2.8

People

People/staff are important. People are the differentiating factor that has helped many 'clicks-and-mortar' companies outperform the virtual companies. In fact, service – before, during and after a sale – is required if repeat business is to be enjoyed. Contact strategies should be developed that give customers choice of contact, but minimize costly interactions with staff. Automated services help but people are also required. Beware of the customer service time bomb. It is a delicate balancing act but bear them both in mind when integrating online and offline marketing activities. Recruitment, training and motivation are required. And remember, happy staff = happy customers = happy shareholders.

2.9 Physical evidence

The aim of this section is to highlight the different aspects of physical evidence a web site can display and check that your web site has them.

WHAT IS ONLINE PHYSICAL EVIDENCE?

As services are intangible customers look for cues such as a well-designed site (as well as endorsements) to give them clues about the quality of the intangible service.

When buying intangible services, customers look for physical evidence to reassure them. In the offline world this includes buildings, uniforms, logos and more. In the online world the evidence is digital. Imagine the impression a broken window would give to a customer. Similarly a web site with a typo sends the same worrying messages. So the web site becomes a significant part of the physical evidence.

In the online world, customers look for other cues and clues to reassure themselves about the organization. So firstly, a reassuring sense of order is required. This means web sites should be designed in an uncluttered style with a consistent look and feel that customers feel comfortable with, as explained in Chapter 6, Site design. But on-site reassurance can extend far beyond this, particularly for an e-tailer, by using:

- Guarantees
- Refund policies
- Privacy policies
- Security icons
- Trade body memberships
- Awards
- Customer lists
- Customer endorsements
- Independent reviews
- News clippings.

Physical evidence should help integrate the online and offline world. Many white goods retailers such as the Carphone Warehouse (www.carphonewarehouse.com) use coupons printed out online which can be redeemed for a discount at a store. This helps conversion-to-sale rates and also tracks how the online presence is impacting offline sales.

Remember that physical evidence emerges in the offline world – if goods and services are delivered offline then the normal physical evidence is required, i.e. professional packaging, paperwork, delivery vehicles and uniforms can all reinforce the right message.

Equally they can damage the brand if they are not managed. Imagine a scruffy delivery person in a filthy broken-down van belching fumes stopping outside your home or office. The offline evidence would damage the online evidence. So, both need to be managed carefully.

Physical evidence

Customers look for cues and clues for reassurance. Web sites can provide these in the form of high quality site design and reassurance through guarantees, refund policies, privacy policies, security icons, trade body memberships, awards, customer lists, customer endorsements, independent reviews, news clippings. Encourage web site visitors to print coupons or white papers as physical evidence to keep your company at the front of their minds.

Offline activities can provide reassurance in the form of professional looking buildings, delivery vans and uniforms. Evidence, whether physical or digital, needs to be managed constantly.

2.10   Process

Process refers to the internal and sometimes external processes, transactions and internal communications that are required to run a business. Excellent execution of these is vital. By the end of this section you will be able to identify the components of process and understand how they need to be integrated into a database. Given that we are sitting on a customer service time bomb (Chapter 8), there is a golden opportunity to develop lifetime customers through deep and engaging customer service processes online.

THE IMPORTANCE OF PROCESS

'Execution, execution, execution' is the new mantra, said Booz, Allen and Hamilton (2003). 'Execution is the missing link between aspirations and results', say Larry Bossiddy and Ram Charan (2004). Excellent processes are where e-commerce ends and e-business begins. Unintegrated e-commerce sites create problems, as witnessed by US online toy stores whose web sites and associated processes did not link into an information system explaining to customers when stocks were unavailable.

Traditional offline services have processes continually on view with the manufacturing process for goods behind closed doors. Online services and their process of production are not as visible since much of the processes operate in systems unseen by the customer. Some of the process, or system, is on view, like menus, form filling, shopping baskets, follow-up e-mails and of course the interactions on web sites. It is on this part of the process and its outputs that customers will judge service.

It seems that many companies have not yet learnt how to optimize these processes – 80% of potential buyers exit before they make their purchase. This suggests ordering is too complicated or confusing, or the system simply doesn't work smoothly.

OPTIMIZING INTERNAL PROCESSES

To understand the importance of process, consider a simple online enquiry and subsequent online sale of a book. How should the system work? Think about which events or actions need to take place for the order to be fulfilled and for the customer to be satisfied.

These are some of the events that need to happen, and they must be backed up by an efficient, seamless process:

- Customer wants to check availability – Does the site show number in stock and when next available if out of stock (see Dabs.com (www.dabs.com) for good practice)?
- Product specification or price is changed – Is the change seamlessly reflected in web site and price lists or catalogues?
- Customer places order – Is the site updated to indicate changed number in stock? Is the customer notified by e-mail that their order has been processed? Is the finance system updated to include the new order within the month's revenue?
- Customer makes e-mail enquiry – Can the system cope when a wave of telephone calls and e-mails hit and respond promptly and accurately?
- Produce dispatched – Is the customer notified of this event by e-mail? Can they track their order if required?

Optimization involves minimizing the people involved with responding to each event and providing them with the right information to serve the customer. Minimizing human resources can occur through redesigning the processes and/or automating them through technology. The problem is that many sites simply do not have efficient systems in place. They lack the logistical and fulfilment infrastructure required to trade online.

Processes continue beyond the sale with after sales service, generating customer feedback, upselling, cross selling, product development and improvement built in as part of the processes.

The front end, customer interface – whether on a web site, interactive TV screen, mobile phone screen or even a telephone sales person – must integrate with the back end systems which are out of sight in the back offices and warehouse. This is easier said than done. Some 50% of the FTSE 1000 companies still do not have a robust and single view of their customers (Mazur 2004).

A well managed process integrates into the business processes and systems which, in turn, shave costs and slash inventories. Some companies take orders and payment immediately and ask third party suppliers to supply directly. So stock (and working capital required to fund stock) is reduced to zero. In fact, because the company receives payment from the customer and doesn't pay the supplier for 30 or 60 days, the company generates surplus cash. This creates negative working capital because instead of having to fund stock with working capital the supply process is so tight it generates its own funds.

E-MARKETING INSIGHT

Wobbly shopping carts blight UK e-commerce

UK e-commerce sites have been slapping customers in the face, rather than shaking them by the hand. Turning consumers away once they have made a decision to buy is commercial suicide.

- 20% of shopping carts did not function for 12 hours a month or more
- 75% failed the standard service level availability of 99.9% uptime
- 80% performed inconsistently with widely varying response times, time-outs and errors – leaving customers at best wondering what to do next and at worst, unable to complete their purchases.

Marketers work hard (and spend a lot) to get visitors onto a site and then subsequently waste all of this effort by irritating the customers with a shopping cart that won't work. Since Leyden highlighted this in 2004, we still find a lot of web sites with 'wobbly shopping carts'. How many bad ones have you experienced, which ultimately force you to abandon your purchase?

E-MARKETING EXCELLENCE

SciVisum identifies failed user journeys

Today, problems with e-commerce performance are typically not downtime affecting the whole the site, but are related to technical problems with particular user journeys and system states. Research by SciVisum in 2007 (SciVisum, 2007) showed that what they referred to as 'invisible errors' are still significant, with one third of the consumer online journeys tested by SciVisum experienced more than 3% error rates, while more than 10% demonstrated extreme inconsistencies in delivery speed of the journey.

SciVisum describe invisible errors as '*Invisible errors are not outages affecting 100% of users, but are problems that impact a percentage of users at any point in time*'. A problem that impacts say 1 in 100 random users on a particular journey is not reproducible by IT teams, and so frequently remains unresolved.

SciVisum's testing adopts a mystery-shopper approach that actually visits the site and attempts to make a user journey every five minutes throughout the day. This allows the company to see what customers see, and makes it possible to identify a range of intermittent problems that impact real users, but that are invisible to any other analysis. These problems include:

- Session swap: where two users see each others' online sessions. Nowhere is this category of problem detected in server or analytic logs.
- Page not delivered errors: because the page is not delivered, there is no log of the error in web analytics.
- Jump back: the user is in error forced back several pages; the new page is itself a valid page, so no errors are logged in analytics or tech logging.
- Page content incomplete: web analytics logs only that a page was delivered, not whether it showed the user what they expected.
- Shopping basket errors: e.g. basket is empty after adding items. Nowhere is this category of problem detected in server or analytic logs.

OPTIMIZING EXTERNAL PROCESSES

Reviewing processes and systems can help radically to redesign supply and distribution chains, and in the process, compete much more effectively.

For many organizations, Jack Welsh's internal slogan 'Destroy Your Business.com' (before the dot-coms do) makes a lot of sense just from the process side alone. Reinvent the business process so it's faster, lighter on resources and, most importantly, makes the customer happy.

Classic marketing empathizes with the customer – what kind of problems, priorities and procedures do they need? What will delight them? Then build the process that caters for the many diverse types of customers out there.

How value chains need to be revised is another aspect of process that is considered in Chapter 9, E-business.

SECTION SUMMARY 2.10

Process

Good processes and systems can create competitive advantage. There's lots of poor processes that kill sales and damage the brand. Processes can have a huge impact on your organization.

2.11   An extra 'P' – partnerships

Perhaps there is a new P in the mix, 'partnerships' or marketing marriages or alliances. With almost two thirds (64%) of the UK top 1000 companies confirming they have staff dedicated to partnership marketing (Craggs, 2002) it is not surprising, a few years later, to find award-winning e-marketing campaigns revealing a common pattern – partnerships. Although increasingly important in the offline world of marketing, clever partnerships are also emerging as keys that open the doors to vast new markets. Hence the emergence of alliance managers. Here are a few examples:

Ford Galaxy teamed up with Tesco and AOL to gain access to a million new online customers within its target audience of 30–44-year-old women with children. Ford also wanted to be associated with brands that have already improved its target audience's lives.

MUtv (the TV channel devoted to Manchester United) partnered with Sky and Century Radio in an attempt to develop its product so it could create an exciting proposition which quickly attracted 379 000 unique users in 98 countries. Combine this with MORI's estimated MUFC global fan base of 70 million and you can see the potential.

In the online world, many e-retailers now have staff dedicated to managing online partnerships, particularly for **affiliate marketing**, which is covered in Chapter 7.

The highly innovative and highly effective partnership between Live 8 Charity and O2, the Mobile service provider, proved that partnerships can achieve what previously seemed impossible.

Situation

The twentieth anniversary of Live Aid saw the hastily prepared Live 8 event snatching global headlines. Live 8 needed to raise over £1 million, promote its concert, create a way of selecting over 100 000 concert ticket holders and then distribute the tickets – all within two weeks. O2 approached Live 8 to run the ticketing process via text. The operator realized that the Live 8 concert was going to be the biggest music event for 20 years and that demand for tickets would outweigh supply.

Objective

1 To develop a fair mechanism to select 130 000 guests for the Live 8 Charity Concert and ultimately distribute 130 000 Live 8 Concert tickets safely and securely in just two weeks.

2 To raise at least £1.6m in revenue for Live 8 (to offset some of the costs of putting on the event and distributing 130 000 tickets quickly and securely at low cost).

Strategy

O2 worked with Mobile Interactive Group (MIG), using its Vote Winner platform to run the competition, having publicized the competition questions and the O2 short-code in all national newspapers and on radio and TV stations.

Tactics

The ticket competition entry mechanic went live on 6 June. In order to meet the requirement for a speedy and fair entry process, a multiple choice question was agreed with Live 8. After seven days the competition closed and 66 500 winners were notified via text message that they had won a pair of tickets.

Action

Each winner was sent a unique PIN which they then had to enter at the O2 Web site. Each text message entered into the competition cost £1.50, all of which went to Live 8. A standard network charge of between 10p and 12p was applied to all messages to cover network costs. O2 didn't make any money from the project. At its peak the system received 611 messages a second, compared to 500 a second for Big Brother (the popular TV show). Within tight deadlines they provided a simple yet effective call to action and an excellent customer experience.

Control

The Live 8 ticketing operation was recorded by the Guinness Book of Records as the largest ever text competition. Nearly 2.1 million people entered and the campaign raised over £3m for the Live 8 Charity Concert for Africa which went on to raise the profile of Africa's plight and win concessions for Africa, including debt cancellation for many countries.

(*Source*: Based on New Media Age Awards 2006 submission).

SECTION SUMMARY 2.11

An extra 'P' – partnerships

We cannot do everything ourselves. Partnerships can help enormously, but they require skilled management.

CHAPTER SUMMARY

1 The marketing mix must be re-examined for the online world since there are many new opportunities to vary the mix to take advantage of the characteristics of digital media.

2 The main elements of the traditional marketing mix are product, price, place, promotion, people, processes and physical evidence. Alternative models such as the 5Is of identification, individualization, interaction, integration, integrity have been developed in recognition of the potential of one-to-one/relationship marketing online.

3 Relationship building and service quality is vital with the trends towards consolidation and commoditization. Building relationships and increasing loyalty is required to increase profitability.

4 **Product**. Products can be extended online by offering new information-based services and interaction with the brand to create new brand experiences.

5 **Price**. Reduction in market prices is caused by online price transparency through purchasing methods such as reverse auction, price comparison and shopping bots. B2B exchanges and hubs will become significant for routine purchase of commoditized products. Marketers will continually have to monitor prices to remain competitive.

6 **Place**. Changes in the place of promotion, purchase, distribution and usage of products are considered when specifying the place element of mix. Disintermediation, countermediation and reintermediation are major marketplace changes which must be responded to. The atomization of content and services through widgets and feed syndication is another trend.

7 **Promotion**. Online options for all elements of the promotional mix from advertising, selling, sales promotion, PR, sponsorship, direct mail, exhibitions, merchandizing, packaging to word-of-mouth should all be reviewed for the promotion part of the mix. Key issues in devising the promotional mix are integration, creativity, globalization and resourcing.

8 **People**. People are a significant contributor to the mix since service quality is a key differentiator online or offline. Organizations need to decide on the best balance of automated online customer service and traditional human service to provide customers with service quality and choice while at the same time minimizing service costs. Online social media enable organizations to recruit customers to help shape their service for other customers through reviews and comments.

9 **Physical evidence**. The quality of the site is the physical evidence online, so it is important to reassure customers buying intangible services through a site that meets acceptable standards of speed and ease of use. This can be supplemented by certification by independent organizations.

10 **Process**. All processes impact customers in terms of product and service quality. In the online context it is particularly important to revise processes by integrating front and back office systems to provide efficient response to customer support requests and fulfilment.

11 **Partnerships**. Marketing marriages and alliances can be potent but need experienced management.

References

Anderson, C. (2006) *The Long Tail: why the future of business is selling less of more*. Hyperion.

Apollo (2007) US consumer research project **Arbitron** and the **Nielsen Company** WARC 15, October.

Bartels, F. (1963) *The History of Marketing Thought*. Richard D. Irwin, Homewood, Illinois.

Berryman, K., Harrington, L., Layton-Rodin, D. and Rerolle, V. (1998) Electronic commerce: three emerging strategies. *The McKinsey Quarterly*, Vol. 1, pp. 152–159.

Booms, B.H. and Bitner, M.J. (1981) Marketing strategies and organizational structures for service firms. In *Marketing of Services*, eds J. Donnelly and W. George, pp. 451–477. American Marketing Association, Chicago.

Booz, Allen and Hamilton, (2003) The four bases of organisational DNA. *Strategy & Business*, Vol. Winter Issue, p. 33.

Bossiddy, L. and Charan, R. (2004) *Execution – the discipline of getting things done*. Crown Business.

Butler, M. (2001) Techno Business. *Winning Business*, January, p. 75.

Clifford, L. (2000) Shatner will fly in Japan; Priceline may not. An interview with Japanese business expert Terri Morrison (co-author *Kiss or Blow – How to do business in 60 countries*). *Fortune*, 2 October.

Cohen, M., Agrawal, N. and Agrawal, V. (2006) Winning in the aftermarket. *Harvard Business Review*, Vol. 84, No. 5.

Colvin, G. (2000) Value Driven, You Might Get Your Next Face Lift Online. *Fortune*, 29 May.

Craggs, J. (2002) *Partnership Marketing Professionals and their Presence in Top British Companies*. CRM Community News.

Customer Management (2007) Customer Loyalty hits rock bottom. *Customer Management Newsletter*, 25th October.

Dyson, E. (1999) www.medialifemagazine.com/newspapers/archives/jan00/news20104. html. 31 December.

Ghosh, S. (1998) Making Business Sense of the Internet. *Harvard Business Review*, March–April, pp. 126–135.

Kotter, J. and Heskett, J. (1992) *Corporate Culture and Performance*. Free Press, New York.

Lautenborn, R. (1990) New marketing litany: 4Ps passes, 4Cs takeovers. *Advertising Age*, 1 October, p. 26.

Leyden, J. (2004) Wobbly Shopping Carts Blight UK e-Commerce. TheRegister.co.uk, 4 June.

Mazur, L. (2004) Poor Profiling. *Marketing Business*, February.

McCarthy, J. (1960) *Basic marketing: a managerial approach*. Richard D. Irwin, Homewood, Illinois.

McMillan, S. (2001) *Next Generation eBusiness*. IBM UK.

MGCC (2004) *Benchmarking Report 2004*. Merchant's Global Contact Centre.

Moore, G. (1999) *Crossing The Chasm*, 2nd ed. Harper Collins.

New Media Age Awards (2006) Centaur, London.

Nielsen, J. (2001) Tagline blues: what's the site about. 22 July. www.useit.com.

Peppers, D. and Rogers, M. (1997) *One to One Future*, 2nd edition. Doubleday, New York.

Queree, A. (2000) *Financial Times*. Technology supplement, 1 March.

Rose, F. (2006) And Now, a Word From Our Customers, *Wired*, 14 December.

SciVisum (2007) SciVisum: Lost Online Sales Study 2007 UK eCommerce sites riddled with 'invisible errors' http://www.scivisum.co.uk/report/lost_sales_2007/index.htm#summary.

Smith, PR (2002) The Marketing CDs www.prsmith.org

Smith, PR. and Taylor, J. (2004) *Marketing Communications – an integrated approach*. Kogan Page.

Toffler, A. (1980) *The Third Wave*. Bantam Books, New York.

Further reading

Bickerton, P., Bickerton, M. and Pardesi, U. (2000) CyberMarketing. *Chapter 6 Exploiting your global niche – the best marketing mix*. Butterworth-Heinemann, Oxford. Chartered Institute of Marketing series.

Chaffey, D., Mayer, R., Johnston, K. and Ellis-Chadwick, F. (2003) Internet Marketing: Strategy, Implementation and Practice. *Chapter 5 The Internet and the marketing mix*. Financial Times/Prentice Hall, Harlow, Essex.

Cumming, T. (2001) Little e, big commerce. *Chapter 6 Set marketing strategies and targets*. Virgin Business Guides, London.

Smith, P.R. and Taylor, J. (2004) Marketing Communications: an integrated approach. *Chapter 1 Marketing and the integrated communications mix*. Kogan Page, London.

Web links

Bized Marketing Mix page (http://www.bized.co.uk/learn/business/marketing/mix). Some in-depth articles on different aspects of the marketing mix and UK case studies.

Bizrate (www.bizrate.com). An example of an online shopping comparison site.

Chevrolet's User generated advertisements article (www.frankrose.com/work2.htm). Frank is a journalist for *Wired* magazine, so there are a range of articles related to innovation in the marketing mix.

Chris Anderson's Long Tail blog (www.thelongtail.com). In-depth blog by the Author of the long tail which relates to the Product element of the marketing mix.

CIM 10 minute guide to the Marketing Mix. (http://www.cim.co.uk/mediastore/10_minute_guides/10_min_Marketing_Mix.pdf). A fairly detailed introduction to the marketing mix with further links.

E-marketing Excellence Book homepage (http://www.davechaffey.com/E-marketing). An index of all e-marketing links for each chapter in this book.

E Digital Research (www.edigitalresearch.com). E Digital Research provides mystery shopping services in the UK.

Introduction to the Marketing Mix (http://www.thetimes100.co.uk/theory/theory--marketing-mix-(price-place-promotion-product)--243.php). The Times 100 – a student and teacher business studies resource centre has a basic introduction to the marketing mix.

New Media Age Awards (www.nmaawards.co.uk). Has awards in innovation across different business sectors.

PaidContent (www.paidcontent.org). Discusses the economics and revenue models for online publishing.

WordSpy: www.wordspy.com/index/Business-Marketing.asp. Introduces the latest marketing and business buzzwords.

Self-test

1 For each element of the marketing mix (7Ps) list two differences introduced by the digital world.

2 How appropriate are the 5Is of identification, individualization, interaction, integration and integrity as a replacement for the marketing mix?

3 What is the principal way in which product can be varied through an online presence?

4 Summarize in one sentence how an online presence can be used to enhance brands.

5 Explain the reasons for price transparency and marketing responses to this phenomenon.

6 Describe the relevance of disintermediation and reintermediation to your organization and actions that have been/should be taken.

7 Summarize online applications of advertising, PR, direct selling and word-of-mouth promotional mix tools.

8 Recommend a channel contact strategy for inbound communications to your organization.

9 How does the concept of physical evidence relate to your organization's web site?

10 Assess how your online presence contributes to the main business processes and to what extent they have been streamlined by the move online.

Chapter **3**

E-models

'The rapid growth of first multi-channel, then digital, then personal video recorders and soon higher-speed broadband are simply the pre-tremors of the real volcanic eruption that technology is about to unleash. At the risk of being overdramatic I would say that most traditional television broadcasters are today standing about the equivalent of one mile from Mount St Helens. When it blows, frankly, that is too close and then it will be too late to run'.

Ofcom chairman Lord Currie's address to the
Royal Television Society quoted in ZDNet (2005)

OVERVIEW

The business world is changing faster than ever before. Old approaches and models are being turned on their head. In this chapter we show how to assess your online marketplace, review new business, revenue and communications models, and develop budget models.

OVERALL LEARNING OUTCOME

By the end of this chapter you will be able to:

- Assess approaches for analyzing your online marketplace
- Appreciate emerging digital revenue models
- Review and select models which are appropriate for your business.

CHAPTER TOPIC	LEARNING OBJECTIVE
3.1 Introduction	Outline the changes to existing and new models
3.2 New models required	Describe the drivers of new models and actions required in response
3.3 E-marketplace models	Understand the role of different intermediaries in influencing online sales
3.4 Online revenue models	Review alternatives for generating revenue, particularly from advertising
3.5 Digital communications models	Describe differences in communications models and how they can be exploited
3.6 Models for assessing communications effectiveness	Assess approaches for reconciling media spend to different digital channels
3.7 Web 2.0 and social network models	Explain the drivers for the increase in Web 2.0 and social networking approaches
3.8 Customer buying models	Summarize changes to buying models and assess their implications
3.9 Customer information processing	Assess differences in customer information processing that occur online
3.10 Loyalty models	Assess the relevance of new loyalty models

3.1 Introduction to e-models

Whether business models, revenue models, communications models or buying models, old models are being replaced by new and revised models. This chapter explores some of the changes to existing models and shows how they can be incorporated into e-marketing planning to make sure you are maximizing your online sales and return on investment. Some of the budgeting models we review are also vital for controlling spend in different online media channels we will cover in Chapter 7, Traffic building.

It is the fluid, flexible and agile businesses that embrace the new models enabled by technology and exploit the opportunities presented by the new economy.

Before exploring the different models, let's clarify what is a model. A model is anything that represents reality. It could be a model aeroplane, a map, a diagram, algebra or a formula. Here, we are particularly interested in descriptive models that describe a process – the current way in which a business operates in its dealings with customers and intermediaries such as media sites or price comparison engines. In Chapter 9, we review changes with other e-business partners like suppliers and distributors.

There are many different implications of change across a variety of models:

- Customers develop new patterns of media consumption and product selection, and brands need to be visible at the right time in the right place as consumers use search engines, review sites and affiliates to choose their preferred supplier. So online marketers need to review their **online marketplace models** to understand their digital marketspace.

- Businesses cross categories, supermarkets become banks, as radical changes to **business models** and **revenue models** are enacted.

- 'Markets become conversations' (Levine *et al.*, 2000), where dialogue between customers, and employee and customers drive the relationships.

- **Value chains** and **distribution channels** are restructured as existing channel partners are bypassed and new channel partners and **value networks** are formed and reformed.

- Your suppliers or distributors may seek new revenue from online ads and affiliate links and this offers new opportunities for you to reach your audience online.

- Marketing becomes transparent as customers manage the relationship with companies rather than the other way around. Systems and control mechanisms are opened up to customers.

- Brand equity changes from being visually driven to interactively driven.

- Businesses can become what Charles Handy calls a 'box of contracts', as many functions are outsourced to form a **virtual business**.

E-MARKETING INSIGHT

The disruptive power of the Internet

Evans and Wurster of Harvard Business School argued in their classic 'Strategies and the New Economics of Information', summarized in Evans and Wurster (1999), that there are three characteristics of information which when combined with **disruptive Internet technologies** can have a major impact on a marketplace. Are you taking advantages of these key aspects of online marketplace models when developing your online strategies?

1 **Reach**. The Internet enables reach to be increased nationally and internationally at low cost through making content on your site available via search engines. For Evans and Wurster, reach also refers to the number of different categories and products you can distribute – what is today referred to as **The Long Tail**. Witness the large range of products available through e-businesses such as Amazon, eBay and Kelkoo.com, and note how existing companies such as easyJet.com and Tesco.com have used the web to extend their product range.

2 **Richness**. The web enables you to give more detailed and timely information about products, prices and availability than through other channels. Broadband now gives great options to add **Rich Internet Applications (RIA)** which offer multimedia interactivity to explore products and offer customization. Encouraging customer interaction through product reviews and forums also adds to the richness of content. Firebox (www.firebox.com) is a great example of a retailer that has exploited this richness.

3 **Affiliation**. In the online marketplace, an organization which has the most and richest links with other compatible organizations will be able to gain a larger reach and influence. That's why we said in Chapter 2 that Partnership is important and should be the 8th P of the marketing mix! Manufacturer 3M (www.3m.com/uk), who have traditionally distributed their products through intermediaries, have taken advantage of new online distribution models through creating a store on Amazon, eBay and using affiliates and price comparison sites to drive visitors to their own e-commerce store (www.3mselect.co.uk).

SECTION SUMMARY 3.1

Introduction to e-models

Models describe the process by which business is conducted between an organization, its customers, suppliers, distributors and other stakeholders. Managers constantly need to review how electronic communications change existing models and offer new models that may confer competitive advantage.

3.2 New models required

What happens when people stop watching TV and stop going to the shops? What happens when a significant proportion of the population, say 10%, stop watching advertisements on TV and the web? They filter out banner ads and junk mail. They also only watch non-commercial TV (e.g. BBC3) or use Personal Video Recorder (PVR) technology like Sky+ to filter out the ads and watch only the programmes, when they want. They also stop shopping in shops because they realize they have better things to do, plus better deals to get by going online instead.

COMMODITIZATION – THE DRIVER OF MANY NEW MODELS

All markets eventually tend towards **commoditization** as competition catches up, matches features, quality and prices. Assuming that prices and quality are similar, then what affects sales volume? We can construct a very simple model which shows that the advertising can differentiate the brands and that distribution can ensure competitive advantage. The model would look like this:

$$A + D = S \ldots \text{Advertising} + \text{Distribution} = \text{Sales}$$

But what if 'A+D' doesn't work for some segments any more? Should the business forget about this small, but growing, percentage of the market and let the market segment move away? Or can it devise new models to try to keep these customers? There is no single right answer here.

Through time, commoditization will further reduce the role of 'A+D'. In time, consumers may use price-driven shopping bots or **searchbots** to scour the web for best deals, brands will suffer as cheapest prices will be chosen every time. Today **price comparison intermediaries** or **aggregators** which accept **XML product feeds** from the retailers, travel companies and banks have become incredibly important in some markets. Are there any new models to deal with this? How can the brand be saved from the price-driven consumers scouring price comparison sites for the best deal? How can a retailer make an impression on the price-sensitive shopper? There are no easy answers here. One option is to change the price positioning of a product with online only rates and features that compare well in some price comparison queries. The other alternative shown by the box below is to remove the listing and use brand advertising to encourage direct visits to the site.

E-MARKETING INSIGHT

The impact of comparison sites

In October 2000, *Revolution* reported a dispute between Abbey National and financial comparison site Moneysupermarket.com. This dispute highlights the positive and negative impact of online comparisons. The bank had reportedly requested that several comparison sites not list them. Simon Nixon, chief executive of Moneysupermarket.com, was reported as saying:

> *'We've all predicted the effect that the Internet will have by giving customers information and choice. If Abbey National is worried about unfavourable comparisons on mortgage rates, then the ball is fairly and squarely in their court'.*

More recently, direct insurer Direct Line (www.directline.com) and Moneysupermarket have joined battle. *The Guardian* (2007) reported on an ongoing spat which saw Direct Line disparaging comparison engines like Moneysupermarket, Confused.com and Go Compare in a multi-million TV campaign. It reported Roger Ramsden, strategy director for Royal Bank of Scotland insurance, which owns Direct Line, as saying:

> *'Direct Line has never been available through a middleman of any sort and never will be, and that's what these [comparison] sites are. They are commercial operations rather than a public service, and the [advertising] campaign is responding to our customers who tell us they are unaware of this and find the sites confusing'*

He does have a point, in that coverage is incomplete. For example, Moneysupermarket covers 80% of the motor insurance market, but does not list quotes from some large insurers such as Norwich Union or other insurers owned by the Royal Bank of Scotland, including Direct Line, Churchill, Privilege and Tesco Personal Finance.

But Richard Mason, director of Moneysupermarket.com, said that Direct Line's campaign:

> *'smacks of complete desperation. We are the new kids on the block and Direct Line don't like it. They have lost their market share since we came on the scene – they were in a position where consumers thought they were competitive and kept renewing their policies. They spent hundreds of millions of pounds on advertising. But now consumers can find cheaper alternatives and are doing so in their droves'.*

Data from Hitwise (2006) supports Moneysupermarket's position. It achieves around a third of its visits from price sensitive searchers looking to compare by typing generic phrases such as 'car insurance' and 'compare car insurance'.

To us, this conflict shows the importance of having a strong brand that consumers will naturally turn to when selecting products. It also shows the continuing importance of offline advertising in shaping consumer perceptions of brands and driving visitors directly to a destination site.

New models required

We need new models to respond to changes in the environment such as reduced TV watching and reduced trips to the shops and the increase in commoditization. We need to think creatively; consider new models; adapt old models; consider mixed mode models and let common sense prevail so that if existing models give the greatest return on investment, then these positions are defended.

3.3 E-marketplace models

It is vital that marketers understand their position in the online marketplace. This is your 'click ecosystem' which describes the flow of online visitors between search engines, media sites, other intermediaries, your competitors and you. Prospects and customers in your online marketplace will naturally turn to search engines to find products, services, brands and entertainment. Search engines act as a distribution system which connects searchers to sites for different phrases. Companies need to analyze consumer use of keyphrases entered from generic searches for products or services, more specific phrases and brand phrases incorporating their brand and competitor names. They also need to assess, using services listed later in this section, which online intermediaries or competitors have the best share of these phrases or which are popular in their own right as well known brands that attract visitors directly.

Online marketplace analysis is a fundamental technique for developing an e-marketing strategy for an organization. It is also useful at an early stage in planning an online marketing campaign to indicate which type of sites to partner with for promotion and the type of search terms which may need to be purchased for pay per click advertising.

To help summarize the linkages and traffic flows in your e-marketplace, we urge you to create an e-marketplace map (Figure 3.1). This shows the relative importance of different online intermediaries in the marketplace and the flow of clicks between your different customer segments, your company site(s) and different competitors via the intermediaries. You need to know which sites are effective in harnessing search traffic, and either partner with them or try to grab a slice of the search traffic yourself, as explained in Chapter 7.

This e-model introduces some concepts we will refer to more in later sections, the main members of the e-marketplace model are:

1 **Customer segments**. Identify different segments to understand their online media consumption, buyer behaviour and the type of content and experiences they will be looking for from intermediaries and your website. Personas are used to understand the preferences, characteristics and online behaviours of different groups as described in Chapters 4 and 6.

2 **Search intermediaries**. These are the main search engines in each country. Typically Google, Yahoo! and Microsoft Live Search, but others are important in some markets such as China (Baidu) and Russia (Yandex). Use audience data from Comscore (www.comscore.com), Hitwise (www.hitwise.com), Nielsen Netratings (www.nielsennetratings.com)

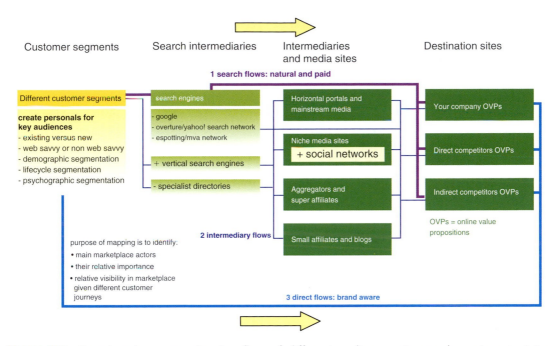

Figure 3.1 E-marketplace map showing flow of different audiences via search engines to intermediaries and destination sites

Websites that received traffic from 'savings account'
Displaying **1** to **10** of **16** websites. **Click Here** to see more websites.

	Website	Volume	
1.	www.moneysupermarket.com	36.82%	
2.	www.hsbc.co.uk	11.05%	
3.	www.abbey.com	<11.05%	
4.	uk.virginmoney.com	<11.05%	
5.	www.rightmove.co.uk	<11.05%	
6.	www.about-savings-accounts.co.uk	<11.05%	
7.	www.rbs.co.uk	<11.05%	
8.	www.best-savings-account.info	<11.05%	
9.	www.icicibankukpromotions.com	<11.05%	
10.	www.lloydstsb.co.uk	<11.05%	

Figure 3.2 Example showing the sites referred by search engines for the phrase 'savings account'. Source: Hitwise (www.hitwise.com)

to find out their relative importance in your country. You will need to know the most important phrases and which sites the visitors are directed to, as shown in Figure 3.2 for example. Tools such as the Google Keyword tool and Google Traffic Estimator (referenced from the link below) are helpful to determine the popularity of phrases. For example, in the financial sector, Moneysupermarket is an important potential partner if you are offering these services and HSBC is successful at achieving visits directly from the search engines for this keyphrase.

3 **Intermediaries and media sites**. Media sites and other intermediaries such as affiliates are often successful in attracting visitors via search or direct since they are mainstream brands. You should assess potential partners in the categories shown in Figure 3.2 such as:

   a **Mainstream news media sites or portals,** include traditional, e.g. *FT.com*, *Times* or Pure play, e.g. Google News, an aggregator of news from other sources

   b **Niche/vertical media sites**, e.g. E-consultancy, ClickZ.com in B2B

   c **Price comparison sites** (also known as aggregators), e.g. Moneysupermarket, Kelkoo, Shopping.com, uSwitch, etc.

   d **Superaffiliates**. Affilates gain revenue from a merchant they refer traffic to using a commission-based arrangement based on the proportion of sales or a fixed amount. They are important in e-retail markets, accounting for tens of percent of sales.

   e **Niche affiliates or bloggers**. These are often individuals, but they may be important, for example in the UK, Martin Lewis of Moneysavingexpert.com receives millions of visits every month. Smaller affiliates and bloggers can be important collectively.

4 **Destination sites**. These are the sites that the marketer is trying to generate visitors to, whether these are transactional sites, like retailers, financial services or travel companies, or manufacturers or brands. Figure 3.1 refers to OVP or Online Value Proposition which is a summary of the unique features of the site, described in more detail in Chapter 4. The OVP is a key aspect to consider within planning – marketers should evaluate their OVPs against competitors and think about how they can refine them to develop a unique online experience.

Well known, trusted brands which have developed customer loyalty are in a good position to succeed online since a common consumer behaviour is to go straight to the site through entering a URL or from a bookmark or e-mail. Alternatively they may search for the brand or URL.

PRACTICAL E-MARKETING TIP

Brand strength

Use web analytics to track the popularity of your brand and how this varies through time with seasonality, offline and online campaigns. You can also see the number of direct visitors arriving straight on the site. You can also access reports showing visitors searching on your brand name, URL, misspellings and in combination with different products. You need to protect your brand from 'brand hijacking' in the search engines, as described in Chapter 7.

THE LONG TAIL MARKETPLACE MODEL (ZIPF'S LAW)

The significance of the Long Tail model was brought to prominence by Chris Anderson's book and his blog (www.thelongtail.com). We introduced it in Chapter 2. Formerly known as Zipf's law, it refers to any large collection of items ordered by size or popularity. It describes how the frequency or popularity of items declines in a regular way. It is also known as the long tail phenomenon since, although a handful of items are very popular, there are many, many others which although not popular individually, collectively can be important if the marketer wants their services to appeal to a range of potential customers. Niche goods and services can be as economically attractive as mainstream goods and services since the potential aggregate size of the many small markets can be large. Furthermore, profitability may be greater on the tail.

E-MARKETING INSIGHT

About Zipf's law

Zipf's law states that in a large collection ordered or ranked by popularity, the second item will be around half the popularity of the first one, and the third item will be about a third of the popularity of the first one. In general:

The kth item is 1/k the popularity of the first.

Zipf's law can be applied to describe the exponential decrease in preferences for using, selecting or purchasing from a choice of items. As the tail is long, it is a mistake to concentrate marketing efforts only on the most popular items since many customers or prospects will have a different behaviour and will have different content or product preferences. The flip side of this logic is that if you have limited resources, you should concentrate your efforts on the head.

Online marketers will encounter the long tail a lot, here are some of the situations and the implications:

1 *Popularity of search terms within a category or for an individual site.* A typical pattern is shown in Figure 3.3. Implication: Keyphrase analysis used to determine search engine optimization and Pay Per Click marketing is most effective when hundreds of potential phrases are analyzed for each customer need rather than only the five or ten top keyphrases.

We have found these tips for targeting the long tail through search include:

- Target keyphrases with four or more keywords through SEO and Pay Per Click. Within SEO, refer to these longer phrases within the <title> of your web page or blog posting
- Use the Google keyword tool (https://adwords.google.com/select/KeywordTool-External) to identify different qualifiers such as 'geography' used to search for a more common phrase, e.g. 'marketing recruitment Manchester' is a geographic qualifier

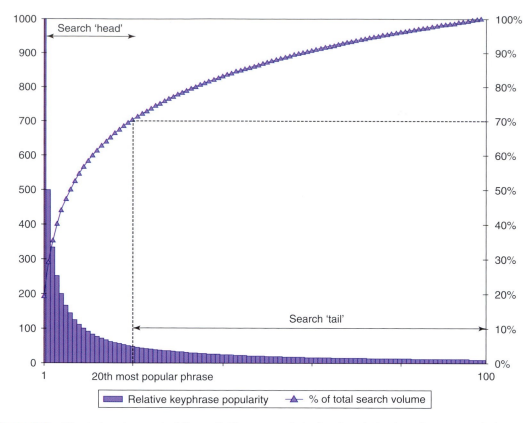

Figure 3.3 Chart showing typical 'Long Tail' pattern of decline in relative keyphrase popularity

- Use synonyms. For example, an article about 'e-marketing' should also reference similar terms such as online marketing, digital marketing and Internet marketing
- Target singular and plural versions – users will search for each.

2 *Popularity of content within a website.* Implication: The more pages you have with different content relevant to your audience, the more likely you are to meet the needs of your diverse audience and the more they will engage with the content. But you should use your web analytics package to identify the top 20 pages which are most visited and then make sure they are effective in communicating your key messages and achieving the actions you are looking for.

3 *The popularity of items purchased from an e-retail site.* Implication: A larger inventory will result in more sales. Higher profit margins are possible for less popular items since consumers may be prepared to pay more for difficult-to-obtain items. Chris Anderson discusses this effect at length in his book.

4 *The popularity of websites in a category measured through unique visitors.* Implication: The e-communications channels we cover in Chapter 7 such as interactive advertising, affiliate marketing and link-building can be used to take advantage of the long tail. Using such techniques to communicate with potential visitors visiting niche sites like blogs and

specialist directories can be a relatively low cost way to achieve reach in comparison to expenditure on the top ten portals of the web or a category.

SECTION SUMMARY 3.3

E-marketplace models

Analysis of your online marketplace can help you understand customer behaviour in order to identify potential search terms for which you should promote your company and also potential partner sites or media buys.

3.4 Online revenue models

A knowledge of the range of options for generating revenue online is useful, both for intermediary sites such as media owners, portals and affiliates, and for transactional sites where the main transactional revenue may be supplemented by ad revenue, for example. It is also useful from a media-buying perspective when promoting your site, since when viewed from the reverse direction these are all options (which we explore further in Chapter 7), that you have for paying for visitors, either when approaching site owners direct or via a media agency. So you need to review the options and select a media mix which delivers the best ROI. We present budgets based on these online media selling/buying models in Chapter 10.

In addition to direct selling online and brokering online sales through an auction arrangement, there are eight main online and revenue models that a budding web entrepreneur or established site owner can use to generate revenue.

1 *Revenue from subscription access to content*. A range of documents can be accessed for a period of a month or typically a year. For example, FT.com has a three tier subscription model according to the types of content you can access varying from £100 to £400 per year.

2 *Revenue from Pay Per View access to documents*. Here payment occurs for single access to a document, video or music clip which can be downloaded. It may or may not be protected with a password or Digital Rights Management.

   For example, we pay to access detailed best practice guides on Internet marketing from Marketing Sherpa.

3 *Revenue from CPM display advertising on site* (e.g. banners ads, skyscrapers or rich media). CPM stands for 'cost per thousand' where M denotes 'Mille'. The site owner such as FT.com charges advertisers a rate card price (for example €50 CPM) according to the number of its ads shown to site visitors. Ads may be served by the site owners' own ad server or more commonly through a third-party ad network service. With display ad networks, space can be bought a lower rate because it is known as a blind ad buy – CPM rates are lower because it is not known where the ads will be placed.

4 *Revenue from CPC advertising on site (Pay Per Click text ads)*. CPC stands for 'Cost Per Click'. Advertisers are charged not simply for the number of times their ads are displayed, but

according to the number of times they are clicked. These are typically text ads similar to sponsored links within a search engine, but delivered over a network of third-party sites such as Google Adsense (www.google.com/adsense), Yahoo! Content Match (http://search-marketing.yahoo.com/srch/contentmatch.php), Microsoft content ads (http://advertising.microsoft.com/advertise/search/content-advertising) or MIVA (www.miva.com). For example, Dave Chaffey's site (www.davechaffey.com) uses Google Adsense by inserting Javascript at different points in the page to automatically serve contextual ads related to the content, so a page about e-mail marketing has ads about e-mail services which can be bought on a CPM (site targeted) or Cost Per Click basis.

For us, the search content networks are one of the biggest secrets in online marketing, with search engines such as Google generating over a third of their revenue from the network. Yet many advertisers don't realize, when they pay for their ads to be displayed in the search results, they may be displayed elsewhere on the web. Google is the innovator and offers options for different formats of ad units including text ads, display ads, streamed videos and now even cost per action as part of its pay per action scheme.

5 *Revenue from Sponsorship of site sections or content types (typically fixed fee for a period) – fixed price deal, CPA or CPC deal.* A company can pay to advertise a site channel or section. For example, bank HSBC sponsors the Money section on the Orange portal. This type of deal is often struck for a fixed amount per year. It may also be part of a reciprocal arrangement, sometimes known as a 'contra-deal' where neither party pays. However it is a negotiated deal, so may also have CPA or CPC elements.

A fixed-fee sponsorship approach was famously used by Alex Tew in 2005, a 21-year-old considering going to University in the UK who was concerned about paying off his university debts. This is no longer a concern since he earned $1 000 000 in four months when he set up his Million Dollar Homepage (www.milliondollarhomepage.com).

6 *Affiliate revenue (typically CPA, but could be CPC).* Affiliate revenue is commission-based, for example I display Amazon books on my site, DaveChaffey.com, and receive around 5% of the cover price as a fee from Amazon. Such an arrangement is sometimes known as Cost Per Acquisition (CPA). Amazon and others offer a tiered scheme where the affiliate is incentivized to gain more revenue, the more they sell. Hence this is often called a pay-per-performance ad deal.

Increasingly this approach is replacing CPM or CPC approaches where the advertiser has more negotiating power. For example, in 2005 manufacturing company Unilever negotiated CPA deals with online publishers, where it paid for every e-mail address captured by a campaign rather than a traditional CPM deal.

However, it depends on the power of the publisher, who will often receive more revenue overall for CPM deals. After all, the publisher cannot influence the quality of the ad creative or the incentivization to click which will affect the clickthrough rate on the ad and so the CPM.

7 *Subscriber data access for e-mail marketing.* The data a site owner has about its customers is also potentially valuable since they can send different forms of e-mail to its customers if they have given their permission that they are happy to receive e-mail either from the publisher

or third parties. The site owner can charge for adverts placed in its newsletter or can deliver a separate message on behalf of the advertiser (sometimes known as list rental). A related approach is to conduct market research with the site customers.

8 *Access to customers for online research.* An example of a company that uses this approach to attract revenue from surveys is the teen site Dubit.

ASSESSING THE BEST FORM OF REVENUE MODEL

Considering all of these approaches to revenue generation together, the site owner will seek to use the best combination of these techniques to maximize the revenue. To assess how effective different pages or sites in their portfolio are at generating revenue, they will use two approaches.

The first is eCPM, or effective Cost Per Thousand. This is a measure of the total revenue the site owner can generate when 1000 pages are served. Through increasing the number of ad units on each page this value will increase. This is why you will see some sites which are cluttered with ads. The other alternative to assess page or site revenue generating effectiveness is Revenue Per Click (RPC) and the similar Earnings Per Click (EPC), actually based on one hundred clicks to make it more meaningful for affiliates who will only generate revenue for a small percentage of clicks out from their sites. Basic revenue model evaluation spreadsheets based on these variables are available from www.marketing-insights.co.uk/spreadsheet.htm.

SECTION SUMMARY 3.4

Online revenue models

There are a bewildering array of online revenue models for media owners to consider, from traditional CPM and fixed sponsorships through to the upstarts CPC and CPA. With contextual advertising options available from the main search networks and with the growth of display ad networks there are now options for all site owners to review their ad revenue options.

3.5 Digital communications models

This section primarily explores how multi-stage communications models are moving into web-based community communications models. Brief reference is also made to other communications models including viral marketing, affiliate marketing and permission-based marketing.

In the last millennium, mass communications models were popular – and the simple model looked like this:

S ——————→ —————— C
Sender   Customer (mass audience)

Then opinion leaders and opinion formers were identified as important elements in communications models. So they were targeted to help encourage word-of-mouth spread. Here the sender sends a message and some of it goes directly to the customer and some is picked up by opinion formers who subsequently pass the message on to customers.

Add in some feedback and interaction and you've got conversations with the arrows also indicating flowbacks to the sender and other customers – a trialogue:

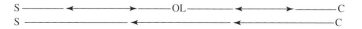

E-MARKETING INSIGHT

Harnessing the trialogue

Walmsley (2007) believes that the main impact of media was not to find new ways to connect brands to consumers as originally anticipated, but in connecting those consumers or 'people', as they like to be called, to each other. So, the age of trialogue has arrived and brands need to reinterpret themselves as facilitators.

Walmsley believes this trialogue will influence every aspect of marketing, from product design through to product recommendation. An example where product design is influenced is Threadless.com, the online t-shirt store, which only carries designs its users have uploaded and manufactures only those that get a critical mass of votes.

The potency of trialogue derives from the opportunity brands now have to talk at people, but to be a small part of billions of their conversations. This is the point where user generated content meets brands – an area fraught with difficulty for the unwary and rich with opportunity for the creative.

Think about who are the opinion formers and opinion leaders in your marketplace. Separate online from offline influencers. They may include business leaders, celebrity users, journalists, public speakers, consultants, professional bodies and awards, influential networks, accrediting bodies, chat room moderators, news groups, etc. Word-of-mouth works much more quickly online than offline.

Now comes the interesting bit. With the Internet came the easier facilitation of customer communities – where customers talk to each other (C2C) and back to the company (C2B).

The flow of communications eventually becomes like a web of communications between customers and opinion leaders – all built around the brand. The company facilitates these conversations. In doing so, it keeps close to customers as it can look and listen to what's being said. It can also communicate easily with the customers and ultimately develop strong

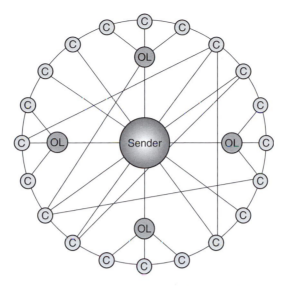

Figure 3.4   A web of conversations – accelerating word-of-mouth. C, customer; OL, opinion leader

relationships. Newsgroups (discussion rooms hosted by the brand), discuss the brand, its applications, problems, issues, ideas, improvements and a broader array of topics linked with some of the brand values. In a sense, a web of conversations is being spun around the brand (Figure 3.4).

Referrals are part of C2C and eventually C2B as the referred customer contacts the business. Viral marketing is an extension of this C2C or P2P model where customers pass the message on. This is accelerated word of mouth. Clever, creative messages with interesting ideas, amazing images, special offers, announcements and invitations are good for viral marketing. For more on viral marketing, see Section 7.7.

Affiliate marketing also spreads awareness of a brand amongst a community of relevant customers, who in turn talk to each other and can spread ordinary or clever viral messages amongst their own communities.

Implicit in all of these communications models is **permission-based marketing**. In this time-compressed, information-cluttered world, customers resent unsolicited SPAM. Excellent e-marketers win permission to send future messages. Now the sender asks permission to send a message. If the customer agrees a message is finally sent. There is more on permission-based marketing in Section 8.2.

ADVERTISING

All the models are changing. None more so than advertising. Advertising agencies are confronted by another big shift in their communications models. They have to move from 'getting attention' to 'giving attention'. This presents new challenges to agencies used to winning attention and creating brand awareness. Now when visitors land on the brand's site, it is the brand who must pay attention.

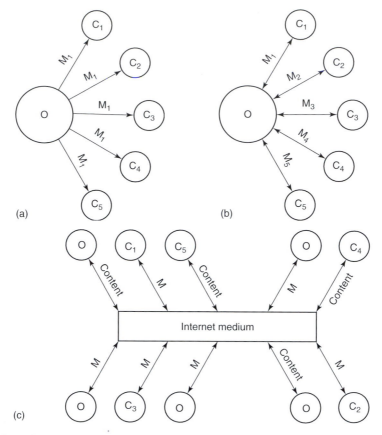

Figure 3.5   The differences between one-to-many and one-to-one communication using the Internet (organization (O), communicating a message (M) and customers (C)). (a) Traditional one-to-many mass marketing communication; (b) one-to-one Internet-based communication; (c) many-to-many communications via the Internet media

Once audiences paid for the media which carried the ads, today many marketers pay the audience for consuming the media (e.g. web-browsing).

E-MARKETING INSIGHT

Chaffey *et al.* (2003) on communication models

Figure 3.5 illustrates the interaction between an organization (O) communicating a message (M) to customers (C) for a single-step flow of communication. It is apparent that for traditional mass-marketing in (a) a single message (M1) is communicated to all customers (C1 to C5). With a web site with personalization facilities (b) there is a two-way interaction with each communication potentially unique. Note that many brochureware sites do not take full advantage of the Internet and merely use the web to replicate other media channels by delivering a uniform message.

SECTION SUMMARY 3.5

Digital communications models

This section explored how multi-stage communications models are moving into web-based community communications models. Brief reference was also made to other communications models including viral marketing, affiliate marketing and permission-based marketing. New models bring new opportunities.

3.6 Models for assessing online communications effectiveness

Online media introduces new challenges in tracking campaign effectiveness. It is rarely the case that a customer will go straight to a site and purchase, or that they will perform a single search and then purchase. Instead, they will commonly perform multiple searches and will be referred by different types of site. One example of this situation is shown in Figure 3.6. This shows how a visitor may be referred to a site several times via different digital communications channels.

Achieving and measuring repeat visits is worthwhile since, according to Flores and Eltvedt (2005), on average purchase intent sees a double digit increase after someone has been to a site more than once.

The task of the online marketer is to try and build the best picture of which channels are influencing sales. This won't be possible if your agencies are using different tracking tools and reporting separately on different media channels, for example, the ad agency reports on display advertising, the search agency on Pay Per Click, the affiliate manager on affiliate sales. Instead it is important to use a unified tracking system which typically uses common

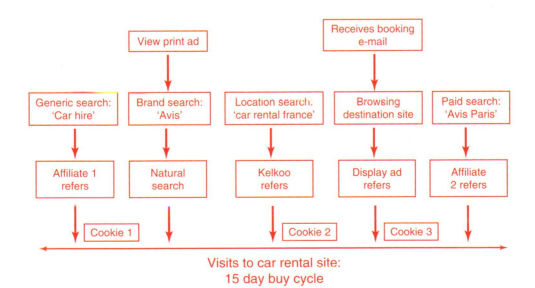

Figure 3.6 Example of a multi-step customer journey resulting in sale for a car hire company

tags across all media channels. Common unified tracking solutions are available from the likes of Atlas, Doubleclick Dart and some of the larger media agencies.

To simplify the understanding of media effectiveness, for companies with a unified tracking method, a common approach is to attribute or credit the sale or other outcome to the last click, in this case, Affiliate 2. This is a good approach in that it avoids double counting – a marketer wouldn't want to credit both Affiliate 1 and Affiliate 2 with 5% commission on basket value. However, it doesn't reflect the role of the mix of media such as display advertising and natural search in influencing sale. A common phenomenon in online advertising is the display advertising **halo effect** where display ads indirectly influence sales. These are sometimes known as 'view-throughs' or post impression effects. A more sophisticated approach is to weight the responsibility for sale across several the different referrers according to a model, so just considering the affiliates, Affiliate 1 might be credited with 30% of the sales value and Affiliate 2 with 70% for example.

E-MARKETING CHECKLIST – YOUR ONLINE TRACKING CAPABILITIES

Here is a checklist to assess your tracking capabilities:

Q1 Do you have unified tracking across all media?
- ☑ What high-level reporting do you have that enables you to compare cost (CPA), value (ROI, ROAS or LTV) and conversion across all media?
- ☑ What granularity do you have, i.e. how far can you break down by:
  - o Media, by referrer type
  - o Category or product(s) initially purchased
  - o Customer type (e.g. size of business/consumer, value or purchase activity over different time periods on lifecycle stages)
  - o Paid and natural search keyphrases – can these be tracked down to campaign, ad group and triggering keyword level in each search network and can these be compared to actual search terms entered by visitors?

Q2 How do you attribute sale to referring media?
Do you use:
- ☑ Last referrer?
- ☑ First referrer?
- ☑ Weighted mix between the two – especially paid search?
- ☑ Have you successfully removed duplication through using common tagging codes?
- ☑ Do you analyze the halo effect of combined media/channel impressions?

Q3 How well do you understand your sales cycle?
i.e. What analysis have you done on sequence and consideration period for searches or affiliate referrals based on 'cookied' visitors i.e. do you understand this pattern?

Which cut-off do you use to assess contribution from different media such as display ads? Usually, a period of 30 days is a standard for a product like a holiday, but it could be shorter for books or CDs, for example.

Q4 Do you assess traffic quality on types of value events (other than sales)?

This is a detailed insight to identify opportunities for further improvement to media and sites – it can be argued it is irrelevant if the cost per acquisition is too high. A simpler approach is bounce rates by media type, i.e. percentage of visitors progressing beyond first page.

Q5 Have you checked the accuracy of your campaign management systems?

Campaigns will be tracked by different sources such as page-tags on a web-analytics system, tags on a campaign management system, ad serving systems or log files. Differences between these should be assessed and minimized, although different data collection will likely always generate discrepancies. The important aspect is to make tracking consistent through time. Tag position on the page can be important and if a page is slow to load then this may not be registered as a click in the analytics system, although the ad-serving system has recorded it. Tags may just be plain wrong through human error, so this also needs to be checked.

E-MARKETING INSIGHT

The display ad halo effect – what do online site visitors do when they see an ad?

Clickthrough rates on ads tend to be very low, with most compilations showing response rates well below 1%. This phenomenon is known as banner blindness. This phenomenon is well known and we consider how to counter it in Chapters 6 and 7, but it is worth considering that not everyone who sees an ad clicks – this is the halo effect.

Research reported by MAD (2007) in the travel market involved asking respondents what their response to an online ad that appealed to them would be. Surely it would be a click? In fact the results broke down as follows:

- Search for a general term relating to the advertisement (31%)
- Go straight to advertiser's site (29%)
- Search for the advertiser's name (26%)
- Click on banner to respond (26%)
- Visit a retail store (4%).

Of course, this methodology shows us reported behaviour rather than actual behaviour, but it is still significant that more than twice as many people are being driven to a search engine by banner advertising than by clicking directly on the banner! This helps explain the halo effect mentioned in the text. The research concludes that paid search marketing needs to be optimized to work with banner advertising by anticipating searches that are likely to be prompted by the banner and ensuring a higher rank for search results. For example a brand featuring a Cyprus holiday offer will generate generic search terms like 'package holiday Cyprus' rather than brand searches.

Models for assessing online communications effectiveness

New tracking models are required to ensure that online media spend is allocated to media which are influencing sales. You need to plan to gain a single de-duplicated unified view of all digital referrers. Once this has been achieved, the next challenge is working out how the combination of digital media consumers have been exposed to impact sales.

3.7 Web 2.0 and social network models

Since 2004 the Web 2.0 concept has increased in prominence amongst website owners and developers, and it is now in the mainstream as a marketing approach which is closely related to social media. The main technologies and principles of Web 2.0 have been explained in an influential article by Tim O'Reilly (O'Reilly, 2005). Web 2.0 isn't a new web standard or a 'paradigm shift' as the name suggests, rather it's an evolution of technologies and communications approaches which have always been possible through the interactive nature of the web, but have grown in importance with the growth in high-speed broadband connections and acceptance of the benefits of social media by consumers. Back in 1997, Hoffman and Novak (1997) foresaw this change when they said:

> *'consumers can interact with the medium, firms can provide content to the medium, and in the most radical departure from traditional marketing environments, consumers can provide commercially-oriented content to the media'.*

Today many well-known startups, such as Digg, Facebook, Flickr and YouTube, which have been purchased for hundreds of millions or even billions of dollars are founded on Web 2.0 principles and many incumbent media owners and existing companies are integrating Web 2.0 applications. So, as part of developing a roadmap for your e-marketing plans, it's important to review the Web 2.0 models and prioritize them for integration into you or your clients sites.

The main characteristics of Web 2.0 are that it typically involves:

- **Supporting participation** – many of the applications are based on altruistic principles of community participation.
- **Encouraging creation of user generated content** – blogs are the best example of this. Another example is the collaborative encyclopedia Wikipedia (www.wikipedia.com) and, of course, YouTube (www.youtube.com) or niche sites like Constant Comedy (www.constantcomedy.com).
- **Enabling rating of content and online services** – services such as delicious (http://del.icio.us) and traceback comments on blogs support this. These services are useful given the millions of blogs that are available – rating and tagging (categorizing) content help indicate the relevance and quality of the content.

- **Ad funding of free services** – web services such as Google Mail/GMail and many blogs are based on contextual advertising such as Google Adsense or Overture/Yahoo! Content Match. Alternatively social networks all offer advertising space (see, for example, www.youtube.com/advertise which offers five different alternatives for brands to interact with their audiences including Display Advertising, Brand Channels, Contests, YouTube Video Ads and YouTube InVideo Ads).

- **Hosted as web services or interactive applications** – examples include Flickr (www.flickr.com), Google maps (http://maps.google.com) or blogging services such as Blogger.com or Typepad (www.typepad.com). However, some Web 2.0 collaborative applications may involve downloading a browser plugin or separate application. For example, Last.fm has a download which enables you to share track listings or 'scroble' of all music you play on your PC so you can find out shared interests and musical recommendations. Virtual World Second Life also requires a large, 30Mb, download.

- **Involve data exchange between sites through XML-based data standards**. For example RSS feeds (which automatically send you update alerts from particular web sites) are based on XML. An attempt by Google to facilitate this which illustrates the principle of structured information exchange and searching is Google Base (http://base.google.com). This allows users to upload data about particular services, such as training courses, in a standardized format based on XML. New classes of content can also be defined.

- **Use rapid application development using interactive technology approaches known as AJAX (Asynchronous JavaScript and XML)** – the best known Ajax implementation is Google Maps which is responsive since it does not require refreshes to display maps.

- **Simplicity in design and style** – many Web 2.0 applications are focused on a single activity such as social networking, mapping or photo sharing. To make the task as easy as possible, they have a simple appearance using design techniques such as simple pastel colour schemes, rounded box corners, gradients and reflections. See http://www.photoshoplab.com/web20-design-kit.html for practical tutorials on these techniques.

WHAT WILL WEB 3.0 BRING AND WHEN?

At the time of writing there is a fair amount of debate as to what **Web 3.0** means and whether we even need the term! It seems as if Web 3.0 is some way into the future since it will require advances in technology and bandwidth to make it a reality. However, the first ripples are here now with the trend to **atomization** and **widgets**. Elements of Web 3.0 will include:

- Increased use of web-based applications and services (like Google word processor and spreadsheets)

- Increased incorporation of syndicated content and services from other sites or a network into a site (using tools such as Yahoo! Pipes and XML exchange between widgets)

- Increased use of streamed video (as suggested by use of YouTube and IPTV services such as Joost)

- Increased use of immersive virtual environments such as Second Life

- Increased exchange of data between social networks fulfilling different needs (as indicated by the recent Google development of OpenSocial)
- Increased use of semantic markup leading to the semantic web envisioned by Sir Tim Berner's Lee over 10 years ago. It seems semantic markup will be needed to develop artificial intelligence applications which recommend content and services to web users without them actively having to seek them and apply their own judgement as to the best products and brands (i.e. an automated shopping comparison service as suggested by the use of standardized data feeds between shopping comparison sites and Google Base).

For us, it is the last of the these which represents the holy grail where we have a 'web that thinks like you' as it has been described.

SOCIAL NETWORK RESEARCH

For us, the impact of **social networks** on media consumption has been the most dramatic trend since the growth of the web itself. At the time of writing, growth rates are phenomenal and there is no sign of this growth abating. Look at this snapshot of the worldwide usage and growth of social network sites in 2007 by audience panel Comscore, which shows the staggering audience size and growth rates of the top networks:

- *MySpace*, 114 million, 72%
- *Facebook*, 52 million, 270%
- *Hi5*, 28 million, 56%
- *Friendster*, 24 million, 65%
- *Orkut*, 24 million, 78%
- *Bebo*, 18 million, 172%
- *Tagged*, 13 million, 774%

This change in media consumption has major implications for how advertisers reach and target these consumers who are now spending less time within mainstream media sites or channels. Brands also need to think about how social networkers discuss their brands and think about how to influence them.

Of course, there are disadvantages in the increasing activity of the web user documented by Keen (2007) in his book *The Cult of the Amateur: How the Democratization of the Digital World is Assaulting Our Economy, Our Culture, and Our Values*. Much of what he says about the lack of editorial control may be valid, but research has always shown that customers value reviews from their peers and particularly their friends. The role of social media and friends, in particular in influencing sales, was highlighted by this research from Forrester (2007):

- 83% – opinion of a friend or acquaintance who has used the product or service
- 75% – a review of the product or service in a newspaper, in a magazine or on TV
- 69% – information on the manufacturers website

- 63% – review by a known expert
- 60% – consumer reviews on a retailer site
- 52% – consumer reviews by users of a content site
- 50% – information at online consumer opinion sites
- 49% – an online review by the editors of a content site
- 37% – information in online chat rooms or discussion boards
- 30% – an online review by a blogger.

This does show there is a hierarchy of trust online starting with known acquaintances, then traditional media and known experts are important, with ratings from consumers rated as relatively untrustworthy. This shows that consumers are well able to apply their own filters and rate the ratings!

We have seen that many of the Web 2.0 approaches involve participation and sharing of information between different applications. The human wish to socialize and share experiences is the real reason behind the success of Web 2.0. This is suggested by Microsoft (2007) research based on interviews and surveys with social networkers who found these motivations for using social networks:

- 59% To keep in touch with friends and family
- 57% I like looking at other people's spaces
- 47% I want to meet people with similar interests
- 46% To express my opinions and views on topics
- 20% It is a good way to date
- 17% Using it for a specific reason, e.g. wedding, job networking

This seems to paint a picture of the web as a substitute for a bar or club! But social networking is not just limited to dating, since people like to express opinions, to discuss and hear the viewpoints of others, whether it's about a consumer electronics product, a fashion brand or a business service. Online marketers need to listen to these discussions to hear viewpoints about their products and shape their actions accordingly. See the list of online reputation management services at the end of the chapter.

E-MARKETING INSIGHT

Nielsen's 90–9–1 rule of participation inequality: encouraging more users to contribute

To encourage online community participation is a challenge since the majority of visitors to a community lurk or don't participate. Usability expert Jakob Nielsen gives examples of participation on Wikipedia (just 0.2% of visitors are active) and Amazon (fewer than 1% post reviews). He says that *'in most online communities, 90% of users are lurkers who never contribute, 9% of users contribute a little, and 1% of users account for almost all the action'.*

He explains:

- *'90% of users are lurkers (i.e., read or observe, but don't contribute).*
- *9% of users contribute from time to time, but other priorities dominate their time.*
- *1% of users participate a lot and account for most contributions: it can seem as if they don't have lives because they often post just minutes after whatever event they're commenting on occurs'.*

While it is isn't possible for a site to turnaround this distortion completely, he does describe some strategies. First, there should be easy methods for a visitor to contribute, clicking a rating or commenting without registering. Second, automate contributions, but show related recommendations or most read articles. Third, provide templates. Fourth, reward users by giving them accolades for contribution and finally promote participation through design or featuring top reviewers.

E-MARKETING INSIGHT

Microsoft digital advertising solutions

Guidelines for advertisers in social networks

With the tremendous increase in social networks over the past few years, there are now many opportunities for advertising within social networks either through buying ad space or more interestingly creating brand space, brand channels or widgets (covered in more detail in Chapter 7) that enable consumers to interact with or promote a brand. The digital advertising part of Microsoft recommends these approaches for interacting with consumers in this space (Microsoft, 2007).

1 *Understand consumers' motivations for using social networks.* Ads will be most effective if they are consistent with the typical lifestage of networkers or the topics that are being discussed.

2 *Express yourself as a brand.* Use the web to show the unique essence of your brand, but think about how to express a side of the brand that it is not normally seen.

3 *Create and maintain good conversations.* Advertisers who engage in discussions are more likely to resonate with the audience, but once conversations are started they must be followed through.

4 *Empower participants.* Social networkers use their space and blogs to express themselves. Providing content or widgets to associate themselves with a brand

may be appealing. For example, during the first six months following the launch of their charity donation widgets to be used on fundraisers blogs and profile pages, 20 000 were downloaded and they became one of the biggest referrers to the Justgiving site (JustGiving, 2007).

5 *Identify online brand advocates.* Use reputation management tools to identify influential social network members who are already brand advocates. Approach the most significant ones directly. Consider using contextual advertising such as Microsoft content ads or Google Adsense to display brand messages within their spaces when brands are discussed.

The golden rule: behave like a social networker

Microsoft recommend this simple fundamental principle which will help content created by advertisers resonate with social networkers: behave like the best social networkers through:

- Being creative
- Being honest and courteous (ask permission)
- Being individual
- Being conscious of the audience
- Updating regularly.

METCALFE'S LAW PROVES THE POWER OF COMMUNITY

Metcalfe's law refers to the power of an interconnected network to enable collaboration and extend the reach of an organization. It originates from Bob Metcalfe, a co-founder and former chief executive of networking company 3Com who said:

> 'The power of the network increases exponentially by the number of computers connected to it. Therefore, every computer added to the network both uses it as a resource while adding resources in a spiral of increasing value and choice'.

More succinctly, the value of a network grows by the square of the size of the network. The community value of the network grows at a rate of n * (n – 1). The bigger the network, the more valuable it is and the more valuable is a new member.

The biggest implication of Metcalfe's law for digital marketing is potentially in the value created from setting up online communities among your organization's staff, partners and customers. For networks set up within companies (intranets) or between partners (extranets), Metcalfe's law suggests value will be increased the more employees or partners are active users.

Initially, the returns on your efforts and investment might be disappointing, but Metcalfe's law dictates that as the network increases in size, returns will grow exponentially. This shows the importance of seeding the network by directly encouraging early adoption before growth becomes organic.

Where communities are created as part of a business proposition, the law shows the importance of supporting the growth of the network through the difficult initial phase until a 'critical mass' of participants is achieved. Many communities never make it through this phase.

E-MARKETING EXCELLENCE

Tapping into the Wikinomics trend

'Wikinomics' is a term brought to prominence by Don Tapscott and Anthony Williams. It explains how businesses can generate business value through using the Internet to facilitate participation by individuals and collaboration individuals.

These are our examples of business initiatives where companies have successfully taken advantage of Wikinomics.

- **Dell Ideastorm** (www.ideastorm.com). Dell customers, or even non-customers, can suggest new products and features. Rightly, Dell have a separate 'Ideas in Action' section where they update consumers on actions taken by the company. As well as improvements to customer service, they have explained how they have introduced systems with a non-Windows Linux operating system in response to suggestions on Ideastorm.

- **Procter and Gamble's Innocentive site** (www.innocentive.com) where freelance scientists, students and academics can work on problems posed by industry and sell solutions in return for cash rewards.

- **Betfair** (www.betfair.com) has successfully introduced an online betting exchange where the company mediates bets with other punters.

- **Zopa** (www.zopa.com) has introduced an online lending exchange.

- **Consumer generated ads from Frito Lay, owners of the Dorito brand**. Doritos used consumer shot videos for its major ad slot at the Superbowl. Doritos solicited ad executions through Yahoo, which hosted a contest for users to vote on their favorite submissions.

- **Ministry of Sound** (www.ministryofsound.com) encourages its web audience to vote on the best tracks and videos for its compilations and, although not a traditional media owner, now includes sponsored links and searches throughout its site to generate additional revenue.

- **Dubit Informer** (www.dubitinformer.com) is part of a teen chat forum site that commissions market research from consumer brands as a significant contributor to its revenue model. Participants get paid or have free product trials in return for their opinions.

- **HSBC** (www.hsbc.co.uk) who responded to groups set up on Facebook criticizing them for introduction of new student banking charges (although not until the case had been featured in the national media).
- **Wikipedia** (www.wikipedia.com). Ironically, arguably the best known example of Wikinomics, an entirely altruistic initiative by its founder, Jimmy Wales, is one of the few sites not to accept contextual advertising which could generate millions of dollars per month.

You can see that Wikinomics can be used for a range of business applications, to create supplementary core revenue through contextual advertising, for market research or as in the case of betting and lending exchanges directly for generating income.

E-MARKETING INSIGHT

Dennis Mortensen on gaining value from social networks

For owners of social networks business objectives will centre around increasing advertising and/or premium membership revenue. To achieve these the performance driver is increased user engagement which occurs as visitors spend more time on the site and return more to the site. So, to assess engagement we need to normalize metrics to create ratios based on:

Social Networking advertising revenue KPI's:

- Advertising revenue
- Visits per week
- Ads served
- Ad units per visit
- Ad CTR (since ad revenue will often be dependent on CPC and CPA deals).

Social Networking user engagement KPI's:

- Anonymous visitors to members conversion rate
- Active member length
- Time since last login
- Total time spent on site.

Using these metrics then brings 'comfort' and control to the Social Media Activities.

Dennis R. Mortensen, COO at IndexTools (http://www.visualrevenue.com/blog).

Web 2.0 and social network models

This section explored the reasons behind the growth of Web 2.0 and social media, namely the wish amongst consumers for participation and social involvement. To tap into communities brands need to plan for more open conversations with consumers, listening carefully and then responding.

3.8   Customer buying models

What goes through a customer's mind moments before they purchase? What stages do they go through when making a purchase? To sell, you have to know how and why people buy. By the end of this section you will be able to select and draw a suitable buying model for online customers.

The choice of model obviously depends on the type of purchase and the type of buyer. We are going to consider an online consumer making a purchase. We will consider two different purchasing scenarios – one for a **high-involvement purchase** (e.g. a car or a PC) and one for a low-involvement routine purchase (e.g. a can of cola). Chapter 4 on e-customers considers these in much more detail. In this short section we'll outline the models in action.

HIGH-INVOLVEMENT PURCHASES

For a high-involvement purchase like a car, customers go through a rigorous buying process from problem identification, to information search, to evaluation, to decision-to-buy through to post purchase.

As we will see in Chapter 4, a good web site (and/or a good interactive advertisement on TV) helps buyers move through all, or most, of these stages in the buying process. Some buyers prefer to browse online and buy offline (or just test drive), while others prefer to test, browse and buy online.

The introductory chapter emphasized the importance of being able to offer this **mixed-mode** of online and offline sales. The integrated database and integrated communications should be able to identify prospects online and close sales offline even if it means delivering a test drive car to the door. Surprisingly, many businesses are still struggling to integrate their databases.

LOW-INVOLVEMENT PURCHASES

Obviously, not all purchases require this much effort. There are many, many low-involvement purchases that we make every day, which do not warrant this kind of effort. Despite being almost 100 years old, and criticized by some, the AIDA model of attention (awareness, interest, desire and action) is still used by many professionals.

There are many buying models such as ATR (awareness, trial and reinforcement), generate awareness, facilitate an easy trial and reinforce it with advertising from then on. There

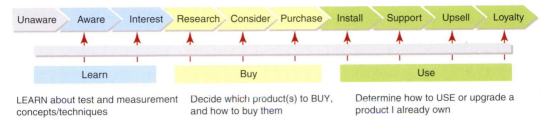

Figure 3.7   Model used to design content and services for the Textronix website (www.tektronix.com)

are many adaptations which web sites can use. The Tektronix Learn-Buy-Use model shows how this approach can be used to deliver relevant content that supports sales and branding objectives.

E-MARKETING EXCELLENCE

Tektronix extends the ATR model

A business-to-business example of applying the ATR model for a high involvement purchase is illustrated by test and measurement provider company Tektronix's (www.tektronix.com) web microsite supporting its e-business suite. It uses the approach shown in Figure 3.7. The site's **online value proposition** used to deliver this experience centres on a resource centre known as MyTek which enables relevant content to be delivered by e-mail throughout the customer lifecycle.

SECTION SUMMARY 3.8

Customer buying models

Online marketers must check to see their online activities (web sites, wap sites, kiosks or other e-tools) accommodate all the stages of the buyer's buying process – whether linear problem solving, AIDA, ATR or others.

3.9 Customer information processing

This section is a short one and leads you into the next chapter on e-customers by raising more questions than answers about online information processing.

There are many models for information processing, some so complex that they render themselves relatively useless in terms of practical application. We are going to look briefly at two of the more practical information processing models – one for display ads and one for web sites: Rossiter and Bellman (1999) developed the ALEA model that describes the online advertising experience as a process whereby attention is gained, followed by learning. If the consumer's emotional responses to the ad content are positively or negatively reinforced, further attention may be paid to the ad and further learning may take place until the brand's attributes are accepted.

This ALEA model is a 'heterarchy' of possible responses and does not specify a definitive sequence except that (1) attention must precede learning and emotional responses, and (2) that learning and emotional responses must precede acceptance.

Rossiter and Bellman (1999) hypothesize that sustained attention is directly related to the evaluative intensity of the consumers' emotional response to a content node encountered during a visit to a web ad.

They also theorize that brand attitude will be directly affected by the appropriateness of the sequence of emotions encountered during a visit to an Internet advertisement and by the appropriateness of the final emotion experienced. Furthermore, they propose that consumers with a high-category need should tend to process the online ad linearly in a 'hierarchy of effects' sequence (a logical pattern of pages) while those with a low-category need should process fewer pages of the site in a random order.

A separate model, Hofacker's model (Hofacker, 2001, see Section 4.6 for more detail), has five stages of information processing which can be used to review the effectiveness of an ad or a promotional container, or overall page template layout on a site:

1 Exposure – is the message there long enough for a customer?
2 Attention – what grabs the attention – movement, colour . . . ?
3 Comprehension and perception – how does the customer interpret the stimulus?
4 Yielding and acceptance – is the information accepted by the customer?
5 Retention – how well can the customer recall their experience?

Each stage acts as a hurdle, since if the site design or content is too difficult to process the customer cannot progress to the next stage. The e-marketer fails.

SECTION SUMMARY 3.9

Customer information processing

Understanding how customers process information helps marketers to communicate more clearly. We have looked at models by Rossiter and Bellman for banner ads and also Hofacker for web sites.

3.10 Loyalty models

Are you loyal to a brand online? Why – what makes you loyal? By the end of this section you will know the components of loyalty.

We know repeat business is, on average, five times more profitable than new business. On the other hand, low loyalty has a high cost as constantly recruiting new customers is expensive.

You need to identify and target your ideal customers and then move them up the ladder of loyalty (Considine and Murray, 1981) so that they become loyal lifetime customers. In fact, move them on to becoming advocates spreading your message. So how do you develop loyalty and strong relations with customers? Quality products, quality service and quality sites are basic prerequisites. In fact satisfying customers should be replaced by delighting customers since many satisfied customers still defect. On top of this we are getting worse at customer service (Cerasale and Stone, 2004). After this comes privacy and security. Respect and protect your customers' privacy. Ensure and reassure them of security. Add value to the relationship and reinforce brand values at every opportunity. Integrate your products and services into your customers' systems. Extend the partnership and share systems – this provides a certain amount of 'lock-in' where customers avoid the disruption caused by changing suppliers.

Going back to 'added value', rewarding customers is one way of adding value to the relationship. There are a number of innovative approaches emerging to reward and encourage online customer loyalty. All involve the visitor being offered some form of reward for buying. Rewards may take a number of different forms, e.g. credits, click miles. Remember there's always room for creativity. Take the Coca-Cola auction. Coca-Cola has amalgamated the loyalty notion with the auction model. In the physical world the potential bidder collects Coke can ring pulls, which once registered can be used to bid for a range of products. Vouchers are another method – visitors to www.richersounds.co.uk can print a 'buy one, get one free' voucher and then visit the store to redeem it. This approach can be used to increase sales and enhance the value of a site by increasing and retaining the user-base.

It is important to explore ways to develop a loyal online customer base. Evidence suggests that site users return to their favourite group of sites, similar to their favourite store. Many emerging pure play companies are relying on the growth of their user base rather than the growth of loyalty among their existing user base. This has yet to be proven as a sound strategic approach, as many companies following this approach have closed as funding has ceased to be available. Eventually, repeat business, lifetime loyalty and relationship marketing will separate the winners from the losers. Loyalty is so important it pops up in every chapter of this book, Section 4.7 giving further details.

The IDIC loyalty model

Peppers and Rogers (1998) have applied their work on building one-to-one relationships with the customer to the web. They suggest the IDIC approach as a framework for using the web effectively to form and build relationships. IDIC stands for:

1 *Customer identification*. This stresses the need to identify each customer on their first visit and subsequent visits. Common methods for identification are use of cookies or asking a customer to log on to a site.

2 *Customer differentiation*. This refers to building a profile to help segment customers. Characteristics for differentiating customers are described in Section 4.9.

3 *Customer interaction*. These are interactions provided on site such as customer service questions or creating a tailored product.

4 *Customer communications*. This refers to personalization or mass-customization of content or e-mails according to the segmentation achieved at the acquisition stage. Approaches for personalization are explained in Section 8.6.

Achieving customer advocacy and Net Promoter Score

Advocacy is another key aspect of loyalty, some argue it is the ultimate measure, with the answer to the Ultimate Question 'would you recommend us' needing to be 'Yes' for as many of your customers as possible. The importance of assessing advocacy and putting in place structures to support it have been highlighted in the concept of the **Net Promoter Score** which has been advocated by Reicheld (2006). This is based on economic analysis of the customer base of a company. For Dell, reports estimate that the average consumer is worth $210 (five year, Net Present Value), whereas a detractor costs the company $57 and a promoter generates $328. The value of promoters is generated by positive word-of-mouth and they also naturally have higher retention and spend rates. At the same time, the influence of detractors needs to be assessed since they can create negative word-of-mouth.

Think about how the Net Promoter Score concept applies to the web. In this chapter, we have seen the increasing importance of social networks and these provide a platform for both Promoters and Detractors. Brands need to think about how they facilitate promotion within the web environment and manage the comments of detractors. An example of the type of problem that can occur is indicated by the Land Rover car brand – a search for this marque shows the message *'DO NOT PURCHASE a Land Rover Discovery 3 – you will live to regret it if you have a similar experience to me as countless other owners have too'* in the natural listings thanks to a critical posting in www.haveyoursay.com. This despite the site owner having approached Land Rover. Maybe time for some **negative SEO** to help reduce the position of this company in the natural listings.

On a positive note, there is a lot a site owner can do to facilitate advocacy within their site, check out our checklist of ideas to consider how to influence and manage online advocacy:

E-MARKETING CHECKLIST – INFLUENCING AND MANAGING ADVOCACY ONLINE

Facilitating online advocacy:

☑ Page template contains 'Forward/recommend to a friend' options

☑ E-mail has 'forward to a friend option'

☑ Enable customer feedback and showcase positive experiences, e-retail sites contain options for rating and commenting on products

☑ Business sites have prominent testimonial and case study sections with pull-outs featuring customer success stories

☑ Sites indicate 'wisdom of crowd' through showcasing top selling products or most read and commented features

☑ Involve customers more in shaping your web services and core product offerings.

Managing online detractors:

☑ Use online reputation management tools (www.davechaffey.com/online-reputation-management-tools) for notification of negative (and positive) comments

☑ Develop a process and identify resource for rapidly responding to negative comments using a natural and open approach

☑ Assess and manage the influence of negative comments within the natural listings of search engines

☑ Practice fundamental marketing principles of listening to customer comments about products and services and aim to rectify them to win back the situation!

SECTION SUMMARY 3.10

Loyalty models

Quality products, quality service and quality sites are basic prerequisites to achieve online customer loyalty. Reward schemes can also be used to enhance loyalty. A plan is needed to facilitate the comments of advocates and manage negative comments by detractors.

CHAPTER SUMMARY

1 Models describe the process by which business is conducted between an organization, its customers, suppliers, distributors and other stakeholders. Managers need constantly to review how electronic communications change existing models and offer new opportunities.

2 New and revised models are required to respond to changes in industry structure and customer behaviour.

3 Analysis of your online marketplace can help you to understand customer behaviour in order to identify potential search terms for which you should promote your company and also potential partner sites or media buys.

4 Online revenue models for media owners to consider include traditional CPM and fixed sponsorships, cost per click models and cost per acquisition affiliate models. Ads can also be displayed as part of a network.

5 Digital media have enabled a change from many-to-one, to many-to-some and to one-to-one communication. Other new communications techniques are viral marketing, affiliate marketing and permission-based marketing.

6 New tracking models are required to ensure that online media spend is allocated to media which are influencing sales. A single de-duplicated unified view of all digital

referrers should be achieved to help understanding of how the combination of digital media consumers have been exposed to impacts sales.

7 Options for utilizing Web 2.0 and social media by a brand should be explored since there is a desire amongst consumers for participation and social involvement. To tap into communities brands need to plan for more open conversations with consumers, listening carefully and then responding.

8 E-marketing must accommodate the linear process for high involvement purchases, mixed-mode buying and traditional models such as AIDA and ATR.

9 Hofacker's customer information processing model of exposure–attention–comprehension and perception-yielding and acceptance and retention is a valuable method of enhancing the communications efficiency of a web site.

10 A quality product, service, web site are basic prerequisites to build customer loyalty. The role of the web in advocacy and negative mentions should be assessed and monitored.

References

Anderson, C. (2006) *The Long Tail, Why the Future of Business is Selling Less of More*. Hyperion, NY.

Baily, P., Farmer, D., Jessop, D. and Jones, D. (1994) *Purchasing principles and management*. Pitman Publishing, London.

Berryman, K., Harrington, L., Layton-Rodin, D. and Rerolle, V. (1998) Electronic commerce: three emerging strategies. *The McKinsey Quarterly*, Vol. 1, pp. 152–159.

Cerasale, M. and Stone, M. (2004) *Business Solutions on Demand*. Kogan Page.

Chaffey, D., Mayer, R., Johnston, K. and Ellis-Chadwick, F. (2003) *Internet Marketing: Strategy, Implementation and Practice*, 2nd edition. Prentice Hall/Financial Times, Harlow.

Considine, R. and Murray, R. (1981) *The Great Brain Robbery*. The Great Brain Robbery, CA.

Daly, J. (2000) Interview with Alvin Toffler. *Business 2.0 Magazine*, 15 September.

Deise, M., Nowikow, C., King, P. and Wright, A. (2000) *Executive's guide to e-business. From tactics to strategy*. John Wiley and Sons, New York.

DTI (2003) *Business in the Information Age – International Benchmarking Study*. Available from http://www2.bah.com/dti2003.

Durlacher (2000) Trends in the UK new economy. *Durlacher Quarterly Internet Report*, November 2000, pp. 1–12.

E-consultancy (2007) Affiliates close ranks after ASOS CEO calls them grubby. Blog posting. http://www.e-consultancy.com/news-blog/362851/affiliates-close-rank-after-asos-ceo-calls-them-grubby.html

Evans, P. and Wurster, T.S. (1999) Getting real about virtual commerce. *Harvard Business Review*, November, pp. 84–94.

Flores, L. and Eltvedt, H. (2005) Beyond online advertising – lessons about the power of brand websites to build and expand brands, Published in proceedings of ESOMAR Online Conference, Montreal, 2005.

Forrester (2007) North American Consumer Technographics Report. February.

Gartner Group (2004) CRM Marketing Business. February.

Guardian (2007) Beware when you compare. Harriet Meyer, Friday June 22, 2007.

Guardian Unlimited. http://money.guardian.co.uk/insurance_/story/0,,2108482,00.html.

Haven, B. (2007) Consumer Trends Survey North America – Leveraging User Generated content, January. Forrester.

Hitwise (2006). Paid and Organic Search: Profile of MoneySupermarket. *Hitwise blog posting.* http://weblogs.hitwise.com/heather-hopkins/2006/09/paid_and_organic_search_profil.html

Hofacker, C. (2001) *Internet Marketing*, 3rd edition. Wiley, New York.

Hoffman, D.L. and Novak, T.P. (1996) Marketing in Hypermedia Computer-mediated environments: conceptual foundations. *Journal of Marketing*, Vol. 60, July, pp. 50–68.

Hoffman, D.L. and Novak, T.P. (1997) A new marketing paradigm for electronic commerce. *The Information Society, Special issue on electronic commerce*, Vol. 13, Jan–Mar, pp. 43–54.

IBM (2001) IBM e-business web site case study.

Jackson, T. (2000) Marketing brainwave falls foul of rule book. *Financial Times*, 14 March, p. 19.

JustGiving (2007) Justgiving Widget version 2.0. Blog posting, July 24th, 2007. http://justgiving.typepad.com/charities/2007/07/justgiving-widg.html

Keen, Andrew (2007). *The Cult of the Amateur: How the Democratization of the Digital World is Assaulting Our Economy, Our Culture, and Our Values*. Doubleday Currency.

Kirkpatrick, D. (2001) Great Leap Forward: From Davos, Talk of Death. *Fortune*, 5 March.

Levine, R., Locke, C., Searls, D. and Weinberger, D. (2000) *The Cluetrain Manifesto*. Perseus Books, Cambridge, MA.

Mad (2007) How online display advertising influences search volumes. Published: 04 June 2007 00:00. MAD Network (*Marketing Week*), Centaur Communications. http://technologyweekly.mad.co.uk/Main/InDepth/SearchEngineMarketing/Articles/f66d813eeab74e93ad8f252ae9c7f02a/How-online-display-advertising-influences-search-volumes.html.

Microsoft (2007) Word of the web guidelines for advertisers: Understanding trends and monetising social networks. Research report.

Nielsen (2007) Participation Inequality: Encouraging More Users to Contribute, AlertBox, October 9, 2006, www.useit.com/alertbox/participation_inequality.html.

Ovans, A. (2000) E-procurement at Schlumberger. *Harvard Business Review*, May–June, pp. 21–23.

O'Reilly, T. (2005) What Is Web 2? Design Patterns and Business Models for the Next Generation of Software. Web article, 30/09/2005. O'Reilly publishing, Sebastopol, CA.

Peppers, D. and Rogers, M. (1998) *One-to-one Field book*. Doubleday, New York.

Reicheld, F. (2006) *The Ultimate Question: Driving Good Profits and True Growth*. Harvard Business School Publishing.

Rossiter, J.R. and Bellman, S. (1999) A Proposed Model for Explaining and Measuring Web Advertising Effectiveness. *Journal of Current Issues and Research in Advertising*, Vol. 21, No. 11, pp. 13–31.

Smith, P. (2004) *Shape The Agenda*. Chartered Institute of Marketing, Jan. 2004 www.shapetheagenda.com.

Tranmit (1999) *Procurement Management Systems: a corporate black hole. A survey of technology trends and attitudes in British industry*. Published by Tranmit, UK. Survey conducted by Byline Research. Report available at www.rswww.com/purchasing.

Walmsley, A. (2007) *New Media The age of the trialogue*. The Marketer, September.

ZDNet (2005) ISPs fear greater Net regulation. 27 January. www.zdnet.co.uk.

Further reading

Deise, M., Nowikow, C., King, P. and Wright, A. (2000) *Executive's guide to e-business. From tactics to strategy*. John Wiley and Sons, New York. Introductory chapters consider buy- and sell-side options and later chapters look at value chain transformation.

Fingar, P., Kumar, H. and Sharma, T. (2000) *Enterprise E-commerce*. Meghan-Kiffler Press, Tampa, FL. These authors present a model of the different actors in the e-marketplace that is the theme throughout this book.

Web links

Andrew Keen's blog (http://andrewkeen.typepad.com) casts a largely cynical view on the social media and Web 2.0 revolution.

Comparison Engines (www.comparisonengines.com). A blog focusing on developments in shopping comparison intermediaries.

Bplans calculators (www.bplans.com/eb/). Includes basic calculators for pay per click and email marketing.

Connected Marketing (www.connectedmarketing.com). Blog and community supporting the book edited by Justin Kirby about approaches to viral marketing and achieving advocacy online.

E-marketing Excellence book homepage (www.davechaffey.com/E-marketing). An index of all e-marketing links for each chapter in this book.

Hitwise blog (http://weblogs.hitwise.com). Sample reports from Hitwise on consumer search behaviour and importance of different online intermediaries.

Marketing Insights online revenue model spreadsheets.

(www.marketing-insights.co.uk/spreadsheet.htm). Excel spreadsheets for modelling visitors volumes and campaign response.

Net Promoter Score Blog (http://netpromoter.typepad.com/fred_reichheld). Blog on achieving advocacy by Fred Reicheld and other specialists in achieving advocacy such as Dr Paul Marsden.

Online reputation management monitoring tools (www.davechaffey.com/online-reputation-management-tools). See also links in Chapter 9, E-business.

Rough Type (www.roughtype.com). Nicholas Carr's blog on how technology is disrupting business models. Carr is formerly editor of the Harvard Business review.

Wikinomics.com (www.wikinomics.com). The blog for the 'Wikinomics' book by Don Tapscott and Anthony Williams.

Self-test

1 Summarize the scope of e-business models.
2 Explain the concept of commoditization.

3 Do you think value networks or the external value chain is a more useful model for defining e-marketing strategy?

4 Explain the relevance of the prosumer concept to the modern marketer.

5 Describe how the B2B marketer can use the concept of e-procurement to enhance sales to existing and new customers.

6 Describe marketing tactics to accommodate changes to the distribution channel for your organization.

7 Outline the changes from traditional mass communication to new communications models.

8 Which e-marketing tactics should be developed to accommodate different buying models?

9 Apply Hofacker's model of customer information processing to your organization's web site.

10 Outline models to help build customer loyalty.

Chapter 4

E-customers

Online customers are changing. Not only do they talk back, they now shout back and even bite back if brands break their promise. Successful e-marketers listen and learn.

OVERVIEW

This chapter looks inside the online customer's mind. We explore customers' issues, worries, fears and phobias, as well as other motivators for going online . . . and how marketers can respond to these behaviours. We also look at on-site behaviour, the online buying process and the many influencing variables. We finish with a look to the future, your future and how to keep an eye on the e-customer.

OVERCOME LEARNING OUTCOME

By the end of this chapter you will:

- Understand online customers and their buying behaviour and how they differ from offline customers
- Overcome the issues and concerns online customers have
- Begin to move e-customers through their online mental stages.

CHAPTER TOPIC	LEARNING OBJECTIVE
4.1 Introduction	Identify the changing customer expectations and how to satisfy them
4.2 Motivations	Evaluate and respond to the factors that encourage users to adopt and stay using the Internet
4.3 Expectations	Determine the facilities that customers require online
4.4 Fears and phobias	Evaluate and manage the fears and phobias that hinder online transactions
4.5 The online buying process	Support the buying process through traditional and digital channels
4.6 Online information processing	Recognize how visitors process information and how marketers can respond to this. Identify the online buying process
4.7 Relationships	Understand how online relationship marketing techniques can develop loyalty
4.8 Communities	Assess the suitability of techniques used to foster online communities and how to build active/lively online communities
4.9 Customer profiles	Describe the profile characteristics of online customers, both B2C and B2B
4.10 Researching the online customer	Assess the process, techniques and measures used to research and assess online marketing effectiveness
4.11 The post-PC customer and virtual worlds	Paint a picture of the future and the new online customer's changing behaviour patterns

4.1   Introduction to e-customers

Understanding customers is fundamental to successful marketing. Good marketers know their target customers inside out and upside down. They are able to put a microscope on their buyers. Understanding online customers is even more important, as the geographic and cultural spread is often much wider. Online customers also have different characteristics and attitudes to both acquiring information and buying online. On top of this, the same person may both think and behave differently online than offline. So overall e-marketers have to watch their online customers even more closely.

Online customers are changing. Not only do they talk back, they now shout back and even bite back if brands break their promises. Today's customers have unlocked 'brand control' from marketers and set up their own brand discussions. Although they are still time-compressed and information-fatigued, they have found a new energy fuelled by Web 2.0 which allows them to fulfil their age old desire to communicate about what interests or concerns them. Customers now have a platform to raise their voices and some of them can't stop shouting!

Customers have been abused by businesses who dump sloppy service on them, again and again. Survey after survey reveals that we have, in fact, got worse at marketing over the last ten years. And customers are angry. They are also increasingly impatient and less forgiving. The clock is ticking. We are sitting on a customer service time bomb.

Surprisingly we've got worse at marketing. We are in an era of declining marketing skills measured by falling customer satisfaction scores as revealed in market after market. Meanwhile automated customer service telephone queuing systems and unworkable web sites have not helped. Robotic answer machines with self service menus dump all the work on the information-fatigued, time-poor customer. Add web sites that don't work, with dead ends, error messages, complicated navigation, and, if you have the patience to struggle through all of that, electronic shopping carts that crash. The customer service time bomb is ticking. The angry customer can be seen lurking amongst the many blogs and hate sites attacking brands. These can fuel an exponential spreading of negative word-of-mouth or ('word-of-mouse').

Research shows that today's customers are less tolerant of bad service, with 80% of consumers saying they will never go back to an organization after a bad customer experience, up from 68% in 2006 (Harris Interactive 2007). Add in customers who talk back and who talk to each other courtesy of new social media or Web 2.0 and the goal posts have moved for many marketers. Social network sites facilitate customer discussions (Coca Cola never asked for rockets, it just happened that customers discovered that mixing Coke and Mentos mints caused an explosive reaction and customers started posting videos of this phenomenon). Customers talk with text and video, some because they want to share opinions, others are hungry for fame (McKinsey 2007) and others want to meet new friends or simply, transcend, to another place.

Customers have unlocked 'control' from communications as **User Generated Content (UGC)** is not totally controllable, as Chevrolet and Nike discovered. Online social networks are here to stay. They will continue to grow in line with the very human need for social contact. Customers have been mobilized by BLOGs, social network sites and invitations to produce User Generated Content.

We are possibly on the cusp of a customer revolution bringing an end to accepting sloppy service and, also, an end to the mass dumbdowned customer. As *Wired* editor and author of *The Long Tail* Chris Anderson says: *'For too long we've been suffering the tyranny of lowest-common-denominator fare, subjected to brain-dead summer blockbusters and manufactured pop. Many of our assumptions about popular taste are actually artifacts of poor supply-and-demand matching – a market response to inefficient distribution'* Chris Anderson (2006). Online digital markets facilitate obscure niche markets as easily as they do mass markets. In the online world it can be as profitable to serve 100 customers, spread across the world, with 100 different digital products as it is to serve 100 local customers one standardized product. This opens a gate to consumer taste which takes it away from the 'tyranny of the lowest dumb down denominator'. Instead of a handful of powerful marketers recommending, and often, determining what is in and what is out – there is now a mobilized customer, generating their own particular recommendations and creating many smaller niche demands.

Although spread across the world, customers with similar interests can communicate and share thoughts through images, audio, video and text anywhere in the world. This means that clusters of customers with similar tastes and interests are connecting with each other to form new global niches and segments. Global markets are here; for example, Manchester United Football Club have an estimated 70 000 000 fans around the world and Al-Jazeera international's English-language TV news service has an audience of 100 000 000 worldwide. As media follows markets, media consumption may go global, therefore marketers must remember that brands with international ambitions must have a consistent global image – production should be international in mind and content rights should be global. Creating content that users can pass on via their networks is an increasingly important channel of communication. But as the Universal McCann 2007 report suggests 'when using these channels it is fundamental that brands and media organizations think global. Multiple local and conflicting brand identities will not work'. In addition localized brand names can often restrict brands from international sales. PR Smith (2004) lists several restrictive brand names including: Sic (French soft drink); Pschitt (French soft drink); Lillet (French soft drink); Creap (Japanese coffee creamer); Irish Mist (in Germany 'mist' means manure); Bum (Spanish potato crisp); Bonka (Spanish coffee); Trim Pecker Trouser (Japanese germ bread); Gorilla Balls (American protein supplement); My Dung (restaurant); Cul toothpaste (pronounced 'cue' in France, which means 'anus'); Scratch (German non-abrasive bath cleaner); Super-Piss (Finnish car lock anti-freeze); Spunk (jelly-baby sweet from Iceland) for more see www.prsmith.org/.

The Internet and broadband, in particular, has changed business dynamics. It has created a level playing field for the smaller niche brands to compete with the established global players. Small brands have access to bigger, global, markets and can communicate directly with customers across the world in new and more meaningful ways – ways never dreamt of ten years ago.

Power will be prised away from those major brands that are not prepared to change. Maybe it will be the database holders who take control. Imagine opening your fridge and as you take the last can of Guinness the fridge asks you if you'd like to replace the beer online automatically with a competitor's new stout? It's the database holder who knows who drinks what beer, when and where, or at least simply records the last beer's bar code as it's taken out of the fridge. The key to accessing the customers' databases embedded in fridges and microwaves, cars, phones and PDAs is not the hardware but the intelligence to know exactly when you might like to replace something with a special offer. The invasion of the infomediary starts here. Microsoft is piloting selling classified ads on its specially designed database (searchable by the company's internet search engine). Amazon is developing its own Internet TV show, 'Amazon Fishbowl' with Bill Maher chatting with guests from the world of books, music and film. Amazon aim to connect artists with new audiences and facilitate any new purchase needs arising.

Along with changing customer needs comes changing media consumption patterns. TV used to be pushed at impassive couch potatoes. The web, on the other hand, was, and still is, a 'pull' medium. Content is pulled down to a computer with a conscious click. This viewer is in control. It turns out that the old heaving mass of supposed slovenly couch potatoes actually like to be active, interactive, even participatory, to influence the programme, its result and even choose the time to view it (as well as enjoy the instant gratification of immediate online purchase and delivery wherever and whenever required). The era of 'appointment-to-view' TV is coming to an end. Perhaps the slothful couch potato may have simply been a function of the absence of interaction (technology) rather than intrinsic defects in human nature? As media technology and audiences move from push to pull, marketers are witnessing a radical increase in consumer sovereignty where informed customers easily compare prices, alert each other to quality issues and brand messages, and challenge marketers directly.

Customers continue to change their media habits, for example, in the EU customers are consuming less TV, newspapers and magazines and more Internet, while radio remains steady (EIAA 2007). eCustomers also have a big appetite for small screens. Consumers around the world use their mobiles, PDA and iPods to consume vast amounts of Internet content. More entertainment is consumed on mobile than on big screens. Total global content on mobile networks (includes games, video and gambling) is worth $31b while Hollywood earns less than $30b in big screens' box offices annually (Ahonen, and Moore 2007).

And some media consumption is changing into media production as user generated content feeds social network sites and millions of blogs. Sydney Pollack (2007) recently observed that *'People are now content creators and not just content consumers. The world has changed radically. They wanna make the content not just watch the content'*. Interestingly, China has the most bloggers (Universal McCann 2007) – perhaps a way of expressing oneself outside a hierarchical structure. Elsewhere, other customers use virtual worlds to meet new people, to break out of their old offline groups and even to escape from their bodies as men become women and women become men or other types of avatars including animals and hybrids in a new virtual world. Some disabled people may find stimulating experiences in new virtual worlds.

Tim Guest (2007) in his book on Second Life suggests that patients suffering from cerebral palsy find virtual worlds like Second Life fulfilling their desire to be free from the shackles of a wheelchair or free from the stigma of being disabled. In this sense the Internet and broadband, in particular, created a level playing field for all customers.

CONSUMERS VALUE PRIVACY AND TRUST

On this new level playing field, privacy, trust and time are emerging as new currencies that have a very high value in customers' minds. They are cautious about giving up private information. They are also busy and don't like wasting time (if you can save your customer time, they will like you even more). They expect you to protect their privacy (hence privacy statements are de rigueur for every web site). Equally, customers resent being asked for too much information or being asked for information when they haven't yet established any relationship – so much so, that many customers just lie when filling in online forms.

You cannot believe all your online surveys since another survey (Adestra 2006) suggests that over half of consumers lied when asked for personal information.

Customers value their privacy. Many customers resent intrusive marketing invading their private time and space. So companies like Cocal Cola invite youth customers into Coca Cola's world of sponsored music instead of invading the customer's space with ads. Customers want to choose when and where they receive information or ads. Having said this, customers welcome relevant help from companies who know how to genuinely save customers time or deliver them new experiences that enhance their lives or their jobs. Customers do like personal, tailored (relevant) communications whether opt-in e-mail or personalized web sites. It has been said that 'enlightened companies remember information for customers, not about them'. This builds trust in the relationship.

Do people trust people more than web sites? Well people trust well known and well respected brands. Why else would you give an unknown American your credit card details and home address (when buying books off Amazon)? In the UK several major brands score higher in trust than the church and police. Well managed brands are trusted as long as their promise is never broken. How do you feel when a web site remembers your name? And when it remembers your preferences? Are we content to have unconscious relationships with brands, robots and machines as well as people? Some sites display team members behind an organization as they feel 'people still buy people'.

Trust is increasingly important as online customers live in a dangerous environment of privacy invasion and identity theft. If mobile subscription fraud is actually easier and more profitable than drug smuggling, then it will attract more criminal behaviour online. Criminal gangs actively target mobile operators as telecoms fraud nears £1bn in the UK alone (Detica 2007); social networking websites can leave both an individual and a business dangerously exposed to fraud. Personal data can be compiled from public profiles that customers post about themselves in social network sites.

Money-rich, time-poor customers need to find information quickly and transact easily. Well designed sites can satisfy impatient customers, build relationships and nurture loyalty through added relevant value. Today, visitors are reducing the number of sites they regularly visit, but they are spending more time on those selected sites. These 'sticky sites' keep visitors longer with relevant material and services that constantly, genuinely, help their customers. In return, customers are prepared to spend more of their 'share of wallet' on a broader range of products from a single site. Growing 'share of wallet' makes sense since it is 'five times cheaper to sell to an existing customer than a new one', in fact online it can be ten times more profitable (Flores and Eltvedt 2005). Brand extensions, web rings, alliances and marketing marriages can extend a product range and satisfy a needy customer simultaneously.

Despite having a wider choice customers are starting to consolidate their choice of preferred web sites. So this creates an opportunity for marketers to develop sticky web sites that keep visitors on the site with easy-to-find, relevant information and services. Ask yourself what is on your site that might attract a visitor to come back a second time and ultimately, regularly revisit the site and develop a strong relationship with the site/brand. Remember the second visit is the start of the relationship game. By getting it right now, there is a possibility of creating competitive advantage by developing a strong relationship with online customers which protects you from the inevitable onslaught of competition.

Finally, watch how B2B companies deliver e-marketing to their customers, because B2B companies are often much more sophisticated than B2C companies at helping their customers. They perfect Scenario Planning to identify how online services can really help customers in their daily lives. Companies like Kingspan Insulated Roof and Wall Systems use their web site to actually help architects design and specify materials they need online quickly and efficiently. Other companies, like National Semi Conductor, have for ten years been giving design engineers (who design component parts for mobile phones and dvd players) access to their 'web-bench' – a sophisticated online design, test and redesign programme that allows them to do in two hours what previously took months. They have over 30 000 design engineers on site generating 3000 orders or referals everyday (one integrated socket for Nokia was 40 milllion units). Learn from best practice wherever you can find it.

E-MARKETING INSIGHT

South Korean innovation

Would you like plastic with your credit?

A completely different mindset applies to customers in other countries. In South Korea, Visa credit card company will ask you on a new Visa card approval on the phone 'do you want plastic with the credit' as the credit card functionality will automatically be enabled on your cellphone and the old fashioned plastic card for your wallet is a free optional extra, only really needed if you travel outside South Korea.

(*Source*: Ahonen and Moore, 2007).

IDEAL CUSTOMERS

Now comes the important and interesting bit – understanding your best customers. Who are your ideal customers? You have good and bad customers. Bad ones continually haggle about prices, pay late, constantly complain, grab all your promotions and leave you as soon as another company comes along. The ideal customers, on the other hand, are the ones that pay on time, give you as much notice as possible, share information, become partners giving you useful feedback. You know the ones – they are a pleasure to work with. But who are they? What makes them different? What do they really want? How can you help them even more? Are they online? Targeting, satisfying and keeping the ideal customer is crucial.

Ideal customers are worth more than you think. Pareto's 80:20 law suggests that 80% of your sales come from only 20% of your customers. Research suggests that your best 20% of customers generate 140% of your profits. This means that many of your other customers generate losses. A company's best customer could be worth 30 times the worst customer. Chris Anderson's (2006) Long Tail theory challenges Pareto and suggests otherwise (see e-marketing insight p. 139).

Regardless, you need to know who are your best customers. Are all of them online? So we need to know our ideal customer's profile – who they are, where they are, what they want, what they spend, any distinguishing characteristics. How do we recognize them on a database? What questions should we ask them about themselves? We need to know them better than they know themselves!

> ## PRACTICAL E-MARKETING TIP
>
> ### Assessing the differences in your online customers
>
> Multichannel businesses should assess the characteristics of their online customers in comparison to their traditional offline audience. How do the demographics differ, how do the length and steps in the buying process differ? How do the purchase patterns differ in terms of category, frequency and value. Then use the differences to develop tactics which suit the online audiences, but also encourage the offline audiences to use your online services before the competitors do!

We need to understand their mindset, their attitudes and aspirations. We also need to know the barriers to buying online – their fears and phobias. We need to know where our proposition sits with their needs, their lives, their jobs – 'their worlds' – both online and offline.

We also need to know their purchasing process – the stages they move through and the information needs they have at each stage. We need to know their information processing stages – how they acquire information (what channels) – how they learn about products and offers, what words they search with, what words (and images) arouse them to take action. How their perception screens out some offers and filters in others.

In general, the online customer is different from the offline customer. The online customer has more power than ever before. Despite living in an information-cluttered and time-compressed world, the online customer is empowered like never before: more information, transparent prices, more rights. They also realize the value of their time and attention. Witness the rise of permission-based marketing and the demise of the effectiveness of intrusion-based marketing. Remember, assumptions you might have about existing offline customers may not apply online. Even the same customer may display different characteristics online and offline.

Engaged Customers = Customer Engagement

We introduced the powerful concept of customer engagement in Chapter 1. If you can understand and influence engagement better than your competitors, then this will help you develop loyalty to a brand and the website.

The ideal customer, or most valuable customer, does not have to be someone who buys a lot. The ideal customer could be an influencer who is a small irregular buyer, but who posts ratings and reviews as his reviews can influence another 100 people. 'Engaged customers' are probably going to become brand zealots if we keep them engaged. Therefore it is important to identify 'engaged customers' and start a brand ambassador programme to further strengthen the relationship and energize their word-of-mouth.

We can monitor the quantity and frequency of blog posts, forum discussions, reviews, profile updates, etc. This identifies opportunities and also acts as an early warning system to any future problems. Consider targeting brand evangelists rather than just purchasers. Some companies actually ask customers to give a product rating or even post a product review as a standard part of their after sales contact strategy. This way the more engaged customers identify themselves by their own self selection.

You should use our engagement checklist (Table 4.1) to determine how involved a customer is with your products or services. A customer who doesn't care about the product is likely to be less committed or less emotionally attached to the firm providing the product. On the other

Table 4.1   Customer engagement checklist

Involvement
1 Does the customer segment buy your product or service more or less frequently compared to your competitors?
2 Does the customer frequently purchase (defined as more than . . . x purchases per month)?
3 Is the customer a frequent visitor to the web site (defined as more than . . .x. . . .visits per month).
4 Does the customer spend above average site visit duration (. . .x minutes) each time they visit your site?
5 Does the customer engage in key service interactions?
   e.g. Choosing and comparing different products
6 Does the customer engage in minor service interactions?
   e.g. Checking status of the account

Interaction
7 Does the customer visit the discussion areas or blogs?
8 Does the customer participate in discussions by posting comments regularly (x . . .per month)?
9 Has the customer written a product review?
10 Has the customer created any other user generated content (including uploading photos or videos)?
11 Has the customer made any connections relevant to the brand in social networks?

Intimacy
12 Does the customer express an opinion in customer service calls?

Influence
13 Does the customer refer other customers to the site?
14 Are you monitoring and acting on engagements in the above areas?

hand, a customer who is engaging is likely to be more emotionally connected to the brand. We need to know about the sentiment, opinion and affinity a person has towards a brand. This is often expressed through repeat visits, purchases, product ratings, reviews, blogs and discussion forums and, ultimately, their likelihood to recommend a friend.

Ask yourself 'how well are we measuring engagement of our different online audiences and then closing the loop by using this data to identify the advocates and deliver more relevant communications'?

E-MARKETING INSIGHT

Pareto V *The Long Tail*

Meet Robbie Vann-Adibé, the CEO of Ecast, a digital jukebox company whose bar-room players offer more than 150 000 tracks – and some surprising usage statistics. He hints at them with a question that visitors invariably get wrong: 'What percentage of the top 10 000 titles in any online media store (Netflix, iTunes, Amazon, or any other) will rent or sell at least once a month?'

Most people guess 20%, and for good reason: We've been trained to think that way. The 80–20 rule, also known as Pareto's principle (after Vilfredo Pareto, an Italian economist who devised the concept in 1906), is all around us. Only 20% of major studio films will be hits. Same for TV shows, games, and mass-market books – 20% all. The odds are even worse for major-label CDs, where fewer than 10% are profitable, according to the Recording Industry Association of America.

But the right answer, says Vann-Adibé, is 99%. There is demand for nearly every one of those top 10 000 tracks. He sees it in his own jukebox statistics; each month, thousands of people put in their dollars for songs that no traditional jukebox anywhere has ever carried. Suddenly, popularity no longer has a monopoly on profitability. The second reason for the wrong answer is that the industry has a poor sense of what people want. We equate mass market with quality and demand, when in fact it often just represents familiarity, savvy advertising, and broad if somewhat shallow appeal. Rhapsody streams more songs each month beyond its top 10 000 than it does its top 10 000. Google, for instance, makes most of its money off small advertisers (the long tail of advertising), and eBay is mostly tail as well – niche and one-off products.

Excerpt from Chris Anderson's (2006) *The Long Tail: Why the Future of Business is Selling Less of More.* Hyperion.

SECTION SUMMARY 4.1

Introduction to e-customers

This chapter explores online customers – who they are, why they go online, their expectations, their fears and phobias. We examine their online buying process as well as their internal mental processes right through to forming relationships and building communities. The chapter finishes with a look at the future – the 'post-PC customer' and shows you how to research the online customer.

4.2   Motivations

By the end of this section you will be able to discuss why customers go online. We will try to lift the lid on online customers' heads, look inside their minds and explore what drives them online. Finally we'll see how we can use this knowledge to get, and keep, more online customers.

Understanding customer motivations is not an option or a luxury. It is an absolute necessity for survival. If you don't know what customers want then how can you satisfy them? If you can't satisfy them, how can you keep them or even attract them in the first place? Without this deep understanding of your customers you're just shooting in the dark and hoping for the best – not the way to run a business.

So we need to know why customers go online. What are their motives? What needs are being satisfied?

WHY DO CUSTOMERS VENTURE ONLINE?

Research presented in Figure 4.1 shows that socializing, catching up on news, shopping/browsing, being entertained and being educated are typical reasons people give for going online. So, socializing through e-mail, chat rooms, blogs and social network sites is the killer application in the B2C markets. Billions of e-mails are sent every day and SMS (text) messages are catching up. Leveraging the strong desire to socialize should not be underestimated. It is one of Maslow's basic defined needs.

The second most popular activity is finding out about products, regardless of whether they are to be purchased online or offline, so we need to facilitate the process of mixed-mode buying – browsing online and buying offline.

Internet users are active, not passive; they enjoy their power and love to exercise it. Comparison shopping puts them in control. The empowered online customer has more knowledge than ever before from sharing information with others and from comparison sites or shop-bots. How well do you know the comparison sites for your products and services? Seek them out and monitor them continuously.

Surprisingly, not all online customers hate real physical shopping. They just like getting good deals and being in control (Windham, 2001). The convenience of online shopping may grow in importance as time-compressed customers realize the time saving nature of online shopping. Time saving can satisfy several needs simultaneously as the time saved can be spent fulfilling a range of unfilled needs.

Incidentally, many products fail to sell in large volumes online since the products don't pass de Kare-Silver's 'electronic shopping test' (see e-marketing insight p. 144) which measures the likelihood of online retail purchases.

Internet activities of adults who have accessed the Internet in the last three months, by sex, UK, 2007

	Men	Women	All
Per cent			
Finding information about goods or services	88	84	86
Sending/receiving e-mails	85	85	85
Using services related to travel and accommodation	65	61	63
Obtaining information from public authorities' web sites	47	43	46
Internet banking	46	43	45
Looking for information about education, training or courses	35	38	36
Playing or downloading games, images, films or music	41	29	35
Other information search or online service	35	33	34
Consulting the Internet with the purpose of learning	35	31	33
Downloading official forms	35	27	31
Reading or downloading online news, magazines	35	25	30
Other communication (use of chat sites, messenger, etc.)	29	26	28
Seeking health-related information	24	31	27
Listening to web radios/watching web television	32	19	25
Sending completed forms to public authorities	29	20	25
Downloading software	34	13	24
Looking for a job or sending a job application	21	21	21
Selling of goods or services (e.g. via auctions)	21	13	17
Telephoning over the Internet/video conferencing	16	8	12
Doing an online course (in any subject)	6	7	6

Figure 4.1   Popularity of online activities in UK. (*Source*: UK National Statistics, 2006)

However, mixed-mode shopping (i.e. online browsing) suggests an effective Internet presence is essential for multichannel business, as shown in Figure 4.2. The data shows that some products such as tickets, books and electrical goods have a much higher conversion rate of browsers to buyers. Of course, the Internet is still having an important although decreasing role in the purchase decision for those who browse online and buy offline as part of mixed-mode buying.

It's simple: if customers can't find the right information about your products and service propositions, then you don't even make it into the 'considered set' of brands being considered by a potential customer.

The third most popular online activity is entertainment. After adult entertainment comes games, music and checking up on the latest news about the favourite band, sports team or celebrity.

It is no surprise that popular sites offer these key activities of socializing, product information, purchasing and entertainment through e-mail and chat, search engines and product guides, shopping, community and games.

For the B2B market, international benchmarking studies (DTI 2003), suggest that the main drivers for adopting e-commerce are cost-efficiency and selling – tapping into the global market. B2B e-marketplaces deliver cost savings through global sourcing, auctions and bids

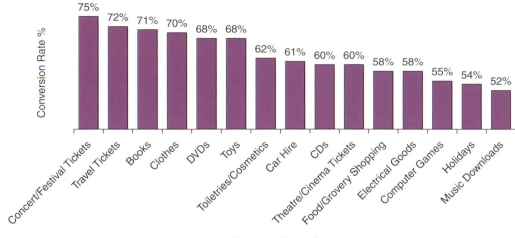

[Base: All Online Shoppers]

Figure 4.2 Percentage of Internet users browsing and buying in Europe during 2007. Conversion percentages are the proportion of all who research the product online who buy online. (*Source*: EIAA, 2007)

as well as reducing supplier numbers, reducing inventories, access to wider/deeper products and services. Enlightened businesses are also using the Internet to get closer to customers, serve them better, build the brand and reach more customers. Some enlightened companies understand how good e-marketing adds value to the brand and many Financial Directors now understand the importance of the brand since IAS 38 (International Accounting Standard) requires companies to value their intangible assets such as brands on the balance sheets when they are acquired (IFR 2005). This motivates B2B organizations to add value and 'sizzle' to their brand via the web site as it not only boosts customer satisfaction scores and builds brand assets, but also boosts market capitalization.

PRACTICAL E-MARKETING TIP

Support satisficing behaviour

When we create online services, we often base our designs for our customer experiences on rational models of how online users behave. However, research such as that by Penn reminds us that, in reality, consumers are often far from rational, they exhibit **satisficing behaviour** where they often act on impulse or make do with imperfect information, so we need to build this into our online designs and our design process by including calls-to-action and content which support slower rational 'maximizer' behaviour and faster, less-rational 'satisficer' behaviour. Some users will just act on impulse, so it should be easy to do that. Ultralase (www.ultralase.com) has a sign-up form on its home page, not hidden deep in the site, similarly Lovefilm (www.lovefilm.com) has used multivariate testing to highlight the 'Free Trial' message rather than the more rational 'Learn More' button which may introduce doubt.

E-MARKETING INSIGHT

Online customers – irrational animals?

We are still not terribly rational customers. As Oscar Wilde once remarked: *'man is a rational animal until he is asked to act within the dictates of reason'*. So it continues the illogical, irrational consumer is still on the rampage. Penn (2005) suggests that if the 'handed down' wisdom is that consumers make rational choices and, moreover, can explain those choices, then brain science suggests, more or less, the opposite. In this alternative view, unconscious processes mediate cognitive rational decision making, leading to a choice which can only be half understood (at best) by introspection. In other words, we can't always say with any reliability why we made a particular choice. Sometimes, we just 'do it', because 'we always do it'.

Penn, D. (2005) Brain Science, That's Interesting, But What Do I Do About It? Market Research Society Conference.

RESPONDING TO CUSTOMER MOTIVATIONS

Once you know why people go online, you can apply a very simple marketing formula:

1 Find out why people buy and what are their aspirations and expectations. Then . . .

2 Reflect the reasons, aspirations and expectations in your communications. This way you give customers what they want instead of what you want.

Of course, you have to be able to deliver the promised benefits. Otherwise repeat sales die, negative word of mouth spreads and the online activities damage the brand. Don't promise what you cannot deliver.

Existing offline customers can be encouraged to go online before they are besieged by other, competitive, online offerings. Remember someone, somewhere, is analyzing and targeting your market right now.

Tempt customers by offering channel choice and, something customers can't get elsewhere, the **online value proposition (OVP)** detailed in Chapters 4 and 6. Tell them how it works and how they can use it. Other motivators such as the social aspect can be used: For home users, and sometimes, for business users also, it is an important social tool enabling conversations with participants known and unknown, from near and far. Also useful member-get-member promotions amongst existing customers help members to help others with useful information about interesting offers. Word-of-mouth and referrals are a powerful tool. Remember, reassurance is vital since security is a major fear and phobia. Section 4.4 later in this chapter explores fears and phobias

We suggest that you consider the 6Cs of customer motivation to help define the OVP (Chaffey, 2004):

1 **Content** – We know that relevant content is still king. Online content should provide something that supports other channels. Often this means more detailed, in-depth

information to support the buying process or product usage. As well as text-based content which is king for business-to-business there is also interactive content which is king for consumer sites and particularly brands. Remember that context is also king. Context provides the right information, personalized for the right segment using the right media to achieve relevance.

2 **Customization** – **Mass customization** of content delivers personalized content viewed as web site pages or e-mail alerts. This is commonly known as personalization or tailoring of content according to individuals or groups – see Siebel.com for a great example.

3 **Community** – Community, these days known as 'social networks'. Online channels such as the Internet are known as 'many-to-many' media meaning that your audiences can contribute to the content. For consumer retail, review sites such as Epinions (www.epinions.com) are important for informing customer perceptions of brands. Similarly in business markets some specialist communities have been set up. For example, e-consultancy (www.e-consultancy.com) has forums and reviews which discuss issues in the supply of e-business services.

4 **Convenience** – Convenience is the ability to easily find, select, purchase and in some cases, use products, from your desktop at any time; the classic 24/7 availability of a service.

5 **Choice** – The web gives a wider choice of products and suppliers than traditional media. The success of online intermediaries such as Kelkoo (www.kelkoo.com) and Screentrade (www.screentrade.com) is evidence of this.

6 **Cost reduction** – The Internet is widely perceived as a relatively low-cost place of purchase. In the UK, Vauxhall have keyed into this perception by offering Vauxhall Internet Price (VIP), in other words lower prices than through dealer-based distribution. Similarly a key component of the easyJet OVP when it launched was single tickets that were £2.50 cheaper than phone bookings. This simple price differential together with the limited change in behaviour required from phone booking to online booking has been a key factor in the easyJet online ticketing channel effectively replacing all other booking modes.

E-MARKETING INSIGHT

De Kare-Silver's electronic shopping test

This assesses the consumer's propensity to purchase a retail product using the Internet. De Kare-Silver suggests factors that should be considered in the electronic shopping test:

1 *Product characteristics.* Does the product need to be physically tried, or touched before it is bought?

2 *Familiarity and confidence.* Considers the degree the consumer recognizes and trusts the product or brand.

3 *Consumer attributes.* These shape the buyer's behaviour – are they amenable to online purchases in terms of access to the technology, skills available and do they no longer wish to shop for a product in a traditional retail environment?

Typical results from the evaluation, where products are scored out of 50 for suitability for electronic commerce, are:

- Groceries (27/50)
- Mortgages (15/50)
- Travel (31/50)
- Books (38/50).

De Kare-Silver states that any product scoring over 20 has good potential, since the score for consumer attributes is likely to increase through time. Given this, he suggests companies will regularly need to review the score for their products.

SECTION SUMMARY 4.2

Motivations

B2C customers are motivated to go online for a range of reasons – social, shopping, entertainment. B2B customers are driven by cost savings, speed and selling. Enlightened companies realize there are other motivators such as enhanced customer relationships. In addition to delivering an excellent product or service, find what motivates your customers and then reflect it through your online and offline communications – a simple formula for success.

4.3 Expectations

By the end of this section you will begin to know how to manage customer expectations. This section reviews what customers expect when they visit a web site and how to deliver these expectations.

WHAT ARE THE ONLINE EXPECTATIONS?

Online customers have raised expectations. They expect higher standards in terms of service, convenience, speed of delivery, competitive prices and choice. They also want, if not expect, to be in control, secure and safe. The problem with raised expectations is that firstly, they are crushed more easily and secondly they can damage the brand if not fulfilled.

Online customers expect fast service and fast delivery. The Internet and everything associated with it suggests speed. If online businesses do not deliver speedily then online customers are disappointed, annoyed, angry and sometimes vociferous. Even if delivery takes the same time as the retail store, the online customers often expect a little more (whether price discount, wider choice or whatever). This is the problem with raised expectations.

Now consider a customer's expectations when buying a book online. Top of the list of online customer expectations is minimizing the time on site and delivering what is promised, but there are many other requirements (see box on customer expectations).

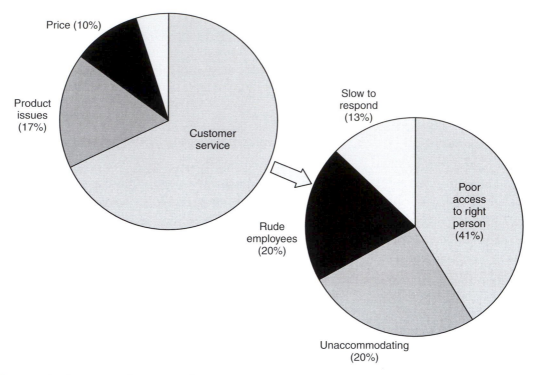

Figure 4.3 Summary of reasons why customers change supplier. (*Source*: Purdue University cross-sector study)

Online customers, quite reasonably, expect things to work – they expect to find what they want easily and buy what they want easily. The Internet is a quagmire for the destruction of both raised expectations and even ordinary expectations.

Sadly, it seems there are many exceptions to perfect service as discussed in the introduction. Customer service is critical, research summarized in Figure 4.3 shows that poor customer service rather than price or features is the number one reason why customers don't remain loyal to a company.

So, the most significant expectations are customer service and we need to work hard to deliver this across the many interactions between company and customer before, during and after the buying process. Section 4.5 discusses the online buying process.

E-MARKETING EXCELLENCE

Customer expectations for an online retail purchase

Our expectations are informed by our peers and by past experience. So when we shop online we expect, or indeed demand, that the experience will be superior to traditional shopping. The list of requirements is long.

1 Easy to find what you're looking for by searching or browsing.

2 Site easy to use, pages fast to download with no bugs.

3 Price, product specification and availability information on site to be competitive and correct, but we probably prefer great customer services to great prices – this is what will keep us loyal.

4 Specification of date, time and delivery to be possible.

5 E-mail notification when order placed and then dispatched.

6 Personal data remains personal and private and security is not compromised.

7 Verification for high-value orders.

8 Delivery on time.

9 Returns policy enabling straightforward return or replacement.

. . . and finally, quick online or offline answers to questions when the expectations above aren't met. This means traceability through databases, someone who knows your order status and can solve your problems.

MANAGING CUSTOMER EXPECTATIONS

Customers' expectations can be managed, met and exceeded. How do we do this? Here are three stages:

1 *Understanding expectations*. Managing the expectations of the demanding customer starts with understanding these expectations. Use customer research and site benchmarking to help this. Use standard frameworks to establish the gap between expectation and delivery and prioritize to solve the worst shortcomings. Use scenarios to identify the customer expectations of using the services on your site.

2 *Setting and communicating the service promise*. Expectations can best be managed by entering into an informal or formal agreement as to what service the customer can expect through customer service guarantees or promises (see box). It is better to under-promise than over-promise. A book retailer that delivers the book in two days when three days were promised will earn the customer's loyalty better than the retailer who promises one day, but delivers in two!

3 *Delivering the service promise*. Commitments must be delivered through on-site service, support from employees and physical fulfilment. If not, online credibility is destroyed and a customer may never return. Detailed techniques on delivering the service promise are given in the following 'Service guarantees and promises' box.

E-MARKETING EXCELLENCE

Service guarantees and promises

These can be made for a range of aspects:

- Information accuracy (product specifications, price, availability and delivery times) must all be accurate. How many customers did the retailer (who mistakenly offered television sets for sale at £2.99) lose when it informed customers who had placed orders that it would not honour the order?
- E-mail response. How long will the company take to respond for different sorts of enquiries?
- Security guarantees. What happens if security is compromised?
- Delivery guarantees. What happens if delivery is late?
- Return guarantees. What happens if the product is unsuitable?
- Price promises. If you are offering the best prices, this should not be an empty promise. If a company uses an *attack e-tailing* approach then frequent comparison with competitors' prices and real-time adjustment to match or better them is required. This approach is important on the Internet because of the transparency of pricing and availability of information made possible through shopping comparison sites such as Kelkoo. As customers increasingly use these facilities then it is important that price positioning is favourable.

Service promises can also be formalized in a service level agreement (SLA). If a business purchases a hosting service from an Internet service provider, its obligations and what it will do if they are not met will be clearly laid out in a service level agreement.

SECTION SUMMARY 4.3

Expectations

Managing customers' expectations is even more challenging in the online world because of raised expectations. We need to:

1 Understand the customer's expectations for service delivery and the gap with current delivery.
2 Make clear service promises through privacy statements, promises and guarantees on security, delivery, price and customer service response times.
3 Deliver the service promise through a fast, easy-to-use site, with competitive pricing backed up by excellent customer service and perfect fulfilment.

Not rocket science – just common sense.

4.4   Fears and phobias

By the end of this section you will understand the fears and phobias that occupy some customers' minds when going online. You will also know how to address these issues.

The average consumer is not fearful of turning on the TV or radio or picking up a telephone. Perhaps the biggest difference about the Internet is the fear associated with it, and as marketers, we have to deal with this. You probably don't have these fears (since you're reading this book). But many of your potential customers do. Now we're going to ask you to do what good marketers are good at – empathise – empathise with customers – imagine how they feel when going online, particularly when going online for the first time, or going to make their first online purchase.

WHAT ARE THE FEARS AND PHOBIAS?

Consider the fears you think your customers might suffer when they think about going online. Security risks such as identity theft and stolen credit card details, hackers, hoaxes, viruses, SPAM and lack of privacy – big brother syndrome – is probably top your list. Others fear having their computer taken over remotely by a malicious or criminal hacker. You may have also noted less significant anxieties such as not knowing what to do, fear of getting lost, fear of too much information or fear of inaccurate information. These fears centre on lack of customer control.

There are also fears about how the Internet will destroy the lives of individuals, families and so the whole of society. Safety needs such as security, protection, order and stability are of great importance in our hierarchy of needs. Finally, we have e-nasties such as cyber stalkers, hate mail, fake mail, mail bombs, cults and paedophiles lurking in children's chat-rooms. The human mind is a complex arena with its realities, its fears and its phobias. Many of these fears are based on reality.

On a more positive note, excellent marketers understand their customers' fears and phobias and take actions to minimize them. The leading e-tailers not only have a great proposition, but they are perceived by the customer as low risk because they eliminate customer fears.

E-MARKETING INSIGHT

Fears diminishing but still strong

Over the years, the UK government has run an omnibus survey which gives great insight into customers' fears and phobias:

- The survey shows that the percentage of individuals who have accessed the Internet in the last three months has increased from 40% to 60%. Of course in the younger age groups the proportion is much higher (16–24 = 90%, 25–44 = 79%,

45–55 = 67%, 55–64 = 48%). This still shows many 'silver surfers' or users over 55, and indicates the potential for growth as the current population ages.

- This still leaves a substantial number who have not used the Internet (40% of households in 2007) who say they do not see a need for the Internet (43%), they have a lack of knowledge or confidence (37%) or costs are too high (11%).

- The main reasons for those not buying online are:

  – Have no need (26%)

  – Prefer to shop in person/see the product (35%)

  – Security concerns (19%).

- It seems as if e-retailers will need to work hard to convince non-adopters to overcome their prejudice, but the potential for success is high.

(*Source*: ONS 2004).

Marketers alone cannot change some of the negative feelings about the Internet. The Internet makes great copy for the newspapers; it seems that the Internet is a scapegoat for many events that occur in modern society, whether this is babies being adopted over the Internet, discontented employees running amok, racism or indeed any immoral or illegal activity.

What marketers can, and must do, is to reassure customers that the problems they perceive are unlikely and act responsibly to minimize the risk of problems happening.

Follow these guidelines to achieve reassurance, gain trust and build loyalty:

1 *Provide clear and effective privacy statements*. Visit the sites of easyJet (www.easyJet.co.uk) and RS components (B2B) www.rswww.com for plain privacy statements which directly address customers' fears and phobias.

2 *Follow privacy and consumer protection guidelines in all local markets*. In 2003 the European Electronic Communications Regulations came into force to supplement existing European data protection laws. The essence of this law, implemented in the UK as the Privacy and Electronic Communications Regulations Act, is to make permission-based e-mail marketing a legal requirement. **Opt-in and opt-out** are both legal requirements for e-mail marketing to consumers (individual subscribers) in the UK. For B2B e-mail communications in the UK this isn't currently a requirement, but it is in many European countries with fines of hundreds of thousands of Euros in some countries. It is also necessary to have clear privacy statements which inform users about **cookies** and **web analytics** tracking.

3 *Make security of customer data a priority*. This is a requirement of data protection law. For example, you should offer the strongest encryption standards possible and use firewalls and ethical hackers to maximize the safety of customer data.

4   *Present independent site certification.* Companies can use independent third-parties who set guidelines for online privacy and performance. The best known international bodies are Truste (www.truste.org) and Verisign for payment authentification (www.verisign.com). Other UK certification bodies include SafeBuy (www.safebuy.org.uk), Webtrader UK (www.webtraderuk.org.uk) and the IMRG Hallmark (www.imrg.org).

5   *Emphasize the excellence of service quality in all communications.* This is explained in Section 4.3 on meeting customers' expectations.

6   *Use content on the site to reassure the customer.* Explain the actions they have taken. Ask them to confirm. Allow them to revoke or cancel an action. Amazon takes customer fears about security seriously judging by the prominence and amount of content it devotes to this issue.

7   *Leading-edge design.* Marketers should challenge their site designers to make the customer experience as easy as possible by customer-centred site design. Intuitive, easy-to-use sites, where customers experience flow, help to counter fears and phobias. Customers become comfortable more quickly and word-of-mouth spreads positive messages.

New approaches are needed to build trust in the networked world since conventional ways of gaining trust such as personal contact are no longer practical. Credibility and trust must be built at Internet speed. Time is of the essence. For some FMCG brands trust was built over two generations, Gap did it in ten years and Yahoo! in five years. In contrast, note that some studies show that trust is also a long-term proposition that builds slowly as people use a site, get good results, and don't feel let down or cheated.

> **SECTION SUMMARY 4.4**
>
> **Fears and phobias**
>
> A headline in a *Harvard Business Review* recently announced: *'Price doesn't rule the web; trust does'.* The typical online customer is fearful and has many anxieties. Companies that succeed in reassuring customers by clearly communicating their security, privacy and ease-of-use backed up by real quality of service will reap the rewards through customer loyalty.

4.5   The online buying process

By the end of this section you will understand the stages buyers go through and how to ensure you address all of these stages online. You simply have to understand how customers use the new media in their purchase decision-making.

The buying process should be catered for both online and offline (**mixed-mode buying**, Chapter 2). Each stage of the purchasing process should be supported both online and offline. Let us consider a 'high-involvement' purchase such as a car or a house. Assuming this follows a simple linear buying model, what occurs at each stage?

1   *Problem recognition.* This can occur through changed circumstances such as a new job, new money or the existing car breaks down, etc. Peer pressure or clever advertising or editorial (online or offline) which highlights the problem (or the need or the want) can also help the customer to recognize it themselves.

2 *Information search*. Having established a need, i.e. the problem is recognized, the customer gathers information. We need to understand how customers gather information – online and offline. Online the web is increasingly used for searching. Remember there is a difference between searching and surfing. Think about the timing and frequency of when online customers seek information. Get the timing and the targeting right and you create 'relevance' which allows the information through the customer's perceptual filters. Get it wrong and your information gets screened out by an uninterested audience.

3 *Evaluation*. We need to use the content on our site to communicate the features and benefits of the brand in what may be a fleeting visit to the site or an in-depth analysis. Independent reports prominently positioned on site may save the buyer from having to search elsewhere. We also need to think about how to cater for different customer buying behaviour according to Internet experience. Remember that search behaviour will differ according to familiarity with the Internet, the organization and its web site.

4 *Decision*. Some car buyers may have already physically test-driven several cars and now want to decide and buy online. Some sites help the decision by offering payment facilities that match the customer's personal financial situation. Once the decision has been made to purchase, we don't want to lose the customer at this stage, so make purchasing slick and simple. And if the customer has anxieties, give them the choice of buying through other channels by prompting with a phone number or a call-back facility.

5 *Action (sale)*. Often an appropriate incentive to 'buy now' either online or offline helps to push the buyer over the edge and into the sale. The purchase can be made online particularly if suitable reassurances are made.

6 *Post sale*. Then the real marketing begins. The sale is only the beginning of the relationship (i.e. relationship marketing and lifetime customers). Lifetime customers generate repeat sales which, in turn, generate much higher profits (some estimates suggest five times higher profits on repeat sales than new customers). Use e-mail and the web site to provide customer service and support.

But think about how the online environment has changed buyer behaviour, generally speaking:

- Search marketing has compressed the cycle – the buying process often starts with a generic search
- Supplier search is now also compressed by visits to comparison sites which often feature well in search engines
- Recommendations from other customers through user-generated content are now an important influencer as we saw in the previous chapter
- Brand has become more important at later decision stages since it provides trust.

Figure 4.4 summarizes how content on site can support the buying process. Produce a map for how your site supports the buying process.

Obviously the process above applies best to high-involvement purchases like a car rather than to low-involvement purchases like a can of cola. Here the model is about awareness, trial and reinforcement (ATR), followed by availability, availability, availability. Rock band, Oasis,

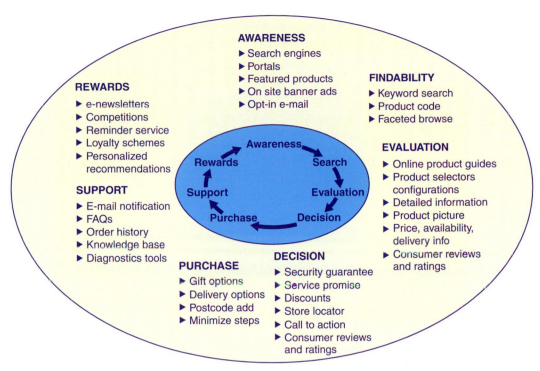

Figure 4.4   The buying process and how it can be supported by site content

followed an interesting ATR approach to promote and sell their CD *Heathen Chemistry*. To satisfy the hunger for previews (before release) and reduce the number of illegal downloads from the Internet . . . seven days prior to the release of the CD, four tracks were offered to *Sunday Times* readers as a cover-mounted CD which was encrypted so it could only be played four times. After that the CD is automatically wiped and the user is directed to HMV.co.uk to buy the album. HMV donate 50 p to Prince's Trust Charity – Big Time Cultural Bank.

B2B buying models have a specification and tender stage built in before sellers can tender or present their bids (and product information). Often, only pre-selected or preferred suppliers' information is considered. Note information search tends to be 'directed' or 'focused' rather than browsing or surfing. In fact five different types of search behaviour have been recognized and we should cater for each in site design and communications, but with the emphasis on the predominant groups.

E-MARKETING INSIGHT

Using the psychology of persuasion

US psychologist Robert Cialdini (Cialdini, 2006) identifies six 'weapons of influence' that you can use to influence site visitors and viewers of ads through use of appropriate messages. The six weapons were originally developed with reference to personal interactions rather than web marketing, but we have summarized them as a checklist in Table 4.2 together with our recommendations on how you can apply them to your web communications.

Table 4.2   Summary of the online implications for Cialdini's six weapons of influence

Influencer	Online marketing implication
☑ 1 Reciprocity	Offer valuable, exclusive content or offers and your audience will remember you and will recommend you through bookmarks, links or by telling their friends. Encourage this behaviour through prompts on the site.
☑ 2 Commitment and consistency	Get initial commitment by encouraging visitors to drill deeper, search, subscribe or engage with product selectors. 'Set their alarm clock' by providing regular reasons to return, such as new promotions, content highlighted on site and within Ezines.
☑ 3 Consensus	Your audience will believe others more than they believe you! So use reviews, case studies, testimonials and rewards as we described in Chapter 2.
☑ 4 Affinity (liking and credibility)	People are persuaded by other people they like or who are like them, so again use recommendations or endorsements by people who are known by your audience or they can relate to.
☑ 5 Authority	Unless you are a well-known brand, you need to prove your authority. So if you are a blogger, for example, you need to show off your authority, expertise and status. Companies need to show off satisfied customers or in the B2B services example, their employees qualifications and reputations!
☑ 6 Scarcity	The fear of loss is more powerful than that of gain, so show site visitors what they could miss. For example, in links to its site in offline communications, in its PPC ads, its e-mail communications and of course on its site, Dell makes use of time-limited offers.

E-MARKETING INSIGHT

Identifying hunters, trackers and explorers

In a report on online retail, benchmarking the user experience of UK retail sites, E-consultancy (2004) identified a useful classification of online shopping behaviour to test how well the web site design matched the different behaviours.

Three types of potential behaviour were identified which are the hunter, tracker and explorer. Note that these do not equate to different people, since according to the type of product or occasion, the behaviour of an individual may differ. Indeed as they research a product they are likely to become more directed.

1 Tracker. Defined as follows:

> *'knows exactly which product they wish to buy and uses an online shopping site to track it down and check its price, availability, delivery time, delivery charges or after-sales support'.*

i.e. the tracker is looking for specific information about a particular product. The report says: 'If they get the answers they are seeking they need little further persuasion or purchase justification before completing the purchase'. While this may not be true since they may compare on other sites, this type of shopper will be relatively easy to convert.

2 Hunter. Defined as follows:

> *'doesn't have a specific product in mind but knows what type of product they are looking for (e.g. digital camera, cooker) and probably has one or more product features they are looking for. The hunter uses an online shopping site to find a range of suitable products, compare them and decide which one to buy'.*

The hunter needs more help, support and guidance to reach a purchasing decision. The report says:

> *'once a potential purchase is found, they then need to justify that purchase in their own minds, and possibly to justify their purchase to others. Only then will confirmation of the purchase become a possibility'.*

3 Explorer. Defined as follows:

> *'doesn't even have a particular type of product in mind. They may have a well-defined shopping objective (buying a present for someone or treating themselves), a less-resolved shopping objective (buying something to 'brighten up' the lounge) or no shopping objective at all (they like the high street store and thought they would have a look at the online site)'.*

The report suggests that the explorer has a range of possible needs and many uncertainties to be resolved before committing to purchase, but the following may be helpful in persuading these shoppers to convert: 'Certain types of information, however, are particularly relevant. Suggested gift ideas, guides to product categories, lists of top selling products and information-rich promotions (What's New? What's Hot?) – these could all propel them towards a purchasing decision'.

Leading companies use web analytics data to see how activity and repeat visits vary through each day, week, month and year. A financial services provider found a traffic peak on Monday lunchtime when people looked to find out more after reviewing alternatives in the Sunday papers. A B2B company found a peak at the start of each month that corresponded with new sales promotions. A monthly competition was launched, timed to coincide with the traffic peak.

Amazingly, research by BT showed that customers seem to use the Internet and telephone more before a full moon, but how marketers can tap into this behaviour is unclear!

The online buying process

We have to support customers through each stage of the buying process: problem identification, information search, evaluation, decision, action and post sales.

We need to think about how we can combine online and offline communications to support the customer through each stage of the buying process and also support mixed-mode buying at each stage. We also need to be self-critical about how we profile customers. What are the underlying variables that might influence the customer's product purchase and usage patterns and can we track these patterns? Techniques to achieve this are described in Section 4.10, Researching the online customer. Finally, some customers want to search, compare and buy online. Others just want to browse. Does your web site accommodate all stages of the buying process?

4.6   Online information processing

By the end of this section you will understand how customers process information – what gets through and what doesn't.

The section is structured around Charles Hofacker's five stages of on-site information processing (Hofacker 2001). The five stages are: (1) Exposure (2) Attention (3) Comprehension and perception (4) Yielding and acceptance (5) Retention. Each stage acts as a hurdle, since if the site design or content is too difficult to process, the customer cannot progress to the next stage. The e-marketer fails.

The best web site designs take into account how customers process information. Good e-marketers are aware of how the messages are processed by the customer and of the corresponding steps we can take to ensure the correct message is received.

The first stage is **exposure**. This is straightforward. If the content is not present for long enough, customers will not be able to process it. Think of splash pages, banner adverts or shockwave animations. If these change too rapidly the message will not be received.

The second stage is **attention**. The human mind has limited capacity to pick out the main messages from a screen full of single column text format without headings or graphics. Movement, text size and colour help to gain attention for key messages. Note though that studies show that the eye is immediately drawn to content, not the headings in the navigation systems. Of course, we need to be careful about using garish colours and animations as

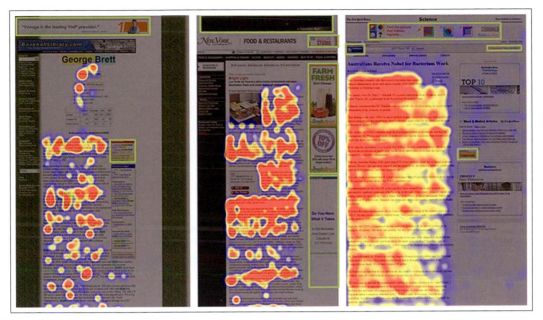

Figure 4.5   Evidence of eyetracking from heatmaps. (*Source*: Nielsen, 2007)

these can look amateurish. Or they can look like loud advertisements which many customers simply screen out as indicated by Nielsen (2007) and Figure 4.5.

Comprehension and perception are the third of Hofacker's stages. They refer to how the customer interprets the combination of graphics, text and multimedia on a web site. The design will be most effective if it uses familiar standards or metaphors since the customer will interpret them according to previous experience and memory. Once relevant information is found, visitors sometimes want to dig deeper for more information.

Fourth, **yielding and acceptance** refers to whether the information you present is accepted by the customer. Different tactics need to be used to convince different types of people. Classically, a US audience is more convinced by features rather than benefits, while the reverse is true for a European audience. Some customers will respond to emotive appeals, perhaps reinforced by images, while others will make a more clinical evaluation based on the text. This gives us the difficult task of combining text, graphics and copy to convince each customer segment.

Finally, **retention** – how well the customer can recall their experience. A clear, distinctive site design will be retained in the customer's mind, perhaps prompting a repeat visit when the customer thinks, 'where did I see that information?' and then recalls the layout of the site. A clear site design will also be implanted in the customer's memory as a mental map which they will be able to draw on when returning to the site, increasing their flow experience.

Sites with excellent design use a range of techniques. Examine Figure 4.6 and read more in Chapter 6 to see how the concepts in this section have been applied.

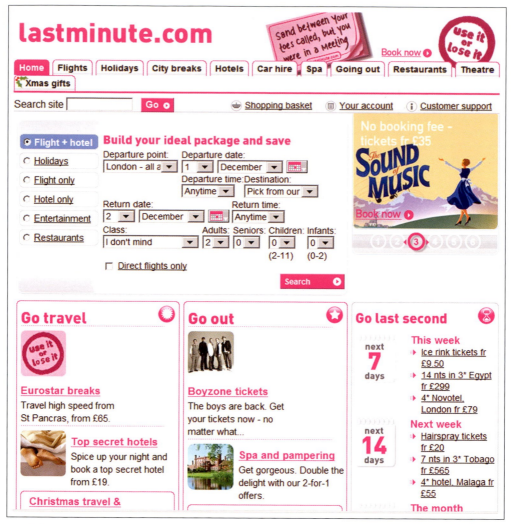

Figure 4.6   Lastminute.com attracts attention

E-MARKETING INSIGHT

Jakob Nielsen on graphics

Jakob Nielsen says:

> 'when they arrive on a page, users ignore navigation bars and other global design elements: instead they look only at the content area of the page' (www.useit.com/alertbox/20000109.html)

Studies show that e-customers are very goal-driven and tend to ignore banner ads while focusing completely on their task. Eye-tracking studies confirm the existence of 'banner blindness' where the user's gaze never rests in the region of the screen occupied by advertising (www.useit.com/alertbox/990221.html).

Nielsen says:

'the most common behaviour is to hunt for information and be ruth-less in ignoring details. But once the prey has been caught, users will sometimes dive in more deeply. Thus, web content needs to support both aspects of information access: foraging and consumption. Text needs to be scannable, but it also needs to provide the answers users seek' (www.useit.com/alertbox/20000514.html)

A good compromise is to have small rectangular animated banner ads to the right of the screen which highlight the special offers. But remember about 'banner blindness'.

SECTION SUMMARY 4.6

Online information processing

Understanding how customers process information through the stages of exposure, atten-tion, comprehension and perception, yielding and acceptance and retention can help us design sites – sites that really help us get our message across and deliver memorable mes-sages and superior customer service.

4.7   Online relationships and loyalty

By the end of this section, you will understand the importance of lifetime customers, rela-tionship marketing and loyalty. You will also know how to begin to explore setting up loy-alty marketing schemes.

Look at the stats. Retaining existing customers is five times more profitable than acquiring new customers. Interestingly Laurent and Eltvedt (2006) suggest that online repeat customers are actually ten times more profitable. Even over ten years ago US corporations were los-ing half their customers every five years (Reicheld 1996). Arguably all markets have accelerated into hypercompetition with more aggressive attrition rates. Even your own opt-in e-mail lists rapidly deteriorate, with estimates suggesting that if your list is left unused for 12 months it can deteriorate up to 66%. Even when active, you lose 5% of your list every three months. The list is most responsive when its freshly recruited i.e. within the first few months.

All marketers know that building long-term relationships with the 'ideal customer' is essen-tial for any sustainable business. Failure to build relationships largely caused the dotcom failures. Research shows that by retaining just 5% more customers, e-companies can boost their profits by 25% to 95%. This section describes techniques to build and maintain rela-tionships with customers using a combination of online and offline techniques.

We want to move customers up what Considine and Murray (1981) originally referred to as the 'ladder of loyalty'. From suspects, to prospects, to customers, to clients, to advocates who are totally loyal and are happy to spread the word about our products and services.

Remember, some customers are more likely to be loyal than others. Companies need to focus on those ideal customers that are likely to become loyal rather than the promiscuous, loss making, customers who grab incentives and run.

Many companies now only proactively market to 'ideal' customers since it has been thought that 20% of existing customers are 'ideal' and generate most of your profits (however see page 133 for an alternative 'Long Tail' view). Some customers break even, while other, disloyal, promiscuous, customers are loss makers. They cost you money. Low loyalty has a high cost.

In *Permission Marketing* Seth Godin (2001) suggests that marketers should 'Focus on share of customer, not market share – fire 70% of your customers and watch your profits go up!' Some companies go further – they actually stop 'bad customers' from becoming customers. They also invest in acquiring and keeping ideal customers. For many businesses it can take at least two years before a company recoups its initial acquisition costs.

So how can we keep customers and form relationships, particularly in the cyber world?

Seth Godin suggests online relationships can be likened to the relationships built through dating, with incentives important at every stage. Lindstrom and Andersen, authors of *Brand Building on the Internet*, encourage e-marketers to think of loyalty as virtual love.

Research summarized by Reicheld and Schefter (2000) showed that acquiring online customers is so expensive (20–30% higher than for traditional businesses) that start-up companies may remain unprofitable for at least two to three years. The research also shows that by retaining just 5% more customers, online companies can boost their profits by 25% to 95%. They say:

> *'but if you can keep customers loyal, their profitability accelerates much faster than in traditional businesses. It costs you less and less to service them'.*

Note that the relationship between customer loyalty and profitability has been questioned, notably by Reinartz and Kumar (2002), who discovered through analysis of four company databases that:

> *'there was little or no evidence to suggest that customers who purchase steadily from a company over time are necessarily cheaper to serve, less price sensitive, or particularly effective at bringing in new business'.*

While few would argue that the cost of acquiring customers is significantly higher than repeat customers and that some customers are unprofitable, care has to be taken with customer selection.

As in any relationship, the early stages are crucial. In relationship marketing the first ninety days are crucial. Maintaining online customer relationships is difficult. Laurie Windham says:

> '*That's what's so scary about customer retention in the online space. We've created this empowered, impatient customer who has a short attention span, a lot of choices, and a low barrier to switching*'.

E-MARKETING INSIGHT

The *Cluetrain Manifesto* on developing online relationships

The authors of the groundbreaking *Cluetrain Manifesto* (Levine *et al*. 2000) kept for posterity as 'read only landmark' at www.cluetrain.com suggest that we should not conceive the Internet as an impassive network of hardware and software, but as a means of creating global conversations within markets – a new dynamic dialogue.

It refers to a large organization being unable to listen or respond to the 'clues' from customers demanding better service and response. Clues include high churn, rising complaints and the success of more responsive competitors.

To illustrate the danger of continuing with push marketing the authors say:

> *Conversations among human beings sound human. They are conducted in a human voice.*

> *Most corporations, on the other hand, only know how to talk in the soothing, humourless monotone of the mission statement, marketing brochure and your-call-is-important-to-us busy signal. Same old tone, same old lies. No wonder networked markets have no respect for companies unable or unwilling to speak as they do.*

> *Corporate firewalls have kept smart employees in and smart markets out. It's going to cause real pain to tear those walls down. But the result will be a new kind of conversation. And it will be the most exciting conversation business has ever engaged in.*

DEVELOPING LOYALTY

So how do you develop loyalty and strong relations with customers?

First, target and acquire the right type of customer – the ideal customer. Second, delight them. Don't just satisfy them. Ground-breaking research by Xerox some years ago revealed that between 65 and 85% of customers who defected from Xerox were actually 'satisfied customers'.

So, we need to excel beyond the five 'primary determinants of loyalty' identified by Reicheld and Schefter (2000):

1 Quality customer support.
2 On-time delivery.
3 Compelling product presentations.
4 Convenient and reasonably priced shipping and handling.
5 Clear trustworthy privacy policies.

And then delight the customer with:

1 *Extra service and added value*. There are a host of other opportunities constantly to delight and surprise the customer. Start by asking, 'What interests, passions and needs do my customers have? How can I help them?' Then see how you can add value. The difficult bit is finding the time to think about these and then the time to implement them. There is no limit to relevant, timely added value ideas – many of which do not cost that much, but have a high value.
2 *Personalization*. Personalization and mass customization can have a high value. They can be used to tailor information in both the web site and opt-in e-mail. Extranets can be used to provide value-added services for key accounts.
3 *Community creation*. Community creation can engage the customer and provide a hook that keeps them returning. It can be used to create a new form of added value built around the brand. Section 4.8 deals with communities.
4 *Integration*. Integration into the customer's own systems (e.g. ERP) reduces duplication of work and increases 'lock-in' which creates a switching cost should a customer ever want to leave.
5 *Incentivization*. Traditional retention methods such as loyalty schemes and sales promotions work well. But remember – be consistent with your page layout so that your customers know where to find the special offers section. Opt-in e-mail can also alert customers to special offers and events. For both B2B and B2C organizations, think about the potential for online events. There are an infinite number of opportunities.

There are many different approaches, but basically they embrace the same principles – focus on good customers, treat them individually and serve them excellently and outstandingly.

E-MARKETING EXCELLENCE

Dell identify loyalty drivers

Reicheld and Schefter (2000) reported that Dell Computer has created a customer experience council that has researched key loyalty drivers, identified measures to track this and put in place an action plan to improve loyalty (Table 4.3).

Table 4.3   Relationship between loyalty drivers and measures to assess their success at Dell Computer. Based on example related in Reicheld and Schefter (2000)

Loyalty drivers	Summary metric
1 Order fulfilment	Ship to target. Percentage that ship on time exactly as the customer specified.
2 Product performance	Initial field incident rate – the frequency of problems experienced by customers.
3 Post sale service and support	On-time, first-time fix – the percentage of problems fixed on the first visit by a service rep who arrives at the time promised.

SECTION SUMMARY 4.7

Online relationships and loyalty

To summarize, we need to keep 'ideal' customers for life by building strong emotional and rational bonds. Constantly find out more about their needs, serve them and then plant seeds and relevant incentives to keep them coming back again and again.

4.8   Communities and social networks

By the end of this section you will understand the benefits of building communities and be able to assess the suitability of techniques used to foster online communities and how to build active/lively online communities that improve brand equity and foster customer retention. We introduced the concept of social networks in Chapter 3 where we looked at the main types of social network and why they have proved so popular.

Man is a sociable animal. Communities or social networks are important. Whether stock-brokers or punks – they tend to group together into communities. Can your brand immerse itself within a community and thereby strengthen its relationship with customers? Communities of buyers, users, lovers, even haters can pop up all over the Internet. Better to work with communities than against them. Wouldn't it be great if you could listen to your customers and prospects talking about your brand and related issues. Imagine occasionally dropping in and asking the community a question.

Imagine them telling you their current and future needs – what they like and don't like about your company. Imagine your brand at the hub of a community? Imagine your customers using your brand as a virtual meeting place? Imagine your customers getting great value from talking to each other?

Community is a key feature of new media that distinguishes them from traditional push media. But why is community important? John Hagel (Hagel and Armstrong 1997) has said:

> '*The rise of* virtual communities *in online networks has set in motion an unprecedented shift from vendors of goods and services to the customers who buy them.*

Vendors who understand this transfer of power and choose to capitalize on it by organizing virtual communities will be richly rewarded with both peerless customer loyalty and impressive economic returns'.

What is the reality behind this vision? How can we deliver the promise of community? The key to successful community is customer-centred communications. It is customer-to-customer (C2C) interaction. Customers, not suppliers, generate the content of the site, e-mail list or bulletin board.

C2C community success and essential power can be gauged by the millions of customers who use Napster and Gnutella to download MP3 music files. Using the peer-to-peer (P2P) approach, these companies created a global swap shop by acting as intermediaries enabling users to exchange files.

E-MARKETING INSIGHT

Durlacher on community

Think about these different types of community, identified by Durlacher at the time of the dotcom boom, but which remain valid today. What content and interaction will occur on each to support them? Which are appropriate to your marketplace?

1 *Purpose* – people who are going through the same process or trying to achieve a particular objective. Examples include those researching cars, e.g. at Autotrader (www. autotrader.co.uk) or stocks online, e.g. at the Motley Fool (www.motleyfool.co.uk).

2 *Position* – people who are in a certain circumstances such as a health disorder or in a certain stage of life such as communities set up specifically for young people and old people. Examples are teenage network Dubit (www.dubit.co.uk) which is used by FMCG brands to research youth market trends and engage opinion formers or sites for the over 50s such as www.over50s.com and www.50connect.co.uk. Travel and financial services group Saga has launched a social network for its audience (www.saga.co.uk, Figure 4.7).

3 *Interest* – this community is for people who share an interest or passion such as sport (www.football365.com), music (www.nme.com), leisure (www.walkingworld.com). See Magicalia (www.magicalia.com) for a range of communities created in the UK.

4 *Profession* – they are important for companies promoting B2B services. Many are successful today, for example, E-consultancy (www.e-consultancy.com) is an online portal for digital media specialists with an active forum, Linked-In (www.linkedin. com) is the biggest B2B social network for professionals, trade papers such as *Construction News* (www.cnplus.co.uk) are the dominant portals for professionals. The community of the CIPD (www.cipd.co.uk/community, Figure 4.8) is a great example of a vibrant community which is used to drive professional membership. Thinking back to Cialdini's Weapons of Influence (Table 4.2); those involved in HR don't want to miss out, they seek affinity and reciprocity.

Figure 4.7   Sagazone (www.saga.co.uk)

Figure 4.8   CIPD community (www.cipd.co.uk/community)

COMMUNITY AND SOCIAL NETWORK BUILDING STRATEGIES

You will notice that most of the community examples are intermediary sites that are independent of a particular manufacturer or retailer. A key question to ask before embarking on a community-building programme is: 'can customer interests be best served through a company independent community'. If the answer to this question is 'yes', then it may be best to form a community that is a brand variant, differentiated from its parent. For example, Boots the Chemist has created Handbag.com as an independent community for its female customers. Another tip, and a less costly alternative, is to promote your products through sponsorship or co-branding on an independent community site or portal. Or at a minimum get involved in the community discussions.

Roger Parker, author of *Relationship Marketing on the Web*, lists eight useful questions to ask when considering how to create a community for your customers:

1 What interests, needs or passions do many of your customers have in common?
2 What topics or concerns might your customers like to share with each other?
3 What information is likely to appeal to your customers' friends or colleagues?
4 What other types of business in your area appeal to buyers of your products and services?
5 How can you create packages or offers based on combining offers from two or more affinity partners?
6 What price, delivery, financing or incentives can you afford to offer to friends (or colleagues) that your current customers recommend?
7 What types of incentives or rewards can you afford to provide to customers who recommend friends (or colleagues) who make a purchase?
8 How can you best track purchases resulting from word-of-mouth recommendations from friends?

What about specific approaches for the B2B community? The B2B community offers great potential for high-involvement business services.

E-MARKETING EXCELLENCE

Overcoming community problems

These are examples of how companies have overcome problems with their communities.

1 *Empty communities.* A community without any people isn't a community. You need to apply your traffic building skills. What is the online value proposition of your community and how are you communicating it? Perhaps it is best if existing brands tap into a third party, independent community rather than starting your own that may not gain critical mass. For example, a baby toy manufacturer is likely to be

better served by getting involved on community sites such as Babyworld (www.babyworld.com) and Babycentre (www.babycentre.co.uk), rather than starting its own community which may never gain critical mass since it is not perceived as neutral.

2 *Silent communities.* A community may have many registered members, but community is not a community if the conversation flags. This is a tricky problem. You can encourage people to join the community, but how do you get them to participate? Here are some ideas.

- Seed the community. Use a moderator to ask questions or have a weekly or monthly question written by the moderator or sourced from customers. Have a resident independent expert to answer questions. Visit the communities on Monster (www.monster.co.uk) to see these approaches in action and think about what distinguishes the quiet communities from the noisy ones.

- Make it select. Limit it to key account customers or set it up as an extranet service that is only offered to valued customers as a value-add. Members may be more likely to get involved.

- Use e-mail. With e-mail groups such as Yahoo Groups (http://uk.groups.yahoo.com) participants don't need to revisit the web site, it is always in their e-mail inbox.

3 Critical communities. Many communities on manufacturer or retailer sites can be critical of the brand. The Egg Free Zone for example (www.eggfreezone.com) from bank Egg had to be closed because of critical comments of its services and retailers. Think about whether this is a bad thing. It could highlight weaknesses in your service offer to customers and competitors, but enlightened companies use communities as a means to better understand their customers' needs and the failings with their services. Community is a key market research tool. Also, it may be better to control and contain these critical comments on your site rather than them being voiced elsewhere in newsgroups where you may not notice them and can less easily counter them. The computer-oriented newsgroup on Monster shows how the moderator lets criticisms go so far and then counters them or closes them off. Particular criticisms can be removed. So, a moderator is clearly needed for any company-run communities.

SECTION SUMMARY 4.8

Communities and social networks

Well-run communities strengthen relationships, trust and loyalty, as well as maintaining brand awareness in the minds of the community members. Communities also allow a unique opportunity to stay close to customers, their concerns, their worries and their desires. Despite these benefits, building an active community can be time consuming, expensive and difficult. Careful moderation and seeding of topics from a subject expert may be required. An alternative approach is to hook up to an established community that has greater independence. Either way, communities are part of the dynamic dialogue and dynamic opportunities that today's marketer enjoys.

4.9   Customer profiles

We need to know who's online. What are their profiles? We need to know each customer segment and the proportion of customers who use various digital channels such as the Internet, interactive digital TV and mobile or other devices:

We need to know the proportion of customers who:

1 Have access to which channel or channels.
2 Are influenced by using which channel or channels.
3 Purchase using which channel or channels.

Let's consider each of these now.

PROFILING B2C CUSTOMERS

1 *Access to channel*. E-commerce provides a global marketplace, and this means we must review access and usage of the Internet channel at many different geographic levels: worldwide, between continents and countries. Also we must evaluate demographic differences in access – the stereotype of the typical Internet user as male, around thirty years of age and with high disposable income no longer holds true. Many females and more senior 'silver surfers' are also active.

   To understand online customer behaviour and how they are likely to respond to messages, we also need to consider the user's access location, access device and '**webographics**', all of which are constraints on site design.

   Finally, we mustn't forget the non-users, who comprise more than half of the adult population in many countries.

2 *Influenced online*. Next we must look at how our audience is influenced by online media. Finding information about goods and services is a very popular online activity, but we need to capture data about online influence in the buying process for our own market.

3 *Purchased online*. Customers will only purchase products online that meet the criteria of de Kare-Silver's electronic shopping test. Research shown in Figure 4.2 suggests that an increasing proportion of people are prepared to buy online. For e-planning you need to know this data for your segment. Although we can use this information when building e-plans and when calculating the channel contribution to revenue, we still need some psychographic information to understand online customers better.

   Many attempts have been made to characterize the online customers in order to tailor the online offering for them (see box 'Information sources for researching customer profiles').

PROFILING B2B CUSTOMERS

That's all very well for B2C, but what about B2B users? How should we profile online business users?

Think about the information you would want to collect when designing an online form to profile registered site B2B users. Users may be asked to enter the following organization characteristics:

- Size of company (employees or turnover)
- Industry sector and products
- Organization type (private, public, government, not for profit)
- Division
- Country and region.

What about buying cycles and budgets? You can also profile customers according to which are hot and which are cold – which are ready to buy and which are not. We also need to know the following customer variables:

- Names
- Role and responsibility from job title, function or number of staff managed
- Role in buying decision (purchasing influence)
- Department
- Product interest
- Demographics: age, sex and possibly social group.

When searching for the ideal customer, what variables or characteristics do you use? What is your profile of your ideal customer?

We can profile business users of the Internet in a similar way to consumers:

1 *The percentage of companies with access.* In most developed countries more than three-quarters of businesses have Internet access, regardless of size, suggesting the Internet is very effective in terms of reaching companies. But does it reach the right people in the buying unit? Not necessarily, as access is not available to all employees.

2 *Influenced online.* Data indicates that the Internet is important in identifying online suppliers, with the majority identifying some suppliers online, especially in the larger companies.

3 *Purchase online.* E-mail and the web are widely used for online purchases, with extranets and EDI less important since these are the preserve of larger companies. Many of the larger blue chip companies only buy online.

Customer profiles

User profiles change as Internet penetration changes. Marketers constantly need to keep a watch on who is online and who is offline – the number of connected customers, the percentage whose offline purchase is influenced online and, of course, the number who buy online. We need to research our customer geographic, demographic and psychographic segments. We also need to know why certain customer segments buy or don't buy.

4.10   Researching the online customer

In our quest to understand online customers, we need to know how to research them. Before that we need to identify what we need to know. In this section we look at the key questions and where to find the answers.

So what do you need to know about online customers? The following are key:

- Who are they – demographics and psychographics?
- What do they want – their needs – why do they buy or not buy?
- How do they buy (online or offline or mixed mode)?
- When do they buy?
- How did they find us or our competitors?

In the context of the site we need to know, in particular, what do visitors need before, during and after they go online and when they arrive at your site? We also need to know what kind of content customers want. One way of finding out is **personas and scenario-based design.**

Modelling personas of site visitors is a powerful technique for helping increase the usability and customer centricity of a web site. Personas are essentially a 'thumbnail' description of a type of person. They have been used for a long time in research for segmentation and advertising, but since the mid-1990s have proved effective for improving web site design. Here are two simple examples for a music publisher wishing to sell music clips and sheet music to a business audience.

Persona 1 – George: George is a 45-year-old violin teacher who has used the Internet for less than a year. He accesses the Internet from home over a dial-up connection. He has never purchased online before, preferring to place orders by phone.

Persona 2 – Georgina: Georgina is a 29-year-old ad exec who has been using the Internet for five years.

You can see that these are quite different types of people who will have quite different needs.

Customer scenarios are developed for different personas. Patricia Seybold in her book *The Customer Revolution* explains them as follows:

> *'A customer scenario is a set of tasks that a particular customer wants or needs to do in order to accomplish his or her desired outcome'.*

You can see that scenarios can be developed for each persona. For an online bank, scenarios might include:

1 New customer – opening online account.
2 Existing customer – transferring an account online.
3 Existing customer – finding an additional product.

Each scenario is split up into a series of steps or tasks before the scenario is completed. These steps can be best thought of as a series of questions a visitor asks. These questions identify the different information needs of different customer types at different stages in the buying process.

The use of scenarios is a simple but very powerful web design technique that is still relatively rare in web site design. Evidence of the use of scenarios and personas in sites are when the needs of a range of audiences are accommodated with navigation, links and searches to answer specific questions. Clear steps in a booking process are also an indication of the use of this approach.

The approach has the benefits of:

- Fostering customer-centricity;
- Identifying detailed information needs and steps required by customers;
- Can be used to both test existing web site designs or prototypes and to devise new designs;
- Can be used to compare and test the strength and clarity of communication of proposition on different web sites;
- Can be linked to specific marketing outcomes required by site owners.

E-MARKETING EXCELLENCE

Dulux use personas to appeal to paint purchasers

We will illustrate the development of personas through a case study from Agency.com available through the IAB (www.iabuk.net). The objectives of this project were to position Dulux.co.uk as 'the online destination for colour scheming and visualization to help you achieve your individual style from the comfort of your home'. Specific SMART objectives were: To increase the number of Unique Visitors from 1M p.a. in 2003 to 3.5M p.a. in 2006; and To drive 12% of visitors to a desired outcome (e.g. ordering swatches).

Effective customer research also uses pre-launch research techniques such as concept testing, competitor benchmarking and usability testing (Chapter 6), as well as post-launch research such as customer profiling and tracking.

TARGET AUDIENCE BASED ON RESEARCH FOR USER-CENTRED DESIGN

- Would be adventurous 25–44 women, online
- Lack of confidence
- Gap between inspiration (TV, magazines, advertising) and lived experience (sheds, nervous discomfort)
- No guidance or reassurance is available currently on their journey
- Colours and colour combining is key
- Online is a well-used channel for help and guidance on other topics
- 12 month decorating cycle
- Propensity to socialize
- Quality, technical innovation and scientific proficiency of Dulux is a given.

Examples of personas developed:

First Time Buyer Penny Edwards, Age: 27, Partner: Ben, Location: North London, Occupation: Sales Assistant

Part Time Mum Jane Lawrence, Age: 37, Husband: Joe, Location: Manchester, Occupation: Part time PR consultant

Single Mum Rachel Wilson, Age: 40, Location: Reading, Occupation: Business Analyst

Each has a different approach to interacting with the brand, for Penny it is summarized by the statement:

> *'I've got loads of ideas and enthusiasm, I just don't know where to start'.*

A storyboard was developed which illustrates the typical 'customer journey' for each persona and these informed the final design (www.dulux.co.uk, Figure 4.9).

E-MARKETING INSIGHT

Using personas and scenarios to inform web site design

These are some guidelines and ideas on what can be included when developing a persona. Start or end with giving your persona a name. The detailed stages are:

1 Build personal attributes into personas:

- Demographic: age, gender, education, occupation and for B2B, company size, position in buying unit.

- Psychographic: goals, tasks, motivation.
- Webographics: web experience (months), usage location (home or work), usage platform (dial-up, broadband), usage frequency, favourite sites.

2 Remember that personas are only models of characteristics and environment:

- Design targets
- Stereotypes
- Three or four usually suffice to improve general usability, but more are needed for specific behaviours
- Choose one primary persona whom, if satisfied, means others are likely to be satisfied.

3 Different scenarios can be developed for each persona as explained further below.

Write three or four, for example:

- Information seeking scenario (leads to site registration)
- Purchase scenario – new customer (leads to sale)
- Purchase scenario – existing customer (leads to sale).

Once different personas have been developed who are representative of key site visitor types or customer types, a primary persona is sometimes identified. Wodtke (2002) says:

> *'Your primary persona needs to be a common user type who is both important to the business success of the product and needy from a design point of view – in other words, a beginner user or a techno-logically challenged one'.*

She also says that secondary personas can be developed, such as super-users or complete novices. Complementary personas are those that don't fit into the main categories and that display unusual behaviour. Such complementary personas help 'out-of-the-box thinking' and offer choices or content that may appeal to all users.

RESEARCH TECHNIQUES

We can divide research techniques into primary data collection where we collect our own data and secondary data where we use published research. For each we need to decide the best combination of online and offline (Figure 4.10). The two main types of primary research are traditional marketing research methods and **web analytics** using server-based or browser-based techniques as shown in Table 4.4. Web analytics give undreamed visibility of customer behaviour, through click streams and page impressions we can find out what a customer is or is not interested in and can measure the response to our online campaigns. We can even use data mining software to profile different online behaviours.

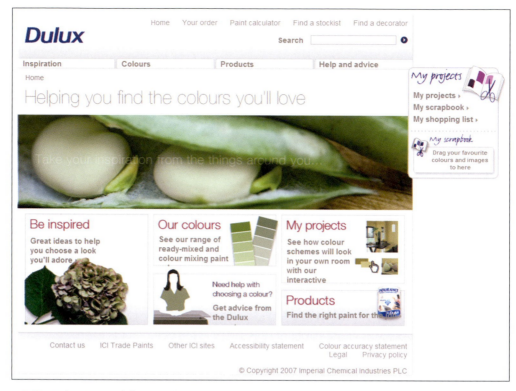

Figure 4.9 Dulux (www.dulux.co.uk)

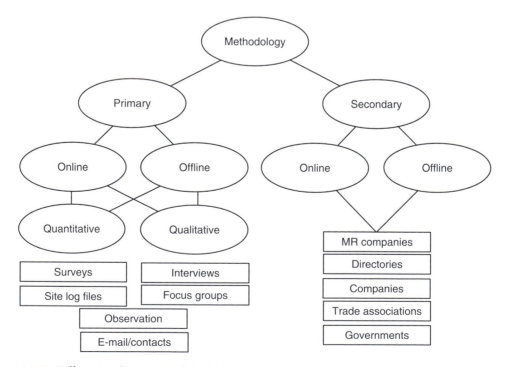

Figure 4.10 Different online research techniques

Table 4.4   A comparison of different online metrics collection methods

Technique	Strengths	Weaknesses
1 Server-based logfile analysis of site activity (web analytics) Examples: www.clicktracks.com www.webtrends.com	• Directly records customer behaviour on site plus where they were referred from • Low cost	• Doesn't directly record channel satisfaction • Undercounting and overcounting • Misleading unless interpreted carefully
2 Browser-based site activity data (web analytics) Examples: www.indextools.com www.google.com/analytics	• Greater accuracy than server-based analysis • Counts all users, unlike the panel approach	• Similar weaknesses to server-based technique apart from accuracy • Limited demographic information
3 Panels activity and demographic data Examples: www.netratings.com www.comscore.com www.hitwise.co.uk	• Provides competitor comparisons • Gives demographic profiling • Avoids undercounting and overcounting	• Depends on extrapolation from limited sample that may not be representative
4 Outcome data, e.g. enquiries, sales, customer service e-mails	• Records marketing outcomes	• Difficulty of integrating data with other methods of data collection when collected manually or in other information systems
5 Online questionnaires Customers are prompted randomly – every *n*th customer or after customer activity or by e-mail	• Can record customer satisfaction and profiles • Relatively cheap to create and analyze	• Difficulty of recruiting respondents who complete accurately • Sample bias – tend to be advocates or disgruntled customers who complete
6 Online focus groups; synchronous recording	• Relatively cheap to create	• Difficult to moderate and co-ordinate • No visual cues as from offline focus groups
7 Mystery shoppers. Example customers are recruited to evaluate the site, e.g. www.emysteryshopper.com	• Structured tests give detailed feedback • Also tests integration with other channels such as e-mail and phone	• Relatively expensive • Sample must be representative

Although initially promising, we should remember the weaknesses of log file analysis indicated in Table 4.4 and consider supplementing them with browser-based analysis methods. For large B2C sites we can also use panel data to give customer numbers and profiles.

To understand the e-customer we can use online versions of traditional marketing research techniques, but more rapidly and cheaper than before. But remember there are many new issues involved with the design and execution of online questionnaires, focus groups and mystery shoppers and we need to assess the strengths and weaknesses of each technique (Table 4.4).

For all research, we must devise a methodology to minimize sample bias. We need to make sure the sample is not made solely of evangelists who love your service or critics who hate it. How do you counter this?

Remember also that the web also offers a fast, lower-cost method of researching the online customer using secondary data. Consider how well your organization uses the web to enhance its market intelligence using the sources given in the web links at the end of the chapter.

SECTION SUMMARY 4.10

Researching the online customer

Today's marketers have the most fantastic opportunity to research customers. We can track customers online, we can ask them questions online and we can have group discussions online. We can gain a closer understanding of online customers. Metrics combine new research techniques such as server log files and traditional techniques such as focus groups and questionnaires. Disciplined marketers will take the opportunity and improve their customer research by mixing online and offline research techniques.

4.11   The post-PC customer

Web access via PCs will decline as a proportion as more people use mobiles, handheld devices, cars, clothes and Virtual Worlds to engage with the Internet. Things are changing. Here's a view of the future, its environment and what the post-PC customer might be like. By the end of this section you will have a glimpse of the future and the customers within it. Let's step into the future now.

The post-PC customer may occasionally accept payment to view some ads. The rest are screened out by both filtering software and PVRs (Section 5.9) wall-to-wall screen TVs. Neither governments nor society permit old style intrusive advertising anymore. No more intrusive evening telephone calls from script reading intelligent agents. It is also illegal to litter anyone's doorstep or house with mail shots and inserts. Heavy fines stopped all that a long time ago. The only ads that do get inside are carried by the many millions of private media owners who rent out their cars, bikes and bodies as billboards.

The tedious task of shopping for distress purchases like petrol, electricity or memory storage is delegated completely to embedded shopping bots. Non-embedded bots spun out of control some years ago when they first appeared in three-dimensional hovering holograms – always at your side, always double checking the best price for hire cars, hotels, even drinks at the bar. Some are programmed to be polite, others aggressive or even abusive. All are programmed to be intrusive whenever anything is being bought. Delays on buses and traffic jams regularly occurred when argumentative bots engaged in lengthy negotiations with bus drivers. Frustration broke out. Bots attacked bots, people attacked bots and bot owners. Eventually bots were banned from buses, planes, trains and several 'peaceful supermarkets'.

Next came the great worm wars. Programming bots so they only buy your brand – for life. But, unlike humans, bots can be re-programmed by a competitor. The advertising agent worm was born. Agent eaters soon followed.

Despite being information-fatigued and time-compressed, the post-PC customer lives a lot longer than many bots. And certainly longer than most of the new brands that seem to come and go. The 150-year-old person has already been born.

Meanwhile, back at the ranch, microwaves insist on offering suggestions of ideal wines to go with your meal, offering instant delivery from the neighbourhood's wired-up 24-hour roving delivery van. Your fridge offers special incentives to buy Pepsi when you run out of Coke (or whichever brand owns or hires the 'infomediary' or the fridge-linked database). Children happily play chess and interact with their opponents on giant vertical screens (which are the side of the fridge). Voice-operated computers are considered noisy and old fashioned as discrete, upmarket, thought-operated computers operate silently, but extremely effectively.

And all the time **Bluetooth** type technology facilitates ubiquitous communications which allows constant interaction between both man and machines, and machine and machine. The tectonic shift will continue.

Think of a world without TV ads, billboards and direct mail – a world where customers choose the information they want to receive. How will businesses reach their target markets in this new environment?

And all the time, the technology, if truly mastered, can free up time to do the important things that give the post-PC customer a genuinely better quality of life.

VIRTUAL CUSTOMERS IN VIRTUAL WORLDS

Now step into today's virtual worlds, where you can leave your body behind and become an entirely new virtual self – man, woman or hybrid. People can explore these 3D interactive opportunities to escape the confines of their bodies and explore the distant reaches of their minds, and meet other people in a new environment where you can play, talk, walk, run, fly, have sex, watch movies and do business all in a virtual, yet real, way. A world free from the dangers of disease – a 'post war, pre-AIDS innocence'. Major businesses are exploring the possibilities with their own virtual islands, offices, shops and community areas as they learn more about the significance of virtual worlds and the 3D environment which gives glimpses of the next stage of web development, Web 3.0.

There are several virtual worlds including Second Life (SL) and Entropia. SL has 7 million claimed members, 83 000 premium residents, with on average 40 000 active at any one time (Keegan, 2007). BBC have screened the Money Programme in Second Life; Sky News have opened a replica of its studio in Second Life; Reuters have a presence there; MTV premiere their TV shows inside Virtual Laguna Beach; Audi offer virtual test drives; IBM have sponsored a ballet; Blarney Pub (in Virtual Dublin) offers virtual Irish Coffees. Virtual World,

Second Life, has just had it's first real world millionaire who made her money from selling property in the virtual world. For more see PR Smith virtual worlds (2007).

Behaviour is a mirror in which everyone displays his own image.

Goethe (1809)

SECTION SUMMARY 4.11

The post-PC customer

As Moore's Law (the observation made in 1965 by Gordon Moore, co-founder of Intel, that the number of transistors per square inch on integrated circuits had doubled every 18 months since the integrated circuit was invented) continues to hold true, the time-compressed, information-fatigued and disloyal, post-PC customer seeks relationships not from brands themselves but from databases that know, understand and seemingly care about them. Witness the virtual girlfriend relationships in Japan. Relationships with shops and vending machines. Oh, and relationships with people – real, quaint, touchy feely, physical people.

CHAPTER SUMMARY

1 Consumers are motivated to venture online for a range of reasons – social, shopping, entertainment. B2B customers are driven by cost savings, speed and selling.

2 We need to understand expectations for service delivery, making promises and then delivering.

3 Online customers have many fears and phobias such as security and privacy. Companies need to reassure that with their services, the risks are minimized.

4 We have to support customers through each stage of the buying process: problem identification, information search, evaluation, decision, action and post sales. We need to account for mixed-mode buying.

5 Understanding how customers process information through the stages of exposure, attention, comprehension and perception, yielding and acceptance and retention can help us design effective sites.

6 Achieving online relationships and loyalty involves defining the ideal customers, understanding their needs and delivering them through the five 'primary determinants of loyalty' of quality customer support; on-time delivery; compelling product presentations; convenient and reasonable pricing; and clear trustworthy privacy policies. We must delight the customer and add value through personalization, community, integration and incentivization.

7 Online communities and social networks can be effective in delivering **stickiness** and understanding customer motivations and fears. A key decision is whether communities are independent of or integral to the brand.

8 Profiling customers involves asking who they are (demographics and psychographics), what they need, why, how and when they buy, and identifying segments.

9 Research involves answering the profiling questions using a combination of online and offline primary and secondary techniques.

10 The post-PC customer. Companies will need to respond to new technologies to offer new forms of customer relationship that deliver customer needs.

References

Adestra (2006) e-data unreliable, *Precision Marketing*, 9 June.

Ahonen, T. and Moore, A. (2007) *Communities Dominate Brands*. Future Text, London.

Anderson, C. (2006) *The Long Tail: Why the Future of Business is Selling Less of More*. Hyperion.

Chaffey, D. (2004) *Article on online value proposition published in the CIM's 'What's New in Marketing?'* September 2004. Available from www.davechaffey.com/E-marketing- Insights.

Considine, R. and Murray, R. (1981) *The Great Brain Robbery*. The Great Brain Robbery, CA.

Cialdini, R. (2006) *Influence, the Psychology of Persuasion*. Collins, 1st Business Edition, New York.

Detica (2006) Criminal gangs actively targeting mobile operators as telecoms fraud nears £1bn in the UK. www.Deticanetreveal.com, 15 November.

DTI (2003) *Business In The Information Age – International Benchmarking Study 2003*. UK.

de Kare-Silver, M. (2000) *eShock 2000*. Macmillan, Basingstoke.

EIAA 2007 *European Interactive Advertising Association Europe*. Online 2006-June 2007.

E-consultancy (2004) Online Retail 2004, benchmarking the user experience of UK retail sites. Available online from www.e-consultancy.com.

Flores, L. and Eltvedt, H. (2005) Beyond online advertising – lessons about the power of brand websites to build and expand brands. Published in *Proceedings of ESOMAR Online Conference*, Montreal, 2005.

Godin, S. (1999) *Permission Marketing*. Simon and Schuster, New York.

Goethe, J. (1809) referred to in *Elective Affinities*, Schifman, L.G. and Kaunk, L.L. (1991) *Consumer Behaviour*, 4th ed. Prentice Hall, International London.

Guest, T. (2007) *Second Lives a journey through virtual worlds*. Hutchinson.

Guggenheim Shenkan, A. and Sichel, B. (2007) Marketing with user-generated content. *McKinsey Quarterly*, November.

Hagel, J. and Armstrong, A. (1997) *Net Gain: Expanding markets through virtual communities*. Harvard Business Press.

Harris Interactive (2007) Customer Experience Impact Report. Bozememan, Mont.

Haven, B. (2007) *Marketing's New Key Metric: Engagement*. Forrester, 8 August.

Hofacker, C. (2001) *Internet Marketing*, 3rd ed. Wiley, New York.

IFR (2005) International Finanacial Reporting Standards (IAS 38).

Keegan, V. (2007) Watch out Second Life: China launches virtual universe with seven million souls. *The Guardian*, 2 June.

Laurent, L. and Harald Eltvedt, H. (2005) Beyond online advertising – lesson about the power of brand web sites to build and expand brands. ESOMAR, Montreal.

Levine, R., Locke, C., Searls, D. and Weinberger, D. (2000) *The Cluetrain Manifesto*. Perseus Books, Cambridge, MA.

Lindstrom, M. and Andersen, T. (2000) *Brand Building on the Internet*. Kogan Page, London.

Lindstrom, M. (2003) Five Steps to Online Trust for Your Brand. Click Z, 18 March.

The New York Times (2005) Read the Tea Leaves: China Will Be Top Exporter, 12 October.

Nielsen, J. (2007) Banner Blindness: Old and New Findings http://www.useit.com/alertbox/banner-blindness.html.

ONS (2004) Office of National Statistics Internet access data from quarterly household survey. www.statistics.gov.uk.

Parker, R. (2000) *Relationship Marketing on the Web*. Adams Streetwise publication, Holbrook, MA.

Penn, D. (2005) Brain Science, That's Interesting, But What Do I Do About It? Market Research Society Conference.

Pollack S. (2007) crea8ivity.com Northern Ireland creative digital hub.

Reicheld, F. (1996) *The Loyalty Effect: The Hidden Force Behind Growth, Profits, and Lasting Value*. Harvard Business School Press, Boston, MA.

Reicheld, F. and Schefter, P. (2000) E-loyalty: Your secret weapon on the Web. *Harvard Business Review*, July–August, pp. 105–113.

Reinartz, W. and Kumar, V. (2002) The Mismanagement of Customer Loyalty. *Harvard Business Review*, July, pp. 4–12.

Smith, P.R. (2007) Virtual worlds, www.prsmith.org.

Smith, P.R. and Taylor, J. (2004) *Marketing Communications – an integrated approach*. Kogan Page.

Universal McCann (2007) Power to the People – tracking the impact of social media wave, 2.0 May.

UK National Statistics (2007) Omnibus Survey, Office for National Statistics. Digital Age compilation.

Windham, L. (2001) *The soul of the new consumer. The Attitudes, Behaviours and Preferences of e-customers*. Allworth Press, New York.

Wodtke, C. (2002) *Information architecture: blueprints for the web*. New Riders, Indianapolis, IN.

Further reading

Godin, S. (1999) *Permission Marketing*. Simon and Schuster, New York. An interesting, influential book which raises direct marketers' hackles.

Seybold, P. (1999) *Customers.com*. Century Business Books, Random House, London. Describes a customer-centric approach to business strategy with many examples drawn from the US.

Windham, L. (2001) *The soul of the new consumer. The Attitudes, Behaviours and Preferences of e-customers*. Allworth Press, New York. The title says it all!

Web links

E-marketing Excellence book homepage (www.davechaffey.com/E-marketing). An index of all e-marketing links for each chapter in this book.

1 Digests of published MR data

ClickZ Internet research	www.clickz.com/stats
Market Research.com	www.marketresearch.com
MR Web (see desk research)	www.mrweb.co.uk
Marketing Charts	www.marketingcharts.com

2 Directories of MR companies

British Market Research Association	www.bmra.org.uk
Market Research Society	www.mrs.org.uk
International MR agencies	www.greenbook.org

3 Traditional market research agencies

MORI	www.mori.com/emori
NOP	www.nopworld.com
Nielsen	www.nielsen.com

4 Government sources

CIA World Fact Book	https://www.cia.gov/library/publications/the-world-factbook
OECD	www.oecd.org
European Government	http://europa.eu.int/comm/eurostat
UK Government statistics	www.statistics.gov.uk, www.ofcom.gov.uk
US Government	www.stat-usa.gov

5 Online audience data

Comscore	www.comscore.com
E-consultancy	www.e-consultancy.com
Hitwise	www.hitwise.com
Mori	www.mori.com/emori
Netratings	www.netratings.com

6 Virtual worlds   www.prsmith.org

Self-test

1 What are the main reasons why customers venture online and how should marketers use this customer knowledge?

2 How should organizations meet the expectations of online customers?

3 Given that the main fears about using the Internet are security and privacy, how should companies reassure customers?

4 Draw a diagram that summarizes the online buying process and actions that can be taken at each stage to help move the customer through the process.

5 Explain what is meant by each of these five stages of on-site information processing: (1) Exposure (2) Attention (3) Comprehension and perception (4) Yielding and acceptance (5) Retention.

6 How can customer loyalty be improved using online tools and techniques for your organization?

7 Explain how to overcome the problem of empty communities, silent communities and critical communities.

8 Identify the key variables by which you need to profile visitors to your organization's web site.

9 What are the research options for determining customers' opinions and feelings about a web presence?

10 How do you think the post-PC customer will live and what will this mean for marketers?

Chapter 5

E-tools

'E-marketing is not only about web sites. Already, in many developed countries, more consumers are accessing interactive digital services through TV and mobile than via the web'.

OVERVIEW

This is where the online world begins to get really interesting. Once we move beyond the PC and into the wireless world of pervasive technology, a whole new vision appears. Always on, everywhere, easy to use, contextual, integrated marketing is exploiting these new technological tools to reach and satisfy customers in new ways.

OVERALL LEARNING OUTCOME

By the end of this chapter you will be able to:

- Assess the marketing opportunities arising from new digital technologies
- Understand the advantages and disadvantages of the many different e-tools
- Begin to integrate e-tools into different platforms and a database.

CHAPTER TOPIC	LEARNING OBJECTIVE
5.1 Introduction	To introduce the e-tools and their significance
5.2 Technology development and customer impact	To show how swiftly technology is advancing
5.3 Interactive digital TV	To understand what iDTV and IPTV is and how it applies within a marketing context
5.4 Digital radio	Understand the relevance and benefits of digital radio
5.5 Mobile devices	To understand the space of mobile devices in a marketing context
5.6 Interactive kiosks	Evaluate the relevance and benefits of interactive kiosks
5.7 Miscellaneous tools	Review the significance of other e-tools
5.8 Repurposing content	Determine the complexities of marketing across integrated digital channels
5.9 Convergence	Assess the significance of the convergence phenomenon
5.10 Integrated campaigns	Define the elements of an integrated campaign

5.1   Introduction to e-tools

Through its short existence, for many, e-marketing has been synonymous with Internet marketing and web marketing in particular. But technology is in constant flux and leading e-marketers look to new technologies to fulfil their objectives. For many years now interactive digital TV and mobile Internet access has been used by more people than the web. Interestingly, China Mobile has more mobile subscribers than the whole US population (Belic 2007) and according to Comscore panel data, use of the web by mobile devices in Japan is equal to that of traditional computer access. So e-tools are becoming increasingly important for marketing to consumers, although they are less important for marketing to businesses.

As the number of e-tools increase, so too does the number of challenges to marketers. This chapter examines the current key e-tools and considers a few more besides. We need to become familiar with all e-tools such as PCs, interactive TV, digital radio, smart phones, interactive kiosks, DVD business cards, wired up clothes and a host of miscellaneous e-tools emerging in the online world. There is a section on each in this chapter. We review different e-tools and consider their advantages and disadvantages, their easy applications and natural integrations.

In some ways it's harder not to integrate the e-tools as they naturally lend themselves to integration, particularly if there is a single seamless database supporting them. A total selling proposition must somehow be maintained across all e-tools and also offline communications tools. The final section, integrated campaigns, addresses this and uses some simple but effective online integrated campaigns as an example of what we're about to see unfold as new forms of 'extended integration'.

Unfortunately content does not generally port easily across to other e-tools, e.g. from web site to mobile, from web site to TV, or even from TV platform to TV platform. This requires repurposing which, in turn, requires resources (skills, budgets and time). Despite the complications there is an e-tools trend towards convergence as 'all devices become equal'. A separate section addresses this. So, let's move rapidly into the changing world of e-tools.

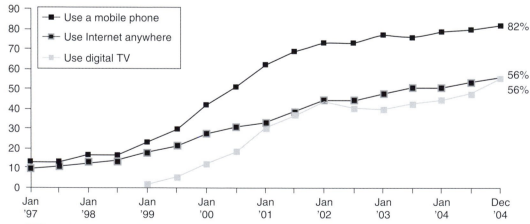

Figure 5.1   Adoption of different technologies over an eight-year period (each bar represents a single year). (*Source*: Svennivig, 2004)

E-MARKETING INSIGHT

The speed of change

Figure 5.1 highlights the speed with which new technologies are adopted by consumers. The challenge for marketers is to select significant new technologies and rapidly deploy services for customers appropriate to the new medium.

SECTION SUMMARY 5.1

Introduction to e-tools

E-marketing involves not only the web access through PCs, but also other tools such as interactive digital TV, digital radio, smart phones, interactive kiosks, CD cards and a host of miscellaneous e-tools emerging in the online world. Marketers need to review the advantages and disadvantages of each and deploy them in integration with other tools, where appropriate, to achieve competitive advantage.

5.2 Technology development and customer impact

Technology continues to evolve, sometimes at a frightening pace. This section explores technology advancement and how it may affect customers' buying behaviour, lifestyles, even life itself.

> *Any sufficiently advanced technology is indistinguishable from magic.*
>
> *Arthur C. Clarke*

From thought-operated computers (see Section 5.7) to intelligent web sites that effectively converse with customers, technology is moving forward rapidly. Many years ago Ray Kurzweil (2001) suggested that we will witness twenty thousand years of progress during the twenty-first century. Kurzweil believes machines will surpass humans and that computing power will continue to grow massively and will soon outstrip the human brain:

> *'Supercomputers will achieve one human brain capacity by 2010, and personal computers will do so by around 2020. By 2030, it will take a village of human brains (around a thousand) to match $1000 of computing. By 2050, $1000 of computing will equal the processing power of all human brains on Earth'.*

In a Web 3.0 world programmes will allow web sites or robots or shopping bots or virtual assistants to converse with customers and actually understand their needs. Heather Havenstein (2005) reported that 'After "reading" 8000 encyclopaedias and novels and accumulating billions of links between words for context, the confabulation architecture – which

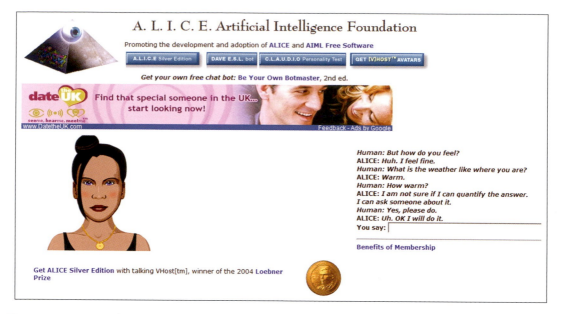

Figure 5.2   ALICE chatbox example

has no software or rules – can generate the end of a sentence that makes some sense after being given the first part of a sentence'. Robert Hecht-Nielsen of Fair Isaacs is developing a cognitive system that can engage with customers by understanding language and adapting through trial and error – similar to how a child learns to hit a baseball.

Nice happy robots will spend as much time as the customer needs, and, as Nielsen says 'they will be polite and fun. It just won't be a person'. They can sift through data and identify patterns much quicker than humans and offer many different tailored promotions targeted to many individuals.

We already have chatbots like Alice in California who responds to references to emotions (http://www.alicebot.org, Figure 5.2) and is offered to webmasters for a fee to add dating or English tutoring or even dating practice to their audiences! Or take George, a British bot, (http://www.jabberwacky.com) who constantly learns new language patterns and facts, and has a capacity to respond to 69 specified emotions, ranging from sarcastic to worried (Rowan 2006). Or meet Anna, a customer service chatbot at Ikea (www.ikea.co.uk) from Artificial Solutions (www.artificial-solutions.com), who will answer your questions and take you to the relevant part of the website in 18 languages.

Change is accelerating and forecasted to, one day, challenge the concept of life and death as we know it. Futurologists such as Ian Pearson at BT predict that:

> *'the next century will see death finally relegated to a mere inconvenience by medical advances and "back up brains" that store all our memories, emotions and thoughts. Such developments will allow us to continue our existence long after our biological bodies have passed away'.*

> *Chartered Institute of Marketing (2006)*

EMARKETING INSIGHT

The law of accelerating returns

An analysis of the history of technology shows that technological change is exponential, contrary to the common-sense 'intuitive linear' view. So we won't experience 100 years of progress in the twentyfirst century – it will be more like 20 000 years of progress (at today's rate).

The 'returns,' such as chip speed and cost-effectiveness, also increase exponentially. There's even exponential growth in the rate of exponential growth. Within a few decades, machine intelligence will surpass human intelligence, leading to The Singularity – technological change so rapid and profound it represents a rupture in the fabric of human history. The implications include the merger of biological and non-biological intelligence, immortal software-based humans, and ultra-high levels of intelligence that expand outward in the universe at the speed of light.

(*Source*: Ray Kurzweil 2001).

Accelerated technology developments are changing the way we live and the way we buy and consume products and services, sometimes in ways that are difficult to forecast, since technology often contains unexpected benefits. Who would have thought that a technology developed in 1992 by Ericsson as a channel for communications between engineers (from PC to mobile) would become 'the symbol of a youth movement; a set of manners and a culture; a way of extracting revenue from TV audiences; the source of a new language; a flirting medium, and a sexual technology, (Carter 2006). Mobile phone text messaging (SMS – Short Message Services) has changed the behaviour patterns of hundreds of millions of people.

Mobile phones have created massive channels to market that themselves have grown vast industries in ways never imagined by many marketers. Mobile phones distribute more content ($31b) than the total global content on the Internet ($25 billion led by pornography and gambling) and more than Hollywood box office's annual $30 billion (Ahonen and Moore 2007). And of course, the humble mobile performs many more functions in other markets, such as in Helsinki where you pay your tram fares by mobile and Japan, where it opens front doors of apartments or Slovenia, where they pay for McDonalds and taxis by mobile.

Add barcode scanning by phone cameras and more possibilities open up, such as wearing your web site on a t-shirt by having a bar code printed on a shirt, a phone camera can photograph this and connect to the web site immediately.

Alternatively, **Proximity Marketing** wireless technology recognizes different customers as they pass by stores that have relevant offers i.e. a special offer is sent to your phone (or any other device that contains a chip – including clothes) as you pass by the DVD store or coffee shop. Rudy De Waele (2006) defines proximity marketing as 'the localized *wireless* distribution of advertising content associated with a particular place. Transmissions can be received by individuals in that location who wish to receive them and have the necessary equipment to do so. Distribution may be via a traditional localized *broadcast*, or more commonly is specifically targeted to devices known to be in a particular area'.

Other e-tools like TV will continue and eventually merge with the PC as IPTV and PCTVs become more popular. As Gary Carter (2006) says 'We are not living through the death of TV. We are living through the death of time and the death of space, and the democratization of the media'. Today's TV is about to liberate content from the limitations of the old linear programme schedule. For example BBC's new strategic vision (Nelson 2007) is driven by programme experiences being built around a new framework of 'find, play and share'. 'Find' means – find and navigate the content through any media when customers want it and go further and deeper into worlds of content. 'Play' means engage simple interactive features which can extend the customer experience. 'Share' means enabling and encouraging audiences to participate, join in, contribute to and discuss and debate their own thoughts, ratings, recommendations and also incorporate/create and share with others. Success in today's Web 2.0 world will come from 'discoverability' and our ability for 'using powerful search algorithms to query our information about programmes, metadata and unearth clips of Churchill using text, voice, face, or other pattern recognition' (Highfield 2006). This is echoed by Antony Lilley (2006) who says:

> *'The root most value online is the connections, not the content. . . . If you can understand how to make connections around content, how to architect experiences from it including how to share it and then maximize its impact on the network then you're going to be popular'.*

SECTION SUMMARY 5.2

Technology development and customer impact

The pace of technology change is accelerating. Marketers must keep pace with it and exploit its rich potential to give much better customer experiences and ultimate competitive advantage as it affects customers' buying behaviour, lifestyles, even life itself.

5.3   Interactive digital TV

TV is the most compelling content channel of all. With over a billion TVs (compared to a few hundred million PCs) you can see how **interactive digital TV** (iDTV) and now **IPTV** has huge potential. Interactive digital TV is here and it's growing at a similar rate to Internet adoption. It's already changing the way audiences use TV with the 'red button' for user interaction now widespread both within programmes and ads. Although still embryonic and clunky, like early use of the web, it is opening up the online world in a new way. In this section we will explore iDTV, its advantages and disadvantages and the key steps towards integrating iDTV into your e-marketing mix.

WHAT IS INTERACTIVE DIGITAL TV?

Some say interactive TV has been around for a long time – children have been using it for over ten years now through games consoles. These have made TV screens interactive and far more engaging than traditional 'linear' TV. But this is not real interactive TV that involves a

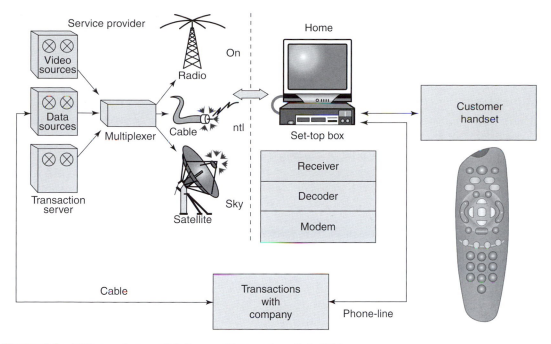

Figure 5.3   Different forms of delivery of interactive digital TV

new digital transmission system instead of standard signals. It converts sound and pictures into computerized digits, which are transmitted through the air by modified transmitters. The digits can be received by standard aerials, satellite dishes or by cable, but have to be decoded and turned into sound or vision (Figure 5.3). This is done either with a separate set-top box, or a decoder built-in to your television (an 'integrated' TV set). Note that only cable gives true two-way digital communications, the other alternatives require the user to dial out via a phone line to make a purchase.

Interactive digital television is different – it delivers more channels, better pictures and more interaction. For marketers this means better targeting and immediate opportunities to sell, to collect data and to develop relationships.

More channels means a huge selection – more than you can ever watch in a lifetime! There is a channel for almost everyone. Many niche TV channels will emerge as markets fragment and splinter into discrete interest groups (or microsegments) such as Manchester United TV or MTV2. More interaction means more shopping, browsing, banking, gambling, games, programme participation, voting, text information services and e-mail, of course. And it's user-friendly – you don't have to be computer literate – it's simple, intuitive navigation through remote control or console should make it easy for everyone to access both pro-grammes and the Internet. No more booting up and logging on, although it seems pedestrian to Internet broadband users. And it is perceived to be a safe, secure and private place to trade. But it can be used to reach adults who do not have an Internet connection. In addition to all of this, all TV stations are now moving towards web access where you can stream TV programmes through your PC (and mobile).

TV is traditionally a '**lean back**' or 'couch potato' medium where relaxation dominates. PCs and the Internet are a '**lean forward**', interactive medium. Perhaps this is why 'mad couch disease' seems to have affected some iDTV producers whose poor screen designs do nothing to nurture the coveted mouse potato! They've forgotten that iDTV is not the web. It is a different experience. A key difference is that iDTV can offer a **return path** – an interaction where the customer sends information to the provider using a phone line or cable, such as voting on a TV programme or placing a brochure request after pressing the red button. However, as Curry (2001) explains, often the return path is not seamless compared to broadband or mobile phone – requiring dial-up and phone charges which restrict its adoption. Surprisingly, this is still true in this age of technological change.

Marketers have, however, a powerful new tool that connects the emotional intensity of TV with instant response and instant buying. In a world of instant gratification, interactive TV makes the perfect fit. As audiences are aroused by films they are simultaneously offered more information or special promotions via the red button. And every response captures data that, in turn, builds a better profile of the household's interests. Advertisements using the red button can potentially offer full sales facilities for the immediate decision makers and store 'more info' requests for viewers who don't want the interruption now but do want the information later. And all the time they're protected by a **walled-garden** required to stop their audiences wandering off and getting lost in the online world.

The implications of IPTV

The cutting edge of IPTV is streamed real-time viewing of hundreds of channels through the two largest offerings, the European Joost (www.joost.com) and the US service Hulu (www.hulu.com) or their myriad competitors such as Babelgum, Vuze or Veoh. Then there is also the IPTV option of digital TV downloaded before playback, as is possible with many traditional broadcasters such as the BBC, Sky or ITV using peer-to-peer distribution from technology providers such as Kontiki (a commercial version of Bit Torrent), where many users download and share small chunks of the programme. With increasing numbers of viewers flocking to IPTV, whether it is streamed broadcasts from traditional TV channels as for Joost (www.joost.com) or end-user mashups on YouTube, one thing is for sure, media fragmentation is accelerating. It will be essential for marketers and ad agencies to learn how to exploit the new IPTV in order to reach these audiences online who may be forsaking traditional media forever – already some digital technophiles have and will never own a conventional TV – all TV is delivered via Internet Protocol!

Providers of IPTV services such as Joost are experimenting with new ad formats, since the days of the 30 second TV spot are gone forever. Research has shown that effective video ads are substantially shorter with brief pre-rolls and interstitial ads between shots the order of the day.

Brand advertisers also have the opportunity to develop their own brief IPTV viral clips to spread their message – witness the 2007 video viral clips from Cadbury and a follow-up spoof from Wonderbra which gained millions of viewers on YouTube.

Clearly, we are at an early stage of the adoption curve, with future opportunities for tailored, addressable ads made possible by direct profiling of members of services such as Joost. Behavioural targeting based on channels viewed and ads responded to are also all possible. But the relative failure of the Microsoft Media Center platform has shown that many households do not want or cannot fathom the benefit of an Internet connected 'gogglebox' in their living rooms. But they will. The only question is when?

E-MARKETING EXCELLENCE

Volvo integrate digital tools for their 'Mystery of Dalaro' campaign

This innovative campaign, supporting the launch of the Volvo S40, was shot in the style of a documentary purporting to be a real account of the Swedish village Dalaro where 32 people all bought a new Volvo S40 on the same day.

But Volvo has now revealed that it is Spike Jonze, the director of the films *Being John Malkovich* and *Adaptation* as well as the legendary Beastie Boys video 'Sabotage', who made the documentary. However it has said that the characters in the campaign are real residents of Dalaro and not actors.

This campaign shows how offline ad executions naturally drive visitors online. During the campaign, visits to the Volvo UK web site doubled and 435 000 digital viewers of the ad selected the red button option to view the documentary via interactive TV.

Those pressing red on iDTV saw a longer eight-minute version of the documentary, made by director Spike Jonze, featuring interviews with residents of Dalaro talking about the spooky phenomenon, and had the opportunity to download brochures, thus interacting much more closely with the brand than was possible before the advent of iDTV. The documentary was also available from the web site which received 96 000 visits with 64% accessing the video and several thousand requesting a brochure.

(*Source*: *Revolution* 19 March 2004) (www.revolutionmagazine.com).

BENEFITS FOR THE MARKETER

Although there are many teething problems, ultimately, interactive TV offers e-marketers a new way of reaching customers. From interactive advertisements, to interactive product placement, to fully interactive programmes, to sponsored programmes, interactive TV presents a host of new opportunities. And it's not just for impulse purchases, but also more considered purchases like cars and computers. In addition to the many advantages for the viewers that include wider choice, convenient shopping, more engaging TV programmes and community participation, there are many advantages for the e-marketer:

1 Direct response mass market advertising
2 Highly targetable

   3 Moves buyers through the complete buying process

   4 Audience engagement through interaction

   5 Brand building and positioning reinforcement

   6 Brand building through community building

   7 Customer-service bottleneck reduction

   8 Security – less risk associated with TV than web sites

   9 Controllable – highly measurable

10 Cost savings.

So iDTV has advantages and disadvantages. However, as the e-marketing insight 'The inter-active viewer: myth or reality?' shows, the convenience of using a PC for digital services seems to be much higher, resulting in greater use. As a result some marketers have sus-pended trial iDTV services in sectors such as banking and travel, and the Sky Active service is now restricted to niche services which can pay their way such as gambling, dating, special offers and directory services. These services target an audience who have iDTV but not a PC, and this audience is large enough to warrant an investment in iDTV.

> **Typical marketing iTV advertisement applications**

Direct response is the most obvious reason for running interactive ad campaigns. This has been used for these applications according to the IDS study of the 600 IA campaigns run up until 2005:

- *Further information* – Mecca Bingo invited viewers to 'Press Red for a free information pack' and many travel and tourism destinations have solicited brochure requests through this mechanism.

- *Sampling* – Brands such as Finish Dishwasher tablets, Coty Rimmel lipsticks, Wilkinson Sword Razors and Total TV Guide have used the sample request format. Results from IDS have so far have indicated that campaigns offering free samples have produced better responses.

- *Donation* – Charities such as the Red Cross, Cancer Research UK, the National Accident Helpline and the NSPCC have used this format. Regular donations can be achieved through entering their account details.

- *Request a call-back* – Dial 4 a Loan and Yes Car Credit have used this approach.

- *Request a test-drive* – Car brands such as Nissan Almera, Lexus and Renault have used this approach.

- *Enter a competition* – IDS notes that some of the highest response rates to date have been achieved with competition offers from Rimmel, Tesco and Walt Disney.

- *Play a sponsored game* – Used by KitKat for the 'Take a break' campaign.

- *Sponsorship of broadcast programmes* – reality TV and pop programmes have successfully used sponsorship combined with Mini-DALS and, of course, SMS voting.

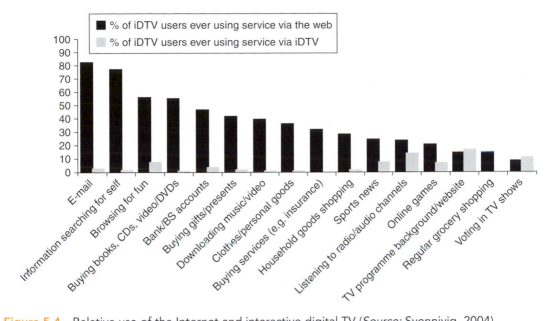

Figure 5.4   Relative use of the Internet and interactive digital TV (*Source:* Svennivig, 2004)

SECTION SUMMARY 5.3

Interactive digital TV

Interactive digital TV can be delivered to a set-top box by cable, satellite or conventional aerial. It offers a large and rapidly growing audience and interactive tools which help engagement and generate a response. Marketing approaches include new programme sponsorship, product placement; advertising opportunities abound in interactive digital TV.

5.4 Digital radio

It's now over 100 years since Marconi made the first radio broadcast. Little has changed up to now. Brace yourself for a whole new world of digital radio. This highly intrusive and highly trusted secondary activity is about to change, forever. By the end of this section, you will understand iRadio's different formats and its advantages and disadvantages as an e-tool.

WHAT IS DIGITAL RADIO?

There are two types of digital radio – digital radio and web radio – both are interactive. Digital radio is also available through iDTV, mobile and in-car.

Digital radio requires buying a new digital radio although it can be streamed just like traditional analogue web radio. Digital radio is often accompanied by a big liquid crystal display. Digital radio is now widely known as **Digital Audio Broadcasting (DAB)** radio.

Web radio or Internet radio is when existing broadcasts are streamed via the Internet and listened to using plug-ins such as Real Media or Windows Media Player. This is an important trend, with radio listener auditing service Rajar reporting that in 2004 nearly 20% of adults had listened to radio on the web. 'Streamies' are people who listen to web radio at home or at work. For many it means logging on to a web radio station and leaving it to play as you work. In fact, once you log on to a station it accompanies you wherever you go on the net – so you can carry on listening wherever you go online. And if you like a particular track you can order it there and then online. Sonic branding!

BENEFITS OF DIGITAL RADIO

According to the World DAB Forum, the trade association promoting DAB, the benefits of DAB for the consumer are:

> *'Aside from distortion-free reception digital sound quality, DAB offers further advantages as it has been designed for the multimedia age. DAB can carry not only audio, but also text, pictures, data and even videos – all on your radio at home and on the move'!*

For example, clips of goals or delivery of electronic programme guides are possible with DAB – an example of media converging.

For the marketer, digital radio is a proven brand builder. It is great for direct response; it increases reach of local radio to global radio; it grows the 'glocal' community; it can build communities around a brand and is a good targeting medium; and like the web it can be personalized by streaming 'radio-tailored' programmes for individual tastes.

A traditional radio campaign will drive listeners to the radio, but if they are listening online they have an instant call-to-action. In 2004, easyJet spent 60% of its non-TV budget on radio and Internet advertising. *Revolution* reported Alistair Buckle, easyJet's head of marketing, explaining: 'a lot of people consume radio in different environments. Most people aren't too far away from web access to book a flight and we wanted to push that impulsive, "come-on, let's fly behaviour"'.

Martin Tod, head of brand and marketing communications at Vodafone UK, says: 'We are big fans of radio and Internet advertising – there is a relationship between the two. It's easier to target radio geographically, and to use the web to reach target audiences and measure direct impact on revenue', *Revolution* (2004).

Let's look at these benefits in terms of the '5Ss of e-marketing'.

Sell

Web radio is radio with a buy button! Cross selling opportunities are enormous. Hear an ad for CDs, concerts or merchandise – click immediately and you have it (eventually just shout 'yes' to your voice activated radio in your car and you'll have a real dialogue)! And web radio reaches often difficult-to-target groups of customers such as young sophisticated international audiences.

Note that such a 'return path' is only available by web radio – with DAB, it is necessary for direct response to be achieved through other e-tools such as a web site or SMS.

Internet radio is great for integrated campaigns. Listeners may first see an ad in the newspaper or on TV, register it but not respond. When they then hear about it online, response is more seamless – they just type in the company or campaign number into their browser. Result! For example, for Christmas 2004 eBay UK ran a treasure hunt to showcase the range of products on sale through clues on the home page which prompted a search. It was advertised both in print and on web radio.

Sizzle

Radio has always been a good brand builder for the marketer. Now it is beginning to offer additional routes via new syndication and content deals which, in turn, may mean new programmes which means new sponsorship opportunities, and even new radio station opportunities. Some radio stations now offer audio ads with a banner ad or 'buy now' button when listening to web radio – you hear the ad – you click the button. Web radio also offers to do partner deals delivering niche radio to other web sites. This adds to the branding and also offers new revenue generating channels as affiliates share ad revenues and merchandise sales from the partner web radio company.

Speak

There is already a dialogue with traditional radio – people phone, e-mail and snail mail in. Now they can click and respond instantaneously and marketers can see what's working and what's not instantaneously. Continue the conversation later or join in a group discussion. This adds lots of 'stickiness' as people stay for many hours with a station and its site. Remember once the listener has logged on to a station, it will accompany them wherever they go on the net so they can carry on listening whatever they're doing online.

> **Serve**

Digital radio allows you to get extra information on a track; buy the track; interact with live shows; vote. This is currently achieved through buttons, but eventually will be via voice-operated systems and a good archive database. Eventually your car radio should be able to do all of this for you, add digital pictures and answer in voice.

E-MARKETING EXCELLENCE

Comet uses Virgin Radio for positioning and response

Virgin Radio website receives over one million unique visitors per month. The Comet campaign is a typical cross-media campaign that uses on-air and web site messaging and interaction.

Campaign objectives

- Support awareness of Comet's Price Promise that they provide low prices all year round.

- Communicate that Comet has great Christmas gifts for all the family.

- Drive traffic to Comet's gift finder at comet.co.uk.

- Create competitive standout through engaging activity.

Implementation

- Listeners were invited to play 'The Price is Right' with Comet in a week-long Drivetime Show promotion.

- Each day, a prize package demonstrating Comet's wide product range was up for grabs with a higher than normal starting price.

- Two listeners then guessed ever-decreasing prices to guess the package's true low Comet price.

- The first listener to get the price right won, or the first to get the price too low lost (and the other won by default).

- On-air mentions directed listeners to Comet's gift finder which was built into a co-branded micro-site on virginradio.co.uk.

- Banner ads and a competition area on the web site directed visitors to gift finder.

(*Source*: Virgin Radio www.virginradio.co.uk).

DISADVANTAGES OF RADIO

So, radio is changing – it might not be called radio in the future. Now let's look at some of the disadvantages of digital radio:

- Bandwidth costs money and the cost of streaming increases in line with the number of listeners.
- Not as sexy as TV. TV adds credibility to a brand – 'as seen on TV'. Radio doesn't quite carry the same impact or credibility.
- Fragmenting audience as number of online stations increase. It therefore requires more work (media planning and media buying) to reach the fragmented audience.

SECTION SUMMARY 5.4

Digital radio

The future of radio is in digital radio and web radio where interaction is possible by responding to on-screen prompts such as voting or e-mail. Digital radio has many advantages including brand-building, impact, direct-response and a few disadvantages including fragmentation. It is highly portable and digital radio, in particular, presents new opportunities to many marketers.

5.5 Mobile (wireless) devices

Although many are cynical about mobiles as an Internet access device, mobile technology is here to stay; it's popular and still evolving at a rapid pace. We are beginning to move beyond the hype, hysteria and disappointment of the early 'mobile Internet', m-commerce and the initial woeful WAP.

With penetration in many western countries already exceeding 80% and estimated mobile use worldwide exceeding two billion, marketers can no longer ignore this potentially powerful new tool. By the end of this section you will understand these developing technologies and know how marketers can use them in different ways.

WHAT ARE MOBILE OR WIRELESS DEVICES?

First let's clarify what's what. In the beginning (1980s) there was the big bulky expensive analogue mobile – the first generation of mobile phones. Then came the second generation – smaller digital mobiles. These almost accidentally created a new phenomenon called text messaging, or SMS (short message service). Then came **WAP, I-mode, GPRS** and **EDGE** all offering greater speed and more interaction. And finally came the third generation, or **3G**, mobiles which use a standard wireless system called **UMTS**.

These advances and their implications for the marketer are summarized in Table 5.1.

Table 5.1   Characteristics of different mobile technologies

	SMS	WAP on GSM	GPRS and 3G	I-mode
Audience size (penetration)	Large	Large	Large	Large in Japan. Launched in Europe
Characteristics	Instnt txt msgs	A new browsing standard	Always on, also offers WAP	Similar to WAP, but introduced in Japan
Speed	9600 bps	9600 bps	GPRS: 56 kbps 3G: 384 kbps	Similar to GSM
Current audience type	Broad range of profiles	Innovators and early adopters	Innovators	Mass market
Audience state of mind	No control – e-mails/text messages interrupt	Some control as there is limited browsing	Some control as there is more browsing	More control as there is lots of browsing
Cost of production (of ad/e-mail/ web site)	Low (text message and e-mail only)	Low–medium (WAP site design and traffic generation)	More costly repurposing	
Message type	Good for urgent messages (time based and location based)	Good for urgent messages (time based and location based)	Good for urgent messages (time based and location based)	Good for urgent messages (time based and location based)
	Limited technical detailed information	Link to more technical detailed information on WAP site	Link to more technical detailed information on site	Link to more technical detailed information on site

Connecting laptops to the Internet can be considered as the first mobile devices and now 3G wireless services are available for remote workers. Today, smart phones are here – they carry chips that allow them to act as a mini PC as well as a phone – you probably have one. Phones now have features built in which are familiar from our PCs such as address books, diaries and have fun features such as MP3 playback and image capture. Live e-mail downloads in the Blackberry devices have taken the business world by storm. Add in **Bluetooth** technology (which allows devices to communicate without wires – as soon as they come into range) and you've got a very powerful interactive device which somehow has moved far beyond being a phone. Maybe this will herald the end of the term 'telephone' as single purpose devices will be deemed archaic. Some marketers are now considering **BlueJacking** which involves sending a message from a mobile phone (or other transmitter) to another mobile phone which is in close range via Bluetooth technology. It has potential for: (1) Viral communication; (2) Community activities (dating or gaming events); (3) Location-based services – electronic coupons as you pass a store.

Whether WAP, I-mode or other form of phone, users can now surf or browse specially built sites, extending the 5Ss benefits derived from web sites, although constrained by the smaller screen and limited graphics.

Now we're moving into location-based marketing where customers receive messages on their mobiles relevant to their geographic location (whether passing a store or arriving in an airport). Add in **voice portals** and things get even more interesting. VPs use speech recognition technology to search and find information from the web and then – the good bit – 'speak it to you' through your phone. No more dialling up, downloading and clumsy mice, all you do is dial a free number and ask the question. A related approach is **unified messaging systems** portals which act as an organizer for text, fax, e-mail and phone messaging.

SMS OR TEXT MESSAGING

Finally don't forget good old text messaging. It is huge, as the e-marketing insight 'How impt is txt msging?' shows!

For the creative marketer who respects opt-in and privacy legislation, SMS has proved a great way to get closer to customers, particularly those in the youth market who are difficult to reach with other media. Here are some of the marketing applications now used by marketers (www.text.it):

1 Text and win
2 Voting and participation on TV
3 Quizzes
4 Games
5 Mobile content (pictures, ringtones, video)
6 Applications (e.g. B2B inventory and order tracking)
7 CRM (can be helpful e.g. if your bank tells you you're just about to be overdrawn, or, imagine if Alex Ferguson calls you with a recording saying 'I love you mate' after Manchester United win a trophy)
8 IVR (Interactive Voice Response connects you to the right department or can direct you to premium rate services in response to TV advertisements)
9 Multimedia messaging (MMS is not fully compatible with all phones yet)
10 Direct ad response (where the mobile is used to text a short code to receive content, messages, coupons)
11 Barcodes (can be sent to mobiles and then used in store to redeem via the standard EPOS system)

12 Location based services (LBS allows shoppers to opt-in to receive offers from nearby stores)

13 WAP portal (the mobile version of a web site)

14 Java portal (content is downloaded in line with your preferences)

15 Mobile search (e.g. Google mobile search)

16 Mobile music (handsets are now designed to play and store music)

17 Podcasting (streamed delivery of a radio programme to a phone with MP3 playing ability)

18 Blogging and RSS feeds (keeps you up to date with all the latest from your favourite web sites and blogs directly into your mobile)

19 Moblogging (blogging from your phone)

20 Bluetooth/infra red.

Chaffey (2005) *What's New In Marketing*.

E-MARKETING INSIGHT

How impt is txt msging?

The UK text messaging total broke through the 4 billion barrier for the first time during December 2006, according to figures by the Mobile Data Association (MDA). December's remarkable total of 4.3 billion takes the overall figure for 2006 to 41.8 billion, surpassing the MDA's prediction of 40 billion and giving a daily average for the year of 114 million.

Person-to-person texts sent across the UK GSM network operators throughout the last month of the year show a growth of 38% on the December 2005 figure of 3.1 billion, and represent an average of 138 million messages per day. On Christmas Day this leapt to 205 million texts, an average of 8 million per hour, with the figure for New Year's Day 2007 even higher reaching a record breaking 214 million, the highest daily total ever recorded by the MDA.

When compared to the mere 42 million messages sent per day five years ago throughout December 2001, it becomes clear just how far the nation has come in embracing text messaging technology which has emerged from a popular craze to becoming an essential communication tool, inclusive to all age groups.

Mobile Data Association 2007.

WI-FI BROADENS WIRELESS INTERNET ACCESS

Wi-fi ('wireless fidelity') is the shorthand often used to describe a high-speed wireless local-area network. Wi-fi can be deployed in an office or home environment where it removes the need for cabling and adds flexibility. Wi-fi access points are now available in major airports and city cafés. We mention it for reference; it does not have additional significant direct marketing applications, but it will increase wireless access to the web. Wi-fi can be accessed from suitably equipped laptops and mobile phones.

BENEFITS OF MOBILE TECHNOLOGIES

In addition to being a new channel to market, mobiles offer marketers many other benefits. In Finland, customers buy flowers, CDs, bid in auctions, buy cola from vending machines and pay for a car wash all with their mobiles. It can be a useful customer support tool, whether reserving airline tickets, checking your bank balance or transferring money. For example, in the UK customers can see and select which airline seats they want from their mobiles (see Section 5.2 Technology development and customer impact for more).

Sales force and other employees can use their mobiles to see client history, get updates about orders and dispatch as well as feeding back research while engineers can access appointments, directions and diagnostic tools. Go Airlines use 'MADS' or text messages to drive traffic to its site. Many airlines let passengers check in via their mobiles. There are some extremely creative approaches to mobile marketing – teaching with text messages is now available via mobile and even the National Blood Service has boosted blood donations using an integrated mobile campaign. Add in disposable mobiles and all sorts of interesting ideas occur to marketers!

You can see how mobiles can help marketers to enjoy all five of the 'S' benefits. The key question to ask is 'How can mobiles help my customers (or distributors, or suppliers, or employees)?'

E-MARKETING EXCELLENCE

I-mode creates a successful wireless proposition

I-mode is a mobile technology to watch in the future. Although I-mode is technology proprietary to NTT Docomo, it has developed a successful proposition.

In Japan, 42 million have subscribed to I-mode since its introduction in February 1999. More recently, over three million elsewhere have subscribed following launches in Germany, The Netherlands, France and Spain, and in 2005 adoption started in the UK. Adoption has been limited to date, due to lack of handsets and competition from local mobile portals such as Vodafone Live! I-mode offers access to entertainment including paid content, games and dating, transaction services such as e-mail, Citibank accounts, Amazon.jp, databases such as travel information and information such as news CNN and local area maps.

There are 85 000 I-mode web sites: a key benefit of I-mode is that content providers create web sites for I-mode using I-HTML, a subset of HTML. This makes it relatively easy to convert any existing web site written in HTML into I-mode content. I-mode also supports Flash and Java based applications and games.

DISADVANTAGES OF MOBILE TECHNOLOGIES

There are several significant hindrances or disadvantages to bear in mind including small screens restricting content; a limited number of web sites; limited content; poorly designed sites; poor coverage causing shopping interrupts and SPAM text messages. Location-based marketing also worries some people as they feel their movements are being tracked – anyone who has seen Tom Cruise in *Minority Report* being followed around a shopping mall by personalized ads will know what we mean. There is also the cost of repurposing – traditional web sites need to be stripped down and repurposed.

SECTION SUMMARY 5.5

Mobile (wireless) devices

Smart phones and Bluetooth technology, text messaging, location-based marketing, voice portals and browser phones didn't exist a few years ago. Today they can help the market achieve all 5Ss, but with the usual caveat – don't SPAM. Phones will get faster, smaller, friendlier and, eventually, become multifunctional devices integrated into most marketers' armoury and many, many customers' lives.

5.6 Interactive self-service kiosks

Interactive self-service kiosks come in all shapes and sizes. Compact and robust, they can be placed virtually anywhere that attracts passing footfall of customers. This makes them ideal not just for sales and marketing, but also for public information purposes and corporate communications. Although they are often known as self-service kiosks, they can also be used in-store by sales staff for demonstrations. By the end of this section you will know how kiosks can help marketers, their advantages and disadvantages.

BENEFITS OF KIOSKS

So how can marketers use interactive kiosks? Let's explore the advantages of kiosks by seeing how they help marketers to enjoy the benefits of the 5Ss. Remember kiosks can have helpful, intelligent, programmes that will eventually converse with customers and, perhaps one day, be seen with great delight as customers see a particular branded kiosk much in the same way as an ATM cash dispenser is often seen with great relief by many customers.

Sell

Kiosks (including vending machines, ATMs and other devices) can widen distribution and ultimately boost sales of both products and services. Kiosks can extend reach to passing footfall of customers. From music kiosks (that create tailored CDs) to in-store kiosks (that extend the range of stock) to bus stop mini-kiosks (that sell theatre tickets) to micro kiosks, or touch pads attached to vending machines (that create virtual outlets) the kiosk is here. And there! In fact they can be anywhere. The key is to think where to put kiosks. Where are the opportunities? Where do your target market congregate? When would they be most likely to buy? When would they like more information?

Serve

An interactive kiosk with full multimedia facilities can do everything a web site can do, better and faster as the media may be already downloaded. Kiosks can provide information, ideas and suggestions, e-mail facilities and ordering facilities. In airports they help passengers to skip check-in queues by printing boarding passes. Kiosks can be particularly valuable if used in 'downtime areas' such as waiting rooms, hospitals, motorway service stations, reception areas, airport luggage halls, even gymnasiums where kiosks can keep the mind off the pain barrier.

Speak

Kiosks can trigger a dialogue with a customer by answering FAQs, engaging interactions and collecting data from customers which, in turn, can be integrated with the Internet or your own office network. Installed in the right place kiosks can grab attention, attract interest and generate data from the ideal customer. But remember if the dialogue is going to continue the marketer must first ask for permission to do so.

Electronically enabled interaction between kiosks and consumer devices is the way of the future. In 2005, drinks brand Carling started delivering information and offers to users of Bluetooth-enabled mobiles when they access a dedicated Carling channel on a series of kiosks in the south west. Users would gain the chance to win tickets to Carling Live gigs in Bristol and London, or a pint of Carling in their local pub.

Save

Kiosks provide physical presence without the associated costs of staff and buildings. Kiosks also provide information and service 24 hours a day, 7 days a week, without the enormous overtime costs of staff. Kiosks can be free-standing and unattended. In Italy, they're even used to pay local taxes. So although initially considered expensive, they can offer cost savings, particularly if they're used to their full potential.

Sizzle

And some of the potential is fulfilled when kiosks simultaneously double up as brand icons and represent the brand in some manner, shape or form. Kiosk design ranges from stunning design-led units that are almost impossible to ignore, to more practical, engineered units. Unlike the Internet, kiosks provide a controlled environment. Protected by a 'walled garden', marketers can connect customers directly to their own site and only their own site or take them beyond if required.

DISADVANTAGES OF KIOSKS

Despite the many advantages, kiosks do have their disadvantages. They can be expensive for different reasons. There is a long lead time and the cost of paying specialists to design and produce them. They require installation and then there are the maintenance costs of electricity, costs of Internet connection, maintenance contracts and support. And of course, they are subject to vandalism. Finally, just as for web sites, they are moving targets requiring updates to content and new design and marketing approaches.

E-MARKETING EXCELLENCE

Vodafone rolls out kiosks worldwide

In the UK, Vodafone deployed 350 interactive kiosks at retail outlets which simulated the Vodafone Live! phone experience including games, e-mail, news and webcam pictures. When not in use, Vodafone ad campaigns can be displayed. The kiosks gave customers the opportunity to research products and allowed sales staff to demonstrate the capabilities of the service. As with web sites, kiosk interactions can be monitored to assess popular applications and products. Customer and branch manager feedback in the UK led to Vodafone rolling out the kiosks worldwide. In New Zealand, displays are state of the art with 50-inch touchscreens showing the shape of the future.

SECTION SUMMARY 5.6

Interactive self-service kiosks

In this section, we have seen how interactive kiosks can sell, serve, save, speak and sizzle. However, they do have some disadvantages such as costs, time, installation, maintenance and vandalism.

5.7 Miscellaneous tools

'A million businesses, a billion people and a trillion devices all interconnected . . .' You've heard it before? Pervasive computing combined with deep computing bringing a new interconnected world. In fact, IBM's Lou Gerstner many years ago said that he dreamed of a world made up of a trillion interconnected intelligent devices, intersecting with data-mining capability – where pervasive computing (embedded chips in doorknobs and clothes) meets deep computing (like the chess playing Deep Blue PC which calculated 200 million moves a second). By the end of this section you will start to see the interconnected future.

Do you remember in Chapter 1 we talked about the wired-up world and how everything in the household was connected to the web, from fridges and freezers to TVs and toys? Do you remember we told you that MIT's Nicholas Negroponte said that by the year 2010 there

Figure 5.5   3D, virtual reality services available from Inition (www.inition.com)

would be more wired-up Barbie dolls than wired up Americans? Teddy bears with mobile phones have since been launched. It's true. The world is becoming connected through a wide range of wireless devices.

Computers in jackets? Phones in ties? Wearable technology has been around for some time (Figure 5.5). US Army and Military Police see wearable computers as an important part of a soldier's arsenal. But it's not just military, industry is also experimenting. Northwest Airlines, Nabisco and General Dynamics are also using wearable computers (connected to their intranets) across different business functions from customer service, distribution centres, and inspection and maintenance. And way before this, in fact in the last century, MIT staff occasionally donned 'hot badges' at parties. After keying in their personal interests, party goers wore the badges and whenever anyone with similar interests came within a few feet then both badges flashed!

Earrings and eyeglasses embedded with instantaneous language translation, speech recognition and speech synthesis so that someone can speak to you in French and you hear it in English all help. And of course cars speak your preferred language. In fact at the end of the last century car computer power (the hidden microcomputers in cars) had more power than all the computers in the first rocket that landed on the moon. Those astronauts were true heroes.

Athletes can be heroes too. Nike have just released a running shoe with a chip in it. Why? Think for a moment why or what possible benefit it might have. The chip in the shoe allows friends or competitors to communicate and race against each other simultaneously even if they are on other sides of the world. Incidentally, Nike also sell a virtual shoe that allows you to move faster in Second Life virtual world.

Then came thought-operated-computers. A glass cone (laced with neurotrophic chemicals extracted from knees to encourage nerve growth) is inserted into the brain's motor cortex. Over a period of a few months, neurones grow and effectively become naturally wired into the brain. This allows disabled people to control a cursor by thinking about moving parts of their body.

Add in some virtual reality and anything becomes possible. Disabled pensioners can play rugby, paraglide the world and meet new people all in a brave new world.

It has been forecast that our whole personalities will one day be downloaded into machines! We're not so sure about this, but we are sure that the embedded chip will be everywhere from your washing machine to your car and everything will be connected to everything else in a seamless wireless way. And the data pulsing through the Internet won't even be seen by humans.

The trick for marketers is first to ask how each device can help my customer, distributors, employees, etc.). Use the 5S checklist. Also ask what proportion of my customers want to use these devices now and in the future? Second, keep all channels integrated on a central database so that customers are reassured as the organization recognizes them regardless of which channel, whether car, TV or running shoe. Third, stay listed with search engines, directories and portals, whether voice portals or automated portals of any description. Fourth, stick close to customers. Use these new tools to listen to customer feedback. Fifth, and finally, don't let the technology blind you. Ensure common sense rules and not the technology! It can pretty much do whatever you want – if you know what you want – which is a good starting point.

DIGITAL SIGNAGE AND PROXIMITY MARKETING

Digital signage is a relatively new, specialist category of digital marketing which already has its own events and trade shows. It combines the awareness raising and mass reach capabilities of traditional advertising with direct response marketing. It can also be used in store (Figure 5.6) and has been used on some of the busiest underground and metro stations.

Digital signage becomes more interactive when it is Bluetooth enabled to encourage download of audio or video clips by **bluecasting** as illustrated by its use in the launch of the album referenced below or to download ringtones (Figure 5.7). This is an example of what is known as Proximity Marketing where wireless technology recognizes different customers as they pass by stores that have relevant offers i.e. a special offer is sent to your phone (or any other device that contains a chip – including clothes). Alternatively ads could be updated in real-time to be customized to the passerby as featured in the film *Minority Report* which

Figure 5.6   Instore digital signage at Ikea (Source: www.beaver-group.com)

gives a nightmare vision of the future, in our opinion, and shows the need for data protection controls!

HSBC Bank used this in a 2007 trial to offer one of its investment products to passers-by to its Canary Wharf branch who had their phones set to discoverable. The risks of this approach can be seen from the writeup in Finextra that was headlined '*HSBC spams passers-by in mobile marketing ploy*'. Although the UK Information Commissioner has acknowledged that the technique isn't covered adequately by privacy rules, obviously care needs to be taken since this technique could easily be seen as intrusive.

Google is also innovating in this area. You may have read of its first forays into Google Classifieds where ads are placed in newspapers and magazines or Google Audio ads where you can place ads across US radio stations. But did you read about the trial of an interactive billboard where an eyetracking technology was used to measure the number of eyeballs viewing the ad. You can see the next steps would be iris recognition technology identifying the passer-by from a global consumer database and then tailoring ads.

E-MARKETING EXCELLENCE

Using Bluecasting to encourage trial of new album

One of the early commercial uses of **Bluecasting** was to support the launch of the Coldplay X & Y album, where a London-based campaign involved 13 000 fans downloading free pre-release video clips, never-before seen interviews, audio samples and exclusive images onto their mobile, via Bluetooth from screens at mainline train stations. In this campaign, 87 000 unique handsets were 'discovered' and 13 000 people opted-in to receive the material, a response rate of 15%. The busiest day was

Saturday June 4th – two days before the official album launch date – when over 8000 handsets were discovered and over 1100 users opted in to receive a video file. The BlueCast systems can deliver time-sensitive contextual content, so, for example, in the morning the user would get an audio clip of the tracks 'Fix You' and be prompted to tune in to Radio One, in the afternoon the clip would be the same but the user would be prompted to watch Jonathan Ross on BBC1.

Figure 5.7 Digital ringtone download via bluetooth (*Source*: Hypertag)

Miscellaneous tools

We need to be responsive to new tools that will be used by customers, distributors or employees. At the moment, some of these futuristic tools include: wearable technology, embedded chips and speech recognition and synthesis.

5.8   Repurposing content

We are witnessing the emergence of a multi-platform culture, where people access online content from a range of different devices or tools. Your customers will use a range of tools for more and more 'moments of interactivity' with your brand. In an ideal world (with unlimited budgets), you would have a presence on all iDTV services, the web, WAP, I-mode, etc. Unfortunately there is no perfect content management system that seamlessly repurposes content for each tool, so for the moment, you've got to do it. Sometimes it's easier to start again and create new content. It will eventually get much easier to create content for multiplatforms, however this section explains how 'traditional' repurposing content for different e-tools occurs, particularly from web to WAP and web to iDTV and TV to IPTV.

What is **repurposing**? The simplest definition of re-purposing is the adaptation of some piece of content for a new purpose to display it on a different e-tool (e.g. from web to iDTV). First, let's look at repurposing from web to WAP.

REPURPOSING FOR WAP

Part of the problem with WAP sites currently is that marketers or site designers and creators often fail to take into account the current limitations of today's mobile devices. WAP is text based. The standard code, WML (wireless mark-up language) is a simple derivative of HTML. So pictures, lavish graphics and sound get stripped out. Many WAP sites seem to be uploaded straight from web sites and therefore the text used is sometimes too long, links are broken or the information is un-navigable on a WAP browser. Today WAP designers have to design for many different mobile devices, each requiring different coding, making development more complex and expensive than simply designing for the two main web browsers and different versions.

REPURPOSING FOR INTERACTIVE TV

Interactive digital television moves TV into the online world and offers many exciting possibilities for the marketer, but also many challenges to transfer content across. Internet content needs to be repurposed for television. You can't take your web site and dump it on iDTV. It's not the web. Content must be 'repurposed', recreated or recoded. Traditional PC-based web sites are 'lean forward' media – designed for lone viewing from two feet away. However software repurposing packages which automatically reformat can assist the process.

iDTV viewing is 'lean back' (relax) medium designed for group viewing from eight feet away on a lower resolution screen. It's a different medium. Even an iDTV ad linked to a micro-site needs large text and large buttons. You won't be able to read a standard web site unless you're practically on top of the set! The problem is exacerbated by different iDTV plat-forms, each based on different technology, making content repurposing highly complicated. Another problem with traditional web sites – they're designed to be accessed with a point and click device, not a remote control. So no scrolling. And of course, iDTV's lower screen resolution adds to the challenge. So remember iDTV is not the web. Its design ethics, visual qualities and viewer usage are entirely different.

So how do you repurpose, say, web site content for iDTV? Same as WAP – strip out all but the text? How do you repurpose text? You don't! You start again and write a new script for voiceover and moving images. Brands need to create TV experiences, not heavy text and graphics. You can of course repurpose cheaply by adding a simple hyperlink button linked to an iDTV microsite. Many TV stations (such as Joost) are now looking to make their pro-grammes available over the Internet via their web sites and links from other social networks like YouTube (BBC work with YouTube).

SECTION SUMMARY 5.8

Repurposing content

Repurposing content for 'other' devices requires an awareness of the problems caused by a lack of repurposing and an ability to think beyond the PC. Most other devices have lower screen resolutions. Many are viewed from a greater distance and have a different style of navigation to the Internet. Exploration of new technologies such as XML and Middleware is required. Think Multi-platform. Create experiences in new environments. Involve your audi-ence. Test, test, test.

5.9   Convergence

It's not so long ago that a phone was a phone and computer a computer. Not any more – **convergence** is here. The cumbersome days of carrying a laptop, a PDA and a phone will go. All of their functions can be carried out by a phone. By the end of this section you will know what convergence means, its fast changing nature and the key to successfully harnessing it.

Convergence means phones will be PCs and TVs, while TVs will be PCs and PCs will be TVs. Handheld devices will be both. The demand for a single device is evident from the numbers of users who already combine the use of devices. Marketers need to think about communicating with users that have multiple devices, for example making web site users aware of mobile and iDTV-based services.

Smart phones carry mini-PCs that combine telephony and computers. 3G phones can stream full motion video. You can watch your football team live on your phone, send e-mails and make some old fashioned telephone calls too. The phone is becoming more than a PC and TV combined. One of the innovators in this field is Nokia who produced the Nokia Communicator which combines a phone with PC and PDA features.

TVs go online and carry out many functions previously considered the domain of the PC. Online TVs with hard drives, memory and interactive online capacity – sounds like TV on steroids.

There's more, phones with flip-down keypads which reveal large screens. Phones with roll-up keypads. Phones with PCs. Phones with dual-mode microbrowser for WAP and HTML access and MP3.

PDAs with voice recognition. PDAs with speakers. PDAs with telephone compatibility almost brings us through the full circle . . .

A PDA is a phone. A phone is a PDA. A PDA is a PC. A PC is a TV. A TV is a PC is a phone. The i-phone embraces all of this in one easy-to-use device.

And don't forget the humble radio – the digital radio can stream data, pictures and audio in your car or in your house. Add voice recognition and the circle seems complete with voice-operated computers, TVs, PCs, radios.

One more thing. Add some **Bluetooth** technology and the e-tools can talk to each other. Radios will not be called 'radios', nor TVs 'TVs'. These 'old world' words will soon be left behind by the lightning quick emergence of media convergence. Moore's Law is on the rampage. What do you think the new devices will be called (we'll have to be more creative than 'personal digital assistants')?

Convergence really means convenience. If customers want to watch, roam, explore, shop, bank or communicate they can now choose whichever tool suits them. In an office it might be a PC. On a train it might be a handheld device. At home it might be a TV or perhaps the fridge, depending on which room you're in.

Key to success will be an underlying integrated database and seamless systems that recognize customers regardless of which 'converged device' they use. So everything is converging with alarming speed. Convergence means convenience. A seamless integrated database must be at the heart of whichever tool or device is used.

CONVERGENCE IN THE HOME

As well as convergence in handheld devices we are starting to see more overlap between PC, TV, iDTV box and DVD player. Many TVs now have the iDTV box built in, perhaps a DVD recorder too. **Personal video recorders (PVRs)** or **digital video recorders (DVRs)** are consumer electronics devices that record television to a hard disk in digital format. Sky+ and TiVo are the two best known PVR/DVR products. Many models are now also offering the facility to record onto DVDs. They enable 'time shifting' features such as pausing live TV, instant replay of interesting scenes, and skipping advertising. At the same time we are seeing PCs that are becoming closer to TVs.

E-MARKETING INSIGHT

Jeff Hawkins on convergence

Jeff Hawkins, founder of Palm and Handspring, believes total convergence is possible. He says:

> 'If you try to integrate a cellphone and a PDA and an e-mail machine and by integration one of them suffers, then people won't buy it. So the trick is, how do you do it right? But I think that's what the world wants. I think you can build a great single device'.
>
> *(Hawkins 2001)*

As CEO of Handspring he has developed devices that incorporate conventional PDA functions such as diary and address books with other features including web access, MP3 players and even GPS navigation.

SECTION SUMMARY 5.9

Convergence

Convergence involves merging technologies into fewer devices. Functions such as speech, TV viewing, text entry, web browsing and listening to music will be available in a single mobile device or a multi-function PC or TV.

5.10 Integrated campaigns

Marketers are beginning to integrate e-tools innovatively. We're going to show you a few examples ranging from TV shows, to cars and cola. These integrated campaigns also integrate the online tools with offline tools such as traditional TV, radio and magazine advertising, direct mail and packaging. By the end of this section you'll be able to 'think integrated' when considering e-tools.

Now consider integrated campaigns for cars. Take Audi, it has used interactive TV, WAP, web and handheld devices. Traditionally car manufacturers use TV for brand building, awareness and reassurance and save the detailed information for a medium you can study such as the press. iDTV can do both. WAP on the other hand can remind them or invite a call back for a test drive, while the web site can take customers through all stages of the buying model from banner ads creating awareness (and/or problem recognition) to web sites that help information search for evaluating and comparing through to booking a test drive. Again offline integration should deliver the test drive car to the door if the request comes from a prospect who fits the ideal customer profile.

As multi-platforms emerge two key issues emerge: security and integration. Security is already a major issue and as multi-platforms are developed security becomes exposed to multiple threats as demonstrated by today's inadequate mobile phone security precautions. Secondly, integrating the database from different tools. If a web site has forms for capturing customer data, or if you have call back technology or even just telemarketing collecting customer data, the data has to be managed so that the data is delivered back into the business, i.e. into the rest of the database.

E-MARKETING EXCELLENCE

MTV use integrated campaign for 'Videoclash'

Here's how MTV used C2B via an integrated campaign to help consumers become prosumers and create a video request TV show. MTV produced their first live television show to be built around SMS text messages. The programme asked viewers to become prosumers by helping MTV produce the most popular programme. Viewers were asked to vote for the video they wanted to see next from a choice of two. Its C2B customers created the product (well at least from a controlled menu). Customers were empowered to play director. Viewer input also became part of the programme as their comments were then run live on MTV while the winning video was played. Messages were sent in via mobile text messages or on the Internet. Using up to 50 characters of text, messages (explaining how the show worked) were sent to yourmobile.com's database and also to teen girl magazine *J17*'s database. Opinion formers were targeted through the fan sites of the artists involved in the show. The programme was explained and the fan sites relayed the information to all their fans. Of course, the artists themselves were also e-mailed. Offline ads in *J17* magazine showed a text message on a phone. Promotional postcards were also distributed in schools in the north-east of England.

Finally, consider Coca-Cola's innovative Coke Auction campaign which combined sales promotions and packaging with the unique online facility of online auctions with offline radio and TV advertisements, with online e-mail viral marketing. Online auctions harness some of the Internet's unique functions. With innovation at the helm, Coca-Cola have somehow converted the normally discarded ring pulls into online currency called unsurprisingly 'Coke credits'. These credits are then used to bid for items from sports tickets to becoming stars in Coke ads (having their faces on the Coke signs) in major advertising venues.

Integrated marketing campaigns used to involve all ten offline communications tools. Today, there's more; they can be integrated with the wide variety of emerging e-tools from web to WAP, to mobile, to kiosks, to iRadio, to iDTV. Use of e-tools in campaigns makes measuring campaign effectiveness easier – we can profile who has sent e-mails or text messages. We're only seeing the start of really interesting integrated campaigns.

In the long-term, information will be 'platform neutral'. Customers will use many different e-tools. This means that marketers will send out messages using many different tools and platforms, as shown in the Tank! e-marketing insight box. Crafting messages that work across many tools is a new skill.

Integrated campaigns, in fact any customer communications, ideally need to integrate with one seamless database. Unfortunately different e-tools have different ways of delivering customer data to your database. Capturing the data in the right way is important. Customers don't care how you do it, but they do expect you to remember their order, request, complaint and background details regardless of which tool they choose.

Finally, a truly integrated business brings data and systems seamlessly together, e.g. if you buy a pair of shoes from an online store you can return them to any of the store's bricks and mortar locations. Total integration is required.

E-MARKETING INSIGHT

Tank! assess the effectiveness of integrated campaign plans

The tank! multi channel testlab was a test set up to determine the best combination, frequency and timing of different media including mail, e-mail, SMS, telephone and web site. Four financial service companies were involved in the test: Abbey, Bristol & West, Tesco Personal Finance and Sainsbury's Bank.

The companies were given a choice of direct mail, SMS, e-mail, outbound telephony and a responsive web site. Their task was to sell a fictitious financial service product, using anonymously branded direct mail as the main communication. They had an opportunity to utilize up to four 'teaser' communications and four 'chaser' communications. They decided the timing and frequency of the communications in the same two-week period. Consumer panellists recruited for the test were primed to assume they were in the market for the product and to respond, but only when the company did enough to convince them to act. This approach has the advantage over traditional research as panellists experienced in real life the communication schedule.

Figure 5.8 shows the winning campaign from Brand M. Points to note relative to other campaigns include:

- E-mail and SMS teaser useful in raising awareness of mail pack.
- E-mail and SMS chaser added to campaign response, creating a second campaign response.
- Initial voice chaser (pack + 2 days) received highest single response of all four campaigns.
- This campaign had the highest number of touches.

(*Source*: Tank! www.tankgroup.com).

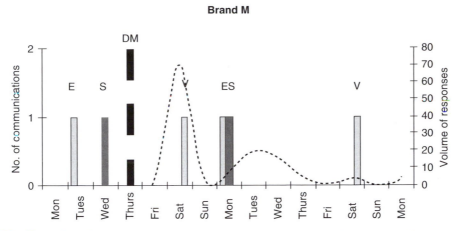

Figure 5.8 Campaign timeline for winning brand in integrated campaign contest (E, e-mail; S, SMS; V, voice; DM, direct mail pack; dashed curve = volume of responses shown on right Y axis). (*Source*: TankOnline, 2004)

E-MARKETING INSIGHT

Amnesty International Multi Channel

Situation and objective

Amnesty International revived its groundbreaking comedy event after a 15-year break. With all the changes there had been in the media world in that time, a new strategy was needed to promote the event.

Strategy

In today's more competitive, media-savvy and cynical environment, the use of digital media and multiple platforms played a fundamental role in reestablishing the event. The strategy behind the promotion was simple – 'Bring the Ball back, everywhere'.

Tactics

This led to the creation of a campaign site, viral films, animations, podcasts, backstage downloads, mobile phone downloads, bluecasts, UGC, social network profiles, blogs and exclusive video for video-sharing sites.

A site was created as the hub for all activity, housed within the main Amnesty website. Four viral films were created as pre-show publicity. Starring a dysfunctional comedy troupe, the films' role was to get a 'non-Amnesty' audience interested in the Ball. The films were seeded in online communities, distributed via mobile phones, and promoted on relevant newsletters and with online partners. A spoof MySpace page was created to extend the idea and engagement, featuring bonus footage, interactive competitions and failed flash mob attempts. Podcasts were used as another platform to distribute a mini-version of the show and were promoted via iTunes and partners like *The Times*. The mobile channel was used by partnering with Channel 4, which allowed people to download John Cleese ringtones, archive material, viral films and other content. SMS was also used to give people a way to join Amnesty while watching the show.

Action

Tremendous attention to detail was required to execute each of the above tactics. Rigorous project management processes were put in place and responsibilities allocated to individuals.

Control

The promotion was highly effective, reinvigorating a property among a youth audience. They said it delivered the message in a clear way for charities and made an effective use of UGC sites in the mix.

New Media Age Awards 2007, Best Use of Multiple Channels

SECTION SUMMARY 5.10

Integrated campaigns

From cars to cola, businesses are beginning to integrate their e-tools. Integration includes: online and offline, databases, systems and processes. Now there's a challenge!

Integrated campaigns use all ten traditional communications tools in conjunction with different forms of traditional media (TV, print, radio) and new media (iDTV, web and iRadio). Each interactive tool can be used to move the consumer through the buying process. Security and database integration are two major issues that need to be addressed.

CHAPTER SUMMARY

1 E-marketing is not restricted to the use of the web and e-mail. It also includes interactions with customers achieved through other access devices such as interactive digital TV, digital radio, mobile phones, kiosks and CD-ROMs. The numbers of users of these services is significant.

2 Interactive digital TV has a rapidly growing audience and opportunities are available for interactive advertising, channel sponsorship or transactional e-commerce.

3 Digital radio is used in conjunction with the web for brand-building and direct response.

4 Mobile devices are widely used for messaging, which gives new opportunities for advertising and location-based services. The facility of browsing through WAP, and multimedia through 3G, will rival the web and iDTV channels.

5 Interactive kiosks can be used to reach an audience who may not access the web frequently. They are at their most powerful when used in-store to offer services tied to loyalty cards.

6 CD-ROMs and interactive business cards can be of value in generating attention about a new service where there is a high-level of access to PCs and detailed or multimedia information needs to be delivered.

7 We must track the introduction of new tools such as interactive technology, speech recognition and synthesis and deploy them where appropriate.

8 Repurposing content for devices other than the web requires careful planning to minimize the costs of repackaging. The cost of repurposing should be considered when deciding which technology platforms to support.

9 Convergence involves multi-functionality built into fewer devices. Functions such as speech, TV viewing, text entry, web browsing and listening to music will be available in a single mobile device or a multi-function PC or TV.

10 Integrated campaigns involve leveraging the ten traditional communications tools across traditional and new media.

References

Ahonen, T. and Alan Moore, A. (2007) *Communities Dominate Brands*. Future Text, London.

Belic, D. (2007) China Mobile Subscribers surpass total population of the United States, *IntoMobile, 7 April.*

Carter, G. (2006) Whose Television is it anyway? Transforming Television: Strategies for Convergence. TRC 2006.

Chaffey, D. (2006) The forgotten digital media – 1. Mobile marketing. *E-marketing insights,* Column 43, January.

Chartered Institute of Marketing (2006) 'Exotic Technologies', Shape the Agenda papers. www.cim.co.uk/shapetheagenda.

Curry, A. (2001) What's next for interactive television. *Interactive Marketing,* Vol. 3, No. 2, October/December, pp. 128–140.

De Waele, R. (2006) October 22nd, in MTrends.org

Duncan, A. (2006) Maximising Public Value in the 'Now' Media World? Excerpts taken from Transforming Television: Strategies for Convergence TRC.

Havenstein, H. (2005) Spring comes to AI winter. *Computer World,* 14 Feb.

Hawkins, J. (2001) Interviews section. tnbt.com. The Next Big Thing. www.tnbt.com.

Highfield, A. (2006) The future role of the BBC as a broadcaster on the web. Excerpts taken from Transforming Television: Strategies for Convergence TRC 2006.

IDS (2005) Interactive TV Survey 2005 – 'Interactive TV – A Maturing Medium.'

Kurzweil, R. (2001) The law of accelerating returns. KurzweilAI.net 7 March.

Lilley, A (2006) New Media Comes of Age. Excerpts taken from Transforming Television: Strategies for Convergence TRC 2006.

Mori (2004) MORI Technology Tracker. Available at www.mori.com/emori/tracker.shtml.

Nelson, S. (2007) Controller of Portfolio and Multimedia, BBC Vision Speech given at BBC Vision in-house Multiplatform Day. *Wednesday 26 September.*

Revolution (2004) Digital finds a new ally in Radio. *Revolution*. December, 2004. www.revolutionmagazine.com.

Rowan, D. (2006) The next big thing: chatbots. *The Times Magazine*, 4 March.

Svennivig, M. (2004) The interactive viewer: Reality or Myth? *Interactive Marketing*, Vol. 6, No. 2, pp. 151–164.

TankOnline (2004) Personal correspondence with Tank Group (www.tankgroup.com).

Further Reading

BBC e-commerce (www.bbc.co.uk/e-commerce). A great summary of the latest applications of technology to boost e-commerce and digital marketing.

The New York Times Technology section (www.nytimes.com/pages/technology). People in the US look to the NYT for the latest innovations in technology and marketing.

Bookmark or subscribe to Trendspotting (www.trendspotting.com) to keep up-to-date with the latest technologies.

Wired magazine (www.wired.com) has traditionally been an earlier proponent of new technologies and how they are marketed.

Web links

Alice in California who responds to emotions (http://www.alicebot.org).

Clickz.com (www.clickz.com/stats). Keep up-to-date with the adoption of digital media worldwide from this searchable aggregator of analyst reports.

Digital radio in the UK, visit www.digitalradionow.com. A summary of services.

Digital Signage blog (http://www.beaver-group.com/v2/home/blog.php). Focuses on developments in digital signage.

E-marketing Excellence book homepage (www.davechaffey.com/E-marketing). An index of all e-marketing links for each chapter in the book.

The World DAB Forum www.worlddab.org. Explains the marketing benefits of DAB with examples of how it is being used around the world.

George (http://www.jabberwacky.com). An example of a British bot.

Howstuffworks (www.howstuffworks.com). Good explanations with diagrams of many new technologies.

IDS Survey www.idigitalsales.co.uk/interactiveadvertising/survey.cfm. Survey about interactive TV.

IntoMobile www.intomobile.com. Mobile phone news and reviews.

IPTV Industry (http://www.iptv-industry.com). A portal focusing on developments in IPTV.

Forrester Marketing Blog (http://blogs.forrester.com/marketing/). Forrester analysts write about developments in technology.

Kiosks.org (www.kiosks.org). Trade association for the mobile kiosks and digital signage industry.

M Trends www.m-trends.org/2006/10/proximity-marketing.html.

Mobile Data Association www.themda.org. Statistics on consumer adoption in UK.

MMetrics (www.mmetrics.com). Research company profiling usage of mobile technology. Research summaries available in press releases section.

Ray KurzweilAI www.kurzweilai.net. Futurologist Ray Kurzweil's blog.

Text.it (www.text.it). Portal from Mobile Data Association with examples of how SMS is used in the UK for consumer and business campaigns.

Text media Centres http://www.text.it/mediacentre/sms_figures.cfm. Latest figures on UK text message adoption.

Trendhunter (www.trendhunter.com). Showcases the latest advances in digital technologies.

TRC www.trcmedia.org.

O'Reilly Radar (http://radar.oreilly.com/). Commentary on the development of web technologies from publishers O'Reilly whose founder Tim O'Reilly coined the term Web 2.0.

TED (www.ted.com). Video showcase of developments in technology and their impact on culture. TED stands for Technology, Entertainment, Design. TED started out (in 1984) as a conference bringing together people from those three worlds.

Whatis.com (www.whatis.com). Succinct explanations of terms for new technologies.

Widget blog (http://blog.snipperoo.com/). Blog focusing on developments in widgets and gadgets.

Self-test

1 Summarize the relative importance, in terms of reach, for all the different e-tools mentioned in this chapter.

2 Describe the different marketing options of interactive digital TV available to a retailer, manufacturer and FMCG brand.

3 Distinguish between digital radio and web radio. How does web radio integrate with PC-based e-marketing?

4 Define the customer value proposition for mobile services. Explain how marketers can work with this proposition.

5 List the different marketing applications of kiosks.

6 Describe the benefits of interactive business cards and CD-ROMs. Which sectors do you think they are relevant to?

7 Summarize how some of the latest technologies, not described in Sections 1 to 6 of this chapter, may influence the future of marketing.

8 Describe approaches to content re-purposing.

9 Explain the relevance of the concept of convergence to marketers.

10 Visit the archive of a new media magazine such as *Revolution* (www.revolutionmagazine.com) and summarize the design and execution of two integrated campaigns using some of the new media described in this chapter.

Chapter **6**

Site design

'Unless a web site meets the needs of the intended users it will not meet the needs of the organization providing the web site. Web site development should be user-centred, evaluating the evolving design against user requirements'.

Bevan (1999)

OVERVIEW

This chapter will make you think about web sites a little differently. We go beyond best practice in usability and accessiblity, to show how to design commercially-led sites which deliver results. Commercially-led site designs are based on creating compelling persuasive experiences which really engage visitors through relevant messages and content, encouraging them to stay on the site and return.

OVERALL LEARNING OUTCOME

By the end of this chapter you will:

- Know what makes an excellent web site
- Be able to review the components of a site when designing an enhancement
- Understand the rules to follow and the mistakes to avoid
- Be able to converse with any web master, marketer or chief executive about improving your web site
- Be able to explore options for added value through dynamic facilities.

CHAPTER TOPIC	LEARNING OBJECTIVE
6.1 Introduction	Identify the main objectives of effective site design
6.2 Integrated design	Ensure web sites are integrated with the rest of the business
6.3 Online value proposition	Develop an online value proposition (OVP)
6.4 Customer orientation	Be able to translate customer needs into web site design
6.5 Dynamic design and personalization	Explore options for added value through dynamic facilities
6.6 Aesthetics	Identify different aspects of aesthetic design
6.7 Page design	Understand and apply best practice for page layout
6.8 Copy writing	Grasp and apply the fundamental principles of copy writing for web sites
6.9 Navigation and structure	Assess best practice for navigation and structure
6.10 Interaction	Assess best practice for interaction (including conversion rates and customer services)

6.1   Introduction to web site design

Web site design = Function + Content + Form + Organization + Interaction

Combining these elements web site design presents a challenge few have mastered since success requires a range of skills. Companies need to harness internal skills and/or use specialist agencies on all of the success factors for web site design which we will review in this chapter:

- *Accessibility* – This should be built into all web sites since it is a legal requirement under disability and discrimination law. An accessible design supports visually impaired site users and other disabled users with limited limb movements. It also helps users accessing the site with a range of different web browsers using different devices such as mobiles or PDAs and it also assists search engine optimization.

- *User-centred design and usability* – With a user-friendly site visitors can find the information they are seeking, have a satisfactory experience and complete actions efficiently. User-centred web site design is an essential approach to ensure the web site meets visitors needs. Research to identify appropriate personas, customer journeys and relevant content is a key activity.

- *Information architecture and findability* – Analysis and design to create a sound system of structure and labelling content in headings and navigation is essential to help findability through standard navigation and on-site search.

- *Search engine optimization (SEO)* – If SEO isn't considered in site design and within content management systems, search robots will be unable to crawl content and the relevance of different pages will be unclear.

- *Web standards* – Complying with standards to produce consistency in the way sites are coded and displayed in different browsers as promoted through the World Wide Web consortium (www.w3.org) and the Webstandards Project (www.webstandards.org).

- *Persuasion to deliver commercial results* – Your design should emphasize specific content and journeys through the site in order for your site to meet its objectives. Users should not be given free rein to visit any content, instead you should prioritize your most valuable content in a similar way to a supermarket using merchandising to promote specific products. We also need to study the psychology of customer engagement (Chapter 1 and 4) to understand the content, messages and visual design that influence customer perceptions (remember Robert Cialdini's six 'Weapons of Influence' from Chapter 4?).

- *Visual design* – The experience of a brand and a site will not be memorable and positive if the visual design isn't energizing and doesn't fit with what the visitor would expect from a brand.

- *Web analytics* – Analysis of site visitor journeys can help improve navigation and conversion to different site goals.

- *Legal requirements* – Site owners need to check they comply with the many laws to control a web presence.

- *Internet marketing planning and improvement process* – The web site must fit within the wider world where it supports different organization goals, integrates with other sales channels and is continuously reviewed and improved to achieve them.

WEB SITE GOALS

Clarifying the key objectives and purpose of the site helps to determine the functions and content of the site. In turn content drives form (the way it looks) and finally form drives the organization of the web site. We will also look at how interaction should be built into the site to improve the visitor experience.

So what is the purpose, or objective, of a web site? First, to help customers, or other stakeholders, ask '*How can my web site help my customers?*' For example:

- Help them buy something they need.
- Help them find information.
- Help them to save money and time.
- Help them to talk to the organization.
- Help them to enjoy a better web experience.

These are the 5Ss Sell, Serve, Speak, Save and Sizzle introduced in Chapter 1, as seen from the customer perspective. Site design can help achieve the 5Ss as follows:

- *Sell* – Growing sales can be achieved through effectively communicating a crystal clear online value proposition and through making e-commerce and lead generation easier.
- *Serve* – We can add value through designing easy-to-use interactive services that help customers to find relevant, up-to-date information quickly.
- *Speak* – We can use the site to converse with and get closer to customers by providing tailored content and designing interactive facilities to create a dialogue or even a trialogue when customers talk to each other, as well as learning about their needs.
- *Save* – Costs are saved through delivering online content and services that may have previously been achieved through print and post or face-to-face service and sales transactions.
- *Sizzle* – An excellent site design helps build the brand and reinforces the brand values through the type of content, interactivities and overall style, tone or feel.

PRACTICAL E-MARKETING TIP

Conversion goals and value events

You should define **conversion goals** for your site to check that you are achieving your objectives. Visits to certain pages such as an e-newsletter registration, where-to-buy or sales confirmation page are more valuable than others.

These are also known as **value events** and you should create a tracking and scoring system to evaluate them by using web analytics 'spotlight page tags' on these goal pages. Google Analytics makes it easy to set up conversion goals and track them and even better show pages or referrers that influence them.

Design priorities do vary, but many companies use the objectives of customer relationship management to serve as objectives for their site:

- *Customer acquisition* – Acquisition means winning customers – converting prospects (visitors) into customers on site.
- *Customer retention* – Retention means keeping customers – ensuring they repeat buy. Timely, personalized and relevant e-mails and offers can bring them back to you via the site.
- *Customer extension* – Extension means extending the share of wallet. Selling other relevant products and services to the same customer. For example, the database can identify similar customers that bought A but not B and then make recommendations.

For each of these, design can help *convert* the visitor to the required marketing outcome. Achieving site **stickiness** increases the chance of achieving these objectives.

PRACTICAL E-MARKETING TIP

Bounce rates

You should use your **web analytics** tools to review **bounce rates** to analyze and improve the effectiveness of landing pages and the quality of referrers to a page.

Bounce rates are the percentage of visitors to a page or site that exit after visiting only a single page. You can also assess duration, as Figure 6.1 shows. The benefit of using these measures is that they vary widely compared to conversion rates, so it is easy to identify your worst and best landing pages.

E-MARKETING EXCELLENCE

Harley-Davidson use the web to achieve diverse objectives

Some sites, like Harley-Davidson (Figure 6.2), are designed with a range of objectives including acquiring new customers through detailed product information about the core product and extended product such as guarantees and rentals; developing additional revenue streams such as rentals, tours and courses and saving through making efficiency gains through helping dealers with warranty claims – thereby generating cost savings and better customer service. Communicating the experience and image possible through owning the brand are important, although this may not always be possible with accessibility goals.

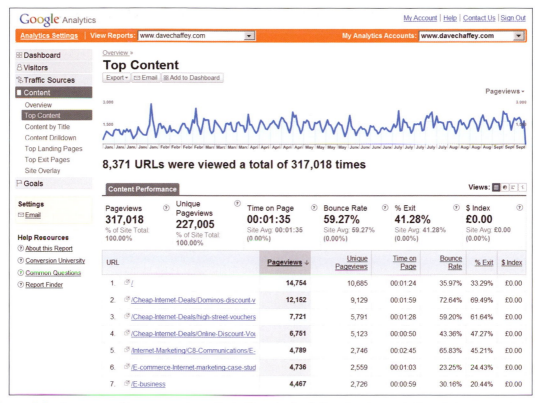

Figure 6.1   Summary of top pages to a site in Google Analytics showing variations in bounce rate

Figure 6.2   Harley-Davidson (www.harley-davidson.co.uk)

So what factors facilitate online sales and encourage visitors back again and again? What are the key variables? A Forrester survey of 8600 US consumers (www.forrester.com) showed that web users believe four main factors encouraged them to return to a site:

1 High quality content.
2 Ease of use.
3 Quick to download.
4 Updated frequently.

Other factors such as coupons and offers and leading-edge technologies were insignificant in comparison. Let's explore these four factors in more detail.

- *Content* is important. It was said in the mid-1990s that 'content is king', but recent thinking suggests that 'context is king'. Having the right information in the right place at the right time – just when you need it – is king. For example, online travel package sites now need much more than plain listings of hotels to compete, they need guest reviews, resort guides and even videos. Quality content helps site visitors make the right decision and also attracts visitors through search engine optimization so increasing brand awareness.

- *Ease of use* is also important. Easy-to-use sites mean good navigation. The form or structure of the site is neither over-complicated nor too big. You never get lost in a good site since it's always clearly signposted. Take sales – the order page should be easily found. E-commerce transactions must be easy to make and provide reassurance about security and privacy.

- *Quick to download*. Good sites also download quickly. Bad sites are cumbersome and slow. Visitors won't wait. Assess performance with services like SciVisum or Site Confidence.

- *Frequently updated*. Good sites stay fresh. They put up new information which is useful, relevant and timely for their audience. They also systematically take out old, out-of-date, information (particularly offers with expiry dates) as this destroys credibility. This is expensive. It takes time, energy and skills to maintain a site. Does your site encourage repeat visits? Does it encourage customers to come back? Does the site offer them genuinely good reasons to return?

E-retailers also need to research what blocks purchase – what causes 'shopping cart abandonment'. Remember that for most e-tail sites, fewer than 10% of new visitors make a purchase. Research presented in Figure 6.3 highlights typical problems. You can see how a combination of technical problems and poor design coupled with inadequate information can hamper the online shopper. Every site can improve its conversion rate by researching the factors that cause abandonment and improving the design to correct problems. Even Amazon still continually needs to refine its site to reduce abandonment and increase average order value.

There is more on all of these issues in the aesthetics, navigation, interaction and copywriting sections in this chapter.

PRACTICAL E-MARKETING TIP

Increasing landing page conversion rate

Remember that many visitors do not enter via your home page, we find often more than half of visitors arrive from search engines and other sources not on the home page but on campaign landing pages. The implication is obvious, designers need to treat every page as the entry point to clearly explain their proposition and aim to convert to action. Here is a checklist of questions to ask to check your landing page effectiveness against specific goals.

☑ *Aim 1 Generate response (online lead or sale and offline call-back)*

Does the page have a prominent call-to-action such as a prominent button above the fold, repeated in text and image form?

☑ *Aim 2 Engage different audience types (reduce bounce rate, increase value events, increase return rate)*

Does the page have a prominent headline and sub-heads showing the visitor is in the right place? Does the page have **scent trail** trigger messages, offers or images to appeal to different audiences? For example, Dell has links on its site to appeal to consumers and different types of businesses. A landing page containing form fields to fill in is often more effective than an additional click since it starts committed visitors on their journey.

☑ *Aim 3 Communicate key brand messages (increase brand familiarity and favourability)*

Does the page clearly explain who you are, what you do, where you operate and what makes you different. Is your online value proposition compelling? Do you use customer testimonials or ratings to show independent credibility? To help with this, use run-of-site messages (on all pages) across the top of the screen or in the left or right sidebars.

☑ *Aim 4 Answer the visitors' questions (reduce bounce rates, increase conversion rates)*

Different audiences will want to know different things. Have you identified personas (Chapter 4) and do you seek to answer their questions e.g. do you use FAQs or messages which say 'Are you a new customer'(so you can explain the proposition)?

☑ *Aim 5 Showcase range of offers (cross-sell)*

Do you have recommendations on related or best-selling products and do you show the full range of your offering through navigation?

☑ *Aim 6 Attract visitors through search engine optimization (SEO)*

How well do you rank for relevant search terms compared to competitors? Do your navigation, copy and page templates indicate relevance to search engines through **on-page optimization**? Review the example of Figure 6.4. This site has effective landing pages because the masthead and left and right sidebars are similar across the site to help communicate key messages consistent with the goals above.

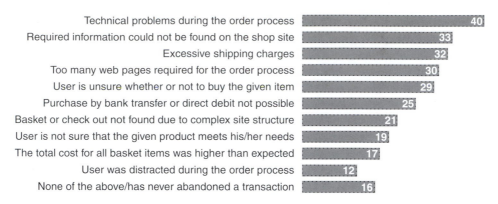

Technical problems during the order process	40
Required information could not be found on the shop site	33
Excessive shipping charges	32
Too many web pages required for the order process	30
User is unsure whether or not to buy the given item	29
Purchase by bank transfer or direct debit not possible	25
Basket or check out not found due to complex site structure	21
User is not sure that the given product meets his/her needs	19
The total cost for all basket items was higher than expected	17
User was distracted during the order process	12
None of the above/has never abandoned a transaction	16

Figure 6.3   Reasons for abandoning online shopping process. (*Source*: Novomind, 2004)

Figure 6.4   Online TEFL (www.onlintefl.com) home page from travel company i-to-i

USABILITY AND ACCESSIBILITY

Effective web site designs are today informed by two key approaches used by professional designers. These are usability and accessibility.

Usability is a concept applied to the design of a range of products which describes how easy they are to use. The British Standard/ISO Standard 'Human Centred design processes for interactive systems' defines usability as:

> *'the extent to which a product can be used by specified users to achieve specified goals with effectiveness, efficiency and satisfaction in a specified context of use'. (BSI 1999).*

You can see how the concept can be readily applied to web site design – web visitors often have defined goals such as finding particular information or completing an action such as booking a flight or viewing an account balance.

In Jakob Nielsen's book *Designing Web Usability* (2000), he describes usability as follows.

> *'An engineering approach to web site design to ensure the user interface of the site is learnable, memorable, error free, efficient and gives user satisfaction. It incorporates testing and evaluation to ensure the best use of navigation and links to access information in the shortest possible time. A companion process to information architecture'.*

In practice, usability involves two approaches. Firstly, **expert reviews** are often performed at the beginning of a redesign project as a way of identifying problems with a previous design. Secondly, **usability testing** which involves:

1 Identifying representative users of the site.
2 Asking them to perform specific tasks such as finding a product or completing an order.
3 Observing what they do and how they succeed.

The use of **personas** and **scenario-based design** which we looked at in Section 4.10 is a key approach to inform usability.

Jakob Nielsen explains the imperative for usability best in his article 'Usability 101' (www.useit.com/alertbox/20030825.html). He says:

> *'On the web, usability is a necessary condition for survival. If a web site is difficult to use, people leave. If the homepage fails to clearly state what a company offers and what users can do on the site, people leave. If users get lost on a web site, they leave. If a web site's information is hard to read or doesn't answer users' key questions, they leave. Note a pattern here'?*

For these reasons, Nielsen suggests that around 10% of a design project budget should be spent on usability, but often actual spend is significantly less.

For a site to be successful, the tasks or actions need to be completed:

- **Effectively** – web usability specialists measure task completion, for example, only three out of ten visitors to a web site may be able to find a telephone number or other piece of information.
- **Efficiently** – web usability specialists also measure how long it takes to complete a task on site, or the number of clicks it takes.

Web accessibility is about allowing all users of a web site to interact with it regardless of disabilities they may have or the web browser or platform they are using to access the site. The visually impaired or blind are the main audience that designing an accessible web site can help, although often the site will become easier to use for sighted users due to clearer navigation and labelling.

This quote shows the importance of the accessibility to a visually impaired user of a web site who uses a screen-reader which reads out the navigation options and content on a web site.

> *'For me being online is everything. It's my hi-fi, it's my source of income, it's my supermarket, it's my telephone. It's my way in'.*

Lynn Holdsworth, screen reader user, Web Developer and Programmer. *Source*: RNIB (www. rnib.org.uk).

Remember that many countries now have specific **accessibility legislation** which you are subject to. This is often contained within disability and discrimination acts. In the UK, the relevant act is the Disability and Discrimination Act (DDA) 1995.

Recent amendments to the DDA make it unlawful to discriminate against disabled people in the way in which a company recruits and employs people, provides services or provides education. Providing services is the part of the law that applies to web site design.

Providing accessible web sites is a requirement of Part II of the Disability and Discrimination Act published in 1999 and required by law from 2002. In the 2002 code of practice there is a legal requirement for web sites to be accessible. This is most important for sites which provide a service. The Code of Practice gives this example:

> *'An airline company provides a flight reservation and booking service to the public on its web site. This is a provision of a service and is subject to the Act'.*

Links on accessibility guidelines and standards are given at the end of the chapter.

E-MARKETING INSIGHT

From AIDA to persuasion marketing

In addition to usability and accessibility, web site designers need to add persuasion into the design mix; to create a design that delivers results for the business.

ClickZ columnist Bryan Eisenberg (www.clickz.com) has been called a 'conversion guru'. He advocates persuasion marketing alongside other design principles such as usability and accessibility. He says:

> *'It's during the wireframe and storyboard phase we ask three critical questions of every page a visitor will see:*
>
> 1 *What action needs to be taken?*
> 2 *Who needs to take that action?*
> 3 *How do we persuade that person to take the action we desire?'*

We can readily apply the AIDA model for advertising to site design to help achieve persuasion. Site designers seek to achieve Attention, then Interest, then Desire, then Action. Although the elements of this model, described by Strong (1925), are often criticized as outdated, many sites use the tried and tested AIDA model as a framework for design objectives. Here AIDA is used to generate a lead from a potential customer.

- *Attention* – The site must grab attention when the visitor first hears about it or even when the visitor actually arrives. We achieve attention through graphics, animation, interaction and easy access to relevant information including a crystal clear OVP (online value proposition).
- *Interest* – Once you have the customers' attention we have to provide more detailed information and incentives to gain interest.
- *Desire* – One approach is using the prefix 'free': free information, free screensaver, free services. Emphasizing the brand values through site design as in Figure 6.1 is another approach.
- *Action* – The call to action, e.g. to ring up, subscribe or order, should be clear and easy to use.

SECTION SUMMARY 6.1

Introduction to web site design

Well-designed sites have clear objectives. The 5Ss can help you to choose objectives. Asking 'How can my web site help my customers?' also helps. But remember the highest priority marketing objectives or purpose should determine the web site design. Well-designed sites have regularly updated, quality content. Both content and context are 'king'. Good sites are also designed for usability and accessibility, but remember the principle of persuasion.

6.2 Integrated design

In this section we look at the importance of integrating the web site into all communications, customer buying modes and with the databases that help to support relationships with customers. We won't explore the ultimate integration into an e-business; this is covered in Chapter 9.

THE WEB AND INTEGRATED MARKETING COMMUNICATIONS

Although web sites do more than just communicate (remember the 5Ss), web sites must integrate with all other communications tools, both online and offline. The web site's brand messages must be consistent with those in offline advertisements and mail-shots. Equally, new offers and major announcements such as awards won should be communicated consistently both online and offline. As the organization and the web site grows this job gets more difficult, but space should be reserved within the page template for these key messages which help show credibility and reinforce perceptions received through other channels.

At a basic level of integrated communications, all offline communications should carry the web site address or **URL** and describe the **online value proposition**. Equally for customers who prefer other forms of contact, the web site should cater for **inbound communications** by carrying telephone, e-mail and fax number. Some sites, however, don't offer e-mail facilities as they don't have the resources to answer e-mails promptly.

The integration of offline and online communications to generate traffic to the web site is described in more detail in Chapter 7 on traffic building.

It is worth remembering, however, that different customers prefer different communication tools, channels or modes, particularly when buying.

THE WEB AND BUYING MODES

The web site should integrate with different buying modes. We must take account of customers' preferences of browsing, comparing, selecting or buying products either online or offline as shown in Figure 6.5. Completing some activities of the buying process offline and some online is referred to as **mixed-mode buying** or **multichannel behaviour**. The site design and offline marketing communications should be integrated to support mixed-mode buying.

Common buying modes include:

- *Online purchase* – Some customers want to search, compare and buy online. Does your web site accommodate all stages of the buying process? Few products can be delivered online so fulfilment is usually offline.

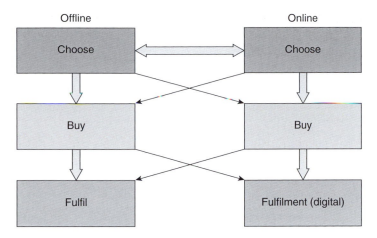

Figure 6.5 Alternative buying modes

- *Online browse and offline purchase* – **Mixed-mode buying** is when customers like to browse, look or research online and eventually purchase *offline* in a real store or in a real meeting. Some of these customers might like to browse online, but purchase via fax or telephone because of security and privacy issues. Does your site have fax forms and telephone numbers for placing orders or taking further enquiries? Does your site integrate with other communications channels? Some sites also have '**call-back facilities**' which allow visitors to request a telephone call from a sales staff to complete the purchase.

▌E-MARKETING EXCELLENCE

How Dell supports mixed-mode buying

Dell supports a common buying mode of:

> ***Offline choose then online choose then offline purchase***

This is done through communications tools that facilitate customer transition from offline to online and vice versa:

- *Offline choose to online choose* – If a customer reads about a particular model of a Dell computer in a magazine, it provides e-codes. These are typed in on the site's 'As Advertised' page, so avoiding the need for the customer to navigate to the particular product page.
- *Online choose to offline purchase* – If the customer decides to proceed with the purchase, but is uncomfortable about providing their credit card details online, Dell facilitate this transition by providing a prominent telephone number on each page. This phone number is web specific, so Dell know that all inbound calls to this number are in response to web research. Dell also uses different web-specific phone numbers on different parts of the site which have different audiences to help connect callers to the right person and track site effectiveness.

HOW SHOULD THE WEB INTEGRATE WITH THE DATABASE?

Mixed-mode buying requires good systems. A web site database should, ideally, be integrated with the old, legacy, database. Enquiries coming in from offline mail-shots or online from the web site should be recorded centrally on the database and subsequently followed up carefully. An integrated database can help sales reps know which web visitors have requested a real visit or a telephone call.

Furthermore, the database and the actual design of the web site can also help to nurture marketing relationships. The database remembers customer names, preferences and behaviours. The days of being able to build an effective web site using simple HTML code are long gone. An integrated database can personalize the experience and make relevant offers that match the needs of particular customer types.

The web site needs to be integrated with databases to deliver facilities such as transactional e-commerce, personalization and customer relationship management.

The database needs to be centralized and seamless as customers access the business via PDAs, WAP watches, interactive TVs, as well as telephones and other offline routes.

The level of integration can go up and down the supply chain so that data is shared and integrated with suppliers, distributors and key customers' own IT infrastructures. Now the business is becoming an e-business (Chapter 9).

E-MARKETING EXCELLENCE

A planned user-centred design approach

Effective web design requires a sound planning approach, success is not simply down to creative skills of the designers. As with many marketing activities, research should be at the core of the web design process, so when briefing and evaluating web suppliers, make sure you gauge the user-centred design process. Don't reinvent the wheel, since there is an established standard for planning a web site improvement project: *ISO 13407: Human centred design processes for interactive systems* (Figure 6.6).

The standard is based on four principles of human-centred design:

1 Active involvement of users and a clear understanding of user and task requirements.
2 Appropriate allocation of function between users and technology, i.e. providing tools which automate user tasks.
3 Iteration of design solutions through prototyping and user review, i.e. test, learn, refine.
4 Multi-disciplinary design meaning the design team should have skills across all design aspects that affect the customer experience and the business results.

The different stages which relate to the techniques we will cover in this chapter are shown in Figure 6.5.

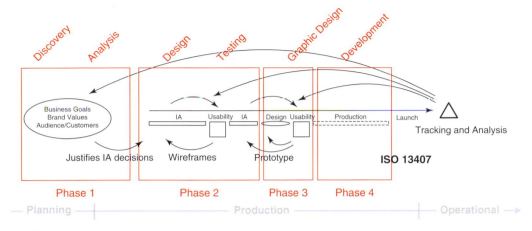

Figure 6.6 User-centred design process showing typical relationship between ISO 13407 and web site design phases. *Source*: Foviance (www.foviance.com)

SECTION SUMMARY 6.2

Integrated design

Web activities on their own won't work. Isolated web sites are ineffectual. They need to be integrated at several different levels:

1 Communications – consistent communications whether online or offline.

2 Buying modes – marketers must facilitate customer transitions between online and offline information sources during the buying process.

3 Databases – databases must be integrated to achieve a consistent view of the customer in order to build long-term relationships.

6.3   Online value proposition

The web gives the ultimate in customer choice. There are millions of sites to choose from and thousands of new domain names are still added every day. How will you stand out?

We saw in the first section of this chapter that good sites have good content, are regularly updated, easy to use and fast to download. In addition to all of these, your site has to have a clear and strong proposition. A proposition to your visitor. A unique proposition. An **online value proposition (OVP)**.

PRACTICAL E-MARKETING TIP

Communicate multiple OVPs run-of-site

You need to communicate your OVP not only on your home page and About Us, but across your whole site through careful design of messages within the masthead and both sidebars, as we saw in Figure 6.4 and will see in Figure 6.7. You also need to develop different OVPs for different audiences – the Dulux site (www.dulux.co.uk) does this well through use of four key personas. E-retailers need to think of their OVPs for different types of buyers from hunters, trackers and through to explorers (Chapter 4).

So reviewing your page template design for OVPs in different site sections during the web design and build process is crucial – you need mockups of all your site sections, not just the home page. This way you can communicate different OVPs to different audiences at different points in the buying process. For example, within the checkout process of a site, visitors need to be reassured about security, additional costs, delivery and returns.

Figure 6.7   Firebox (www.firebox.com) exhibits a clear, detailed online value proposition

Why should a customer visit, stay and even revisit your site? What does your site propose to visitors? Can you summarize the proposition for your site? Try to identify the proposition as you visit other web sites. Can you summarize their OVPs? Refer to Chapter 2, Remix, since the OVP will refer to different aspects of the marketing mix. The OVP should be clearly evident to the visitor. If you don't clearly know why a customer should visit and revisit your site, how likely is it that customers will understand?

The OVP is similar to the traditional unique selling proposition used in advertising, although advertising executives can have great debates about how the cyber world is different. Ideally, we need to try to find a proposition that explains what your organization or site is offering that:

- is different from your competitors
- is not available in the real-world
- makes a difference to your customers' lives.

At the very least the proposition should clearly show the services you are offering and your credibility to deliver.

You then need to devise a tag line that accompanies your brand identity and URL to drive home your web proposition in all communications, both web-based and real world.

E-MARKETING EXCELLENCE

Examples of B2B and B2C OVPs

For a business-to-business OVP, see RS (www.rswww.com) which describes itself as 'Europe's leading distributor of electronic, electrical and industrial components'. It then has these elements of its proposition listed on the home page, using numbers to make their point, with hyperlinks to more detailed proof.

- 262000 products at your fingertips
- Easy, online ordering
- Free next day delivery
- Free technical help
- Lower prices for larger orders.

Consumer gift and gadget site Firebox (www.firebox.com, Figure 6.7) is more about the brand experience than functional benefits. Firebox cleverly use visual design, and merchandising techniques like Top 20s and What's New listings in the sidebars to show an appealing range of products which are it's OVP. Today a key part of their OVP is **user generated content** including where customers send in photos, videos or written descriptions of their experiences with the product. This has become so effective that functional benefits such as next day delivery, security and order tracking are less prominent than previously – the idea is to make the product so desirable, that functional benefits become less important.

So, we have our proposition. What next?

1 First we need to leverage the proposition in traffic building. The proposition can be combined with the **URL** or web address and be in all advertising, as an e-mail signature and included in all marketing collateral.

2 We need to state clearly the proposition on-site. Many sites are designed so that their proposition is prominent on the home page and may be referred to on every page at the top or top left as part of the organization's identity. Others make the visitor work too hard to understand the proposition.

3 We need to deliver on the proposition through all interactions a customer has including online and offline fulfilment and service.

The following section on customer orientation examines what customers want, what's important and what's affordable.

E-MARKETING INSIGHT

Different views on the value proposition

These comments epitomize traditional meanings of the 'value prop' which can all be translated into an online environment.

A conventional view of the value proposition is provided by Knox *et al.* (2003) in their review of approaches to customer relationship management. They say a value proposition is:

> *'an offer defined in terms of the target customers, the benefits offered to these customers, and the price charged relative to the competition'.*

Similarly, Rayport and Jaworski (2004) suggest that construction of a value proposition requires consideration of (1) Target segments, (2) Focal customer benefits, (3) Resources to deliver the benefits package in a superior manner to competitors. However, branding advocates believe that the value proposition is more than the sum of product features, prices and benefits. They argue that it also encompasses the totality of the experience that the customer has when selecting, purchasing and using the product. We will see that these customer experiences and also service quality are very important online. For example, Molineux (2002) states that:

> *'the value proposition describes the total customer experience with the firm and in its alliance partners over time, rather than [being limited to] that communicated at the point of sale'.*

To summarize, we can say that:

1 The offer forming the OVP should be developed specifically for specific target customer segments (see the Firebox example in Figure 6.7).

2 The OVP is not limited to the customer experience on-site but involves how it links to other channels as part of a multi-channel buying process.

3 The product or service offer and experience that form the OVP must be based on in-depth research of which factors govern purchase and loyalty behaviour and refined according to actual experience of the OVP by customers.

What should be specific elements of an OVP? Remember from Chapter 4 the six Cs that e-customers demand: Content, Customization, Community, Convenience, Choice and Cost reduction. These can all be built into the OVP.

SECTION SUMMARY 6.3

Online value proposition

In addition to good content, regular updates, ease-of-use and downloads, good sites need to have clear and strong online value propositions. OVPs require a lot of thought and refining. The hard work is rewarded as a good OVP distinguishes your site and also, simultaneously, helps to focus the marketing effort and the customer's mind.

6.4   Customer orientation

Defining, first, the purpose of your web site and second, your audience, are fundamental stages of web site development. The answers drive the kind of content required; content drives the form required and form drives the structure of the site. Usability and accessibility as defined at the start of this chapter are also a key element of customer orientation.

There are many different types of audiences including your competitors, shareholders, employees, the press and customers, to name a few (Table 6.1). **Customer orientation** is about trying to achieve the impossible – trying to provide content to appeal to a wide range

Table 6.1   Different types of web site audience

Customers vary by	Staff	Third parties
New or existing prospects	New or existing	New or existing
Size of prospect companies (e.g. small, medium or large)	Different departments	Suppliers
Market type, e.g. different vertical markets	Sales staff for different markets	Distributors
Location (by country)	Location (by country)	Investors
Members of buying process (decision makers, influencers, buyers)		Media students

of audiences. It's also about prioritizing your content for your key audiences and their key needs. Look at www.cisco.com, www.ibm.com and www.ni.com as examples of B2B sites that efficiently connect their audience with the information they need. In this section we focus on the core audience – different types of customer.

As far as customers are concerned, you must remember that your web site exists for one reason and one reason only – to help customers. The big question is 'how can my web site help my customers?'

A customer-orientated web site starts with customers and their needs. The site will not only fulfil basic customer needs, it may even delight customers by fully understanding and satisfying the different needs which different customers have. So ask customers! Try thinking about the types of services you can offer customers. Identify their key tasks and goals and make these options prominent. These may be services you offer already such as giving the status of an order, new added value services that don't cost much, or there may be new services that customers can operate themselves. Also ask customers what they think of your existing site. Ask them how you can improve your web site – what would they like to see there?

Rosenfeld and Morville (2002) suggest four stages of research that help achieve customer orientation:

1 Identify different audiences.
2 Rank importance of each to business.
3 List the three most important information needs of audience.
4 Ask representatives of each audience type to develop their own wish lists.

Customer orientation can create competitive advantage. Customer-orientated web sites are relatively rare compared to product-orientated web sites. Product-orientated web sites tend to show lots of products (or services) and their features. Benefits are buried, as are any attempts to identify customer needs. Product benefits are never matched to specific customer needs. These sites never ask 'How can I help my customer?'

Although we have said we want to provide content to appeal to a wide range of audiences, providing detailed content to all audiences may well be undesirable (since our messages to priority target segments may be diluted) or impractical (resources are limited). So we need to ask which key audiences should we concentrate resources on? A good starting point is to ask the question, 'Who is my ideal customer?'

E-MARKETING INSIGHT

Defining contexts of use

Nigel Bevan of usability specialists Serco refers to customer orientation in terms of contexts of use. He suggests designers should ask:

- Who are the important users?
- What is their purpose for accessing the site?

- How frequently will they visit the site?
- What experience and expertise do they have?
- What nationality are they? Can they read English?
- What type of information are they looking for?
- How will they want to use the information: read it on the screen, print it or download it?
- What type of browsers will they use [and at which screen resolutions]? How fast will their communication links be?
- How large a screen/window will they use, with how many colours?

(*Source*: Bevan 1999).

E-MARKETING EXCELLENCE

Customer orientation in practice

Figure 6.8 is an example of the principle of customer orientation in action. In the first edition of *eMarketing eXcellence*, we noted that retail site DIY.com is targeted at a range of users of DIY products, so it was designed around three zones: products, advice and inspiration. Experts who know what they want go straight to the product section and buy what they need. Less experienced users with queries on what to purchase can gain advice from an expert just as they would in store and novices may visit the inspiration zone which includes room mock-ups with lists of the products needed to create a particular look.

Usability testing and assessing web analytics has shown B&Q that most customers simply need to be connected with a product as quickly as possible. There is a prominent search box at the centre of the screen with a detailed directory list of product departments forming the main navigation below the search box. In the second edition we saw how products were in the navigation on the left, but today B&Q has exposed more products within each department on the home page. This helps findability (fewer clicks) and is also good for SEO since the product is linked and included within the home page which has the highest PageRank. Key user tasks are now available to the Advice and Services options which are available both above and below the fold and are more prominent deeper into the site (Figure 6.9). Finally, on the right of the screen, there is a promotional area, which is not given too much prominence, so as not to distract key journeys, but it will appeal to price sensitive shoppers as they scan the page.

An alternative approach is used by Guinness (www.guinness.com) who at the time of the first edition had three site zones '*like it, live it, love it*'. This has now transformed to: 'Knowing (education for students), Seeing (ads) and Doing (web store and downloads).

As well as customer segments, we also need to think about how the backgrounds of visitors to our site will vary. Visitors have different levels of familiarity with the Internet, your organization, your products and your site. Customer-orientated web sites are built to accommodate all of these different levels of **familiarity**.

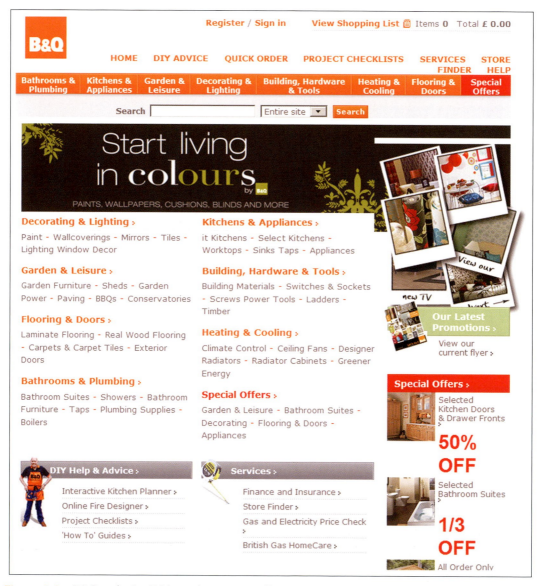

Figure 6.8   B&Q web site DIY.com home page illustrates customer orientation (www.diy.com)

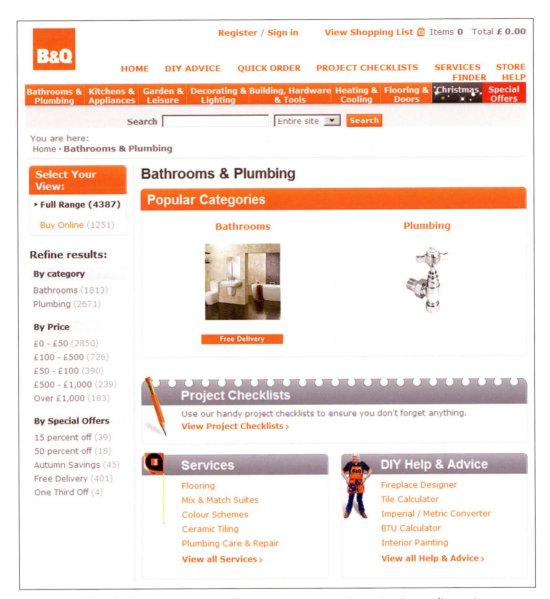

Figure 6.9   B&Q web site category page illustrates customer orientation (www.diy.com)

E-MARKETING INSIGHT

The four familiarities

Research by Forrester (Figure 6.10) suggests that users pass through different stages of familiarity and confidence as they use different Internet facilities. Site design should try to accommodate this by allowing for users with different levels of experience. Remember that thousands of people still use the Internet for the first time every day and it may be the first time they have visited your site – so they will be on your site, trying to find their feet.

We can identify other forms of familiarity that good sites take account of. Our 'four familiarities' are:

1 *Familiarity with the net.* See above.

2 *Familiarity with your organization.* For those who don't know, you need content to explain who you are, your OVP and a statement of credibility through 'About us' options and customer testimonials.

3 *Familiarity with your products.* Even existing customers may not know the full range of your product offering. Many companies have parts of pages or post-transaction pages to educate customers about the range of products.

4 *Familiarity with your site.* Site maps, Search and Help options are 'must have', not 'nice to have' options for a web site since you may lose potential customers if you cannot help them when they go astray.

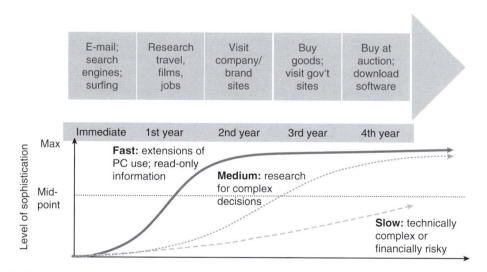

Figure 6.10   Stages of familiarity with the Internet. (*Source*: Forrester Technographics (www.forrester.com))

SECTION SUMMARY 6.4

Customer orientation

A customer-oriented site provides easy access to content and services tailored for a range of audiences. But resources for content development should be targeted at ideal customers.

Site design should allow for different levels of experience or familiarity amongst its audience including familiarity with the net, the organization, its products and its web site.

6.5   Dynamic design and personalization

The most important sound in the world is your own name. Remembering customer names and their needs is a personal thing. Web sites can get personal. Internet-based personalization delivers customized content and services for the individual either through web pages, e-mail or push-technology. In this section we are going to look at what **personalization** is and what its components are. This topic is also reviewed from a different perspective in Section 8.6 where the concepts of **customization, mass customization** and **individualization** are explained.

Today's marketers have a dream opportunity – to personalize their services, and web sites in particular. Web technology, combined with database technology, increase the marketer's memory so that any number of customers can be recognized, preferences remembered and served immediately. Cookies are the key to web personalization. When a new visitor arrives on a site, a **cookie** or small text file is placed on their computer which contains an identifier unique to them (it does not contain personal data as is commonly thought – this is securely stored in a database). When they return they are recognized by the cookie and a personal message is automatically displayed within the page template according to their profile. Although some users do delete their cookies, if they are openly used with the option to 'remember me', then can provide a seamless, personalized experience, of which Amazon is arguably still the best example. Remember sites are legally obliged to ask the visitor's permission to add cookies.

Personalization also helps to Sell, Serve, Speak and Sizzle:

- *Sell* – personalization can make it easier for customers to select their products. A customer of an online supermarket does not want to select a new shopping basket of goods each time they shop. Example: Tesco (www.tesco.com).
- *Serve* – a customer who uses an online travel booking service does not want to have to key in the same journey details if it is a common itinerary. Instead personalization enables them to save their itinerary. Example: Expedia (www.expedia.com).
- *Speak* – through personalization a customer can select the type of communications they want to receive from a company as part of permission marketing. For example, a customer may just want to hear about major product launches via e-mail, but not receive a weekly e-mail. Example: Amazon (www.amazon.co.uk).
- *Sizzle* – all of the above can help add value, strengthen the brand and develop the relationship. Example: Dulux (www.dulux.co.uk). The Dulux brand enables visitors to save colour swatches and products to a scrapbook or project area for later access.

Note though that we missed out Save, since web-based personalization tends to be expensive to create and maintain. A less-costly, e-mail-based approach may be best for many companies. Personalized e-mails can be pushed out to customers reminding them and helping them in many different ways.

Chartered Institute of Personnel and Development use a personalized home page container

This example shows that some relatively simple personalization approaches can be effective. The CIPD (www.cipd.co.uk) reserve part of their home page, known as a content container or portlet to deliver personalized messages to its visitor. For un-registered visitors, the absence of a cookie triggers a Welcome message (Figure 6.11). Return visitors receive a general campaign promotion, perhaps about a HR conference. Registered visitors and members are welcomed by name and receive micro-targeted messages such as recommended qualifications and training which are integrated with personalized e-mail, direct mail and phone communications.

But remember that personalization can create barriers since passwords and log-ins are required and easily forgotten. But they can be managed. This is where **cookies** work well if permission is sought during registration, but remember the legal requirements for using cookies. Cookies identify customers and provide a link to stored data about their preferences without the need for passwords.

E-mail or direct mail reminders of passwords and the site OVP can be used. You will also need personalized opt-in e-mail which offers an alternative route to keeping the dialogue alive.

OPTIONS FOR PERSONALIZATION

Personalization can occur through displaying different information depending on customer specific or dynamic environment variables. Examples, many of which are illustrated by Figure 6.11, include:

- *Customer or company name*. A site can be personal on a simple level by referring to returning customers by name (using cookies).
- *Date or time*. Updating the date or time on site using **JavaScript** can be used to highlight a dynamic, up-to-date online presence that is worth returning to.
- *Country*. Sites can identify the origin of a visitor based on their **IP address** and deliver content accordingly. IBM.com automatically **redirects** customers to their own country site. Amazon recommends a local site if a visitor is on .com.
- *Customer preferences*. Personalization of content on a web site can be set up by a customer clicking or selecting different types of content. This can be used to build data collected via registration forms, questionnaires, cookies and of course purchases.
- *Recommendation algorithms*. This approach often known as **collaborative filtering** uses automatic prediction (filtering) about the interests of a visitor by collecting preference information from different users. This is arguably the most effective personalization since it is unobtrusive; Amazon is the best known example since it gives recommendations of

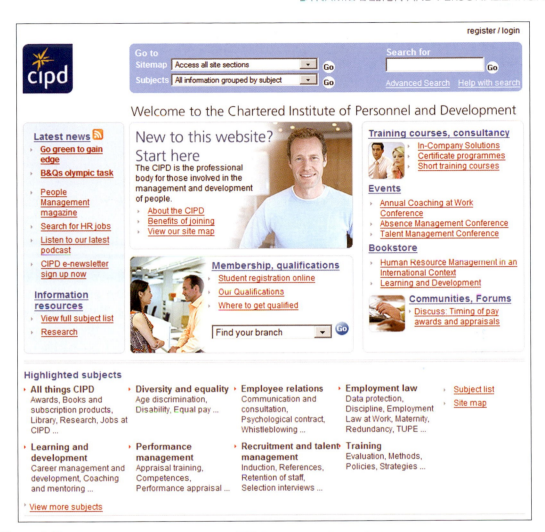

Figure 6.11   Personalization container on CIPD home page (www.cipd.co.uk)

books based on past purchases by customers with similar interests without requiring the user to register their preferences using techniques described in IEE (2003). The basic approach outlined in the paper is:

```
For each item in product catalog, I₁

    For each customer C who purchased I₁

        For each item I₂ purchased by customer C

            Record that a customer purchased I₁ and I₂

    For each item I₂

        Compute the similarity between I₁ and I₂
```

- *News and events*. Results, surveys or press releases can be automatically posted to the site.
- *Viral personalization*. Here a user interacts with a site and personalized video clips are delivered based on a lookup of keywords typed by visitors. Try it for this Burger King viral (www.subservientchicken.com). This approach was also used on the Mini Aveaword campaign where it was combined with e-mail to send a personalized video clip urging a friend to try the mini based on their geography, gender, job, hobbies, name and sexual preferences (straight or gay, etc.). This degree of personalization was both highly entertaining and effective – the word-of-mouth generated many additional sales during the campaign period.
- *Referrer string*. Content can potentially be personalized according to which site the visitor previously visited and in particular the keyphrase typed into a search engine, e.g. an insurer has used the type of insurance searched for to tailor messages for new visitors.
- *Location*. Internet phones enabled with WAP make it possible to send promotions to a customer as they pass a shop. Whether this is desirable is another matter!
- *Multivariate real-time, conversion optimized personalization*. Some systems use a combination of the variables above and then use a series of promotional containers to present the most relevant promotion which is predicted to have the highest clickthrough rate, conversion rate or average order value for an individual customer. The best known of these approaches is Omniture Touch Clarity (www.touchclarity.com), which is used by portals such as MSN to encourage subscription, travel companies like Lastminute.com for holiday products and banks such as HSBC to encourage product quotes. The power of such techniques is indicated by the trial on the Lastminute.com home page which increased home page sales by 200%!

Note however that personalization can be expensive to implement. It requires complex software and up-to-date databases. As such it is most commonly used by retailers and major media owners who hope to have frequent interactions with customers and can demonstrate the returns. However, we predict that lower cost personalization approaches will become widespread.

SECTION SUMMARY 6.5

Dynamic design and personalization

Personalization delivers customized services through web pages and e-mail and rich media-containers. Personalization can be triggered through several dynamic variables including: customer preferences, dates, events and locations. The jury is still out on the value of personalized web sites. It may work for some situations such as media sites, portals or complex e-tail catalogue sites. Remembering names shows respect. Recognizing customers and their preferences sows seeds of good relationships and better business. The database is vital to this.

6.6   Aesthetics

Aesthetics = Graphics + Colour + Style + Layout and Typography

As we noted at the start of this chapter, effective web site design includes both form and function. Form means the aesthetics created by the visual design and function means interaction, navigation and structure. In this section we're going to look at aesthetics – its components

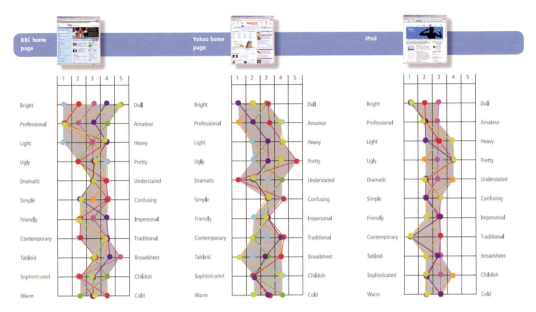

Figure 6.12 Emotional response testing example. *Source*: cScape (www.cscape.com)

and the constraints. A site with powerful aesthetic appeal can help communicate a brand's essential values. The use of graphics, colour, style, layout and typography create aesthetics. Together these create a personality for the site.

SITE PERSONALITY

Words we could use to describe site personality are just as for people: formal, fun or engaging, entertaining or professional and serious. These should be consistent with brand. Emotional response testing can be completed by comparing well-known sites in a category against existing or proposed site sections as part of user-centred design. Figure 6.12 shows the power of this technique.

How would you describe the character of your site? Is this how you want to be seen or positioned? Is it consistent with the target audience? What do they think? Have you asked your customers what they think?

Contrast Figure 6.13 and Figure 6.14 and think about how their personality and emotional response will be consistent with their audience. Note that since the first edition, the two sites have become more similar with less use of imagery on the Egg site and more on the Cisco site. This is part of a process that has been referred to as 'web site undesign'. Increased use of text at the expense of graphics has been driven by a wish to improve usability, accessibility and search engine optimization. However, with increased broadband usage, sites like Cisco are making more use of rich media in a hybrid design which has Flash elements in the main container on the home page and use of video and audio within its interaction network. Note how both sites use the right sidebar for their navigation. This is unconventional, but will have the benefit that promotions in the centre and left of screen will be viewed since this is where visitors naturally look.

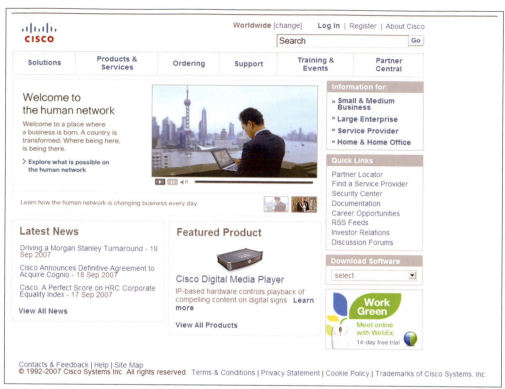

Figure 6.13   Cisco B2B site – networking products (www.cisco.com)

Figure 6.14   Egg B2C site – financial products (www.egg.com)

SITE STYLE

Some sites are information intensive and other sites are graphics intensive. **Information-intensive sites** may appear cluttered because of the amount of text blocks, but the intention is to make best use of screen real estate and project an image of information depth and value to the visitor. Retail sites often fall into this category. Tests by Amazon have shown that they generate best average order value with a design with many containers in left and right sidebars and with the option to scroll several times – there is simply more opportunity to connect a diverse audiences with relevant products and promotions as they scan and scroll. With **graphics-intensive sites** there is relatively little text; graphics and animations are used to create an impression. FMCG brand sites often use this approach with an introductory graphical screen or splash screen. Again contrast Figure 6.13 and Figure 6.14 and think about the extent to which they are information or graphics intensive.

WHAT ARE THE DESIGN CONSTRAINTS?

There are many design constraints or challenges under which web designers operate. Unfortunately the list of constraints is long and sometimes neglected, to disastrous effect:

1 *Modems and download time*. Although broadband access is growing rapidly, at the time of writing a significant proportion of home users in many countries still have a dial-up connection. Good designers optimize graphics for fast downloading and then test using a slow modem across phone lines. Remember the top sites download in less than a second. Also remember the eight second rule of thumb that shows the majority of initial visitors to a site will not hang around to wait for it to download if it takes longer than this.

PRACTICAL E-MARKETING TIP

Decreasing download times – does your site pass the four second rule

Research from Akamai (2006) shows that content needs to load rapidly – within four seconds otherwise site experience suffers and visitors will leave the site. The research also showed, however, that high product price/shipping costs and problems with shipping were both considered more important than speed. However, for sites perceived to have poor performance, many shoppers said they were less likely to visit the site again (64%) or buy from the e-retailer (62%).

These practical tips for designers developed by accessibility specialist Trenton Moss of Webcredible (Webcredible, 2004) show how approaches to coding pages can make a difference. So make sure your site designers optimize for speed, not simply focusing on visual design.

1 Lay out your pages with CSS (Cascading Style Sheets), not tables
2 Don't use images to display text

3 Call up decorative images through CSS

4 Use contextual selectors (use classes to format)

5 Use shorthand CSS properties

6 Minimize white space [within code], line returns and comment tags

7 Use relative call-ups

8 Remove unnecessary META tags and META content

9 Put CSS and JavaScript into external documents

10 Use / at the end of directory links.

2 *Screen resolution.* Today a relatively small proportion of users have lower screen resolutions of 640 × 480 or 800 + 600 pixels; the majority have 1024 + 768 pixels or greater. But if designers use resolutions much greater than the average user, the screens may be difficult to read for the majority. **Fluid designs** may be best for retail sites where the design maximizes the space on the screen – fitting more above the fold on higher screen resolutions. However designers of brand sites often prefer **fixed designs** where they have more control over the visuals. Some site designs such as Kelkoo give users the choice.

3 *Number of colours.* Some users have monitors capable of displaying 16 million colours giving photo-realism while others may only have the PC to set up to display 256 colours.

4 *Browsers.* Different types of **web browsers** such as Microsoft Internet Explorer, Mozilla Firefox and Apple Safari and different versions of browsers such as version 6.0 or 7.0 may display graphics or text slightly differently. An e-commerce site tested under one browser may fail completely under another. Make sure your designers test their designs against different versions of web browsers using a tool like Browsercam (www.browsercam.com). Many don't but should!

5 *Plug-ins and download time.* If the site requires **plug-ins** that the user doesn't have you will be cutting down the size of your audience by the number of people who are unable or unprepared to download these plug-ins. Only use standard plug-ins such as Macromedia Flash or Windows Media Player which are pre-installed on PCs.

6 *Font sizes.* Choosing large fonts on some sites causes unsightly overlap between the different design elements. The facility for the user to change font size is required for accessibility, so test tolerance of a design for text resizing.

7 *Platform.* Sites are increasingly viewed via mobile phones or handheld devices like the Play Station Plus. Different stylesheets can be provided for different platforms or view modes such as printing or without images. But effectively, web pages have to be repurposed for mobile use.

As a result of these constraints, design of web sites is a constant compromise between what looks visually appealing and modern and what works for the older browsers, with slower modems, i.e. the *lowest common denominator*.

What are the implications of all these constraints? Although many professional site designers will work within these constraints, it is best to be up front about target platforms you are targeting. The briefing or requirements specification should specify the target environments such as screen resolutions, browsers and platforms.

VISUAL DESIGN

As the e-marketing insight box below shows, first impressions are important whether it's meeting in the real world or via a web site. The visual design of a site is important to establishing trust and sets the tone for the future experience.

The biggest error with visual design is getting the balance wrong. Designers need to create a balanced visual design which is visually appealing, but also works for accessibility, usability, persuasion and branding! One way to help achieve this is to use different parts of the screen to achieve these elements. It used to be said by Jakob Nielsen himself that 'Flash is 99% bad, but it is increasingly common to use Flash elements to engage an audience and to show the brand experience'. Take a look at sites from chocolate brand www.divinechocolate.com, Business software companies like www.salesforce.com or www.microstrategy.com which use a Flash banner, or PR company Ketchum (www.ketchum.com) which has an overlay of a team member literally engaging the audience. However, using a site which is 100% Flash is still rarely a good idea since there is little content for search engines to crawl except for niche entertainment sites such as games.

COLOUR

The combination of colours used is important since they create a feeling about the site and brand. Colour schemes need to be right, i.e.

- Right for a personality which fits the target audience
- Right for a colour scheme that fits the brand
- Right for usability and accessibility.

Different colour temperatures evoke different feelings between warm reds and oranges and cold blues and greens which can be helpful to give a more professional look. Of course, each colour has a different meaning or symbolism. For example, in western cultures, red is vibrant, passionate indicating love and danger while blue contrasts and indicates reliability. But you need to be careful about local interpretation. See http://www.princetonol.com/groups/iad/lessons/middle/color2.htm for examples of colour symbolism in different cultures.

Complementary colours which are opposite each other on the colour wheel need to be used carefully and may cause problems with accessibility. The primary complementary colours are: red and green; blue and orange; and yellow and purple. Contrasting colours which are not necessarily opposite each other on the colour wheel tend to produce a vivid (if not garish) effect. When considering text on a background colour, for accessibility, high contrast is positive and tinted background boxes are also useful for highlighting content you want visitors to read such as a call-to-action. The Unilever corporate site (www.unilever.com) shows how a dominant colour can be used in each site section and this site also makes use of contrast.

Another issue to consider is white space (or background tints). White space can increase the visual appeal of a page and increase usability. However, it is again a balance since the site visitor will need to scroll down more for content.

But whatever colour scheme you use, you need to make sure it's tested for accessibility, for example through colour blindness simulators such as http://www.etre.com/tools/colourblind-simulator/ which tests for the three types of colour blindness (Protanopia, Deuteranopia, Tritanopia).

E-MARKETING INSIGHT

How long do you have to make an impact?

Research suggests visitors can decide ultra-fast on whether they like a site, not in two seconds, but 50 milliseconds (that's 0.05 of a second). Summarizing the research by Gitte Lindgaard (Lindgaard *et al.*, 2006) of Carleton University in Ottawa, published in the *Journal of Behaviour and Information Technology*, says:

> *'The lasting effect of first impressions is known to psychologists as the 'halo effect': if you can snare people with an attractive design, they are more likely to overlook other minor faults with the site, and may rate its actual content more favourably.*
>
> *This is because of "cognitive bias", People enjoy being right, so continuing to use a website that gave a good first impression helps to "prove" to themselves that they made a good initial decision'.*

The research by Lindgaard *et al.* (2006) presented volunteers with a glimpse of web pages previously rated as being either easy on the eye or particularly jarring, and asked them to rate the websites on a sliding scale of visual appeal.

Even though the images flashed up for just 50 milliseconds, roughly the duration of a single frame of standard television footage, their verdicts tallied well with judgements made after a longer review.

Further research by Haynes and Zambonini (2007) has shown a curve of visitors to museum sites that shows a peak (of visitors clicking) at about 2–3 seconds after page load. So, this is a good indication of how long you have to get your message across. Based on this, a boxing analogy seems apt – you need to achieve a one-two punch. First you need a high impact home page, which is relatively simple, but then follow-up with a knockout punch on a second-level page or further down the main page which is the detailed proposition which prompts conversion through the range of benefits, features and testimonials that your offer is so good it will convince visitors to buy.

Figure 6.15 shows how DVD Rental company Lovefilm (www.lovefilm) uses a similar approach with a relatively simple message greeting visitors at the top of the page and encouraging trial, but with more details further down the page or via a main navigation menu option to 'Learn more'. This is another great example of how to develop a strong OVP for an online service. It is backed up by extensive multivariate testing of the design and messaging which works best.

TYPOGRAPHY

The power of typography in adding to the visual appeal and persuasive power of a website is often underestimated. Here are some practical tips to consider.

PRACTICAL E-MARKETING TIP

Typography do's and don'ts

Here is an example of some general traps to avoid when using fonts.

The XYZ Company offer you the opportunity to take part in our online competition exclusively for customers who have made several purchases over the last year.

E-consultancy (2007) recommends these approaches to typography best practice.

1 Use a consistent typography throughout a site. This will typically be enforced through cascading stylesheets.

2 Limit the use of different font types and sizes.

3 San-serif font styles such as Arial or Verdana tend to work best on the web, as they look sharper on the screen and are therefore easier to scan and read (unlike print where the reverse is true). Sans-serif is by far the most popular approach online. But a visit to the *New York Times* (NYT.com) shows that the use of serifed fonts can make the site appear more distinguished – it affects the site personality.

4 Left justified text works best in web browsers and is best for legibility.

5 The widespread use of images for rendering text in headlines and navigation is today generally discouraged for accessibility and search engine optimization reasons (search engines read text, not images), but exceptions includes text used in branding, promotions and certain sites where an immersive experience is required.

6 Where images are used for text captions, alternative text commonly known as 'alt tags' should be provided for accessibility reasons.

7 Create separate design requirements and a test schedule for the rendering of fonts in different browsers.

Figure 6.15   Lovefilm site (www.lovefilm.com)

CHECKLIST FOR EXCELLENCE IN WEB TYPOGRAPHY

☑ **1** Never use underline in body text as a reader will think it's a hyperlink.

☑ **2** Avoid extensive use of italics as it is difficult to read on screen, but they can add variety.

☑ **3** Agree a standard for capitalization of headlines and link text. Generally, sentence case: 'Amazing new product released' is best since it is most scannable. Title case 'Amazing New Product Released' and all caps is ugly (and more difficult for readers to scan). However, all caps can be attention grabbing if selectively used.

☑ **4** Headlines longer than three or four words may work best for SEO purposes, so ensure font type size is not too large to support this or allow the design to support wrapping or sub-headlines.

☑ **5** Remember that many web browser users will increase their type sizes, so check that the design renders gracefully as type is enlarged (at least by a small amount).

☑ **6** The difference between heading point sizes has a distinctive effective on design. Use a small difference between them for a smooth effect and a large difference for a more distinct design.

☑ 7 Where possible, avoid pages where the text content stretches across the full width of the browser, especially in fluid layout designs. Splitting the content into columns will vastly increase readability and is more in line with how people read articles and content in newspapers and magazines

☑ 8 Standard fonts should be specified in the stylesheet(s), which allows a designer/developer to specify the font order in which the web browser should try and render the size. Using CSS also allows for simple and quick site-wide changes to the fonts displayed.

☑ 9 sIFR (or Scalable Inman Flash Replacement) is available for implementing non-standard fonts in site headings. sIFR (http://www.mikeindustries.com/sifr/) is an SEO friendly approach for using more imaginative typography on sites. For headings which are important for SEO and the main application of sIFR, the text is still specified as <h1>, <h2>, etc.

SECTION SUMMARY 6.6

Aesthetics

Aesthetics comprises graphics, colour, style and personality. Many web sites indulge in over-elaborate graphics and ignore their audiences' capability, and patience, to view them. Web designers must consider the constraints of variable modems, screen resolutions, colour displays, browsers and of course audiences. Many designers don't like designing for the lowest common denominator, but it does give you the widest audience.

6.7 Page design

In this section we will explore the components of good page layout. Page layouts are implemented within **Content Management Systems** as **page templates**. Typically the design will be more effective if there is a different page template for different site sections which have different objectives. But it is necessary for different layouts to be consistent, so following throughout a website for consistency are usually:

- Company name and logo for identity (this should link to homepage).
- Menu (and submenus) for navigation.
- Footer for reference to copyright and privacy information (usually in small text).
- Page title for content, e.g. product information.

Using a capable CMS is essential to the consistency and management of any large site since it will enable **content owners** in different parts of the organization to update the content they are responsible for. Some good open source CMSs are now available such as Plone (www.plone.org) which is used for the page templates for Dave Chaffey's e-marketing portal (www.davechaffey.com) making it easy to add new articles and news items.

A good page template design will achieve:

- An aesthetic, visually pleasing layout
- Clear emphasis of different content types
- Visual hierarchy showing relative importance of different content through size
- Prioritization of marketing messages and calls-to-action for different audiences and products for persuasion purposes
- Clear navigation options to a range of content, services and visitor engagement devices.

A mistake often made is to use a symmetrical design in which page elements don't stand out, instead, **persuasive design** advocates that users should be guided on relevant paths by larger page elements. A good rule of thumb is to achieve 'Focus on Five' key areas of screen (or 6 or 7) as shown by the design of Figures 6.13 and 6.14.

Wireframes are used by web designers to indicate the eventual layout for web page templates by showing where navigation elements and different types of content will appear on the page. The example wireframe in Figure 6.16 shows that the wireframe is so called

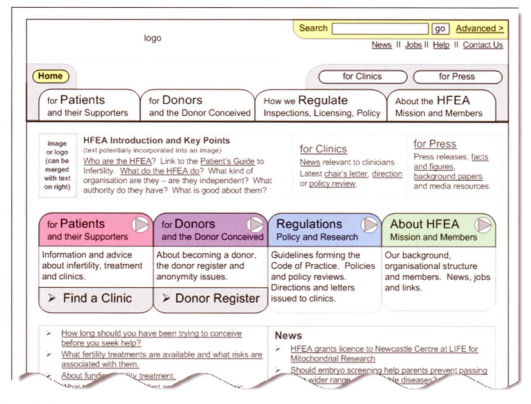

Figure 6.16   Example wireframe. *Source*: © Bunnyfoot 2007 (www.bunnyfoot.com). With client permission. This and other examples are extracts from a full user-centred design project that Bunnyfoot performed with the HFEA (www.hfea.gov.uk) in 2006

because it just consists of an outline of the page with the 'wires' of content separating different areas of content or navigation shown by white space. Wireframes are essential for agencies and clients to discuss the way a web site will be laid out without getting distracted by colour, style or messaging issues which should be covered separately as a creative planning activity.

Wodtke (2002) describes a wireframe (sometimes known as a schematic) as:

> *'a basic outline of an individual page, drawn to indicate the elements of a page, their relationships, and their relative importance'.*

As well as the position of navigation, wireframes should also consider announcements or special offers, which can be more effective if they occupy a consistent position on screen. Examples include: links to product and service information; special offers or promotions; incentives to register; contact phone numbers; company news and PR.

The limited space on a page requires: concise writing (more so than brochures); chunking or breaking text into units of five to six lines at most; use of lists with headline text in a larger font; generally never including too much on a single page. The art of writing succinctly for the web is addressed in Section 6.8 on copy writing.

E-MARKETING INSIGHT

Users spend most of their time on other sites

Jakob Nielsen says:

> *'Users spend most of their time on other sites. This means that users prefer your site to work the same way as all the other sites they already know . . . Think Yahoo and Amazon. Think "shopping cart" and the silly little icon. Think blue text links' (Nielsen 2000b).*

Web site designers face a difficult challenge in that they want their site to be memorable and differentiated from competitors. On the other hand, for ease of use, standardization of web features that users are familiar with is desirable. Think about the merit of these features of standardization:

- Widely used standards for labels such as Home, Main page, Search, Find, Browse, FAQ, Help, About us and Contact us.
- Logo top left, hyperlink to home pages.
- Main menu left margin or at top.
- Signposts of content at top or top left of page.
- Don't use non-standard text hyperlinks e.g. non-underlined links.

Using eyetracking to improve page layout design

According to Lucy Carruthers, usability consultant at Foviance (www.foviance.com), the benefits of eyetracking are as follows:

> *'Usability evaluations typically involve think-aloud protocols – whereby users describe their thoughts and actions as they carry out a set of tasks. This gives the facilitator a good view of the reasoning and driving factors behind the participant's actions.*
>
> *However, some types of behaviours are difficult to measure efficiently with think-aloud alone because participants may not be able to verbalize part of their thought processes and/or because some behaviours never reach consciousness.*
>
> *With eye tracking, however, we can provide insights into web design based on rigorous quantitative measures that are not possible using more traditional usability techniques'.*

The heatmap example in Figure 6.17 show that the location of headings and content pods will influence where people look. You can also see that the first part of headings and paragraphs are particularly important as visitors scan the page.

Bear in mind when evaluating a page template that eyetracking studies of gaze trails typically show that visitors eyes follow this path:

- Start in the centre
- Move to top left
- Move to top centre
- Move down the right column or navigation if present
- Move to the bottom of the page.

However, these general patterns are influenced by the layout.

Page design

Consistent layout is important. Key messages, menus, links, page size and frames versus tables all need to be considered carefully for effective web use.

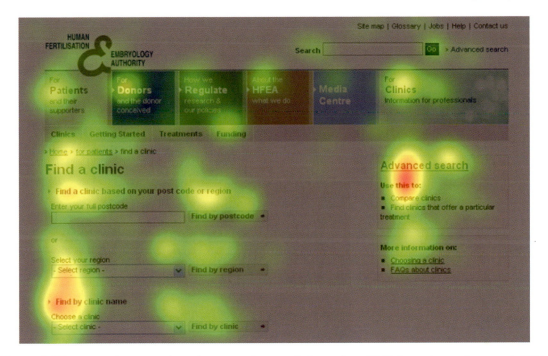

Figure 6.17   Example eyetracking heatmap *Source*: © Bunnyfoot 2007 (www.bunnyfoot.com). With client permission. This and other examples are extracts from a full user-centred design project that Bunnyfoot performed with the HFEA (www.hfea.gov.uk) in 2006

6.8   Copywriting

Copywriting for the web is an evolving art form, but many of the rules for good copywriting are as for any media. This section explores the basic rules.

Possibly the most important rule is don't assume your visitors have full knowledge of your company, its products and services. Remember the four familiarities described in Section 6.4. So, don't use internal jargon about products, services or departments and avoid indecipherable acronyms!

So what should you do? How should you write copy for your web site? A simple mnemonic for web copywriting is CRABS; aim for Chunking, Relevance, Accuracy, Brevity and Scannability.

Chunking, Brevity and Scannability go together. Many visitors briefly scan pages looking for headlines, followed by short, brief, digestible chunky paragraphs of five or six lines maximum which can be hyperlinked to further detail for those that want to 'drill down' for more information. Other visitors scan, move on and quickly find what they need elsewhere on the site. Section 6.9 on structure and navigation explores this in more detail.

In addition to chunky, brief and scannable, the copy must be relevant and useful to the target audience. This is where 'content is king' becomes 'context is king' – relevant information available at the right time in the right place. The copy must satisfy their needs and not yours, i.e. start with benefits instead of features. You can create benefits out of features by adding the three magic words: 'which means that . . .' after a feature.

Remember that you are copywriting not only for your human audience, but also the search engine spiders or robots which read (index) the words you use in your copy. So words used should include keyphrases that users are likely to search on within search engines (see Chapter 7 on search engine optimization).

And as with any genuinely good writing, it must be accurate to win credibility and loyalty in the long term. Don't promise what you cannot deliver. Do not cheat customers. It kills repeat business as well as new, referred business.

So, use CRABS (chunky, relevant, accurate, brief and scannable) to write good web copy. And remember, don't leave the best until last because, first, readers who scan will miss it, and, second, some readers won't scroll.

You should also check how persuasive your copy is against Cialdini's Six 'Weapons of Influence' which we referenced in Chapter 4.

And last but not least – don't forget nomenclature, or names, used for headings and sign-posting. Different nametags and signposts can give a very different feeling. Eyetracking research (www.poynter.org) suggests that on the web, customers' eyes are drawn first to the headings rather than the graphics. Test different headings to see which give the best **clickthrough**.

E-MARKETING INSIGHT

Gerry McGovern's top ten rules of copywriting

These are ten copywriting rules from Gerry McGovern (www.gerrymcgovern.com). As you read through these, think about whether these rules apply for other media and also whether your organization achieves them on your web site.

1 *Be honest*. Paper never refused ink. Web sites never refused hype. If you can't deliver within twenty-four hours, then don't promise to.

2 *Be simple, clear and precise*. Time is the scarcest resource, so never use five sentences when one will do. Avoid jargon. People are confused enough today.

3 *State your offer clearly*. What exactly is it that you sell?

4 *Tell them about your products' limitations*.

5 *Have a clear call to action*. If they like what you have to offer how do they go about buying it?

6 *Tell them quickly if they're not a customer you can supply*. There's nothing I find more frustrating than finding out at the last moment that they can't deliver.

7 *Edit! Edit! Edit*! There has never been an article that cannot be made shorter.

8 *Give them detail*. If they feel like finding out more about a particular product feature, then give them that opportunity. (That's what hypertext is for!)

9 *Write for the web.* Avoid the customer having to download Word documents, Powerpoints or PDFs unless offered as an alternative for convenience. (Note that Google and other search engines do now index these documents.)

10 *Leave it at nine!* If you want to create a 'Ten Rules' but can only find nine, leave it at nine.

BEST PRACTICE E-MARKETING TIP

A/B and multivariate testing

Your creative experience and skill in copywriting will only take you so far. For key pages, such as the home page and landing pages you should trial different versions of pages with different copy, different visuals and different calls-to-action using **A/B testing** to determine which best achieves your goals of conversion or average order value. **Multivariate testing** enables simultaneous testing pages for all combinations and variations of page elements that are being tested. These enable selection of the most effective combination of design elements to achieve the desired goal. The Lovefilm home page (www.lovefilm.com) for example, was optimized using this technique using a system known as Maxymiser (www.maxymiser.com) and Google has it's own page optimization tool (http://services.google.com/websiteoptimizer) for landing pages related to AdWords campaigns.

SECTION SUMMARY 6.8

Copywriting

Copywriting for web sites is different to brochures and mail shots – think CRABS – chunky, relevant, accurate and brief. Write for scannability and watch the detail – even words used in signposts create a different feel or personality to the site.

6.9   Navigation and structure

Ease of use = Structure + Navigation + Page layout + Interaction

Ease of use is number two of the key factors that make customers return to web sites. To achieve ease of use we need to structure our site so that users can easily navigate. **Navigation** describes how users move from one page to the next using navigational tools such as menus and hyperlinks. We also need a suitable page layout that makes it easy for visitors to find information on the page and the right types and amounts of interactivity, as described in separate sections.

This section examines structure and navigation to ensure that first, all sections of your web site are easily accessible, and second, visitors enjoy the satisfying experience of finding what they want.

SITE STRUCTURE

Web site **structure** is the big picture of how content is grouped and how different pages relate to others. Without a planned structure, a site can soon end up as a 'spaghetti site'. This may leave visitors dazed, disorientated, confused and frustrated. If they cannot achieve **flow control**, they may not return.

A planned site structure with clear hierarchies will allow the user to build up a 'mental map' of the site. As we will see later, this can be reinforced by clear sign-posting and labelling.

There is a formal process that professional site designers use to create an effective structure known as an **information architecture**. Rosenfeld and Morville (2002) point out the importance of designing an information architecture when they say:

> '*It is important to recognize that every information system, be it a book or an intranet, has an information architecture. "Well developed" is the key here, as most sites don't have a planned information architecture at all. They are analogous to buildings that weren't architected in advance*'.

They describe an information architecture as:

1 '*The combination of organization, labelling and navigation schemes within an information system.*
2 *The structural design of an information space to facilitate task completion and intuitive access to content.*
3 *The art and science of structuring and classifying web sites and intranets to help people find and manage information.*
4 *An emerging discipline and community of practice focused on bring principles of design and architecture to the digital landscape*'.

Rosenfeld and Morville (2002)

Creating an information architecture requires specialist techniques. For example **card sorting** or **web classification** categorize web objects (i.e. documents and applications) in order to facilitate user task completion or information goals. **Blueprints** are then produced which show the relationships between pages and other content components, and can be used to portray organization, navigation and labelling systems. They are often thought of, and referred to, as site maps or site structure diagrams and have much in common with these, except that they are used as a design device clearly showing grouping of information and linkages between pages, rather than a page on the web site used to assist navigation.

The depth of the site is one aspect of creating an information architecture. This is important since it will determine the number of clicks a user has to make to find the information they need. The balance is between shallow and deep.

Which of Figure 6.18 (a) or (b) would you say is best? Most would agree that a shallow site structure is best since it takes fewer clicks for the customer to find the information they

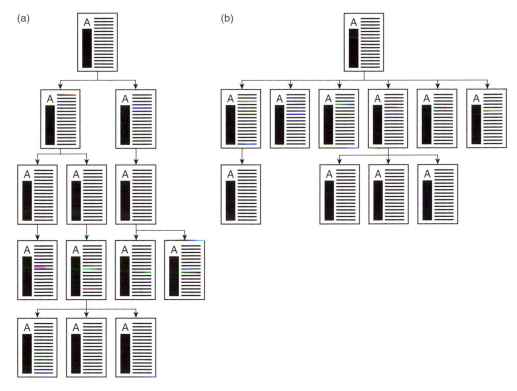

Figure 6.18   Alternative site structures: (a) deep, (b) shallow

need. A good rule of thumb is that, even for a large site, **three clicks** should be sufficient to enable the user to find their area of interest. Placing an order should never be more than three clicks away. How deep is your site?

However, site design is an art, not a science. If you selected the deep structure you will have had your reasons – the user has more simple choices at each stage in comparison with the shallow structure. In fact, the correct answer is probably a compromise between the two!

ACHIEVING FLOW

Good web designers try to enable 'flow'. Flow is a concept that describes the degree of control or power a consumer has over the site. If customers can easily find the information they want through clicking on menu options and graphics they will feel in control and this will be an enjoyable experience. We can use buttons and hyperlinks within copy to help achieve flow, but this is often neglected.

Site designers need to provide a choice for site visitors in browse mode or search mode. Many retail sites now use **faceted navigation** such as that shown in Figure 6.9 where the number of options in each category or sub-category are shown. Retail sites also invest in **search analytics** to assess and improve the conversion rates from searches to sale. They will assess, for example, how many searches result in zero results following different types of product searches.

NAVIGATION RULES

Here are three navigation rules for a navigational template that is used throughout the site:

1 *Keep it simple*. Not too many buttons. Psychologists who have analyzed the behaviour of computer users in labs say the magic number is seven (or fewer). Any more than seven and the user will find it difficult to choose. Seven or less keeps it simple. You can use nesting or pop-up menus to avoid the need for too many menus or too many menu items. Simplicity is necessary to avoid confusing the user.

2 *Be consistent*. Consistency is helpful since we want to avoid a user seeing different menus and page layouts as they move around the site. For example, the menu structures for customer support should be similar to those for when browsing product information.

3 *Signposts*. Signposts help visitors by telling them where they are within the web site.

Cater for customers at different stages of the buying process – some want to see more, some want to try a sample and some want to buy right now. So 'See, Try, Buy' options can help. These can be presented in different formats – particularly when catering for customers who prefer to receive information in different formats e.g. video (demonstration), text (often a PDF article) or actually speaking to a human (call-back technology). We also need to clearly label the different folders or directories on the site so they act as a reference point for describing particular types of content on the site. A **URL strategy** specifies how different types of content will be placed in different folders.

A further example is where site owners have to make a decision how to refer to content in different countries – either in the form of sub-domain:

http://<country-name><company-name>.com

or the more common

http://www.<companyname>com.com/<country-name>.

E-MARKETING INSIGHT

Jakob Nielsen on navigation

Nielsen (2000c) suggests that the designer of navigation systems should consider the following information that a site user wants to know:

- *Where am I?* The user needs to know where they are on the site and this can be indicated by highlighting the current location and clear titling of pages. This is *context. Consistency* of menu locations on different pages is also required to aid cognition. Users also need to know where they are on the web. This can be indicated by a logo, which by convention is at the top or top left of a site.

- *Where have I been?* This is difficult to indicate on a site, but for task-oriented activities such as purchasing a product it can show the user that they are at the nth stage of an operation such as making a purchase.

- *Where do I want to go?* This is the main navigation system which gives options for future functions.

NAVIGATION TYPES

Most web sites have several types of navigation. These include:

- *Global navigation* – These are site-wide navigation schemes. Examples for a B2B site are: Products, Solutions, Clients, Support. They often occur at the top or bottom of a site, but may occur down the side.
- *Local navigation* – More detailed navigation to find elements in an immediate area – for example, Products may be broken down further.
- *Contextual navigation* – Navigation specific to a page or group of pages which may be in the body copy or in slots such as Related products.
- *Breadcrumbs* – Used to indicate where the visitor is on the site. For an example see: http://www.davechaffey.com/E-marketing. As you navigate around this site you will see, just below the top menu, a list of pages showing where you are and allowing you to easily visit a higher point in the structure. These are so named from the trail of breadcrumbs Hansel and Gretel left in the forest to go back to their house.

On a customer-facing web site, there are a number of alternative approaches to navigation. The most important are:

- Product-based
- Organization-structure based
- Visit-based: first time/repeat visitor
- Task-based or need related
- Relationship-based: customer/non-customer
- Customer type based
- Company need
  - calls-to-action
  - campaign related
  - branding.

How many of these are appropriate to your web site? How many are you missing? Note that many companies only adopt some of these, with the product-centric or organization structure common. Often key navigation approaches may be missed such as task, relationship or customer type-based. It is always a balance between accommodating a range of audience needs and avoiding confusing visitors through too many navigation options.

E-MARKETING EXCELLENCE

Navigation at the BBC

The BBC site (www.bbc.co.uk) is a great example of a site that achieves consistency, simplicity and context and has a clear URL strategy. Visit the site and navigate around different areas such as News (www.bbc.co.uk/news), Sport (www.bbc.co.uk/sport), Football (www.bbc.co.uk/sport/football) and Radio 1 (www.bbc.co.uk/radio1). You will see that there is clear signposting at the top of each page, which part of the site you are on and there are changes in colour and style associated with each part of the site. You will also notice that the site has a well thought through information architecture with each section having a clear URL.

SECTION SUMMARY 6.9

Navigation and structure

So navigation and structure can in themselves satisfy or dissatisfy customers. You need a strong information architecture. Well thought through navigation options are needed to promote flow experiences. Keep the page layout simple, consistent and clearly signposted, and you're on your way to success.

6.10 Interaction

Interaction helps to engage web site visitors by giving them some two-way communications plus greater involvement and control over their web experience. This section explores the types and benefits of interactions.

DIFFERENT TYPES OF INTERACTION

We can identify several basic interactive mechanisms:

- A simple mouse click on an image or an arrow to find more information or to look at the next item in a sequence (mouse event).
- Placing the mouse over a text menu option may give feedback by changing the colour of the text (mouse rollover).
- Selection from drop-down boxes.
- Drag and drop.
- Typing requirements into a box and then searching through a catalogue.
- Slider, same choice: small, medium or large.

Remember also that there are many other types of interactions that add value to the user experience such as simulations, calculators, crosswords, quizzes, helpful information and turbine optimizers (Chapter 1).

Good interactions reinforce brand values – like Fedex's delivery update service. In addition to all of these automated interactions, web sites can also have real staff interaction, e.g. where

call-back technology invites a customer to request phone contact, **live chat sessions** or **co-browsing** involving a real-time web dialogue.

Now consider how interactions and two-way communications can help move a customer through several stages of the buying process, which was introduced in Chapter 4.

1 *Learning*. Help customers learn about you – your company, your products, features and their benefits. Interaction helps a customer to learn because involvement deepens the learning process. Interactive techniques include:

- Simulations or interactive demonstrations of products, e.g. the National Instruments Product advisor (www.ni.com/advisor).
- Animations that explain different features or benefits of a product (e.g. www.nike.com).
- Tailoring – by product category or segment, e.g. Dell asks users to state whether they are a small, medium or large company. The site tailors itself accordingly (www.dell.com).
- Selection choice – online toy e-tailers allow selection by age of child, by type of toy and by brand (for example, www.fisherprice.com).
- Downloads of detailed technical sheets often presented as **PDF** files, e.g. Business-to-business resources libraries with whitepapers to support different people involved in the buying decision for a complex product.
- Testimonials or case studies, e.g. www.accenture.com has client successes for each of its offerings.
- 'E-mail a friend' facility. This can be used to alert a colleague or make them aware of a product or service.

2 *Deciding*. There are many kinds of interactions that can help customers to choose your product. Here's a small selection:

- An **interactive product selector** or sales adviser (Figure 6.19). This will help customers choose between different options if it is well-designed.
- **Call-back facility**. Human advice may be helpful in guiding the user through selection. To achieve this, some sites include call-back facilities where a customer types in their name and phone number and specifies a time when the company should ring back.
- **Chat facility**. Some companies also include chat facilities where a human customer service representative types an immediate response to the customers' queries. This approach is more efficient than bouncing e-mails between suppliers and customers over a long period. LivePerson (www.liveperson.com) illustrates this type of interaction. Co-browsing or screen-sharing can also help.
- **On-site search engines**. These help customers find what they're looking for quickly. They are popular features and some companies have improved conversion to sale greatly by improving the clarity of the results they return. Site maps are a related feature.
- **'E-mail a friend' facility**. This can be used to alert a colleague or friend or to help accelerate a shared decision on a purchase within an organization.

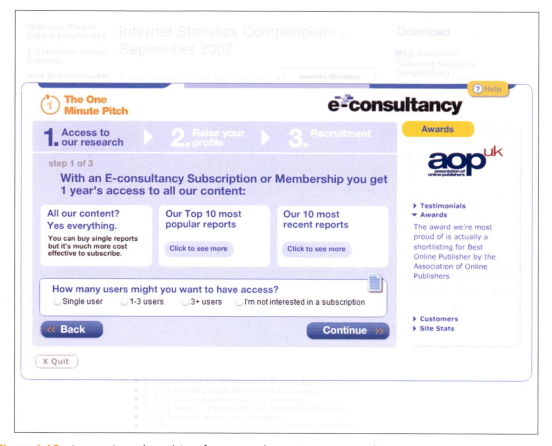

Figure 6.19 Interactive sales adviser for e-consultancy (www.e-consultancy.com)

Some e-tailers such as Lands' End (www.landsend.com) use a range of communications techniques to interact with the customer, including e-mail, call-back and chat (Lands' End live) – all helping the customer to decide.

Customer rating systems. Incorporating star ratings and comments can add authenticity to a site and help increase conversion rates. Additional, fresh content can also help with SEO. See Superbreak (www.superbreak.com) for an example.

3 *Buying*. Leading the customer through the purchase can help break down reluctance to buy online or **shopping cart abandonment** as shown by Figure 6.3. Established e-tailers use techniques such as:

- Leading the customer through the purchase in clearly numbered stages.
- Minimizing the number of stages.
- Offering an incentive to 'buy now'.
- Understanding purchasing objections and information needs at each stage of the checkout process and providing appropriate information within the checkout area.
- Location selection tool – find your nearest dealer by typing in a postal or ZIP code.
- Voucher systems that are printed out on a customer's printer, then redeemed in store.

- Including a phone number on site to encourage purchase by phone where the customer prefers this.
- Detailed content to reassure about security and privacy.

This remains an important, but hugely challenging, area despite the use of techniques such as usability analysis and web analytics.

4 *After-sales support.* After-sales support techniques for interactive support include:

- Searchable FAQs – easyJet (www.easyJet.com) have worked at improving their FAQs by analyzing online and offline customer service queries and then presenting FAQs when the customer selects the 'Contact us' option.
- Interactive support tools – Epson allow customers to diagnose their problems with printers by prompting them to select their problem from pre-configured choices and then suggesting solutions (www.epson.co.uk/support).
- Customer feedback – After customers have used the interactive support tool they have the option of interacting via a questionnaire on how useful the support was.
- The methods used for product selection, namely call-back, chat or community discussion forums, can also be used. Some companies such as Cisco have found that customers can help solve other customers' problems.

Increasingly interaction such as product selectors (Figure 2.3) is delivered using a **Rich Internet Application (RIA)** using techniques such as **Ajax** (Asynchronous Javascript and XML) and/or Flash. While these applications can provide a compelling customer experience, care has to be taken with respect to search engine optimization (SEO) since the search engines may not index and link to specific product pages as readily.

Finally, all the interaction techniques we have reviewed in this section can also be viewed as a means of collecting marketing research. Web stats or web logs from your site reveal customer preferences, responses and problems.

E-MARKETING EXCELLENCE

Using interactions for research

Consider these examples of how interactions can be used to gather customer intelligence:

- *Customer preferences* – For example, Dell can see the proportion of users clicking on 'small, medium and large' customers' to gain an appreciation of the role of the Internet in reaching these segments.
- *Responses to promotions* – When the Carphone Warehouse analyzes response to online vouchers they can analyze regional differences in use of the Internet and response to promotion.
- *Customer problems* – Epson can use information from its interactive support tool to find out the type of problems customers experience with products and feed this information through into both customer service and new product development.

SECTION SUMMARY 6.10

Interaction

Appropriate interactions add satisfaction, value and flow to the web site. They help customers to learn about features and benefits, choose products and enjoy better after-sales service. It's worth considering!

CHAPTER SUMMARY

1 Site design should be determined by clear marketing objectives. Key concepts for an effective design are usability, accessibility and persuasion.

2 Web site design needs to be integrated with other marketing activities, in particular outbound and inbound communications, buying modes and databases.

3 Each site should have a clear online value proposition (OVP) that differentiates the site from competitors, and defines services not available in the real world which positively impact the customer's lives. The OVP should be communicated offline, online and on the site itself and should be delivered.

4 Customer orientation involves grouping access to content and services that meet the needs of an audience made up of different stakeholders and customer segments with different familiarity with the net, the organization, its services and its site.

5 Customized services can be delivered through personalization of web pages and e-mail. These help build relationships as data can be gathered about customers' needs and services provided that these match needs more closely.

6 Site aesthetics are an important consideration in design since the combination of graphics, colour, style, layout and typography define a site's personality and style, which are important in branding. Designers have to work under the constraints of and test for many technology variations including download speed, screen resolution, browsers and plug-ins.

7 Page layout is important to providing a clear consistent message throughout the site. This is achieved through standard locations for menus, logos, names, signposts and content.

8 Copywriting for the web shares much in common with other media. 'CRABS' highlights the importance of Chunking, Relevance, Accuracy, Brevity and Scannability.

9 Ease of use is achieved by creating a sound information architecture and then designing navigation tools and structures that enable a smooth flow for site visitors. Minimizing clicks to find content, simplicity, consistency and signposts can all help achieve this.

10 Providing interactive content in addition to static content can help support the customer throughout the buying process through product selection tools, callback facilities and direct or indirect customer service tools.

References

Akamai. (2006) Akamai and Jupiter Research Identify '4 Seconds' as the New Threshold of Acceptability for Retail Web Page Response Times. Press release, Nov 6th 2006. http://www.akamai.com/html/about/press/releases/2006/press_110606.html.

Bevan, N. (1999) Usability issues in web site design. *Proceedings of the 6th Interactive Publishing Conference*, November 1999. Available online at www.usability.serco.com.

British Standards Institute (1999) BS 13407 Human Centred design processes for inter-active systems. British Standards Institute.

E-consultancy (2007) Best Practice Guide to Effective Web Design Improving your online customer experience through results-led web design and development. Lead author: Dave Chaffey. Published, May 2007 by E-consultancy at http://www.e-consultancy.com/publications/web-design-best-practice-guide/. Free download available.

Haynes, J. and Zambonini, D. (2007) Why Are They Doing That!? How Users Interact With Museum Web sites. In *Museums and the Web 2007: Proceedings*, eds J. Trant and D. Bearman, Archives & Museum Informatics, Toronto. Published March 31, at http://www.archimuse.com/mw2007/papers/haynes/haynes.html.

IEEE (2003) Amazon.com Recommendations Item-to-Item Collaborative Filtering by Greg Linden, Brent Smith, and Jeremy York of Amazon.com. *IEEE Internet Computing*, January–February, pp. 76–80.

Knox, S., Maklan, S., Payne, A., Peppard, J. and Ryals, L. (2003) *Customer Relationship Management: Perspectives from the Marketplace*. Butterworth-Heinemann, Oxford.

Lindgaard, G., Fernandes, G., Dudek, C. and Brown, J. (2006) Attention web designers: You have 50 milliseconds to make a good first impression! *Behaviour & Information Technology*, Vol. 25, pp. 115–126.

Lynch, P. and Horton, S. (2002) *Web style guide. Basic design principles for creating web sites*, 2nd edition. Yale University Press.

Molineux, P. (2002) *Exploiting CRM. Connecting with customers*. Hodder & Stoughton, London.

Nielsen, J. (1999a) Web Research: Believe the Data. *Jakob Nielsen's Alertbox*, 11 July. www.useit.com/alertbox/990611.html.

Nielsen, J. (1999b) Ten Good Deeds in Web Design. *Jakob Nielsen's Alertbox*, 3 October. www.useit.com/alertbox/991003.html.

Nielsen, J. (2000a) *Designing Web Usability*. New Riders Publishing, USA.

Nielsen, J. (2000b) End of Web Design. *Jakob Nielsen's Alertbox*, 23 July. www.useit.com/alertbox/000623.html.

Nielsen, J. (2000c) Details in Study Methodology Can Give Misleading Results. *Jakob Nielsen's Alertbox*, 21 February. www.useit.com/alertbox/990221.html.

Novomind (2004) E-commerce research by Novomind/Faz Institute. Hamburg, Germany, 27 October. www.novomind.com.

Rayport, J. and Jaworski, B. (2004) *Introduction to E-commerce*, 2nd edition. McGraw-Hill, New York.

Rosenfeld, L. and Morville, P. (2002) *Information Architecture for the World Wide Web*, 2nd edition. O'Reilly, Sebastopol, CA.

Strong, E.K. (1925) *The Psychology of Selling and Advertising*. McGraw-Hill Book Co., New York.

Webcredible (2004) Article by Trenton Moss, November 2004. Ten ways to speed up the download time of your web pages. http://www.webcredible.co.uk/user-friendly-resources/web-usability/speed-up-download-time.shtml.

Wodtke, C. (2002) *Information architecture: blueprints for the web*. New Riders, Indiana-polis, IN.

Further reading

E-consultancy (2007) Best Practice Guide to Effective Web Design Improving your online customer experience through results-led web design and development. Lead author: Dave Chaffey. Published, May 2007 by E-consultancy at http://www.e-consultancy.com/publications/web-design-best-practice-guide/. Free download available.

Eisenberg, B. and Eisenberg, J. *Call To Action: Secret Formulas to Improve Online Results*. Wizard Press, Austin, Tx. Many practical tips on improving conversion for e-commerce sites.

Van Duyne, D., Landay, J. and Hong, J. (2007) *The Design of Sites. Patterns, Principles, and Processes for Crafting a Customer-Centered Web Experience*, 2nd edition. Addison-Wesley, Reading, MA. An in-depth analysis of web site design with many examples. All web site designers will learn some new tips from this book

Krug, S. (2000) *Don't Make Me Think*. New Riders. A commonsense introduction to this topic.

Mill, D. (2005) *Content is King. Writing and editing online*. See www.writingediting.co.uk. An excellent guide for European audiences covering all aspects of writing and editing from web pages to ads to search engines.

Nielsen, J. (2000) *Designing Web Usability*. New Riders Publishing, USA. The original classic book on web site design. Now superseded by others in this list, but see Nielsen's latest book, *Prioritizing Web Usability*.

Rosenfeld, L. and Morville, P. (2002) *Information Architecture for the World Wide Web*, 2nd edition. O'Reilly, Sebastopol, CA. A structured, fairly academic description of how to approach information architecture.

Lynch, P. and Horton, S. (2002) *Web style guide. Basic design principles for creating web sites*, 2nd edition. Yale University Press. A great online resource available at: www.webstyleguide.com.

Web links

A List Apart (www.alistapart.com). 'Explores the design, development, and meaning of web content, with a special focus on web standards and best practices'.

Boxes and Arrows (www.boxesandarrows.com). A collection of best practice articles and discussions about Information Architecture.

Disability and Discrimination Act. Code of practice including reference to web sites available from www.disability.gov.uk/dda.

E-consultancy Web Design Best Practice (www.e-consultancy.com/publications/web-design-best-practice-guide).

E-marketing Excellence book homepage (www.davechaffey.com/E-marketing). An index of all e-marketing links for each chapter in this book.

Jakob Nielsen's UseIt (www.useit.com). Detailed guidelines (alertboxes) and summaries of research into usability of web media.

User Interface Engineering. Articles on usability that often provide a counterpoint to those of Nielsen. (www.uie.com).

Royal National Institute for the Blind web accessibility guidelines (www.rnib.org.uk/accessibility).

Sitepoint (www.sitepoint.com). Online publisher with a range of blog articles in all web design categories.

Step Two (www.steptwo.com.au). This design company has introductory outlines and more detailed articles on information architecture and other aspects of usability.

UsabilityNet (www.usabilitynet.org). A portal about usability with good links to other sites and an introduction to usability terms and concepts.

Usability News (www.usabilitynews.com). A compilation of articles from different sources, plus jobs and events.

Webby Awards (www.webbyawards.com). The Oscars for the web – international.

Web Standards Project (WASP) (www.webstandards.org) – a consortium that promotes web standards.

Worldwide Web consortium web accessibility guidelines (www.w3.org/WAI).

Self-test

1 Explain the linkage between site design and marketing objectives.

2 Describe a scenario where on-site and offline marketing communications can be integrated to support mixed-mode buying.

3 Explain how OVP differs from USP and define the OVP for your organization.

4 How would you assess whether a web site had good customer orientation?

5 Describe the benefits of different types of personalization.

6 What are the constraints on using graphical elements to produce a site with strong visual appeal?

7 Draw a diagram summarizing the main page elements of your organization's web site.

8 Write down six rules for effective web copywriting.

9 Explain the concept of flow.

10 Describe the link between web site design and supporting customers through stages of the buying process.

Chapter **7**

Traffic building

'*If you build it, they will come*'. This famous line proved true in the 1989 film *Field of Dreams*, but unfortunately, it doesn't apply to web sites. If you want to maximize visitors to your site and to acquire new customers online you have to work hard to master the full range of online and offline marketing communications tools or digital media channels.

Sadly it's not always the best products that succeed but rather reasonably good ones that (a) everyone knows about and (b) everyone can easily find when they need them. The same is true of web sites. This chapter shows you how to build traffic – how to acquire the right visitors to your site in order to achieve the right marketing outcomes for you. You will receive a briefing on the different digital communications channels including search engine marketing, online PR, online partnerships, interactive advertising, opt-in e-mail and viral marketing. We will also show you that to succeed with your online communications also means gaining different forms of visibility on partner sites which are themselves successful in traffic building.

OVERALL LEARNING OUTCOME

By the end of this chapter you will be able to:

- Evaluate the range of options for traffic building
- Develop a plan to balance the options for traffic building
- Identify success factors for different online communications tools
- Review options for achieving positive representation on third-party sites.

CHAPTER TOPIC	LEARNING OBJECTIVE
7.1 Introduction	Assess different options for traffic building
7.2 Search engine marketing	Use different approaches to improve a site's listing in search engines including search engine optimization (SEO) and pay per click (PPC)
7.3 Online PR	Manage your reputation online through supporting journalists and maximizing your representation on portals and social networks
7.4 Online partnerships	Use link-building, affiliate marketing ,and online sponsorships to exploit the network effect of the Internet
7.5 Interactive advertising	Identify the elements of a successful online display ad campaign
7.6 Opt-in e-mail	Build traffic and relationships through opt-in e-mail
7.7 Viral marketing	Assess the relevance of viral marketing
7.8 Offline traffic building	Create a balance between offline and online promotion techniques
7.9 Control	Monitor the effectiveness of traffic building
7.10 Resourcing	Construct a traffic building plan

7.1 Introduction to traffic building

Generating traffic is vital to achieving e-marketing objectives, no matter whether the aim is sell, speak, serve, save or sizzle (see Chapter 1). What are the key characteristics of effective traffic building? In this section we will introduce three key aspects of traffic building:

1 *Targets* – specific objectives for traffic building need to be developed before embarking on a traffic building campaign. Traffic building objectives are essentially tactics to achieve wider e-marketing objectives.

2 *Techniques* – traffic building involves combining new online **digital media channels** and traditional offline communication techniques to promote the web site proposition and so encourage visits. Achieving the correct mix of traffic building techniques is vital, but difficult. Use your **web analytics** systems as your ally to understand which elements of your communications mix are effective. As Figure 7.1 shows, web analytics tools like Google Analytics, which is an excellent free tool we recommend for small-to-medium businesses, show the range of traffic sources and you can even drill down to find individual sites or search terms by which visitors find your site.

3 *Timing* – when should traffic building occur? Smart e-marketers include both specific campaigns, perhaps to launch a site, new product or promotion, but they also make investment in a continuous process of attracting visitors by search or affiliates. After all, online customers are looking for products, services and experiences throughout the year, not only when your campaign is live.

Figure 7.1 Google Analytics report showing information on relative importance of different traffic sources or referrers

E-MARKETING EXCELLENCE

Alliance and Leicester ringfence budget for continuous traffic building

Speaking to *New Media Age* (2006), Graham Findlay, Customer Acquisition Manager at bank Alliance and Leicester said:

> '*A big part of my team's job is to continually monitor traffic to and from our sites. We work to maintain the bank's profile. Some of our competitors don't always have a full online presence, settling instead for bursts of activity. That's certainly not our strategy'*.

This sentiment is backed up through investment in search and affiliate marketing. The article reported that Alliance and Leicester have increased their Search Engine Marketing budget from 2001 (£10 000) to £3million in 2006 as part of a £13 million budget. About search he says:

> '*I believe there's volume to be made from search and it's only right that a direct bank like us features in the top listings through search'*.

TARGETS

Typical traffic targets include the quantity, quality and cost of traffic. Although a successful site is often referred to in terms of quantity, such as the number of visitors, it is the traffic quality that really indicates the success of each **referrer,** that is the site or channel which is delivering visitors via your traffic building campaign.

Remember that generating traffic is not limited to driving visitors to your own web site. Traffic-building can also be effective on the third-party sites that your audience use. For example, a manufacturer of nappies may decide to create or sponsor a microsite on a third-party site such as www.babyworld.com or www.babycentre.co.uk. See the box 'Lexus achieve opt-ins through *Guardian* microsite' as an example of this type of microsite campaign. This case also shows the marketer can track online campaigns to assess their return on investment.

Traffic quality can be assessed by asking two questions about site visitors. First, are they within the target audience for the web site? Second, do they respond in line with the communications objectives, i.e. do they engage with your content, do they receive the key messages about your brand and convert to the site outcomes you require? Remember from Chapter 6 that **bounce rate** is an excellent way to compare the quality of different referrers to different **landing pages**.

Cost can be considered in terms of the cost of getting the visitor to the site, and the cost of achieving the outcomes during their visit. Experienced online marketers control their traffic building through managing the cost per acquisition (CPA) (sometimes called Cost Per Action). Depending on context and market, CPA may refer to different outcomes.

Typical cost targets include:

- cost per acquisition – of a visitor (**Cost Per Click, CPC**)
- cost per acquisition – of a lead
- cost per acquisition – of a sale (**allowable customer acquisition cost**).

CPA is typically equivalent to cost per sale (CPS) but may also apply to cost per visitor, lead or enquiry or other type of outcome since direct product sales are not practical or appropriate for all web sites. For a car manufacturer, for example, CPA might refer to the cost of generating a brochure or test drive request.

The value of sales should also be considered. Online retailers calculate sales value in terms of the value from the first sale (**average order value, AOV**) and campaign **return on investment (ROI)**. Companies should also model **customer lifetime value (LTV)**. Leading e-marketers select online referrers (i.e. choice of portal) not only by minimizing CPA, but also through maximizing new visitors with the highest potential LTV.

Costs and value should be compared for different sources of traffic such as **referrals** of visitors from **online adverts** on different sites or different search keyphrases. To be able to measure cost per action effectively, we need to be able track a visitor from different referrer sources from when they first arrive on the web site through to when the action (sale or enquiry) is taken. This is sometimes referred to as 'tagging visitors'. Costs are considered further in Section 7.10 on resourcing.

E-MARKETING EXCELLENCE

Lexus achieve opt-ins through *Guardian* microsite

In 2004, Toyota invested £200 000 in a sponsored microsite campaign to support the launch of the Lexus RX300 SUV. The site, themed around how we use our time, was connected with the Proms and other summer events. The site achieved 90 000 page impressions and also registered more than 5500 competition entries with a 48% opt-in to future communications from Lexus – so database building through direct response was one of the results, and this is not usually achieved through offline sponsorship. A prominent brochure request panel was also used, but this proved less successful achieving only 73 requests. Likewise a PDA initiative only gathered 30 e-mail addresses. The effectiveness of the sponsorship was increased by a range of ads targeting relevant content on the *Guardian* site and through e-mail ads of which 700 000 impressions were served. Another success factor of the microsite was its topical focus on our lack of time today, with editorial titled 'Too tired for sex' driving interest from elsewhere in the site and other media.

This case shows the importance of monitoring cost per acquisition of a lead, so that e-marketers can refine future work.

(*Source*: Interactive Advertising Bureau UK www.iabuk.net).

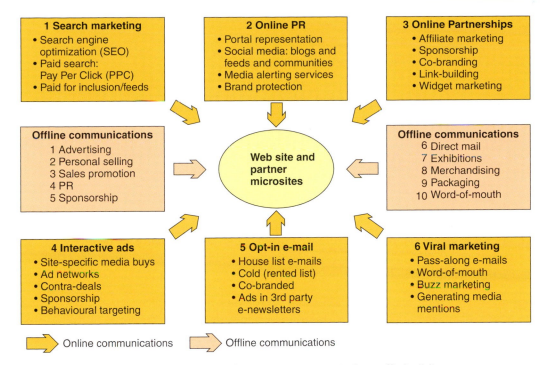

Figure 7.2   Options available in the digital communications mix for traffic building

TECHNIQUES

The traffic building techniques we will cover are summarized in Figure 7.2. These are now commonly referred to by agencies as digital media channels (or digital channels for short). Figure 7.2 will give you a good framework for planning your traffic-building or digital marketing campaign activities. The skill in traffic building is using the correct mix of online techniques such as viral marketing, affiliates and search engine optimization which best fits the media consumption of your audience. The promotional mix for traffic building typically includes a range of online and offline techniques, each with their own strengths and weaknesses, which will be explored in later sections of this chapter. Van Doren *et al.* (2000) provide an overview of the range of techniques.

TIMING

Traditional advertising is based around campaigns that run for a fixed duration. Specific campaigns are also used for traffic building. These are often tied into a particular event such as the launch or relaunch of a web site. For example a banner advert campaign may last for a period of two months following a relaunch. In addition to campaigns there are also **continuous traffic building activities**. Companies should ensure that there is sufficient investment in continuous online marketing activities as shown in Figure 7.1 including search marketing, affiliate marketing and sponsorship.

E-MARKETING INSIGHT

Gordon Pincott of Millward Brown on site promotion

Pincott (2000) suggests there are two key issues in site promotion. First there should be a media strategy which will mainly be determined by how to reach the target audience. This will define the online promotion techniques described in this chapter and where to advertise online. Second there is the creative strategy. Brown says that 'the dominant online marketing paradigm is one of direct response'. However, he goes on to suggest that all site promotion will 'influence perceptions of the brand'.

SECTION SUMMARY 7.1

Introduction to traffic building

Targeting, techniques and timing are three key aspects of traffic building and their relevance should be assessed for all techniques described in this chapter. It is traffic quality, not quantity, that really indicates the success of a traffic building campaign. Traffic quality is high if site visitors are within the target audience for the web site and if they respond in line with the communications objectives.

7.2   Search engine marketing

Search engine marketing is arguably the most important digital marketing channel for customer acquisition. We all now naturally turn to a search engine when we are seeking a new product, service or entertainment. We also turn to search when we become familiar with a new brand either through offline advertising or direct mail or through other digital channels such as graphical display ads.

In our experience, some transactional sites can generate over half of all their new business through search, although this will depend how well-known a brand is. For a well-known brand, users may navigate directly to a site via the URL, but they will often use the search engine to enter the brand name URL or brand and product (known as a navigational search).

PRACTICAL E-MARKETING TIP

Assess your brand health in search

Assess how many of your visitors arrive at your site on brand-related searches and how this varies when you run cross-channel campaigns. You will need to protect your brand from brand-hijacking where affiliates or competitors may advertise on your brand names if you don't take steps to protect it.

The importance of effective search marketing is suggested by Figure 7.3. The graph on the left shows that you really have to be on the first of the **search engine results pages (SERPS)**. The chart on the right shows that the first few positions are important in driving visitor volume for the search phrases you are targeting.

We will now review the three main search engine marketing techniques for making a company and its products visible through search engines:

1 Search engine optimization (SEO)

2 Paid search marketing or Pay Per Click (PPC)

3 Trusted feed including paid-for-inclusion.

SEARCH ENGINE OPTIMIZATION (SEO)

Search engine optimization (SEO) involves achieving the highest position or ranking practical in the **natural or organic listings** on the search engine results pages after a specific combination of keywords (or keyphrase) has been typed in. In search engines such as Google, Yahoo! and MSN Search, the natural listings are on the left as shown in Figure 7.4(a), although there may also be sponsored links above these. The position or ranking is dependent on an algorithm used by each search engine to match relevant site page content with the keyphrase entered. There is no charge for these listings to be displayed or when a link relevant to your site is clicked upon. However, you may need to pay a search engine optimization firm to advise or undertake optimization work to make your web pages appear higher in the rankings.

How are the search engine results pages produced?

To optimize your position in different search engines, it is essential to understand the basis on which SERPS are generated and ordered. Marketers who understand the ranking

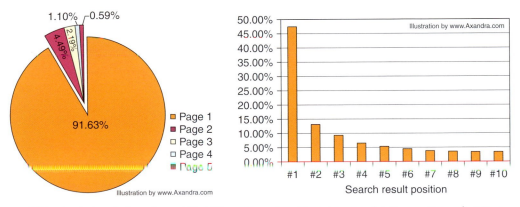

Figure 7.3 Analysis of data from US AOL users using Google.com. (a) Proportion of visitors who look at different number of pages; (b) Proportion of visitors who click on the results according to position on first page. Number of visitors received according to position of result

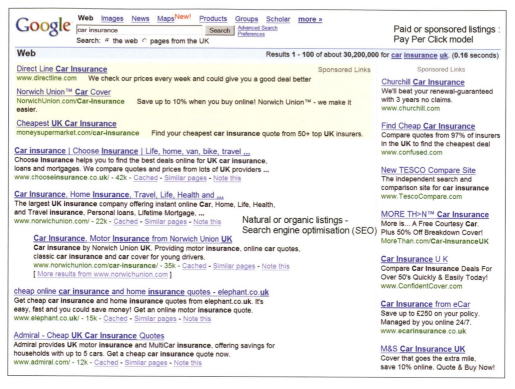

Figure 7.4 (a) Google search engine results page for keyphrase 'car insurance'

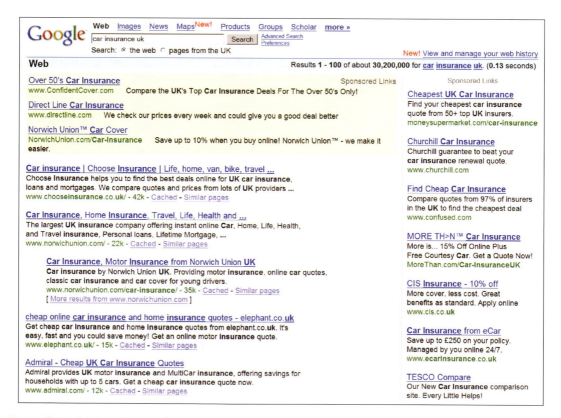

Figure 7.4 (b) Google search engine results page for keyphrase 'car insurance uk'

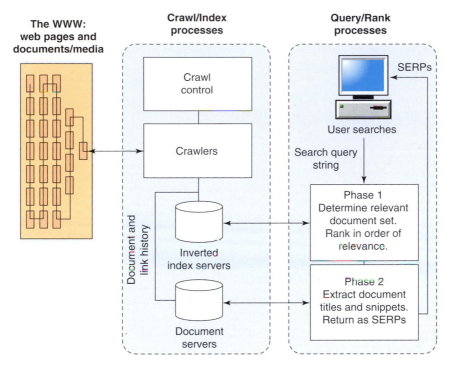

Figure 7.5   Stages involved in producing a search engine listing (*Source*: E-consultancy 2007)

processes can boost their position higher than their competitors and so achieve higher levels of traffic. We believe that SEO is too important to just be left to an agency and success in search involves training content owners and editors within a company to create content which fits the criteria used by search engines to assess relevance. Figure 7.5 shows that search technology involves these main processes:

1 **Crawling**. The purpose of the crawl is to identify relevant pages for indexing and assess whether they have changed. Crawling is performed by **robots** (bots) which are also known as **spiders**. These access web pages and retrieve a reference URL of the page for later analysis and indexing.

> ### PRACTICAL E-MARKETING TIP
>
> Each robot leaves a signature in the web server **log file** of the site it visits with a unique user agent string such as 'Googlebot/2.1'. SEOs can use this signature to assess whether or how frequently a page is being crawled by different robots. Site owners can also use the Google Webmaster tools to assess index inclusion and also identify errors such as pages that aren't crawled, perhaps because of a limitation of the content management system or broken links.

2 **Indexing**. An index is created to enable the search engine to rapidly find the most relevant pages containing the query typed by the searcher. Rather than searching each page for a query phrase, a search engine 'inverts' the index to produce a lookup table of the documents containing particular words.

PRACTICAL E-MARKETING TIP

Index inclusion

You can check that you are registered with a search engine and your **index inclusion** or number of pages included in the index by:

1 Reviewing **web analytics** data which will show the frequency with which the main search robots crawl your site.

2 Using web analytics referrer information to find out which search engines your site visitors originate from, and the pages they use.

3 Checking the number of pages that have been successfully indexed on your site. For example, in Google the search 'inurl:www.davechaffey.com' or 'site www.davechaffey.com' lists all the pages of Dave's site indexed by Google and gives the total number in the top right of the SERPS.

4 Using the webmaster tools from Google and Yahoo! referenced at the end of the chapter.

Sites wishing to reach an international audience should should check index inclusion for different countries, particularly across different English language versions of sites such as Australia, Canada, United Kingom and United States. Typically, using a separate local company domain such as www.company.fr or www.company.de which is also hosted locally in a country is often the most reliable approach for Google.

New sites without any external links indicating their reputation tend to be less trusted than existing sites (a phenomenon sometimes known as the 'Google Sandbox effect') which means that great care should be taken by startup companies or new marketing campaign sites since these cannot compete effectively with similar sites in a sector which have more backlinks. For a campaign microsite, it is often best to host the campaign on the main company site even if a separate campaign URL is used which redirects to the site content.

---

3 **Ranking or scoring**. The indexing process has produced a lookup of all the pages that contain particular words in a query, but they are not sorted in terms of relevance. Ranking of the document to assess the most relevant set of documents to return in the SERPs occurs in real-time for the search query entered. First, relevant documents will be retrieved from a runtime version of the index at a particular data centre, then a rank in the SERPs for each document will be computed based on many ranking factors, of which we highlight the main ones below.

4 **Query request and results serving**. The familiar search engine interface accepts the searchers query. The users' location is assessed through their IP address and the query is then passed to a relevant data centre for processing. Ranking then occurs in real-time for a particular query to return a sorted list of relevant documents and these are then displayed on the Search Results Page.

Google uses around 200 factors or signals within its search ranking algorithm. These include positive ranking factors which help boost position and negative factors or filters which are used to remove search engine spam from the index where SEOs have used unethical approaches to game the Google index. We will explore the most important ranking factors in a moment.

Site submission

How do you submit a new site? The good news is that registration with many search engines is free if you find the 'Add a URL' page (e.g. www.google.com/addurl.html) where you supply your home page URL and Google will then automatically index all the linked pages. It is recommended that automated submission tools are not used since these can be considered a **search engine spamming** technique. In fact, if you have links from other companies that are already indexed by a search engine, many search engines will automatically index your site without the need to submit a URL.

Keyphrase analysis

The key to successful search engine optimization and pay per click is achieving **keyphrase** relevance since this is what the search engines strive for – to match the combination of keywords typed into the search box to the most relevant destination content page. Notice that we say 'keyphrase' (short for keyword phrase), rather than 'key word' since search engines such as Google attribute more relevance when there is a phrase match on a page. Despite this, many search companies and commentators talk about optimizing your 'keywords' and in our opinion pay insufficient attention to **keyphrase analysis**.

You can see from comparing Figure 7.4(a) with Figure 7.4(b) that some well-known companies are visible for one search phrase, but not the other. Other companies who have done the appropriate analysis are visible for both.

The E-consultancy (2007) best practice guide recommends these stages for analysis and goal-setting:

A. *Demand analysis*. Identifying the popularity of each search term, its relevance to the products or services qualified by the 'intent of the searcher' indicated by the phrase and the competition on it. We recommend using two free Google tools, the Google Keyword Tool and Google Traffic Estimator which are great for giving estimates on the popularity of searches for different products and brands online. A list of keyphrase analysis tools in different categories, including these, is kept updated at http://www.davechaffey.com/seo-keyword-tools. You can see an example of the output from the Google Keyword Tool for terms related to car insurance in Figure 7.6

Keywords	September Search Volume ?	Advertiser Competition ?
car insurance		
cheap car insurance		
cheaper car insurance		
car insurance uk		
car insurance quote		
car insurance quotes		
cheapest car insurance		
classic car insurance		
car insurance online		
compare car insurance		
short term car insurance		
car insurance companies		
best car insurance		
car insurance for young drivers		
car insurance comparison		
car insurance for women		
direct car insurance		
car insurance company		

Figure 7.6 Variation in popularity of searches on terms related to car insurance. (*Source*: Google Keyword tool)

Other sources for identifying keyphrases include your market knowledge, competitors' sites, key phrases from visitors who arrive at your site (from web analytics), the internal site search tool. When performing the keyphrase analysis we need to understand different qualifiers that users type in so that we can target them in our SEM. For example, this list of seven different types of keyphrases is taken from an Overture representative talking at Search Engine Strategies in 2004. We have added examples for 'car insurance':

1 *Comparison/quality* – compare car insurance
2 *Adjective (price/product qualifiers)* – cheap car insurance, woman car insurance
3 *Intended use* – high mileage car insurance
4 *Product type* – holiday car insurance
5 *Vendor or brand* – Churchill car insurance
6 *Location* – car insurance uk
7 *Action request* – buy car insurance
8 *Provider type* – car insurance company, car insurance supermarket.

B. *Performance analysis*. This assesses how the company is currently performing for these phrases. With the right tracking tools and tags, it should be possible to report average position in natural or paid listings; Click volume referred from search; Click quality (conversion rates and ideally bounce rates to compare landing page effectiveness); Outcomes (sales, registrations or leads); Costs (CPC and CPA); profitability (based on cost of sale or lifetime value models).

C. *Gap analysis*. Identifies for each phrase and product where the biggest potential for improvement is, so you can target your resources accordingly.

D. *Set goals and select keyphrases*. You should identify the different types of keyphrase you want to be visible for. Particularly important are the strategic keyphrases which are critical to success.

> ### Improving search engine ranking through SEO

Although each search engine has its own algorithm with many weighting factors that change through time, fortunately there are common factors that influence search engine rankings. The challenge for SEOs is that there are many ranking factors. In a May 2006 presentation, Alan Eustace (a Senior VP of Engineering at Google) said that Google uses over 200 'signals' to assess the relevance of a page for a particular query! We will simplify it to the most important factors which can be managed, these are:

1 On-page optimization
2 External linking
3 Internal link-structures.

Let's look at these in a little more detail:

1 **On-page optimization**. The most basic test of relevance by the search engines is the number of times the phrase appears on the page.

However, there are many other factors that can also be applied. In its guidance for Webmasters, Google states: '*Google goes far beyond the number of times a term appears on a page and examines all aspects of the page's content (and the content of the pages linking to it) to determine if it's a good match for your query*'.

These other factors include:

- Frequency
- Occurrence in headings <h1>, <h2>
- Occurrence in anchor text of hyperlinks
- Markup such as bold
- Density (the number of times)
- Proximity of phrase to start of document and the gap between individual keywords
- Alternative image text (explained below)
- Document meta data (explained below).

> **Alternative image text**

Graphical images can have hidden text associated with them that is not seen by the user (unless graphical images are turned off or the mouse is rolled-over the image), but will be seen and indexed by the search engine.

For example text about a company name and products can be assigned to a company logo using the 'ALT' tag or attribute of the image tag as follows:

<IMG NAME = 'Logo' SRC = 'logo.gif' ALT = 'Car insurance'>.

Due to search engine spamming this factor is assigned limited relevance, although it is still worthwhile for images that link to another page within the site. However, it is best practice to use this approach for significant images since it is also required by accessibility law and screen-readers used by the blind and visually impaired read-out the ALT tags.

> **Document meta data**

The three most important types of meta data are the document <title> tag, the document 'descriptions' meta tag and the document 'keywords' meta tag. You should try to make these unique for each page on your site(s) since otherwise Google may assess the content as duplicate and some pages may be down-weighted in importance.

  i *The document title* The <title> tag is arguably the most important type of meta data since each search engine places significant weighting on the keyphrases contained within it AND it is the call-to-action hyperlink on the search engine results page. If it contains powerful, relevant copy you will get more clicks and the search engine will increase position in the listing accordingly relative to other pages which are getting fewer clicks.

 ii *The 'description' meta tag* A meta tag is an attribute of the page within the HTML <head> section which can be set by the content owner.

The 'description' meta tag denotes the information which will typically be displayed in the search engine results page. If it is absent or too short relevant 'snippets' will be used from within the body copy, but it is best to control your messages.

So, the page creator can modify this to make a stronger call-to-action in the search engine listings as in this case:

<meta name = 'description' content = 'Direct Line offers you great value car insurance by cutting out the middleman and passing the savings directly on to you. To find out if you could save, why not get a car insurance quote? Breakdown Cover Insurance also available'.>

 iii *The 'keywords' meta tag* The Meta keywords meta tag is used to summarize the content of a document based on keywords. Some unscrupulous SEOs can still be heard to say to potential clients ('we will optimize your meta tags'). But this is a waste of time today since the keywords meta tag is relatively unimportant as a ranking factor (Google has never used them) although these keywords may be important to internal search engines.

Example:

<meta name = 'keywords' content = 'Car insurance, Home insurance, Travel insurance, Direct line, Breakdown cover, Mortgages personal loans, Pet insurance, Annual holiday insurance, Car loans, uk mortgages, Life insurance, Critical illness cover'>

2 External linking. Boosting externals links is vital to your SEO efforts although it is less easy to control and often neglected. The founders of Google realized that the number of links into a page and their quality was a great way of determining the relevance of a page to searchers, especially when combined with the keyphrases on that page. Although the Google algorithm has been upgraded and refined continuously since then, the number and quality of external links is still the most important ranking factor.

While natural links will be generated if content is useful, a proactive approach to link-building is required in competitive markets. We recommend these steps to help boost your external links. There are more link-building tips in Section 7.4.

i *Identify and create popular content and services*. The starting point for both natural and pro-active link-building has to be to think of the value of your site and different types of content or services on different pages. The acid test is whether your visitors will bookmark a page of your content or tell a friend about it. Think not only about the home page, but also other pages within the site.

By creating more valuable content and then showcasing them within your navigation, or grouping it within a few pages such as a 'Useful Resources' or a more extensive 'Resource Centre' you can encourage more people to link to your content naturally, or approach them and suggest they link not only to the home page, but directly to the useful tools that have been created.

PRACTICAL E-MARKETING TIP

Prompting social bookmarking

Use social bookmarking tools such as Delicious (http://del.icio.us) or AddThis (www.addthis.com) or review top entry pages into your site from web analytics to identify content which existing visitors find valuable. Yahoo! uses Delicious and Google uses Google Bookmarks to assess popular content.

ii *Identify potential partner sites*. There are several options to find partner sites. It is helpful to try to identify the types of sites that you may be able to link with, for example:

- Directories of links (often less valuable)
- Traditional media sites
- Niche online-only media sites
- Trade associations
- Manufacturers, suppliers and other business partners
- Press release distribution sites
- Bloggers including customers and partners
- Social networks.

Look for sites that offer links. There are often free options such as specialist directories.

Method 1. Google Searches on keyphrases

To identify directory type sites, search for these phrases on Google for different keyphrases

1 <keyphrase> + directory
2 <keyphrase> + 'Add URL'
3 <keyphrase> + 'Submit site'
4 <keyphrase> + 'Add Listing'
5 <keyphrase> + 'Links'
6 <keyphrase> + 'Where to buy'/'Stores'/'Suppliers'

Method 2. Use Yahoo Site Explorer to find links of competitors

Enter URL into https://siteexplorer.search.yahoo.com and then select Show Inlinks 'Except from this sub domain' as below.

Method 3. Use Google related syntax

Once seed sites have been identified, the Google 'related:' syntax can be used to find additional links. The Google related syntax typically identifies sites which share links in common. So competitor sites or media sites may both be present.

3 Contact partner sites

A typical sequence is:

- Step 1. Write e-mail encouraging link (or phone call to discuss from someone inside the company will often work best).
- Step 2. Follow-up link.
- Step 3. Setup links.

PRACTICAL E-MARKETING TIP

Link anchor text and 'nofollow' in title

When setting up links it is important to use specific suitable anchor text for the link. Links deep into the site, specific to a particular product are often more valuable. It is also worth remembering that Google won't follow links which have the rel= 'nofollow' link on them, so check for these.

PRACTICAL E-MARKETING TIP

Finding out who links to you, and your competitors

The best free way to find link associations for you and competitors is the Yahoo! Site Explorer. (https://siteexplorer.search.yahoo.com) can be used to check the number of pages within the Yahoo! index and identify links from other sites. For your own site, we would strongly recommend using the Google Webmaster tools (www.google.com/webmasters/ which provides a useful set of tools just for sites owned and verified by their owners including internal and external links. It is also possible to use tools such as Advanced Link Manager (www.advancedlinkmanager.com) to show links. Note that using the 'link:site' syntax in Google to see the number of quality links into a page on your site as judged by Google is inaccurate, it only gives a selection of links. Of course you should also use your web analytics system to find who links to you and which generates the most traffic.

THINK LINK-QUALITY NOT LINK-POPULARITY

Today, Google assesses not just number of links into a page, but also uses the concepts of hubs and authorities to assess the relevance of a page about a particular topic. This approach was originally described by Google engineers Bharat and Mihaila (1999). Essentially, a hub page (actually referred to as 'Expert page' in the paper) is a page which contains many quality outbound links about a particular topic. An authority page, referred to as a 'target' in the paper contains many inbound links about a topic. Expert pages (hubs) are given more weighting to identify authority pages.

The context or theme of the linking page is also very important, with the search engines needing to determine hubs and authorities based on an assessment of the context of the link for the page based on the phrases it contains.

In the Bharat paper there is a direct indication of the factors used to assess the theme of a page. They suggest the importance to good ranking, of a searchers keyphrases occurring in:

- The page title phrase (part of on-page optimization described in last month's article)
- Headings within documents (again on-page optimization)
- Hyperlink anchor text (the words making up the hyperlink).

We describe different approaches to link-building in Section 7.4 Online partnerships.

3 **Internal link-structures**. Many of the principles of external link-building can also be applied on your own sites. This is often a missed opportunity since here you have the benefit that you have control of the linking, although the impact is less than links from external sites. The most important principle is to include keyphrases used by searchers within the anchor text of a hyperlink to point to relevant content. It's also important to

consider how you can increase the number of internal links to pages which you want to rank well. A meshed structure with lots of interlinks can work better than a simple hierarchy.

PRACTICAL E-MARKETING TIP

Analyzing pagerank and internal backlink distribution

PageRank varies across a site. The home page is typically highest, with each page deeper within the site having a lower PageRank. There are several implications of this. First, it is helpful to include the most important keyphrases you want to target on the homepage or at the second level in the site hierarchy. Second pages that feature in the main or secondary navigation (text link menus referencing the keyphrase in the anchor text are best) are more likely to rank highly than pages deeper in the site that don't have many internal backlinks because they are not in the menu. Third, you need to review whether there are pages deeper within the site which feature products or services that are important which you need to rank for. If so you need to find a method of increasing the number of backlinks (internal or external), perhaps by including a link to the them in the footer or sidebars of the site which are separate from the main navigation. Google webmaster tools has reports on internal and external links which are excellent diagnostic tools.

PRACTICAL E-MARKETING TIP

Improve your link anchor text

The importance of hyperlink anchor text isn't always realized by content authors, with many sites having hyperlinks which read 'click here' or 'read more' rather than referring to the target document's content. This is often a constraint/feature of content management systems, but body copy links can be used to refer to the target document using a meaningful link such as, 'read more about search engine optimization best practice (http://www.e-consultancy.com/publications/seo-guide/) which is also better from a user experience point-of-view.

E-MARKETING CHECKLIST – INTERNAL LINK-BUILDING CHECKLIST

☑ 1 *Links from standard navigation.* These are most effective if text-based rather than image menus. As well as the main navigation categories, conventionally across the masthead, providing more navigation links within the left or right sidebars can help indicate to search engines the themes of pages.

☑ 2 *Links from ancillary navigation (e.g. page footers).* These can be varied in different site sections.

☑ **3** *Links from document listings*. (Including publishing search results or lists of news items.)

☑ **4** *Sitemaps*. These are useful for both human visitors and search robots – Google recommends creating these. They are most effective if broken down into different categories which are themed about specific topics.

☑ **5** *Body copy*. See the e-marketing best practice tip.

☑ **6** *Image links*. These were discussed in the section on document meta data.

PAID OR PAY PER CLICK (PPC) SEARCH MARKETING

Paid search marketing or Pay Per Click (PPC) is similar to conventional advertising; here a relevant text ad with a link to a company page is displayed when the user of a search engine types in a specific phrase. A series of text ads usually labelled as 'sponsored links' are displayed to the right of the natural listings in Figure 7.4 (a) and (b). Although many searchers prefer to click on the natural listings, a sufficient number do click on the paid listings (typically around a quarter or a third of all clicks) so that they are highly profitable for companies such as Google and a well designed paid search campaign can drive a significant amount of business for the search companies.

Each of the main search engines has its own advertising programmes:

● Google Adwords (http://adwords.google.com)
● Yahoo! Search Marketing (http://searchmarketing.yahoo.com, formerly Overture)
● Microsoft adCenter (http://adcenter.microsoft.com)
● MIVA Pay Per Click, Pay Per Call and Pay Per Text (www.miva.com).

Each of these programmes has to be managed individually through an online service or alternatively large campaigns can be managed and evaluated through a **bid management service**.

There are two significant differences between PPC and conventional advertising which are its main advantages:

1 *The advertiser is not paying for the ad to be displayed*. Cost is only incurred when the ad is clicked on and a visitor is directed to the advertiser's website. Hence it's a **Cost Per Click (CPC) model**! However, there are increasingly options for paid search marketing using other techniques, Google also offers CPM (Site targeting) and CPA (Pay Per Action) options on its **content network** where contextual ads are displayed on third-party sites relevant to the content on a page.

2 *PPC advertising is highly targeted*. The relevant ad with a link to a destination web page is only displayed when the user of a search engine types in a specific phrase (or the ad appears on the content network, triggered by relevant content on a publishers page), so there is limited wastage compared to other media. Users responding to a particular key-phrase or reading related content have high intent or interest and so tend to be good quality leads.

The relative ranking of these 'paid performance placements' is not simply based on the highest bidded CPC for each keyword phrase as is often thought by those unfamiliar with CPC. Additionally Google, and now the other search engines, also take into account the quality of the listings. Within Google this is known as the **Quality Score**.

E-MARKETING INSIGHT

Mastering Quality Score

Understanding the Quality Score is the key to successful PPC marketing. You should consider its implications when you structure the account and write copy. Google developed the Quality Score because they understood that delivering relevance through the sponsored links was essential to their user's experience, and their profits. In their AdWords help system (Google, 2007), Google explains:

> *'The AdWords system works best for everybody; advertisers, users, publishers and Google too when the ads we display match our users' needs as closely as possible. We call this idea "relevance".*
>
> *We measure relevance in a simple way: Typically, the higher an ad's Quality Score, the more relevant it is for the keywords to which it is tied. When your ads are highly relevant, they tend to earn more clicks, move higher in Ad Rank and bring you the most success'.*

The current formula for the Google Quality Score is:

Quality Score = (keyword's clickthrough rate, Ad Text Relevance, Keyword Relevance, Landing Page Relevance and other methods of assessing relevance)

So, higher clickthrough rates achieved through better targeted creative copy are rewarded as is relevance of the landing page (Google now sends out AdBots-Google to check them out). More relevant ads are also rewarded through ad text relevance which is an assessment of the match of headline and description to search term. Finally, the keyword relevance is the match of the triggering keyword to the search term entered.

If you have ever wondered why the number of paid ads above the natural listings varies from none to three, then it's down to the quality score – you can only get the coveted positions for keywords which have a sufficiently high quality score – you can't 'buy your way to the top' as many think.

In addition to performance-based payment and well targeted prospects, PPC has other advantages:

1 *Good accountability.* With the right tracking system, the ROI for individual keywords can be calculated.

2 *Predictable.* Traffic, rankings and results are generally stable and predictable. This contrasts with SEO.

3 *Technically simpler than SEO.* Position is based on a combination of bid amount and quality score, whereas SEO requires long-term, technically complex work on page optimization, site restructuring and link-building.

4 *Speed.* PPC listings get posted quickly, usually in a few days (following editor review). SEO results can take weeks or months to be achieved. Moreover, when a website is revised for SEO, rankings will initially drop while the site is reindexed by the search engines.

5 *Branding.* Tests have shown that there is a branding effect with PPC, even if users do not click on the ad. This can be useful for the launch of products or major campaigns.

However, these disadvantages need to be managed:

1 *Competitive and expensive.* Since Pay Per Click has become popular, some companies may get involved in bidding wars that drive bids up to an unacceptable level. Some phrases such as 'life insurance' can exceed £10 per click.

2 *Inappropriate.* For companies with a lower budget or a narrower range of products on which to generate lifetime value, it might not be cost-effective to compete.

3 *Needful of specialist knowledge.* PPC requires a knowledge of configuration, bidding options and of the reporting facilities of different ad networks. Internal staff can be trained, but they will need to keep up-to-date with changes to the paid search services.

4 *Time consuming.* To manage a PPC account can require daily or even hourly checks on the bidding in order to stay competitive. This can amount to a lot of time. The tools and best practice varies frequently, so to keep up-to-date is difficult.

5 *Irrelevant.* Sponsored listings are only part of the search engine marketing mix. Many search users do not click on these.

Managing Pay Per Click

Different advertisers bid on particular key words through a web-based management interface provided by the network to achieve the listing that they want. The structure of Google AdWords account management is shown in Figure 7.7. Setting up a sound account structure is important since it determines how closely you can target your paid search activities.

Campaigns provide a way to manage ads for related products. You should set a daily budget, which will often correspond to budgets for different product groups (categories) and geographies. Generic search terms and brand terms often also have their own campaigns compared to more specific product campaigns. Within each campaign Ad Groups will be set up which contain keywords that will trigger the ad to be displayed when it is searched upon. Advertisers decide on the maximum Cost Per Click (CPC) they are prepared to pay for each keyword or Ad Group. Figure 7.8 shows an example of an Ad Group created for a model of mobile phone. In this case there is a single keyword which when typed will trigger a targeted message for which different versions can be served for testing.

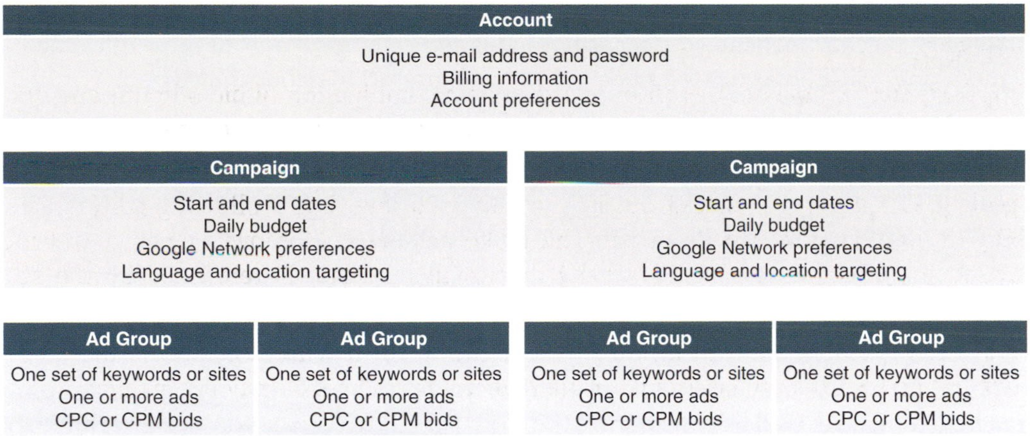

Account

Unique e-mail address and password
Billing information
Account preferences

Campaign	**Campaign**
Start and end dates	Start and end dates
Daily budget	Daily budget
Google Network preferences	Google Network preferences
Language and location targeting	Language and location targeting

Ad Group	**Ad Group**	**Ad Group**	**Ad Group**
One set of keywords or sites	One set of keywords or sites	One set of keywords or sites	One set of keywords or sites
One or more ads	One or more ads	One or more ads	One or more ads
CPC or CPM bids	CPC or CPM bids	CPC or CPM bids	CPC or CPM bids

Figure 7.7   AdWords account structure

Keyword	Status [?]	Current Bid Max CPC	Clicks	Impr.	CTR	Avg. CPC	Cost	Avg. Pos
Search Total	Enabled	Default £0.40 [edit]	41	727	5.6%	£0.36	£14.47	5.5
Content Total [?]	Not enabled		2	797	0.2%	£0.34	£0.68	5.8
"mda pro"	Active	£0.40	40	688	5.8%	£0.36	£14.35	5.2
(1 Deleted Keywords)			1	39	2.5%	£0.12	£0.12	10.2

Reporting is not real-time. Clicks and impressions received in the last 3 hours may not be included here. Lower CTRs for content ads do not adversely affect your campaign. [?] Inactive for search keywords have a Quality Score and Max CPC which are too low to trigger ads on searches for Google or the search network but they remain active for content impressions. These keywords may occasionally accrue search clicks as we re-assess their quality. [?]

Ads (3 Deleted Ads, 14 Clicks, 1.2% CTR, £0.33 Avg. CPC)   + Create New Ad: Text Ad | Image Ad   Back up to keywords

Free MDA Pro
6 months Half Price Line Rental!
Free UK delivery.
fonetasticmobile.co.uk
17 Clicks | 8.2% CTR | £0.37 CPC
Served - 13.6% [more info]
Edit - Delete

MDA Pro : Free
6 months Half Price Line Rental!
Free UK delivery.
biz.fonetasticmobile.co.uk
12 Clicks | 6.0% CTR | £0.37 CPC
Served - 13.0% [more info]
Edit - Delete

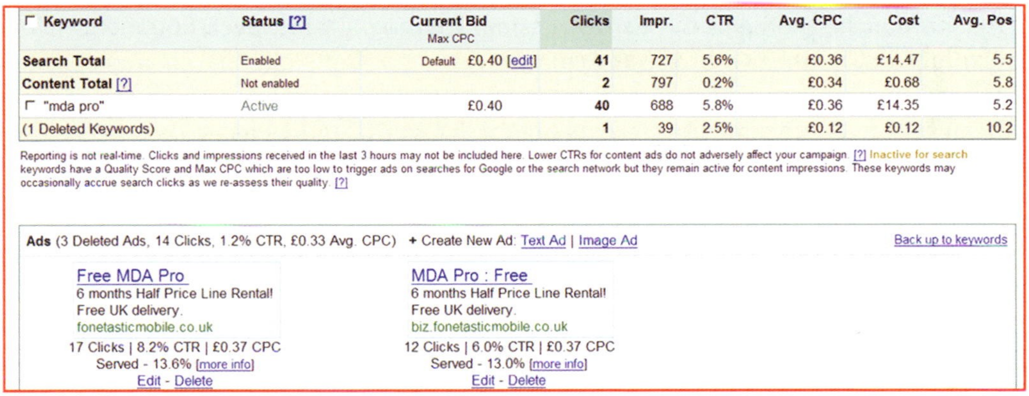

Figure 7.8   An example of an Ad Group within the Google AdWords campaign management tool

---

BEST PRACTICE E-MARKETING TIP

Google AdWords account structure

Your ads will tend to be more relevant to searchers if you create many focused Ad Groups in each campaign which each target a particular type of searching. Each Ad Group shouldn't have too many diverse, unrelated keywords since you will be less able to deliver relevance so your clickthrough rate will be low and your price bid will have to be high compared to competitors to get the listing position you need. A good rule of thumb is 10 to 20 maximum keywords per Ad Group.

Figure 7.8 shows how easy it is to test alternative creative/copy – check that your agency have developed the best messages through testing. To save time you can use dynamic content insertion to tailor the ad. For example, in Google, the syntax {Keyword: <Default phrase>} is used to activate this 'dynamic keyword insertion' feature when defining the ad headline or description. This typically results in greater relevance and higher clickthrough rates since the phrase entered matches that typed.

It is also useful to create separate campaigns for the content network, then you can treat this differently by using different messages. As a first time advertiser, it is usually best to switch off the content network initially, so you can concentrate on getting advertising right within the main search results.

With PPC as for any other media, media buyers carefully evaluate the advertising costs in relation to the initial purchase value or lifetime value they feel they will achieve from the average customer. As well as considering the Cost Per Click (CPC), you need to think about the conversion rate when the visitor arrives at your site. Clearly, an ad could be effective in generating clickthroughs or traffic, but not achieve the outcome required on the web site such as generating a lead or online sale. This could be because there is a poor incentive, call-to-action or the profile of the visitors is simply wrong. One implication of this is it will often be more cost-effective if targeted microsites or landing pages are created specifically for certain keyphrases to convert users to making an enquiry or sale. These can be part of the site structure, so clicking on a 'car insurance' ad will take the visitor through to the car insurance page on a site rather than a home page. This is not a form of advertising to use unless the effectiveness of the web site in converting visitors to buyers is known.

Table 7.1 shows how Cost Per Click differs between different keywords from generic to specific. It also shows the impact of different conversion rates on the overall CPA. It can be seen that niche terms that better indicate interest in a specific product such as 'women's car insurance' demand a higher fee (this may not be true for less competitive categories where niche terms can be cheaper). The table also shows the cost of PPC search in competitive categories. Advertising just on these four keywords to achieve a high ranking would cost €33 000 in a single day! Some advertisers target lower positions in the SERPs, since visitors are better value and lower cost.

Table 7.1 Variation in cost per click for different key phrases in Google UK, 2004

Keywords	Clicks/Day	Average CPC	Cost/Day	Average position	CPA @ 25% conversion	CPA @ 10% conversion
Overall	5714	€5.9	€33,317	1.3	€23.4	€58.4
'insurance'	3800	€5.4	€20,396	1.3	€21.5	€53.7
'car insurance'	1700	€6.6	€11,119	1.2	€26.2	€65.5
'cheap car insurance'	210	€8.4	€1757	1.1	€33.5	€83.7
'women's car insurance'	4.1	€10.5	€43	1.0	€42.2	€105.4

The cost per acquisition (CPA) can be calculated as follows:

$$\text{Cost per acquisition} = (100/\text{Conversion rate \%}) \times \text{Cost per click}$$

Given the range in costs, two types of strategy can be pursued in PPC search engine advertising. If budget permits, a premium strategy can be followed to compete with the major competitors who are bidding the highest amounts on popular keywords. Such a strategy is based on being able to achieve an acceptable conversion rate once the customers are driven through to the web site. A lower-cost strategy involves bidding on lower cost, less popular phrases. These will generate less traffic, so it will be necessary to devise a lot of these phrases to match the traffic from premium keywords.

Optimizing Pay Per Click

Each PPC keyphrase ideally needs to be managed individually in order to make sure that the bid (amount per click) remains competitive in order to show up in the top of the results. Experienced PPC marketers broaden the range of keyphrases to include lower volume phrases. Since each advertiser will typically manage thousands of keywords to generate clickthroughs, manual bidding soon becomes impractical.

Some search engines include their own bid management tools, but if you or your agency is using different Pay Per Click services such as Overture, Espotting and Google, it makes sense to use a single tool to manage them all. It also makes comparison of performance easier too. **Bid management software** such as Atlas One Point (www.atlasonepoint.com) and BidBuddy (www.bidbuddy.co.uk) can be used across a range of PPC services to manage keyphrases across multiple PPC ad networks and optimize the costs of search engine advertising. The current CPC is regularly reviewed and your bid is reduced or increased to achieve a goal of profitability or sales volume.

More sophisticated bid management tools such as Efficient Frontier use historical click, cost, impression and position data to model the whole campaign in a portfolio-style approach similar to those used by stock market traders. For each keyword and each position, these tools predict the required bid, the actual CPC (cost per click), the click volume and the conversion rate.

As more marketers have become aware of the benefits of PPC, competition has increased and this has driven up the Cost Per Click (CPC) and so reduced its profitability. We will soon reach the point where those bidding at the top will be the companies with the most efficient web sites for conversion to outcome and the highest potential lifetime value for cross-selling.

Making your ad creative effective

We have seen how important creative ad copy is to quality score and minimizing costs. Compare our tips checklist against the ads in Figure 7.4. Your copywriting techniques need to work within the many editorial guidelines.

E-marketing best practice checklist – effective paid search ad creative

☑ **1** Deliver relevance by including search term keywords in headline and body

☑ **2** Be specific on the offer

☑ **3** Include specific benefits e.g. free delivery, costs

☑ **4** Differentiate – explain what is unique about your offering

☑ **5** Include numbers as appropriate since they stand out when visitors scan the page

☑ **6** Use CAPS (Capitalize first letters and use acronyms where appropriate)

☑ **7** Space can be good – sometimes relatively short text can have a higher impact

☑ **8** Use characters (sensibly): !, ?, :, &

☑ **9** Be quirky!

☑ **10** Use distinctive words

☑ **11** Try to squeeze in a call-to-action

☑ **12** Capitalize display URLs (the web address shown) and consider including a sub-folder that highlights the product or a benefit.

Beware of the fake clicks

Whenever the principle of PPC marketing is described to marketers, very soon a light bulb comes on and they ask, 'so we can click on competitors and bankrupt them'. Well actually no. The PPC ad networks detect multiple clicks from the same computer (IP address) and say they filter them out. However, there are techniques to mimic multiple clicks from different locations such as software tools to fake clicks and even services where you can pay a team of people across the world to click on these links. It is estimated that in competitive markets one in five of the clicks may be fake. While this can be factored into the conversion rates you will achieve, ultimately this could destroy PPC advertising. We believe that, in the longer term, PPC will move to something similar to an affiliate model where marketers only pay when a sale or some other outcome on a site occurs.

TRUSTED FEED

This form of search advertising is less widely used, so we will only cover it briefly. In trusted feed, the ad or search listings content is automatically uploaded to a search engine from a catalogue or document database in a fixed format which often uses the XML data exchange standard (see http://www.w3.org/XML). This technique is mainly used by retailers who have large product catalogues for which prices and product descriptions may vary and so potentially become out-of-date in the SERPs. A related technique is **paid for inclusion (PFI)**. Here, PPC ads are placed within the search listings of some search engines interspersed with the organic results. In paid inclusion, the advertiser specifies pages with specific URLs for incorporation into the search engine organic listings. There is typically a fixed set-up fee and then also a PPC arrangement when the ad is clicked on. A crucial difference with other PPC types is that the position of the result in the search engine listings is not paid according to price bid, but the normal algorithm rules of that search engine to produce the organic listings. The service most commonly used for PFI is Yahoo! Sitematch. Note that Google does not offer trusted feed in its main search results at the time of writing (but it does offer a free XML feed to its main Google product search shopping catalogue).

SECTION SUMMARY 7.2

Search engine marketing

Ensure you employ someone who is knowledgeable to optimize your position with search engines. Remember, the main techniques are:

1 Ensure your sites are included in the indexes of the main search.
2 Complete keyphrase analysis to identify phrases relevant to your market.
3 Start a search engine optimization initiative. This may involve restructuring your site to make it more accessible to search engines and including relevant keyphrases in the body copy, title tag and other page elements.
4 Maximize quality links from and to different sites – run a link-building campaign.
5 Review the relevance of pay per click advertising and trusted feeds and be sure to devote sufficient resources to deliver ROI from these.

7.3 Online PR

Online PR or e-PR leverages the network effect of the Internet. Remember the term 'Internet' is a contraction of 'interconnected networks'! Mentions of your brand or site on other sites are powerful in shaping opinions and driving visitors to your site. Furthermore, as we saw in the section on search engine optimization, the more quality backlinks there are from other sites to your site, the higher your site will be ranked in the natural or organic listings of the search engines.

Ranchhod *et al.* (2002) identify four key differences between online PR and traditional PR:

1 *The audience is connected to organizations.* Previously, there was detachment – PR people issued press releases which were distributed over the newswires, picked up by the media and then published in their outlets. These authors say:

> 'the communication channel was uni-directional. The institutions communicated and the audiences consumed the information. Even when the communication was considered a two-way process, the institutions had the resources to send information to audiences through a very wide pipeline, while the audiences had only a minuscule pipeline for communicating back to the institutions'.

2 *The members of the audience are connected to each other*. Through publishing their own web sites or through e-mail, information can be rapidly distributed from person to person and group to group. The authors say:

> *'Today, a company's activity can be discussed and debated over the Internet, with or without the knowledge of that organization. In the new environment everybody is a communicator, and the institution is just part of the network'.*

3 *The audience has access to other information*. Often in the past, the communicator was able to make a statement it would be difficult for the average audience member to challenge – the Internet facilitates rapid comparison of statements. The authors say:

> *'It takes a matter of minutes to access multiple sources of information over the Internet. Any statement made can be dissected, analyzed, discussed and challenged within hours by interested individuals. In the connected world, information does not exist in a vacuum'.*

4 *Audiences pull information*. This point is similar to the last one. Previously there were limited channels in terms of television and press. Today there are many sources and channels of information – this makes it more difficult for the message to be seen. The authors say:

> *'Until recently, television offered only a few channels. People communicated with one another by post and by phone. In these conditions, it was easy for a public relations practitioner to make a message stand out'.*

There are many activities that need to be proactively managed as part of online PR which we have summarized in Figure 7.9. We recommend you create a plan for e-PR in four key areas:

1 *Search marketing activities (SEO)*. We have covered these in the previous section. As the diagram suggests, many of the other techniques involve creating **backlinks** which will also assist with this.

2 *Brand engagement activities*. Engagement is all about creating interaction or dialogue with online audiences to help understand audience needs and potentially influence them. This may be on your own site or on third-party sites through **business blogs** and communities which we will discuss more below.

3 *Buzz-building activities*. Here we use online and social media to create a noise about a campaign or message and then help the message to spread through viral marketing as described in Section 7.7. Naturally, web addresses should also be quoted for all offline PR activity to complete the campaign's objective in driving traffic to the site. This activity will include communicating with media (journalists) online who increasingly use the Internet as a new conduit to access press releases through e-mail alerts and RSS feeds. Options include setting up a press-release area on the web site; creating e-mail alerts about news which journalists and other third parties can sign up to; and submitting your news stories or releases to online news feeds. Examples include: PR Newswire (www.prnewswire.com);

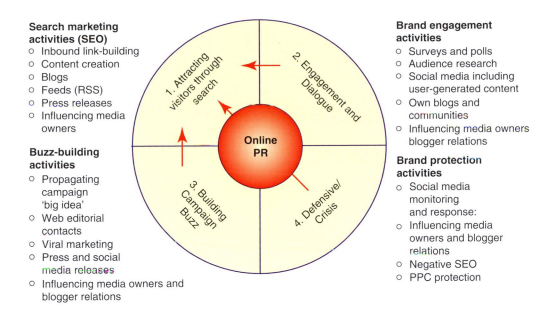

Search marketing activities (SEO)
o Inbound link-building
o Content creation
o Blogs
o Feeds (RSS)
o Press releases
o Influencing media owners

Buzz-building activities
o Propagating campaign 'big idea'
o Web editorial contacts
o Viral marketing
o Press and social media releases
o Influencing media owners and blogger relations

1. Attracting visitors through search

2. Engagement and Dialogue

Online PR

3. Building Campaign Buzz

4. Defensive/ Crisis

Brand engagement activities
o Surveys and polls
o Audience research
o Social media including user-generated content
o Own blogs and communities
o Influencing media owners blogger relations

Brand protection activities
o Social media monitoring and response:
o Influencing media owners and blogger relations
o Negative SEO
o PPC protection

Figure 7.9 Online PR options

Internetwire (www.internetwire.com/iwire/home); PressBox (www.pressbox.co.uk); PRWeb (www.prweb.com) and Business Wire (www.businesswire.com). **Widgets** can also be used to extend your reach and build buzz as described in the box below.

4 *Defensive and crisis PR*. Defensive PR overlaps with many of the activities mentioned above. It is necessary to track the health of a brand online through reputation management tools and then respond accordingly. Crisis PR involves a proactive approach to manage a potentially negative incident such as hardware which has a major flaw or an oil company that has a major incident.

BEST PRACTICE E-MARKETING TIP

Monitor your online reputation

Simple free online reputation management tools including Googlealert (www.googlealert.com) and Google Alerts (www.google.com/alerts) will alert you when any new pages appear that contain a search phrase such as your company or brand names. You can also read our full listing of the main suppliers of online reputation management (www.davechaffey.com/online-reputation-management-tools).

CREATING BUSINESS BLOGS AND FEEDS

Web logs or **'blogs'** are best known as an easy method of publishing personal web pages which are online journals or diaries. But the power of business blogs, which are created by

Figure 7.10   As seen on screen (http://blog.asos.com) blog

people within an organization, is often underestimated. Let's take a look at the some examples and the benefits which are:

- Showcases a company's expertise on a topic – commonly used by analysts, example for Forrester Marketing blog (http://blogs.forrester.com/marketing). Blogs can also showcase the quality of a suppliers data, the approach taken by Hitwise (http://hitwise.com).
- Gives the company views on issues, so useful for reaching journalists who today scour the web for stories, for example CIPR blog, PR Voice (http://prvoice.typepad.com/pr_voice/).
- Can help attract visitors from searchers on the different categories that are blogged on, for example B2B Marketing Agency-B2B International (www.b2binternational.com/b2b-blog) has a great blog.

Business blogs can be created by individuals, but they are often best with features from different columnists on different types of topics. This way, different columnists can specialize on different features or viewpoints just as for a magazine. If you think this way, they are a means of making an e-newsletter more interactive and more topical.

Blogging software is incredibly good value, with many free tools. It is relatively cheap if setup on a separate domain as for the ASOS blog (Figure 7.10) which is effectively a low-cost in-house magazine. It can become more expensive, the more closely integrated it is with the main site since this will require additional development costs for coding. A good template style that reflects the brand is important, but these themes can often be applied using similar cascading style sheets to the main brand, and therefore should not be expensive to create because of the limited number of page types.

The main blogging tools for marketing blogs in rough order of popularity are:

1 Movable Type (www.movabletype.org) from Six Apart is a download for management on your servers. Paid service.
2 Typepad (www.typepad.com), also from Six Apart who offer as an online service similar to most of those below which is easier for smaller businesses. Paid service.
3 Blogger (www.blogger.com), purchased by Google some time ago – the best free option?
4 Wordpress (www.wordpress.com) – open source alternative for download. Highly configurable. Used by many personal bloggers.
5 Other open source CMS are more often used for corporate sites, e.g. Plone, Drupal and Mambo or corporate content management systems such as Microsoft Office SharePoint server.

The blogging format enables the content on a website to be delivered in different ways. We'll use the e-consultancy blog as an example, since this has a lot of rich content which can be delivered in different ways:

- By topic (in categories or topics to browse) – example – online PR category
- By tag (more detailed topics – each article will be tagged with several tags to help them appear in searches) – example 'blogs and blogging' tag
- By author (features from different columnists who can be internal or external) – example – guest column from Andrew Girdwood on SEO
- By time (all posts broken down by the different methods above are in reverse date order). This shows the importance of having a search feature on the blog for readers to find specifics – this is usually a standard feature.

These features are great from a usability viewpoint since they help visitors locate what is most relevant to them. They are also great for SEO, since they provide pages focused on a particular topic, e.g. online PR, which are regularly updated with fresh content. That said, there are many basic blogs which don't have any other option than breaking down by archives.

We think there are surprisingly fewer good examples of blogs used in consumer space. The key difference here is there are great opportunities for getting non-company people to blog. Here are some examples:

- Amazon.com now has blogs for its 'artists'.
- *The Telegraph* has recently enabled users to create their own blogs, so helping increase engagement and generate content on additional topics.

- Thomson Holidays have a blog (http://thomsonholidays.blogs.com/my_weblog) which gives a more visual way of showcasing new offers and packages than flat plain press releases.
- Celebrity fashion store ASOS has a blog (http://blog.asos.com) discussing new ranges and fashions.
- Ford created a soap opera blog – Where are the Joneses.

There are also risks to blogs which may have put many companies off blogging, but these can be countered:

1 *Damage to reputation.* Non-company staff or even company staff can write negative posts or comments or defame others – moderators are needed or a signup process which limits contributors. Alternatively, comments can even be switched off although you lose the benefits of interactivity.

2 *SEO spam.* The Thomson blog has some SEO spam comments with links in the post name to other sites. The impact of these can be limited by using captchas to prevent signup and using the rel='nofollow' tag on hyperlinks, or preventing hyperlinks.

3 *Poor levels of traffic.* If you prominently label your blog on your site then you should get a proportion of traffic to visit and maybe they will bookmark the blog. Blogs often get bookmarked more than the main company site since visitors want a reminder to return. Blogs should attract natural search activity, but as with any SEO activity they require the keywords of posts to reflect searcher behaviour and they need work to attract links-in.

PRACTICAL E-MARKETING TIP

Options for setting up and creating marketing blogs

To summarize, here is is a checklist of ten options to consider when creating a blog for marketing.

☑ 1 *Moderation*: Either open or closed to comments, with or without a moderator. Star rating of posts is a good option.

☑ 2 *Frequency*: Five to 20 posts per month would be typical for a company site unless posted in multiple categories for a new site.

☑ 3 *Authorship:* Do you have a single author – head of company, different contributors or guest contributors?

☑ 4 *Topics:* For usability and SEO, remember to place blog postings of a main blog in categories enable tagging by different keywords. Alternatively you may separate blogs on different topics.

☑ 5 *Integration with web site including SEO.* Links to the blog should be clearly labelled as blog across run-of-site. Article categories should reflect keyphrases you are optimizing for on the main site. Keyphrases within categories and individual posts should show up clearly in <h1> and <title>.

☑ **6** *E-mail digest/e-newsletter integration.* Can you include some blog postings in your e-newsletter or how can the two overlap?

☑ **7** *Linking to third-party sites.* You have the choice of using the rel='nofollow' on comments – I would advise this to discourage comment link spam. See rel='nofollow' definition. Also consider the availability of plug-ins to make blog management easier.

☑ **8** *Images and rich media.* Blogs should easily allow images or videos to be integrated. The CIPD blog focuses on topical podcast interviews.

☑ **9** *RSS Feeds and syndication.* **Really Simple Syndication (RSS)** is an extension of blogging where a blog, news or any type of content is received by specialist reader software integrated with a browser (e.g. Firefox Live Bookmarks) or e-mail package (we recommend Attensa for Outlook). These offer a method of receiving news that uses a different broadcast method to e-mail, so is not subject to the same conflicts with SPAM or SPAM filters. Feeds should be made available for the blog overall or different categories for interested readers to subscribe to. RSS feeds also enable you to distribute your content for use on other sites – so my feeds are included on the Amazon site for example.

☑ **10** *Next Steps/Monetization.* Since blogs like that from ASOS are often set-up on a separate sub-domain (http://subdomain.company.com) with a different style, links through to the site may not be clear. It will help if links to the main site (or ads) are in the left or right sidebars or at the top/bottom of each post where they will be most visible. Also remember links back to the main site from within the blog stories – the ASOS blog links to search results for particular fashion items for example.

E-MARKETING INSIGHT

Use PR to increase PR

Mike Grehan, a UK search engine marketing specialist, stresses the importance of the web to PR. He puts it this way (Grehan, 2004):

> *'Both online and off, the process is much the same when using PR to increase awareness, differentiate yourself from the crowd and improve perception.*
>
> *Many offline PR companies now employ staff with specialist online skills. The web itself offers a plethora of news sites and services. And, of course, there are thousands and thousands of newsletters and zines covering just about every topic under the sun.*
>
> *Never before has there been a better opportunity to get your message to the broadest geographic and multi-demographic audience. But you need to understand the pitfalls on both sides'.*

In the article he also emphasizes the importance of link-building activities to build Google PageRank – the 'PR' referred to in the title.

PORTALS

Understanding **your online marketplace and different portals** on which to gain visibility is important to successful online PR and link-building. We described an approach to this in Section 3.3.

SECTION SUMMARY 7.3

Online PR

1 Online PR is maximizing favourable mentions of your company, brands, products or web sites on third-party web sites that are likely to be visited by your target audience.

2 An important part of this is online reputation management, which is controlling the reputation of an organization through monitoring and controlling messages placed about that organization.

3 There are four main differences between online PR and traditional PR: the audience is connected to the organizations; the members of the audience are connected to each other; the audience has access to other information; audiences pool information.

4 Activities that can be considered as online PR include: communicating with media (journalists) online; link-building; blogs and RSS feeds; managing how your brand is presented on third-party sites; creating a buzz – viral marketing.

7.4 Online partnerships

We showed in Chapter 2 that partnerships are an important part of today's marketing mix. The same is true online. Resources must be devoted to managing your online partners. Many large organizations have specific staff to manage these relationships. In smaller organizations it is often neglected – a big missed opportunity. There are three key types of online partnerships that need to be managed: link-building, affiliate marketing and online sponsorship. All should involve a structured approach to managing links through to your site.

LINK-BUILDING

Link-building is a key activity for search engine optimization. It's simple logic! More quality links from relevant sites mean more quality visitors and more marketing outcomes.

Here is our checklist of six best practice approaches to link-building:

☑ 1 *Achieve natural link-building through quality content* – Through creating 'must-have' resources and guides and using social bookmark tools such as www.addthis.com to encourage visitors to bookmark these documents creates inbound links from sources such as Delicious.

☑ 2 *Request inbound-only or one-way links from partners* or through running a link-building campaign.

☑ **3** *Reciprocal linking* – **Reciprocal links** are agreed between yourself and another organization. These are less valuable than one-way links, but from trusted sources are usually better than no links at all. Use the Yahoo Site Explorer (https://siteexplorer.search.yahoo.com) to identify potential link partners by assessing your own or rival sites.

☑ **4** *Buying links* – Directories and link purchase exchanges (these are not recommended since such sites are widely believed to be penalized by Google when identified). However, Google is unlikely to be able to identify agreements between site owners . . .

☑ **5** *Creating your own external links* – On blogs and in community forums – not typically successful since many forums have introduced an attribute tag on outbound links known as rel='nofollow' which means that the search engine can potentially ignore these links.

☑ **6** *Generating buzz through PR* – Optimize and distribute your press releases or create articles which contain links back to your site which can be syndicated to third-party sites.

E-MARKETING INSIGHT

Ken McGaffin on why linking matters

McGaffin (2004) provides a great introduction to link building. The main principle of link building is as he says:

> *'Create great content, link to great content and great content will link to you'.*

However, a structured link building campaign is also needed to maximize the number of quality inbound or backlinks which are from sites that have a high page rank and from pages with the right content and anchor text. Ken McGaffin recommends these stages in his report at www.linkingmatters.com:

1 *Who links to you now*? Set up Google Webmaster Tools for the best indication of links.

2 *Who links to your competitors*? Use the Yahoo! Site Explorer.

3 *Which sites could link to you*? It helps to categorize the types of site when building links, you will have relationships with many already. For example, directories, media sites, customers, partners and suppliers.

4 *Understand why external sites would link to you.* It also helps to list all the types of content that could encourage links. In particular, content which naturally attracts links, which is known as **linkbait**. Examples include helpful tips, insightful articles and even lists of useful links (don't be afraid to link out from a site). Viral content that people will discuss in blogs is particularly valuable.

5 *Set objectives.* Ask how much you hope to improve your PageRank, the number of links you will seek to gain and how this translates to visitors and competitive positions. This is particularly difficult since one quality link may be more worthwhile than ten poor quality ones which could be discounted by the search engines, or even damage your reputation.

6 *Make sure your site is link friendly*. You should have a URL strategy which means clear URLs that others can use on their site. Facilitating social media is part of this with many sites now having options to bookmark a site with Delicious or Google Bookmarks.

7 *Which links are on your site*? Having sections or articles with links out can encourage others to link to you. It is sometimes suggested that **reciprocal links** are 100% bad, but this is not the case so long as they are not part of link-exchanges. It is also sometimes suggested that links out are 100% bad, but this is not the case if they are useful for visitors and they can lead to you being seen as a hub by search engines.

8 *Ask for inbound links*. Although Ken and link-building experts such as Eric Ward (www.ericward.com) will rightly say that the best links are natural and generated by valuable content, obtaining links proactively is still a key aspect of link-building.

9 *Track and improve*. See the box on tools listed below.

But remember that it is link quality, not link quantity – you need to gain links from sources which the search engines trust.

AFFILIATE MARKETING

Affiliate marketing is the ultimate form of marketing communications since it's pay-per-performance – it's a commission-based arrangement where the merchant only pays when they make the sale or get a lead. Compare this to the wastage with traditional advertising or direct mail! It can also drive a volume of business in a range of sectors – many banks, travel companies or online retailers get more than 10% of their sales from a well-run affiliate marketing programme. It's not so suitable though for business products or lower priced consumer products since it won't be sufficiently profitable for the affiliates.

Figure 7.11 summarizes the affiliate marketing process. To manage the process of finding affiliates, updating product information, tracking clicks and making payments, many companies use an **affiliate network** or **affiliate manager** such as Commission Junction (www.cj.com)

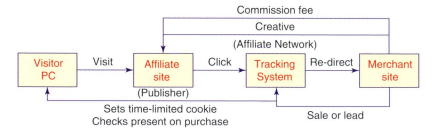

Figure 7.11   The affiliate marketing model (note that the tracking software and fee payment may be managed through an independent affiliate network manager)

or Trade Doubler (www.tradedoubler.com). Since the affiliate network takes a cut on each sale, many merchants also try to set up separate relationships with preferred affiliates often known as 'super affiliates'.

Many of the benefits of affiliate marketing are closely related to search engine marketing since affiliates are often expert at deploying SEO or PPC to gain visibility in the natural search results. The main benefits of affiliate marketing are:

- Gain more visibility in the paid and natural listings of the SERPs (increase 'share of search').
- Can use different affiliates to target different audiences, product categories and related phrases.
- Affiliates may be more responsive than your in-house or agency terms in terms of algorithm changes for SEO or changes in bidding approaches for PPC. They are also great at identifying gaps in your search strategy. For example, they may be quicker at advertising on new products, or may use keyphrase variants that you haven't considered.
- Enables you to reach customers on generic phrases (e.g. 'clothing') at a relatively low cost if the affiliates secure better positions in natural listings.
- Increase the reach of your brand or campaign since affiliate ads and links featuring you will be displayed on third-party sites.
- Can be used to generate awareness of brand or new products for which a company isn't well known.
- Use of affiliates reduces the risk caused by temporary or more fundamental problems with your SEM management.
- Pay per performance – the costs of acquisition can be controlled well.

But there are substantial disbenefits to an affiliate marketing programme which arise from the fact that your affiliates are mainly motivated by money. It follows that some of them may use unethical techniques to increase their revenue. Potential disadvantages are:

- *Incremental profit or sales may be limited*. You may be cannibalizing business you would have achieved anyway as shown in the e-marketing excellence box below.
- *Affiliates may exploit your brand name*. This is particularly the case where affiliates exploit brand names by bidding on variations of it (for example 'Dell', 'Dell Computers' or 'Dell laptop') or by gaining a presence in the natural listings. Here there is already awareness. It is important to prevent this and many affiliate programmes exclude brand bidding although affiliates can have a role in displacing competitors from the listings for brand terms.
- *May damage brand reputation*. Your ads may be displayed on sites inconsistent with your brand image such as gambling or pornography sites. Alternatively creative may be out-of-date which could be illegal.
- *Programme management fees*. If using an affiliate network to manage your campaigns they may take up to 30% of each agreed affiliate commission as additional 'network overridge'.
- *Programme management time*. Affiliate marketing is found on forming and maintaining good relationships. This cannot be done through the agency alone – marketers within a company need to speak to their top affiliates.

E-MARKETING EXCELLENCE

Is affiliate marketing right for us?

The disadvantages of affiliate marketing mean that some marketers may avoid or stop using affiliate marketing.

Dabs marketing director Jonathan Wall explains how dabs.com reappraised their use of affiliate marketing. He said:

> *'We stopped all our affiliate and price-comparison marketing in February because we wanted to see what effect it had on our business and if we were getting value for money.*
>
> *It was proving a very expensive channel for us and we've found [stopping] it has had virtually no effect, because we're seeing that people will still go to Kelkoo to check prices and then come to our site anyway. It's like they're having a look around first and then coming to a brand they know they can trust. We're continuing with paid-for search on Google, but that's all we're doing with online marketing at the moment'.*

More recently, in 2007, affiliates were famously described by Nick Robertson, the CEO of online designer clothing store ASOS as *'grubby little people in grubby studios'*.

E-MARKETING INSIGHT

So just who are these affiliates?

Since affiliate marketing is about relationship marketing, you need to understand your audience. E-consultancy 2007 had some interesting insights on this audience who were:

- 83% male
- 73% are spare time affiliates
- 49% earned less that £500 a year from affiliate marketing
- Of affiliates where affiliate was their main job: 61% earned at least £20 000 a year; 10% earned more than £750 000!

Of the high earners known as super-affiliates some are small businesses, others are wealthy individuals. With the 80:20 rule active here you have to spend time working with the 20% of your affiliates (actually fewer) who will generate over 80% of the sales.

Of promotion techniques 74% favoured Search Engine Optimization (SEO) and 38% favoured paid search. SEO is rated most effective by 43%, with paid search second at 22%. Affiliates are typically signed up with multiple affiliate networks. Only 15% of affiliates are signed up with just one network.

Travel and Flights is the most popular sector for affiliates, followed by Entertainment and Music.

BEST PRACTICE E-MARKETING TIP

Watch your EPC!

Success in affiliate marketing is based on selecting the right commission levels for different products which have different levels of awareness and will have different lifetime values for the retailer. The affiliates or publishers are obsessive about their **Earnings Per Click (EPC)**. EPC stands for Average Earnings Per Click (EPC) and is usually measured across 100 clicks since an average is needed over this number of clicks.

This is a crucial measure in affiliate marketing since an affiliate will compare merchants on this basis and then usually decide to promote those with the highest EPC which will be based on the commission levels and the conversion rates to sale for different merchants. It also depends on the **cookie expiry period** agreed on the time between when a visitor clicks the affiliate link and the sale is accredited to the affiliate. Common times are 7, 30 or 90 days. A longer cookie period will result in a higher EPC. Of course, you don't typically want to pay multiple affiliates for a single sale – although that will boost your EPC. Instead, it is usually the last referring affiliate who is credited or a mix between first and last.

You can compare your EPC for different products against competitors using the affiliate networks, which is valuable insight which you may miss if all is outsourced. You may also be able to use this to benchmark your conversion rates.

For example, at the time of writing, this is how Tesco.com used affiliates for different products:

- E-diets commission from £12 on 1–9 sales to £20 on 61+sales.
- Wine at 2% on lowest tier to 3% on the Gold tier of sales of >£2,500.
- Grocery and utilities – flat fee of £5.

Fees are relatively low on groceries for which Tesco.com is well known, but less so for diets and wine where awareness of the product offering may be lower or competition higher.

DIFFERENT CATEGORIES OF AFFILIATE SITE

Online marketers also need to be selective in choosing the right forms of affiliate marketing – not all may be desirable. These are the options of affiliate marketing models for you to consider.

1 *Aggregators* – These are the big comparison sites like Kelkoo, Shopzilla and MoneySupermarket. These aren't strictly affiliates since most charge per click, but Google Product Search (formerly Froogle) is a free option and you should definitely consider creating a product feed for some of these comparison sites.

2 *Review sites* – You'll know the CNet reviews or maybe startups like Reevoo or Review Centre. These all link to merchants based on cost per click or cost per acquisition deals.

3 *Rewards sites* – With names like GreasyPalm or QuidCo you get the idea. These split the commission between the reward site and their visitors.

4 *Voucher code sites* – MyVoucherCodes or Hot UK Deals are typical. If you have some great deals to entice first time shoppers you should generate business, although many search by well-known brand.

5 *Uber-bloggers* – Martin Lewis's MoneySavingExpert.com is an incredibly popular site due to his PR efforts and great content. Although he has no ads, he is an affiliate for many sites he recommends.

6 *Everyone else* – They don't tend to be high volume super-affiliates like all the above, but they're collectively important and you can work them via affiliate networks like Commission Junction or Tradedoubler. They often specialize in SEO or PPC. Don't expect this option to be easy since affiliates often only promote a few well-known merchants who maximize their Earnings Per 1000 Clicks (EPC).

WHAT ARE WIDGETS?

Widgets are different forms of tools made available on a website or on a user's desktop. They either provide some functionality, like a calculator or they provide real-time information, for example on news or weather.

They are often placed in the left or right sidebar, or in the body of an article. They are relatively easy for site owners to implement, usually a couple of lines of Javascript, but this does depend on the content management system. The ad for Amazon on the right is a static affiliate marketing widget referencing a particular book, but Amazon have other options which update in real-time to show bestsellers or the latest deals.

E-MARKETING INSIGHT

Different types of widgets?

A widget is a badge or button incorporated into a site or social network space by its owner, but with content typically served from another site. They deliver content such as up-to-date information or even mini applications. There are now many types which offer to help a site owner spread their message beyond their own site. In a word, they're about reach. You can encourage partners to place them on their sites and this will help educate people about your brand, possibly generate backlinks and also engage with your brand when they're not on your site (which is the majority of the time). They offer your partner sites the opportunity to add value to their visitors through the gadget functionality or content, or to add to their brand through association with you (co-branding).

1 *Web widgets*. Web widgets have been around for years for affiliate marketing, but they are getting more sophisticated enabling searches on a site, real-time price updates or even streaming video.

2 *Google gadgets*. Different content can be incorporated onto a personalized Google homepage.

3 *Desktop and operating system gadgets*. Vista, the new Microsoft OS, makes it easier to create and enable subscription to these widgets and place them into sidebars.

4 *Social media widgets*. You see these everywhere, for example to encourage site visitors to subscribe to RSS or to bookmark the page on their favourite social media site like Delicious, Digg and Technorati.

5 *Facebook applications*. Facebook have opened up their API (application programming interface) to enable developers to create small interactive programs that users that can add to their space to personalize it. Charitable Giving site Just Giving has a branded API with several hundred users.

ONLINE SPONSORSHIP

Online sponsorship is not straightforward. It's not just a case of mirroring existing 'real world' sponsorship arrangements in the 'virtual world'. There are many additional opportunities for sponsorship online which can be sought out, even if you don't have a big budget at your disposal.

Ryan and Whiteman (2000) define online sponsorship as:

> *'the linking of a brand with related content or context for the purpose of creating brand awareness and strengthening brand appeal in a form that is clearly distinguishable from a banner, button or other standardized ad unit'.*

For the advertiser, online sponsorship has the benefit that their name is associated with an online brand that the site visitor is already familiar with. So, for users of the ISP Wanadoo, with whom they are familiar, sponsorship builds on this existing relationship and trust. Closely related is online 'co-branding' where there is an association between two brands.

Paid-for sponsorship of another site, or part of it, especially a portal for an extended period, is another way to develop permanent links. Co-branding is a lower-cost method of sponsorship and can exploit synergies between different companies. The e-marketing excellence box featured in Section 7.1 'Lexus achieve opt-ins through *Guardian* microsite' shows that sponsorship does not have to directly drive visitors to a brand site – it may be more effective if interaction occurs on the media owner's microsite.

A great business-to-business example of online sponsorship is offered by WebTrends who sponsor the customer information channel on ClickZ.com (www.clickz.com/experts). They combine this sponsorship with different ads each month offering e-marketers information about different topics such as search marketing, retention and conversion marketing through detailed whitepapers and 'Take 10' online video presentation by industry experts which could be downloaded by registered users. The objective of these ads was to encourage prospects to subscribe to the WebTrends WebResults e-newsletter and to assess purchase intent at signup enabling follow-up telemarketing by regional distributors. WebTrends reported the following results over a single year of sponsorship:

- List built to 100 000 WebResults total subscribers.
- 18 000 'Take 10' presentations.
- 13 500 seminar attendees.

E-MARKETING INSIGHT

How effective are online sponsorships?

A study by Performance Research (2001) compared differences in the perception of the online audience to banner ads and sponsorships. Respondents were shown a series of web page screens; for each, half of the respondents were shown a similar version with a banner advertisement, and the remaining half were shown a nearly identical image with web sponsorship identifications (such as 'Sponsored by', 'Powered by' and 'in association with').

The results were illuminating. Of the 500 respondents, ratings for different aspects of perception were:

- Trustworthy (28% for sponsorships to 15% for ads)
- Credible (28% to 16%)
- In tune with their interests (32% to 17%)
- Likely to enhance site experience (33% to 17%)
- More likely to consider purchasing a sponsor's product or service (41% to 23%)
- Less obtrusive (66% to 34%).

SECTION SUMMARY 7.4

Online partnerships

We reviewed three key types of online partnerships:

1 Link-building; obtaining links from third-party sites to a company site. This should be performed in a structured manner to maximize visitors from third-party sites and to help increase page rank within Google.

2 Affiliate marketing; a commission-based arrangement where referring sites are paid a fee for sales, leads or visitors. It is potentially a large source of quality traffic for e-retailers.

3 Online sponsorship; a long-term arrangement to associate a brand with a site, or part of a site.

Widgets can be applied to extend your reach via each of these three arrangements.

7.5   Interactive advertising

A visitor who clicks on an **interactive (banner) ad** at an ad site is then **referred** through to the site of the company who paid for the banner ad which links through to a **destination site** as indicated by Figure 7.12. Many organizations link interactive ads to a specific campaign **microsite**. This provides content tailored to the campaign that appears immediately on clickthrough without the distractions of a link to the standard site. The microsite can be independent of the media owner site, or it can be part of it, which can potentially improve response.

But ad clickthrough rates for non-video formats average a CTR of less than 0.2%. The microsite approach is somewhat ineffective. Instead, today, the name of the game is interaction and engagement. Many ads will encourage the media site visitor to interact through a prompt to 'rollover' and another Flash creative will be loaded which may offer a clear brand message rendered in large font, a response form such as an insurance quote or a request to obtain a SIM or a game or poll. The effectiveness of the ad campaign can then be assessed through the **IR** or **Interaction Rate** which will typically be ten times higher than the clickthrough rate if the targeting, offer and creative is right.

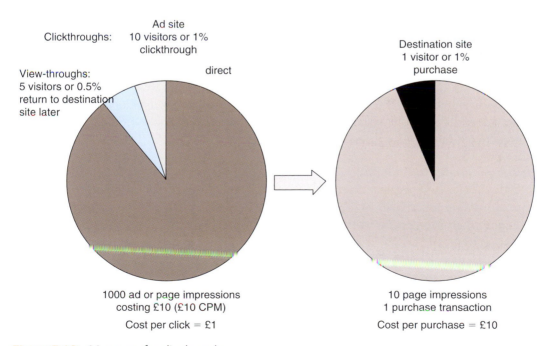

Figure 7.12   Measures for display ads

Although display advertising is often thought of simply as a traffic building technique, there are several alternative objectives which were first summarized by Cartellerieri *et al.* (1997):

- *Deliver content*. Information on-site to help communicate a company's offering.
- *Enable transaction*. An e-tailer intending to use banner ads to increase sales.
- *Shape attitudes*. An advert that is consistent with a company brand or that features a new product can help build brand or product awareness. Research services such as Dynamic Logic (www.dynamiclogic.com) are used by savvy online advertisers to assess the effectiveness of creative in terms of traditional branding metrics such as message association, brand awareness and purchase intent.
- *Solicit response*. An advert may be intended to identify new leads or as a start for two-way communication.
- *Encourage retention*. The advert may be placed to remind about the company and its service.

Some marketers have had a bad experience of online advertising, and certainly there are weaknesses to be aware of including:

1 *Poor and diminishing clickthrough rates*. Partly as a result of banner blindness, there has been a dramatic decline in average clickthrough rates (CTR) from 25% on the first banner in 1994 which simply said click here, to an average of 0.1%, although higher for rich media as video streamed ads.

2 *Relatively high costs*. Relative to some other online marketing tools, such as search engine marketing and affiliate marketing which also have the advantages of being performace-based, interactive advertising costs can be relatively high, with media costs around £10 per thousand ads served (£10 CPM), plus creative costs.

3 *Branding effect difficult to quantify*. Although it is possible to pre-test and post-test online advertising effectiveness, there are relatively few providers in this area. It is a relatively costly discipline.

But before you move on to the next section, online advertising has developed a lot from the early banners and CPM only deals. Consider these advantages of today's display advertising, for example for a car manufacturer:

1 *Ads highly targeted*. Media buyers can select the right site or channel within a site to reach the audience (e.g. a specialist online car magazine or review site or the motoring channel within an online newspaper or TV channel site). Audiences can also be targeted via their profile through serving personalized ads, or ad in e-mail if visitors have registered on a site.

2 *Ad networks can reduce costs*. Ad networks from suppliers such as Blue Lithium or 24–7 Media give advertisers the options of advertising across a network of sites to reach a particular demographic, e.g. female 18–25, but at a lower cost since the actual site used for the ad placement isn't known (hence these are sometimes known as blind network buys). Lower CPMs are achievable and in some cases CPC or CPA payment options are available. Site owners such as publishers use ad networks since it gives them a method of gaining fees from unused ad inventory which has not sold at premium rates.

3 *Behavioural re-targeting options*. It is well known from traditional media campaigns, that the impact of an ad in terms of its ability to shape brand awareness, ad recall and purchase intent is dependent on the ad frequency or the number of times it is seen on average. This effect can be magnified if an ad is served preferentially to someone who seems to have an interest in a topic from the content they consume. Effectively the ad follows the viewer around the site. For example, if someone visits the car section of a site, then the ad is served to them when they view other sections of the site. Retargeting can work across an ad-network too and can even be sequential, where the messages are varied for an individual the more times they are exposed to the ad. Search retargeting offers the option to display an ad after a visitor has searched on a particular term such a car marque. Tracking of individuals is achieved through use of **cookies**.

4 *New ad formats can increase response*. In the early days of online advertising, most ads were simply banners of 468 × 60 dimension. Today if you view ads served by rich media companies such as Tangozebra (www.tangozebra.com) in their labs, you will see that there is a wealth of Flash-based ad formats including expandable banners and skyscrapers where if the user rolls-over the ad, then a new ad can be triggered which might include a streamed video clip, audio, a personalized message or a form prompting someone to order a brochure, book a dealer appointment or perform a search on a site. Effectively the ads are serving a microsite or delivering their web site through an advert!

E-MARKETING EXCELLENCE

Online video advertising best practice

Online video can generate higher response rates of 1–4% according to the compilations of ad serving companies such as Ad Tech (www.adtech.de), but they need to use the right approach to influence more. Research by Dynamic logic summarized in Admap (2007) understandably advises 'Keep it short and simple'. They say: '*While a repurposed 30-second TV commercial may be of some benefit, shorter units may have an even greater impact. Short ads may reach a broader audience by communicating a simple message before viewers have the opportunity to become irritated or impatient and stop the player*'.

Online ads are one of the main revenue models for online media owners so there is a lot of research into how to make them effective. Here we will summarize the issues involved in interactive advertising by setting out five questions to ask when working with agencies when first exploring interactive advertising.

Q1. Mix of offline and online media (are we spending enough?)

The first question to ask is how much are you spending on online elements of campaigns, or, put another way – what is your optimal media mix to increase awareness and purchase intent within your target markets?

Table 7.2   Optimum media mix suggested by XMOS studies

Brand	TV %	Magazine %	Online %
Colgate	75	14	11
Kleenex	70	20	10
Dove	72	13	15
McDonald's	71	16 (radio)	13

Source: IAB (2004)

For any given campaign, media selection and the proportion of spend on online media will often be left to the media planner. But, depending on the agency used, they may play it safe by putting the ad spend into what they are familiar with and what may be most rewarding – offline media. Many **cross-media optimization studies (XMOS)** have shown that the optimal mix for low-involvement products is surprisingly high, with online advertising at 10–15% of total spend.

E-MARKETING INSIGHT

XMOS studies show importance of online spend

XMOS research is designed to help marketers and their agencies answer the question 'What is the optimal mix of advertising vehicles across different media, in terms of frequency, reach and budget allocation, for a given campaign to achieve its marketing goals?' The mix between online and offline spend is varied to maximize campaign metrics such as reach, brand awareness and purchase intent. Table 7.2 summarizes the optimal mix identified for four famous brands. For example, Dove found that increasing the level of interactive advertising to 15% would have resulted in an increase in overall brand awareness of 8%. The proportion of online is small, but remember that many companies are spending less than 1% of their ad budgets online meaning that offline frequency is too high and they may not be reaching many consumers.

Q2. Are we exploiting the full range of ad formats?

The classic 468×60 rotating GIF banner ad is virtually dead – many online veterans suffer from 'banner blindness' – we simply filter out this content. Media owners now provide a choice of larger, richer formats which web users are more likely to notice. Research has shown that message association and awareness building is much higher for Flash-based ads, **rich media** ads and larger format rectangles and skyscrapers. Visit the rich media ads at www.eyeblaster.com or www.tangozebra.com and you will agree that they definitely can't be ignored.

Other online ad terms you will hear include 'interstitial' (intermediate adverts before another page appears); and superstitials (pop-up adverts which require interaction by the user to close them down). Online advertisers face a constant battle with users who deploy pop-up blockers, or, less commonly, ad-blocking software. This is one reason why, in the UK in 2004, 40% of online ad-spend is in PPC – it is more visible – it can't be blocked (yet). Some media sites such as *The Guardian* now charge a premium for those users who don't want to see ads.

Q3. Are your ad buys smart?

Banner advertising is purchased for a specific period. It may be purchased for the ad to be shown or served on:

- The run-of-site (the entire site) and roadblocks
- A relevant section of site
- According to keywords entered on a search engine (the PPC model described earlier in the chapter).

Payment is typically according to the number of customers who view the page as a cost per thousand (CPM or CPT) ad or page impressions. Typical CPM is in the range of £10–£50. Other options that benefit the advertiser if they can be agreed are: per clickthrough, e.g. Valueclick (www.valueclick.co.uk) or per action such as a purchase on the destination site.

Placements on individual pages are also important – an ad is less likely to be viewed below the fold or in a masthead which is above the main menu of a site. Placements which are integrated with the content tend to be most effective and increasingly editorial is bought as part of the deal.

BEST PRACTICE E-MARKETING TIP

Frequency

As for other media, repeated exposure of a web user to an ad will make it more effective until the point of diminishing returns where each of view of the ad doesn't have any additional impact. Research suggests that campaigns should be capped at four. Ask your ad agency to report not only on the average frequency, but also on the frequency distribution.

Q4. Are you using all the targeting options?

Online ads can be targeted through:

1 Purchasing on a site (or part of site) with a particular visitor profile
2 Purchasing at a particular time of day or week

3 Online behaviour – the ultimate in **dynamic ad targeting** according to types of content used. For example FT.com using software from Revenue Science can identify users in eight segments: business education, institutional investor, IT, luxury and consumer, management, personal finance, travel and private equity.

Banner ad networks provide the facility to advertise on a range of properties and target in a range of ways, as shown in the e-marketing excellence box.

Effective online advertisers build in flexibility to change targeting through time. Best practice is to start wide and then narrow focus – allow 20% budget for high performing ad placements (high CTR and conversion).

E-MARKETING EXCELLENCE

Options for targeting advertising

Leading online media owners such as MSN (www.msn.com) and FT (www.ft.com) offer a range of options for targeting:

1 Content targeting. Placement of advertising message on a particular interest site or within an entire interest category such as: automotive, business and finance or health.

2 Behavioural targeting. An audience can be targeted according to how they use the web or an individual site. For example, advertisers can select business users by delivering advertisements on Monday to Friday between 9 am and 5 pm, or leisure users by targeting messages in the evening hours. Ads can be targeted according to the types of content viewed, even when in a different part of the site.

3 User targeting. This enables advertisements to be placed according to specific traits of the audience including their geographic location (based on country or post code), domain type (e.g. educational users with addresses ending in .edu or .ac.uk can be targeted), business size or type according to SIC code or even by the company they work for based on the company domain name. This is possible where users create a profile on a site such as Yahoo! (www.yahoo.com) or FT (www.ft.com) or through automated analysis of the type of content they consume.

4 Tech targeting. This is based on user hardware, software and Internet access provider.

Q5. Are you using creative effectively?

Avantmarketer (www.avantmarketer.com) summarizes these tips for effective online creative:

- Brand the first frame with a brand identity (or the top of skyscrapers).
- Tell a story, but each frame should stand alone.

- Ditch 'Click here!', instead use an action verb such as 'Sign-up now' or 'Download our whitepaper' (many would advise using 'Click here' for some ad types).
- Use high contrast.
- Keep it simple – only use a few elements in ad creative.
- Include a human face where possible.
- Flash makes producing higher impact ads more practical.

Choosing creative for different ad placements is difficult to predict and requires hard work. In an iMediaConnection interview, ING Direct VP of Marketing, Jurie Pieterse highlighted:

> *'Another lesson we learned is the importance of creative. It's critical to invest in developing various creative executions to test them for best performance and constantly introduce new challengers to the top performers. We've also learned there's no single top creative unit – different creative executions and sizes perform differently from publisher to publisher'.*

iMediaConnection (2003)

Finally, consider your options for online sponsorship which is closely related to interactive advertising (online sponsorship is covered in Section 7.4 Online partnerships).

SECTION SUMMARY 7.5

Interactive advertising

Interactive advertisements can help build site traffic, but also have a role in building brand recognition. Rich media and large format ads are effective in targeting visitors through placements on specialized portals and dynamic or behavioural ad targeting. Acquiring customers by banners paid for by CPM is relatively expensive and alternative forms of promotion or payment according to results is preferable.

7.6 Opt-in e-mail

Savvy e-marketers understand that **opt-in e-mail** is a powerful online communications tool. As with direct mail it is most widely used for direct response, but e-newsletters in particular can also achieve branding objectives. It enables a targeted message to be pushed out to a customer to inform and remind and they are certain to view at least the subject line within their e-mail inbox, even if it is only to delete it. Contrast this with the web – a pull medium where customers will only visit your site if there is a reason or a prompt to do this. But there is a problem; in the minds of many Internet users, e-mail is evil. It is **SPAM**, unsolicited e-mail sent by unscrupulous traders. Some say SPAM stands for 'Sending Persistent Annoying E-mail', but it actually originates from the Monty Python sketch. Remember that SPAM is now outlawed in many countries.

To achieve the potential benefits of opt-in e-mail, marketers should take careful measures to avoid SPAM. This section explains how to achieve this.

Opt-in is the key to successful e-mail marketing. Customer choice is the watchword. Before starting an e-mail dialogue with customers, companies must ask them to provide their e-mail address and then give them the option of 'opting into' further communications and selecting their communications preferences, for example the frequency of e-mail and type of content. Privacy law in many countries requires that they should proactively opt-in by checking a box (showing consent in some way). E-mail lists can also be rented where customers have opted in to receive e-mail.

Opt-in e-mail options for customer acquisition

For acquiring new visitors and customers to a site, there are three main options for e-mail marketing. From the point of view of the recipient, these are:

1 *Cold e-mail campaign.* In this case, the recipient receives an opt-in e-mail from an organization who has rented an e-mail list from a consumer e-mail list provider such as Experian (www.experian.com), Claritas (www.claritas.com), IPT Limited (www.myoffers.co.uk) or a business e-mail list provider such as Mardev (www.mardev.com), Corpdata (www.corpdata.com) or trade publishers/event providers such as VNU. Although they have agreed to receive offers by e-mail, the e-mail is effectively cold. For example, a credit card provider could send a cold e-mail to a list member who is not currently their member. It is important to use some form of '**statement of origination**' otherwise the message may be considered SPAM. Cold e-mails tend to have higher CPAs than other forms of online marketing, but different lists should still be evaluated.

2 *Co-branded e-mail.* Here, the recipient receives an e-mail with an offer from a company they have a reasonably strong affinity with. For example, the same credit card company could partner with a mobile service provider such as Vodafone and send out the offer to their customer (who has opted-in to receive e-mails from third-parties). Although this can be considered a form of cold e-mail, it is warmer since there is a stronger relationship with one of the brands and the subject line and creative will refer to both brands. Co-branded e-mails tend to be more responsive than cold e-mails to rented lists since the relationship exists and fewer offers tend to be given.

3 *Third-party e-newsletter.* In this visitor acquisition option, a company publicizes itself in a third-party e-newsletter. This could be in the form of an ad, sponsorship or PR (editorial) which links through to a destination site. These placements may be set up as part of an interactive advertising ad buy since many e-newsletters also have permanent versions on the web site. Since e-newsletter recipients tend to engage with them by scanning the headlines or reading them if they have time, e-newsletter placements can be relatively cost effective.

Opt-in e-mail options for customer retention

For most organizations, e-mail marketing is most powerful for developing relationships with customers as part of e-CRM. We explore options for using e-mail marketing to build relationships with customers through Chapter 8 and specifically in Section 8.5.

MAD use sequential e-mail to assist conversion

MAD (www.mad.co.uk) is a marketing-specific portal accessed through online subscriptions. It offers a trial one-month subscription to its service. During this period, a series of e-mails is used to help convert the prospect to a full subscription. E-mails are sent out at approximately 3, 10, 25 and 28 days to encourage a subscription before the trial lapses.

E-MAIL MARKETING SUCCESS FACTORS

Effective e-mail marketing shares much in common with effective direct e-mail copy. We suggest you use the mnemonic 'CRITICAL' as a checklist for e-mail marketing success factors. CRITICAL is a checklist of questions to ask about your e-mail campaigns (Chaffey, 2006). It stands for:

- *Creative* – This assesses the design of the e-mail including its layout, use of colour and image and the copy (see below).
- *Relevance* – Does the offer and creative of the e-mail meet the needs of the recipients?
- *Incentive* (or offer) – The WIFM factor or 'What's in it for me?' for the recipient. What benefit does the recipient gain from clicking on the hyperlink(s) in the e-mail? For example, a prize draw is a common offer for B2C brands.
- *Targeting and timing* – Targeting is related to the relevance. Is a single message sent to all prospects or customers on the list or are e-mails with tailored creative, incentive and copy sent to the different segments on the list? Timing refers to when the e-mail is received; the time of day, day of the week, point in the month and even the year; does it relate to any particular events. There is also the relative timing – when is it received compared to other marketing communications – this depends on the integration.
- *Integration* – Are the e-mail campaigns part of your integrated marketing communications? Questions to ask include: are the creative and copy consistent with my brand? Does the message reinforce other communications? Does the timing of the e-mail campaign fit with offline communications?
- *Copy* – This is part of the creative and refers to the structure, style and explanation of the offer together with the location of hyperlinks in the e-mail.
- *Attributes* (of the e-mail) – Assess the message characteristics such as the subject line, from address, to address, date/time of receipt and format (HTML or text). Send out Multipart/MIME messages which can display HTML or text according to the capability of the e-mail reader. Offer choice of HTML or text to match user's preferences.
- *Landing page* (or microsite) – These are terms given for the page(s) reached after the recipient clicks on a link in the e-mail. Typically, on clickthrough, the recipient will be

presented with an online form to profile or learn more about them. Designing the page so the form is easy to complete can affect the overall success of the campaign.

Designing direct e-mail copy is as involved as designing direct mail and many similar principles apply. Effective e-mail should:

- Grab attention in subject line and body.
- Be brief and be relevant to target.
- Be personalized – Not Dear Valued Customer, but Dear Ms Smith.
- Provide opt-out or unsubscribe option by law.
- Hyperlink to web site for more detailed content.
- Have clear call-to-action at the start and end of the message.
- Be tested for effectiveness.
- Operate within legal and ethical constraints for a country.

SECTION SUMMARY 7.6

Opt-in e-mail

E-mail is an effective push online communications method. It is essential that e-mail is opt-in, otherwise it is illegal SPAM. Consider options for customer acquisition including cold e-mail, co-branded e-mails and placements in third-party e-mails. For house list e-mails, experiment with achieving the correct frequency, or give customers the choice. Consider automated event triggered e-mails. Work hard on e-mail design and maintaining up-to-date lists. Stay within the law.

7.7 Viral marketing

Ideally, viral marketing is a clever idea, a shocking idea, or a highly informative idea which makes compulsive viewing. It can be a video clip, TV ad, a cartoon, a funny picture, a poem, song, political or social message, or a news item. It's so amazing that it makes people want to pass it on.

Viral marketing harnesses the network effect of the Internet and can be effective in reaching a large number of people rapidly in the same way as a computer virus can affect many machines around the world.

Like most buzz words 'viral marketing' means different things to different people. A viral marketing execution certainly needs to create a buzz to be successful. The two main forms of viral marketing are best known as 'word-of-mouth' and 'word-of-mouse'. Both rely on networks of people to spread the word. Viral marketing also occurs in social networks.

To make a viral campaign happen, Justin Kirby of viral marketing specialists DMC (www.dmc.co.uk) suggests there are three things that are needed (Kirby, 2003):

1 Creative material – the 'viral agent'. This includes the creative message or offer and how it is spread (text, image, video).
2 Seeding. Identifying web sites, blogs or people to send e-mail to start the virus spreading.
3 Tracking. To monitor the effect and to assess the return from the cost of developing the viral agent and seeding.

We distinguish between these types of viral e-mail mechanisms.

1 *Pass along e-mail viral*. This is where e-mail alone is used to spread the message. It is an e-mail with a link to a site such as a video or an attachment. Towards the end of a commercial e-mail it does no harm to prompt the first recipient to forward the e-mail along to interested friends or colleagues. Even if only one in 100 responds to this prompt, it is still worth it. The dramatic growth of Hotmail, reaching ten million subscribers in just over a year, was effectively down to pass-along as people received e-mails with a signature promoting the service. Word-of-mouth helped too.

   Pass-along or forwarding has worked well for video clips, either where they are attached to the e-mail or the e-mail contains a link to download the clip. If the e-mail has the 'WOW!' factor, of which more later, a lot more than one in 100 will forward the e-mail. This mechanism is what most people consider to be viral, but there are the other mechanisms that follow too.

2 *Web facilitated viral (e-mail prompt)*. Here, the e-mail contains a link/graphic to a web page with 'e-mail a friend' or 'e-mail a colleague'. A web form is used to collect data of the e-mail address to which the e-mail should be forwarded, sometimes with an optional message. The company then sends a separate message to the friend or colleague.

3 *Web facilitated viral (web prompt)*. Here it is the web page such as a product catalogue or white paper which contains a link/graphic to 'e-mail a friend' or colleague. A web form is again used to collect data and an e-mail is subsequently sent.

4 *Incentivized viral*. This is distinct from the types above since the e-mail address is not freely given. This is what we need to make viral really take-off. By offering some reward for providing someone else's address we can dramatically increase referrals. A common offer is to gain an additional entry into a prize draw. Referring more friends gains more entries to the prize draw. With the right offer, this can more than double response. The incentive is offered either by e-mail (option 2 above) or on a web page (option 3). In this case, there is a risk of breaking privacy laws since the consent of the e-mail recipient may not be freely given. Usually only a single follow-up e-mail by the brand is permitted. So you should check with the lawyers if considering this.

5 *Web-link viral*. But online viral isn't just limited to e-mail. If you click on any of the links in this article – that can also be considered to be online viral marketing or you could call it online PR. Links in discussion group postings or **blogs** that are from an individual are

also in this category. Either way, it's important when seeding the campaign to try to get as many targeted online and offline mentions of the viral agent as you can.

> ### E-MARKETING INSIGHT
>
> **Seth Godin and the ideavirus**
>
> Godin (2001) writes about the importance of the ideavirus as a marketing tool. He describes it as 'digitally augmented word-of-mouth' and viral marketing is seen as one form of the ideavirus. What differences does the ideavirus have from word-of-mouth? First, transmission is more rapid, second, transmission tends to reach a larger audience and third, it can be persistent – reference to a negative comment about a product or a service on a site such as Epinions (www.epinions.com) remains online to be read at a later time. Godin emphasizes the importance of starting small with a niche audience he describes as a 'hive' and then using advocates in spreading the virus – he refers to them as 'sneezers'.

SECTION SUMMARY 7.7

Viral marketing

With viral techniques, traffic is built either through using e-mail (virtual word-of-mouth) or real-world word-of-mouth to spread the message from one person to the next.

7.8   Offline traffic building

In this section we will see that offline communications are a key component of the e-communications mix. Companies need to decide on whether advertising is *incidental* or *specific*; whether specialist messages need to be communicated and the mix of techniques used. All ten offline communications tools from Smith and Taylor (2004) can and should be used to build online traffic. These ten tools are referred to in Table 2.1. They are: advertising, selling, sales promotion, PR, sponsorship, direct mail, exhibitions, merchandising, packaging, and word-of-mouth – all can be used to communicate or promote in the online or offline world.

How significant is offline promotion? After evaluating the range of online promotion techniques available, you may be asking yourself, 'if all these online techniques are effective, why do companies spend so much on offline advertising?' In fact, the spend on online advertising is dwarfed by spend on advertising in traditional media such as print, TV and radio. In 2007, the UK Internet Advertising Bureau research showed that online ad spend had exceeded 15%, but 85% spend offline is still significant! At the start of the new millennium, global online advertising spend was around 1% of total advertising. On average, it has still not reached double figures, but some leading adopters are now spending more than 10% of their budget online.

PRACTICAL E-MARKETING TIP

Assessing the effectiveness of offline communications as a traffic driver

Web analytics is again your ally in assessing the effectiveness of offline ad spend. You should consider how you will track campaign effectiveness before you start. Some options include:

- Landing page entries direct to the URL promoted in the campaign.
- Number of visitors to site arriving after searching on your brand name or products, campaign names mentioned in the ad (some of these searches will be influenced by offline spend too).
- Increment in number of direct visitors to the site or section of site promoted in campaign compared to business (i.e. same period last month or last year).
- Number of visitors arriving from new-links to the site referencing the campaign.

To summarize, a key decision for e-marketers is deciding on balance of spend between online and offline promotion, as we will see in Section 7.10 on resourcing.

WHAT ARE WE COMMUNICATING OFFLINE?

Important aspects of the online brand to communicate are:

- The URL (of course). In print, using a sub-folder in URL www.domain.com/campaign name can help direct users to the relevant section.
- Online value proposition (see Section 6.3). The ad creative should give a specific benefit for immediately visiting the site.
- Traditional brand values.
- Sales promotions and offers.

Let us now briefly consider four of the main tools, advertising, word-of-mouth, PR and direct mail.

Advertising

Early attempts by many traditional clicks-and-mortar companies to advertise their online offering were limited to **incidental advertising** where the company's web site address was added as a footnote to the advert with no attempt to explain the online proposition or drive a web response. For dotcoms, it is vital to use offline advertising to communicate their online value proposition in specific adverts and traditional companies are increasingly using this approach as more sales are achieved online. Online recruitment agency Monster.com saw its traffic quadruple in the 24 hours following adverts in the prime US Superbowl spot. Many organizations now run **web response ad campaigns** where one of the main objectives is to achieve web site visits. The web may be used to request a sample, enter a competition, find further information or if appropriate, buy online. Enlightened FMCG brands are now using offline advertising in conjunction with the web to get customers to interact with their brand, profile them and add value.

Word-of-mouth

Word-of-mouth is a powerful technique of offline promotion. An urban myth is that if someone successfully buys a book online they will tell ten other people, but if fulfilment is poor, they will tell 20 people! Offline communications techniques such as PR and advertising should be aimed at stimulating word-of-mouth and online viral techniques can also promote this.

PR

PR is a powerful and relatively low-cost form of offline communications. There is good demand amongst the general and specialist media for stories about e-everything. PR can leverage events such as site launches and relaunches with new services, particularly when they are first in a sector. Press releases can be issued through normal channels, but using e-mail linked to the full story on the web site to get information to the journalists faster. Options for getting mentions on the new online-only news sources should be explored. Some defensive, reactive PR may be necessary by scanning press releases on other company sites. The scope for PR stunts related to web sites is limitless. In the US a town, Half.com, has been renamed to be the first dot-com town.

Direct mail and physical reminders

Physical reminders about web site offers are important since most of our customers will spend more time in the real-world than the virtual world. What is in our customers' hands and on their desk top will act as a prompt to visit your site and overcome the weakness of the web as a pull medium. Examples include brochures, catalogues, business cards, point of sale material, trade shows, direct mail sales promotions, postcards (in magazines), inserts (in magazines), password reminders (for extranets).

E-MARKETING INSIGHT

Understanding the opportunities of integrating digital media channels

Digital media, as with other media, are most effective when combined with a range of media. A useful way of characterizing the benefits of integrated communication are the 4Cs of Pickton and Broderick (2000):

- *Coherence* – different communications are logically connected.
- *Consistency* – multiple messages support and reinforce, and are not contradictory.
- *Continuity* – communications are connected and consistent through time.
- *Complementary* – synergistic, or the sum of the parts is greater than the whole!

To help you think of the opportunities for integrating digital media into your communications, refer to Table 7.3.

Table7.3 Marketing communications terminology

Marketing communications term	Definition	Examples
Medium (media)	'Anything that conveys a message.' The carrier of the message or method of transmission. Can be conceived as the touchpoint with the customer.	Broadcast (television, radio), press, direct mail, cinema, poster, digital (web, e-mail, mobile).
Discipline	'A body of craft technique biased towards a facet of marketing communication'. These are traditionally known as 'promotion tools' or the different elements of the communications mix.	Advertising, direct marketing, public relations, market research, personal selling, sales promotion, sponsorship, packaging, exhibitions and trade shows.
Channel (tools)	The combination of a discipline with a medium.	Direct mail, direct response TV, television brand advertising. Digital channels: different forms of search marketing, affiliate marketing, display advertising, e-mail marketing, social media, blogs and feeds.
Vehicle	A specific channel used to reach a target audience.	TV (ITV, Channel 4), newspaper (*Sun*, *Metro*, *Times*), magazine (*Economist*, *Radio Times*), radio (Virgin Radio, BBC radio 5) and their web equivalents. Different search engines such as Google fit, or aggregators such as MoneySupermarket fit here.

When discussing marketing communications, there are many ways to refer to the different facets of campaigns that marketers can control.

Within a team working on a campaign, it is helpful if there is clarity about the opportunities for integrating different media and different agencies involved at the outset. For terminology, the approach recommended by Jenkinson and Sain (2000) of the Centre for Integrated Marketing Communications (CFIM) is sound. They say:

> 'A variety of concepts and terms are used across both academics and practitioners. For example, within our research into media neutral planning, some people referred to media, some to contact points or channels as methods of distributing communication. Similarly, some referred to tools and others to channels, disciplines or methods as the techniques by which the media could be used'.

In practical terms, a sound process is essential for integrating and refining different media throughout the campaign. The checklist developed by ISBA/IPA (2007) is helpful.

☑ 1 Briefing and strategy: all agencies briefed together and strategy agreed upfront
☑ 2 Budgets: discuss, budget accurately and allow for contingencies
☑ 3 Roles and responsibilities: a single point of approval works best
☑ 4 Timings and project planning: plan early
☑ 5 Design and development: stretch yourselves
☑ 6 Tracking and measurement: measure only what matters
☑ 7 Trafficking and campaign launch: plan for quality assurance testing
☑ 8 Produce back-up inventory: saves white space embarrassment – and money
☑ 9 Optimization, reporting, updates: monitor and nurture your campaign in-flight
☑ 10 Learning from analysis of results: test and refine.

E-MARKETING INSIGHT

Jay Walker of Priceline on offline promotion

Jay Walker, co-founder of Priceline.com, a cybermediary for consumer products, has said: 'Priceline.com has been about building a brand as opposed to building traffic. In advertising, you're building a larger context around who you are as a company. To do that, online advertising just doesn't cut it'. In its first 12 months, in the dotcom boom, Priceline.com spent $40 million to $50 million on old-media advertising and it's one of the dotcom survivors.

SECTION SUMMARY 7.8

Offline traffic building

Specific offline communications are vital to traffic building for both dotcoms and clicks-and-mortar companies. Traditional advertising, PR and direct mail are all essential to communicate the URL and IVP. Remember that although we have reviewed online and offline traffic building techniques separately, they need to be part of integrated e-marketing communications.

7.9   Control

This section summarizes how the offline techniques described in other sections of this chapter can be harnessed together and their effectiveness can be assessed. We explore: measuring traffic origin, content and quality. It is closely linked to Section 7.10 on resourcing which explains how the different techniques should be balanced. Key control questions that managers need to answer are:

1 *How is budget allocated?* This is covered in more detail in the resourcing section where it will be seen that often the typical amount spent on online and offline promotion is similar.

2 *How is the contribution of different promotional tools calculated?* The contribution can only be calculated if the right control processes are in place. Using data from server log files the following referrals can be measured directly: affiliate sites, banner ads, partners and links. Market research can be used to estimate customer acquisition from other sources such as: traditional advertising, word-of-mouth and PR.

3 *What is the cost of acquisition?* The cost of customer acquisition is important when assessing each promotion technique. As mentioned above, cost of acquisition can be measured as the cost of acquiring a visitor to site, the cost of acquiring a lead or a customer who makes a purchase. The suitability of each measure will depend on the type of site, but for media sites selling advertising space, cost of visitor acquisition would be most relevant and for e-tailers, cost of customer acquisition will be relevant.

4 *What is traffic quality?* Traffic quality is dependent on whether visitors are within the target group of customers and their propensity to buy. A key measure for traffic quality is **conversion rate** which is calculated by dividing the number of new customers by new visitors. **Repeat visits** are also important to traffic quality. To see whether these objectives are being achieved, customers need to be **tagged** through time, but remember the privacy law implications. **Web analytics** are one method of achieving this (see Table 7.4).

Table 7.4   Relative effectiveness of different forms of marketing communications

Media	Budget (%)	Contribution (%)	Effectiveness
Print (off)	20	10	0.5
TV (off)	25	10	0.25
Radio (off)	10	5	0.5
PR (off)	5	15	3
WoM (off)	0	25	Infinite
Banners (on)	20	20	1
Affiliate (on)	20	10	0.5
Links (on)	0	3	Infinite
Search engine registration (on)	0	2	Infinite

Identifying the contribution from different referrers

With a little forethought, it is possible to collect good information about the contribution of traffic from different referrers. Here are some suggestions:

- Don't link through to the home page, but use a microsite specific to each campaign or referrer (sometimes called a CURL, or campaign specific URL).
- Use a different web page or directory for different advertisers, e.g. www.name.com/promotion_name, if necessary a number of pages can be used for different referrers, which then **redirect** through to a common page.
- Enable the referrers option in the server log file (see below) to collect information about the relative importance of different referrers.
- Ask the customer how they were referred through conventional or online questionnaires.

WEB ANALYTICS

Valuable information on the effectiveness of promotion is available from **web analytics tools**. These software tools record 'site statistics' such as the volume of traffic, its source (referring sites) and which content is popular on site including **clickstreams** of each visit.

Two alternative technical approaches are commonly used to capture this information. Traditionally, server-based tools such as WebTrends were popular, particularly for large enterprise sites. These work by summarizing, across different time periods, all the events recorded in a transaction log file every time a web page or graphic is downloaded for viewing by a site visitor. More recently, browser-based measurement tools such as Google Analytics, Omniture, Visual Sciences or Indextools have become more popular since these are more accurate. Browser-based tools work by including a small piece of Javascript in each page which records the page view on a separate (remote) server. Browser-based tools such as that shown in Figure 7.8 have the advantage that information can be accessed in real-time and visits to pages are recorded each time a page is viewed. This contrasts with the server-based approach where repeat visits may not be identified if the pages have already been loaded and are cached by the browser or a server. A combination of tools is often used since server-based tools are best for managing server load, page errors and identifying crawling by search robots.

The most valuable type of information available from web analytics systems to improve your traffic building includes:

1 *Referring sites*. The proportion of visitors from different sites indicates the relative importance of referrers. This is useful for identifying potential link-partners. You can also segment site visitors by different types of visitors to see which drive the most valuable traffic.

2 *Referral time*. The most popular days and times of arrival of visitors can be used to plan the timing of future campaigns such as e-mail campaigns.

3 *Search engine keywords*. Search engine keyphrases indicate the behaviour of customers trying to find your site and can be used to assess the success of your SEM efforts.

4 *Conversion rates*. Conversion to key outcome pages such as registration pages or purchase pages can be calculated to understand the effectiveness of site design, messaging and incentives. In Google Analytics these are called 'Goal Conversion pages'. Once you have identified them and set a monetary value against them, you can assess the value of different referrers and pages in driving this value.

5 *Stickiness*. The duration of visitors on different pages of your site can be used to assess whether visitors are finding what they require. Assessing the **bounce rates** of different landing pages and different referrers is also really helpful information that can be used to refine campaigns and site copy and creative.

6 *Repeat visits*. During a campaign we need to see whether the proportion of visitors on the site are new or existing customers. Cookies or registration on a web site need to be used to estimate repeat visitors. Here there are relatively few new users, so a banner campaign is probably not currently active and most visitors are looking for technical support.

E-MARKETING INSIGHT

Eric Peterson demystifies web analytics

Eric, an analyst specializing in web analytics, defines it as:

> 'Web analytics is the assessment of a variety of data, including web traffic, web-based transactions, web server performance, usability studies, user submitted information (i.e. surveys), and related sources to help create a generalized understanding of the visitor experience online'.

Note that in addition to what are commonly referred to as 'site statistics', sales transactions, usability and researching customers' views through surveys are also included. The definition could also refer to comparison of site visitor volumes and demographics relative to competitors using panels and ISP collected data.

We believe, though, that the definition can be improved further – it suggests analysis for the sake of it – whereas the purpose of analytics should be emphasized. Our definition is:

> 'Web analytics is the customer-centred evaluation of the effectiveness of Internet-based marketing in order to improve the business contribution of online channels to an organization'.

(*Sources*: Peterson 2004, www.davechaffey.com).

PANEL DATA AND AUDITING

In addition to measuring traffic directly from a site, it is also possible to use **panel data** to estimate your traffic, break it down by socio-demographic characteristics and compare it to competitors. A panel member is profiled in terms of socio-demographics and software is installed on their PC to monitor the sites they visit. Examples of online panel data providers are Nielsen Netratings (www.netratings.com) and Comscore (www.comscore.com). Similar data is available from Hitwise (www.hitwise.com) which aggregates data from ISPs it has signed agreements with to show the relative popularity of sites (online audience share) within a sector. Hitwise is particularly valuable since it gives information on competitors such as which keyphrases they rank well for, which traffic sources drive visitors and click-streams showing sites their audience visit before and after the site.

SECTION SUMMARY 7.9

Control

Control activities should target assessing the effectiveness of promotion campaigns against objectives of: traffic volume; traffic quality (marketing outcomes); cost of visitor and customer acquisition for different promotional techniques. Log file analyzers and panel data are important in making this evaluation.

7.10   Resourcing

Resourcing is about achieving the correct balance of investment between traffic building and other e-marketing activities. Other aspects of resourcing that must be balanced are between online and offline promotion and between campaign and continuous traffic building activities.

Table 7.3 provides an example of the promotional mix for a fictitious company. There are a range of promotional techniques comprising the total budget. Which would you say are most cost effective in terms of their contribution to revenue? It is apparent that the lower-cost methods shown at the bottom of the table including affiliates, word-of-mouth, PR and link building are all effective.

Watson *et al.* (2000), although dated, does suggest the different levels of effectiveness of media for digital marketing. Therefore, constant monitoring of integration is crucial.

BALANCE BETWEEN TRAFFIC BUILDING AND OTHER E-MARKETING COSTS

You also need to be clear about what is the right balance between expenditure on:

1 Web-design or creation
2 Service or maintenance
3 Traffic building (promotion).

It has been suggested that many European sites have allocated resources between design, service and traffic in the ratio 5 to 2 to 1. However, for many US sites, these were in the order 1 to 2 to 5, i.e. with the emphasis firmly on traffic. You need to review carefully what is right for your business.

Deciding on the best communications mix for an online campaign is perhaps more of an art than a science, because there are so many elements (which we introduced at the start of this chapter) which should influence your decision. When selecting each digital marketing channel, you should assess its:

- *Cost per acquisition* (CPA). You will naturally be looking to minimize this, it will depend on the combination of media costs, delivery of the right target audience and conversion rates.
- *Volume.* More campaign expenditure will typically go into the channels that drive volume, often paid search which can also have a well controlled CPA. Having a low CPA channel is not helpful if it doesn't drive volume because it is not possible to purchase sufficient media.
- *Conversion.* Not all digital channels convert equally, for example paid search tends to convert slightly more highly than natural search since searchers have sought out the paid ad. Similarly paid search tends to convert better than display ads since with the former searchers have higher intent and are more directed while with display ads, they may have clicked more out of impulse.
- *Flexibility.* Important for larger campaigns, is it possible to build in tests and amend the creative to gain better results, as is the case with paid search and display ads.
- *Frequency.* Does the channel enable you to re-target to repeat messages as is the case with behavioural retargeting and paid search?
- *Risk.* Is it a tried and tested channel which you can be confident of delivering results? Viral marketing, for instance, or renting an e-mail list are both high-risk strategies, display advertising and paid search lower risk.

E-MARKETING INSIGHT

Zed media on assessing the right online marketing mix

Selection of the right type of e-tools will vary according to whether your campaign is focused on creating direct response, which is more typical for transactional categories such as finance, travel and retail or whether awareness is more important, which is more typical for many business-to-business categories or consumer goods. Figure 7.13 shows how one agency estimates mix can vary according to type of campaign. You can see that for direct response, paid search and affiliate marketing are often most suitable with lower budgets, while display advertising is a relatively small part of the mix. This is reversed for awareness campaigns.

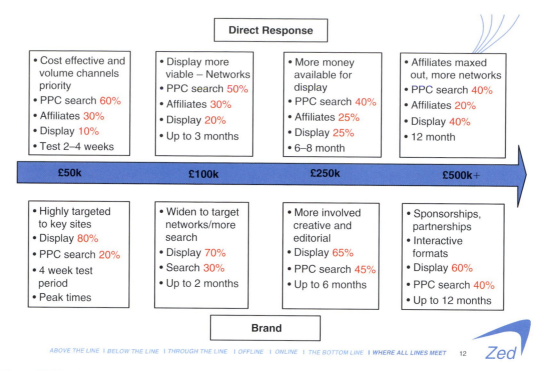

Figure 7.13 Options for varying the mix for direct response and brand awareness campaigns

BALANCE BETWEEN ONLINE AND OFFLINE PROMOTION

Defining the correct balance between investment in online and offline promotion is another key aspect of resourcing. The appropriate balance is determined by many factors, but the most important is the percentage of sales that are informed or completed online. In the foreseeable future investment in offline communications will still dominate overall, because of its power in creating awareness and demand for brands which will often then give rise to site visits.

BALANCE OF CAMPAIGN AND CONTINUOUS TRAFFIC BUILDING

It would be a mistake to spend an entire promotion budget on campaigns. A proportion should be left for expenditure required every month of the year for search engine re-registration and updating; updating copy to improve search engine positions; link building; managing long-term sponsorship arrangements and direct opt-in e-mail.

SECTION SUMMARY 7.10

Resourcing

Resourcing is about achieving the right balance of: promotion, service and design; online and offline promotion and campaign activities and continuous traffic building. For campaigns, resourcing decisions include: banner run length, ad-weighting, targeting and campaign size.

CHAPTER SUMMARY

1 Traffic building or visitor acquisition is dependent on defining the appropriate *targets* of traffic quantity and quality, using the correct combination of online and offline *techniques* and using both campaign-based and continuous *timing*.

2 An organization's presence on a range of search engines should be achieved and then optimized by using specialist techniques such as rewriting copy, redesign and link-building. Pay per click marketing can be essential to achieve visibility in competitive markets.

3 Organizations should consider their online reputation and visibility by reviewing options for online PR and their representation on a range of portals: horizontal, vertical and geographic.

4 You should review your potential online partners to drive visitors by link-building, affiliate marketing and online sponsorship.

5 A wide range of different types of interactive ads, including skyscraper, large rectangle and rich-media formats, can be used to refer traffic to the site and can also be used for brand building.

6 Opt-in e-mail is an effective method of communications since it is a push method delivering information to the mail inbox of the audience. E-mail options include newsletters, promotional campaigns and as a conversion tool.

7 Viral e-marketing techniques involve transmitting a marketing message using word-of-mouth or online word-of-mouth (e-mail and chat).

8 Offline communications are essential to achieve reach amongst an audience to increase awareness and explain the Internet value proposition.

9 Control supported by web analytics software should be in place to assess the effectiveness of promotional campaigns against objectives of traffic volume, traffic quality and cost of acquisition.

10 Resourcing issues involve budgeting a suitable expenditure on site creation, maintenance and advertising; getting the right balance between the mix of online and offline promotional techniques and campaign-based and continuous traffic building.

References

Admap (2007) The effectiveness of online video advertising, Suzanne Moorey-Denham and Ann Green, March 2007, pp. 45–7.

Atlas DMT (2004) The Atlas Rank Report: How Search Engine Rank Impacts Traffic. Available from Research Insights, http://www.atlasdmt.com/insights.

Bharat, K. and Mihaila, G. (1999) Hilltop: A Search Engine based on Expert Documents http://www.cs.toronto.edu/~georgem/hilltop/.

Cartellerieri, C., Parsons, A., Rao, V. and Zeisser, M. (1997) The real impact of Internet advertising. *The McKinsey Quarterly*, Vol. 3, pp. 44–63.

Chaffey, D. (2006) *Total E-mail Marketing*, Second edition. Butterworth-Heinemann, Elsevier, Oxford.

E-consultancy (2007) Search Engine Optimisation Best Practice Guide. Available from www.e-consultancy.com.

Farris, J. and Langendorf, L. (2001) Engaging customers in e-business, How to build sales, relationships and results with e-mail. White paper available online at www.e2software.com.

Godin, S. (2001) Unleashing the ideavirus. Available online at: www.ideavirus.com.

Google (2007) Understanding the Quality Score, Google Help Center. http://adwords.google.co.uk/support/bin/answer.py?answer=10215.

Grehan, M. (2004) Increase your PR by increasing your PR. *E-marketing News*, November. http://www.e-marketing-news.co.uk/november.html#pr.

Hoffman, D.L. and Novak, T.P. (2000) How to acquire customers on the web. *Harvard Business Review*, May–June, pp. 179–188. Available online at: http://ecommerce.vanderbilt.edu/papers.html.

IAB (2004) XMOS research centre. Interactive Advertising Bureau (www.iab.net/xmos).

iMediaConnection (2003) Interview with ING Direct VP of Marketing, Jurie Pieterse http://www.imediaconnection.com/content/1333.asp.

ISBA/IPA (2007) Best practice guide for online campaign development http://www.isba.org.uk/isba/news/article.jsp?ref=526.

Jenkinson, A. and Sain, B. (2003) Getting words clear – Marketing needs a clear and consistent terminology. Available from Centre for Integrated Marketing (www.integratedmarketing.org.uk).

Kirby, J. (2003) Online viral marketing: next big thing or yesterday's fling? *New Media Knowledge*, March. http://www.nmk.co.uk/knowledge_network/kn_item.cfm?ItemID54884&ThreadID546.

McGaffin, K. (2004) Linking Matters. How To Create An Effective Linking Strategy To Promote Your Web Site. Published at www.linkingmatters.com.

New Media Age (2006) Banking on Search. *New Media Age*, 16.03.06.

New Media Age (2005) Product placement. By Sean Hargrave. New Media Age. www.nma.co.uk. 12/05/05.

Performance Research (2001) Performance Research Study 'Mastering Sponsorship On-Line'. http://www.performanceresearch.com/web-based-sponsorships.htm.

Peterson, E.T. (2004) Web Analytics Demystified: A Marketer's Guide to Understanding How Your Web Site Affects Your Business. Available from www.webanalyticsdemystified.com.

Pickton, A. and Broderick, D. (2000) *Integrated Marketing Communications*. Financial Times/Prentice Hall, Harlow.

Pincott, G. (2000) Web site promotion strategy. White paper from Millward Brown Intelliquest. Available online at www.intelliquest.com.

Ranchhod, A., Gurau, C. and Lace, J. (2002) On-line messages: developing an integrated communications model for biotechnology companies. *Qualitative Market Research: An International Journal*, Vol. 5, No. 1, pp. 6–18.

Ryan, J. and Whiteman, N. (2000) Online Advertising Glossary: Sponsorships. ClickZ Media Selling channel, 15 May.

Smith, P.R. and Taylor, J. (2004) *Marketing Communications – An integrated approach*, 4th edition. Kogan Page, London.

Van Doren, D., Fechner, D. and Green-Adelsberger, K. (2000) Promotional strategies on the World Wide Web. *Journal of Marketing Communications*, Vol. 6, pp. 21–35.

Watson, R., Zinkhan, G. and Pitt, L. (2000) Integrated Internet Marketing. *Communications of the ACM*, Vol. 43, No. 6, pp. 97–102, June.

Williamson, D. (2001) Lastminute.com sets off Easter campaign. *Revolution*, 4 April.

Further reading

Hoffman, D.L. and Novak, T.P. (2000) How to acquire customers on the web. *Harvard Business Review*, May–June, pp. 179–188. Available online at: http://ecommerce.vanderbilt.edu/papers.html.

Web links

A4UForum. See www.a4uforum.co.uk. Used by affiliates to discuss approaches and compare programmes.

Atlas DMT Research Insights, (www.atlasdmt.com/insights). Detailed research on effectiveness of search marketing and advertising such as impact of frequency and reach on ad effectiveness.

ClickZ (www.clickz.com). An excellent portal for the online marketer to learn more, with channels for different e-tools such as e-mail marketing, search and ad buying.

Dave Chaffey Digital Marketing Strategy Guides (www.davechaffey.com/guides). A summary of strategy and tools available for the full range of digital marketing channels.

Dave Chaffey's keyword suggestion tools (www.davechaffey.com/seo-keyword-tools). The latest version of a range of free and paid tools for natural and paid search.

Doubleclick Knowledge Central (www.doubleclick.com/knowledge_central). US, European and Asian trends on responsiveness to advertising campaigns.

E-consultancy (www.e-consultancy.com). One of the best sources for details about traffic building tools such as search and affiliates. Includes specific channels on each with buyers' guides and best practice guides.

E-marketing Excellence book homepage (http://www.davechaffey.com/E-marketing). An index of all e-marketing links for each chapter in this book.

Google Webmaster tools (www.google.com/webmasters) provides a useful set of tools for sites verified by their owners including index inclusion, linking and ranking for different phrases in different locations.

E-metrics (www.emetrics.org). Articles and insights about web analytics collated by Jim Sterne of Target Marketing.

IMediaConnection (www.imediaconnection.com). 'State of the art' articles and guidance on interactive advertising techniques.

Ken McGaffin's Linking Matters (www.linkingmatters.com) gives a basic summary of a commonsense approach to link-building which covers some of the approaches above.

Searchenginewatch (www.searchenginewatch.com). This is the premier source for keeping up-to-date on the significance of different search engines and the techniques they use.

Search Engine Land (www.searchengineland.com). Blog by Danny Sullivan, the leading commentator on the search engine industry, containing updates on all major and many minor developments.

Yahoo! Site Explorer (https://siteexplorer.search.yahoo.com) can be used to check number of pages within the Yahoo! index and identify links from other sites.

Self-test

1 Define appropriate measures for traffic building quantity and quality for a campaign for your organization's site.

2 Distinguish between the operation of a search engine and a directory. What are the implications for promotion of a company?

3 List the relevant portals your company *should be* and *is* represented on. Include horizontal portals, vertical portals and geographical portals.

4 What approaches should be used in a link-building campaign?

5 Assess the relevance of banner advertising to your organization through reviewing their advantages and disadvantages.

6 Summarize the elements of effective opt-in e-mail.

7 List the different types of viral marketing campaigns for which you have been a recipient. Which could be effective for your own organization?

8 Explain why offline communications are significant. What should be their aims?

9 Review the suitability of different forms of measuring the effectiveness of a web campaign including server log file analysis, traditional market research and audience panels.

10 Audit the current balance of online and offline traffic building techniques used in your organization, producing a summary as for Table 7.1.

Chapter **8**

E-CRM

'What self respecting marketer would subject his organization's valuable customers to lengthy phone queues as they wait to talk to someone about their phone bill or bank account and then, when they finally get through, be unable to properly hear the person on the other end of the line'.

Wright (2007)

OVERVIEW

Online customer relationship management is packed with fundamental common sense principles. Serving and nurturing customers into lifetime customers makes sense as existing customers are, on average, five to ten times more profitable. At the heart of this is a good database – the marketer's memory bank, which if used correctly, creates arguably the most valuable asset in any company. In this chapter we show how to develop integrated e-mail contact strategies to deliver relevant messages throughout the customer lifecycle.

OVERALL LEARNING OUTCOME

By the end of this chapter you will be able to:

- Apply basic Customer Relationship Management principles in the online world
- Appreciate the careful planning required to create the perfect database
- Begin to develop and nurture a properly integrated, multi-channel database.

CHAPTER TOPIC	LEARNING OBJECTIVE
8.1 Introduction	Understand the significance of e-CRM
8.2 Relationship marketing	Explain the basic principles of relationship marketing and the importance of coherent contact or communications strategies
8.3 Database marketing	Grasp the basic principles of database marketing
8.4 E-CRM	Specify what new media add to CRM
8.5 Profiling	Know how to approach profiling
8.6 Personalization	Know the options for personalizing web sites, opt-in e-mails, prices and promotions.
8.7 E-mail marketing	Develop a strategy for managing inbound e-mail, outbound e-mail marketing campaigns and e-newsletters.
8.8 Control issues	Develop a control strategy
8.9 Cleaning the database	Assess approaches to database cleaning
8.10 Making it happen	Outline a plan to achieve e-CRM

8.1 Introduction to CRM

This section introduces **e-CRM**, explains what it is, how it is inextricably linked with database marketing, why e-CRM is so important to delivering competitive advantage, yet often underused, and how the other sections in this chapter fit together.

So first, what is e-CRM? Customer Relations Management with an 'e'. Ultimately, e-CRM cannot be separated from CRM, it needs to be integrated, and seamlessly. However, some organizations do have specific e-CRM initiatives or staff responsible for e-CRM. Both CRM and e-CRM are not just about technology and databases, it's not just a process or a way of doing things, it requires, in fact, a complete customer culture.

In many ways there's nothing new here since good marketers have been taking care of their customers for many decades now. What is new is the lack of CRM in the fast moving online world:

- A world where customer expectations are often higher than those of the offline world.
- A world where customers' raised expectations are regularly crushed by previously successful offline companies.
- A world where customer e-mails are left unanswered for days.
- A world where immediate responses are expected, but more often than not, are not delivered.
- A world where satisfying customers is simply not enough to keep them.
- A world of consolidating relationships. . . . where surfers visit fewer sites but spend longer with them.

We are sitting on a customer service time bomb. Vast numbers of faulty web sites, millions of customer e-mails ignored, customer data lost and companies don't even know who their customers are let alone answer their e-mails. Half the FTSE 100 cannot profile their own customers. Two thirds of European companies cannot track customer relationship history. Half of all CRM projects fail. More than two thirds of all IT projects fail. The few CRM systems that do work focus on value restoration (dealing with complaints) rather than value creation (enhancing the customers experience). And all the while customer expectations are rising.

CONSUMERS ARE FEELING BAFFLED, BERATED AND BETRAYED

Processes companies have for handling customer feedback are often weak and fragmented and are not supported by systems . . . customers prefer to stand in queues in banks rather than deal with automated telephone systems.

Professor Merlin Stone (2004)

Has anything changed since 2004?

It gets worse. Overall, CRM is going backwards. Products have got better (rust proof cars), but service has got worse. 'Customer satisfaction is declining in just about every market I've looked at over the last 15 years. Yet more money is being spent than ever before measuring customer satisfaction. Most things marketing people do tend to be of no value whatsoever' (Earls 2004). Mark Earls believes that 'Much of the time we produce things which are of no value to anyone'.

Constant cost cutting and operational failings have shifted the emphasis of many CRM programmes from value creation to value restoration. Fujitsu have found that 50%–70% of calls to call centres are for value restoration (Mitchell 2004) – repairing something that the company has not done correctly e.g. late delivery, out of stock, wrong delivery, poor product quality).

38% of major UK companies ignore incoming customer e-mails. This seems ridiculous. It is. Egain's State of Customer Service study found that 38% of 'major UK companies' don't bother to respond to e-mails despite the fact that their numbers are increasing. Retailers had the best track record, responding to 70% of e-mails, but telecoms had the worst – 58% of e-mails were simply ignored (Egain 2007).

The list continues. 50% of the FTSE 1000 do not know who their customers are, i.e. they cannot profile their own customers (MORI 2003). Has it improved since? 66% of European companies cannot track customer relationship history (Smith 2004). 50% of companies lose crucial customer information when staff leave (as the information is held on palmtops, lap tops and mobiles). 50% of CRM projects fail, that is, they completely fail to live up to expectations, while another 20% substantially fail to live up to expectations (Gartner 2004).

Microsoft recently looked at a high growth economy, Ireland, and found that most executives lack the information needed to enable effective decision-making, which means that companies are flying blind (Microsoft 2006). Perhaps part of the problem is that we marketers allow CRM projects to be included under the broad heading of IT projects. IT is not an end unto itself. It simply is a process to help run a business. However, the numbers are even worse here. 74% of IT projects failed in 2005 – this, surprisingly is the same percentage as in Standish Group and Gartner Group's 1980 survey (Tranfield and Braganza 2007). Why? Partly scope creep (constantly adding extra requirements into the brief) partly lack of buy-in from staff who fear change and partly lack of training. Motivation and training programmes are required to bring people on board. This was recognized as a problem a few years ago when a Business Europe.com survey revealed that 25% of marketing professionals record customer details incorrectly and 40% of marketing professionals do not share customer contacts with colleagues. Training and motivation are critical components in any CRM programme.

In addition, old CRM systems were effectively automated selling systems that took little or no account of what customers actually wanted. Danger bells should start ringing when an IT consultant offers a front end automated solution that cuts costs and streamlines operations and processes because this does not necessarily make marketing more effective.

'But new technologies are being implemented with the overriding aim of driving efficiencies and cost savings rather than enhancing the customer service. A strong

marketing director who is respected through out the organization can, at worst, ensure that the customer is not adversely affected by a new IT investment, and, at best, ensure that the investment delivers tangible customer benefits'.

Wright (2007)

THE GOLDEN OPPORTUNITY

The good news is that this presents a golden opportunity to create competitive advantage by developing an integrated CRM system that adds value to customers' experiences, brings them closer to us, listens to them, collects data and serves their needs better than ever before. Organizations like McKinseys are forecasting the 'after sale market' (after sales service, consultancy, training) to be where many companies will find new growth. This emphasizes the critical importance of CRM systems that work for customers first and the company second.

A key e-CRM concept is **Sense and Respond marketing**. The Sense, Respond, Adjust approach of delivering relevant, **contextual marketing** communications through monitoring customer behaviour. E-CRM enables digital marketers to create a multi-channel marketing process of:

- Monitoring customer actions or behaviours (clicks on specific e-mails or website offers) and then. . .
  - Reacting with appropriate messages either online, for example through an e-mail follow-up, or offline, for example, a phone or direct mail follow-up to encourage response
  - Monitoring response to these messages and continuing with additional reminder communications and monitoring.

The secret is to put the time into defining rules and testing automated follow-up communications which match the context. For example, an online shopper who has purchased a product can be sent a series of welcome e-mails in the context of their purchase to encourage future purchases (Figure 8.1).

SOME e-CRM BENEFITS AND CHALLENGES

There is e-CRM software which enhances our ability to understand customers and enquirers, their needs, names, interests and a lot more. We can get closer to them. Speak with them. One of the 5Ss – the five fundamental benefits of e-marketing.

A dynamic dialogue that is instantaneous, relevant, value adding and information gleaning:

- recognizes and remembers each customer by name and need
- answers questions often automatically and ideally, personally
- asks questions, collects information and builds a better profile, particularly of those, ideal, lifetime customers.

The real potential advantage of online marketing lies in its potential to build relationships and create long-term value. Companies who have risen to the challenge of E-CRM have a

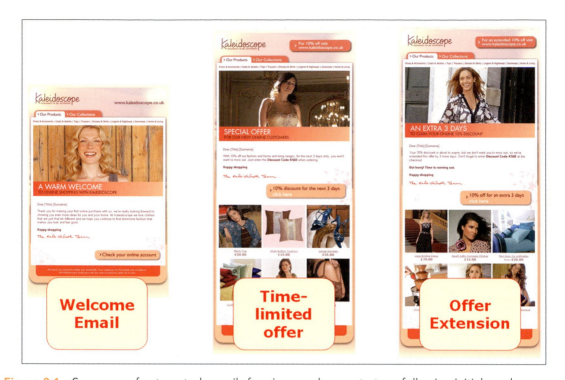

Figure 8.1 Sequence of automated e-mails forming a welcome strategy following initial purchase

'360 degree view of their customers'. This in turn generates real loyalty from lifetime customers who readily share valuable data with you.

Have you got the software to exploit the valuable data you can collect from customers? Most don't. Have you got the processes in place to ensure excellent service – that keeps customers coming back for more? On average purchase intent sees a double digit increase after someone has been to a site more than once (Flores and Eltvedt 2005). Keeping existing customers coming back for more is more profitable than acquiring new customers. Flores and Eltvedt suggest it is ten times more profitable to serve an existing customer than recruit a new one. It therefore makes a lot of sense to nurture the captured customers into lifetime friends. CRM and e-CRM helps to keep ideal customers. Customer retention can be improved by improving CRM. The returns on this investment are large.

All of this is a new business environment. This is completely different to just a few years a go. The time-compressed, information-fatigued, impatient customer is unforgiving. 80% of consumers will never go back to an organization after a bad customer experience, up from 68% in 2006 (Harris Interactive 2007). Combine this with customers who talk back and who talk to each other courtesy of new social media or Web 2.0 and the goal posts have moved for many marketers. Social network sites facilitate customer discussions (Coca Cola never asked for rockets, it just happened that customers discovered that mixing Coke and Mentos mints caused an explosive reaction and customers started posting videos of this phenomenon). User Generated Content (UGC) is not totally controllable, as Chevrolet and Nike discovered (see the customer bites back in eCustomers). Web 2.0 is here to stay. It will grow in line with the very human need for social contact. Customers have been mobilized by blogs, social network sites and invitations to create UGC to name but a few Web 2.0 tools. The old CRM customer dialogue has evolved in the customer trialogue (see eModels).

> *'The hardest lesson to learn is that there are smarter people not working for your company than there are working for your company'.*

> *Michael Boreel referring to customers and other stakeholders (including pressure groups) who generate content outside of your control and all about your brand.*

The online world presents new challenges when nurturing customer relationships. This e-CRM chapter has sections on the key elements including two introductory-level sections on CRM itself and Relationship Marketing, Database Marketing as well as Personalization, Profiling, Managing Incoming e-mails and Implementing e-CRM.

Remember CRM, or e-CRM in particular, is not about technology, it's not just a process or way of doing things, it requires, in fact, a complete customer culture. The challenge is yours.

Given these benefits of e-CRM, many companies have attempted to implement CRM technologies to help give a 'single view of the customer'. The challenge of CRM is that it is not just an immense technological challenge, but it is also a challenge because of the change management needed for changes in process and the role of staff.

E-MARKETING EXCELLENCE

Boots 'Change One Thing' campaign

This example shows how e-CRM can be built into a marketing campaign. In this campaign the web site, database of customer preferences and e-mail marketing were at the core of an integrated campaign based around the big idea of self-improvement.

Offline communications delivered by TV and print ads plus editorial coverage were used to inspire an audience to take on a personal challenge such as losing weight or giving up smoking at the start of the year. These communications were used to drive visitors to the web where they could then select their challenge and interact with others with the same challenge.

E-mails were sent to remind participants and help them sustain the challenge. Automated, personalized e-mails (and texts) were sent throughout the lifecycle of the relationship. For example to:

1 Engage existing customers already signed up to e-newsletters.
2 Encourage customers to select a personal challenge.

3 Drive to site to encourage them to commit to challenge and update their progress.

4 Encourage social interaction – share experience, encourage others.

5 Subscribe to text reminders services to remind when weakspot, e.g. time of day.

However, this campaign highlights a risk with short-term campaigns. A microsite was set up to maintain this dialogue, but if you went there mid year, the microsite has been taken down and visitors are asked to wait until next Christmas! This shows the importance of obtaining resource to continue the dialogue and continue the momentum of a campaign. It is often best to integrate such campaigns into the main website to deliver continuity and to help build awareness of the full online brand experience and other product offerings.

SECTION SUMMARY 8.1

Introduction to CRM

Customer Relationship Management is well established as an approach to acquiring customers and then retaining them to develop a higher life-time value for each customer. Managing CRM online and integrating it with offline CRM activities introduces new challenges. We need to think about how we can use online tools to have a more dynamic dialogue with the customer, answering their questions, understanding their needs, profiling them and then delivering appropriate services and communications.

8.2   Introduction to relationship marketing

By the end of this section you should be able to see how relationship marketing and permission-based marketing are essential to CRM and e-CRM.

What is **Relationship Marketing**? Marketing is all about relationships. Relationships with customers, lapsed customers and potential customers. There are also relationships with suppliers, partners and even internal audiences (staff). So although relationship marketing involves more than just customers, we're focusing on customers – CRM-Customer Relationship Management. True CRM involves treating each customer differently according to their characteristics as described in the e-marketing insight box below.

Relationship marketing shifts marketing away from short-term **transactional marketing** (with its one-off sales) towards developing longer lasting relationships which, ideally, develop into lifetime customers. This obviously generates more profitable repeat business as well as increased share of wallet or customer share.

E-MARKETING INSIGHT

Peppers and Rogers on building one-to-one relationships

Peppers and Rogers, authors of the now classic one-to-one marketing book (1999), have applied their work on building **one-to-one** relationships with the customer to the web. They suggest the IDIC approach as a framework for using the web effectively to form and build relationships. IDIC stands for:

1 *Customer identification.* This stresses the need to identify each customer on their first web site visit and subsequent visits. Common methods for identification are use of cookies or asking a customer to log on to a site.

2 *Customer differentiation.* This refers to building a profile to help segment customers into groups which share characteristics and can be evaluated according to company value. Peppers and Roger suggest Most Valuable Customers, Most Growable Customers and Below Zero Customers.

3 *Customer interaction.* These are interactions provided on site such as customer service questions or creating a tailored product.

4 *Customized communications.* This refers to personalization or mass-customization of content or e-mails according to the segmentation achieved at the acquisition stage.

PERMISSION MARKETING

Building relationships is a delicate affair. Marketers have to gain permission firstly, then trust and ultimately, loyalty. It's all common sense stuff. Stick to basic marketing tenets of identifying, anticipating and satisfying customer needs relentlessly helps to build relationships. But how do you do this? Firstly, adopt a 'permission based marketing', approach as developed by the now classic *Permission Marketing* by Seth Godin (Godin 1999). There are several steps towards permission marketing:

1 *Gaining Permission.* The first step is to get customer's permission to give them information. Winning this permission, in the customer's time-compressed world, is a valuable asset, so a range of offers will be more powerful, as shown by the Ultralase example in Figure 8.2.

2 *Collaboration.* Marketing is a collaborative activity – where marketers help customers to buy and customers help marketers to sell. The customer forum and testimonials used by Ultralase are an example of this.

3 *Dialogue-trialogue.* A dialogue emerges whether via web site e-mails, discussion rooms, real conversations in focus groups or even real meetings between customers and sales reps, as well as amongst customers themselves (trialogue).

Permission marketers develop the relationship and win further permission to talk on a regular basis. Some excellent permission-based marketers actually get permission to place

Figure 8.2   The design of the Ultralase laser eye treatment provider emphasizes gaining permission (www.ultralase.co.uk)

orders on the customer's behalf. Other permission-based marketers even deliver right into the customers buildings without the customer opening the door! They become part of the customer's systems.

In developing the relationship there are a series of stages through which the customer moves. There are several approaches one of which is the Ladder Of Loyalty (Considine and Murray, 1981) from Suspects to Prospects to Customers to Clients to Advocates.

When a customer 'opts-in' for further e-mail, they give permission to be e-mailed. This is a first step in using their permission to develop the relationship. Do not abuse this permission. Do not pass their details on to other marketers. Ensure your future contact with the customer always adds value.

Remember you have to respect this relationship – this special permission you have. It is a moral and legal requirement to offer the customer the option to 'opt-out'. The number of existing customers that opt out from further contact is known as the 'churn rate'. Obviously good marketers watch the churn rate closely, and try to understand why it varies.

The concept of permission marketing is best summarized by three magic words. Seth Godin said:

> '*Permission marketing is . . . anticipated, relevant and personal*'

He goes on to describe the essential concepts of permission marketing as 'Dating the Customer':

1 Offer the prospect an incentive to volunteer [Achieve opt-in]
2 Using the attention offered by the prospect, offer a curriculum over time, teaching the consumer about your product or service [Enable the customer to learn more]
3 Reinforce the incentive to guarantee that the prospect maintains the permission [Offer opt-out, but minimize the likelihood for this]
4 Offer additional incentives to get even more permission from the consumer [Learn more about the customer through time]
5 Over time, leverage the permission to change consumer behaviour towards profits [Deepen the relationship through converting from prospect to customer and trialist to loyalist].

E-MARKETING INSIGHT

Victor Ross on permission marketing

Not everyone sees permission marketing as a marketing panacea – interruption marketing is still required to start the dialogue. Victor Ross, a fellow of the Institute of Direct Marketing, says in reviewing Seth Godin's *Permission Marketing* (Ross, 2001):

'This book and the concept behind it need to be debunked before they gain cult status'. He suggests that much of the approach is not new: 'the large number of direct marketers who start the selling process with an ad offering information, and take it from there with a graduated programme of data collection and follow-ups will wonder how it is they have been practicing permission marketing for all this time without knowing'.

Despite this, we believe that Seth Godin's *Permission Marketing* is a significant contribution since it highlights the importance of a key principle of digital marketing in a clear and colourful way.

MANAGING THE DIALOGUE THROUGH CONTACT STRATEGIES

Too much contact can wear out the relationship. The key to building the best relationship is to have the right number of contacts of the right type at the right time for specific customers. This is a **contact strategy**. Determining which kinds of customers and enquirers get which sequence of contacts. Most organizations require coherent contact strategies spanning across online and offline. For example some garages maintain contact with their customers via e-mail, or SMS, sending them reminders when their car is due for a service. If no response is generated then this triggers a prompt for staff to make a phone call to see whether the customer still wants to receive reminders. Other organizations ask their customers how they prefer to be updated about special offers, reminders and announcements.

Table 8.1 Example template for e-mail contact strategy

Message type	Interval/trigger condition	Outcomes required	Medium for message/ Sequence
1 Welcome message	Guest site membership sign-up Immediate	• Encourage trial of site services • Increase awareness of range of commercial and informational offerings	E-mail, post transaction page
2 Engagement message	1 month: Inactive (i.e. <3 visits)	• Encourage use of forum (good enabler of membership) • Highlight top content	E-mail, home page, side panels deep in site
3 Initial cross-sell message	1 month active	• Encourage membership • Ask for feedback	E-mail
4 Conversion	2 days after browsing content	Use for range of services for guest members or full members	Phone or e-mail

The database stores their preferred media (including – if e-mail – whether text or HTML is preferred) and ensures that they are contacted in the preferred manner. So organizations vary their contact strategy depending on how customers (and prospects) react.

Your contact strategy should define an initial **welcome strategy** when the prospect is first added to the database based on the best interval and sequence of messages as shown in Table 8.1. The contact strategy should then be extended for later stages in the customer lifecycle with messages designed to convert them to purchase (from shopping basket abandons), encourage repeat purchases, trial of new products or reactivate customers when their interest wanes.

An automated e-mail sent by a business-to-business supplier two weeks after a customer has registered initial interest in the company. Such e-mails can help companies educate customers about their offering and engage them through digital assets such as a calculator – which fits the permission marketing model of 'learning more through time'. Renault is a good B2C example of a welcome strategy. Over the initial six month period of purchase consideration, they use a container or content pod within their e-newsletter to deliver personalized information about the brand and model of car the prospect is interested in. This is updated each month as the customer gets to know the brand better and the brand gets to know the customer better!

For another example, see how Tesco's contact strategy varies according to new customers' responses to previous contacts in Section 8.4 page 369 and Section 8.5 for other contact strategies. Some organizations consider some web facilities as part of the dialogue, e.g. an on-site search engine preceded with a friendly face or question 'tell us what you are looking for'. Virtual assistants, real-time live web chat and call-back facilities also facilitate a dialogue. Ironically some under resourced companies, whilst holding customers in a telephone queue suggest that they might prefer to get a quicker answer online at the web site. Online contact varies as web sites carry FAQs, blogs (with clearly labelled topics) and sometimes customer forums actually facilitate self servicing by the customer amongst customers. Some of these are also mentioned in Section 2.8 Delivering online service. Markets are always changing, so your communications need to be flexible and capable of individualized, personalized, responses.

Don't forget that relationships have traditionally been two-way conversations (dialogues). Today they are trialogues with customers talking to each other, generating PR, informing ads, designs and discussions about products. It involves as much listening as talking, e-mailing, mobile messaging, telesales, advertising, etc. Watch clickthroughs on different e-newsletter topics, news pages, special offers and forums as well the incoming flow of communications. Give the customer a chance to talk to you and each other, taking the time to listen and tell the other party how what they have told you has been acted upon, or at least heard! Today's marketers listen a lot more.

Tell customers what they have told you, maybe in the form of order acknowledgement or consolidated feedback from surveys, etc. Show them how this has changed what you do/ how you do it is an important part of building a relationship. All part of the ongoing dialogue. Remember 'Markets are conversations'! Database driven marketing allows the dialogue to become a dynamic dialogue – responsive, relevant and fast moving.

E-MARKETING INSIGHT

Practical e-permission marketing guidelines

It is now over seven years since Seth Godin launched his permission marketing mantra. So, we need to ask, 'how can the original principles of *Permission Marketing* be applied by today's online marketer'? We would emphasize these key developments of permission marketing principles, what we call 'e-permission marketing principles'.

1 *'Offer selective opt-in to communications'*. Offer choice in communications preferences to the customer to ensure more relevant communications. Some customers may not want a weekly e-newsletter, rather they may only want to hear about new product releases. Remember opt-in is a legal requirement in many countries. Four key opt-in options, selected by tick-box are:

- *Content* – news, products, offers, events
- *Frequency* – weekly, monthly, quarterly, or alerts
- *Channel* – e-mail, direct mail, phone or SMS
- *Format* – text vs HTML.

2 *Create a 'common customer profile'.* A structured approach to customer data capture is needed otherwise some data will be missed, as is the case with the utility company that collected 80 000 e-mail addresses, but forgot to ask for the postcode for geo-targeting! This can be achieved through a common customer profile – a definition of all the database fields that are relevant to the marketer in order to understand and target the customer with a relevant offering. It sounds obvious, but. . .

3 *Offer a range of opt-in incentives.* Many web sites now have 'free-win-save' incentives to encourage opt-in, but often it is one incentive fits all visitors. Different incentives for different audiences will generate a higher volume of permission, particularly for business-to-business web sites. We can also gauge the characteristics of the respondent by the type of incentives or communications they have requested, without the need to ask them.

4 *'Don't make opt-out too easy'.* Our view is that we often make it too easy to unsubscribe. Although offering an easy opt-out or unsubscribe is now a legal requirement in many countries due to privacy laws, a single click to unsubscribe is perhaps making it too easy, the relationship is over too abruptly. Instead wise permission marketers like Amazon or First Direct have the option of more granular communications preferences where it is possible to unsubscribe, but also to control the frequency and type of e-mail content received. If customers definitely want to unsubscribe, then this is made easy, with the option of commenting on the reason for the unsubscribe and many do, providing useful information on improving e-CRM for others.

The use of 'My Profile' can be tied to the principle of 'selective opt-in' – you could call it selective opt-out.

5 *'Watch don't ask'.* The need to ask interruptive questions can be reduced through the use of monitoring of clicks to better understand customer needs and to trigger follow-up communications. Some examples:

- *Monitoring clickthrough to different types of content or offer.*
- *Monitoring the engagement of individual customers with e-mail communications.*
- *Follow-up reminder to those who don't open the e-mail first time.*
- *Monitoring the day and time of typical clickthrough to send e-mails when the customer is most receptive.*

6 *Create an outbound contact strategy.* Online permission marketers need a plan for the number, frequency and type of online and offline communications and offers. This is a contact or touch strategy. The contact strategy should indicate

1 Frequency (e.g. minimum once per quarter and maximum once per month).
2 Interval (e.g. there must be a gap of at least one week or one month between communications).

3 Content and offers (we may want to limit or achieve a certain number of prize draws or information-led offers).

4 Links between online communications and offline communications.

5 A control strategy (a mechanism to make sure these guidelines are adhered to is for example using a single 'focal point' for checking all communications before creation dispatch).

Source: This is a summary of an article by Dave Chaffey for *What's New in Marketing* (www.davechaffey.com/E-marketing-Insights)

SECTION SUMMARY 8.2

Introduction to relationship marketing

Relationship marketing is at the heart of e-CRM. It requires a longer-term perspective, a lifetime value perspective built on upon permission, trust and listening and responding to customers to build longer, lasting success.

8.3   Database marketing

The database and **database marketing** is at the heart of e-CRM. By the end of this section you will understand what a database is, the complications that can arise, the types of data fields and the importance of linking it all to a clear marketing programme.

It has been said that 'The driving force underlying modern CRM systems is the customer database'. The repository of information on customers and prospects from all sources and channels – whether web sites, interactive TV, sales reps or customer service staff.

The database and profiling software is a vital part of e-CRM since it enhances our ability to understand customers and enquirers, their needs, names, interests and a lot more. We can get closer to them.

It helps achieve the dynamic dialogue of permission marketing which:

- recognizes and remembers each customer by name and need
- answers questions often automatically and, ideally, personally
- asks questions, collects information and builds a better profile, particularly of those ideal lifetime customers
- delivers communications which are instantaneous, relevant and value adding.

WHAT IS STORED IN THE DATABASE?

A database is more than a list of names. A database is distinguished by the amount and quality of relevant marketing data held on each customer or prospect. It should identify best ('ideal') customers and worst customers. The worst customers have 'negative value' these are customers who claim early on insurance, are bad debtors, or just an intensive user of free services. There are two types of information kept on a database which a simple mailing list does not provide: historical data and predictive data. Smith and Taylor (2004) describe **historical data** as 'transactional' or 'back' data which includes names addresses, recency and frequency of purchases, responses to offers and value of purchases. They say **predictive data** identifies which groups or subgroups are more likely to respond to a specific offer. This is done through statistical scoring: customer attributes (e.g. house type, business type, past behaviour, etc.) are given scores that help to indicate their future behaviour.

This begs the question – what kind of data, or 'fields' should be captured? In addition to capturing a customer's name and address, there are obviously other kinds, or 'fields', of data worth capturing for firstly, a B2C business and then, secondly, a B2B business. **FRAC** is a useful mnemonic. It stands for: Frequency, Recency, Amount and Category of purchase.

For example, RFM analysis can be applied for targeting using e-mail according to how a customer interacts with an e-commerce site. Values could be assigned to each customer as follows:

Recency:

1 – Over 12 months

2 – Within last 12 months

3 – Within last 6 months

4 – Within last 3 months

5 – Within last 1 month

Frequency:

1 – More than once every 6 months

2 – Every 6 months

3 – Every 3 months

4 – Every 2 months

5 – Monthly

Monetary value:

1 – Less than £10

2 – £10–50

3 – £50–£100

4 – £100–£200

5 – More than £200

Customers can be combined in different categories and then appropriate message treatments sent to encourage purchase. Simplified versions of this analysis can be created to make it more manageable, for example a theatre group uses these nine categories for its direct marketing:

Oncers (attended theatre once)

- Recent oncers   attended >12 months
- Rusty oncers   attended <12>36 months
- Very rusty oncers   attended 36+ months

Twicers:

- Recent twicer   attended >12 months
- Rusty twicer   attended <12 >36 months
- Very rusty twicer   attended in 36+ months

2+ subscribers:

- Current subscribers Booked 2+ events in current season
- Recent   Booked 2+ last season
- Very rusty   Booked 2+ more than a season ago

There is a lot of other useful data worth collecting, such as promotions history (responses to specific promotions), share of wallet or customer share (potential spend), timing of spend and more. In B2B, we are interested in business type (SIC codes), size of business, holding companies and subsidiaries, competitive products bought, etc. You can segment customers by their activity or responsiveness levels and then develop strategies to engage them. For example, Novo (2003) recommends the use of **hurdle rates** which are the percentage of customers in a group (such as in a segment or on a list) who have completed an action. Hurdle rates can then be used to compare the engagement of different groups or to set targets to increase engagement with online channels as the examples of hurdle rates below show:

- 20% of customers have visited in past six months
- 5% of customers have made three or more purchases in year
- 60% of registrants have logged on to system in year
- 30% have clicked through on e-mail in year.

Whether B2C or B2B, managing the activity levels of your subscribers is key – you need to manage e-mail list decay.

E-MARKETING INSIGHT

Managing e-mail engagement decay

It is inevitable that e-mail list subscribers have their highest levels of engagement with a brand when they are first added to a database and that this will decay through time. Dom Yeadon of The Marketing Bureau (www.tmb.uk.com) has analyzed a sample of B2C and B2B lists that show the extent of e-mail list decay. He summarizes the implications of the research as follows:

- You could lose 5% of the whole list every 3 months
- Your list loses 2/3rds of its value in 12 months
- Fresh e-mails (0 to 3 months old) are each worth three times as much as older e-mails (12 months old)

Dom suggests you can evaluate your e-mail list value based on a formula based on different aspects of e-mail response:

$$\text{Engagement Index} = (D \times V \times CTR \times 100)$$

where D = Deliverability, V = Views (Opens) and CTR = Clickthrough rate

He gives these examples:

- E-mail engagement index, 0–3 months = 11
  - Delivery rate = 90%
  - Views = 35%
  - Clickthroughs = 36%
- E-mail engagement index, 9–12 months = 4
  - Delivery rate = 73%
  - Views = 31%
  - Clickthroughs = 18%

So what do about e-mail decay?

E-MARKETING BEST PRACTICE CHECKLIST – LIST DECAY

Here is our checklist for managing e-mail list decay:

☑ Develop a welcome programme where over the first three to six months you deliver targeted auto-triggered e-mails to educate subscribers about your brand, products and deliver targeted offers.

☑ Think about how you can reactivate list members as they become less responsive.

☑ Segment list members by activity (responsiveness) and age on list. Assess your level of e-mail list activity (ask what percentage of list members haven't clicked within the last three to six months – if they haven't, they are inactive and should be treated differently, either by reducing frequency or using more offline media).

☑ Follow-up on bounces using other media to reduce problems of dropping deliverability.

☑ Best practice when renting lists is to request only e-mails where the opt-in is within the most recent six to nine months when subscribers are most active.

WHICH SOFTWARE TOOLS ARE REQUIRED?

Every organization has lots of useful data on its customers. This can be very simple and well organized, or incredibly complex, usually the latter. Unfortunately many organizations have several databases, each set up at different times with no ability to cross-reference the data within them. Typically, there is the old '**legacy**' database or customer contact management system for traditional direct mail and a completely separate database for web site visitors containing registration information in a profile and purchase information for an e-commerce site. There is usually a separate system for managing e-mail marketing which contains customer profile details and information on how they responded to each campaign.

CHOOSING AN E-MAIL MARKETING SYSTEM

There are several options for sending marketing e-mails to customers.

1 *Standard office software*. For example, using Microsoft Outlook. We don't recommend this option since it is only really practical for relatively small lists since each contact has to be added and removed manually. No tracking is available with this approach and all bounced e-mails have to be processed manually.

2 *Desktop mailer software*. With this approach e-mail lists are managed and e-mails broadcast using a software application running on the user's PC. Most of the software tends to be from US suppliers like Infacta GroupMail (www.infacta.com, with a separate tracking package GroupMetrics) and Gammadyne Mailer (www.gammadyne.com/mmail.htm). These have the advantage of low cost and there is no fee for each message sent. They offer some personalization and now have additional tracking packages. A similar option for small business is sales and contact management software which can also be used for e-mail management and tracking contact history, like Act from Sage (http://www.act.com) and Goldmine from Frontrange (http://www.frontrange.com).

3 *List-server software*. For businesses requiring higher volumes of e-mail broadcast from an internal server there are options such as Lyris (www.lyris.com). Such tools have many options for personalization, tracking and automation of contact strategies, but if hosted internally will require support from IT and there may be problems with deliverability if the reputation of the broadcaster becomes compromised. Some of the e-mail service providers mentioned in the next section such as Email Reaction (www.emailreaction.com) and EmailCenter (www.emailcenteruk.com) also provide the capability for their ASP solutions to be installed in-house.

4 *E-mail service providers (ESPs)*. ESPs are web-based services that can be used by a client to manage their own e-mail activities. Rather than buying software that you host and manage on your server, the software is effectively used on a subscription basis and runs on another company's server. In other words it provides all the technical infrastructure that is needed to run the campaign, but managed by an outside company. You can see a list of the most commonly used tools at www.davechaffey.com/email-tools. From a user experience point-of-view, the user logs in to a web-based 'booth' and is then able to create the e-mail, select the targeting, broadcast and track the results in real-time.

5 There are four main requirements or tasks involved with managing e-mail campaigns and e-newsletters. Here is our checklist of issues to consider for selecting an e-mail service provider.

> ### E-MARKETING BEST PRACTICE CHECKLIST – CHOOSING AN E-MAIL SERVICE PROVIDER

The main e-mail management activities are:

1 *Creating the content*.
   - ☑ Are pre-defined templates available?
   - ☑ Is there an integrated WYSIWYG editor in which content and images can be edited within a template, or does it require a separate web editing programme like Dreamweaver?
   - ☑ Can different permissions be assigned to limit access according to skill level?
   - ☑ How easy is it to add a personal salutation?
   - ☑ How easily can dynamic content be included according to database criteria?
   - ☑ Can e-newsletters be easily archived on site?
   - ☑ Can e-newsletter features be provided as RSS feed if required?

2 *Managing the list*.
   - ☑ Can subscriptions and unsubscribes be managed through a website?
   - ☑ Are bounces managed such that the marketer only receives genuine replies, not undelivered messages and out-of-office autoreplies, etc?
   - ☑ Do the standard database fields work for basic activity?
   - ☑ Is it easy to add new fields to the standard fields?
   - ☑ What are the options for integrating with other databases of customer/campaign/sales information? The options to achieve data integration are:
     - Ad-hoc import/export process, i.e. customer profile information for personalization is exported from the customer database before a campaign as required and changes to communications preferences are updated after each campaign.
     - Regular batch synchronization process, system can be set up to exchange data at a regular time – daily, weekly or monthly.
     - Real-time synchronization process, direct communications are set up to occur between the e-mail database and customer database using application programming interfaces (APIs).

3 *Broadcasting the message*.

☑ Is smart-broadcasting used to reduce the volume to avoid a high volume spam signature?

☑ Is there a unique IP address available for every campaign (not essential and sometimes expensive)?

☑ Can autoresponse notifications be easily setup?

☑ Can pre-defined automated touch strategy e-mails be setup for behavioural or contextual marketing (sense and respond)?

☑ Can future e-mail broadcasts be scheduled (e.g. for next day)?

4 *Tracking/reporting the results*.

☑ Is deliverability and response tracked by ISP/web mail provider to identify problems.

☑ Is closed-loop reporting of inbox delivery and complaints integrated with ISP/web mail providers?

☑ How easy is it to setup up A/B or multivariate testing cells?

☑ What metrics are available (after the click), i.e. tagging on the website to show number and type of pages accessed? Can the tagging integrate with a web analytics system?

☑ Can response be tracked at an individual level?

☑ Can response be tracked across time/multiple campaigns?

☑ Can response be tracked for different demographic profiles?

☑ Is there text and/or visual reporting on which links were clicked?

☑ Can viral pass alongs be easily monitored?

☑ Can response be integrated using the options (a) to (c) above?

Then comes the really interesting software – **data mining** software that drills down into the data warehouses to find correlations and profiles buried deep within the layers of data. Data mining can reveal surprising correlations, some of which help to profile their own customers and then look for similar types elsewhere.

There is an increasing growth in complex database generation because of the obvious links between data capture and web marketing – when you have a visitor to your web site you have a great opportunity to capture data about that visitor, especially if you use **cookie** technology. But remember data captured for data's sake does not make a good database. What will you do with the data? If, for example, key predictive data identifies a customer who is likely to defect – what is the strategy? How will you separate offers between ideal and negative value customers? It is important to be clear about why you are creating a database in the first place. If there are no clear objectives then the database is an expensive, unused toy.

Rohner (2001) says '*Without a corresponding marketing programme, database marketing should not be introduced*'. You must be clear what you want to do with the database. What kind of **contact strategy** will you have? A sequence of **opt-in** e-mails, snail mails, telephone calls, personal visits or what? What kind of responses and offers will be date triggered (e.g. three months after purchase), event triggered (e.g. Christmas time), purchase triggered (bought

Item but not Item B). What is the sequence of contacts for each of these? Be clear about what you want to achieve with your e-CRM system?

Active database marketers know that databases deteriorate over time, people die, change job, move house. So the database asset has to be maintained, cleaned or updated. The cleaning process costs resources, but is crucial if the database is going to be used to its optimum. See the section on 'cleaning the database'.

Finally, it is essential to have a seamless, integrated database that works across all different platforms. So a customer is recognized and remembered and serviced in a personalized way whether they access the company by telephone, web site, interactive TV or mobile phone. Integrating the databases presents a big challenge.

E-MARKETING EXCELLENCE

Abbey cares about data and cuts costs and gets closer to customer

Abbey Bank treats data as a critical corporate asset and has a board level agreed strategy and method for managing it. The bank has created a 'data superstore' (data warehouse) that can be accessed by any authorized user or application within the bank.

By using Avellino Discovery, in the first two years, Abbey:

- Achieved more efficient integration of Abbey Bank data into the central data architecture which delivered £1 million (US$1.5m) Net Present Value (NPV).

- Migrated data into the central data architecture faster and with more accuracy. The total benefit is estimated at £2.5 million ($4m) NPV.

- Completed data-cleansing activities achieving £1.7 million ($2.7m) in savings.

- Achieved more accurate bad debt provisioning and credit scoring which has led to well over £10 million ($16m) in NPV benefits.

'We estimate that Avellino Discovery has delivered benefits to the bank worth some £15.2m,' said Christine Craven, Head of Retail Information at Abbey National.

'Without Discovery, we estimate that it would take around five man-years to manually check the 29 million records that need migrating [from the data warehouse] into a new customer database,' said Christine. 'With Discovery automating much of the process, we estimate this activity will instead take around three man-months.'

Jean Knight, head of information quality at Abbey National, says the old system took 40 hours to analyze one field in five million records. The bank is introducing new software that takes just three hours to complete the same task.

(*Source*: Based on Avellino case studies www.avellino.com).

Database marketing

Although the database and database marketing is at the heart of e-CRM it goes way beyond simply collecting data. You now know the importance of linking the database to a clear marketing programme; the types of data fields – the complications that can arise; how mining can help to profile different types of customers (including best and worst) and the importance of maintaining and cleaning the database. A carefully planned, integrated and managed database can reap huge rewards.

8.4 E-CRM

This section shows how e-CRM draws on the basic principles of CRM, relationship marketing and database marketing. By the end of it you will also know how to (a) list the CRM stages and (b) keep the relationship alive.

WHAT DOES THAT 'e' ADD TO CRM?

Relationship Marketing is about building relationships with all external parties involved in marketing. CRM focuses specifically on the relationship with customers and e-CRM focuses even further on the electronic relationship with customers.

CRM software is used to manage these electronic relationships. Ebner *et al.* (2002) define this software as 'the systems that allow companies to plan and analyze marketing campaigns, to identify sales leads, and to manage their customer contacts and call centres'.

More specifically, here is an e-CRM checklist which shows the options for an e-CRM programme.

E-MARKETING BEST PRACTICE CHECKLIST – MANAGING AN e-CRM CHECKLIST

☑ Using the *web site for customer development* from generating leads through to conversion to an online or offline sale using e-mail and web-based information to encourage purchase.

☑ *Managing e-mail list quality* (coverage of e-mail addresses and integration of customer profile information from other databases to enable targeting).

☑ Applying automated triggered *e-mail marketing* to support contact strategies aimed at customer development (welcome, purchase, upsell, cross-sell and after sales) as shown by the Tesco.com example below.

☑ *Data mining* to identify new segments and improve targeting.

☑ Providing online personalization or *mass customization* facilities to automatically recommend the 'Next-best product'.

☑ Providing *online customer service facilities* (such as Frequently Asked Questions, Call-back and Chat support).

☑ Managing *online service quality* to ensure that first time buyers have a great customer experience that encourages them to buy again.

☑ Managing the *multi-channel customer experience* as they use different media as part of the buying process and customer lifecycle, i.e. providing clear linkages and seamless transition between online and offline channels or touchpoints as part of the relationship.

These facets of e-CRM means that marketers can potentially deliver cheaper, faster and more flexible CRM. *Cheaper* since although software can be expensive initially if it is carefully chosen and utilized fully, it can deliver significant savings particularly when much of the dialogue is both personalized and automated. *Faster* since much e-CRM is automated and so responses are almost instantaneous, e.g. when visitors register on a web site acknowledgement is now almost instantaneous. Similarly when placing orders via web sites most sites now automatically respond by acknowledging the order immediately. Many e-customers expect this now. *More flexible* since CRM systems should be readily updated to accommodate new products and new promotion techniques for new media.

The CRM software also enables permission marketing to be achieved – from the customer's point of view it means that the relationship, and communications in particular, are *more relevant*, *more tailored* and often *more interactive*.

With its customer orientation, CRM helps marketers, by growing longer lasting customer relationships. So both lifetime value and customer share grow. The best relationships are those where both partners feel they are equal and can build respect for each other through mutual understanding. From the customer's point of view it means that the relationship, and communications in particular, are more relevant, tailored and often interactive. Speedy responses and considered responses are always appreciated by customers. In fact complaining customers can become friends for life if their problems are dealt with swiftly and professionally. So it follows that resources, the **3Ms**, have to be allocated towards monitoring customer feedback and dealing with the specific non-standard problems on a one-to-one basis. For example, many companies have found online chat (Live Person) and telephone call-back systems activated when customers fill in an online form are effective for moving customers from a virtual world relationship to a more involving real-world relationship with contact centre staff. However, such systems are resource intensive and customer expectations must be met so that they don't have to wait for that chat session or phone call.

E-CRM software is also important to *automate* the way the dialogue with the customer is initiated and then the relationship built through a series of targeted, tailored, timed e-mail and direct mail communications. The e-marketing excellence box – Tesco.com automates relationship building – shows how this is achieved.

E-MARKETING EXCELLENCE

Tesco.com automates relationship building through web, e-mail and direct mail

Tesco.com uses software to monitor events which occur in the customer lifecycle. The examples below show that a sequence of follow-up communications are triggered after an event. Communications after event 1 are intended to achieve the objective of converting a web site visitor to action; communications after event 2 are intended to move the customer from a first time purchaser to a regular purchaser and for event 3 to reactive lapsed purchasers.

Trigger event 1: Customer first registers on site (but does not buy)

- Auto-response (AR) 1: Two days after registration e-mail sent offering phone assistance and £5 discount off first purchase to encourage trial.

Trigger event 2: Customer first purchases online

- AR1: Immediate order confirmation
- AR2: Five days after purchase e-mail sent with link to online customer satisfaction survey asking about quality of service from driver and picker (e.g. item quality and substitutions).
- AR3: Two weeks after first purchase – Direct mail offering tips on how to use service and £5 discount on next purchases intended to encourage reuse of online services.
- AR4: Generic monthly e-newsletter with online exclusive offers
- AR5: Bi-weekly alert with personalized offers for customer.
- AR6: After two months – £5 discount for next shop
- AR7: Quarterly mailing of coupons

Trigger event 3: Customer does not purchase for an extended period

- AR1: Dormancy detected – Reactivation e-mail with survey of how the customer is finding the service (to identify and problems) and a £5 incentive.
- AR2: A further discount incentive is used in order to encourage continued usage after first shop after a break.

KEEPING THE RELATIONSHIP ALIVE

Think about your own relationship. What makes it work? All relationships can get stale unless you work hard at it. This means your web site needs to be updated and kept fresh and tailored – your offerings need to be more attractive than the competition. How can you keep the relationship alive – without changing so much that you are no longer the organization they wanted to have a relationship with in the first place? DRAMA – that's how!

- *Dialogue.* An organization should offer customers ways to talk to them – every message sent should allow for a response. Every unsolicited communication from them should receive a swift and relevant response. The organization MUST show that it listens and can talk and tell too!

- *Relevancy.* The beauty of e-CRM is that mass communication can be personal and made relevant to the recipient, indeed the customer's expectation of relevance will be so high that it is dangerous to send bulk messages that are not tailored to that one person's/company's needs.

- *Accuracy.* e-CRM opens the door for poor information management as does any other form of direct communication – but this time the problem might well have originated with the customer themselves, e.g. they mis-spell a name, enter digits incorrectly, etc., when data is captured. Data must be checked, must be updated and must be kept 'clean'. Equally, any information you give to customers must be double checked (as in all good communication) to ensure total accuracy.

- *Magic.* This is what makes the difference! The extra dimension that makes people want to be your customer. There is much talk of Customer Delight – go one better and aim for Customer Amazement!!! The Internet allows for special effects, deliveries of technically advanced packages of information presented in very appealing ways – animation, sound, interaction, prizes, incentives, collection schemes – these are all pretty much expected by customers nowadays, so what will you do that is different? Will it be your creative execution? The links with famous personalities whom you sponsor or hire? The very personal touch of a one-to-one advisor whether delivered by a virtual **avatar** adviser (Figure 8.3)

Figure 8.3   Avatar delivered by IKEA (www.ikea.co.uk)

or a human online chat. MAGIC is what should be the goal – and never guess what it might be, carry out research to find out what your customers want it to be.

- *Access.* 'I feel like we're drifting apart!' Don't let your relationship wither due to lack of contact, but also be sure you are not smothering the relationship with over-attentiveness! If you have a scheme to get your customers to visit you regularly (let's say they have to visit you every week for a year to collect all the cards in a deck of cards to be able to get an opportunity to have a free trip to Las Vegas, you must keep them going with spot prizes, because a year is a very long time to wait!) then be sure there is something worth seeing when they do visit! Getting someone to access your site is one thing – entertaining them, informing them, having what they want when they get there is something else – and cannot be ignored.

So now let us get down to the nitty-gritty of e-CRM – what are the specific stages? There are many different approaches to the CRM or e-CRM stages or cycle such as the Ladder of Loyalty or the customer development cycle of selection, acquisition, retention and extension. Here is another approach to the CRM cycle.

1 *Attract!* Obviously this is where traditional off-line communication as well as on-line communication about your offering is being designed to bring customers to your site. From TV advertising to banner ads and hot-spots, getting them to your site will only be possible if (a) they know what you are offering and are interested (b) they know where you are and how to get to you.

2 *Capture Data.* The Internet is a splendid mechanism for capturing data – the prospect has the keyboard and screen in front of them and you can incentivize the giving of data.

3 *Get Closer.* Get to know them better. It is not surprising that there is reluctance on the part of many individuals to give personal data away to an Internet screen. So it is often better to gather more information about a person slowly and over time, as the trust builds between you and them.

4 *Embrace Them.* Make your customer feel loved! Approach them with offers, prizes, rewards, incentives and information as well as experiences that show them you are thinking about THEM.

5 *Golden Handcuffs.* Once you get them to show some loyalty, build a system whereby things are too good for them to leave! Tailored information or services to suit them specifically. Or services that integrate with the customers own systems or lifestyle. These switching costs make leaving less likely.

SECTION SUMMARY 8.4

e-CRM

e-CRM draws on the basic principles of CRM, relationship marketing and database marketing. There are a clear set of stages in CRM development. You have to work hard at keeping the relationship alive (DRAMA). There are many benefits including lifetime customers and increased share of wallet which help to grow your business.

8.5 Profiling

Profiling helps you to know your customers better. By the end of this section you will know what profiling is, how it works and how it can help marketers.

Profiling can combine explicit data (customer information collected from registrations and surveys) and implicit data (behavioural information gleaned from the back end, i.e. through the recorded actions of customers on your site). Good strategies continually combine both implicit and explicit data. It is important to have a clear understanding of the target markets, the characteristics that define each segment and how you want to serve each segment. For example, certain car buyers might have different demographic profiles, show interest in particular features (pages) of a car and request a test drive. If this group of visitors (or segment) fits the ideal customer profile then they may get a DVD and an immediate incentive to buy now. Whereas another group, or segment, of visitors with a less likely profile may only get an e-newsletter once a month.

We can observe visitors as they leave an audit trail of what they did, what they looked at and for how long. As the cookie enables us to trace which pages you access, we can establish your profile according to what you're interested in (pages visited × duration spent there), everything you put into your shopping basket and ultimately what you did or did not buy.

> ### BEST PRACTICE E-MARKETING TIP
>
> **Review response by segment**
>
> Don't only review the overall response to your e-mail campaigns as measured by open, click and purchase rates. Drill-down deeper and see how well different segments respond to different offers or features in a newsletter – then you will know how well the relationship is working with different groups of customers.

The database can help you to find out who your most profitable customers are and whether they have any similar characteristics (e.g. came from a certain type of site, search engine, searched using a particular key phrase or spent a certain amount of time on particular pages). It makes sense to build up profiles of both customers and enquirers and segment them according to their different interests/enquiries/requirements or purchases.

The better the profiling the better the results because the more accurately you target your marketing efforts on particular profiles or segments, the less your efforts will be wasted. Different customers have different needs. It is actually easier to satisfy them if you divide them into groups sharing similar needs (segments) and then treat each segment differently.

The more you know about customers the better. It's a simple as that. Therefore a well used database as part of a CRM system can create a competitive advantage as you grow your own mini monopoly (customers on your database).

Today, we can build sophisticated consumer profiles based on previous purchasing decisions and even identify the consumer hierarchy of criteria, whether quality, speed of delivery, level of service, etc. This enables us to target tailored offers that match the specific needs of segments on our database. Get this right and this 'virtuous cycle' delivers superior service and simultaneously creates competitive advantage that protects our customers from the inevit-able, new, competitive offers looming on the horizon.

WHICH INFORMATION IS NEEDED FOR PROFILING?

Who is your customer? This is a classic marketing question. Do you really know who they are? What are your customers' key characteristics? What characteristics separate your **ideal customers** from your average customers? What is the profile of your ideal customer? Is it different from your worst, **negative value customers**? Surprisingly, many companies can-not answer these questions. If you don't know your customer profiles how can you (a) sat-isfy them better and (b) find other customers like them?

A **customer profile** can take everything you know about the customer and everything you know about people who are like that customer. It can then be layered with all the psychological and sociological theory that suggests how that person will react to a specific offer or promotion. This helps you to tailor offers that work better for both your customers and your business.

APPROACHES TO PROFILING

Profiling is a continuous activity. Continually collecting customer information, mining it and using it to profile and target more successfully. It is crucial to know what fields or data should be collected.

A simple example of this is the classic, timeless, grandfather clock story. A marketer with a huge database decided to market a limited edition upmarket grandfather clock. After some consideration they targeted 45–65 year olds, upper income, living in large detached houses. They ran a test mailing which generated 60 orders. They then used the 60 responses to build a better profile of the actual customer. Using a more accurate customer profile, they then targeted a different segment of their database and sold every single clock!

Profile data can be gathered from several sources: internally from the customer's own input on a web form, tracking mechanisms and questionnaires or externally from research companies and data bureaux. Data can be complex and of massive volume – it might be that you have to hire a computer bureau to crunch the data to turn it into useful information. An example of building a profile through an online conversation with customers is given in the box 'Tektronix build customer intimacy with virtual conversations with their customers'.

One of the toughest jobs is to know which data matters most – especially where there is conflicting data. Some customers will give you incorrect information – consciously or uncon-sciously. You have to come up with ways to:

1 acquire the information in the first place, and
2 then make it useful to your organization validation.

The issue of the invasion of privacy is a difficult one. Laws, ethics and codes of practice come into play. Ethics have a role but the main arbiters of 'how much contact is too much contact', are the customers themselves. They will show you how ready they are to be communicated with by their response. You have to gain their permission.

Asking for information is a delicate affair. You cannot be too greedy. Beyond the basic information, you may need to offer incentives for more information or simply wait for the relationship to develop and permission to ask for more. But remember customers value their privacy. Let your customers see your privacy policy posted clearly on your web site and any other access point customers may have with you.

Of course, it is one thing to collect profile information, it is quite another to use it and derive value from it. Marketing Business (2004) noted that it's increasingly acknowledged by organizations of all sizes, shapes and sectors that their most valuable asset is their customer information. Ironically, it also seems to be one of the least understood and most poorly managed areas. It was reported that 50% of FTSE 1000 companies still do not have a robust and single view of their customers. Often, no one is in overall charge of the data and there is a failure to invest in developing processes and systems to help staff contribute to data collection, quality and usage. Far too often, the same message and creative is sent to everyone on a list.

E-MARKETING EXCELLENCE

Tektronix build customer intimacy with virtual conversations with their customers

B2B test and measurement company Tektronix (www.tektronix.com) uses e-mail as a strategic communications tool to build relationships with its customers. Tektronix uses regular e-newsletters and periodic personalized e-mail 'e-blasts' about products launches and promotions based on a detailed personal 'MyTek' profile. Tektronix also uses a novel form of e-mail marketing to create greater intimacy with its customers. This uses technology from I-OP (www.i-op.com) to generate a dialogue with the e-mail recipient rather than complete a simple online form.

The goal in using e-mail in this way is to:

- Increase registration form completion rates to get more leads
- Pre-qualify leads so the sales team don't waste their efforts
- Build intimacy by educating leads with useful materials on products that are right for them.

When the customer receives an e-mail it links to a form titled 'A virtual conversation with Tektronix' (Figure 8.4). They are then led through a series of questions on different forms to help better understand their characteristics and needs, offering relevant whitepapers in return. The questions are carefully tuned so that different customers see different questions and are offered different whitepapers according to their interests. With these 'skip patterns' the average respondent sees around 8 questions although there may be 20 or so in total.

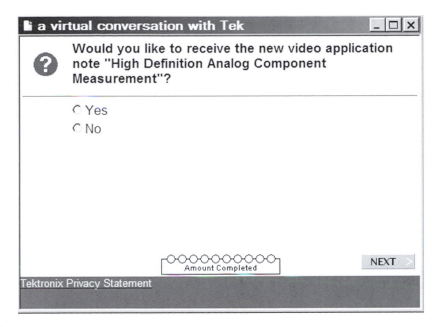

Figure 8.4   E-mail dialogue for Tektronix. (www.tektronix.com)

SECTION SUMMARY 8.5

Profiling

Profiling helps you to:

- see your customers more clearly
- identify customer segments
- separate your best from worst customers
- make more tailored tempting offerings relevant to specific customer profiles
- build lifetime relationships
- enjoy lifetime value.

8.6   Personalization

Specialized software combined with an up-to-date and well-cleaned database allows marketers to personalize communications such as e-mails, voice mails (voice activated e-mails), snail mails (traditional direct mail), SMS text messages (for mobiles) and most interestingly, web sites – personalized web sites. Chapter 6 Web Design includes a section dedicated to personalized web sites.

WHY PERSONALIZATION?

The most important sound in the world is . . . your own name! We all appreciate it when people remember our names. It's personal. It's a compliment – an expression of respect. By the end of this section you'll know how personalization helps to build relationships and the issues that arise. Some call it affectionately 'the personal touch', when a restaurant remembers your favourite wine or preferred table. The database enhances the marketers memory of customer names, needs, interests and preferences.

Personalization enhances the relationship. Personalized web pages help to create a sense of ownership. Not of the customer by the marketer, but of the site by the customer!

When you make a customer feel that their home page is truly theirs, that the offers you make available to them are theirs, that the information they access is put together just for them, then you allow the customer to own you.

This enhanced service helps to sell while also providing the platform for ongoing dialogue ('Speak') and enhancing the brand personality. So personalization delivers four of the 5Ss benefits of e-marketing. Which 'S' is missing? Save – personalization software does cost money. And the larger the customer base gets the more complex the personalization becomes. For this reason many organizations stick with a less sophisticated mass web site.

APPROACHES TO PERSONALIZATION

There are three distinct approaches to personalization: customization, individualization and group-characterization. **Customization** is the easiest to see in action: it allows the visitor to select and set up their specific preferences. **Individualization** goes beyond this fixed setting and uses patterns of your own behavior (and not any other user's – they know it's you because of your login and password choices) to deliver specific content to you that follows your patterns of contact.

In **group-characterization** you receive a recommendation based on the preferences of people 'like' you, using approaches based on collaborative filtering and case-based reasoning.

Mass customization is where different products, services or content is produced for different segments – sometimes hundreds of different segments.

Personalization is different. It is truly one-to-one, particularly when not only the web site and communications are personalized but the product is personalized.

E-MARKETING INSIGHT

HSBC uses personalization to deliver tailored propositions

When HSBC Bank International (HBIB) refined its website it wanted to use personalization with the goal of delivering specific offers and servicing to different customer segments and encouraging customers to move into more valuable segments. This would enable it to capitalize on sales opportunities that would otherwise be missed. *New Media Age* (2007) reported that this was a challenge since '60% of total weekly visitors to offshore.hsbc.com log on to the internet banking service, HSBC wanted to market to them effectively while they were engaged in this task, disrupting their* *banking experience without infuriating them'*. Business rules were created to serve promotions dependent on the type of content accessed and the level of balance in the customers' account.

HSBC was successful in meeting its goals and the results show the benefit of personalized, targeted banners. On average, *New Media Age* reported that the new banners had an 87.5% higher clickthrough rate than non-personalized banners (6.88% versus 3.67%). The number of savings accounts opened via Internet banking increased by 30% (based on six months pre- and post-launch). And the number of non-Premier customers upgrading to Premier accounts (requiring a balance of £60 000 or more) increased by 86% (based on four weeks pre- and post-launch of the targeted banners).

The concept appears powerful, but as with everything there are always exceptions where things go wrong – Murphy's Law – what can wrong will go wrong! Here's two examples where personalization goes wrong – passwords and personalized products. Take personalized sites – many of them require users to log in with a password which they inevitably lose. So the personalization is lost in frustration of having to remember, find or recreate a password. Many visitors give up and leave the site. The use of cookies here can avoid the need for passwords and log-ins. Note privacy laws now require e-marketers to explain the use of cookies within the privacy policy and seek permission before placing a cookie on the end-users PC. Now consider personalized products and possible problems . . . consider Nike's web site which invited customers to personalize or make their own shoes by stitching on their own personal logo. One customer filled out the online form, sent the $50 and chose 'sweatshop' as a personal logo. Nike refused. The publicity soared.

E-MARKETING INSIGHT

Gartner on personalization

There are many options for online personalization – these are some, from simple to complex, recommended by Gartner (www.gartner.com). How many of these do you use?

- Addressing customers personally:
  - Address customers/prospects by name in print communication
  - Address customers/prospects by name in electronic communication
- Real-time personalization:
  - Keyword query to change content
  - Clickstream data to dynamically change web site content
  - Collaborative filtering to classify visitors and serve content

- Customer-profile personalization:
  - Geographic personalization to tailor messages in traditional media
  - Demographic personalization to tailor messages in traditional media
  - Give web site visitors control over content from set preferences
  - Demographic personalization to tailor online messages
  - Geographic personalization to tailor online messages
  - Registration data to change web site content.

E-MARKETING INSIGHT

Overpersonalization leads to over familiarity

Although personalization is important, it is possible to overpersonalize. UK Online For Business reported that American Express call centres discovered that customers resented being greeted in person until they had said who they were; the practice was swiftly discontinued.

Likewise e-CRM systems make it possible to identify an individual responding to an e-mail and downloading product information or a price list on a web site. While a follow-up phone call is obviously well timed, the call needs to be scripted carefully. It sounds like big brother if you say 'we see you downloaded a pricelist this morning'. Much better to talk more generally about checking to see whether the customer needs any assistance in selecting a product.

SECTION SUMMARY 8.6

Personalization

There are pros and cons for the different levels of personalization. To summarize: It requires resources. It requires a well-kept database. It does create a feeling of ownership. It does have some specific challenges (Murphy's Law), but can, if well executed, enhance customer relationships.

8.7   E-mail marketing

A coherent e-mail marketing programme which helps build relationships needs to combine excellence both in devising effective outbound e-mail campaigns and managing incoming e-mails to satisfactorily resolve customers' questions.

OUTBOUND E-MAIL MARKETING

E-mail is most widely used as a prospect conversion and customer retention tool using an opt-in house-list of prospects and customers who have given permission to a company to contact them. For example, Lastminute.com has built a house list of over ten million prospects and customers across Europe. Successful e-mail marketers adopt a strategic approach to e-mail and develop a contact or **touch strategy** that plans the frequency and content of e-mail communications.

Think of the many benefits of e-mail marketing which show why it has been called 'direct mail on steroids':

1 *Relatively low cost of fulfilment.* The physical costs of e-mail are substantially less than direct mail.
2 *Direct response medium encourages immediate action.* E-mail marketing encourages click-through to a website where the offer can be redeemed immediately, this increases the likelihood of an immediate, impulsive response.
3 *Faster campaign deployment.* Lead times for producing creative and the whole campaign life-cycle tends to be shorter than traditional media.
4 *Ease of personalization.* It is easier and cheaper to personalize e-mail than real physical 'snail' mail.
5 *Options for testing.* It is relatively easy and cost effective to test different e-mail creative and messaging.
6 *Integration.* Through combining e-mail marketing with other direct media which can be personalized such as direct mail, mobile messaging or web personalization, campaign response can be increased as the message is reinforced by different media.

E-MARKETING BEST PRACTICE CHECKLIST – PRACTICAL TIPS FOR E-MAIL MARKETING

But e-mail marketing brings its own peculiar set of challenges that need to be managed. Your e-mail programme will fail if you are not managing these issues adequately:

☑ *Deliverability.* The difficulty of getting messages delivered through different internet service providers (ISPs), corporate firewalls and webmail systems. Make sure you check your deliverability into the inbox using a tool like Lyris Email Adviser for different webmail services your customers may be using like Hotmail or Gmail. The two main reasons your carefully crafted e-mail may be classified as SPAM is due to use of spam words within the e-mail subject or body (use the Lyris content checker to see whether your copy is classified as SPAM www.lyris.com/resources/contentchecker) or if the reputation of your e-mail sender is poor due to complaints or the broadcast characteristics are consistent with spam (high volumes, sent rapidly, check your reputation using SenderScore (www.senderscore.org)). The better your reputation then the less likely you are to be blocked for using copy such as 'free' or 'limited offer' which have proven effectiveness.

☑ *Renderability*. A horrible word! It refers to the difficulty of displaying the creative as intended within the in-box of different e-mail reading systems. The most common problem here is if e-mail creative is all image-based and so is not displayed by default in the e-mail reader as an anti-spam measure. In this case the e-mail will be meaningless unless it is has a powerful subject line, so response rate will fall. Instead, best practice is to use the approach shown in Figure 8.5 which uses body copy which is still clear when images are blocked with hyperlinks highlighting value and encouraging clicks. It also uses alternative text for images (the same alt tags as we mentioned for accessible web pages in Chapter 6) to highlight offers and what the e-mail is about. Finally, at the top of the e-mail there is a link *'Can't see this e-mail? Click here for a web version'* which some recipients may prefer. An additional problem is that different e-mail readers display e-mails

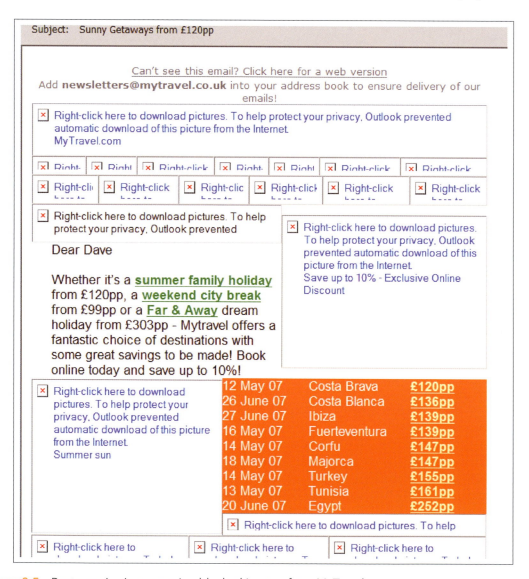

Figure 8.5   Best practice in countering blocked images from MyTravel

slightly differently, so they need to be coded and tested to look their best across different e-mail readers which are even less standardized than different web browsers!

☑ *E-mail response decay*. E-mail recipients are most responsive when they first subscribe to an e-mail. It is difficult to keep them engaged. We discussed this issue and approaches to counter it, such as a defined welcome strategy, earlier in this chapter.

☑ *Communications preferences*. Recipients will have different preferences for e-mail offers, content and frequency which affect engagement and response. Some list members will naturally prefer more frequent e-mails. These can be managed through communications preferences.

☑ *Resource intensive*. Although e-mail offers great opportunities for targeting, personalization and more frequent communications, additional people and technology resources are required to overcome issues such as testing, deliverability and renderability.

OPTIONS FOR E-MAIL MARKETING

When developing an e-mail marketing programme, there are several options to be reviewed. Our checklist of options for using outbound e-mail marketing as part of e-CRM include:

☑ *Conversion e-mail* – someone visits a web site and expresses interest in a product or service by registering and providing their e-mail address although they do not buy. Automated follow-up e-mails can be sent out to persuade the recipient to trial the service. For example, betting company William Hill found that automated follow-up e-mails converted twice as many registrants to place their first bet compared to registrants who did not receive an e-mail.

☑ *Regular e-newsletter type* – consider options of different frequency such as weekly, monthly or quarterly with different content for different audiences and segments.

☑ *House-list campaign* – these are periodic e-mails to support different objectives such as encouraging trial of a service or newly launched product, repeat purchases or reactivation of customers who no longer use a service. Although a newsletter is a good place to start with e-CRM, a problem with newsletters is that amongst the different features, your main message maybe diluted, so you need a standalone e-mail or 'e-blast' to have maximum impact.

☑ *Event-triggered e-mail sequence* – these tend to be less regular and are sent out as part of an automated touch strategy to assist with customer development.

Think about which approaches you use now and which others you may consider. You can read more about how e-mail is used strategically as part of Customer Relationship Management in *Total E-mail Marketing* (Chaffey 2006). We reviewed options for using e-mail marketing for acquiring customers and creative best practice in Chapter 7.

MANAGING INCOMING E-MAILS

Surprisingly, many major blue chip companies insult their customers by ignoring or mismanaging their incoming e-mails – lose sales, raise anger and damage the brands which they have spent fortunes building. By the end of this section you will know how to reduce the incoming quantity, reduce the workload of outgoing responses while growing strong customer relations.

Incoming e-mails can be sales enquiries, complaints, after sale service requests and much more. They provide a direct conduit the marketplace. Having made the effort to create a dialogue you need to have the systems, procedures and resources in place to manage this new communications channel. You must have systems in place that:

1 Receive, sort and route the incoming e-mails.
2 Generate an automatic 'message received' response or not, depending on what you have decided is best for your customers.
3 Provide a suitable response regardless of the quantities.

This all sounds very simple, but it demands good planning and foresight. The quantity of incoming e-mails can be reduced, without jeopardizing the relationship by:

1 FAQ's allow for many issues to be dealt with without the customer contacting you directly.
2 Search facilities allow customers to find out more about a topic without having to contact you directly.
3 Linked websites and other locations can allow customers to research a topic across the web without having to contact you directly. It is worth looking at other web sites and their FAQs.

Even once you have removed many of the most repetitive reasons for e-mail, there will still be some incoming communication that can be dealt with through fairly standard answers. This is where pre-prepared standard template responses come in!

And template responses can be used without human input thanks to intelligent software that matches words in incoming e-mail to potential responses. So, for example, when the right count of critical words matches a certain topic, a specific relevant standard template response is sent. It can even be personalized. There are arguments for and against this type of response. It would be nice to think that nothing could match the way in which a human responds to another human, but this is not always the case.

When using real customer service or e-CRM staff, you need well trained, knowledgable staff who, if they don't know the answer to a question at least know where to look to find it. There are always some e-mails that require a human response – so don't ignore human training as well as system design! And if your site has real-time text messaging facilities which gives live e-mail answers or call-back facilities where you request a telephone call, remember these require different skills – e-mail skills and telephone skills.

Staff need to be managed. They need to be set goals for response, set performance standards, trained, motivated and monitored. Ignore people management at your peril.

E-mail marketing

Systems help to categorize incoming e-mails. FAQs reduce the workload. Standard templates reduce workloads. Intelligent systems also use standard templates. Real staff also answer e-mails. They need to be trained and managed . . . if incoming e-mails are going to help customer relations to blossom.

8.8   Control issues

In this section we examine six typical e-CRM control issues that confront marketers reguarly: Inexperience, Unintegrated systems, Information Overload, High Churn Rate, Spiralling Cleaning Costs and Changing Regulations. By the end of this section you will know how to begin to deal with them.

1   *Inexperience.* You have to start good management from within, but there is no reason why you can't try to learn some lessons from outside too! Some of these forms of advice come free, others have a fee attached. The best way to learn about the sort of information that is available for those setting up and managing database and e-CRM systems is to visit some of the organizations who offer such services.

2   *Unintegrated Systems.* Having systems and sub-systems that don't talk to each other – either online or offline – is one of the most common challenges, and one that has to be overcome without all the data, on all the systems, having to be recreated! The expensive way to tackle this is to get in new hardware and software and 'recapture' all the data. A better way is to work with a company that has the skills, scope and track record to do the job. There are many companies who offer to integrate your systems.

3   *Information Overload.* Information overload means too much data. Even when your databases are integrated the amount of data can grow too large to manage properly. Again, by using systems or data that have been designed to solve this issue you can break down seemingly huge tasks into a series of smaller, more manageable tasks. This eases workflow and aids planning. For example, business-to-business company Actel provides its sales account managers with an e-mail every Monday morning listing prospects or customers to follow-up who have engaged with an e-mail the previous week. Even better, the list indicates which products they are interested in through summarizing links clicked or web pages visited. A simpler example is to include a field in the database which shows the date the customer last responded or interacted with an e-mail, so it is possible to see how long ago they were last active.

4   *High Churn Rate.* Imagine this. Everything it seems is working well, but the 'churn rate', or customer defection rate, is high. The result of high churn rate is high recruitment costs and high data capture costs, as well as increasing the required rate of cleaning. One solution is to investigate the reasons for the high churn rate, e.g. are your introductory offers too good to miss, but your subsequent offerings not meeting customer expectations.

5 *Spiralling Cleaning Costs*. Cleaning costs can escalate. Remember that a dirty database is a bad database. It is essential to maintain the integrity of the database. However, there can be pressure to reduce cleaning costs by either de-duplicating less often or less thoroughly. Whilst the relentless search for cost savings is constant, cutting costs here could well be your most expensive false economy.

6 *Changing Regulations*. Industry rules and regulations keep changing or evolving (e.g. privacy laws) and therefore stop you being as creative as you would like. CRM and especially the e-CRM industry can only survive and thrive if it has the confidence of the customers. Every practitioner should strive to protect and enhance that trust in all their dealings. Don't forget to read up on the changing laws and regulations, particularly if you attract international customers.

E-MARKETING EXCELLENCE

Richard Beal of Direct Line on a single data view

According to *Financial Times* (2000a) Richard Beal believes that the key to effective control of CRM lies not in trying to enforce one single view of the customer (although Direct Line does have a large database of customer information). He uses a Japanese *kaizen* or continuous improvement approach, but this does not involve huge teams of call centre agents employing a single approach to callers, but small groups of staff trying out different ways of handling calls.

For Richard Beal the strategic goal of this CRM project is cross-selling. Direct Line has expanded into home insurance and now offers loans via the Internet. This approach gives it the ability to identify a loan application that comes from a customer who might also benefit from one of its credit card schemes. The Chordiant software it uses allows a customer to bounce between web contact and a telephone conversation. Direct Line believes this flexibility is the key to converting queries into sales.

Richard Beal says *'We have found that people want a hybrid, they will commence an inquiry over the Internet, but do not feel comfortable carrying out the whole transaction online'*.

SECTION SUMMARY 8.8

Control issues

Be aware of some of the e-CRM issues that lie ahead of you including Inexperience, Unintegrated systems, Information Overload, High Churn Rate, Spiralling Cleaning Costs and Changing Regulations. Now is the time to learn more about dealing with them if you are to enjoy excellent customer relations.

8.9   Cleaning the database

The database is arguably a company's greatest asset yet it can turn into a liability if not maintained properly. By the end of this section you'll know why and how it can be done.

Your database is an asset. You must maintain its integrity. Like all assets it needs to be maintained otherwise it becomes a liability – harassing uninterested people, duplicating e-mails and snail mails, calling people the wrong name – effectively making a nuisance of yourself and damaging your brand, not to mention wasting time and money. Horror stories abound.

The excuse that you have an old system or worse, several old and unintegrated systems, which present too big a task is a weak, although understandable excuse. Some organizations manage to put off setting up effective cleaning systems for years by having some sort of committee or group looking into a new super-system, costing the project and then realizing that technological developments have moved ahead.

And all the time, the working group has been costing huge sums of money to operate and very little, if anything, has been invested in keeping the databases in question clean and up-to-date. This is a very poor, but frequently observed, business practice. You must try to keep cleaning, even whilst discussions about changes and upgrades continue.

APPROACHES TO CLEANING DATABASES

There are many methods of keeping databases clean, some are proactive and some are responsive.

Let's start with the minimum requirement – responsiveness. Respond to changes in data. It needs to be updated continually. And remember, as with any communication, online or offline, the recipient should be given the chance to inform you either (a) how their information should be corrected or (b) if they want to be taken off your database. The web site is an obvious place to achieve this, through a communications preferences or customer profile form, but this facility is only usually offered by e-tailers.

Maybe the members of your database want to tell you that they didn't like a specific mail shot, that they continue to receive three copies of something from you, that they do not wish to receive e-mails about pet insurance but they do about car insurance, or even more unusual items that you cannot imagine. To maintain a good relationship, you must be flexible and allow for a wide-ranging dialogue. This requires good systems and procedures, as well as trained customer service staff.

A free-flowing and flexible dialogue can be encouraged by: freephone numbers, dedicated web pages, a dedicated e-mail address and mailback/faxback special request sheets. The aim is to get any unusual request into the system quickly and accurately, allow someone to have responsibility for checking that it is routed within the organization to the right place/person and to be able to follow-up should the database member request it.

> **PRACTICAL E-MARKETING TIP**
>
> You can use a data bureau to manage the process of matching or appending profile data from different databases or de-duplicating common customer records. They can also correct e-mail addresses, postcodes and other information through referencing other data sources. Another alternative is to use specialist list cleaning software such as WinPure (www.winpure.com) in-house.

Sometimes it's not enough to listen – you have to go out and ask. Being proactive means you have much better databases because you take responsibility for your data being correct.

So:

- Regularly contact (by mail or e-mail) inactive database members.
- Regularly scan your records for possible duplication.
- Regularly cross-reference your new records against your old.

As with all business processes, you can do the cleaning yourself in-house, or subcontract, or outsource, the service – i.e. you can buy in the planning and design and then run it yourself, etc. There are many companies that specialize in software that manages customer relationships via mail, e-mail, telephone and sales force. It is worth having a look at some of them.

SECTION SUMMARY 8.9

Cleaning the database

The database is an asset. It needs to be maintained and cleaned. You can do it yourself in-house or subcontract outside. You can be responsive through customers helping to clean the database and you can be proactive by actively cleaning yourself. Either way, cleaning is essential if your database is to remain an extremely valuable asset.

8.10   Making it happen

Given the list of failed CRM projects . . . how do you make it happen – how do you establish excellent e-CRM? Many organizations have to start from scratch. By the end of this section you'll know what's involved when setting up an e-CRM system.

It is quite common for a inter-disciplinary team to be developed to create a database marketing and e-CRM system. They will have to develop project teams made up of the users of the system, analysts to understand their requirements, technical staff to create the system and a project manager with sufficient time to devote to the job.

When choosing a CRM system you need to consider the current and future scale; how it can now, and in the future, integrate with other systems (like invoicing and debt collection) and

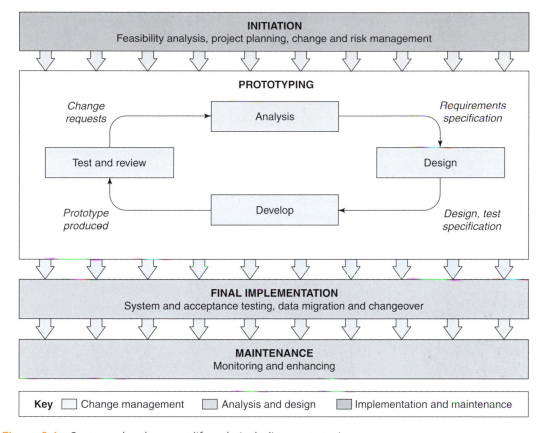

Figure 8.6 Systems development lifecycle including prototyping

of course your budget which includes 3Ms – men and women – people who will be involved in data capture, analysis and use; money – budget required for software license plus training and motivation schemes (to ensure staff buy into the new system); minutes (time required to specify the brief, source it, test it, modify it, train the team and roll it out).

Systems development should follow a structured approach, going through several stages as shown in Figure 8.6. Note though that, just as for web site development, prototyping is the most effective approach since it enables the system to be tailored through users experience of early versions of the system. Beware of 'scope creep'. Ultimately, CRM is an attitude as much as a system. Success depends on a customer culture where all staff always ask 'how can we help the customer?' (Table 8.2).

US marketers need to improve our skill sets. We need to get better at speaking the language of IT and develop a greater understanding of how technology can translate into improved customer knowledge and ultimately an 'improved customer experience'. As Hooly Wright says 'IT people use scary language, and marketers step back from it. But if marketers constantly brought conversations back to the benefits for the customer, that would help build a common language around the customer and put technology back in its place'.

Table 8.2 E-marketing best practice checklist – CRM

Do you have a real CRM culture?	Yes/No

Customer Culture

1   Do all of your company staff understand your brand values and customer service goals?
2   Do you write brand values and customer service goals into job specs?
3   Do you reward staff based on achieving brand values and customer service goals?
4   Do your executive directors meet customers regularly and is customer satisfaction discussed at board level?
5   Do your managers present 'learnings' from the marketplace (particular customer learnings) annually?
6   Are you riding the right trends?
7   Does your web site facilitate different visitors who are at different stages, i.e. who want to (a) Learn More (b) Try a Sample/Trial (c) Buy Now.
8   Does your web site facilitate different visitors that prefer information in different modes (a) PDF (b) Video (c) Link to More Pages (d) Telephone.
9   Does your web site facilitate different buyers' preferred mode of buying including (a) Telephone (call back facility) (b) e-mail (c) Direct order.

Contact Strategy

10 Do all incoming e-mails receive either a same day response or at least an auto-response? Do you set expectations for response time and then deliver on them?
11 Do you treat new subscribers to your e-newsletter differently? Do you use a welcome strategy?
12 Do you practice 'Right Channelling' – upweighting e-mail communications for customers who prefer receiving e-mail web communications and who prefer web services?
13 Do you have a refined e-contact strategy with defined touchpoints reflecting position in customer lifecycle, e.g. survey five days after first purchase, one year after subscribing, etc.
14 Do you promote and assess advocacy (e.g. forward to a friend e-mails, members get member promotions).
15 Do you acknowledge all customer complaints and have a process for following up?
16 Do you acknowledge all customer suggestions and have a process for following up?

Satisfaction Improvement – analysis and testing

17 Do you use usability testing on your web site? If a retailer, do you use online mystery shoppers? Have you surveyed customers experience on the web and e-mail programmes recently?
18 Do you review customer profiles, motivations and buying process regularly?
19 Do you analyze, and act on, reasons for customer defections (including identifying the customer signals indicating imminent defection)?
20 Has your customer satisfaction scoring criteria changed in the last three years?

Treat 'Don't Know' as a 'No'. Then count your 'Yes's'
0–13 you are not really building true CRM into your business.
14–17 you are becoming a CRM driven business with some room for improvement.
18–20 you are an excellent 'marketing driven business'.

As they say: 'Front end is fun. Back end is business'. Marketers are reasonably good at developing web sites (front end), but we have to become experts with the database and the eCRM systems (back end) required to build continual success.

MANAGING THE DATABASE

The database is the core of the CRM system. The database administrator/manager (DBA) has many responsibilities here:

1 *Database Design*. Ensuring the design is effective in allowing customer data to be accessed rapidly and queries performed.
2 *Data Quality*. Ensuring data is accurate, relevant and timely.
3 *Data Security*. Ensuring data cannot be compromised by attacks from inside or outside the organization.
4 *Data Backup and Recovery*. Ensuring that data can be restored if there are system failures or attacks.
5 *User Coordination*. This involves specifying who has access to the information retrieval and who has access to information input. Too many uncontrolled inputs mean files get changed and deleted by too many different people. The database spins out of control.
6 *Performance monitoring*. Checking the system is coping with the demand placed on it by users.

There's one more part of the DBA's job – to communicate with clarity to the whole of the rest of the organization the advantages of database marketing.

COSTS AND TIMESCALES

When it comes to the crunch question of 'how much does it all cost?', there are many variables to consider:

1 The set-up costs of the system
2 The type of system
3 The scope of the system
4 The size of the system
5 The choice made about the DBMS(Database Management Systems)
6 The maintenance programme
7 The use you make of it!
8 Where your physical database management system is geographically located.

It is a complex job, but once all these variables are taken into consideration, a task breakdown can be performed and analysis, design, set-up, maintenance and running schedule of costs can be calculated.

What's missing? Staff – customer service staff. They are a key component, particularly when handling wide ranging, non standard, requests or complaints. Here's a crucial question. How many customer service staff should you employ? How many customer service staff, do you think, AOL employs? Well AOL has created a customer service army of 6000 employees and contract workers who handle technical questions and inquiries (Newell, 2000). How many customer service staff do you need?

The other key question is 'how long does it take to set up an e-CRM system?' The variables are similar to cost:

1 Time allowed for investigative stage
2 Time allowed for design
3 Time for writing programmes
4 Time for data capture/reassessment/input
5 Time for trials, piloting, testing and de-bugging.

SECTION SUMMARY 8.10

Making it happen

An effective CRM programme needs a strong project manager who can unite the business and technical team members. A defined database administrator is also required who will champion the system and own it to ensure appropriate data quality, security and performance. Planning using the systems development lifecycle provides a framework for costing, scheduling and monitoring the project. Remember also that CRM programmes should never end; they evolve.

CHAPTER SUMMARY

1 **e-CRM** operates in an environment where customers demand quality services from organizations. Since it is technology based it can be used to increase the speed, frequency and relevance of interactions, while remembering that human contact is the best for some situations.

2 **Relationship marketing** involves a long term rather than transactional approach to customers. It is built on building up permission, trust, listening and then responding to customers.

3 **Database marketing** is key to e-CRM since the database can be used to understand customer needs through profiling and data mining, segment customers and manage integrated marketing and direct marketing campaigns.

4 **e-CRM** provides DRAMA – Dialogue, Relevancy, Accuracy, Magic and Access to marketing communications. A good approach to the CRM cycle is attract, capture data, get closer, embrace and golden handcuffs.

5 **Profiling** helps to identify groups of customers and rank them according to their importance to the company. Appropriate communications and offers can then be developed for these groups with the aim of building long-term relationships with them.

6 **Personalization** refers to tailoring of a range of communications from e-mails to web sites. These can be individual (one-to-one) or to segments (mass customization). Personalization can occur due to user selection (customization), marketing rules (individualization) and group characterization such as collaborative filtering.

7 If **incoming e-mails** are mismanaged, this can destroy customer relationships. Procedures must be put in place to sort and route the incoming e-mails, notify receipt and provide a suitable response. Contact strategies such as FAQ and using the phone where appropriate can minimize the volume of e-mails and maximize the clear-up rate.

8 Control must occur to avoid e-CRM problems such as Inexperience, Unintegrated systems, Information Overload, High Churn Rate, Spiralling Cleaning Costs and Changing Regulations.

9 Cleaning the database is important to minimize marketing costs and improve relationships. Approaches are responsive where customer requests are implemented rapidly and proactive where regular planned cleaning occurs.

10 An effective CRM programme needs a strong project manager to achieve staff involvement across the business and ensure the implementation is well planned, so delivering on time. A good quality database administrator is important to champion the system and to deliver data quality, security and performance.

A final checklist covering all aspects of E-CRM is provided in Table 8.2.

References

Boreel, M. (2007) Sogeti IT Consultancy Marketing Age, March.

Broadvision (2001) Case study of Aviall (www.broadvision.com).

Chaffey, D. (2006) *Total e-mail marketing*, 2nd edition. Butterworth-Heinemann, Oxford.

Considine, R. and Murray, R. (1981) *The Great Brain Robbery*. The Great Brain Robbery, CA.

Earls, M. (2002) *Welcome To The Creative Age – bananas, business and the death of marketing*. John Wiley.

Earls, M. (2004) Gone Bananas. *The Marketer*, 3 June 2004.

Egain's State of Customer Service (2007) *New Media Age*, 31 May.

Financial Times (2000a) Direct Line: Strategic goal of this CRM project is cross-selling. Financial services case study by Michael Dempsey. *Financial Times*, 7 June.

Financial Times (2000b) Enterprise: a seamless electronic environment. *Financial Times*, 7 June 2000. http://www.ft.com/ftsurveys/spb2f6.htm, http://www.ft.com/ftsurveys/spb2f2.htm

Flores, L. and Eltvedt H. (2005) Beyond online advertising – lesson about the power of brand web sites to build and expand brands. ESOMAR, Montreal 2005.

Gartner Group (Feb 2004) reported in *Marketing Business*.

Godin, S. (1999) *Permission marketing*. Simon and Schuster, New York.

Harris Interactive (2007) Second annual Customer Experience Impact Report, a Harris Interactive study sponsored by RightNow(R) Technologies.

Information Week (2001) Scaling Up: Prudential's Very Large Database Pays Off. *Information Week*. January 15th. http://www.informationweek.com/820/database.htm.

Laurent, L. and Harald Eltvedt, H. Beyond online advertising – lesson about the power of brand web sites to build and expand brands. ESOMAR, Montreal 2005.

Marketing Business (2004) Detica IT Survey Nov 2003 reported by Laura Mazur in *Marketing Business,* Feb 2004.

McKim, B. and Hughes, A. (2001) How to measure CRM success. Database Marketing Institute, March 9. www.dbmarketing/articles/Art198.htm.

Mertz, S. (2005) *Software to keep customers happy. The Times,* 1 December.

Microsoft (2006) *Customer Driven Productivity – A Study on CRM Practice in Ireland.* Microsoft Business Solutions Microsoft Ireland. Published February.

Mitchell, A. (2004) Heart of the Matter. *The Marketer,* 3 June 2004.

MORI (2003) 'Managing your Customer Insight Capability and the Drivers for Change' – Client Managed, Cosourced, Insourced or Outsourced – a survey of UK FTSE 1000 organisations' commissioned by Detica.

Murphy, D. (2004) The Truth About CRM. *Marketing Business,* Feb.

Newell, F. (2000) *Loyalty.com.* McGraw Hill.

New Media Age (2007) Impulse Buying. Emma Rubach 30.08.07. *New Media Age.* www.nma.co.uk.

Neumeier, M. (2007) Zag The #1 Strategy for high performance brands. AIGA New Riders.

Novo, J. (2003) *Drilling Down: Turning customer data into profits with a spreadsheet.* Available from www.jimnovo.com.

O' Neill, B. (2001) Seeking definition. *The next big thing.* www.tnbt.com. March 7 2001.

Peppers, D. and Rogers, M. (1999) *One-to-one field book.* Currency/Doubleday, NY.

Pond, J. (2007) Don't Call Us. *The Marketer,* July/Aug.

Rohner, K. (2001) *Marketing in the cyber age – the why, the what and the how.* Wiley, New York, NY.

Ross, V. (2001) Review of Permission Marketing by Godin (1999). *Interactive Marketing,* Vol. 2, No. 3. Jan/March 2001.

Siebel (2001) BMC Software case study from Siebel web site: http://www.siebel.com/case_studies/HighTech/BMC.pdf.

Smith, P. and Taylor, J. (2004) *Marketing Communications – an integrated approach,* 4th edition. Kogan Page, London.

Smith, P.R. (2004) The ticking customer service time bomb, www.prsmith.org.

Stone, M. (2004) in an interview with P.R. Smith.

Tranfield, D. and Braganza, A. (2007) Businss Leadership of Technological Change – five key challenges facing CEOs. Chartered Management Institute.

Wright, H. (2007) Reclaiming the customer high ground. *The Marketer,* July/August.

Further reading

Ebner, M., Hu, A., Levitt, D. and McCrory, J. (2002) How to rescue CRM. *The McKinsey Quarterly,* 2002, Number 4.

Godin, S. (1999) *Permission marketing.* Simon and Schuster, New York. An interesting and influential book.

Newell, F. (2000) *Loyalty.com*. McGraw Hill. An accessible book with US examples of the principle of loyalty.

Reicheld, F. and Schefter, P. (2000) E-loyalty: Your secret weapon on the Web. *Harvard Business Review*, July–August 2000, pp. 105–113. An essential, short summary of achieving customer loyalty using online techniques.

Seybold, P. (1999) *Customers.com*. Century Business Books, Random House. London. Describes a customer centric approach to business strategy with many examples drawn from the US.

Web links

ClickZ (www.clickz.com/experts). E-mail channels. Clickz has expert articles within its channels on deliverability, e-mail optimization and creative.

CRMGURU (www.crmguru.com). Forum, plus some white papers.

Database Marketing Institute (www.dbmarketing.com). Great practical guidelines and presentations on traditional database marketing and online marketing using e-mail and web personalization.

Email Marketing Tools (www.davechaffey.com/email-tools). A compilation of tools for managing e-mail broadcast and deliverability.

Email Marketing Strategy Guide (http://www.davechaffey.com/guides/email-marketing-strategy-guide). Everything you need to know about e-mail marketing on a single page.

Email Experience Council (www.emailexperience.org). A US organization with compilations of practical tips on e-mail marketing.

E-Loyalty (www.e-loyalty.com). An introduction to achieving online loyalty by Ellen Reid-Smith.

MyCustomer.Com (www.mycustomer.com. Portal focusing on traditional and online CRM.

JimNovo.com (www.jimnovo.com). A specialist on online CRM, Jim's site has many practical insights about analyzing and following up according to online purchase behaviour including the excellent 'Drilling Down' guide.

Net Promoter Score Blog (http://netpromoter.typepad.com/fred_reichheld). Blog on achieving advocacy by Fred Reicheld and other specialists in achieving advocacy such as Dr Paul Marsden.

Peppers and Rogers One to One marketing (www.1to1.com). Contains interesting articles, case studies and supplier guides.

Self-test

1 How do database marketing, relationship building, direct marketing and CRM relate to each other?

2 Describe different staged approaches to relationship building.

3 Explain the concept of data mining.

4 How do we use DRAMA to keep customer relationships alive?

5 How, when and why should profiling occur for an organization you are familiar with.

6 Summarize the benefits and disadvantages of personalization.

7 Describe the management issues of incoming e-mails.

8 Explain these six issues of e-CRM control: six typical e-CRM control issues that confront marketers regularly: Inexperience, Unintegrated Systems, Information Overload, High Churn Rate, Spiralling Cleaning Costs and Changing Regulations.

9 Describe approaches to database cleaning.

10 Produce an outline list of the main activities that need to occur for e-CRM implementation and maintenance.

Chapter **9**

E-business

'Businesses have invested heavily in ICT of all sorts over the last three years, and in many cases found themselves with an expensive depreciating asset, and less than hoped for benefits. Businesses are now seeking to use ICTs more shrewdly to unlock business value'.

DTI (2003)

The dot-com disasters still scare many professionals. Clicks-and-mortar companies generally outperform pure-play Internet companies. Why didn't these new e-businesses survive? Where did they go wrong? The answer is that they weren't e-businesses. They weren't even businesses since many were ignorant of business essentials such as the need to integrate front-office systems with back-office systems, keep close to customers, deliver real added value, have clear propositions, carefully target the right customers, etc. This chapter clarifies what is meant by e-business; a much misunderstood concept.

OVERALL LEARNING OUTCOME

By the end of this chapter you will:

- Know what an e-business really is – what its components are
- Understand the risks, resources and rewards associated with running an e-business
- Be able to avoid the key mistakes.

CHAPTER TOPIC	LEARNING OBJECTIVE
9.1 Introduction	Understand the context of e-business
9.2 E-business architecture	Identify the components of an e-business architecture
9.3 An e-business value framework	Distinguish between and understand links between buy-side, sell-side and in-side e-business
9.4 Buy-side applications	Define the opportunities and marketing relevance of buy-side applications
9.5 In-side applications	Define the opportunities and marketing relevance of in-side applications
9.6 Sell-side applications	Define the opportunities and marketing relevance of sell-side applications
9.7 Creating the e-business	Identify the main elements of moving to e-business
9.8 E-business security	Outline the main risks and solutions to e-business security
9.9 E-business success criteria	Specify criteria for e-business success (ensuring an e-business transition works)
9.10 E-business failure criteria	Specify criteria for e-business failure (including why new systems fail)

9.1   Introduction to e-business

This chapter explores the challenges and changes involved in creating an e-business. For many, these are uncharted waters.

We've talked about the difference between e-commerce (selling online), e-marketing (marketing online) and e-business (running a business electronically) in chapter one. Now we are going to explore the major task of developing an e-business. Firstly, remember that **e-business** impacts absolutely everything about a business! It is far bigger than **e-marketing**. But what exactly is it? What does e-business entail? What are the components, the issues and the obstacles facing e-business? This chapter addresses all these questions and more. By the end of this first section you will know exactly what it is and will be able to discuss it comfortably with colleagues.

So what exactly is e-business? There are several definitions. Deloitte and Touche Consulting Group use this definition:

> *'The use of electronic networks for business (usually with web technology)'.*

Here's IBM's definition:

> *e-business (e' biz' nis) 'The transformation of key business processes through the use of Internet technologies'.*

Technology can transform key business processes out of the old **value chain** and into new, dynamic, **value networks**. This involes integration, automation and extension of processes both inside and outside a company. This usually means letting go – handing over information and empowerment to employees, strategic partners, customers, distributors and other stakeholders.

The old value chain started with the purchasing of raw materials and then moved to the production of goods and services, their distribution, marketing, sales and after sales service. The new **value networks** reshuffle the sequence so that customers, distributors and partners are involved more as the business integrates into a flexible, faster moving, customer driven extended network of online partners. We will explore this initially using the business value framework.

Creating an e-business offers a golden opportunity to analyze and improve your whole business – its operations, processes and procedures as well as strategic partners – a fresh opportunity to re-engineer a company.

Perhaps one of the greatest impacts of the Internet is that it has forced many business to rethink all of their 'cherished perceptions and ideas'. Building an e-business helps managers to adopt what the Zen Buddhists call 'the beginner's mind'.

Having said that, the term, 'e-business' probably won't exist in a few years as most businesses will be using 'e-business' as part of their normal procedures. But reviewing business processes and re-engineering of companies will continue long after e-business has integrated itself into the business architecture.

But what's normal tomorrow is not necessarily normal today. E-business can create new business models that take little notice of convention.

In this chapter, we will show you how value networks have replaced the old value chain model. We will break it down into a simple business value framework that will help you to build an e-business architecture. We will take this further and help you to make this happen, i.e. how to create an e-business.

We will also help you assess whether your e-business idea will make a profit. We will show you why many e-businesses fail and how to avoid failure with the help of a handy checklist.

Beyond the risk assessment of a new e-business, there are other risks in the online world. Could your board of directors be taken to court on the grounds of negligence if proper security measures and/or proper back-up systems are not in place? We will address these other issues in subsequent sections.

Finally, please note that e-business should never be seen as an end in itself. Like a web site (which is a small part of e-business), it is a journey not a destination. You primarily create them – to help customers, followed by suppliers, partners and distributors. Combine this with a drive for continual improvement and you can see why it's an ongoing journey.

Evolutionary stages

This journey takes most organizations through several evolutionary stages. Most organizations' web sites evolve from the early stage, one-way communications sites sometimes called brochure-ware (listing products and prices) to two-way sites that can interact with customers via making sales transactions and having two-way communications whether sales, e-mails, discussions or automated interactions. Today, we add in Web 2.0 (collaborative facilities) and it becomes a lot more interesting (more later). The web site may then further evolve into an e-business system with the web site often at the hub of all processes. This is sometimes referred to as a web centric business.

A five year analysis of leading consumer web sites supports the notion that websites are transitioning from a mere spoke in the marketing wheel to the hub itself (Flores and Eltvedt 2005).

Web sites are moving beyond just helping customers to helping internal staff (intranet), external customers, distributors, suppliers and strategic partners (extranet). Now add two additional dimensions, an intranet, for internal staff information and processes, and an extranet integrating with suppliers, distributors, and customers, and the web centric approach makes a lot of sense.

Less than ten years ago the idea that airline companies would, one day, allow customers to book their own flights, select their own seats and even check themselves in – all from outside the airport – would have been considered lunacy. Today airlines extend their extranet to allow customers to self service themselves. Equally, the idea that banks would one day allow customers to access their account balance from a competitor bank and withdraw cash outside a secure building from a 'hole in the wall' in a busy street in any country would have seemed absurd. Today bank and airline extranets have opened up inner operational systems to customers in ways never thought possible only a few years ago.

Web 2.0 stage

Web 2.0 helps organizations to create online communities (both internal and external), social networks and collaborative groups. Recent research reveals that more and more companies are using the extranet's collaborative facilties of Web 2.0 to engage customers in NPD and self ser-vicing (sharing solutions). Today, many organizations use collaborative product development tools, such as initiating discussions in blogs to test ideas, or virtual development tools involving customers in the use of collaborative design tools (allowing external designers and engineers to collaborate using a company's exclusive development software), or testing how well products sell within virtual worlds. Many organizations (two-thirds of McKinsey survey 2007) use online tools to involve their customers in product development. Each industry sector is different, e.g. both financial services and manufacturing, for example, focus on testing concepts and screening ideas, while those in high tech focus on generating new ideas (McKinsey 2007). Some organizations are realizing that Web 2.0 is not just about having a new dialogue between the brand and the customer, but having a 'trialogue' where customers talk to each other and the brand can then be a small part of billions of conversations. Customers want to talk to each other, to participate and to create and to hear what other customers have to say. Witness book reviews, uploading photos in Flickr, writing comments on people's walls in Facebook, reading blogs, posting comments and on it goes.

> *This is the point where user generated content meets brands – an area fraught with difficulty for the unwary and rich with opportunity for the creative.*
>
> Walmsley, A. (2007)

The extranet helps to integrate suppliers, distributors and stakeholders efficiently into the value network. An organization's intranet has huge potential to increase operational efficiencies and boost team work. However, if it isn't sold properly to senior management, and consequently senior management doesn't engage, then mis-management is almost inevitable. Well managed intranets deliver time – the most limited of all three key resources (3Ms – men, money and minutes/time).

Intranets help staff to carry out basic tasks such as finding product information; finding experts; locating forms and processes. New research suggests that intranets, and in particular Web 2.0 facilities also improve employee collaboration. However this requires constant care and attention. Your intranet is not a massive heaving 'rough-and-ready' library where stuff gets stored. Caution is urged when considering using Wikis for internal document storage as, without very careful management, they can grow to become a heaving mass of unedited and only partially organized information.

Gerry McGovern says: 'Your intranet can be a goldmine, so don't sell it like a coalmine. The gold-dust of the intranet is productivity. A great intranet will save time whenever a staff member carries out a common task. These time savings will lead to greater operational efficiency and a more competitive organization (saving five minutes here and two minutes there)' McGovern (2007). It can seem difficult to sell the importance of the intranet to senior management but persevere, because, as McGovern says, it is the 'essence of the organization'. Since the dawn of business, finding information, processing it and retrieving it has been critical to running any business – so too the intranet is becoming more and more critical to many organizations today.

Even e-business can learn from history – sixteenth century Florentine philosopher, Niccolo Machiavelli, once said: 'There is nothing more difficult to take in hand, more perilous to conduct, or more uncertain in its success, than to take the lead in the introduction of a new order of things'.

Interestingly, a recent (2007) experiment in Venice found that a free wireless hot spot had the same effect as free water hundreds of years ago – both created a community around the available resource. A once quiet unused area became a thriving busy bubbling community collecting water, or more recently using a free wireless hot spot.

You can learn from others and adopt best practice demonstrated in this chapter. You must, however, be prepared to change your ways of doing business; the business environment and models are changing profoundly. American business guru, Peter Drucker, once said: 'A time of turbulence is a dangerous time, but its greatest danger is the temptation to deny reality'. So let's get on with it and explore e-business.

E-MARKETING INSIGHT

A capability model for e-commerce

A detailed stage model which businesses can use to benchmark their e-commerce capabilities was developed by E-consultancy (2005). Capabilities which should be evaluated are:

- Strategy process and performance improvement
- Structure of organizational location of e-commerce
- Senior management buy-in
- Marketing integration
- Online marketing focus.

A summary of this E-consultancy research is presented in Table 9.1. This was based on research designed to identify the challenges faced in managing e-commerce and the approaches used. The first phase involved interviews with e-commerce/digital marketing managers at: Alliance & Leicester, BCA Interactive, BP, Carphone Warehouse, DTI, Henderson Global Investors, Lloyds TSB, MTV, MyTravel, Orange, Ordnance Survey, Shell, Sony, TUI and Wheel. Phase 2 was designed to validate the results of Phase 1 and to assess the overall maturity of e-commerce management in the UK. Phase 2 of the research involved an online survey of a wider range of UK organizations with turnover from less than £500 000 to over £10 million.

Table 9.1 Stage model of E-commerce adoption based on E-consultancy research. *Source:* E-consultancy (2005)

E-commerce capability level	(A) Strategy process and performance improvement	(B) Structure: organizational location of e-commerce	(C) Senior management buy-in	(D) Marketing integration	(E) Online marketing focus
1 *Unplanned*	*Limited.* Online channels not part of business planning process. Web analytics data collected, but unlikely to be reviewed or actioned.	*Experimentation.* No clear centralized e-commerce resources in business. Main responsibility typically within IT.	*Limited.* No direct involvement in planning and little necessity seen for involvement.	*Poor integration.* Some interested marketers may experiment with e-communications tools.	*Content focus.* Creation of online brochures and catalogues. Adoption of first style guidelines.
2 *Diffuse management*	*Low-level.* Online referenced in planning, but with limited channel-specific objectives. Some campaign analysis by interested staff.	*Diffuse.* Small central e-commerce group or single manager, possibly with steering group controlled by marketing. Many separate web sites, separate online initiatives, e.g. tools adopted and agencies for search marketing, e-mail marketing. E-communications funding from brands/businesses may be limited.	*Aware.* Management becomes aware of expenditure and potential of online channels.	*Separate.* Increased adoption of e-communications tools and growth of separate sites and microsites continues. Media spend still dominantly offline.	*Traffic focus.* Increased emphasis on driving visitors to site through Pay Per Click search marketing and affiliate marketing.

(Continued)

Table 9.1 (Continued)

E-commerce capability level	(A) Strategy process and performance improvement	(B) Structure: organizational location of e-commerce	(C) Senior management buy-in	(D) Marketing integration	(E) Online marketing focus
3 Centralized management	*Specific.* Specific channel objectives set. Web analytics capability not integrated to give unified reporting of campaign effectiveness.	*Centralized.* Common platform for content management, web analytics. Preferred-supplier list of digital agencies. Centralized, independent e-commerce function, often a profit-centre, but with some digital-specific responsibilities by country/product/brand.	*Involved.* Directly involved in annual review and ensures review structure involving senior managers from Marketing, IT, Operations and Finance.	*Arms-length.* Marketing and e-commerce mainly work together during planning process. Limited review within campaigns. Senior e-commerce team-members responsible for encouraging adoption of digital marketing throughout organisation.	*Conversion and customer experience focus.* Initiatives for usability, accessibility and revision of content management system (including search engine optimization) are common at this stage.
4 Decentralized operations	*Refined.* Close co-operation between e-commerce and marketing. Targets and performance reviewed monthly. Towards unified reporting. Project debriefs.	*Decentralized.* Digital marketing skills more developed in business with integration of e-commerce into planning and execution at business or country level. E-retailers commonly adopt direct channel organization of which e-commerce is one channel. Online channel P + L sometimes controlled by businesses/brands, but with central budget for continuous e-communications spend (search, affiliates, e-communications).	*Driving performance.* Involved in review at least monthly.	*Partnership.* Marketing and e-commerce work closely together through year. Digital media spend starts to reflect importance of online channels to business and consumers.	*Retention focus.* Initiatives on analysis of customer purchase and response behaviour and implementation of well-defined touch strategies with emphasis on e-mail marketing. Loyalty drivers well known and managed.

5 Integrated and optimized	Multi-channel process.	Integrated.	Integral.	Complete.	Optimization focus.
	The interactions and financial contribution of different channels are well understood and resourced and improved accordingly.	Majority of digital skills within business and e-commerce team commonly positioned within marketing or direct sales operation. Supporting process of 'frontend' systems development skills typically retained in a central e-commerce team which is more likely to be a cost centre.	Less frequent/in-depth involvement required. Annual planning and six monthly or quarterly review.	Marketing has full complement of digital marketing skills, but calls on specialist resource from agencies or central e-commerce resource as required. Online potential not constrained by traditional budgeting processes.	Initiatives to improve acquisition, conversion and retention according to developments in access platform and customer experience technologies. May use temporary multi-disciplinary team to drive performance.

E-MARKETING EXCELLENCE

Yorkshire Water revises business processes

As part of the move to e-business, Yorkshire Water implemented SAP R/3 and SAP Business-to-Business Procurement with the aim of increasing the efficiency of business processes, e-procurement and improved supplier management.

Systems development manager Dave Murphy explains how change was achieved:

> *'We ran a whole series of different computer systems which had been written by our own staff in the late eighties. They were heavily tailored to Yorkshire Water's needs and they were held together by bits of string and sticky tape'.*

SAP was chosen as the result of a selection procedure since around 87% of business requirements were fulfilled by the software. Murphy says:

> *'To bridge the gap between 87% and 100%, Yorkshire Water preferred to adapt its business processes rather than the software. We didn't customize the software package because we realized that these business changes were a good thing'.*

To give an indication of the areas of the business affected by the change, the following modules were implemented in a ten month period:

- Sales and Distribution (SD)
- Financials (FI)
- Controlling (CO)
- Materials Management (MM)
- Project System (PS)
- Time Sheet (CATS)
- Payroll
- Human Resources (HR)
- Asset Accounting (AA).

(*Source*: SAP web site www.sap.com/uk).

SECTION SUMMARY 9.1

Introduction to e-business

E-business is bigger than e-marketing. It involves using technology to facilitate improvements to business processes and increase the efficiency of internal and external information flows with customers, suppliers and distributors. Rigid value chains are changed to flexible, responsive value networks.

9.2   E-business architecture

The e-business architecture brings together the systems, processes and applications used by all parts of the business. The e-business architecture connects these different processes, or applications, across both internal departments and external partners.

'Applications are like building blocks – they have to be put together carefully and systematically' to create a solid e-business architecture.

Kalakota and Robinson (2000) say that good e-business design integrates applications so they 'work together like a well oiled machine to manage, organize, route and run a business'.

This e-business architecture transforms data into useful information available to the right person at the right time in the right place – which these days means anyplace – anywhere in the world. For example, using workflow technology can achieve 'intelligent routing' of an important e-mail query from a key account customer to someone who can act on it swiftly. It's easy to see how excellent information creates competitive advantage.

WHICH BUSINESS ARE YOU IN?

E-business is more than just transplanting existing business practices and processes into online applications. It is disruptive. The Internet and e-business certainly have the capacity to disrupt the old ways of doing business. E-business provides a golden opportunity to rethink the whole business – how it operates, who does what, where and when. E-business affects every aspect of a business.

Take the value chain – it's no longer valid. Even newer, customer focused, non-linear businesses are realizing that only parts of a company create real value and generate profit, while other parts don't. In other words some bits are profitable and other bits lose money.

So many businesses find other companies that can do those bits or certain processes better and out source, or subcontract, seamlessly with a new strategic partner. Ultimately, a business can become what Charles Handy calls 'a box of contracts'.

This drives a big question: What are the core competencies? They are those core skills that your business is better at than any one else. E-business may involve some businesses becoming modular, or molecular – shrinking back to their core competencies while outsourcing everything else. For example, about 70% of Cisco's hardware goes directly from connected partner producers to customers without Cisco ever seeing it. E-businesses form 'business webs' or **value networks** – a connected box of contracts. These value networks of production, distribution and service partners are glued together by the Internet. The Internet has revolutionized the global supply chain and inventory management for many companies.

Here is a slightly dated, although still, for many, shocking statement from John Hagel at the World Economic Forum, (*Fortune*, 2001):

> *'Companies that design and brand their own products, build and package them, and deliver them to their customers will soon no longer exist'.*

This then begs the question – 'what business am I in?' Established companies are not even sure what their core competencies are. Worse still, they no longer know who, where or what competition is. 'Who is my competitor?' is a difficult question, even if you do know what business you are in you may not know who's competing against you, as today's competition is boundary-less, category-less and now sometimes just a minute part of the value network (or the old value chain). For example, different collaborators may form a consortium to bid for an engineering contract, which will be difficult for their competitors to counter since they have limited knowledge about this new organization.

The weak links in the old value chain are now being picked off by new 'plug-and-play' companies (who are better at a specific process within the value network) and who offer themselves as partners in an extended network – the value network – a kind of loose confederation. As businesses move towards value networks they minimize physical infrastructure and non-critical assets to create 'zero gravity' (zero physical assets which tie them down). This ultimately forces the question we raised in Chapter 1 'what business am I in?' This causes major shocks to established businesses. Plug-and-play companies can almost pop up overnight and slice your market up and by time you've woken a chunk of the market is gone.

Right now, as you read this, there are analysts from Tokyo to Toronto and Bombay to Beijing analyzing industry by industry, sector by sector where there are weak links in the old value chain. They identify the weak links (unprofitable bits) and offer to replace them with their services – all linked seamlessly via secure systems. Most CEOs know that certain parts of their old value chain are not as profitable as other parts. In fact some parts of their value chain lose money and other parts make money. So when a proposal is made by a trustworthy supplier, often on the other side of the world, to replace this weak link with a much more efficient automated system which reduces error and associated costs whilst simultan-eously saving overheads and seamlessly linking into the rest of the company's systems, it is difficult to avoid the proposal. Save costs, increase effectiveness. It is here that CEOs ask difficult questions like 'which bit are we really good at?' 'Should we outsource and connect with strategic partners globally?' This then brings the tricky question – 'what business am I in?'

If you think that's tough, here's what wakes CEOs up in the middle of the night in a cold sweat: realizing someone has just broken the locks of the old business model and opened up a whole new way of doing business. The Internet facilitates this. Combine this with the boundaryless, categoryless nature of business today and it is difficult to see who is the competitor. All markets are now global markets attracting international competitors into the back yard of old secure marketplaces. Competitors who are often categoryless, i.e. capable of moving into markets with apparent ease. Once upon a time supermarkets sold groceries and petrol stations sold petrol. Today supermarkets sell groceries, petrol, financial services, books, videos, office equipment, clothes, furniture. And petrol stations sell groceries, newspapers, DVDs, hot coffee and croissants. As they say, 'once upon a time eBay and iPods were typos and Google was a number. Who is my competitor? What market place am I in? What business am I in?

As businesses become 'boxes of contracts', more and more functions such as design, manufacturing, operations, distribution, sales and customer service are outsourced. Although e-business systems facilitate the seamless connection between various stakeholders and value contributors, be wary of the outsource fiends who want to outsource everything, including customer service and customer relationship management, as this, we feel, is too important to let go.

Responding to the worry that e-business is complex, one way of simplifying it is to consider a basic framework which simplifies and clusters many of these applications together. The next section explores this in more detail.

Meanwhile just remember the e-business architecture must deliver a fast, error free, integrated service that is secure, robust, reliable and scalable. Not much to ask!

E-MARKETING INSIGHT

The Internet's chameleon qualities

The importance of pooling the skills of the workforce will grow and new ways of building on the learning that happens in companies will be discovered. Happily, the communications revolution presents new opportunities to do this. It also presents new challenges. For example, Internet technologies help to spread and share ideas, but they also allow ideas to move easily beyond a company, creating a need for protection. However, too much protection of intellectual property rights can stifle innovation so governments and companies need to be able to strike a balance between openness and protection (Cairncross 2002).

E-MARKETING INSIGHT

Beyond the value chain concept

Chaffey (2004) suggests that although the value chain concept still helps to start the thought process about increasing business efficiency and customer value, it has inherent weaknesses:

1 Most applicable to manufacturing rather than services.
2 A one-way chain involving push, ignores need to highlight customers needs (through market research) and responsiveness through innovation and new product development; e.g. Cisco have feedback forms and forums on their site that enable them to collect information from customers and channel partners that can feed through to new product development.
3 Tends to ignore the value of value networks.

SECTION SUMMARY 9.2

E-business architecture

Constructing the e-business architecture means somehow bringing together the systems, processes and applications from all parts of the business, both inside and outside. Not much to ask!

9.3   An e-business value framework

We're going to use a basic e-business framework as an overview of some of the components and key processes that are required to run a business.

Let us keep it simple. Let us ignore legal departments, accounting, HR and IT departments and assume that they have to be integrated into any business system. So, let's just break up the business into those aspects that perform Buy-side, In-side and Sell-side processes (Figure 9.1). This identifies three key areas in which to achieve e-business performance. There are other approaches to this. But for now, let's just stick with this simple model.

BUY-SIDE E-BUSINESS

The buy-side is B2B – buying raw materials and/or services. It can include procurement, inbound logistics, and warehousing. Here, the business's **extranet** is used to open up certain aspects of the business (applications and data) to an exclusive audience of carefully selected suppliers to allow: faster and easier trade with suppliers, manufacturers and/or distributors; collaboration with suppliers, manufacturers and/or distributors so that they move from 'independence to interdependence', sharing data to improve operational efficiency and ultimately customer satisfaction.

Reduced working capital is achieved as efficient systems allow 'just-in-time' deliveries thereby avoiding having vast quantities of cash tied up in stock (working capital) as shown by the example of Shell Chemical in Section 3.4. This is an 'extended enterprise' where partner suppliers and distributors work much more closely together. Supply chain management applications are commonly used.

INSIDE E-BUSINESS

The in-side is sometimes known as B2E – business to employee – involving internal processes and communications. This could be manufacturing, management or operations. Here the **intranet** empowers employees by opening up access to key information and applications. Any of these internal processes can be outsourced. Excellent B2E systems are vital if a small core internal team is going to run a tight ship.

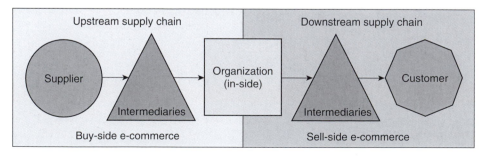

Figure 9.1   A simple e-business value framework

Now the intranet can be used to: improve communications between business and employee as employees can find information more easily and communicate with each other via discussion groups; evolve from competency to 'responsive knowledge workers'; use Web 2.0 collaboration and knowledge management tools. Typical applications used here are business analytics or intelligence, knowledge management and decision support tools and/or **enterprise resource planning** (ERP) applications. Many of these are extended into partners, i.e. extended ERP – Dell and Ford.

SELL-SIDE E-BUSINESS

The sell-side involves processes and applications that help sell to and service customers, whether directly or indirectly through intermediaries. E-CRM applications and Selling Chain Management applications are commonly used. Here the **extranet** provides exclusive use to strategic intermediary partners such as distributors and also to key account or registered customers. Extranets can be used to:

- Sell to customers directly and indirectly through intermediaries.
- Move from online occasional sales to lifetime loyalty relationships.
- Serve and manage customer relations better.
- Speak to them individually and tailor one-to-one offerings drawn from the database.

There are also many applications:

- CRM
- ERP
- Supply Chain Management
- Selling Chain management
- Operating Resource Management
- Enterprise Application Integration (EAI)
- Business Analytics
- Knowledge management
- Decision support applications.

Remember that isolated, standalone applications will soon be history. For new e-businesses, options for **business models** and **revenue models** will also have to be reviewed. Some of the options for business models are shown in the box 'Paul Timmers on business models' and for revenue models in the box 'Yahoo! revenue models'. **Revenue models** specifically describe different techniques for generation of income. For existing companies, the standard revenue model is the income from sales of products or services. This may be either for selling direct from the manufacturer or supplier of the service or through an intermediary who will take a cut of the selling price. Other options for generating revenue include selling advertising space and **affiliate** revenues.

Paul Timmers on business models

Approximately ten years ago Timmers (1999) identified no less than eleven different types of business model that can be facilitated by the web, as follows:

1 *E-shop* – marketing of a company or shop via web
2 *E-procurement* – electronic tendering and procurement of goods and services
3 *E-malls* – a collection of e-shops such as the now defunct BarclaySquare. This model didn't prove sustainable. The nearest equivalent is Price comparison sites, such as Pricerunner (www.pricerunner.com), which link through to different e-shops.
4 *E-auctions* – these can be for B2C, e.g. Ebay (www.ebay.com) or B2C, e.g. QXL (www.qxl.com)
5 *Virtual communities* – these can be B2C communities, such as Xoom (www.xoom.com) or B2B communities, such as Vertical Net (www.vertical.net). These are important for their potential in e-marketing and are described in the Focus on Virtual Communities section in Chapter 6.
6 *Collaboration platforms* – these enable collaboration between businesses or individuals, e.g. Yahoo Groups! (www.yahoo.com) services.
7 *Third-party marketplaces* – marketplaces such as EC21 (www.ec21.com)
8 *Value-chain integrators* – offer a range of services across the value-chain
9 *Value-chain service providers* – specialize in providing functions for a specific part of the value-chain, such as the logistics company UPS (www.ups.com)
10 *Information brokerage* – providing information for consumers and businesses, often to assist in making the buying decision or for business operations or leisure
11 *Trust and other services* – *an example is* Truste (www.truste.org) which authenticates the quality of service provided by companies trading on the web.

Yahoo! business and revenue models

Chaffey (2004) describes three different perspectives for considering business and revenue models (shown in Figure 9.2). It can be seen that Yahoo! has been one of the more successful Internet **pureplays** since it has developed a range of revenue sources through growth and acquisition.

1 *Marketplace position perspective.* Here Yahoo! is both a retailer and a marketplace intermediary.
2 *Revenue model perspective.* Yahoo! has commission based sales through Yahoo! shopping and also has advertising as a revenue model.
3 *Commercial arrangement perspective.* Yahoo! is involved in all three types of commercial arrangement shown.

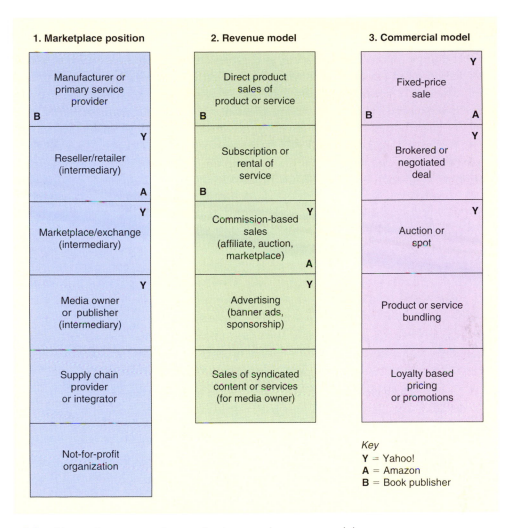

Figure 9.2 Alternative perspectives on business and revenue models

An e-business value framework

A simple business framework for assessing e-business change is:

- buy-side e-business – extranets used for buying raw materials and or services. It can include procurement, inbound logistics, and warehousing

- in-side e-business – intranets used for optimizing internal processes and communications. This could be manufacturing, management or operations.

- sell-side e-business – extranets used for exclusive use to strategic intermediary partners such as distributors and key account or registered customers.

Together these elements of the framework help to optimize supply chain management

9.4   Buy-side applications

Internet technology can be used to open up the purchasing, in-bound logistics, stock management and reordering system to an exclusive audience of carefully selected suppliers who gain direct access to the company's back office systems via the exclusive external Internet, the company's extranet. This way, the organization gets to trade with suppliers, manufacturers and/or distributors more accurately, more swiftly and more easily, as cumbersome paperwork processes are abandoned and faster, easier, smarter systems are opened up to supply partners. Advanced supply chain integration becomes easier with e-business technology. This, in turn, strengthens the partnership relationship.

Chaffey (2004) suggests that stage models can be developed for the buy-side in the same way that those have been produced for the sell-side (Section 1.12). The following levels of sophistication in *product sourcing applications* can be identified:

- *Level I*. No use of the web for product sourcing and no electronic integration with suppliers.
- *Level II*. Review and selection from competing suppliers using intermediary web sites, B2B exchanges and supplier web sites. Orders placed by conventional means.
- *Level III*. Orders placed electronically through EDI, via intermediary sites, exchanges or supplier sites. No integration between organization's systems and supplier's systems. Rekeying of orders necessary into procurement or accounting systems.
- *Level IV*. Orders placed electronically with integration with companies procurement systems.
- *Level V*. Orders placed electronically with full integration of company's procurement, manufacturing requirements, planning and stock control systems.

As part of strategy development, the current level can be identified and then target levels set for the future.

PARTNER RELATIONSHIP MANAGEMENT

Rather than the 'them and us' of buyers versus suppliers, the 'partners' develop common goals and common measures to monitor their joint performance. This creates an atmosphere of collaboration and co-operation where opportunities and problems are identified and solved together.

Both the supplier and buyer move from 'independence to interdependence' sharing data to improve operational efficiency and ultimately, customer satisfaction. The original organization now builds a network of trusted partners, a network or an '**extended enterprise**', where partner suppliers and distributors work much more closely together courtesy of web technology.

DRIVING FORCES FOR PRM

Forming such buy-side links can be proactive. Some companies, like GEC, will not trade with suppliers if they cannot both integrate and trade online. In return, the buyers can easily relay current sales and stock levels in real-time to suppliers. For example, a supermarket (buyer) can collect, analyze and disseminate sales and other data via the Internet to its suppliers. Within seconds information on actual sales, store inventory and shelf space is available to suppliers (via a standard browser). It can be downloaded right into the supplier's own ERP (enterprise resource planning) spreadsheet and other systems.

This data can also be used in sophisticated forecasting systems which combine historical trends with current sales demand to predict how much will be bought. This in turn helps both the suppliers and the retail stores to improve promotional planning as they can monitor early responses to, say advertising campaigns, more quickly. This in turn, facilitates further collaboration particularly if joint promotions or exclusive promotions are created. The partnership grows stronger. They can even have newsflashes about specific product sales.

All very exciting stuff, but you can probably guess what can be a major barrier to all of this ... culture – organizations not used to sharing data and accessing each other's ERPs ... security risks and fears associated may require a gigantic cultural leap. We look at this in more detail in the section on 'Creating an e-business'.

There is one other interesting point, in fact a new phenomenon created by tight online supply chain management, and that is – **negative working capital**. Working capital refers to money tied up in stocks and debtors, money which is required to run a business. It is possible for a company to reduce stock by having suppliers deliver as and when orders come in. This '**just-in-time**' delivery obviously reduces stock and the cash it ties up. In addition cash is boosted if customer payments are taken (when the order is placed) before paying suppliers. This creates negative working capital.

E-MARKETING EXCELLENCE

Daimler Chrysler opens up

Daimler-Chrysler opened its employee suggestion box scheme to its external suppliers. As a result it received thousands of suggestions to improve efficiency, and is measuring the benefit in billions – not millions – of dollars!

E-MARKETING EXCELLENCE

Virgin Atlantic Airlines select Tranmit Sprinter

Nick Wildgoose, Head of Purchasing, says:

> 'In evaluating IT systems, we have several criteria in mind including ease of use, which is vital to user acceptance, and ease of integration, which is key to minimizing disruption and costs. Tranmit's product satisfied these criteria, but also allowed us to implement a solution that reflected the reality of the marketplace. Whether our suppliers generate invoices on paper or electronically we need to be able to push ahead in line with our commitment to innovation and service. This software allows us to do that without leaving our business partners behind'.

> **E-MARKETING INSIGHT**
>
> **Dell and Ford and the Extended Enterprise**
>
> When Dell receive an order from Ford Motor via the PremierPages extranet, Dell knows immediately what type of worker is ordering and what kind of PC is required. Dell assembles the hardware and installs the software including Ford-specific configuration code that's stored at Dell. That's an integrated supply chain as part of the Ford or Dell Extended Enterprise.

SECTION SUMMARY 9.4

Buy-side applications

Perfect information about customers, distribution partners and supplier partners can tighten the supply chain and create competitive advantage.

9.5 In-side applications

This section explores how web technology can help the besieged employee to do a better job. How the business can communicate more easily with employees and how employees can communicate with the organization and work with each other more easily.

This is crucial as grand strategies don't work if they are poorly executed. Some estimates suggest that up to 40% potential return on marketing spend is lost by employees. In some cases these staff are the brand builders engaged in hundreds of millions of 'brand moments'. Staff communications become even more important here.

The internal Internet, the **intranet**, can change the way people work together; replace cumbersome paper based systems; reduce information overload; create 'responsive knowledge workers'; use collaboration and knowledge management tools to make better decisions. On top of this an e-HR department can create virtual classrooms to support 'just-in-time learning' and longer more structured learning involving both individuals and collaborative team efforts. However, careful consideration needs to be given to avoid drowning in a sea of e-mails that clog systems and people. Knowledge management is key to success.

With over 1000 new books published every day, hundreds of thousands of new web pages every day and a growing number of e-mails, it's not surprising that many managers feel overwhelmed by information. In the US it's a medical condition known as 'information fatigue syndrome'. Here is an actual case where managers had too much information and a paper based system that didn't work. They sought an intranet solution.

E-MARKETING EXCELLENCE

Novartis select autonomy for knowledge management

John McCulloch, Manager, Executive Information Systems says:

> *'Novartis is a world leader in pharmaceuticals, healthcare, agribusiness and nutrition. That means we handle a vast amount of complex information daily, both from internal and external sources. Until now, that has cost us a great deal of time and money in manual processes, but Autonomy's technology can automate the whole process from start to finish. We are delighted to be bringing the technology on board'.*

Novartis implemented Autonomy Portal-in-a-Box™ to provide an automated infra-structure for the handling and personalization of the complex information generated internally, as well as research papers, market intelligence and breaking news from outside. The system not only aggregates and personalizes an enormous amount of content without incurring high labour costs, in the form of staff, to read, manually tag and hyperlink each piece of information, but also dynamically and continuously understands individual needs and preferences in order to deliver compelling and timely content.

Personalization occurs by automatic profiling of employees by analyzing the ideas in the text they read and write in company documents, e-mail and web sites visited. Important information is automatically delivered to top managers by alert flashing icons, based on their interests and professional expertise, as soon as it is available, without the user having to waste valuable time actively searching for it.

Source: Autonomy web site (www.autonomy.com)

E-MARKETING EXCELLENCE

ASDAs intranet

ASDA supermarket had the information management problems of unreliable distri-bution of documents to 230 stores; too much information, managers complained of being 'inundated' with communication while frustrated by loss and late arrival of cer-tain documents. Managers wanted information in a format that could be searched, and the facility to share their ideas with their colleagues without simply increasing the volume of e-mail.

An intranet that was created that was intended to add value to communications from a user's point of view by identifying and prioritizing applications with most business benefit. It also optimized the cost and time taken for authors to create information – real emphasis was placed on sustainability of applications. A further aim was to encourage a broad church of ASDA house departments to become involved in the development programme – build internal awareness. The intranet gave staff access to:

- Merchandise briefs
- Daily weather forecasts
- Press releases and internal announcements
- HR policies
- Customer service information
- Checkout queue length reports
- Store performance self assessment systems
- Peer-based discussion groups.

Staff are also encouraged to add to and amend the information – authors of textual information are assisted by background routines that automatically validate the completion of fields, create hypertext links, index documents for the search facility and delete obsolete documents. Workflow processes facilitate quality control and approval of material prior to publication.

SECTION SUMMARY 9.5

In-side applications

In-side applications use intranets to share knowledge amongst employees while avoiding problems of information overload.

9.6 Sell-side applications

The sell-side involves processes and applications that help to both sell and service customers, whether directly or indirectly.

Sell-side applications include transactional e-commerce functionality, **e-CRM** programmes, the potentially huge online affiliate programmes and collaborative functionality that turns customers into 'prosumers' – designers and producers who eventually consume their own product. (Note: CRM is also considered in Sections 3.10, 4.7 and 8.4.)

First, consider eCRM and how relationship marketing helps nurture lifetime customers whose repeat sales generate much higher profits than new customers. Managing the customer relationship makes cross-selling and upselling helpful rather than intrusive.

In many ways CRM is not anything new since good marketers have always taken care of their customers. What is new is the lack of CRM in the fast moving online world. A world where the higher expectations of online customer are regularly crushed by sloppy e-marketing.

Surprisingly, excellence in the offline world is often forgotten in the online world even by major players: e-mails are left unanswered for days.

So major efforts are required to keep online customers loyal. Have you got the processes in place to ensure excellent service? Do you remember customers, their names, needs, past preferences when they contact you? Is there a seamless system that recognizes customers whether they access you through iTV, iKiosks, web radio, mobile phones or good old traditional PC accessed Internet web sites? Does your system help you to paint a total picture of each online customer?

Have you got the software to exploit the valuable data you can collect from customers? Most organizations don't. The reality is that many companies have a diverse range of incompatible applications combined with dirty data (unclean data).

It therefore makes a lot of sense to nurture the captured customers into lifetime friends, particularly if they're ideal customers. The returns on this investment are high.

The online world presents new challenges when nurturing customer relationships. One particular challenge is the tension between security and customer convenience – the hassle of hard to remember passwords versus easy access.

Affiliate marketing

Given that distribution is the most important element of the marketing mix, e-business offers a host of distributor options including **portals**, **hubs**, **metamarket switchboards**, **infomediaries**, **shopping bots**, web links and **affiliates**. Each of these routes to market can create competitive advantage (if managed correctly). An affiliate programme is an easy and effective option when used on a small scale with a handful of trusted organizations who refer business or visitors to your site. As it grows it requires careful management to operate and ensure all affiliate partners get paid on time for referring or creating links that bring customers to your site.

Affilliate programmes have created one of the biggest model changes in the online world as they can convert customers or third parties into sales agents or affiliates. Witness Amazon's network of 900000 affiliate links from their customers' web sites; a powerful network of virtual middlemen that creates a protectable competitive advantage. Affiliate marketing is considered more in Section 7.4.

Combine this vast affiliate network with Amazon's infinite shelf space and its real-time information about buying trends and public opinion and suddenly a new economic model emerges – *The Long Tail* (Chris Anderson 2004). Millions of tiny niche markets for previously obscure products and services suddenly become profitable. Some organizations take it further by not only letting the customers make recommendations and reviews, but actually modifying and creating products online – this the world of the prosumer.

Prosumers – where the 'sell-side' meets the 'in-side' (new product development)

The now, very old, linear model of 'design and build, brand it, sell it', is being replaced by a more dynamic mode that involves customers in new product development and suppliers

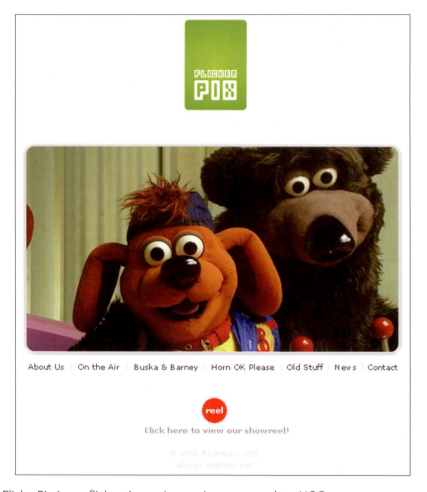

Figure 9.3   FlickerPix (www.flickerpix.com) – a unique approach to UGC

in the ordering process. Instead of a linear production process with customers at the end of it, the new model actually has feedback and input from customers coming in much earlier, more frequently, in fact as an integral part of the production process. In some cases it's called UGC – user generated content, e.g. YouTube or even just web sites encouraging customers to post interesting comments and ideas about tips on using the product. This is UGC.

Arguably, the ultimate UGC is a BBC Northern Ireland radio show that attracted such humorous callers encouraged by an equally humorous host, that they were able to use the dialogues (recorded on air) and create a cartoon show using the actual sound recordings from their audience. Produced by Flickerpix, 'On The Air' (Figure 9.3), it can be seen on YouTube and www.crea8ivity.com.

Chapter 5 has an interesting example of how MTV used text messages and the web to create a show based on the customers' votes. But look around you and observe 'people TV' in action. It uses real people/customers/audience as the stars of the production (reduces costs). Audiences then take control and vote for who should stay or go. The web cam keeps running. The hits keep counting and the show goes on, partly created and largely controlled by the

Figure 9.4   Constant Comedy (www.constantcomedy.com)

customer. Another innovative company constantcomedy.com hosts videos of amateur comedians who then get voted on or off by online audiences (Figure 9.4).

Prosumers can create and partially create products and services. Look around you and you'll see it happening. From TV, to toys, to cars and computers. Customers are increasingly involved in the production process. Cars are no exception when it comes to the prosumer. Visitors can assemble and order their own car online. The customers fill in the order form and specification forms (not the sales rep). More interestingly, BMW actually had customers' online help to design and choose a final version of one marque.

We all know how clever Dell, IBM and many others are at integrating their production process right into their customers' own internal systems so that customers can order directly online what they need, when they need it. The box 'Barbie and the young prosumer' illustrates another example of using the web to involve the customer in NPD.

SECTION SUMMARY 9.6

Sell-side applications

Sell-side applications include e-commerce, e-CRM, affiliate programmes and collaborative prosumers. E-CRM is all about common sense, yet so many major companies abandon common sense and treat customers dismally. The database is an asset that must be maintained and used to enhance relationships.

9.7 Creating the e-business

So how do you create an e-business? How do you go about it? Here are seven steps to e-business.

1. ESTABLISH THE VISION

Creating an e-business requires a clear vision of where you want to be. How you want your business to grow, expand, extend and operate in a new collaborative environment. One thing that must be absolutely clear is the vision – what you want the e-business to do and what benefits it will bring.

After that you find the technology and team to implement this. Not the other way around. Technology should not drive the vision – customer needs and partner collaboration requirements should drive the vision. Technology will do whatever it is asked. Do not let technology control the vision. You control the technology. You control the vision.

For example, vision could include:

1 Information online for customers and suppliers
2 Interact and transact externally online
3 Deploy IOCTs in their internal processes
4 Deep pervasive integration between their internal systems and those of customers and suppliers.

2. GET SENIOR MANAGEMENT SUPPORT AND RESOURCE

Creating an e-business, whether a brand new, pure play dot-com or a mixed mode click-and-mortar (online and offline) business requires careful consideration, research, planning, testing, implementation – a lot of energy and effort. It requires a dedicated team fully supported by top management.

One measure of this is whether there is budget available for the resources required even just to research it – as this requires time, people and money. Top management support is a must otherwise emotions, tensions and energy are unnecessarily aroused, exhausted and frustrated. Another senior management challenge is to create a culture that welcomes change rather than resists it: a culture of shared responsibility where empowered employees own their own employability.

3. SELECT A PROJECT TEAM AND ANALYZE REQUIREMENTS

You need a strong project leader and a cross-functional team from inside and outside the organization. Task the group with identifying what the requirements of the e-business might be – what processes need to link together – who needs to link with whom – what information they need and when. Run 'discovery workshops'. Allow partners access to internal systems in real-time. Project management skills are essential.

4. REVISIT VALUE NETWORK AND CORE COMPETENCIES – WHAT BUSINESS ARE WE IN?

This is the big one. Businesses are breaking up their old value chains and reconstructing themselves around their core competencies – their 'global core'. The other parts of the old chain (whether logistics, procurement, HR or even marketing) are fulfilled by a web of strategic partnerships. There appears to be a not-so-subtle shift from the delivery of work to the co-ordination of work. Focusing on core competencies forces managers to ask a fundamental question – what business are we in? Remember the 'outsource fiends'? There are many issues arising around 'down sizing' and outsourcing including dying concepts such as staff loyalty and staff morale.

5. DESIGN E-BUSINESS ARCHITECTURE

Having decided what business you're in and what your core competencies are, the next question is 'What are the processes involved in running the business?' What needs to be linked to what? The value network reaches beyond the enterprise and into the extended enterprise's network of collaborative partners – suppliers, distributors, producers and others. Whether extended to outside strategic partners or kept within the e-business architecture the network has to create a seamless flow of information between different functions and departments; both inside and outside the company itself. Does the front end integrate with the back end? Can it be built stage-by-stage. Is it scalable? Is it robust and secure? What is the risk assessment?

6. DEVELOP, PILOT, TRAIN AND ROLL-OUT

The integrated applications obviously have to be developed – although many of them are off-the-shelf. The danger of tailor-made or proprietary applications can take so long that they emerge as 'still-born' solutions – out-of-date before released. The systems are tested rigorously, bugs extracted, staff are trained and eventually the e-business is ready to roll out. One of the delicate roll-out issues that has to be addressed early is whether to integrate the e-business with the main business, separate it but keep it in the same premises or spin it off as a separate company and reintegrate it later. Staff buy-in is essential. Time, money and effort has to be spent bringing them on board otherwise they resist and resent the new e-business systems.

7. BENCHMARK, MEASURE AND MONITOR

As mentioned earlier, e-business, like a web site, is not a destination it is a journey. A journey towards continual improvement. So the whole operation is regularly reviewed, benchmarked and reported for improvements. New technology will continue to roll out – better, faster, easier, seamless and sensible. Remember Moore's Law. The key is not to constantly update bits and pieces, as it can be disruptive to have the processes changing all the time without the staff buying into the idea. So good management skills are required to harness the technology and the delicate continual drive towards constant improvement . . . to constantly delight customers and partners.

How long do you think a major e-business project might take to go through all these stages? Answer: 24–56 weeks for a large company; 10–16 weeks for a small company.

SECTION SUMMARY 9.7

Creating the e-business

The seven steps to becoming an e-business are:

1 Establish the vision
2 Get senior management support
3 Identify requirements
4 Revisit value network (and core competencies)
5 Design e-business architecture
6 Develop, pilot, train and roll-out
7 Benchmark, measure and monitor.

9.8 E-business security

There are thousands of hackers, vandals and viruses at large at any given time. It's disturbing whether you are concerned about the privacy of your personal data, or the potential risk to your organization. Businesses and customers get damaged. Kids, conmen, criminals and competitors, not to mention pressure groups, political groups, government intelligence agencies and many more want to break through security systems.

In the corporate world, popular targets for activists include: large corporations, news outlets, banking/finance, hate groups, political sites, e-commerce, personal/credit card data, computer security sites. What's left?

The excitement of building a new dynamic e-business combined with the race to market exposes many companies to significant new risks. This is the case since the extended enterprise opens up systems and data to external parties. Poorly designed systems thrown together by technical whizz-kids often ignore the wide variety of risks lurking out there.

Organizations can be accused of negligence for breaches of privacy/security. In the UK, the Information Commissioner has announced that his office will take a tougher line with organizations that have privacy breaches. So apart from damaging customers trust in your organization, security lapses can end company directors up in court, if they are deemed to be negligent in their responsibilities towards good security. Having anti-virus software and a 'secure server' are not sufficient, as they only provide minimal protection against 'very few of the threats that your web site will see'. In fact Web 2.0 can actually make it easier for security breaches.

Although usability and accessibility are popular issues, we don't see much about security. Good web site management needs to build in security policies, security reviews, security testing and auditing, as well as planning for business continuity in case of 'disaster recovery' and emergencies. Remember the earlier security is discussed, the cheaper it becomes to manage risks. Also integrate security into any testing programmes.

E-BUSINESS SECURITY THREATS

Check the list of different types of security breaches. You will know of some of these risks, but who is responsible for managing the threats to your organization and are they covering all the bases? These are some of the threats:

- *Credit card fraud*. Imagine having your card details sucked into cyberspace and used by someone else. Or imagine customers denying receipt of goods delivered. Almost half of Visa's card disputes are Internet-related. Elsewhere it's higher. For the e-tailer the percentage of fraudulent purchases on sites can run to double figures. On top of this returns can be high. Phishing attacks where SPAM e-mails encourage users of secure services, such as banks, to divulge their security detail are still widespread because some new consumers fall for them.

- *Distributed denial of service (DDOS)*. This effectively denies access to your site when hackers flood network routers from lots of different sites with an overwhelming amount of traffic to targeted web sites. They effectively shut down the sites.

- *Cyber graffiti*. Hackers can alter your web site, insert nasty images, false information, false testimonials and even direct customers to another site. Non-hackers can put up rogue sites sounding very similar to your own and attract lots of your customers. Spot the difference between: Investsmartindia.com and Investmartindia.com.

- *Botnets or alien computer control*. If you have a permanent Internet connection (cable or ADSL), you're constantly open and vulnerable to the outside world. Any hacker can easily gain access to your computer by using network scanning tools which track poorly protected systems. Then an alien or remote third-party software controls your PC and together forms a botnet of 'Zombies' used for phishing scams or DDOS. If you know the right contacts you can hire a botnet at a few cents per PC!

- Your web site is used to *host and distribute other unauthorized software*, some of which may damage other users' computers (even a simple response form for an enquiry could have some hidden code placed by a hacker so that it deletes database information or sends emails to everyone in your address book). Remember social media Web 2.0 can increase your vulnerability to hackers.

- *Chat room undesirables*. Even without permanent connections, your chat rooms can be invaded by uninvited and unwanted third parties such as racists. They post obscene messages or more subtle racist arguments to often vulnerable audiences. In 2001 Telextext had to close its SMS-based chat service because of racist taunting by rival football fans.

- *Intellectual property theft*. On top of this, theft of intellectual property happens all the time – software, music, information downloaded, copied and passed on. Sometimes it's duplicated and sold commercially by unauthorized pirates. Worse still, pirating is effectively legal in some countries where there is no IPR law.

- *Competitive information*. Another type of intellectual property also gets stolen – sensitive company information, particularly competitive information and databases of customers.

- *Anything that damages your data can have huge legal implications,* since without properly used back-up systems directors can be liable for any damage to their own business caused by a virus.

E-marketing fright

From: ealym@tiscali.it

To: paul@multimediamarketing.com

Subject: A Trojan Horse is on your PC

Hi, I am from Belgium and you'll don't believe me, but a Trojan Horse is on yor PC. I've scanned the network ports on the internet. (I know, that's illegal) And I have found your pc. Your pc is open on the Internet for everybody! Because the services. exe Trojan is running on your system. Check this, open the task manager and try to stop that! You'll see, you can't stop this Trojan. When you use win98/me you can't see the Trojan.

On my system was this Trojan too!

And I've found a tool to kill that bad thing.

I hope that I've helped you too!

Sorry for mybad English!

greets.

This was an e-mail received by PR Smith – threats, hoaxes and real problems are everywhere.

Apart from damage done to the business, security violations can also end in downstream negligence litigation.

We see much more about usability and accessibility nowadays than several years ago, but who asks about security?

E-BUSINESS SECURITY SOLUTIONS

Good security starts with a security policy. Do you have one? System security is part of a wider security policy that should include physical (lost laptop, stolen pc) and procedural security (to avoid disaffected employees deliberately formatting a disc or sending information out).

It's good to build security into the design of an e-business early as it's hard to retrofit security to an operational system under attack. 'Design security in rather than inspect security breaches out'.

Tough decisions are required, e.g. convenience and security don't always work together; passwords are a nuisance but do offer at least a minimal level of security. Equally, risk can be reduced by asking customers to pre-register before purchasing anything or clearing payment before goods are despatched.

There are many other technological, physical and procedural controls required:

- *Contracts*. Clauses that define the security processes to be used may have to be incorporated into contracts with companies you do business with online.
- *Trend and exception monitoring*. Visa contact cardholders if any 'out of character' purchases are made and AmEx offer temporary numbers that are valid for a predetermined (1–2 hours) shopping period and amount.
- *Public key technology and cryptography*. Web servers and browsers can be set up easily to encrypt or seal all communications. Public key encryption basically confirms the identity of an individual or company as established by an intermediary trusted by your company; it proves a transaction originated with that individual or company, so it cannot subsequently be denied (often called non-repudiation) and seals data, such as transactions or e-mails, to prevent the contents being altered.
- *Intrusion detection routines*. These scan for attacks such as denial of service or access to a site via a competitor. They are often part of a **firewall** solution which is a specialized server at the gateway to a company that is used to keep out unwanted intruders.
- *Virus scanners*. These should be set up to monitor continuously and kept updated to the latest version.
- *Audit trails*. You need to record good audit trails of key events, with particular security related events and transaction records. Do you audit the information that should be retained to help resolution of disputed electronic transactions?
- *Back-up*. Back-up is crucial if your business depends on being online. Do you have good back-up and recovery procedures? Is your web site content stored separately?

The best systems in the world aren't going to help if people don't use them properly. A security solution is only as strong as its weakest link and lapses such as assigning 'no brainer' passwords like 'password' or the day of the week create gaping holes for even the most novice hacker.

E-MARKETING INSIGHT

Some common sense security guidelines

Here's some simple common sense advice from the Institute of Public Relations:

1 Turn on anti-virus software (and update it)
2 Know the original creator of e-mails with attachments
3 Know the purpose of the attachment before opening it

4 Don't be fooled by e-mail virus hoaxes

5 Update IRC Internet chat software products

6 Be wary of newsgroups and mail lists

7 Keep informed

8 Be paranoid

9 Write-protect floppys before inserting into other users' computers

10 Back-up, back-up, back-up!

SECTION SUMMARY 9.8

E-business security

There are many security challenges out there including:

- Credit card fraud
- Distributed denial of service
- Web site defacing
- Computer viruses
- Populate your chat rooms
- Intellectual property theft
- Sensitive data theft.

Fortunately there are many solutions, from firewalls to filters and encryption. But remember constant vigilance is required in this fast changing online world.

9.9   E-business success criteria

By the end of this section you will understand the key characteristics of successful e-businesses. In this section we review nine criteria. The more of these criteria you can score in the better: creating an e-business is like a decathlon.

Starting an e-business or repurposing an existing one is not like starting an ordinary business; but many of the criteria for success are the same for non-e-businesses . . . good business principles and practice are applicable anywhere . . .

THE NINE SUCCESS CRITERIA

1 *A clicks-and-mortar parent provides cash flow and resources.* Despite popular opinion, many dot-coms are now profitable or at least forecasting profitability! Most of them, however, are not standalone e-businesses, but clicks-and-mortar businesses. This is no surprise: it merely shows that 'mothering' works; the e-business is brought into this world and

nurtured by a caring parent which allows it to develop its individuality before eventually it becomes self-supporting and leaves home.

That parent could be an existing model business: big retailer develops online sales; big service company develops online customer relationship management system, or the parent is an investor group providing financial succour and ideally some business acumen and skills too.

Besides the e-businesses in profit already (capable of leaving home . . .), many more are approaching profitability. So what makes the successful ones work?

2 *An existing brand provides brand awareness and a customer base*. Building on existing brands: most companies now realize their brand equity is transferable to e-business. In fact, customers are so wary of the plethora of unheard-of online suppliers – it is reassuring for them to find a traditional brand.

3 *Existing management team and structure*. Existing management and organizational structures can help if it means your e-business doesn't have to resource, from day one, all the functions needed to run a business, but which don't directly lead to the creation of value: personnel, finance, property, perhaps even IT. Even so, you need a management that is quick-witted and flexible and capable of allowing the e-business venture to grow somewhat off the cuff: rigid adherence to a plan can cause it to fail.

4 *Value network already in place*. The value network must be in place from supply-side to customer service, fulfilment and despatch. Or if it isn't, focus on putting it in place; or maybe a bit of both: Tesco's online shopping relies in part on the existing supply chain (buying goods, distributing them to supermarkets) and in part on a new added element (staff to pick orders from shelves, vans to provide delivery service).

5 *If not, ability to find suppliers and partners to create the value network for fulfilment*. Creating the value network is a tricky call for traditional retailers who are geared up to hand you a bag of goods at a till, but have no infrastructure to handle orders, pick stock from shelves, pack and despatch and then handle your phone enquiry three days later. The successful e-business gets this right: where the e-business value network is different from the one in the mother business, they create the network ... get fulfilment wrong and you can damage the reputation of the mother business too.

6 *E-business enables re-engineering of existing business*. Business process re-engineering (BPR) might be a partial by-product of building an e-business. Or it could be a business opportunity in itself: e-business enables the traditional firm to re-engineer itself and achieve new scale – for example Vacuum-Cleaners Direct which grew from £170K sales to over £1m. So, get it right and you can transform a small business into, well, at least a not so small business. And all because there is now a better product/service for the customer. Whether you have expanded the market or simply shifted market share in your direction . . . do you care?

7 *Realistic pace of development*. Develop at a realistic pace and do not try to grow too fast too soon – Tesco deliberately ran the service only from certain flagship stores until they had all parts of the value network running smoothly.

8 *E-business operates in a marketable niche*. Consider operating in an existing or new niche – as value networks get more complex and as e-businesses find there are missing components,

there are opportunities to be the provider of these. You can create an e-business which has its own virtues as a niche activity, particularly if the e-business enables you resolve problems of marketing and distribution because it is the best way to target your customers.

9 *Additional benefits of bricks-and-mortar*. What else can a bricks-and-mortar mother-business bring to the e-business?

- Confidence for investors: they can smell and taste a real business and recognize the brand; as pure-play dot-coms started to fail, investors got over the greedy rush and worried about the potential failure of non-recognized brands.

- More than likely, a solid cash flow to give the e-business working capital.

- More than likely, purchasing power through scale and therefore lower costs compared to new-start rivals.

Finally, like any business venture, you need to get the three Ts right . . . timing, timing and timing.

ENSURING SUCCESSFUL E-BUSINESS TRANSITION

More than lending support, the CEO must take ultimate responsibility for a major transition into an e-business. Most IT projects fail not because of IT failure, but because of management failure to manage. Weak management of business change as opposed to inability to install technology causes failure.

Here are some tips for the CEOs facing this daunting challenge.

E-MARKETING BEST PRACTICE CHECKLIST – IMPLEMENTING E-BUSINESS

1 **Have a clear vision.** See how all the processes fit together. See the single picture for all change initiatives and have a clear understanding of how the effects of decisions made in one division or project can affect another department. Effectively, all processes and 'established work patterns' are for review/scrutiny. This requires sensitive and strong leadership skills.

2 **Manage risk.** Whether the robustness of leading technology, the ability of suppliers and vendors to meet deadlines, recruiting and retaining people with the right skills, training staff in new skills or simply acquiring sufficient technical understanding and knowledge or the security issues surrounding the migration data and services outside of the organization (into the extranet), risks need to be identified and planned for carefully. What early warning signals do you need? What regular update information do you need?

3 **Plan for resistance.** We have a neurotic resistance to change. The authors note how, midway through a workshop, when we ask delegates to stand up and swap seats with someone else, how people dislike this very small change. Assess the organization's 'readiness for change'. Game playing and organizational politics are 'standard responses to poor leadership from the top' (Tranfield and Braganza 2007).

4 **Communicate internally.** Allocate time for internal marketing, i.e. communicate the overall vision and outcomes (benefits and changes required) of this transition. Reinforce business outcomes such as 'how far this puts you ahead of the competition and fits with your brand differentiator'.

5 **Develop shared understanding.** Remind staff of the overall business benefits. Develop shared ownership by clearly defining roles, responsibilities and challenges. Get the team to define crystal clear metrics.

6 **Motivate the team.** Remember 'Change programmes generate angst and absorb a lot of energy. The Chartered Management Institute's rule of thumb suggests that levels of motivation stretch to about 18 months and that projects beyond this require renewal. Several organizations now use a '90 day change management cycle' (Tranfield and Braganza 2007).

7 **Train the team.** Allow time, money and human resource for training all staff members. Systems are only as good as the input data. Inaccurate data collection or erroneous data input creates useless systems.

8 **Allow for testing.** Time is often the most limited resource. CEOs under pressure to get new operational systems up and running and showing an early return on investment means time periods required for testing and modifying systems often get squeezed.

9 **Celebrate success.** As they say 'Nothing succeeds like success'. When the systems are up and running don't forget to thank all the team and find some way of celebrating this success.

Managing change requires taking a holistic view of large quantities of detail. 'I normally have in my office, for our stores, a planner with every single person in store and how much capacity they have to change. Then we have how much that capacity for change we're using in any one period, actually planned down to the week' Tesco's John Browett.

E-MARKETING INSIGHT

IBMs seven primary components of e-business management

IBM (2001) suggest these are the main components required for e-business management

1 Mission – purpose and approach to managing e-business

2 Organization – structure and reporting relationships and connections between e-business resources and their counterparts in other areas of the enterprise

3 Roles and responsibilities to define work activities of groups and individuals

4 Processes that define the sequence of activities and outcomes

5 Measures to ensure accountability and improvement

6 Policies for achieving standards

7 Content model to provide consistency and quality of content.

Morgan Stanley Dean Witter also provides a checklist of success criteria for subscribers to its Internet Market Study Service:

- Sustainable market position with first mover advantage
- Clear broad distribution plans; reach and market share
- Insane customer focus
- Insane customer focus!
- Stickiness and customer loyalty
- Rapidly growing customer base
- Opportunity to increase customer 'touch' points
- Extensible product lines
- Annuity-like business with sustainable operating leverage assisted by barriers to entry
- Low-cost infrastructure and development
- Strong business momentum.

SECTION SUMMARY 9.9

E-business success criteria

From this section you now know some of the factors which markedly improve the chances of success. First of these is having a clicks-and-mortar parent to provide succour, resources, economies of scale, investor confidence; you should be able to make a virtue of existing management structures and expertise . . . but it is not vital provided you establish the value network you need and create a niche in which to operate and offer a significant value/service proposition to your customers.

9.10   E-business failure criteria

Some dot-coms are now profitable. That means most are not, and that excludes the already failed ones! There are lots of casualties out there. You won't have got this far without having read of the many spectacular failures: Boo.com, Clickmango, eToys. There is even an influential web-site that tracks failing e-businesses and marks their downfall (www.disobey.com/ghostites). What's gone wrong? By the end of this section you'll know why they failed and how failure could have been avoided. The reasons given are also typical in e-business failure – you will be able to apply these tests to your own or another company's plans and assess the risk factors and then be able to revise the plan to increase the chances of success.

We will show you why they failed and how failure could have been avoided. But long before anyone thought of e-business, it was an accepted truth that most new businesses fail. So before you consider the e-biz aspects of your e-business, ensure that the non-e specific aspects are all working and on-track.

THE NINE FAILURE CRITERIA

1 *Bad idea in the first place; there is no market.* Much of the talk of the new economy is about new **business models** and **revenue models** (see Section 9.3). Clearly, if these fail the business will fail. The important patterns in failure all have to do with time: you run out of cash, the environment changes, investor appetite changes, markets change, morale changes. But that doesn't mean you can't control these to a great extent. Many dot-coms did not have crystal clear propositions which actually satisfied real needs. A clever bit of web technology is not a proposition, a solution nor even a product.

2 *Bad production or delivery.* Above all though, is failure down to the product or service itself? Was it just a bad idea in the first place; sometimes there is a gap in the market because there really is no market (the proverbial 'taking coals to Newcastle . . .'). However the ideas may have been good, but wrecked by bad production or delivery.

3 *Management inexperience or inflexibility.* If management is a key to success it can also be a key to failure: e-business bosses are typically younger than leaders of traditional companies. They may lack business experience in key areas, and failure results. Equally, traditional managers often can't cope with fledgling enterprises: they lack the flexibility, creativity and sheer nerve to do anything other than stick to Plan A. The e-business has to be able to respond to trend changes and rapidly alter plans. Sometimes investors are their own worst enemies – lack of financial control at boo.com – whose fault was that?

4 *Failure to create a niche.* Failure to create a niche and stick to it until it works: to move from profit-seeking to profit making, you need to sell more not spend more. Too many e-businesses do the latter: opening European offices, further developing the technology without addressing the reasons why they are not making profits. Going for the niche is all very well, but customers are pragmatists and expect to see a whole product: they won't buy your brilliant idea if you can't manufacture it, sell it, deliver it and service it. Hence the failure so far of schemes to reward Internet usage.

5 *Trying to create the e-business in isolation from the whole of the value network.* One solution is to address the value network problem: should the new e-business try and create the entire network or reel in partners and associates with specialisms in each segment? Maybe even embrace suppliers as partners?

6 *Company focused on the product or service and not on the customer's needs.* If the e-business failed to focus on customer need business failure is guaranteed. It is too easy in the flush of enthusiasm for a new idea to forget to ask: does any one want to buy this?

7 *Product/service badly marketed.* Underestimate the marketing and you'll fail; this is the myth of 100 million users. Without a mother business to fall back on, there is a lot of marketing to do. Thus you now find a www address on almost every product label and every newspaper and outdoor advert. Remembering marketing's four Ps – product, price, placement and promotion. Market leaders are not always the best of breed of a product, but they are nearly always the best marketed.

8 *Investor panic*. Numerous examples show that investor enthusiasm can rapidly evaporate if results are not delivered.

9 *Technology not ready or not delivering*. Technology solutions take time to develop and redefine if not delivering, in the meantime the brand and revenue stream will be damaged.

E-MARKETING INSIGHT

Michael Porter on strategy and the Internet

Michael Porter attacks those who have suggested that the Internet invalidates his well known strategy models. He says:

> *'Many have assumed that the Internet changes everything, rendering all the old rules about companies and competition obsolete. That may be a natural reaction, but it is a dangerous one . . . decisions that have eroded the attractiveness of their industries and undermined their own competitive advantages'.*

He gives the example of some industries using the Internet to change the basis of competition away from quality, features and service and towards price, making it harder for anyone in their industries to turn a profit.

In reviewing industry structure, he reinterprets the well-known five forces model concluding that many of the effects of the Internet, such as commoditization are damaging to industry. He reiterates the importance of six fundamental principles of strategic positioning:

1 The right goal: superior long-term return on investment.

2 A value proposition distinct from those of the competition.

3 A distinctive value chain to achieve competitive advantage.

4 Trade-offs in products or services may be required to achieve distinction.

5 Strategy defines how all elements of what a company does fit together.

6 Strategy involves continuity of direction.

(*Source*: Porter 2001).

E-MARKETING INSIGHT

Seth Neiman on failures caused by running out of time

Seth Neiman, Cross-Venture Partners in a letter to Red Herring

> *'There are some very important patterns in failure, and they all have to do with time. Failure in a start-up happens when you run out of cash and depends on whether or not you can get more. In addition, the environment*

can change, investor appetite can change, markets can change, and morale can change. So the patterns are embedded in the way a company spends its time and, of course, its cash. The easiest way to waste time is to constantly change strategy and the execution plan driving it. Start-ups have to be incredibly agile in their reactions, but the senior team must separate momentary tactical shifts from real strategic change. If they don't, they will draw a zigzag line to their goal and waste time and money along the way'.

SECTION SUMMARY 9.10

Why did the dot-coms become dot-bombs?

In this section we have examined some of the reasons why dot-coms fail, from bad basic ideas, no market, no value network, no managerial experience, no marketing – it would almost be a joke if people's jobs, lives and careers were not at stake!

Why new systems fail

IT systems, deployed intelligently, enable organizations to make major leaps in productivity, customer service, and even redefine competition within specific sectors, while delivering new business benefits that can secure a business's survival and growth. However this is rarely the case. Why do so many well intentioned attempts at developing a complete e-business or components of an e-business fall into difficulties? 74% of IT projects failed in 2005 – this, surprisingly is the same percentage as in 1980 (Standish Group and Gartner Group). So many IT projects fail because of IT overemphasis, scope creep, demotivation and lack of training. Installation is different from implantation.

IT projects fail, firstly, because they're called 'IT projects'. Informational technology facilitates business processes. IT is not an end in itself. IT is not isolated technology. It is information technology that simply serves a purpose or helps to fulfil a process for non-IT people. So the first problem is technology people taking control, instead of CEOs or marketing people taking control and driving the deliverables.

The second problem is scope creep. Making additional requests to the already agreed brief or specification is called scope creep. This has knock on effects of causing delays and running over budget. Once extended implementation time frames creep in, alarm bells should start ringing. Scope creep occurs when inadequate specifications are drawn up in the first place. Inadequate specifications emerge when too few departments are involved in shaping the specification. Multifunctional teams are required. These include anyone either using the output or the input into the system. These teams then define all that is required of the project. The twin traps of limited exploitation of business benefits and extended implementation timeframes jeopardize many projects – as does lack of training and motivation schemes.

Demotivation occurs when regular processes are disrupted and new processes are imposed without explaining how this will help the customer, the business and the member of staff to do their job better. Well managed projects take motivation seriously. Managers understand how threatening new processes can be. Successful projects also invest in training to ensure that staff fully know how to use the new processes. Installation is different from implementation (which involves communication, motivation, training, testing).

Stop using the term 'IT Projects' as a shorthand for what is actually business transformation involving changing organizational design, people and processes (two of the Marketing Mix's 7Ps).

'The new borders are between people who have skills and those who don't, who speak the right language and those who don't, and who are flexible and those who resist change. These factors will separate success from failure in the future' Andy Green, CEO BT Global Services.

CHAPTER SUMMARY

1 E-business is larger than e-marketing. It involves using technology to facilitate improvements to business processes and increase the efficiency of internal and external information flows with customers, suppliers and distributors.

2 An e-business architecture needs to be defined that brings together systems, processes and applications from across the business.

3 The development of an e-business framework should consider both buy-side, sell-side and in-side applications.

4 Buy-side applications involve setting up extranet links for e-procurement and supply chain management to reduce costs and optimize delivery of a service or a product. New purchasing approaches such as auctions may be used.

5 In-side applications involve creating intranets to improve knowledge management and assist in decision making to improve business performance.

6 Sell-side applications involve creating extranets to manage distributor channels (partner relationship management) or directly manage the relationship with the customer (customer relationship management).

7 Steps in creating the e-business are defined: 1. Establish the vision; 2. Get senior management support; 3. Identify requirements; 4. Revisit value network (and core competencies); 5. Design e-business architecture; 6. Develop, pilot, train and roll-out; 7. Benchmark, measure and monitor.

8 There are many security threats to the e-business such as fraud, theft and accidents. Security solutions such as firewalls, encryption and back-up should be put in place to counter these.

9 Nine e-business success criteria are defined. They are: the presence of a clicks-and-mortar parent providing cash flow and resources; an existing brand to provide brand awareness and a customer base; an existing management team and structure; value network already in place; ability to find suppliers and partners to create the value network for fulfilment; e-business enables re-engineering of existing business; realistic pace of development; e-business operates in a marketable niche and additional benefits of bricks-and-mortar.

Ensuring successful e-business transition includes: have a clear vision; manage risk; plan for resistance; communicate internally; allocate time for internal marketing; develop shared understanding; motivate and train the team; allow for testing; celebrate success.

10 Nine e-business failure criteria are defined, many which have resulted in the death of dot-coms. They are: bad idea in the first place – there is no market'; management inexperience or inflexibility; failure to create a niche; trying to create the e-business in isolation from the whole of the value network; company focused on the product or service and not on the customer's needs; product/service badly marketed; investor panic and technology not ready or not delivering.

11 Why so many new 'IT' systems fail: because of IT overemphasis, scope creep, demotivation and lack of training. Remember, installation is different from implementation.

References

Anderson, C. (2006) *The Long Tail: Why the Future of Business is Selling Less of More*. Hyperion (an updated version of the original 2004 article forms part of Chapter 1 of the Long Tail).

Bea Systems http://www.Vnunet.Com/Vnunet/News/2198074/Business-Bosses-Unimpressed-Web.

Cairncross, F. (2002) *The Company of the Future: How the Communications Revolution is Changing Management*. Harvard Business School Press.

Cairncross, F. (2000) eManagement – Inside the machine. *The Economist,* 18 November.

Chaffey, D. (2004) *E-business and e-commerce management: Strategy, implementation and applications,* 2nd edition. Pearson Education, Harlow, UK.

Deise, M., Nowikow, C., King, P. and Wright, A. (2000) *Executive's guide to e-business. From tactics to strategy.* John Wiley and Sons, New York, NY.

DTI (2003) *Business In The Information Age – International Benchmarking Study*. Available from http://www2.bah.com/dti2003.

E-consultancy (2005) Research Report. Managing an E-commerce team. Author Dave Chaffey.

Flores, L. and Eltvedt, H. (2005) Beyond online advertising – lessons about the power of brand web sites to build and expand brands. Published in *Proceedings of ESOMAR Online Conference,* Montreal.

Fortune (2001) Great Leap Forward: From Davos, Talk of Death by David Kirkpatrick. *Fortune,* Monday, 5 March.

IBM (2001) Managing e-business: The Top ten myths. Whitepaper at www.ibm.com/services/whitepapers.

Kalakota, R. and Robinson, M. (2000) *e-business, Roadmap for Success*. Addison Wesley, Reading. MA.

Lister, J. (1999) *Pointing employees in the same direction. Building a successful e-Business,* CBI/Caspian.

McGovern, G. (2007) Intranets: Getting Senior Management's Attention. 26 August, Gerry McGovern Newsletter, Gerry McGovern.Com.

McKinsey (2007) How Companies Are Marketing Online: A McKinsey Global Survey.

Porter, M. (2001) Strategy and the Internet. *Harvard Business Review*, March, pp. 63–78.

Timmers, P. (1999) *Electronic commerce strategies and models for business-to-business trading*. John Wiley, Series on information systems, Chichester, England.

Tranfield, D. and Braganza, A. (2007) Business Leadership of Technological Change – five key challenges facing CEOs. Chartered Management Institute.

Walmsley, A. (2007) New Media – the age of the trialogue. *The Marketer*, September.

Williams, I. (2007) European bosses unimpressed by Web 2.0. 05 Sep 2007. vnunet.com http://www.vnunet.com/vnunet/news/2198074/business-bosses-unimpressed-web.

Further reading

Chaffey, D. (2004) *E-business and e-commerce management: Strategy, implementation and applications*, 2nd edition. Pearson Education, Harlow, UK. Free updates at www.davechaffey.com/E-business. Part 1 describes e-business concepts, Part 2 describes approaches to e-business strategy for buy-side, sell-side and in-side e-commerce and Part 3 describes practical issues of implementation such as change management and user-centred design.

Deise, M., Nowikow, C., King, P. and Wright, A. (2000) *Executive's guide to e-business. From tactics to strategy*. John Wiley and Sons, New York, NY. Suggests approaches to e-business according to four snapshots and their impact on organizations, people, processes and technology. The snapshots are: channel enhancement, value chain integration, industry transformation and convergence.

Kalakota, R. and Robinson, M. (2000) *e-business. Roadmap for Success*. Addison Wesley, Reading. MA. Good introductory book on approaches to e-business divided into buy-side and sell-side.

Web links

BRINT (A business researchers interests) Ebiz (www.brint.com/ebiz/). Well established management portal providing articles, news and discussion groups.

Constant Comedy (www.constantcomedy.com).

Crea8ivity.com (www.crea8ivity.com). Northern Ireland's creative digital hub that features constant comedy.com and unique examples of a new wave of digital content companies.

E-consultancy.com (www.e-consultancy.com). A digest of whitepapers and articles about managing e-business and e-commerce.

E-marketing Excellence book homepage (www.davechaffey.com/E-marketing). An index of all e-marketing links for each chapter in this book.

Flickerpix (www.flickerpix.com) produced arguably, the ultimate, UGC programme 'On–Air'.

Flickr photo sharing site www.flickr.com.

IBM (www.ibm.com/services/whitepapers/). A digest of whitepapers including: Managing E-business: Top ten myths. What's your best e-business model.

IT Toolbox (www.ebusiness.ittoolbox.com). Resources including whitepapers and supplier information.

Threadless User Generated T-Shirts (www.threadless.com).

YouTube (www.youtube.com).

Self-test

1 Devise an explanation of e-business for a colleague in the context of your organization.

2 What are the key elements of an e-business architecture?

3 Explain buy-side, in-side and sell-side components of the e-business framework.

4 Describe how buy-side enhancements could improve your organizational performance.

5 Describe how in-side enhancements could improve your organizational performance.

6 Describe how sell-side enhancements could improve your organizational performance.

7 What are the important e-elements of an e-business strategy?

8 Summarize the main security threats to your business and describe solutions to each threat.

9 Make notes on the nine e-business criteria for success explaining which are missing or not relevant to your business.

10 Outline the factors that may contribute to e-business failure (including IT projects failure).

Chapter **10**

E-planning

'There's no point rowing harder if you're rowing in the wrong direction'.

Ohmae (1999)

E-marketing planning involves marketing planning within the context of the e-business e-environment. So, not surprisingly, the successful e-marketing plan is based on traditional marketing disciplines and planning techniques, adapted for the digital media environment and then mixed with new digital marketing communications techniques. This chapter shows you how to create a comprehensive e-marketing plan, based on the well-established principles of the SOSTAC® Planning System (PR Smith, 1993).

OVERALL LEARNING OUTCOME

By the end of this chapter you will be able to:

- Draw up an outline e-marketing plan
- Analyze the situation
- Draw up realistic objectives
- Begin to develop sensible strategies
- Develop appropriate tactics
- Execute the tactics with detailed action plans
- Control, monitor, measure, report and adjust.

CHAPTER TOPIC	LEARNING OBJECTIVE
10.1 Introduction	Describe the context and main components of an e-plan
10.2 Situation analysis	Assess your performance within the online and multichannel marketplace
10.3 Objectives	Model and define SMART commercial and communications objectives for the e-marketing plan
10.4 Strategies	Explain the difference between strategy, objectives and tactics, and devise e-strategies
10.5 Tactics	Select the relevant digital communications channels that can be deployed as part of tactics
10.6 Actions	Create an outline e-marketing implementation plan
10.7 Control	Build a review process into your plans based on web analytics and management dashboards
10.8 Resources	Identify the key internal and external resources required and allocate these to achieve your e-marketing objectives

10.1   Introduction to e-marketing planning

By the end of this chapter you will know what an e-marketing plan is, its key components and how they fit together. Without a realistic plan, an organization drifts unknowingly and can end up anywhere – usually sinking, without cash and without direction – just like so many of the 'dot-bombs'.

Planning is essential. It helps you to stop constant fire-fighting, desperately searching for funds, panicking and paying higher prices (like rush rates). Planning puts you in control and reduces stress. It also gives direction to the team so they can work in harmony.

There are many types of plans. Corporate plans and business plans incorporate the long-term corporate strategy which includes diversification and acquisition strategies, systems and funding. Then there are marketing plans that must help to fulfil the overall corporate objectives; and e-marketing plans which have to integrate with the offline, traditional marketing plan.

E-marketing plans do not occur in isolation, but are most effective when integrated with offline marketing communications channels such as phone, direct-mail or face-to-face selling. Online channels should also be used to support the whole buying process from pre-sale to sale, to post-sale and the continuing development of customer relationships.

Although the e-marketing plan can span right across an organization's functions (e.g. customer feedback, customer service, product enhancement, sales, finance/payment, delivery, administration and marketing), e-marketing plans tend to be linked strongly to marketing communications plans. The reality is that any e-marketing plan needs to be part of a marketing communications plan and it should also be part of a broader marketing plan. Needless to say the e-plan should also fit in with the overall business plan.

For a traditional business, an overall corporate or business plan covers systems, procedures, resources and structure, while a marketing plan covers the sales, distribution, communications and delivery of the product or service.

Figure 10.1 shows the typical relationship between different plans. The corporate plan guides the marketing and e-business plan, both of which in turn, guide the e-marketing plan. The plans are integrated so that developing the e-marketing plan may give insights that help to impact strategy in other plans. The e-marketing plan can highlight and review opportunities for business growth by targeting new audiences, new geographic markets or through introducing new products and services. Companies who have successfully used the web to grow sales have used a cost-effective web presence coupled with the right investment in digital media to exploit new opportunities. For example, airline easyJet and business-to-business retailer RS Components have launched new services in many countries where sales are serviced online.

> **Long- versus short-term plans**

Many organizations have short- and long-term plans or roadmaps. Ultimately they must integrate the goals, the timeframes and resources required. We can distinguish between short-term (1 year) plans, medium-term (2–3 year) plans and longer-term (3–5 year) plans. All these plans can use SOSTAC®. For example all these plans include strategy and tactics sections. Strategy gives clear guidance and direction for all subsequent tactical details. Strategy for a

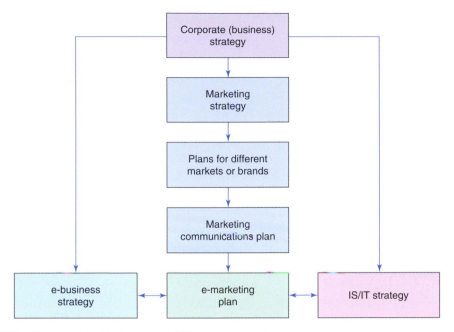

Figure 10.1 The relationship between different types of plans

short-term plan summarizes how the one-year objectives will be achieved, while strategy for a long-term plan summarizes how the long-term objective will be achieved.

Some feel that strategy is by definition deemed to have a longer term and more enduring perspective while tactics are shorter term and more flexible.

Longer-term e-marketing plans should place emphasis on three key areas. First, early identification of significant changes/trends in the macro-environment and changes to competitive forces in the micro-environment. Second, developing and communicating value propositions for customers using online services as part of their buying process. Third, definition of the technology infrastructure and database architecture to deliver these value propositions.

New technologies, such as a customer relationship management systems and integrated databases to deliver customized communications, can take several years to specify, select and implement and so need to go on a long-term roadmap. Database, CRM, integration of e-business architecture and business processes are all long-term when making plans and major decisions.

The shorter-term operational e-marketing plan can then address the mix of communications techniques, such as search marketing and online advertising (Chapter 7), used to acquire new customers and the tools used to engage and retain customers online, such as incentive programmes and customer contact strategies delivered through opt-in e-mail marketing integrated with traditional direct media such as phone and direct mail.

SOSTAC® PLANNING

To help you, we'll structure this chapter by using a simple aide mémoire, called SOSTAC. **SOSTAC®** is used by thousands of professionals to produce all kinds of plans – corporate plans, marketing plans, e-marketing plans, even advertising plans.

SOSTAC stands for: Situation analysis, Objectives, Strategy, Tactics, Actions and Control (see Figure 1.1):

- *Situation analysis* means 'where are we now?' For multi-channel marketers, how many of your customers are buying or influenced online? What is the growth forecast? What are your competitors doing? What is the impact of the new intermediaries? What's working for them? What seems to work online and offline and what seems not to? How have you performed online? What's changing in the online world?

- *Objectives* means 'where are we going, or where do we want to be?' Why go online? What are the benefits, what is the purpose of going to all of this effort? Remember the 5Ss? Good objectives are quantified and also contain strict timescales.

- *Strategy* means 'how do we get there?' Strategy summarizes how to fulfil the objectives. How will sales and other brand goals be delivered? Which trends are we responding to? Which segments will be targeted with which propositions? Which media mix will be used to acquire new customers and which contact strategy will be used for customer retention and share of wallet growth?

- *Tactics* are the details of strategy. Breaking the tactical e-tools into more detail. Highlighting, on say, a Gantt chart, exactly which tactics occur when, e.g. execution of Pay Per Click ads or a series of opt-in e-mails. What level of integration should there be between tools, database and e-CRM? Tactics explain how to implement the strategy.

- *Actions* are the details of tactics. What actions have to be taken to create a banner ad, an interactive TV ad, an opt-in e-mail campaign? Each is a mini project. Everything degenerates into work! Arguably, this is the weakest part of the planning process for most companies (as identified by Bossidy and Charan 2004). Internal marketing is often the weakest link where managers forget to allocate time and resources to explain and motivate their own staff to execute the actions better.

- *Control* questions whether you know if you are succeeding or failing – before it is too late. This is where web analytics systems regularly measure and monitor the key online measurables – visitors, durations, enquiries, subscriptions, sales, conversion rates, churn rates, loyalty levels and more. Control needs to be built into a plan, i.e. who reports on specific control criteria (e.g. usability testing, web stats analysis and external trend spotting) and how frequently.

BEST PRACTICE E-MARKETING TIP

Integrated e-marketing planning

Your planning devices should integrate situation analysis, goal-setting, strategy, tactics and control. Table 10.1, for example, shows how the e-SWOT of situation analysis can be used to generate ideas for corresponding strategies and tactics which can then be prioritized and selected as part of strategy definition. Another toolkit to facilitate integrated planning is to create a table with rows for different goals with columns for corresponding objectives, drivers (based on situation analysis), strategies and KPIs used for control.

Table 10.1   An example of Internet SWOT analysis showing typical opportunities and threats sometimes presented by the Internet for an established multichannel brand. It also acts as a strategic option generator and review toolkit

The organization	Strengths – S 1 Existing brand 2 Existing customer base 3 Existing distribution	Weaknesses – W 1 Brand perception 2 Intermediary use 3 Technology/skills (poor web experience) 4 Cross-channel support 5 Churn rate
Opportunities – O 1 Cross-selling 2 New markets 3 New services 4 Alliances/ co-branding	SO strategies Leverage strengths to maximize opportunities = attacking strategy **Examples:** 1 Migrate customers to web strategy 2 Refine customer contact strategy across customer lifecycle or commitment segmentation (e-mail, web) 3 Partnership strategy (co-branding, linking) 4 Launch new web-based products or value-adding experiences, e.g. video streaming	WO strategies Counter weaknesses through exploiting opportunities = build strengths for attacking strategy **Examples:** 1 Counterrmediation strategy (create or acquire) 2 Search marketing acquisition strategy 3 Affiliate-based acquisition strategy 4 Refine customer contact strategy (e-mail, web)
Threats – T 1 Customer choice (price) 2 New entrants 3 New competitive products 4 Channel conflicts 5 Social network	ST Strategies Leverage strengths to minimize threats = defensive strategy **Examples:** 1 Introduce new Internet-only products 2 Add value to web services – refine OVP 3 Partner with complementary brand 4 Create own social network/customer reviews	WT Strategies Counter weaknesses and threats: = build strengths for defensive strategy **Examples:** 1 Differential online pricing strategy 2 Acquire/create pure-play company with lower cost-base 3 Customer engagement strategy to increase conversion, average order value and lifetime value 4 Online reputation management strategy/e-PR

Your e-marketing plan should also be reviewed and revised frequently. Quick reactions are required. If something isn't working – find out why and change it. Constantly improve. In addition to regular detailed measurements, review your overall plan once a quarter and be prepared to revise and re-present it to senior management every six months.

Don't forget, a plan without resources will fail. So you need to budget for the 3Ms, the three key resources. These are:

- Men (and women) – human resources
- Money – budgets
- Minutes – time scales and time horizons for production, delivery, service, etc.

All aspects of SOSTAC® must be thought through. The next sections will take you through each of the SOSTAC® and 3M aspects. At the end, you will be able to plan your e-marketing with confidence.

SECTION SUMMARY 10.1

Introduction to e-marketing planning

E-marketing plans must support, and be integrated with, corporate/business plans and marketing plans. SOSTAC® stands for: Situation analysis, Objectives, Strategy, Tactics, Actions and Control.

10.2 Situation analysis

Situation analysis is the first part of the e-marketing plan. It explains 'where are we now?' After this you can define where you want to go (see Section 10.3 Objectives). We need to analyze both internally and externally – internally within the organization, and externally, the business environment affecting our online business situation.

The traditional tried and tested analytical areas are:

- *KPIs* – key performance indicators which identify the business's success criteria, results, data and measurements against benchmarks.
- *SWOT analysis* – identifying internal strengths, and weaknesses, as well as external opportunities and threats.
- *PEST* – political, economic, social and technological variables that shape your marketplace.
- *Customers* – how many are online, how many prefer iDTV – are there new channel segments emerging?
- *Competitors* – who are they? New online **pure-play** adversaries or the same old '**bricks-and-clicks**' competitors as always?
- *Distributors* – are new, online, intermediaries (e.g. affiliate networks) emerging while old offline distributors migrate their services online?

Figure 10.2 is a checklist of the different types of management information that should feed into your situation analysis.

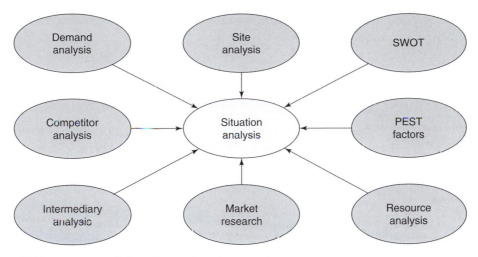

Figure 10.2   Elements of situation analysis for e-marketing

INTERNAL ANALYSIS

The internal analysis looks at key performance indicators (KPIs). Common KPIs used to assess online activities include:

- Enquiries or leads
- Sales
- Market share
- ROI (Return on Investment)
- **Online revenue or service contribution** (see Section 10.3).

Other KPIs include:

- **Unique visitors** – the number of separate, individual visitors who visit the site (typically over a month).
- **Conversion rates** to different goals – the percentage of visitors converting to subscribers (or becoming customers). This is critical to e-marketing. Let's take an example. Say 2% of 5000 visitors to a site in a month convert to 100 customers who place an order. £10 000 cost divided by 100 conversions gives £100 cost per order. Now imagine you can double your conversion rate, or better still quadruple it to 8%, you then get £25 cost per order. The leverage impact caused by improved conversion rates is huge – revenues go up and percentage of marketing costs go down. We saw in Chapter 2 how you should should define and score different conversion goals for different types of outcomes.
- Total numbers of **sessions** or **visits** to a web site (forget '**hits**' – these are a spurious measure, since when a web page is downloaded to the PC, a number of separate data transfers or hits takes place, usually one for each HTML and graphics file. Techies need to measure hits because this helps them plan the resources needed to run the sites efficiently; you as an e-marketer should measure **page impressions** because that's the

real measure of customer traffic to your site and for an advertiser equates with other familiar measures such as 'opportunities to view').

- **Repeat visits** – average number of visits per individual. Total number of sessions divided by the number of unique visitors. Update your site more often and people come back more often. **Cookies** can help track repeat visits. Remember to get permission before placing any cookies on someone else's PC.

- **Duration** – average length of time visitors spend on your site (but remember that for some areas of the site, such as online sales or customer service, you may want to minimize duration). A similar measure is number of pages viewed per visitor. Also see the box on the much abused term '**stickiness**'.

   Most popular pages or most popular product – can be identified by seeing which pages attract the most traffic for the longest duration. Some large e-commerce and media sites watch this every day or even hourly. When they see something popular they lift the offer onto the home page to boost traffic even more for a period.

- **Subscription rates** – numbers of visitors subscribing for services such as an opt-in e-mail and newsletters.

- **Churn rates** – percentage of subscribers withdrawing or unsubscribing (after you have emailed them).

- **Click through rates (CTR)** – from a banner ad or web link on a site other than your own.

All of the preceding KPIs can be quantified and used as objectives, which can be constantly measured. The control section explains how frequently each KPI is measured and by whom.

Costs also need to be analyzed. These metrics are also considered as part of control (Section 10.7). Internal analysis will also review the success of an organization's resources, processes and structure in delivering customer value, satisfaction and loyalty. Market research of customers and partners will be needed to determine their opinions.

Remember that numbers out of context are meaningless. Sales of £1 m – is this good news or bad news? If last year's sales were £500 K then this is good news but if they were £2 m then this is bad news. Imagine the previous year's sales were £500 K, this year's sales are £1 m and the market had quadrupled in size? Although your sales have doubled your market share has halved! This is bad news in the long run. So remember all indicators are relative – leading, backwards and across. Leading to show what future results will be, backwards over time – to see the trend compared to similar periods and across your industry – to see how competitive you are.

E-MARKETING EXCELLENCE

Use of independent auditing by Handbag.com for KPIs

Handbag.com use the ABC Electronic auditing service (www.abce.org.uk). This is used to prove the reach and engagement of the audience with the site for potential advertisers.

Additional KPI ratios of engagement through time can be derived from this data and for any site which uses a web analytics system, for example average page views per visit and average number of visits per visitor. These can be related to site enhancements and marketing campaigns that occur at different times.

Table 10.2   Audited traffic volume and engagement figures for Handbag.com
(*Source*: www.abce.org.uk)

Period	Page imps	Visits	Users
01/05/07–31/05/07	22,044,640	2,149,692	1,452,290
01/10/06–31/10/06	20,719,734	1,812,981	1,162,614
01/09/05–30/09/05	28,479,908	2,118,030	1,322,786
01/01/05–31/01/05	28,115,600	1,756,921	986,695
01/01/04–31/01/04	24,291,888	1,633,173	876,031
01/10/03–31/10/03	21,429,504	1,535,139	821,701
01/03/03–31/03/03	18,459,340	1,315,567	651,261
01/09/02–30/09/02	14,172,543	1,522,195	570,440
01/05/02–31/05/02	11,268,505	1,461,764	529,412
01/10/01–31/10/01	6,320,845		509,625
01/05/01–31/05/01	5,041,864		403,282
01/11/00–30/11/00	2,874,798	733,218	367,071
01/07/00–31/07/00	2,041,367	580,241	312,158

E-MARKETING INSIGHT

Neil Mason of Applied Insights on measurement frameworks

As a consultant who helps customers improve their online business performance, Neil advocates the use of an online performance management framework to help focus an organization on its most important digital marketing KPIs or the 'measures that matter'. Table 10.3 shows an example summarizing metrics for improving performance in different parts of the customer lifecycle from acquisition to retention. The rows indicate different forms of tracking metrics and performance drivers which will influence higher-level metrics such as the customer-centric Key Performance Indicators (KPIs) and business value KPIs. In the bottom two rows we have also added in typical strategies and tactics used to achieve objectives which shows the relationship between objectives and strategy. Note though that this framework mainly creates a focus on efficiency of conversion, although there are also some effectiveness measures such as reach, profit and advocacy. We have added strategies and tactics to show how these should be based on achieving goals set in measurement. Use this as a checklist to assess which goals are relevant for you at the Objective setting stage of SOSTAC and KPIs used to assess performance at the Control stage using web analytics and management dashboards which include visual summaries of the KPIs.

Table 10.3   Sample online performance management grid for e-retailer (*Source*: adapted from Neil Mason's (www.applied-insights.co.uk) Acquisition, Conversion, Retention approach

Metric	Visitor acquisition	Conversion to opportunity	Conversion to sale	Customer retention and growth
Tracking metrics	• Unique visitors • New visitors	• Opportunity volume	• Sales volume	• E-mail list quality • E-mail response quality • Transactions churn rate
Performance drivers (diagnostics)	• Bounce rate • Conversion rate: new visit to start quote	• Macro-conversion rate to opportunity and micro-conversion efficiency	• Conversion rate to sale • E-mail conversion rate	• Active customers % (site and e-mail active) • Repeat conversion rate for different purchases
Customer centric KPIs	• Cost per click and per sale brand awareness	• Cost per opportunity • Customer satisfaction	• Cost per sale • Customer satisfaction • Average order value (AOV)	• Lifetime value • Customer loyalty index • Products per customer • Advocacy (net promoter score)
Business value KPIs	• Audience share	• Order (n, £, % of total)	• Online originated sales (n, £, % of total)	• Retained sales growth and volume
Strategy	• Online targeted reach strategy • Offline targeted reach strategy	• Lead generation strategy	• Online sales generation strategy • Offline sales impact strategy	• Retention and customer growth strategy • Advocacy
Tactics	• Continuous communications mix • Campaign communications mix • Online value proposition	• Usability • Personalization • Inbound contact strategy (customer service)	• Usability • Personalization • Inbound contact strategy (customer service) • Merchandising • Triggered e-mails	• Database/list quality = opt-out/ churn rate • Targeting • Outbound contact strategy (e-mail) • Personalization

STRENGTHS AND WEAKNESSES

A situation analysis usually includes an analysis of strengths and weaknesses. For a multi-channel business, the e-marketing plan should focus on comparing the strengths and weaknesses of the digital channel with other channels, i.e. it is an *Internet-Specific SWOT or e-SWOT*. An example e-SWOT is shown in Table 10.1. What do you think are your online strengths and weaknesses? Which tactical tools are you particularly good at? You may review the following:

- Customer database – is it large, live, clean and integrated? Can you deliver personalized communications (one-to-one) through every communications tool both online and offline?
- Online customer care – is it sloppy or outstanding? Has your speed of response or speed of resolution increased or decreased? Do you measure it?
- Web site – is it a user-centred design that is effective in converting visitors to outcomes? Do you use customer scenarios and usability testing?
- Integrated database – does it link all online and offline tools together?
- Opt-in e-mail campaigns – are these generating results?
- Web links – are **referrals** being generated from a range of sources?
- Display ads or sponsorship – are clickthrough rates and customer acquisition costs favourable?
- Mobile marketing – what are your experiences (if relevant) with mobile phone campaigns?
- Interactive TV – if it's relevant to your marketplace, have you any experience with it?

EXTERNAL ANALYSIS

The external analysis includes analyzing customers (Creating personas, Chapter 4), benchmarking competitors and the uncontrollable opportunities and threats. E-marketing is overflowing with new opportunities and threats thrown up by the constant waves of change. We showed a number of tools you could use to assess your online marketplace in Table 10.1. You should create an e-marketplace map as we showed in Chapter 3 (Figure 3.1) to understand the dynamics and interactions of different customer types with search engines, different intermediaries and competitors. You can also use the Big 5 social media sites to explore customer types, brands, competitors from a different perspective. These include Wikipedia. org – the user-generated online encyclopedia; Flickr www.flickr.com user generated pictures of products and their ads; YouTube www.youTube.com customer reviews and critiques, advertisements, spoof advertisements (including 'User generated Dis'Content' (or negative advertisements), press conferences highlights; Digg dig.com tech-news community – votes on stories they think are most interesting; Del.icio.us, an online favourite folder where members share their finds with other members. In addition Google Alert and Google News track brands, companies and people or trends, and deliver the headlines daily or weekly into your inbox. Lastly, the wayback machine www.archive.org allows you to see old web pages from 1996 – if you were interested in tracking how an organization or a brand is changing over time.

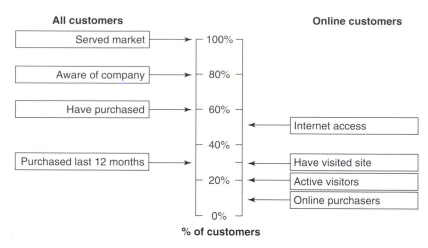

Figure 10.3 Assessing customer adoption of online services

Consider customers, how are they changing? How many are online? Which segments? Do you have a similar proportion of your customers buying online? If not, why not? Figure 10.3 shows the type of picture you need to build up of customer activity showing demand for your online services. This compares the role of online channels, such as the web site, as a means of reaching, influencing and directly delivering sales. We need to ask – How many buy exclusively online? How many browse online and shop offline? How many use price comparison sites? How many are happy to give you permission to e-mail them, text message them or even snail mail them? Are the numbers changing? You should repeat this activity for different segments requiring different products. It is also useful for multichannel businesses to compare the demographic profile of their online B2C or B2B audiences with their traditional offline audiences, as this should inform strategies to encourage adopters or non-adopters of digital channels to purchase more.

What do your competitors offer on their web sites that you don't? Who are they? Are there new online players entering your market? What are their differentiators?

A further issue is distributors such as online intermediaries. Are there new intermediaries you could partner with, are your competitors already working with them?

So, effectively, the analysis is not a one-off annual analysis. It's an ongoing observation of your marketplace known as **environmental scanning** which includes regularly checking stats, web sites, customer surveys and reading reports.

OPPORTUNITIES AND THREATS

The OT in SWOT, the external 'opportunities and threats', are churned up by the relentless tide of change. They can be from the PEST factors:

- Political laws or regulations that affect your online marketing (such as the UK PECR – Privacy and Electronic Communications Regulations).
- Economic – variables impact all markets.

- Social – the trends that shape future online behaviour.
- Technology – are you abreast with developments – have you got an overview of the emerging technology?

External opportunities and threats are also posed or presented by changes in aspects of the marketplace such as customer behaviour or new strategies pursued by intermediaries or competitors. We advocate summarizing the results of your situation analysis through an Internet-specific SWOT analysis.

BEST PRACTICE E-MARKETING TIP

Perform an e-SWOT to identify and select optional strategies

The form of SWOT shown in Table 10.1 is recommended since it not only summarizes the current situation, but can be used to help to develop strategy by placing optional strategies on it. It is not important which cells the strategies are placed in, some may overlap, but it is a method of formulating and then selecting strategies. Remember the first strategy someone thinks of is rarely the best one. Hence strategic options need to be considered before choosing the best strategy.

SECTION SUMMARY 10.2

Situation analysis

Your situation analysis should include KPI; customers; competitors and intermediaries; as well as the uncontrollable PEST factors. Now you know where you are, the next section will help you to determine your online destiny – where you want to go (your objectives).

10.3 Objectives

While the situation analysis explains 'where you are now', objectives clarify where you are going – where you want to be. By the end of this section you'll know what are the realistic objectives of an e-marketing plan, and what benefits each of these objectives can yield for your business.

There are five broad benefits, reasons or objectives of e-marketing. These can be summarized as the 5Ss (see Chapter 1 for a description and Table 1.1). You must decide whether all or only some are going to drive your e-marketing plan.

- *Sell* – Grow sales (through wider distribution to customers you can't service offline or perhaps a wider product range than in local store, or better prices).
- *Serve* – Add value (give customers extra benefits online; or product development in response to online dialogue).

- *Speak* – Get closer to customers by tracking them, asking them questions, conducting online interviews, creating a dialogue, monitoring chat rooms, learning about them.
- *Save* – Save costs: of service, sales transactions and administration, print and post. Can you reduce transaction costs and therefore make online sales more profitable? Or use cost-savings to enable you to cut prices, which in turn could enable you to generate greater market share?
- *Sizzle* – Extend the brand online. Reinforce brand values in a totally new medium. The web scores very highly as a medium for creating brand awareness and recognition.

Specific objectives are created for each. Consider sales – a typical objective might be:

> *'To grow the business with online sales, e.g. to generate at least 30% of sales online within six months'.*

Or

> *'To generate an extra £100 000 worth of sales online by December'.*

These objectives can be further broken down, e.g. to achieve £100 000 of online sales means you have to generate 1000 online customers spending on average £100. If, say, your conversion rate of visitors to customers was a high of 10% then this means you have to generate 10 000 visitors to your site. You can use the KPIs (key performance indicators) mentioned in Section 10.2 to help you quantify the main objectives and the subsequent detailed objectives.

Specific targets for the **online revenue contribution** for different e-channels should be set for the future as shown in Figure 10.4 and illustrated in the box on Sandvik Steel. Objectives should be set for the percentage of customers who are reached or influenced by each channel (or brand awareness in the target market) and the percentage of sales to be achieved through the channel. The online revenue contribution should also consider **cannibalization** – are online sales achieved at the expense of traditional offline channels?

Another major objective might be to build brand awareness, e.g. to create brand awareness among 50% of our target market through online activities. Equally it might be to use the online opportunity to create some excitement around the brand ('sizzle'). Interactive TV and text messaging come to mind, as do reactive viral marketing techniques.

Another major online objective might be to consolidate relationships and increase loyalty from 50 to 75% among a high-spending customer segment during the year.

There are many types of objectives. They will, of course, be underpinned by either financial objectives (sales, profit margin, cash flow), or communication objectives (positioning, branding, awareness, e-CRM . . .).

Whatever the objective, it ultimately has to be measurable. Therefore your objectives need to be quantifiable and to have a deadline.

Online Media Mix mode - based on % budget - with example of 'average' clickthrough rates

Overall budget	£100 000

	Media costs					Media volume/response				Conversion to Opportunity			Conversion to Sale			
	Setup/ creative Mgt costs	CPM	CPC	Media costs	Total cost	Budget %	Impressions or names	CTR	Clicks or visits	CRO	Opport-unities	CPO (cost per lead)	CRS	Sales	% of sales	CPS (CPA)

External online media

Online ad buys (CPM)	£0	£10.0	£5.00	£10 000	£10 000	10%	1 000 000	0.2%	2000	10.0%	200	£50.00	10.0%	20	1%	£500.0
Ad network (CPC)	£0	£20.0	£1.00	£20 000	£20 000	20%	1 000 000	2.0%	20 000	10.0%	2000	£10.00	10.0%	200	10%	£100.0
Paid search (CPC)	£0	£10.0	£0.50	£30 000	£30 000	30%	3 000 000	2.0%	60 000	10.0%	6000	£5.00	10.0%	600	30%	£50.0
Natural search (Fixed)	£0	£0.5	£0.05	£5000	£5000	5%	10 000 000	1.0%	100 000	10.0%	10 000	£0.50	10.0%	1000	50%	£5.0
Affiliates (CPS)	£0	£10.0	£1.00	£5000	£5000	5%	500 000	1.0%	5000	10.0%	500	£10.00	10.0%	50	3%	£100.0
Aggregators (CPS)	£0	£0.0	£0.00	£0	£0	0%	0	1.0%	0	10.0%	0	£0.00	10.0%	0	0%	£100.0
Sponsorships (Fixed)	£0	£100.0	£33.33	£10 000	£10 000	10%	100 000	0.3%	300	10.0%	30	£333.33	10.0%	3	0%	£3333.3
Online PR (Fixed)	£0	£100.0	£10.00	£10 000	£10 000	10%	100 000	1.0%	1000	10.0%	100	£100.00	10.0%	10	1%	£1000.0
E-mail lists (CPM)	£0	£10.0	£1.00	£10 000	£10 000	10%	1 000 000	1.0%	10 000	10.0%	1000	£10.00	10.0%	100	5%	£100.0
Total/Average	£0	£6.0	£0.50	£100 000	£100 000	100%	16 700 000	1.2%	198 300	10.0%	19 830	£5.04	10.0%	1983	100%	£50.4

Internal online media

In-house e-mail list/CM	£1000	£0.0	£0.33	£0	£1000	n/a	100 000	3.0%	3000	15.0%	450	£2.22	30%	135	n/a	£7.4
Own-site ads (other footfall)	£1000	£0.0	£0.05	£0	£1000	n/a	1 000 000	2.0%	20 000	10.0%	2000	£0.50	25%	500	n/a	£2.0
Total/Average	£2000	£1.8	£0.09	£0	£2000	n/a	1 100 000	2.1%	23 000	10.8%	2450	£0.82	15.8%	635	n/a	£3.1

| **Overall total/Average** | £2000 | £5.7 | £0.46 | £100 000 | £102 000 | n/a | 17 800 000 | 1.2% | 221 300 | 11.2% | 22 280 | £4.58 | 18.2% | 2618 | n/a | £39.0 |

Figure 10.4 An e-communications mix for an annual plan or an e-campaign. Blue cells in the spreadsheet can be changed for what-if analysis.

Source: Marketing Insights (www.marketing-insights.co.uk/spreadsheet.htm)

Finally be realistic about what is achievable – interactive technology means e-marketing offers enormous potential for data gathering and analysis, but many advertisers and marketers expect just too much!

So ask, are your objectives well-defined and properly thought through? Are they SMART? Specific, Measurable, Achievable, Realistic and Time-related.

E-MARKETING EXCELLENCE

Sandvik Steel sets detailed objectives by markets and segments

Way back in 2001, *The Financial Times* (Fisher 2001) reported a range of variations in online revenue contribution. At the time of the article, only a small part of all orders were transacted over the web. Nordic countries are leading the way. Around 20% of all orders from Denmark are online, as are 31% of those from Sweden. The proportion in the US, however, is only 3%, since most business goes through distributors and is conducted by EDI (electronic data interchange). Over the next six months, the company hopes to raise the US figure to 40% and in two years, between 40 and 50% of total orders are planned to come via the web.

Annika Roos, marketing manager at Sandvik Steel, was reported as saying: 'by the end of December, 2001, we want a confirmation from at least 80% of key customers that they consider the extranet to be a major reason to deal with Sandvik. Our aim is to have 200 key customers using the extranet at the end of June 2001'.

SECTION SUMMARY 10.3

Objectives

The 5Ss (Sell, Serve, Speak, Save and Sizzle) are a useful starting point for objectives. Ultimately objectives have to be SMART. Finally objectives help you to focus on where you want to get to. Now you're ready to move on to how to get there, the next section shows you just how to do this – Strategy.

10.4   Strategy

There is much confusion about the difference between strategy and tactics. Strategy summarizes 'how do we get there?' Objectives specify 'where do we want to go'. Strategy summarizes how to achieve the objectives and guides all the subsequent detailed tactical decisions. Strategy is influenced by both the prioritization of objectives (sell, serve, speak, save and sizzle) and of course, the amount of resources available (see Section 10.8). It should embrace the aspects previously discussed: OVPs, contact strategies (databases and technology required) and overall trends affecting the marketplace. Strategy should also exploit distinctive competitive advantage. Play to your strengths (assuming the market/customers want your strengths).

BEST PRACTICE E-MARKETING TIP

Ensuring strategies support objectives

To help ensure that strategies support objectives, you should create a linkage between the two as shown in Table 10.1, which also shows related tactics to deliver the strategies.

Strategy is crucial. Get it wrong and all your hard work is wasted. As Kenichi Ohmae (1999) said 'There's no point rowing harder if you're rowing in the wrong direction'. Hard work is wasted if the strategy is wrong. Take some examples of absurd strategies. Imagine building an amazing WAP site, but none of your customers use WAP phones. Or imagine building a transactional web site to take orders yet the majority of your market only browses online and always shops offline. Or missing the early adopters in your target market by avoiding interactive TV advertising. Or, worse still, reaching them through interactive TV but not having the back office systems and fulfilment services required to, say, deliver pizzas within 30 minutes, or offer a test drive the next day. Dominos Pizza has successfully used interactive TV to reach its online audience and then created the infrastructure to serve them. Integrating procedures and redesigning business processes is strategic and tends to be longer term.

Strategy summarizes how the objectives will be achieved. So let us say the overall marketing objective is to achieve a 50% increase in sales. The strategy that rolls out could be based on expanding the marketplace and securing new customers, attacking a particular competitor's customers or simply reducing churn (lost customers) and getting more of your existing customers to re-order. Three different strategies: one for market expansion, one for competitor attack and one for customer retention.

BEST PRACTICE E-MARKETING TIP

Model your strategy options

The sales and profit delivered by each prong of the strategy (e.g. acquisition, retention or new product introduction) should be modelled using available information on customer and marketplace demand for products. Different scenarios should be reviewed to check your strategies will deliver the objectives. This will be an iterative process with models revised during the goal setting and strategy selection and tactics.

For example, Figure 10.4 shows a model for assessing the best online communications mix based on the KPIs for different digital communications channels which we described in Chapter 8. A fuller model would also have margin and profit added.

For online e-retailers or any online transactional business, it is also essential to model lifetime value as shown per the example in Figure 10.5 (a) and (b).

So what goes into an e-marketing strategy – whatever it takes to achieve your objectives. The e-marketing strategy focuses on what you're going to do in the 'e' world. It can include propositions (which summarize the online mix). Will your online proposition be different to your offline proposition? Or integrated? Can you succinctly tell your boss what your strategy is? Strategy helps it all to fit together and avoids ad hoc tactical patchworks which usually, in the end, cause more complications. For some strategists, strategy is all about establishing an integrated database between your web site and all other communications points. For others it is developing the web site from one-stage to two-stage to three-stage e-marketing (e.g. fully integrated automated database-driven linking opt-in e-mail and direct mail). Others develop an Internet strategy, an intranet strategy and an extranet strategy. These are longer-term strategic perspectives. For a few, e-marketing strategies are just about traffic building – a shorter-term strategic perspective.

Ideally an experienced strategist would create strategy by thinking purely about how to achieve the objectives with the resources available. Having generated several strategic options, the best strategy is carefully chosen and this then eventually cascades down into the tactical details. However, in reality, because there is little good solid experience of making strategies, many practitioners tend to move to what they're good at – tactics, e.g. display ads, search marketing and opt-in e-mail. Having developed a range of exciting tactics, they then sit back and try to make sense of it all or try to tie it all together, summarize it and then call it a traffic strategy (retrospective strategy making)! This can work if (a) it all integrates sensibly (b) you can test it against at least another two strategic alternatives.

Other strategists draw from marketing warfare, e.g. full frontal attack (comparative marketing on web sites); flanking attack using the web site to highlight areas of weakness among competitors (surround bigger players by creating an array of micro sites and web rings around an area so that smaller players cannot complete). See the e-marketing insight box 'Timothy Cummings on competitive strategies' for more.

Refer back to Table 10.2 to review alternative digital marketing strategies generated through an Internet SWOT analysis. Note how strategies tend to fall into these three types, which are used for selecting your options:

1 Acquisition-focused communications strategies.
2 Retention-focused communications strategies.
3 Market and product development or marketing mix related strategies related to new markets, products, new pricing, new partnerships or new intermediaries (place), etc.

STRATEGIC QUESTIONS

Some of the questions that an e-marketing strategy can answer are:

- What segments are being targeted online? Who is the target market?

	A	B	C	D	E	F
1	New customers in Year 1	100 000				
2	Margin	15%				
3		Year 1	Year 2	Year 3	Year 4	Year 5
4	Customers (new)	100 000	50 000	27 500	16 500	10 725
5	Retention rate	50%	55%	60%	65%	70%
6	Average revenue per annum	£100	£110	£120	£130	£140
7	Total revenue	£10 000 000	£5 500 000	£3 300 000	£2 145 000	£1 501 500
8	Net profit	£1 500 000	£825 000	£495 000	£321 750	£225 225
9	Discount rate	1.000	0.860	0.740	0.636	0.547
10	NPV Contribution	£1 500 000	£709 500	£366 102	£204 633	£123 198
11	Cumulative NPV contribution	£1 500 000	£2 209 500	£2 575 602	£2 780 235	£2 903 433
12	Lifetime value at net present value	£15	£22	£26	£28	£29

(a)

	A	B	C	D	E	F
1	New customers in year 1	100 000				
2	Margin	0.15				
3		Year 1	Year 2	Year 3	Year 4	Year 5
4	Customers	=B1	=B4*B5	=C4*C5	=D4*D5	=E4*E5
5	Retention rate	0.5	0.55	0.6	0.65	0.7
6	Average revenue per annum	100	110	120	130	140
7	Total revenue	=B4*B6	=C4*C6	=D4*D6	=E4*E6	=F4*F6
8	Net profit	=B7*$B$2	=C7*$B$2	=D7*$B$2	=E7*$B$2	=F7*$B$2
9	Discount rate	1	0.86	0.7396	0.636	0.547
10	NPV Contribution	=B8*B9	=C8*C9	=D8*D9	=E8*E9	=F8*F9
11	Cumulative NPV contribution	=B10	=B11+C10	=C11+D10	=D11+E10	=E11+F10
12	Lifetime value at net present value	=B11/$B$1	=C11/$B$1	=D11/$B$1	=E11/$B$1	=F11/$B$1

(b)

Figure 10.5 (a) Lifetime value model. Blue cells in the spreadsheet can be changed for what-if analysis. (b) Lifetime value model showing formulas corresponding to Figure 10.5 (a). Blue cells in the spreadsheet can be changed for what-if analysis and orange cells. *Source*: Marketing Insights (www.marketing-insights.co.uk/spreadsheet.htm)

- Should new or existing products be sold into all existing segments and markets, or can specific or new segments and markets be targeted? Different options are often reviewed using the Ansoff matrix shown in Figure 1.9.
- Source of differentiation – what is the **online value proposition**? See Figure 10.6 for how the details of an OVP are explained on a 'learn more' page for those who aren't convinced to immediately start a trial. Another question to ask for multichannel organizations is can new digital products or services be developed to compete with pureplays?

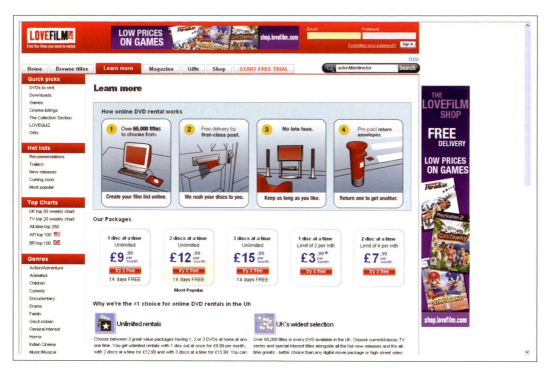

Figure 10.6 LoveFilm explain the details of their OVP on their 'Learn More' page (www.lovefilm.com/learn)

- How do we deal with competition? See the box 'Timothy Cummings on competitive strategies'.

- What level of interaction on site – brochure, two-way interactive sales support, online sales, fully personalized CRM or reviews and Web 2.0 interactions. What stage of 'e'volution is required? Will the other stages follow in subsequent years?

- What level of database integration is required? Can the customer be dealt with as a recognizable individual with unique preferences regardless of how the customer comes into contact, e.g. web, WAP, iDTV, telephone call centre, etc.?

- Will the online channels complement the company's offline channels or will it replace them? See 'Complement or replace?' below.

- Web sites or WAP sites or both? How important are these compared to other channels to market? What major website enhancement initiatives will increase customer engagement against goals of enhanced conversion rates, average order value or lifetime value?

- How relevant are interactive TV or mobile marketing?

- Focus of customer communications for acquisition – what is emphasis on affiliates, aggregators, natural search, paid search, display ads, social networks for the company.

- Focus of customer communications for retention – does the customer contact strategy need to be refined?

COMPLEMENT OR REPLACE?

An e-marketing strategy should define the level of resources directed at different channels. Essentially, the question is 'will the online channels complement the company's other channels or will it replace other channels'? Gulati and Garino (2000) describe it as 'Getting the right mix of bricks and clicks'. If it is believed that sales through digital channels will primarily replace other channels, then it is important to invest in the technical, human and organizational resources to achieve this. A replace strategy was chosen by airlines such as easyJet and Ryanair who now sell over 90% of their tickets online. To assess the replace versus complement strategy alternatives, Kumar (1999) provides a framework. He suggests that replacement is most likely to happen when:

1 Customer access to the Internet is high.
2 The Internet can offer a better value proposition than other media (i.e. propensity to purchase online is high).
3 The product can be delivered over the Internet (it can be argued that this is not essential).
4 The product can be standardized (the user does not usually need to view to purchase).

If at least two of Kumar's conditions are met there may be a replacement effect. For example, purchase of travel services or insurance online fulfils criteria 1, 2 and 4.

STRATEGIC COMPONENTS – STOP AND SIT

One way to remember some of the key components of marketing strategy is the acronym STOP and SIT. First of all, strategy must be focused on crystal clear *Segments (S)*, and the selected *Target markets (T)*. *Positioning (P)* is a fundamental part of the overall customer proposition or offering, e.g. what exactly is the product, its price and perceived value in the marketplace? Can this be summarized into a strong proposition? STP is a fundamental part of any marketing strategy. Assuming it helps to fulfil the *Overall objectives (O)*, then the remaining components are *Sequence or Stages (S)*, *Integration (I)* and *Tools (T)*.

Sequence and stages embrace a couple of strategic e-issues. Sequence means should there be a sequence of tools, e.g. which comes first, a web site before interactive TV before mobile? In addition it is imperative to develop credibility before raising visibility, e.g. develop a credible web site that works before raising visibility and generating a lot of traffic. More importantly, should the business have a series of online stages of web evolution (see the evolutionary stages of Quelch and Klein (1996) in Section 1.12.) Are the web site processes and databases integrated and accessible for other transactions, whether WAP, iDTV or telephone? Can the online activities be integrated with the offline processes and databases? Or should it have a substantial web site at all – for FMCG goods, perhaps just microsites attached to other portals are most appropriate. These are strategic questions for the online marketer.

Figure 10.7   RS (www.rswww.com) appeal to different audiences

B2B organization RS http://rswww.com (Figure 10.7) has thought through their segmentation and uses different terminologies in **scent trails** to appeal to different audiences. As well as different industrial applications, they refer to the larger audience with the question '*Order to place over £1000*'?.

E-marketing strategy guides the choice of target markets, positioning and propositions which in turn guide combination of the optimum mix, sequence of e-tools (such as web sites, opt-in e-mail, e-sponsorship, viral marketing), service level and evolutionary stage (from brochure-ware sites to two-way interactive sites to fully integrated e-business systems). One ultimate (medium- to long-term) part of e-marketing strategy is the development of the dynamic dialogue (including a contact strategy) and the eventual full use of the integrated database potential. Regardless of how the customer comes into contact, he or she must be dealt with as a recognizable individual with unique preferences. This affects customer retention which, in itself, is a strategic decision (e.g. to improve customer retention levels requires a complete integrated database and contact strategy as explained in Chapter 8).

The overall balance of the marketing mix is strategic while the details of the mix are tactical. For example deciding whether to heavily discount prices and raising a high profile in a broad array of down-market online web sites and communities is strategic. The tactical details would list the sites and communities and relevant prices in detail.

So the components of e-marketing strategy can include:

- Segments, trends in the market place – how the strategy embraces these
- Target markets, positioning and propositions

- Positioning and ultimately, online value propositions
- Crystal clear objectives (does the strategy fulfil what you want to achieve online?)
- Evolutionary stage (what stage you want to be at)
- Online marketing mix (particularly place (partnerships) and service levels)
- Optimum mix of tactical digital media channels (search affiliates, display ads, social networks, etc.)
- Dynamic dialogue and contact strategies to retain customers
- User-generated content, community and social networking tactics (on own site and third party sites). For example, should consumer reviews be included as part of the proposition and how are these managed. For example, online travel agent pureplay TravelRepublic (www.travelrepublic.co.uk, Figure 10.8) has incorporated customer reviews onto its own site. Other travel companies have developed **widgets** to be incorporated within social networks such as Facebook
- Online brand reputation management (positive and negative), with a focus on social networks through online PR tactics, particularly if engaging in User Generated Content (whether reviews, ads, product ideas or just discussions)
- Integrated database (recognize and remember each customer whether via web or telephone).

Figure 10.8   TravelRepublic (www.travelrepublic.co.uk) reviews

Remember STOP and SIT, the components that any marketing strategy should include. Segmentation, Targeting and Positioning – fundamental to any strategy – state very clearly who you're after and how you'll be positioned (this can include varying propositions for different target markets, or can you state the OVP?). 'O' for objective – don't forget objective – the strategy shouldn't simply restate the objective but should fulfil the objective. 'S' for Sequence of activities, how everything integrates and time scales (are there a series of stages or key dates?). Now can you summarize all that into a few strategic options? A good e-marketing strategy is more than just communications, it integrates into the guts of a business (value propositions and modus operandi/processes). Ultimately it should outline clearly (and succinctly) how the objectives will be achieved.

UNFOCUSED STRATEGY

E-marketing strategy is lacking in many businesses. This contributes to ad hoc tactical approaches that are short term and often unfocused. Here's a selection of examples of some elements of e-marketing strategies that do not constitute a full strategy. You will see vastly different approaches to this crucial aspect of planning:

'by creating a seamless interface between online and offline, integrated by the underlying database . . .'

'by moving through the three evolutionary stages over an 18-month period means the race is on to get our e-strategy on track . . .'

'integrate website, database and CRM to efficiently automate a two-way dialogue between customers and our business. . . .'

'by establishing a presence on several different portals . . .'

'to own a particular content sector online rather than try to sell a specific product'.

Unilever took a major strategic shift to change Persil from a product-centric portal (product information) to a customer-centric portal (two main sections: Time In and Time Out – lifestyle and time for yourself – relaxation, minding your skin, diet and kids, time with kids . . . tips for a happy family . . . get creative with kids section . . .). This is an online brand experience integrated into TV, press and Internet campaigns.

You can see how each of these statements fits particular components from STOP and SIT.

Implicit in all strategic choices is resource. The strategy will in the end be constrained by the resource available and its allocation (see Section 10.8). For example, when trying to allocate resources between web site design, web site service and web site traffic generation, whichever strategy you choose, try to generate a few strategic alternatives before deciding the final e-marketing strategy. Remember the first strategy that comes to mind is not necessarily the best one.

You may generate different propositions (with different mixes) for different markets. This is perfectly acceptable. But ensure each strategy includes the key components (STOP and SIT) and works within the limited resources available (3Ms). Finally determining how much you are prepared to invest in either acquiring a customer or retaining an existing one is a useful exercise as it is strategic in so far as it influences your contact strategy, integrated database, sequence of messages across a variety of tools, as well as forcing you to think beyond the short term, one-off transactional sale.

E-MARKETING EXCELLENCE

Hamleys selects a niche strategy

Financial Times (2000) describes how Hamleys (www.hamleys.com) has used the web to acquire new customers from overseas markets – the majority of its sales are in the US, despite its London base. Instead of simply increasing sales to existing customers, the site has given Hamleys the opportunity to attract new customers who, according to the article, spend more on an average visit to the site than visitors to the London shop. The strategy used was to target customers looking for specialist collectibles that were difficult to obtain elsewhere, such as Steiff bears and die-cast figures. While its London store stocks around 40 000 toys, the site offers only a small fraction of that number. There are already numerous toyshops online offering cheap, plentiful toys aimed at the mass market. A visit to the current site suggests that the strategy has been revised since the article was written.

E-MARKETING INSIGHT

Timothy Cummings on competitive strategies

Cummings (2001) applies well-known military strategies to e-marketing. The strategies are not exclusive. They are:

1 *Full-frontal attack*, e.g. use of comparative marketing on web sites.
2 *Flanking attack*, e.g. use the web site to strike at areas in which competitors are weak such as price or service.
3 *Surround and cut-off*, e.g. larger companies use their resources to provide web site communications that are targeted at micromarkets. Smaller companies cannot compete with the resources needed.
4 *Blocking attack*, e.g. closing out competitors by offering additional services to customers.
5 *Guerrilla attack*, e.g. direct attack of competitors using guerrilla tactics such as online PR. The easyJet online competition to guess the losses of rival airline Go is an example of these tactics.
6 *Niche defence*, e.g. specializing through providing superior content or services to competitors.

7 *Territorial defence*, e.g. developing leading communities for particular segments or countries in advance of a competitor.

8 *Mobile defence*, e.g. developing new online functionality that is one step ahead of the competitors.

9 *Stealth defence*, e.g. minimizing web content about a new service, so existing players find it difficult to find out about the new service. The service is promoted through direct sales, networking and word-of-mouth.

10 *Diplomatic nous*, e.g. partnering with content providers to increase the value of your site compared to competitors.

One of the best books on e-marketing strategy was written over two thousand years ago by Tsun Tzu, a Chinese military genius who was conscious of the environment and understood the importance of alliances and market intelligence (translated by Wing, 1989).

SECTION SUMMARY 10.4

Strategy

Strategy is the big picture. It summarizes how you're going to get there. STOP and SIT combined with resource allocation (constraints) present at least some of the components required as part of an e-strategy.

Now you're ready to move on to the details of strategy – tactics. The next section explores them in more detail.

10.5 Tactics

Tactics are the details of strategy. You need to list all the e-tools you plan to use, in the sequence or stages set out in the strategy.

THE DIFFERENCE BETWEEN STRATEGY AND TACTICS

Tactics tend to be short term and flexible, whereas strategy is longer term and more enduring. But tactics must also be developed only after the strategy is agreed and set. It is tempting to do the reverse: have a bright idea for a new marketing initiative or a new service offering and rush it into play without a strategic context. Tactics don't drive strategy. You don't plan the journey until you have decided where you want to go.

It is easy to muddle strategy and tactics. Here's an easy example: let's say your strategy is to create an effective e-CRM programme (because one of your objectives is to increase repeat sales and reduce customer churn). To deliver this strategy, you decide to have four tactics – four moments of contact with each customer over the next six months: these will be an e-mail acknowledging the order, a follow-up e-mail to check delivery was OK, a real Christmas card, and a personalized e-mail and newsletter. These are the detailed tactics that support the strategy.

Your plans will need to be set down clearly. The best tool for this is a Gantt chart that lists all the tactical activities across all the e-tools throughout the weeks and months of the planning period, so you can see what's happening when.

Also your strategy will have gone through approval and budget processes and will be set for a defined period, whereas your ability to make swift and effective tactical responses to the changing environment will be a key factor in determining your success. This is especially so in e-business and e-marketing, where change happens so quickly. For example you may know at the start how you plan to implement the strategy; but what if a competitor steals a march, or an e-tool you were planning to use fails? You must think on your feet, be first to react.

E-MARKETING TACTICS

E-marketing tactics focuses on deciding the optimum marketing mix. This was described in detail in Chapter 2 ReMix. Here we simply look at decisions about the choice of tactical e-tools. Do you recall the physical e-tools at your disposal? They include platforms such as PCs and lap-tops, iDTV, i-radio, mobiles and hand-held devices, kiosks and miscellaneous devices discussed in Chapter 5. And then there are traffic tools such as banner ads, text messages, opt-in e-mail, viral marketing, search engine optimization – all discussed in Chapter 7.

Which of these tools are you going to use to implement the strategy? And will you be aware enough of the technology to adopt or abandon e-tools as and when necessary?

Now let's look at the e-marketing-specific tactical e-tools.

The web site

A web site could be pure brochureware, or a mechanism for creating and managing a dynamic dialogue with the customer, or a vehicle for generating sales. Don't denigrate brochureware that enhances the brochure. With appropriate use of Flash and similar products, and increasing installation of broadband, an online brochure can become a virtual experience. Imagine a cruise holiday web site that gives you video of the cabin you might be staying in or a property sale site where you can get a virtual tour of the house you might buy . . . properly-done brochureware needn't be as soporific as it normally is. Remember: good tactics will still need good execution!

Interactive advertising and sponsorship

Advertising your wares on other online media properties can promote your brand, create market awareness or bring traffic to your door. You can also sponsor a well-targeted portal; or if a market you want to reach is well covered by some other company running an opt-in e-mail newsletter, you could advertise on this.

Opt-in e-mail

We all receive e-mail from a variety of commercial sources; besides the pure junk you receive, there are a number of companies you deal with who offer opt-in e-mail – 'Would you like to receive more information on our company and our products'? Used sensibly, as companies from Amazon to Symantec do, this is very effective. Amazon will e-mail you when a book you might like is published. Customers can receive e-mails to alert them when their favourite band is on tour, or when there's an unmissable holiday offer. If the frequency is too high then Amazon will reduce the frequency so that messages have higher impact or customers can edit their communications preferences. With reasonable software at your end, opt-in e-mail is an extremely effective way to market. There are even opt-in e-mail products you could usefully use yourself (see Web links at the end of this chapter).

PRACTICAL E-MARKETING TIP

Automated event triggered e-mails

Don't forget the importance of devoting resource to planning your contact strategy to support the customer lifecycle (see Chapter 8) for different audiences you are targeting. For example, cosmetics brand Clinique (www.clinique.co.uk, Figure 10.9) has different e-mails for its male and female audiences and has a cleverly crafted welcome strategy that explains its OVP and encourages trial of its online services and products.

Customer relationship management tools

If you then provide benefits or added value information through the opt-in e-mail service . . . you can develop an integrated database of customers and prospects which can be exploited in further ways: send them gifts, invite them to enter contests, run a free draw for tickets to a sports or cultural event you sponsor . . . the trick is to use the connection with the customer to create ongoing relationships which give you regular access points where you can deliver a marketing message. CRM online presents one of the greatest challenges to the marketer, particularly as 50% of CRM projects fail (Gartner Group, 2004).

But before you choose your e-tools, you need to really understand what each can and cannot do; there is no short-cut to spending time on the web and on interactive TV and exploring other e-marketers' activities!

CONTROLLING TACTICS

Who has control of tactics and implementation is a big question and the e-marketer must win the ownership argument. Take the web site: is it controlled by marketing or by technical or some other function? Many web sites actually damage brands with their broken links, dead ends, cumbersome downloads, out-of-date content, impossible navigation and unanswered e-mails (see 'Sloppy e-marketing' in Section 1.5). No e-marketer would let this

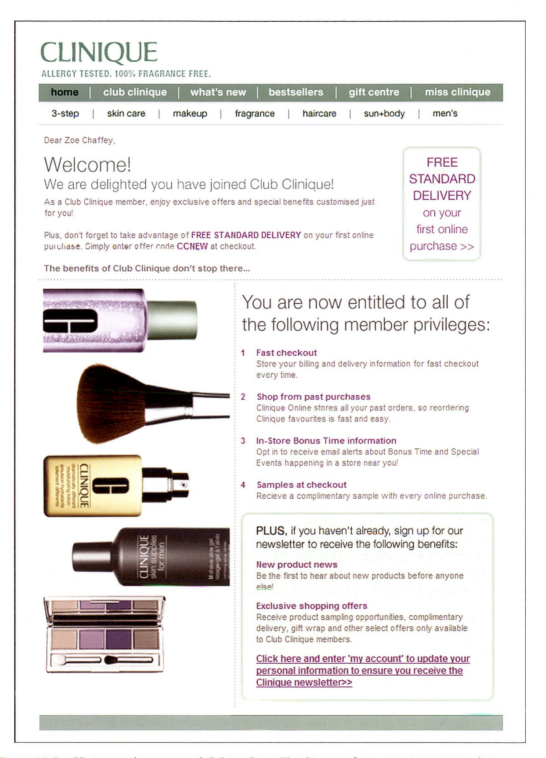

Figure 10.9   Clinique welcome e-mail. Subject line – Thanking you for registering at www.clinique.com, From address: Clinique registration [infocl@clinique.co.uk]

happen. You can usually tell from a site whether the webmaster is a 'techie' or a marketer. Many sites skip the cardinal rule of asking customers what they would like on a web site. Then having put it up, they forget to check to see if they got it right. Regular reviews should not be devoted to reviewing the latest technology but rather, they should be focused on customer reviews. As an e-marketer, you'll want a site that is easy on the eye and clear to the reader and lightning fast to download. If that means dispensing with some of the techies' zanier ideas . . . well the customer will thank you for it!

E-MARKETING EXCELLENCE

Pepsi use a range of e-tools

The e-marketing strategy of Pepsi UK focuses on using push techniques (opt-in e-mail) to keep the customers in a dialogue and provide offers to stimulate sales. The tactical e-tools used are:

- Pepsi web site to gather customer e-mails.
- Sponsorship of other sites, e.g. Pepsi Chart.
- Regular opt-in e-mails, e.g. Pepsi Chart predictions.
- Opt-in e-mail promotions, e.g. Win a holiday.
- E-mail requests to participate in online survey.
- E-mail a friend a Christmas themed animation.

Offline communications are also used to capture e-mail addresses and provide information about the online services.

E-MARKETING INSIGHT

Willcocks and Plant on tactics to achieve differentiation

Willcocks and Plant (2000) describe two dimensions to 'sustain the e-advantage through differentiation' that can be considered as e-marketing tactics:

- Merchandise dimension – for a car this includes its characteristics such as performance, image and options. The web site can use content to differentiate by describing what the offer will do for the customer, or aura – what the offer will say about the customer.
- Support dimension – differentiating features which help them in choosing, obtaining and using the offering. For a car, examples include availability of information, ease of test drive, ordering a brochure and the purchase mechanism via the web site. Personalization and expertise available via the web site can help enhance the support dimension.

Tactics

Tactics are the details of strategy. Tactics list the events and e-tools that will be used over time. Now you have a tactical plan (Gantt chart) – now make it happen. The next section, 'Actions' shows you how.

10.6 Actions

Everything degenerates into work – strategies and tactics eventually cascade into actions which become work that has to be carried out and eventually checked for any mistakes. According to John Stubbs, former executive director of the Chartered Institute of Marketing, up to 40% of marketing expenditure is wasted through poor execution.

As mentioned in Chapter 1, we are swimming in a sea of sloppy marketing and e-marketing. It is not surprising that Bossiddy and Charan (2004) suggest that 'execution is the missing key between aspirations and results'. So, the action stage, or execution, may be the weakest link in the planning process.

Tactics break down into actions. In fact a series of actions, for example to build a web-site or run an online advertising campaign. Each tactic becomes a mini project.

You need to produce a project action plan for each project, with key steps allocated to specific people with specific timescales. Good project management skills are essential. Apply more Gantt charts, or critical path analysis, flow charts or whatever project management approach is best. Most e-marketing plans would not necessarily go into this level of detail. These project action plans need to be drawn up at some stage, whether in the appendix or the main plan.

Each tactical e-tool requires careful planning and implementation. Whether building a web site, a banner ad, an interactive TV ad, a viral campaign or an opt-in campaign, good project management skills and diligent attention to detail is required.

It is at this stage that you build your web-site or commission the creatives to produce your banner ad campaign, devise the e-mail campaign or get the techies to design the database which will be populated by customer data generated by your feedback systems.

TYPICAL E-MARKETING ACTIONS

Think about the sort of actions you might be pursuing for achieving different web site objectives:

1 *Traffic building actions*. To generate visits and/or traffic to your web site, portal or iDTV channel you will probably be using links or banners on other sites, sponsoring other online activities, possibly using competitions or creative content ideas to generate interest. You'll need creative input and a budget to buy media space.

2 *Actions to achieve customer response*. To capture user enquiries – thus turning visitors into sales prospects, capturing data, using enquiry data to analyze customer needs, plan development – you'll need a response mechanism for customers to enter their data online and a database logging and processing the data as it comes in.

3 *Actions to gain sales*. For collecting sales orders: use iDTV or the web site to generate actual sales, handle money transactions and initiate order processing systems.

4 *Fulfilment actions*. Efficient data transfer to warehouse to get product off the shelf and into the box for despatch . . . Orders might be one-off products or subscription services. More software and hardware solutions to implement here: ideally, dovetail into parents' existing systems used for mail order and phone order businesses – then you know that the processes that are invisible to the customer have been installed, tested and proven already.

5 *E-CRM actions*. To build better relationships by creating dialogue with customers . . . you might be running online polls, using rewards and competitions to secure commitment and response; you could also set up and moderate an online user group: in this way you empower customers by means of interactivity – feedback, listen to customer response and visibly act on it. Staff training and motivation (incentive systems) are crucial.

Success in all these actions requires good implementation. The best strategy in the world will achieve nothing if it is not implemented well. Good implementation only happens if you plan well and use your resources well. First of all you have to communicate to get the plan approved and supported from above and below. Among the activities are going to be: project management schedules, meeting deadlines, meetings, memos, phone calls, chasing people, careful preparation, constant checking and attention to vast volumes of details. Free lunches and tickets to Wimbledon come but rarely!

RISK MANAGEMENT

Action, or implementation, also requires an appreciation of what can go wrong from cyber libel to viruses, to mail bombs, hackers and hijackers, to cyber squatting and much more . . . contingency planning is required. What happens when the server goes down or a virus comes to town? What happens if one of the e-tools is not working, or is not generating enough enquiries? Something has to be changed. **Risk management** involves:

- Brainstorming a list of all the things that could go wrong.
- Assessing their impact and likelihood.
- Creating contingency plans for the highest impact and most probable risks.
- Continuous review, revising and refining during campaign execution.

Use post-implementation reviews to learn from the successes and failures for the next project. Note, in addition to the usual KPIs, Procter and Gamble asks their managers to report on their 'learning' from the market place.

This may seem obvious, but it takes time. Do you take the time?

Actions

Good project management skills are essential during the implementation or action stage. You are now ready to control your destiny by building control mechanisms into your e-plan.

10.7   Control

Are you feeling lucky? Without control mechanisms, e-marketing depends on luck. It's a bit like playing darts in the dark. How do you know if you are hitting the target or are just shooting blindly and wildly? How do you know if you're targeting the right customers? Who are they? What do they like and not like? How many of them become repeat customers? Which e-tool works best? How much does each customer actually cost you? By the end of this section you'll be able to answer these questions and begin to take control of your destiny instead of spinning out of control. Control also includes monitoring your competitors – what they're doing; what they're repeating; what works for them; what they're stopping doing.

THE CONTROL PROCESS

Good marketers build in control systems to ensure they know what's working and what's not, early rather than late. Why wait until the end of the year? Why not have a system in place to keep track of key performance indicators?

You have done the work – implemented the tactics, performed the actions . . . now, is the plan working? Have you achieved the objectives, is the strategy working, did you choose the right tactics . . . have you spent the money and time wisely? To find out you must measure and review what you did – performance measurement. To do this, you need to determine what data you will look at each day, each week, each month, each quarter. This is the Control section of the e-marketing SOSTAC® cycle. Remember we agreed in Section 10.2 that your objectives had to be SMART: Specific, Measurable, Achievable, Realistic and Time-related. Now we test whether they were!

Time has to be made for a regular review of what's working and what's not – performance diagnosis. Good marketers have control over their destinies. They do not leave it to chance and hope for the best. They reduce risk by finding what works and what doesn't. Then, your e-tactics, or even strategy, can be changed through corrective action if necessary. Your plan should specify the frequency of reporting required, as well as who takes appropriate actions arising.

And you don't want to wait for the year end to find out something isn't working. If something is wrong, you need to have control systems (reviews) in place so that you find out and correct the problems early rather than late. Equally, if something is working unbelievably well, you need to know so you can learn and perhaps accelerate the success.

Figure 10.10 summarizes key issues in the control process for e-marketing.

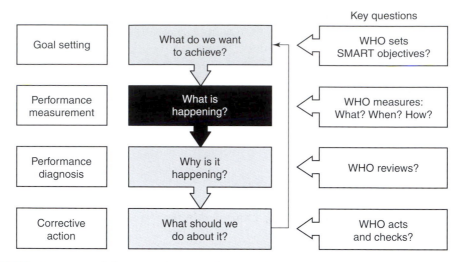

Figure 10.10 Summary of the control process for e-marketing planning

THE METRICS

Performance is measured against detailed targets based on the objectives and strategy.

So you need to measure the KPIs that were detailed in Section 10.2, Situation analysis and Section 10.3, Objectives. For example, for a web site they might be:

- Sales (number of and source of)
- **Online revenue contribution**
- Subscriptions (number of and source of)
- **Conversion rates to different types of conversion goals**
- Enquiries (number of and source of)
- Number of **unique visitors**
- Number of **repeat visitors**
- **Average duration** (proportion of active or engaged visitors)
- Most popular pages
- **Churn rates**
- **Termination rate** or **attrition rate**
- **Source of traffic (and particularly the source of traffic which has the highest conversion rates)**
- Awareness levels.

So where do you get this information? Many of the metrics concerning visitor behaviour are available from **web analytics**. Collection by other information systems or processes is required for key measures such as sales, subscriptions, conversion and attrition rates. Standard practice should ensure data from the different sources is compiled into a monthly or weekly report that is delivered and reviewed by the right people. Decide which metrics need to be reviewed daily, weekly or monthly, and by whom. The e-marketer must know which tools are working. That's why 'source of' sales or enquiries is useful – if a particular banner ad doesn't pull customers drop it and try another until you find one that does.

Remember all forms of measurement (or metrics) cost money – you'll have to factor in budgets and resources for the following mechanisms:

- Monitoring customer awareness
- Monitoring customer satisfaction
- Monitoring customer attitudes.

Other forms of control like sales analysis require only that you allocate quality time. So how do you know if things are going well? Some objectives are easy to state and easy to measure. Existing recording systems in the organization will produce the data to answer the question: if the objective is to grow sales . . . what was the target for growth and the timetable for achieving it . . . and did you make it?

PERFORMANCE DIAGNOSIS

Some objectives require more careful study, in fact, when you set objectives and define strategy, you should already be thinking: what would be considered a successful outcome and how are we going to monitor performance and measure this?

If the objective is to create a dominant web-based brand (first stage) and then to make a profit within 18 months on advertising sales and sponsorship . . . what criteria can you set to define success, and how will you then measure against these criteria? You may need to implement data recording systems and develop analysis tools within the action plan.

Similarly, if the objectives revolve around getting closer to customers – customer relationship management or CRM – your measurement tools must be carefully defined and implemented.

Consider how the motor industry has adapted to the Internet. Many manufacturers are dealing direct with consumers, not only in terms of information provision but even order-taking: some dealerships should be worried, the process of disintermediation is going to squeeze them out. But how should industry measure its success? By counting sales and sales leads directly generated by the Internet – that's the easy bit. And also by measuring conversion rates for people who visit the web-site and choose your car when they subsequently go to a dealer. This is hard to measure so you need to be capturing customer feedback scientifically and measuring levels of customer satisfaction – that's the difficult part.

CORRECTIVE ACTION

Corrective action is used to revise the strategies and tactics to ensure the objectives are achieved. Or perhaps the objectives need revising? To minimize the need for corrective action good marketers can monitor e-tools before they are rolled-out through testing, testing and testing. E-marketers can reduce risk with relevant information so that their decisions are based upon fact instead of blind luck. This applies even to web site development – researching concepts and usability testing helps to ensure the design is right and you don't have high termination rates.

So which of the e-tools are giving the best return on investment? Why?

Good marketers also have contingency plans. What happens if Plan A doesn't work? What happens if the competition cut prices? Or worse still, what happens if the server goes down and your network crashes? Do you have a second server? Good marketers think things through.

On a more positive note, good marketers react quickly to emerging opportunities and threats. As mentioned earlier some companies, when checking the daily web stats, spot a lot of additional traffic on a particular page or a particular item being purchased more frequently, then highlight the page or the product on the main home page to boost even more traffic/conversions during a period until they spot some other, more popular page, emerging.

E-MARKETING INSIGHT

Chaffey on key areas of e-marketing metrics

Chaffey *et al.* (2003) suggest that control should consider the effectiveness of e-marketing in five key areas of the 'WebInsights' framework shown in Figure 10.11. Each e-marketing channel, such as web or interactive TV, should be considered separately against traditional channels using this framework.

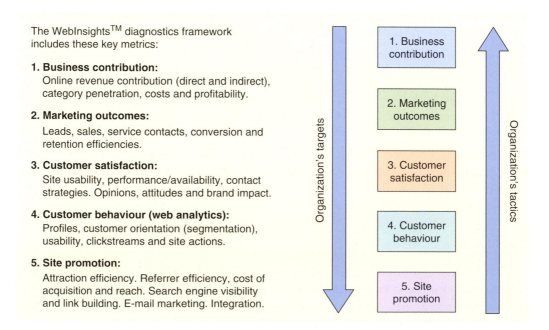

The WebInsights™ diagnostics framework includes these key metrics:

1. **Business contribution:**
   Online revenue contribution (direct and indirect), category penetration, costs and profitability.

2. **Marketing outcomes:**
   Leads, sales, service contacts, conversion and retention efficiencies.

3. **Customer satisfaction:**
   Site usability, performance/availability, contact strategies. Opinions, attitudes and brand impact.

4. **Customer behaviour (web analytics):**
   Profiles, customer orientation (segmentation), usability, clickstreams and site actions.

5. **Site promotion:**
   Attraction efficiency. Referrer efficiency, cost of acquisition and reach. Search engine visibility and link building. E-mail marketing. Integration.

Organization's targets

1. Business contribution
2. Marketing outcomes
3. Customer satisfaction
4. Customer behaviour
5. Site promotion

Organization's tactics

Figure 10.11   Key metrics from the Chaffey (2003) framework for assessing e-marketing effectiveness

SECTION SUMMARY 10.7

Control

Control is about monitoring whether your objectives are being achieved and then modifying the tactics and actions to ensure they are.

10.8   Resources – men, money and minutes

Budgeting for the delicate balance of resources required to run an online operation is a science not yet fully understood by many. The late Professor Peter Doyle simplified this critical issue when he said: 'The resource allocation decision is the choice of which products and markets offer the best opportunities for investment'.

We are going to consider resource allocation among different products, markets and e-marketing tools by splitting the resource issue into three components – the 3Ms: men (and women, the human resource), money (budgets) and minutes (time scales and time horizons for production, delivery, service, etc.).

MEN (AND WOMEN)

How many bodies are required to deal with incoming e-mail enquiries and outgoing telephone calls triggered by the 'call-back' facility on the web site? Or can it be automated and personalized? How much time to allow and notify customers of deliveries? How much time to set up a project and integrate with the existing (legacy) database systems, etc.? There are some key questions in the area of people resources. Even at times when many tech companies are shedding staff, really able people who know what they are doing in terms of website design, e-commerce delivery, e-business strategy, online media sales, etc. are not in huge supply. So you will have to call on a mixture of internal resources and external skills to deliver your plans.

It is often said that a company's greatest assets walk out the door each night – i.e. the people.

Human resource allocation can be critical: if you can find existing resources to fulfil some of the e-marketing requirements, then you keep costs down and that reduces pressure on revenues.

Outsourcing or Insourcing

To outsource or not to outsource – that is the question. Outsourcing continues to grow in popularity both in major strategic aspects of e-marketing and also in shorter-term tactical aspects of e-marketing. In Chapter 3, we explained how value networks and their dependence on excellent outsourcing management skills are becoming increasingly popular. Here are a few specific outsourcing questions to consider.

So you need to update your web site – do you do it in-house or contract out to an agency? And what balance should you strike between resources allocated to building the site and those required to maintain it on a regular basis, leaving a pot aside for a complete review and upgrade in three, six or nine months? Do not forget traffic – resources are also required to build traffic. Remember out-of-date web sites can damage brands: who will trust your airline if the offers on the web site have expired? Resourcing for promoting the web site is reviewed in Section 7.10.

Other resources to consider are telesales: are additional staff required or can the in-house team do it? Who will do the e-marketing research? Who is going to analyze the data you get from the customer feedback, and who is going to produce the recommendations? Is it the existing team, or a new position? If customers show there is need to change procedures, do we have the people to react and respond?

Don't underestimate the ability of customers to consume your people resources: if you offer an e-mail response mechanism, who is going to answer the incoming e-mails? But if you don't answer them, or don't even offer an e-mail response . . . how will your customers view this? Pretty badly is the answer!

MONEY

Of course, to a large extent the people resources at your disposal will be a function of the money resources. So once you have calculated the people requirements for your e-marketing plan . . . you need to work out how to get them: you need to find the skills, and you need the budget to pay for them.

Marketing costs money; e-marketing is no different. Your e-marketing plan must include a budget covering the costs you will incur and a clear benefit statement – what will the return on the investment be?

Be aware that the very nature of e-marketing is that you may be expected to demonstrate a clear relationship between investment and return: if your budget is allocated in order to create an online service that generates sales, then you'll have to create a model showing the ratio of e-marketing cost to sales return.

And be realistic in your expectation: if revenues fall short of the plan, you should assume this will put pressure on the money resources left at your disposal! You may have to trim costs on the web-site or reduce the online marketing spend.

Try therefore to get some sliding scale agreed, so that there is also an upside: develop plans for additional marketing activity if sales are going well so you can quickly up a gear and build on the success.

But with e-marketing you also have some opportunities to generate some income: can you get sponsors for your web site or sell some banner ads? Can you partner with suppliers of other products and get them to give you a cut of their income? If you can do any of these, you can then approach the budget decision makers and negotiate to be able to spend some or all of the income you generate.

Also don't forget the obvious: work out what you could usefully do for free. You may find a complementary business prepared to exchange banners and links, you must certainly ensure you are well represented on search engines. Look around the web for opportunities to promote your sites and services or acquire names for your database which won't cost you a penny.

A specific warning too: don't underestimate the resources required to maintain a web site. Too often, companies go out and spend vast sums getting designer-rich agencies to build flashy and complex sites and then find that when it comes to updating the content and answering the customers, there is no resource left to cover this.

MINUTES

Time is often the tightest of the resources: there seem to be not enough hours in the day or days in the week, and when you have the impetus of a plan to implement, there is always more that could be done.

Of course the e-marketing world is used to shorter timescales: you might need three months to prepare a TV campaign or twelve months to create a new pack; but you could build a new web site in a lot less time. Or could you? How long would competitor analysis, focus group discussions, concept testing and usability testing take? Even simple banner ads take time to prepare. The creatives required for an online banner campaign are generally less complex than those for a print campaign; and of course booking times are shorter: you can in theory plan, design and deliver an online campaign in a matter of days.

So get the balance right: recognize that e-marketing has an expectation of being able to think, plan, react, change and respond quickly; that's the fun and excitement, and also the power, of e-marketing. But don't be bullied into skimping on the planning and research and design and development just because timescales have been made arbitrarily or are artificially short.

E-MARKETING INSIGHT

5:2:1 Versus 1:2:5

It has been suggested that UK companies tend to adopt a ratio of 5:2:1 (design to service to traffic building), whereas the ratio tends to be 1:2:5 ratio in the US. The US approach makes sense as there's no point having a wonderful (expensive) web site if no customers or prospects bother to visit. In addition, as mentioned earlier, popular sites are frequently updated during maintenance (service) and quick to download even in a download world. As a final example of an organization that we think has this balance right, see Figure 10.12 – The Barbican website which combines usability with innovation in rich and social media.

Figure 10.12   The Barbican site (www.barbican.org.uk)

E-MARKETING INSIGHT

Gulati and Garino (2000) on restructuring to obtain resources

Gulati and Garino (2000) identified a continuum of strategic approaches from integration to separation. They describe the choices as:

1 *In-house division (integration).* Example: RS Components Internet Trading Channel (www.rswww.com)
2 *Joint venture (mixed).* The company creates an online presence in association with another player.
3 *Strategic partnership (mixed).* This may also be achieved through purchase of existing dot-coms, for example, in the UK, Great Universal Stores acquired e-tailer Jungle.com for its strength in selling technology products and strong brand while John Lewis purchased Buy.com's UK operations.
4 *Spin-off (separation).* Example: Egg bank is a spin-off from the Prudential financial services company.

These authors give the advantages of the integration approach as being able to leverage existing brands, to be able to share information and achieve economies of scale (e.g. purchasing and distribution efficiencies). They say the spin-off approach gives better focus, more flexibility for innovation and the possibility of funding through flotation. For example Egg has been able to create a brand distinct from Prudential and has developed new revenue models such as retail sales commission. They say that separation is preferable in situations where:

- A different customer segment or product mix will be offered online
- Differential pricing is required between online and offline
- If there is a major channel conflict
- If the Internet threatens the current business model
- If additional funding or specialist staff need to be attracted.

SECTION SUMMARY 10.8

Resources – men, money and minutes

Your e-marketing plan must provide properly for the resources you will need to deliver:

- Men (and women) – You need to work out what people resources you will need and how to acquire these in a market where core skills are not abundant.
- Money – You need adequate budgets in order to achieve your plans; this will include a forecast for the return on investment and a plan to be able to adjust costs if sales figures are higher or lower than expected.

- Minutes – Your e-marketing plan must contain timescales, schedules and deadlines. And if you want it to work, your actions will stick to them!

CHAPTER SUMMARY

1 E-marketing plans must support and be integrated with corporate or business plans and marketing plans. SOSTAC® stands for: Situation analysis, Objectives, Strategy, Tactics, Actions and Control.

2 Situation analysis is the first part of the e-marketing plan. It explains 'where are we now'? It reviews internal resources and e-marketing performance and external factors such as customer, competitor and intermediary activity. It also reviews the PEST factors – Political, Economic, Social and Technology.

3 SWOT analysis is used to summarize Strengths, Weaknesses, Opportunities and Threats.

4 Objectives are set to define the direction of the plan. Objectives can be constructed by reviewing the 5Ss of Sell, Serve, Speak, Save and Sizzle. Objectives must be checked to ensure they are they SMART: Specific, Measurable, Achievable, Realistic and Time-related.

5 Strategy summarizes how the objectives will be achieved. The key components are highlighted by STOP and SIT (Segments (S), Target markets (T), Overall objectives (O), Positioning (P) and Sequence or Stages (S), Integration (I) and Tools (T)).

6 Tactics define how the strategy will be achieved. It describes the e-tools used and how they will be sequenced through time.

7 Action equals implementation plans. Actions should be defined to build traffic, gain customer response, gain sales and fulfil them if appropriate and foster e-CRM. Risk management should be used.

8 Control gives a feedback loop starting with monitoring whether the objectives are achieved, assessing what the problems are and then revising the strategies, tactics and actions as appropriate.

9 Resources can be planned through the 3Ms of men (and women, the human resource), money (budgets) and minutes (time scales and time horizons for production, delivery, service, etc.).

References

Bossiddy, L. and Charan, R. (2004) *Execution, the discipline of getting things done*. Crown Business.

Chaffey, D. (2004) *E-business and e-commerce management. Strategy, implementation and practice*, 2nd edition. Pearson Education, Harlow.

Chaffey, D., Mayer, R., Johnston, K. and Ellis-Chadwick, F. (2003) *Internet Marketing: Strategy, Implementation and Practice*, 2nd edition. Prentice Hall/Financial Times, Harlow.

Cummings, T. (2001) *Little e, big commerce – how to make a profit online*. Virgin Publishing, London.

Cutler, M. and Sterne, J. (2001) E-metrics. Business Metrics for the New Economy. Research report from NetGenesis (www.netgen.com).

Doyle, P. (1994) *Marketing Management and Strategy*. Prentice Hall, London.

Financial Times (2000) Hamleys: Where to buy a gold-plated model of James Bond's Aston Martin. *Financial Times*, http://www.ft.com/ftsurveys/spbf9a.htm.

Fisher, A. (2001) Sandvik – The challenge of becoming an e-business. *Financial Times*, 4 June.

Gartner Group (2004) CRM. *Marketing Business*, February.

Gulati, R. and Garino, J. (2000) Getting the Right Mix of Bricks and Clicks for your Company. *Harvard Business Review*, May–June, pp. 107–14.

Iconocast (2001) Upfront Market Reflects Ad Weakness. E-mail Strategy, Pt. I (12 July). www.iconocast.com.

Kumar, N. (1999) Internet distribution strategies: dilemmas for the incumbent. *Financial Times Special Issue on Mastering Information Management*, No. 7. Electronic Commerce.

Neumeier, M. (2007) *Zag – The #1 Strategy of High Performance brands*. AIGA New Riders.

Ohmae, K. (1999) *The Borderless World: Power and Strategy in the Interlinked Economy*. Harper Business, New York.

Quelch, J. and Klein, L. (1996) The Internet and international marketing. *Sloan Management Review*, Spring, pp. 61–75.

Simons, M. (2000) Barclays gambles on web big bang. *Computer Weekly*, 13 July, p. 1.

SOSTAC® was created by P.R. Smith in 1993. SOSTAC® is a registered trademark of P.R. Smith. See www.PRSsmith.org for more.

Smith, P.R. and Taylor, J. (2004) *Marketing Communications – An Integrated Approach*, 4th edition. Kogan Page.

Smith, P.R., Berry, C. and Pulford, A. (1999) *Strategic Marketing Communications – new ways to build and integrate communications*, revised edition. Kogan Page.

Willcocks, L. and Plant, R. (2000) Business Internet Strategy: Moving to the Net. In *Moving to E-business*, eds L. Willcocks and C. Sauer. Random House.

Wing, R.L. (1989) *The Art of Strategy (translation of Sun Tzu, c. 480–221BC, The Art of War)*. Aquarian Press, Wellingborough, Northants.

Further reading

Chaffey, D., Mayer, R., Johnston, K. and Ellis-Chadwick, F. (2005) *Internet Marketing: Strategy, implementation and practice*. Financial Times/Prentice Hall, Harlow, 3rd edition. This book covers a structured approach to e-planning in detail, with Chapters 2 and 3 looking at situation analysis and Chapter 4 at Internet marketing strategy.

Web links

Avinash Kaushik's blog (www.kaushik.net). Avinash is an expert in web analytics and his popular blog shows how web analytics should be used to control and improve return on e-marketing investments.

DaveChaffey.com (www.davechaffey.com). Articles about e-planning and detailed guidance on implementation of e-marketing plans.

E-consultancy (www.e-consultancy.com). Discussion and articles about e-planning.

Marketing Sherpa (www.marketingsherpa.com). Case studies and news about e-marketing planning.

Epikone (www.epikone.com/resources). A specialist web analytics blog and e-book giving guidance on how to tailor Google Analytics.

Neil Mason of Applied Insights www.applied-insights.co.uk – blog featuring Neil's insights related to measurement and control of e-marketing.

New Media Age (www.nma.co.uk). A UK digital marketing trade weekly which has interviews with practitioners discussing their strategic approach to digital marketing.

Revolution magazine (www.revolutionmagazine.com). Articles and interviews with e-planners useful for reviewing different strategies.

PR Smith.org (www.prsmith.org) – the originator of SOSTAC® – more information on SOSTAC®.

The wayback machine www.archive.org allows you to see old web pages from 1996.

Wikipedia.org (www.Wikipedia.org) – the user-generated online encyclopedia has useful content on marketing and e-marketing planning.

YouTube www.youTube.com customer reviews and critiques, advertisements, spoof advertisements and some videos on marketing and e-marketing planning.

Self-test

1   Summarize the relevance of the elements of a SOSTAC® e-plan for your organization.

2   What are the main factors of situation analysis that should be reviewed in the areas of internal and external review?

3   Summarize objectives for your organization for each one of the 5Ss.

4   What are the elements of strategy summarized by STOP and SIT?

5   Write down each of the e-tools used as part of tactics that are most relevant to your organization.

6   Which specific actions are required for you to build traffic, gain customer response, gain sales and fulfil them if appropriate and foster e-CRM?

7   What are the key measures of the effectiveness of your online presence?

8   Specify the main resource types required to develop an online presence.

Glossary

3G   Third generation of mobile phone technology based on UMTS standard with high speed-data transfer enabling video calling and download.

A/B Testing   A/B or AB testing refers to testing two different versions of a page or a page element such as a heading, image or button. The alternatives are served alternately with the visitors to the page randomly split between the two pages. Hence it is sometimes called 'live split testing'. Changes in visitor behaviour can then be compared using different metrics such as clickthrough rate on page elements like buttons or images or macro-conversion rates, such as conversion to sale or sign-up. AB Testing is aimed at increasing page or site effectiveness against key performance indicators including clickthrough rate, conversion rates and Revenue per visit. Since it doesn't consider combinations of variables tested, for best uplift *multivariate testing* is increasingly used.

Acceptance (of customer)   One of Hofacker's five stages of web site information processing. Does the customer accept (believe) the message?

Accessibility legislation   Legislation intended to protect users of web sites with disabilities including visual disability.

Acquisition cost   Total promotional cost to gain a new customer.

Aggregators   A site featuring a range of product or service listings from suppliers, for example a price comparison intermediary. Prices are usually updated by suppliers using *XML* feeds. Google product search is an example of an aggregator.

Ad network   A collection of independent web sites of which each has an arrangement with a single advertising broker to place banner advertisements on a CPM, CPA or CPA basis.

Aesthetics of site design   Graphics + Colour + Style + Layout + Typography.

Affiliate marketing   A commission-based arrangement where referring sites (publishers) receive a commission on sales or leads by merchants (retailers).

Affiliate networks   Brokers known also as affiliate managers who manage the form of links, tracking and payment between a merchant and a range of affiliates.

AIDA model   Attention, Interest, Desire, Action. A hierarchy of responses model to communications.

ALEA model   Attention, Learning, Emotional response and Acceptance. A hierarchy of responses model to communications.

Allowable customer acquisition cost (CPA)   The maximum acceptable cost for gaining a new customer typically based on consideration of the initial profitability or lifetime value for gaining that customer type.

Animated ads   A *GIF or Flash* file is used to present a sequence of several different image frames to the viewer.

Anti-aliasing   A technique to smooth the edges of curves or fonts in graphic images such as *GIF* or *JPEG*.

ARG (Alternative Reality Game)   A story that takes place over time and has a beginning, middle and an end as opposed to a persistent world created in massively multiplayer games.'

ATR model   Awareness, Trial and Reinforcement.

Atomization   Describes a concept where the content on a site is broken down into smaller fundamental units which can then be distributed via the web through links to other sites. The use of widgets and the distribution of content via RSS feeds are examples of atomization. The small units of content contributed by participants within a social network can also be considered atomization.

Attention   One of Hofacker's five stages of web site information processing. Can the site attract the customer's attention?

Attrition rates   Percentage of site visitors that are lost at each stage in making an online purchase.

Average order value (AOV)   The average amount spent for a single checkout purchase on a retail site for a particular customer group, e.g. first time purchasers.

Auctions   A buying model where traders make offers and bids to sell or buy under certain conditions.

Auditing   An independent body verifies the number of *page impressions* and *visitors* for a *web site*.

Autoresponders   Software tools or 'agents' running on a *web server* which automatically send a standard reply to the sender of an e-mail message.

Backlinks   Hyperlinks which link to a particular web page (or website). Also known as inbound-links. Google PageRank and Yahoo! WebRank are methods of enumerating this.

Bandwidth   Bandwidth indicates the speed at which data is transferred using a particular network media. It is measured in bits-per-second (bps).

Banner adverts   A typically rectangular graphic displayed on a web page for purposes of brandbuilding or driving traffic to a site. It is normally possible to perform a *click-through* to access further information from another web site.

Banner adverts, animated   Early banner adverts only featured a single advert, but today they will typically involve several different frames which are displayed in sequence to attract attention to the banner and build up a theme, often ending with a call to action to click on the banner.

Behavioural targeting   Personalised, relevant messages are delivered for example by email or web which relate to a customers current interests. For example, if they review a specific product online then they may receive an email or be served an ad which relates to their interest. Also known as *contextual marketing*.

Behavioural retargeting   Ads are displayed elsewhere on a site or other sites in an ad network after a customer has interacted with an initial ad or related content. A series of relevant adds developing the message can be displayed through behavioural re-targeting.

Bid management software   Software or web based services which partially automate the management of paid search advertising across a range of paid search networks by applying rules to display ads for specific keyphrases at particular bids, positions and times to achieve specified business aims such as ROAS, ROI, Profitability, etc while minimizing cost.

Blog   An online diary regularly updated by an individual or group with topical news and views.

Bluejacking   Sending a message from a mobile phone or transmitter to another mobile phone which is in close range via *Bluetooth* technology (without the user's permission).

Blueprints   Show the relationships between pages and other content components, and can be used to portray organization, navigation and labelling systems.

Bluetooth   A standard for wireless transmission of data between devices, e.g. a mobile phone and a *PDA*.

Breadcrumbs   An indication of position in site structure which also allow users to go up a level within the site.

Broadband   A term referring to methods of delivering information across the Internet at a higher rate by increasing *bandwidth*, e.g. fibre-optic cable access.

Bounce rate   Proportion of visitors to a page or site that exit after visiting a single page only, usually expressed as a percentage.

Brochureware   A web site in which a company has migrated their existing paper-based promotional literature onto the Internet without recognizing the differences required by this medium.

Browser safe palettes   A set of 216 standard colours designed to achieve colour consistency on different web browsers where the display colours are set to 256 colour.

Business cards (interactive)   A CD-ROM of a similar size to a business card containing company and product information.

Business models   A summary of how a company will generate revenue identifying its product offering, value-added services, revenue sources and target customers.

Business-to-business (B2B)   Commercial transactions between an organization and other organizations.

Business-to-business (B2B) exchanges   Virtual locations with facilities to enable trading between buyers and sellers.

Business-to-consumer (B2C)   Commercial transactions are between an organization and consumers.

Buy-side e-commerce   E-commerce transactions between a purchasing organization, its suppliers and partners.

Call-back   A direct response facility available on the web site for a company to contact a customer by phone at a later time as specified by the customer.

Cannibalization   Sales achieved via an e-commerce site replace sales traditionally via other channels.

Card sorting or web classification   The process of arranging a way of organizing objects on the web sites in a consistent manner.

Channel conflict   A significant threat arising from the introduction of an Internet channel is that while *disintermediation* gives the opportunity for a company to sell direct and increase profitability on products, it can also threaten existing distribution arrangements with existing partners.

Churn rate   The percentage rate at which customers stop/lapse in use of a service or product.

Clicks and mortar   A business combining an online and offline presence.

Clickstream   A record of the path a user takes through a web site. Clickstreams enable site designers to assess how their site is being used.

Click-through   A click-through (ad click) occurs each time a user clicks on *banner adverts* with the mouse to direct them to a *web page* with further information.

Click-through rates (CTR)   The click-through rate is expressed as a percentage of total ad impressions, and refers to the proportion of users viewing *banner adverts* who click on them. It is calculated as the number of *click-throughs* divided by the number of ad impressions.

Cloaking   Serving different pages to a visitor than those indexed by a search engine. This is unethical, but surprisingly common. One example is using hidden text on the site that can't be seen by visitors, another is serving different pages to the searchers to those served to search engine robots by identifying the type of visitor.

Co-branding   An arrangement between two or more companies where they agree jointly to display content and perform joint-promotion using brand logos or a *banner advert*. The aim is that the brands are strengthened if they are seen as complementary. This is a reciprocal arrangement which can occur without payment.

Co-browsing   Customers screen can be viewed by the call-centre operator in combination with *callback* or *realtime chat*.

Co-buying   Group buying enabling a reduction in price for a volume purchase.

Collaborative filtering   Profiling of customer interests coupled with delivery of specific information and offers, often based on automatic assessment of the interests of groups of similar customers.

Commoditization   Products are selected primarily on price due to minimal differences between competitive products.

Comprehension   One of Hofacker's five stages of web site information processing. Does the customer understand the message as intended?

Contact strategy   A defined sequence of integrated communications delivered by personalised email and web contacts plus traditional media such as direct mail and phone. Contact strategies will help provide contextual communications throughout the customer lifecycle or for different phases in a campaign.

Content   Content is the design, text and graphical information which forms a *web page*. Good content is the key to attracting customers to a web site and retaining their interest or achieving repeat visits.

Content management system (CMS)   A software tool/web application for creating, editing and updating documents accessed by intranet, extranet, or Internet.

Content network   Sponsored links are displayed by the search engine on third-party sites. Ads are paid for on a PPC basis or on a CPM basis.

Content owners   Company staff, usually within the business who are responsible for updating content.

Contextual ads   A paid search technique where ads embedded within a publishers site are displayed on the **content network** according to the type of content. For example, an ad placed on a page about email marketing techniques will be related to email marketing services.

Contextual marketing   Personalised, relevant messages are delivered for example by email or web which relate to a customers current interests. For example, if they review a specific product online then they may receive an email or be served an ad which relates to their interest. Also known as *behavioural targeting*.

Continuous traffic building activities   Communications activities such as affiliate marketing, search engine marketing and online sponsorship intended to drive visitors to the site which tend not to occur in short burst campaigns, but across the year.

Convergence   A trend in which different hardware devices such as TVs, computers and phones merge and have similar functions.

Conversion goal   A page on the site such as e-newsletter registration or sales confirmation for which a visit shows that a business objective is being met. Site owners should track number of conversion goals and the pages or referrers that influence them. Also known as a *value event*.

Conversion rate   Percentage of site visitors that perform a particular action such as making a purchase.

Cookie   Small text files placed on an end-user's computer to enable web sites to identify the user. They enable a company to identify a previous visitor to a *web site*, and build up a profile of their behaviour. They do not contain personal data which is securely held in a database and looked up via the unique identifier (customer code) in the cookie.

Cookie expiry period   The time stated in an affiliate marketing programme between when a visitor clicks the affiliate link and the sale is credited to the affiliate. Common times are 7, 30 or 90 days. A longer cookie period will result in a higher EPC.

Cost per acquisition (CPA)   The cost of acquiring a new customer. Typically limited to the communications cost and refers to cost per sale for new customers. May also refer to other outcomes such as cost per quote or enquiry.

Cost per click   The cost of each click from a referring site to a destination site, typically from a search engine in pay per click search marketing.

Cost per thousand (CPM)   Cost per 1000 *ad impressions* for a *banner or display advert*.

Countermediation   A response to *reintermediation* where an established organization creates or purchases a rival portal that is positioned as independent or part of an existing brand.

Customer Engagement   Repeated interactions that strengthen the emotional, psychological or physical investment a customer has in a brand.

Customer lifetime value (LTV)   A modelled future value of customers over a set number of years based on future purchases and customer acquisition and management costs.

Customer orientation   Providing content, services and offers on a *web site* consistent with the different characteristics of the audience of the site.

Customer preferred channel   Customer prefers a particular channel for certain activities, e.g. phone to purchase, e-mail for support.

Customer-to-business (C2B)   Customer is proactive in making an offer to a business, e.g. the price they are prepared to pay for an airline ticket.

Customer-to-customer (C2C)   Interactions between customers on a web site, e.g. posting/reading of topics on an electronic bulletin board.

Customer scenarios   Alternative tasks or outcomes required by a visitor to a web site. Typically accomplished in a series of stages of different tasks involving different information needs or experiences.

Customer unions   The same as *co-buying*.

Data mining   Searching organizational databases in order to uncover hidden patterns or relationships in groups of data. Data mining software attempts to represent information in new ways so that previously unseen patterns or trends can be identified.

Data warehouse   Data warehouses are large database systems containing detailed company data on sales transactions which are analysed to assist in improving the marketing performance of companies.

Database driven marketing   The process of systematically collecting data about past, current and/or potential customers, maintaining the integrity of the data by continually monitoring customer purchases, by inquiring about changing status and using the data to formulate marketing tactics and foster personalized relationships with customers.

Destination site   Frequently used to refer to the site that is visited following a *click-through* on a banner advert. Could also apply to any site visited following a click on a *hyperlink*.

Digital audio broadcasting (DAB) radio   Digital radio with clear sound quality with the facility to transmit text, images and video.

Digital media channel (digital channels)   Different forms of digital media used for online promotion such as affiliate marketing, paid search and display advertising.

Digital rights management (DRM)   The use of different technologies to protect the distribution of digital services or content such as software, music, movies, or other digital data.

Digital signage   The use of interactive digital technologies within billboard and point of sale ads. For example, videos and bluetooth interaction.

Digital value   Offers or services that can only be accessed or delivered online.

Direct response   Usually achieved in an Internet marketing context by banner ads, *callback services* or *e-mail marketing*.

Directories   A directory provides a structured listing of registered web sites in different categories. They are similar to an electronic version of the *Yellow Pages*.

Disruptive Internet technologies   New Internet-based communications approaches which change the way in which information about products is exchanged which impacts the basis for competition in a marketplace.

Disintermediation   The removal of intermediaries such as distributors or brokers that formerly linked a company to its customers. It enables a company to sell direct to the customer by 'cutting-out the middleman'.

Dithering   The browser renders the nearest match to a colour when the site designer has used a colour which is not in the *browser safe palette* and the user's monitor is set to 256 colours.

Doorway pages   Pages deliberately created which are optimized for particular key phrases or search engines in order to increase listings in SERPS which often re-direct to other pages in sites. Typically they are entry points that are not part of the main navigation. They are considered to be an unethical approach known as search engine spamming. Ethical search marketers instead create search entry pages that are part of the main site navigation which are themed around particular phrases customers are likely to use.

Dynamic ad targeting   Specific ads are served in real-time to visitor clusters according to their characteristics and behaviour assessed by content types viewed.

Earnings per Click (EPC)   An important measure that an affiliate uses to determine the value of each merchant or pages on their site. It stands for Average Earnings Per Click (EPC) and is usually measured across 100 clicks since an average is needed over this number of clicks.

E-business   All electronically mediated information exchanges, both within an organization and with external stakeholders supporting the range of business processes.

E-commerce   All electronically mediated information exchanges between an organization and its external stakeholders. Can refer to purchase transactions only.

Effective cost per thousand (eCPM)   A measure of the total revenue the site owner can generate when 1000 pages are served.

EDGE   Evolved Data for GSM Evolution. Intermediate mobile standard between *GSM* and *UMTS*.

E-mail   Push sending of messages or documents, such as news about a new product or sales promotion.

E-mail inbound   E-mails received by a company from customers and other stakeholders.

E-marketing   Achieving marketing objectives through use of electronic communications technology.

Enterprise application integration (EAI)   The middleware technology that is used to connect together different software applications and their underlying databases is now known as 'enterprise application integration (EAI)'.

Enterprise resource planning   Software providing integrated functions for major business functions such as production, distribution, sales, finance and human resources management.

Environment scanning   The process of continuously monitoring the environment and events, and responding accordingly.

E-procurement   The electronic integration and management of all procurement activities including purchase request, authorization, ordering, delivery and payment between a purchaser and a supplier.

Expert reviews   Often performed at the beginning of a redesign project as a way of identifying problems with a previous design.

Exposure   One of Hofacker's five stages of web site information processing. Does the customer see the message?

Extended enterprise   Functions of an organization *outsourced* as part of a *value network*.

Extranet   Formed by extending the *intranet* beyond a company to customers, suppliers, collaborators or even competitors. This is password protected to prevent access by general *Internet* users.

Faceted navigation   Used to enable users to rapidly filter results from a product search based on different ways of classifying the product by their attributes or features. For example: by brand, by sub-product category, by price bands.

Fast moving consumer goods (FMCG)   The term says it all.

Findability   An assessment of how easy it is for a web user to locate a single content object or to use browse navigation and search system to find content. Like usability it is assessed through efficiency – how long it takes to find the content and effectiveness – how satisfied the user is the experience and relevance of the content they find.

Firewall   A specialized software application mounted on a server at the point the company is connected to the Internet. Its purpose is to prevent unauthorized access into the company from outsiders.

Fixed layout   The screen design has a fixed number of pixels width unlike a fluid layout or adaptive layout which dynamically resize according to minimum screen resolutions.

Fluid designs   An adaptive web page or email design which makes use of all horizontal space as screen resolution increases. Fixed layouts have a fixed width in pixels.

Focus groups   Online these follow a bulletin board or discussion group form where different members of the focus group respond to prompts from the moderator and each other.

FRAC A data analysis technique based on assessing the Frequency, Recency Amount and Category of purchases by customers.

Frames A technique used to divide a *web page* into different parts such as a menu and separate content.

General Packet Radio Services (GPRS) A standard offering mobile data transfer and WAP access approximately five to ten times faster than traditional GSM access.

Geographical portal A *portal* limited to a single country, area or city.

GIF (Graphic Interlaced File) GIF is a graphic format used to display images within a *web page*. An interlaced GIF is displayed gradually on the screen building up an image in several passes.

Globalization The increase of international trading and shared social and cultural values.

Google dance A periodic change to the search engine algorithm weighting that affects rankings and so causing companies' positions in the SERPS to change, sometimes dramatically.

Graphics-intensive sites Sites in which white space or large images are mainly used to convey the message rather than text.

Group characterization Web site communications are based on grouping people's preferences as part of *mass customization*.

Halo effect The role of one media channel on influencing sale or uplift in brand metrics. Commonly applied to online display advertising, where exposure to display ads may increase clickthrough rates when the consumer is later exposed to a brand through other media, for example sponsored links or affiliate ads. It may also conversion rates on a destination sites through more exposure to the brand and message.

Hit A hit is recorded for each graphic or block of text requested from a *web server*. It is not a reliable measure for the number of people viewing a page.

Horizontal portal A *portal* with a wide audience or *reach* offering general services, e.g. Yahoo!, MSN.

HTML HTML (hypertext markup language) is a standard format used to define the text and layout of a *web page*. HTML files usually have the extension .HTML or .HTM.

Hubs Alternative term for *B2B exchange*.

Ideal customer Preferred customer who is targeted due to their potential for a profitable relationship.

I-MODE A successful mobile standard originating in Japan that enables transfer of colour images between phones.

Incidental advertising Offline advertising where the web address is incidental to the main aim and creative.

Index inclusion Ensuring that as many of the relevant pages from your domain(s) are included within the search engine indexes you are targeting to be listed in.

Indirect online contribution Assesses the influence of the web site in generating offline purchases.

Individualization Tailoring of content or offer to individual preferences.

Infobots Software tools that collect information from the web for their users according to predefined preferences.

Infomediaries   An *intermediary* business whose main source of revenue derives from capturing consumer information and developing detailed profiles of individual customers for use by third parties.

Information architecture   The combination of organization, labelling, and navigation schemes comprising an information system.

Information-intensive sites   Sites in which text is mainly used to convey the message rather than white space or large images.

Interactive banner ads   Banner ads where the user can type in information and receive a response, for example loan interest for a particular loan.

Interactive business cards   A CD-ROM of a similar size to a business card containing company and product information.

Interactive kiosks   Fixed site access to information about an organization and its services through a PC simplified through touch-screen access.

Interactive radio   Access to radio via a web site or digital radio.

Interaction rate (IR)   The proportion of ad viewers who interact with an online ad through rolling over it. Some will be involuntary depending on where the ad is placed on screen, so it is highly dependent on placement.

Intermediary   Online sites that help bring different parties such as buyers and sellers together. Pay a similar role to traditional brokers or channel partners.

Internet   The physical network that links computers across the globe. It consists of the infrastructure of network servers and communications links between them that are used to hold and transport information between the clients and servers.

Internet value proposition   See *Online Value Proposition*.

Interstitial ads   Ads that appear between one page and the next.

Intranet   A network within a single company which enables access to company information using the familiar tools of the *Internet* such as *web browsers* and *e-mail*. Only staff within a company can access the intranet, which will be password protected.

IP address   The unique address of a computer accessing the Internet or a server used to host information (e.g. 207.68.156.58).

IPTV (Internet Protocol Television)   Digital television service is delivered using Internet Protocol, typically by a broadband connection. IPTV can be streamed for realtime viewing or downloaded before playback.

JPEG (Joint Photographics Experts Group)   A graphics file format and compression algorithm best used for photographs.

'Just-in-time'   An approach to operations management where inventory holding is minimized by manufacturing according to immediate demand.

Key performance indicators (KPIs)   Key measures collected to assess whether an organization's objectives are achieved.

Keyphrase   The combination of keywords typed into a search engine by a user.

Keyphrase analysis   A structured approach to identifying and selecting relevant combinations of keywords for *SEO marketing* and *PPC marketing*.

Keyphrase density   The percentage importance of a keyphrase in comparison with the total number of words within a title, meta tag or web page.

Knowledge management   Techniques and tools for disseminating knowledge within an organization. Knowledge is used to apply staff experience to problem solving.

Lean back medium   Used to describe traditional TV.

Lean forward medium   Used to describe interactive TV or web usage.

Legacy systems   Old IT systems on which an organization is reliant, but they do not meet the current organizational requirements.

Lifetime value (LTV)   The estimated value of a customer or group of customers integrated across their past, current and future revenue.

Link anchor text   The text used to form the blue underlined hyper link viewed in a web browser defined in the HTML source. For example: Visit Dave Chaffey's web log is created by the HTML code: <A HREF = "http://www.davechaffey.com">Visit Dave Chaffey's web log </A>

Link building   A structured activity to include good quality hyperlinks to your site from relevant sites with a good Page Rank.

Linkbait   Valuable content on a site that is naturally attracts links and is probably designed to do that – a process known as linkbaiting.

Link farms   Interlinked sites set up to increase Page Rank. Considered to be *search engine spamming*.

Live chat sessions   A user asks questions of a company representative by typing into their browser. The representative replies in real-time.

Localization   Designing the content of the *web site* such that it is appropriate to different audiences in different countries.

The Long-tail   The Long-tail concept describes a frequency distribution showing the typical decline in popularity of items within a sector when a consumer has a choice in selecting these items. In search, the most common generic search terms (of the search head) for a site or market sector have much higher volumes than the less common phrases, which together are important in generating qualified visitors. The tail in retail refers to the capability of less popular products to generate sales and profitability.

Mass customization   Using technology to create tailored marketing messages or products for individual customers or a group of similar customers yet retain the economies of scale of mass marketing or production.

Measurement   A process that collects metrics to indicate the effectiveness of Internet marketing activities in meeting e-marketing objectives.

Meta tags   Text within an *HTML* (hypertext markup language) file summarizing the content of the site (content meta-tag) and relevant keywords (key-word meta-tag) that are matched against the keywords typed into search engines.

Meta-market switchboards   Third-parties that provide a single point of contact and deliver a range of services between customers and suppliers.

Microsite   Specialized *content* that is part of a media owner web site, e.g. ad specific content for a company on an independent portal.

Middleware   Software used to facilitate communications between business applications including data transfer and control.

Mixed-mode buying   The process by which customer switches between online and offline channels during the buying process.

MMOG (massively-multiplayer online games) Online games like World of Warcraft with multiple players.

Modems Device used to connect to the Internet via phone lines. Converts signals from digital to analogue.

Multichannel behaviour Customers use different traditional media or locations (phone, store, direct mail) in combination with different digital media (web, mobile, IPTV) to inform their purchase decision.

Multivariate testing Multivariate testing enables simultaneous testing pages for all combinations and variations of page elements that are being tested. These enables selection of the most effective combination of design elements to achieve the desired goal.

Natural or organic listings The pages listing results from a search engine query which are displayed in a sequence according to relevance of match between the keyword phrase typed into a search engine and a web page according to a ranking algorithm used by the search engine. Placements in the natural listings are targeted through *Search Engine Optimisation (SEO)* activity.

Navigation Navigation describes the methods of finding and moving between different information and pages on a web site. It is governed by menu arrangements, site structure and the layout of individual *Web page*s.

Negative working capital Working capital refers to money tied up in stocks and debtors. If *Just-in-time* delivery occurs and customer payments are taken in advance of supplier payment, negative working capital can be created.

Negative SEO A company aims to decrease the ranking of other sites (usually indirectly) by gaining more favourable mentions above a negative listing in the natural search engine results.

Net Promoter Score A measure of the number of advocates a company (or website) has who would recommend it compared to the number of detractors.

Offline promotion Offline promotion uses traditional media such as TV or newspaper advertising and word of mouth to promote a company's *web site*.

One-to-one marketing Communication and tailoring of offer at an individual level.

Online marketplace model A description of the main audiences, intermediaries and destination sites within a specific market. It is used to assess consumer behaviour, competitor strength and the role of different intermediaries in influencing consumer purchases and media consumption.

Online PR Maximizing favourable mentions of your company, brands, products or web sites on third-party web sites that are likely to be visited by your target audience.

Online promotion Online promotion uses communication via the *Internet* itself to raise awareness about a *web site* and drive traffic to it, e.g. *hyperlink*s from other *web sites, banner adverts* or targeted *electronic mail (e-mail)*.

Online reputation management Controlling the reputation of an organization through monitoring and controlling messages placed about the organization.

Online revenue contribution An assessment of the extent to which the *Internet* contributes to sales is a key measure of the importance of the Internet to a company.

Online surveys Surveys on-site through pop-up questionnaires.

Online value proposition Defines an organization's online offering distinct from offline or competitor offering.

On-page optimization Writing copy and applying markup such as the <title> tag and heading tags <h1> to highlight to search engines relevant keyphrases within a document.

Onsite search engine Search engine specific to a single site to help users find content.

Opt-in e-mail The customer is only contacted when they have explicitly asked for information to be sent to them (usually when filling in onscreen *forms*).

Opt-out The customer is not contacted subsequently if they have explicitly stated they do not want to be contacted in future. Opt-out or *unsubscribe* options are usually available within the e-mail itself.

Outsourcing Contracting an outside company to undertake e-marketing (or any) activities.

Page impressions A *page impression* denotes one person viewing one web page.

Page template A defined layout that is used throughout the site for different page categories (e.g. category page, product page, search page).

Page Rank An index used to assessed the interconnections between web pages. A trademark of Google. Based on 'link popularity' or the number of inbound links and the Page Rank of the linking sites.

Paid for inclusion (PFI) The advertiser specifies pages with specific URLs for incorporation into the search engine organic listings. There is a setup fee and/or annual fee and pay per click charge.

Panel Members are recruited in order that their TV or web usage can be measured.

Panel data Includes time and duration of access and content accessed for different geodemographics.

Partner relationship management Management of marketing activities performed by downstream (or upstream) channel partners.

Pay per click (PPC) search marketing Refers to when a company pays for text ads to be displayed on the search engine results pages when a specific key phrase is entered by the search users. It is so called since the marketer pays for each time the hypertext link in the ad is clicked on.

Permission-based marketing Customers agree (*opt-in*) to be involved in an organization's marketing activities usually as a result of an incentive.

Personas A summary of the characteristics, needs, motivations and environment of typical web site users.

Personal digital assistants (PDAs) Digital organizers with a touch screen that can be used to access the Internet and personal productivity applications.

Personal video recorder (PVR) or digital video recorder (DVR) Home consumer electronics device that records television shows to a hard disk in digital format.

Personalization Delivering customized content for the individual either through *web pages*, *e-mail* or *push technology*.

Person-to-person (P2P) *Intermediaries* such as Napster which enable individuals to share information or files, similar to *C2C*.

Persuasion marketing (Persuasive design) Using design elements such as layout, copy and typography together with promotional messages to encourage site users to take follow particular paths and specific actions rather than giving them complete choice in their navigation.

Plug-in A program that must be downloaded to view particular content such as an animation.

Portals A web site that acts as a gateway to the information on the Internet by providing search engines, directories and other services such as personalized news or free e-mail.

Price comparison intermediaries   Sites like MoneySupermarket (www.moneysupermarket.com) and Shopping.com, Expedia which allow a user to specify the features of the product they are looking for and then finds the best deals from participating suppliers.

Price transparency   Prices can be readily compared by purchasers using the Internet, particularly through *shopping bots*.

Privacy   Concerns that affect an individual's or company's personal details.

Profiling   Determining the customer key characteristics to enable *segmentation*.

Promotion   *Online promotion* uses communication via the Internet itself to raise awareness about a site and drive traffic to it. This promotion may take the form of links from other sites, banner adverts or targeted e-mail messages. *Offline promotion* uses traditional media such as TV or newspaper advertising and word of mouth to promote a company's *web site*.

Proximity marketing   Marketing messages are delivered in real-time according to customers presence based on the technology they are carrying, wearing or have embedded. Bluecasting is the best known presence example where messages are automatically pushed to a consumers Bluetooth enabled phone or they request audio, video or text content to be downloaded from a live advert. In the future ads will be able to respond to those who view them.

Prosumer   Typically 'proactive consumer', but see the range of definitions on pages 59–60.

Pureplay   An online only organisation with no physical high-street present or distribution as opposed to a multichannel or bricks and clicks organisation which will have both an online and offline customer-facing presence. They may still use offline communications such as direct mail and advertising and have staff to manage inbound enquiries.

Quality Score   Influences a Pay Per Click ads' position on Google and the Google Network. It also partly determines your keywords' minimum bids. In general, the higher your Quality Score, the better your ad position (Ad Rank) and the lower your minimum bids (the bid needed to trigger an ad).

Reach   The audience size of a web site as a percentage of total possible audience.

Really Simple Syndication (RSS)   An extension of blogging where a blog, news or any type of content is received as a "feed" by specialist RSS reader software such as RSS reader (www.rssreader.com). It offers a method of receiving news that uses a different broadcast method to e-mail, so is not subject to the same conflicts with SPAM or SPAM filters.

Realtime chat   A customer support operator in a call-centre can type responses to a site visitor's questions.

Reciprocal links   Two organizations agree to link to each other's sites.

Redirects   A temporary web page or address is used, often for measurement purposes, before the required page is served to the user.

Referrals   The number of links from other sites.

Referrers   A previously visited site from which the user followed links to reach the current site. Includes all the main digital media channels such as search engines, affiliates and display ads. Can also refer to offline referrers such as print ads.

Reintermediation   The creation of new intermediaries between customers and suppliers providing services such as supplier search and product evaluation.

Relationship building   Consistent application of up-to-date knowledge of individual customers to product and service design which is communicated interactively in order to develop a continuous and long-term relationship which is mutually beneficial.

Repeat visits   A *tagged* visitor is recorded as visiting a site again.

Representation   Defines all the locations on the Internet where an organization is referred to or purchases can be made. Includes own web site and intermediary sites.

Repurposing   Porting content from one digital platform to another, for example, web to interactive digital TV.

Return path   An interaction where the customer sends information to the provider using a phone line or cable.

Return on investment (ROI)   A measure of the value derived from a marketing campaign (or any business activity) compared to its costs. There are many forms of ROI equation, but they can be simplified to: Profit generated from activity divided by amount spent on activity (over a defined period of time).

Revenue models   Different options for generating revenue from an online presence including sale, affiliate, subscription and advertising.

Reverse auctions   The buyer places a request for tender or quotation (RFQ) and many suppliers compete, decreasing the price with the supplier with the lowest price winning the contract.

Rich Internet Applications (RIA)   Interactive applications which provide options such as product selectors or games. They may incorporate video or sound also. Typically built using technologies such as Adobe Flash, Ajax, Flex, Java or Silverlight.

Rich media adverts   *Banner adverts* that are not static, but provide animation, sound or interactivity. An example of this would be a banner advert for a loan in which a customer can type in the amount of loan required, and the cost of the loan is calculated immediately.

Roadblocks   Where an advertiser buys all the available advertising space on a particular page.

Robots   A software tool employed by *search engines* to regularly index web pages of registered sites. Can also refer to any automated agent.

Satisficing behaviour   Consumers do not behave entirely rationally in product or supplier selection. They will compare alternatives, but then may make their choice given imperfect information.

Scenarios   See *Customer scenarios*.

Scenario-based design   Site design and testing is based on common path or flow of events or activities performed by visitors.

Scent trails   Cues such as text and image hyperlinks and page labels that web browsers follow to find content or services when navigating a sight typically associated with directed information seeking.

Screen resolution   Number of pixels (dots) displayed, e.g. 800 across by 600 vertical.

Search analytics   The evaluation of the effectiveness of on-site search in order to increase its effectiveness.

Search bots   Software agents that search the web for information based on keywords.

Search engine   A specialized website that uses automatic tools known as *spiders* or *robots* to index web pages of registered sites. Users can search the index by typing in keywords to specify their interest.

Search engine optimization (SEO)   A structured approach used to increase the relative ranking position of a company or its products in search engine *natural* or *organic* results listings on *search engine results pages* for selected *keyphrases*.

Search engine results pages (SERPS)   The pages generated and displayed by a search engine after a search engine user types in their key phrase.

Search engine spamming   Unethical actions deliberately taken by marketers to mislead the search engines and give a higher ranking such as repeated use of *keyphrases* and use of *link farms, doorway pages* and *cloaking*. Search engines may penalize if they detect spamming.

Second layer selling   Product is sold via an intermediary.

Secure Electronic Transaction (SET)   A standard for public-key encryption intended to enable secure e-commerce transactions lead-developed by Mastercard and Visa.

Secure Sockets Layer (SSL)   A commonly used encryption technique for scrambling data as it is passed across the Internet from a customer's web browser to a merchant's web server.

Security   Security attributes include:

1 *Authentication* – are parties to the transaction who they claim to be? This is achieved through the use of digital certificates.

2 *Privacy* and *confidentiality* – is transaction data protected? The consumer may want to make an anonymous purchase. Are all non-essential traces of a transaction removed from the public network and all intermediary records eliminated?

3 *Integrity* – checks that the message sent is complete, i.e. that it isn't corrupted.

4 *Non-repudiability* – ensures the sender cannot deny sending the message.

5 *Availability* – how can threats to the continuity and performance of the system be eliminated?

Segmentation   Identification of different groups within a target market in order to develop different offerings for the groups.

Sell-side, e-commerce   E-commerce transactions between a supplier organization, intermediaries and its customers.

Sense and Respond marketing   Monitoring customer actions or behaviours and then reacting with appropriate messages and offers to encourage desired behaviours.

Share of wallet   Amount of customer income spent at a single organization as a proportion of all expenditure in a category, e.g. financial services.

Shopping bots   Software agents that find the lowest price for a specified product.

Short message service (SMS)   Also known as text messaging between mobiles.

Social network   A site enabling community interactions between different consumers (C2C model). Typical interactions including posting comments and replies to comments, sending messages, rating content and tagging content in particular categories. Well-known examples include Bebo, Facebook, MySpace and Linked-In.

SOSTAC®   SOSTAC® is a simple planning system covering Situation Analysis, Objectives, Strategy, Tactics, Action and Control. SOSTAC® was created by P.R. Smith in 1993. SOSTAC® is a registered trademark of PR Smith. See www.PRSmith.org for more.

SPAM   Unsolicited e-mail (usually bulk mailed and untargeted).

Spamming   Bulk sending of SPAM.

Specific advertising   Offline ads that specifically highlight the *online value proposition*.

Spiders   Automatic tools known as spiders or robots index registered sites. Users search by typing keywords and are presented with a list of pages.

Spotlight tags   An outcome page on a site is marked as valuable for use in Management Information reports. The tag is usually script which effectively updates a counter that this page has been viewed, often using a single pixel image referenced by the web analytics system.

Spotlight was originally a proprietary terms of Doubleclick DART, which has now been replaced by floodlight tags. These terms are now used more generally.

Statement of origination   A message in an opt-in e-mail showing who has sent the message and why they have permission to send it.

Static ads   *Banner ads* that are not *animated*.

Stickiness   An indication of the duration of how long a visitor stays on a site.

Strategy, e-marketing   Definition of the future direction and actions of a company defined as approaches to achieve specific objectives.

SWOT   Internal strengths and weaknesses, external opportunities and threats.

Superstitials   Pop-up adverts that require interaction to remove them.

Tagging visitors   Tracking of origin of site visitors, their actions and spending.

Touch strategy   The sequence, frequency and content of outbound communications such as e-mail and direct mail.

Traffic building   The use of *online promotion* and *offline promotion* techniques to increase the audience of a site (both new and existing customers).

Trialogue   The interaction between company, customer and other customers facilitated through online community, social networks, reviews and comments.

Unified message service   *Portal* offering combined access to mobile, landline and e-mail messaging, e.g. e-mails can be heard by phone.

Uniform resource locator (URL)   A unique web address in the format, for example, http://www.company.com.

Unique visitors   The number of individuals who visit a web site in a fixed time period.

UMTS   Universal Mobile Telecommunications System. The standard for *3G mobile access*.

URL rewriting   A technique used to make complex web addresses for pages associated with dynamic content such as product catalogues or news articles visible to search engines.

URL Strategy   A defined approach to forming URLs including the use of capitalisation, hyphenation, domain canonicalisation and sub-domains for different brands and different locations. This has implications for promoting a website offline through promotional or vanity URLs, search engine optimisation and findability. A clean URL which fits many of these aims is http://www.domain.com/folder-name/document-name. Care must be taken with capitalisation since Linux servers parse capitals differently from lower case.

User Generated Content (UGC)   Web users rather than the site owners create content. Example include Wikipedia, personal blogs and reviews of products and companies.

Usability   An engineering approach to website design to ensure the user interface of the site is learnable, memorable, error free, efficient and gives user satisfaction. It incorporates testing and evaluation to ensure the best use of navigation and links to access information in the shortest possible time.

User testing   Representative users are observed performing representative tasks using a system.

Value chain   A model for analysis of how supply chain activities can add value to products and services delivered to the customer.

Value Event   A visit to a web page such as e-newsletter registration or sales confirmation which indicates that a business objective is being met. Also known as a conversion goal. Site owners should track number of conversion goals and the pages or referrers that influence them. Also known as a value event.

Value networks   The links between an organization and its strategic and non-strategic partners that form its external value chain.

Vertical integration   The extent to which supply chain activities are undertaken and controlled *within* the organization.

Vertical portal   A *portal* with specialized content, often for a vertical market.

Viral marketing   E-mail is used to transmit a promotional message to another potential customer. 'Online word of mouth'.

Virtual assistants   Different types of software agents such as shopping bots and infobots.

Virtual business   An organization which uses information and communications technology to allow it to operate without clearly defined physical boundaries between different functions. It provides customized services by outsourcing production and other functions to third parties.

Virtual communities   A customer-to-customer interaction delivered via e-mail groups, web-based discussion forums or chat.

Virtual integration   The majority of supply chain activities are undertaken and controlled *outside* the organization by third parties.

Visitor session   One visit by a single customer. Visit ends after no activity for 30 minutes. The number of unique visitors is always less than visitor sessions.

Visits, site   The number of visits to a web site in a fixed time period.

Voice portals   Portals that can be accessed by phone to hear information such as news or e-mails.

Web 2.0   Refers to a collection of web services which facilitate certain behaviours online such as community participation and user-generated content, rating and tagging.

Web 3.0   Next generation web incorporating high-speed connectivity, complex cross-community interactions and an intelligent web where applications can access data from different services to assist searchers.

Web accessibility   Designing web sites so that they can be used by people with visual impairment or whatever browser/access platform they use.

Web analytics   Techniques used to assess and improve the contribution of e-marketing to a business including reviewing traffic volume, referrals, clickstreams, online reach data, customer satisfaction surveys, leads and sales.

Walled garden   Access is limited to a selection of online stores – characteristic of interactive digital TV.

Web browsers   Browsers such as Netscape Navigator or Microsoft Internet Explorer provide an easy method of accessing and viewing information stored as *HTML* (hypertext markup language) web documents on different *web servers*.

Web log file   A log file analyser is a software tool used to summarize the information on visitor activity in a log file which contains a line defining the page, access time and *IP address* of the visitor.

Web pages   A single page of a *web site*.

Web response ad campaign   An offline print or TV campaign where one of the main campaign objectives is to encourage ad viewers to visit the web site. For example, to request a sample, enter a competition, find further information or buy online.

Web servers   Used to store the *web pages* accessed by *web browsers*. It may also contain databases of customer or product information which can be queried and retrieved using a browser.

Webographics   The web access characteristics of users such as place of access, connection speed and experience.

Welcome strategy   The sequence of personalised emails, web messages and offline communications intended to educate the customer about a brand and develop a relationship.

Widget   A badge or button incorporated into a site or *social network* space by its owner, but with content typically served from another site. Content can be updated in real time.

Wi-Fi ('wireless fidelity')   A high-speed wireless local-area network enabling wireless access to the Internet for mobile, office and home users.

Wireframe   Also known as schematics, a way of illustrating the layout of an individual webpage.

Wireless application protocol (WAP)   Offers Internet browsing from mobile handsets. Mainly text-based sites developed in wireless markup language (WML).

World wide web   A medium for publishing information on the Internet. It is accessed through *web browsers* which display *web pages* and can now be used to run business applications. Company information is stored on *web servers* which are usually referred to as *web site*.

XML or eXtensible Markup Language   A standard for transferring structured data, unlike HTML which is purely presentational.

XML Product feeds   A standard format of product feature and pricing information that is uploaded by merchants to price comparison intermediaries to enable listing of all products in their catalogue.

XMOS (cross-media optimization studies)   XMOS research is designed to help marketers and their agencies answer the question 'What is the optimal mix of advertising vehicles across different media, in terms of frequency, reach and budget allocation, for a given campaign to achieve its marketing goals?' The mix between online and offline spend is varied to maximize campaign metrics such as reach, brand awareness and purchase intent.

Yielding   One of Hofacker's five stages of web site information processing. Does the customer accept (believe) the message?

Index